POLAND

Chapters by John Lawrence Angel, Eldon R. Burke, Joseph C. Gidyński, Malbone W. Graham, Oscar Halecki, Zygmunt Karpiński, Jan K. Kasprzak, Robert J. Kerner, Manfred Kridl, Felix Roderick Labuński, Stephen P. Mizwa, Frank T. Nowak, Julia Swift Orvis, Irena Piotrowska, Jerzy Radwan, Joseph S. Roucek, Bernadotte E. Schmitt, Stanisław Strzetelski, Wojciech Świętosławski, S. Harrison Thomson, Leopold Wellisz, Edmund Zawacki, Henryk Zieliński

Edited by BERNADOTTE E. SCHMITT

ANDREW MacLEISH DISTINGUISHED SERVICE PROFESSOR OF MODERN HISTORY IN THE UNIVERSITY OF CHICAGO

UNIVERSITY OF CALIFORNIA PRESS
BERKELEY AND LOS ANGELES · 1945

UNIVERSITY OF CALIFORNIA PRESS
BERKELEY AND LOS ANGELES
CALIFORNIA

◇

CAMBRIDGE UNIVERSITY PRESS
LONDON, ENGLAND

PRINTED IN THE UNITED STATES OF AMERICA
BY THE UNIVERSITY OF CALIFORNIA PRESS

GENERAL WŁADYSŁAW SIKORSKI

PRIME MINISTER AND COMMANDER IN CHIEF, 1939–1943

TO THE MEMORY OF

WŁADYSŁAW SIKORSKI

1881–1943

PATRIOT, SOLDIER, STATESMAN

The United Nations Series

THE UNITED NATIONS SERIES *is dedicated to the task of mutual understanding among the Allies and to the achievement of successful coöperation in this war and in the coming peace. In the measure that the United Nations understand one another they will march triumphantly through total victory to lasting peace.*

The University of California offers this series as a part of its contribution to the war effort of this state and nation and of the nations united in the greatest conflict known to history, and it heartily thanks the editors of the respective volumes and their collaborators for their devoted service in this cause and for their effort to present an honest, sincere, and objective appraisal of the United Nations.

ROBERT J. KERNER
General Editor

Editor's Preface

WHEN I BEGAN *to study history some forty years ago, the partition of Poland shocked me more than any other single episode about which I read. Not only was the cynicism of its authors disgusting, but, prior to 1914, there seemed no prospect that Poland would ever again exist as a free and united nation. Consequently, the reëstablishment of Poland in 1919 gave me great personal satisfaction, and I was much pleased when the University of California Press, in the autumn of 1942, invited me to serve as the editor of the present volume. The volume was planned and its contributors were selected by me in consultation with the General Editor. In the autumn of 1943 I entered upon some special work, and since then the editorial task has devolved largely on Professor Robert J. Kerner, who has devoted untiring energy to completing the book and seeing it through the press. It is only because of his generous coöperation that the publication of the volume on Poland has been assured.*

The Poland of 1919–1939 will provide a valuable "case study" for political scientists. After being partitioned and ruled by foreigners for more than a century, the Poland which emerged in 1919 faced a unique task—to integrate into a single homogeneous nation a people which had been living under these different political, economic, and social systems. That considerable progress was made is attested by the many chapters in this volume. On the other hand, twenty years did not allow sufficient time in which to complete so vast an undertaking, and Poland was unable to resist the onslaught of 1939.

In the perspective of twenty-five years, it now seems clear that the high hopes of 1919 were defeated by three circumstances. In the first place, Poland failed to devise a satisfactory foreign policy.

Lying between Germany and Russia, both its traditional enemies and both much stronger, Poland tried to play one off against the other but succeeded only in uniting them against itself. Secondly, the Polish Government failed to satisfy the national minorities which comprised nearly one-third of the population of the country. Thirdly, the democratic political regime established in 1921 was gradually replaced by a semidictatorship which, after the death of Marshal Piłsudski in 1935, proved inadequate to the needs of the country.

Just what form Poland will assume after the war is, of course, uncertain. But clearly the German menace will be destroyed and the alliance of Russia apparently will be available, if the Poles desire it. Furthermore, Poland will, in all probability, lose the greater part, if not all, of its minorities. Finally, all indications point to the determination of the Polish people to establish a genuinely democratic political, economic, and social system. This Poland will be smaller than the Poland of 1919–1939, but it will be more homogeneous and probably, therefore, both more stable and more secure. The friends of Poland are entitled to believe that, as the national anthem proclaims, "Poland is not lost forever!"

BERNADOTTE E. SCHMITT

Contents

PAGE

The Polish National Anthem, *Poland Is Not Lost Forever* xxi

Translated by S. DE JASTRZĘBSKI

PART ONE: LAND AND PEOPLE

CHAPTER I

Poland and Europe: Geographic Position . 3

By OSCAR HALECKI, Ph.D.

Professor of Eastern European History, Graduate School, Fordham University, 1944–; director and editor of *Bulletin,* Polish Institute of Arts and Sciences in America, 1942–; Professor of Eastern European History, University of Warsaw, 1919–, Dean, Faculty of Arts, 1920–1921, 1930–1931; expert, Polish Delegation to Peace Conference, Paris, 1919; member, League of Nations Secretariat, Geneva; first secretary, Committee on Intellectual Coöperation, 1921–1924, and chief of section on university relations, International Institute of Intellectual Coöperation, 1925–1926; assistant delegate of Poland, League of Nations Assembly, 1924; President, Polish University in Exile, Paris, 1939–1940; visiting professor to many American and Canadian universities, 1940–1942; fellow, Polish Academy (Cracow) and of section of Social Sciences and Letters (Warsaw and Lwów); member, Institut de France (Paris), Royal Historical Society (London); commander, Polonia Restituta, also Saint Gregory; officer, Legion of Honor (France); author of numerous publications, among them: *History of the Polish-Lithuanian Union* (1919–1920, 2 vols.); *Poland in the Time of the Jagiełłons* (1928); *Un Empereur de Byzance à Rome* (1930); *A History of Poland* (French edition, 1933, English edition, 1943); *The Crusade of Varna* (1943); co-editor, *Cambridge History of Poland* (1941); and contributor of many articles in learned foreign and American journals.

CHAPTER II PAGE

Anthropology of Poland: Prehistory and Race 10

By John Lawrence Angel, Ph.D.

Associate in Anatomy and Physical Anthropology at the Baugh Institute of Anatomy, Jefferson Medical College, Philadelphia; Instructor in Anthropology, University of California, Berkeley, 1941–1942, and University of Minnesota, Minneapolis, 1942–1943; Harvard Traveling Fellow (Greece), 1937–1939; author of "Geometric Athenians," *Hesperia,* Supplement II (1939); "Physical Types of Ancient Corinth," *American Journal of Archaeology,* v. 45 (1941); "Classical Olynthians," Appendix in D. M. Robinson's *Excavations at Olynthus,* Part XI, *Necrolynthia,* Baltimore (1942); "Ancient Cephalonians," *American Journal of Physical Anthropology,* N.S., v. 1 (1943); "A Racial Analysis of the Ancient Greeks," *American Journal of Physical Anthropology,* N.S., v. 2 (September, 1944).

PART TWO: HISTORICAL BACKGROUND

CHAPTER III

The Formation of the Polish State 31

By Frank T. Nowak, Ph.D.

Professor of History, Boston University; adjutant of Interallied Commission to Eastern Europe, 1919; awarded Congressional citation as Captain, U. S. Army and medal for work in American Relief Association (Poland), 1919; author of *Medieval Slavdom and the Rise of Russia* (1930); co-author, *Great Men and Women of Poland* (1941).

CHAPTER IV

Poland as a European Power 40

By Oscar Halecki

CHAPTER V

Partitioned Poland, 1795–1914 49

By Julia Swift Orvis, Ph.D.

Alice Freeman Palmer Professor of Modern European History, emeritus, Wellesley College; executive secretary, Society to Eliminate Economic Causes of War (1918–1923); author of *A Brief History of Poland* (1916).

CHAPTER VI PAGE

Rebirth of Poland, 1914–1923 70

By Bernadotte E. Schmitt, Ph.D., LL.D., Litt.D.

Andrew MacLeish Distinguished Service Professor of Modern History, University of Chicago; Guggenheim Fellow, 1927; Pulitzer Prize winner, 1931; Professor of Diplomatic History, Institut Universitaire de Hautes Etudes Internationales, Geneva, 1931–1932; member of Polish Institute of Arts and Sciences in America; author of *England and Germany, 1740–1914* (1916); *The Coming of the War 1914* (1931); *Triple Alliance and Triple Entente* (1934); *The Annexation of Bosnia* (1937); *From Versailles to Munich* (1939); *What Shall We Do with Germany?* (1943); "Europe, 1919–1939," *Encyclopedia Britannica* (1944); and of numerous articles in learned journals; co-author, *Czechoslovakia, Twenty Years of Independence* (1940) and *Cambridge History of Poland* (1941); editor of *Journal of Modern History* (Chicago, 1929–), *Cambridge Modern History*, new series (1935–), and of *Some Historians of Modern Europe* (1942).

PART THREE: POLITICAL DEVELOPMENT

CHAPTER VII

Constitutional Development of Poland . . 89

By Joseph C. Gidyński, J.D.

Engaged in research in sociology and law; judge, Poznań; member, Examining Committee, Bar Association, Poznań; member, Board of Editors, *Ruch Prawniczny, Ekonomiczny i Sociologiczny;* general secretary and member, Board of Polish Sociological Institute; author of *The Problem of Unjust Enrichment* (Poznań, 1926, in Polish) and of numerous legal and sociological articles in *Legal, Economic, and Sociological Movement* (University of Poznań), *Court Gazette* (Warsaw), and *Lawyers' Journal.*

CHAPTER VIII

Polish Political Parties 104

By Malbone W. Graham, Ph.D.

Professor of Political Science, University of California, Los Angeles; member, European Conference of American Professors of International Law and Relations, 1926; Lecturer, N. W. Harris Institute, University of Chicago, 1935; Faculty Research Lecturer, 1933; Commander, Order of Gediminas (Lithuania); Vigesimal Medal of Finland, 1939; member of numerous American learned societies; author of *New Governments of Central Europe* (1924); *The Controversy*

PAGE

between the United States and the Allied Governments Respecting Neutral Rights and Commerce, 1914–1917 (1924); *New Governments of Eastern Europe* (1927); *The Soviet Security System* (1929); *The League of Nations and the Recognition of States* (1933); *In Quest of a Law of Recognition* (1933); *The Soviet Union and Peace* (1935); *Diplomatic Recognition of the Border States:* Part I, *Finland* (1936), Part II, *Estonia* (1939), Part III, *Latvia* (1931); co-author, *Czechoslovakia, Twenty Years of Independence* (1940); editor, *The Renaissance of Asia* (1941); *Frontiers of the Future* (1941); *The Meaning of the War to the Americas* (1941); *Africa, the Near East and the War* (1943); *The Southwest Pacific and the War* (1944); and contributor of numerous articles in learned journals.

CHAPTER IX

Polish Politics, 1918–1939 123

By MALBONE W. GRAHAM

CHAPTER X

Minorities 148

By JOSEPH S. ROUCEK, Ph.D.

Chairman, Department of Political Science and Sociology, Hofstra College; Penfield Fellow, New York University; knight, Star of Rumania; knight, Order of the Crown, Jugoslavia; associate editor, *World Affairs Interpreter, New Europe;* author of *The Working of the Minorities System under the League of Nations* (Prague, 1928); *Contemporary Rumania and Her Problems* (1932); *The Politics of the Balkans* (1939); co-author of *Our Racial and National Minorities* (1937); *Contemporary World Politics* (1939); *The Sociological Foundations of Education* (1942); *The Twentieth Century Political Thought* (1944); and contributor of numerous articles in learned journals.

PART FOUR: ECONOMIC AND SOCIAL DEVELOPMENT

CHAPTER XI

Poland's Economy between Two World Wars 169

By HENRYK ZIELIŃSKI

Head, Economic Division, Office of Postwar Research Agency of the Polish Government; formerly in Polish diplomatic service; author of articles in Polish periodicals covering demographic, social, and economic problems, and of various pamphlets concerning population problems.

CHAPTER XII PAGE

Industry, Foreign Trade, and Communications 184

By LEOPOLD WELLISZ, B.L.

Economist; Vice-Chairman, Polish-American Chamber of Commerce; author of *Adam Mickiewicz, Juste et Caroline Olivier—Les amis romantiques* (Paris, 1933); *Felix Stanisław Jasiński, graveur* (Paris, 1934); *Foreign Capital in Poland* (London, 1938); *Une amitié Polono-Suisse* (Lausanne, 1942; "Problems of Post-war Reconstruction of Poland," *World Economics* (March, 1944).

CHAPTER XIII

Poland's Monetary and Financial Policy, 1919–1939 206

By ZYGMUNT KARPIŃSKI, D.R.E.

Manager, Bank Polski (Bank of Poland); to 1939 Chief of Foreign Exchange Control in Poland; author of numerous articles and pamphlets on economic and monetary problems in Polish journals.

CHAPTER XIV

Agricultural Reconstruction in Poland . . 219

By JERZY RADWAŃ

Director, Agrarian Department, Polish Government in London; Chief, Provincial Offices for Parcellation and Agricultural Improvements, Polish Ministry of Agriculture, 1921–1939; Director, Commassation Department, 1932–1939; author of series of articles on agrarian problems published in Poland and France.

CHAPTER XV

Social Progress in Poland, 1918–1939 . . . 232

By JAN K. KASPRZAK, Ph.D.

In Consulate General of Poland, New York; to 1932 Professor, Teachers' College, Warsaw; official, Polish Ministry of Foreign Affairs, 1932–1938; attaché, Polish Embassy, Ankara, 1938–1940; author of articles in Polish journals on political and social problems.

PART FIVE: CULTURAL DEVELOPMENT

CHAPTER XVI PAGE

Religious Life 247

By Oscar Halecki

CHAPTER XVII

Education 257

By Wojciech Świętosławski, D.Chem., Ph.D., (h.c.)

Research Fellow, Mellon Institute; Professor of Physical Chemistry, Warsaw Polytechnic, 1918–; Rector, 1928–1929; member, Polish Academy and since 1935 its Vice-President; Senator, 1935–; Minister of Education, 1935–; Director, Coal Department, Warsaw Chemical Research Institute; author, among many others, of *Chemia Fizyka* (1923–1934) 4 vols.; *Thermochemie* (1928–1934); *Ebulliometry* (1936), (later editions, 1937–); *Coke Formation Process and Physico-Chemical Properties of Coals* (1944); and of numerous scientific articles in various languages.

CHAPTER XVIII

Science and Scientific Institutions 274

By Wojciech Świętosławski

CHAPTER XIX

Polish Literature 284

By Manfred Kridl, Ph.D.

Visiting Professor of Slavic, Smith College; Professor of the History of Polish Literature, University of Wilno, 1932–1939; author of *Literatura Polska Wieku XIX* (1925–1931, 5 vols.); *Adam Mickiewicz et la France* (1930); and other works.

CHAPTER XX

The Fine Arts 311

By Irena Piotrowska, Ph.D.

Specialist in history of art; graduate studies, Ecole du Louvre, Paris; scholar on the National Cultural Fund for Studies in Italy, 1929–1930; delegate for United States to the Society for the Expansion of

PAGE

Polish Art Abroad (TOSSPO, Warsaw), 1938–1939; among other publications, author of *Christophorus Boguszewski and the Poznań School of Painting at the Beginning of the Seventeenth Century* (1928); *Problems of Contemporary Polish Painting* (1935); and articles in Polish and American art periodicals.

CHAPTER XXI

Music 323

By Felix Roderick Labuński

Composer and historian of music; student of Marczewski and Maliszewski (Warsaw) and of Dukas and Migot (Paris); Director, American Section, International Society for Contemporary Music (New York); President, Association of Young Polish Musicians, Paris, 1930–1934; Head, Department of Classical Music, Polish Radio, Inc. (Warsaw); Professor of Music, Marymount College, 1940–1941; lectured on history of music at numerous American institutions; composer of "Triptyque Champêtre" for orchestra (winner of Warsaw Competition, 1930); "The Birds" for soprano and orchestra; "Suite" for string orchestra (performed at Festival of I.S.C.M., San Francisco, 1942); "Polish Cantata" for soli, chorus, and orchestra; "God's Man" ballet; and numerous works for chamber music, piano, violin, and voice; contributor to *International Cyclopedia of Music and Musicians* (1939); *Great Modern Composers* (1941); and to numerous leading foreign and American journals devoted to music.

CHAPTER XXII

The Polish National Spirit 328

By Edmund Zawacki, Ph.D.

Head, Department of Polish, University of Wisconsin.

PART SIX: POLISH-AMERICAN RELATIONS

CHAPTER XXIII

Polish-American Cultural Relationships . . 347

By Stephen P. Mizwa, A.M., LL.D.

Secretary and Executive Director, Kościuszko Foundation; Assistant Professor of Economics, Drake University, 1921–1924; President, Alliance College, 1930–1932; author of *Nicholas Copernicus, 1543–1943* (1943); and editor of *Great Men and Women of Poland* (1941), and of *Nicholas Copernicus: A Tribute of Nations* (1944).

CHAPTER XXIV PAGE

Polish-American Political and Economic Relations 365

By ELDON R. BURKE, Ph.D.

Research Adviser for the Brethren Service Committee; Associate Professor, Ball State Teachers College, 1937– (on leave); author of *The Polish Policy of the Central Powers During the World War* (Doctoral dissertation).

PART SEVEN: FOREIGN RELATIONS

CHAPTER XXV

Foreign Relations 377

By S. HARRISON THOMSON, Ph.D., Litt.D.

Professor of Medieval History, University of Colorado; Traveling Fellow, American Council of Learned Societies, 1933–1935; Czechoslovak State Prize, 1944; member, Polish Institute of Arts and Sciences; edited, *Mag. Johannis Hus Tractatus Responsivus* (1927); and *Johannis Wyclif Summa de Ente* (1930); editor of *Progress of Medieval Studies in the United States and Canada* (1936–), *Journal of Central European Affairs* (1940–), and of *Medievalia et Humanistica* (1942–); author of *The Writings of Robert Grosseteste, Bishop of Lincoln 1235–1253* (1940); *Czechoslovakia in European History* (1943); and of articles in *Medium Aevum, English Historical Review, Isis, Revue Bénédictine*, etc.; co-author of *Czechoslovakia, Twenty Years of Independence* (1940); and *Contemporary Europe* (1941).

PART EIGHT: SECOND WORLD WAR AND AFTER

CHAPTER XXVI

Poland and the War 427

By STANISŁAW STRZETELSKI

Director in Polish Ministry of Information, France, 1939–1940; counselor, Polish Ministry of Foreign Affairs, 1919; founder and editor of the daily *Wieczór Warszawski* and the weekly *Kronika Polski i Świata;* Deputy in Parliament, representing Warsaw County as member of the National Party in the Opposition.

PAGE

Epilogue 457

By Robert J. Kerner, Ph.D., LL.D., Litt.D.

Sather Professor of History, University of California, Berkeley; general editor, The United Nations Series; American contributing editor, *The Slavonic Review* (London), 1924–1940; member, Board of Directors, Polish Institute of Arts and Sciences in America; member, Board of Directors, Russian Economic Institute; foreign member, Royal Bohemian Society of Letters and Sciences (Prague); foreign member, Šafařík Learned Society (Bratislava); corresponding member, Rumanian Academy; awarded Czechoslovak State Prize for Literature (1941); commander, Order of the White Lion (Czechoslovakia); officer, Order of the Star (Rumania); member, Expert Staff, Colonel House Inquiry and American Commission to Negotiate Peace, Paris, 1917–1919; Faculty Research Lecturer, 1943; author of *Slavic Europe* (1918); *Social Sciences in the Balkans and Turkey* (1930); *Bohemia in the Eighteenth Century* (1932); (with Harry N. Howard) *The Balkan Conferences and the Balkan Entente* (1936); *Northeastern Asia* (1939, 2 vols.); editor and co-author, *Czechoslovakia, Twenty Years of Independence* (1940); author of *The Urge to the Sea* (1942); *The Russian Adventure* (1943); and of numerous articles in learned journals.

BIBLIOGRAPHY

A Selected Bibliography 467

INDEX

Index 479

List of Illustrations

FACING PAGE

General Władysław Sikorski, Prime Minister and Commander in Chief, 1939–1943 iii

Ignacy Jan Paderewski, Prime Minister, 1919 74

Marshal Józef Piłsudski 82

Władysław Raczkiewicz, President of the Republic of Poland, 1939– 102

Bank of National Economy, Warsaw 206

Nativity at Łowicz 250

Public School in Królewska Huta 258

Wooden Heads 326

Head of Old Mountaineer 342

Wooden Chapel 438

Stanisław Mikołajczyk, Prime Minister, 1943–1944 454

MAPS

PAGE

Poland, 1919–1939 5

Dismemberment of Poland Prior to 1918 170

Frontiers of Poland 459

POLISH NATIONAL ANTHEM*

Poland Is Not Lost Forever

Poland is not lost forever,
While our lives remain,
What the foe by force did sever,
Force shall soon regain!

March! March! Dombrowski,
From fair Italia's plain,
Under thee, our native land,
We shall soon greet again!
Under thee, our native land,
We shall soon greet again!

Jeszcze Polska nie zginęła,
Póki my żyjemy;
Co nam obca prze moc wzięła,
Mocą odbierzemy.
Marsz, marsz, Dąbrowski,
Z ziemi Włoskiéj do Polskiej!
Za twoim przewodem
Złączym się z narodem!

Translated by S. DE JASTRZEBSKI

---

* James Duff Brown (and Alfred Moffat), *Characteristic Songs and Dances of all Nations* [words by Wybitski; tune probably by Ogeński, 1765–1835], (London, Bayley and Ferguson, 1901), p. 153.

Part One

LAND AND PEOPLE

CHAPTER I

Poland and Europe: Geographical Position

BY OSCAR HALECKI

ANY POLITICAL MAP of Europe between the tenth century and the present time, except for the period from 1795 to 1918, shows a large and independent country called Poland, lying east of Germany, which it separates from Russia. This country does not always occupy the same place on the map. Early losses in the west have been compensated since the fourteenth century by an expansion in the east and this, in turn, was considerably reduced when Poland recovered its independence after the First World War. Always, however, the question rises, to which part of the European Continent does Poland belong? The question is presented in two different forms: sometimes, whether Poland belongs to central or to eastern Europe; but usually, whether Poland is a part of western or eastern Europe.

In either form that initial question is misleading. If Europe were divided into two sections only, opposing the west to the east, two different points of view would have to be distinguished. Geographically Poland belongs rather to the eastern part and its racial origin seems to confirm such an opinion, because very frequently eastern Europe is more or less identified with the Slavic world, whereas western Europe is considered as a community of Romance and Germanic nations. But, in spite of any territorial or ethnographic considerations, Poland is so closely connected through its culture with the Latin West that such a simplified classification proves to be entirely wrong.

The limits between western and eastern Europe being always highly controversial, a third geographical unit called central Europe is frequently distinguished between them. But its boundaries, especially in the east, are still harder to determine; and as undoubtedly Germany is the main part of central Europe, just as Russia is the main part of eastern Europe, there often appears a tendency to identify central Europe with Germany and eastern Europe with Russia, a tendency which was greatly favored by the political situation in the century before 1914. This resulted in a total neglect not only of Poland, but of all the other nations between those two Great Powers.

In order to understand the real position of these in-between nations, and especially of Poland which is the largest among them and occupies a central place—a key position, as has often been pointed out—not merely two or three but four constituent parts of the European Continent must be distinguished. Their names, necessarily artificial and relative, are irrelevant; what really matters is the fact that proceeding from west to east, the four great countries of France, Germany, Poland, and Russia are met; these form four distinct territorial units and therefore are indispensable pillars of any continental order or equilibrium.

As far as Poland is concerned, modern geographical research has abandoned the idea that it was something like a transition between Germany and Russia and has clearly demonstrated that it ought to be considered as an independent whole, stretching from the Baltic to the Carpathians. Its geographical unity has been shaped by intimate connections among the river basins on its territory. For that very reason the problem of its access to the sea has always been of outstanding importance. A country whose geographical backbone has always been the basin of the Vistula, could not possibly develop normally without possessing the mouth of at least that river with the adjacent shore, inhabited since time immemorial by a population of Polish stock. And as a matter of fact, only a temporary foreign conquest lasting from 1308 to 1454, and much later the First Partition of Poland (1772), deprived it of such an access to the Baltic. At an earlier period that access had even included the mouth of the Oder and, at the time of Poland's greatest power, reached as far as the Gulf of Riga, whereas its direct and secure access to the Black Sea did not last more than a few decades in the fifteenth century.

Although the sea and the Carpathian Mountains were Poland's

natural frontiers in the north and the south respectively, it never had and for obvious geographical reasons cannot have any natural frontier either in the west or in the east. In the great European

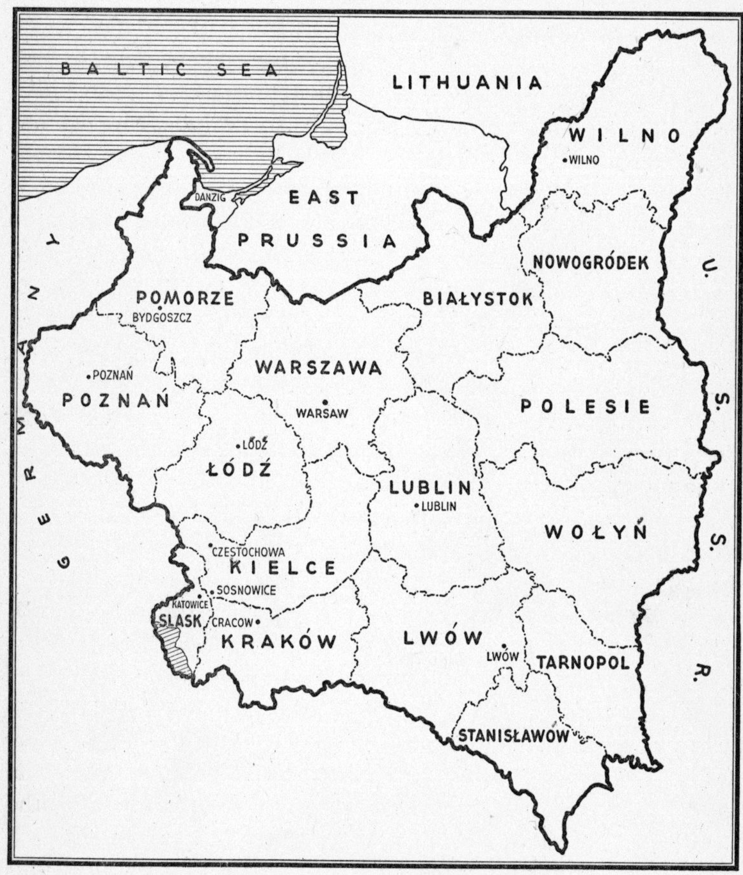

POLAND, 1919–1939

Shaded area acquired from Czechoslovakia in the Munich Crisis, 1938

plain where Poland is located, even the largest rivers are quite inadequate to serve as boundaries, and create ties rather than limits between the lands on both sides. Thus it has become commonplace to emphasize the fact that these long, open frontiers have been a permanent source of weakness for Poland. There is of course a great deal of truth in such statements, but still they are overstatements involving a dangerous geographical determinism—dangerous, because of the possible conclusion that in such a position no state could have any chance of maintaining its independence. Yet, in spite of frontiers so difficult to defend, Poland had existed as an independent state for more than eight hundred years before the partitions, and for centuries had played the part of a great power; and if contemporary Poland after twenty years of independence has been overrun by its neighbors, it only shared the fate of several other countries, including those which had strong natural boundaries.

Moreover, those "indefensible" frontiers in many instances have proved to be unexpectedly persistent. Such is, for instance, the case of the main sector of Poland's western frontier, which did not suffer the slightest change from the middle of the fourteenth century to the partitions at the end of the eighteenth, and reappeared without essential modifications in 1919. Even the so-called "corridor" had existed, broader than after 1919, from 1466 to 1772. In the east where the situation was entirely modified by the Polish-Lithuanian Union of 1386, there had been only a few territorial changes before the middle of the fourteenth century. The new frontier of 1386 lasted without substantial changes until 1500, and none occurred during the last century before the partitions. What proved decisive was not so much the geographical position of Poland, as the political situation without and Poland's strength within.

It might seem that Poland always has had the same neighbors—the Germans in the west and the Russians in the east, both hostile. Such was not true. First of all, in prehistoric times, i.e., before the middle of the tenth century, the western neighbors of the Poles were closely related Slavic tribes, which separated them from the Germans; its eastern neighbors were other Slavic tribes, which had not yet been united by the Varangians into a political unit called Russia. Therefore, the Poles could live quietly for centuries while creating their national state which, when mentioned for the first time, already was a strong political entity developed under favorable conditions of security. It is true that these conditions changed as early as the second half of the tenth century with the first German and the first Russian invasion. The former took place in 963, one year after the founding of the Holy Roman Empire of the German nation, and as long as that Empire remained powerful its eastern policy was a grave danger to Poland. But even then, despite its unfavorable frontiers, Poland had defended its independence more successfully than had Bohemia with its natural boundaries; and since the breakdown of the unity of the Empire, the individual German states were no real threat, until one of them, the nearest neighbor, created in the eighteenth century the imperialistic military power of Prussia. In the east, the unity of the old Kievan Russia did not last long enough to endanger Poland seriously; and it took many centuries before Muscovy, transformed into the gigantic Russian Empire, could make attempts at Poland's destruction in coöperation with its western partner.

In the meantime, Poland found itself face to face with other dangers, coming from different sides, which were not connected with the open frontiers either in the west or in the east. For more than two hundred years the Teutonic Order, having created a German colony on the Baltic, menaced Poland from the north. This colony, the present East Prussia, not only narrowed down and temporarily even cut off Poland's access to the sea, but by uniting with the Mark of Brandenburg gave rise to modern Prussia, which encircled Polish territory from two sides. Moreover, not to mention the Swedish invasions from the other side of the Baltic, the Turkish danger which during more than two hundred years had handicapped Poland's policy came from the south; and the Tartar invasions from the southeast molested Poland even in times of its greatest power, cutting it off from the Black Sea.

These dangers were much more the consequence of historical events in Poland's neighborhood than of its geographical position. However, it was because of its geographical position between central and eastern Europe that Poland had to bear the heavy burden of protecting the central and western parts of the Continent against the chronic onslaught of the European and Asiatic East; at the same time, its immediate western neighbors, hostile as they were, separated Poland from its natural allies in the extreme western part of Europe. Moreover, Europe as a whole has never succeeded, up to the present, in creating an international order guaranteeing the security of any nation, regardless of its geographical location. The most serious attempt made in this direction since the Middle Ages, the settlement of 1919, based upon the League of Nations and the idea of collective security, was therefore of particular interest to Poland and its final failure particularly harmful to that country.

Consequently, Poland, past and present, had to look for possibilities of regional coöperation with other countries that were in a similar geographical position. The most striking example was the case of the old Grand Duchy of Lithuania. This state originally, just as the Lithuania of today, occupied only a small section of the European plain in the northeastern part of Poland. In the fourteenth century it had expanded over almost all the White-Russian and Ukrainian lands, the former territory of the Kievan state which was developing in an entirely different way from later Muscovite Great Russia. Common defense was the natural basis of Poland's union with the Grand Duchy of Lithuania which, like itself, reached from a narrow sector of the Baltic shore to the steppes near the Black Sea, without any natural frontiers either in the west or in the east.

The Polish-Lithuanian Union, which lasted from 1386 to the partitions four hundred years later, had created a commonwealth strong enough to overcome all the difficulties resulting from the unfavorable geographical position of both its constituent parts. But this union also brought about a fundamental difference between the purely ethnographic Poland of the earlier Middle Ages, in the basins of the Oder and the Vistula, and the historical Poland, including not only the basins of the Niemen and the Dniester, but reaching as far as the Dvina and the Dnieper, and sometimes even beyond these rivers.

In its frontiers of 1939, although larger than the purely Polish ethnographical territory, Poland was considerably smaller than the old Republic before the First Partition of 1772, having only 150,000 instead of almost 300,000 square miles. Nevertheless, it was one of the largest states in Europe, the sixth in size after Russia, Germany, France, Spain and Sweden. With more than thirty-five million inhabitants, it was also the sixth European state in population, coming after Russia, Germany, Great Britain, Italy, and France.

Having again a natural frontier in the south, the Carpathian Mountains, and an access to the Baltic Sea in the north (although much narrower than before the partitions), Poland found itself again between its two old neighbors: Germany, more closely united than ever before, and Russia, which as the Union of Soviet Socialist Republics included most of White Russia and the Ukraine. But the reborn Polish Republic had common frontiers also with four smaller states which, like itself, had been reconstituted after the First World War—Czechoslovakia and Rumania in the south, Lithuania and Latvia in the north. And in spite of territorial controversies with two of them, there was an obvious community of interest between Poland and all these countries located in the same geographical region of Europe.

CHAPTER II

Anthropology of Poland: Prehistory and Race

BY JOHN LAWRENCE ANGEL

POLAND MOST CONVENIENTLY may be divided into a number of north-to-south ecologic zones, funneling westward down from the sprawling river-netted and forested Russian plateau into the fertile sandy loam of the plains of Prussia, the Netherlands, and southeastern England—plains now largely flooded by the southern third of the North Sea, though lying too high for the Baltic. The Polish plains make up the most important ecologic zone of Poland, and their north-to-south zoning is emphasized by the east-west direction of moraines and river valleys from the Scandinavian glaciers of the last glaciation. South of these plains is a range of crystalline heights stretching southeast from the St. Croix Mountains near Kielce, west of the Vistula, to the plateau of Podolia and the Black Earth country between the southern Bug and Dniester rivers. South of this also are the loess plains of Galicia, centered on the triangle outlined by the upper Vistula and San rivers, stretching west into Upper Silesia and southeast into the Ukraine. And the final zones are the foothills and crests of the Carpathians, Tatras, and Beskids stretching from southeast to northwest and continued by the Sudetens after a loess-plain gap.

Environment.—Three more major geographical features influence the distribution and movement of cultures and races in Poland, modifying the smooth pattern of east-west population movements and north-south distribution zones which the geography outlined above implies. On the east the Pripet marshes and woods channel immigrations into the southeast from the Black Earth and the Ukraine, and into the northeast from the forest belt of Russia and the east Baltic regions. The March-Upper Oder and Waag-Vistula valleys allow immigration from Moravia-Bohemia and the Danube to the south of Poland, in addition to the broad routes of movement from Brandenburg or Silesia along the Oder, Warta, and Notec valleys to the Vistula. The route from the south fits with those south-north routes of the Warta, Vistula, and Bug rivers which established themselves during the retreat of the Würm glaciers, cutting across north-south zoning and contributing to a diagonality of migrations across the Polish sector of the north European plain. Thus, although the basic cultural and racial distribution in Poland is a north-south zoning, the irregularities just mentioned at many periods transform the actual distribution into a checkerboard.

During the height of the first phase of the last, or Würm, glaciation, the climatic zoning which was revealed by a study of insect and larger fauna was very marked. The southern plain, bare of the ice sheet, was a tundra zone succeeded by a narrow belt of loess steppe to the south, by a thin line of forest at the foot of the Carpathians, and by Alpine meadows and scrub leading to the frosty heights of the mountains. The climate was primarily continental. During the long winter, steppe animals and the men who hunted them took refuge in the Carpathian foothill valleys from the quiet, windless cold of snow-covered steppe and tundra zones. In spring unstable west winds brought warm rains which helped the melting snow to feed the grass of luxuriant prairies now traversed by great herds of grazing bison, horse, and mammoth—herds forced southward up into the rich Alpine meadows or into Moravia by the dry dust storms which were swept steadily southward by north winds at the height of summer. Then, in early winter, after a cool autumn, ocean winds again brought rain, followed by snow, at which time the low-pressure area of the ice sheet spread out over Poland.

After the third (Pomeranian) advance between about 18,000 and 15,000 B.C., the Würm glaciers receded in irregular and slow stages and the Polish climate became warmer and less continental. Between 8500 and and 7500 B.C. a rapid rise in temperature occurred, and birch and pine forests marched down from the southern foothills and mountains into the plains. During the rapid rise of land coincident with removal of the basins which had been cut by glaciers north of Poland, the Baltic formed the Ancylus Lake; the

North Sea was still north of Dogger Bank, and a warm and dry climate was typical, with strong winds which heaped the glacial sands of the central and northern Polish plains into shifting and treeless dunes. This Boreal climate lasted from immediately before the final retreat of the glaciers (Ragunda: 6800 B.C.) to about 5600 B.C. at which time the eustatic rise in sea level overran the Skagerrak and the Cattegat to begin the high levels of the Litorina Sea in the Baltic. The North Sea flooded the Thames-Rhine valley, and deciduous trees became dominant over pines in forests spread thickly over the plains. With high sea levels and temperature this was the Atlantic phase of wet, oceanic climate for all northern Europe, with temperatures considerably higher than at the present time, with moist, west winds, and with a newly channeled Gulf Stream promoting the spread of deciduous forest and the formation of peaty soil over the sand dunes.

By 2000 B.C. the climate had become cooler and drier, with irregularly "normal" sea levels in the Baltic, reduction of forests and of marshland, and resumption of dune formation during the sub-Boreal period. A wetter, more oceanic climate labeled sub-Atlantic lasted irregularly from soon after 1000 B.C. to 500 A.D. with the formation of another soil layer over the dunes which had been covered again by shifting sands blown up during the medieval dry phase. The present climate of Poland is definitely more maritime than that of the prairies of the Ukraine.

Culture.—The history of man's development in the north European plain may be divided into three economic phases, each concluding with a relatively rapid increase in population at the climax of an accelerating cycle of change. (1) During the bulk of the Pleistocene period a slowly evolving food-gathering economy reached its climax, at the end of the Würm glaciation, in a communal hunting culture of considerable achievement and of material and ethnic complexity, with a population density greater than that of any surviving hunting group. (2) After the ultimate introduction of peasant agriculture from the Near East in the early third millennium B.C., the basic farming economy was enriched by importation of specialized metalworking techniques, with a consequent reflected climax in trade, and a rise in pastoral warfare, with great ethnic movements at the beginning and the end of the phase, and with a population perhaps one-fifth its present density. (3) After the fall of the Roman Empire the center of civilization began its shift northwestward and, during the great spread and feudalizing of the Slavic-speaking peoples, the increase of population in Poland as well as in western Europe had gradually accelerated through the discovery and use of an increasing number of new metallurgical techniques culminating in the present industrial and martial civilization of the Europeans.

It is often assumed that, during the first two interglacial periods of the Pleistocene, food gatherers who used implements made predominantly from flakes rather than from cores of flint inhabited the north European plain. However, positive traces of them have been found only at the western end of the plain where they contrast with the northernmost extension of Eurafrican "core industries" which derived ultimately from the Near East.

The earliest definite evidence for Paleolithic man in Poland comes from the lowest levels of caves near Cracow (Kraków) and Skaryce in Galicia, where a Micoquian "core" industry suggests a date at the close of the last interglacial period and an ethnic movement from western Europe. This is followed by thick Mousterian strata in other caves in the general Cracow region. The Mousterian strata here spans the first maximum of the Würm glaciation, accompanied by a consistent combination of tundra and woodland fauna, which ended in a typical late Mousterian development with small, flatly flaked hand axes as well as with flaked tools with "stepped" retouch of edges. This late Mousterian presumably overlaps the Chatelperronian (Early Aurignacian) of western Europe, and at some Polish sites a mixture of Upper Paleolithic artifacts with Mousterian is suggested.

The Upper Paleolithic is distinguished from the earlier hand-ax and flake industries by its almost exclusive use of long, smoothly struck blades of flint both for knives and projectile points, and the development of a number of special "gravers" to work wood or bone into tools. The Upper Paleolithic of Poland occurs in open loess sites near Cracow and near Rovno (Równe) in the Volhynian as well as in the Galician caves, and is sufficiently attached to the East Gravettian (Upper Aurignacian) marked by La Gravette and tanged points so that a migration from south Russia is indicated.

As in the west European Aurignacian-Gravettian-Magdalenian sequence, a Solutrean interlude is noted from the occurrence in both cave and loess sites of bifacially flaked, leaf-shaped points, some of which might have been evolved locally from modification of Mousterian techniques. This occurs at the height of the second Würm advance, accompanied by a cold-steppe fauna, and is followed during the third Würm advance by an evolved Gravettian culture, with increasing use of bone and a definite western, Magdalenian influence shown in an arrow straightener and in other engraved bone objects of a geometric style not typically western. These late Gravettian sites occur in the dune country between the Vistula and Pilica rivers, and indicate the start of the northward movement of Paleolithic survivors which occurred with the retreat of the ice.

Like the animals on which they lived, the Gravettian hunters must have migrated seasonally from loess steppes to Carpathian foothills, living alternately in open camps and at the edges of caves. Possibly they may also have used earth lodges like those of their Russian and Moravian contemporaries. They lived largely on the flesh of the mammoth, bison, antelope, and horse as well as on that of the woolly rhinoceros, cave bear, and reindeer which had been killed with projectiles perhaps shot from the bow, or killed by the spear, or even by being trapped or corralled in numbers great enough to suggest the coöperation of an entire community. In general, life must have been comparable with that of the Plains Indians of the North American grass-covered prairies before the introduction of the horse.

This parasitism on herbivores was relentlessly reduced and was ended by the northward march of forests, when the first reindeer, and then elk, red deer, and boar were the only big game available, and the hunters of Galicia moved north to the area of the Polish dunes. They used some microliths, and flint-blade tools similar to those of the Gravettian, but which often had flat, Solutrean-like flaking especially around the tang of an arrowpoint. This culture is called Swiderian, after the type site of Swidry on the middle Vistula, and stretches southeast into the Ukraine, northeast into Lithuania, and west into Brandenburg almost into contact with a parallel development there. This happened during the pre-Boreal period, and the Swiderian populations lasted certainly into Boreal times, when intruding hunters enter Poland from the southwest to compete successfully for occupancy of the treeless dunes and sandy areas of the now increasingly forested Polish plains. There were the Tardenoisian hunters who introduced into Europe the North African (or Spanish) technique of making composite tools and weapons from wood or bone holders set with rows of sharp flint chips, slivers, or microliths—the latter small, geometric flints, made in the typical Tardenoisian by breaking a long flint blade into sections of trapezoid shape. In Boreal times Tardenoisian hunters spread sparsely into Poland, increasing during Atlantic times, but always inhabiting only sandy areas where they could camp in their small and sunken huts, clear of the surrounding forests. Avoiding Galician loess the Tardenoisian hunters spread from Upper Silesia and the Kielce region east of Volhynia (Wołyń) and north to the Baltic shores into contact with the great forest and fen culture of the north European plain—the Maglemosean.

The Maglemosean culture was created by those hunters of the Hamburgian (late Gravettian) of north Germany who, having developed a tanged-point and almost Microlithic culture like the Swiderian (Ahrensburg), invented first the antler (Lyngby) and then the flint-and-antler pick and ax, and learned also some Microlithic techniques from the Tardenoisians. They lived in summertime in camps scattered across the great stretch of lowland and fenland which extended from Estonia via southern Scandinavia and Dogger Bank to eastern England, and ranged south only as far as the edge of the plain. Though they could cut enough trees to make boats and floors for marsh dwelling, no stone or antler (or even bronze) axes really were adequate to use for felling trees in the forests. Maglemosean fishermen and fowlers netted fish in the Polish rivers along the south shore of the Ancylus Lake (Baltic), speared pike and other fish with bone spear points equipped with notches, barbs, flint microlith insets, curved leister prongs, or even barbed harpoon heads, and assisted by their domestic dogs, shot or trapped birds and deer with spears and sometimes with arrows. The Maglemoseans decorated their bone objects with geometric patterns, perhaps derived from the Magdalenian bone decoration already noted in the late Gravettian of the Polish dune country. Their domination of north Poland vanished when the Maglemosean was split into pieces by the flooding of the North Sea and the now salty Litorina Sea (Baltic) during the Atlantic period. And scattered flint axes, picks, and coarse blades have been found in the Warta-Pilica region, and in northeast Poland and Volhynia in contact with similar but as yet ill-defined Russian industries.

About 2800 B.C., during the anticlimax for the Tardenoisian and post-Maglemosean hunting peoples of Poland, the first peasants began to push into the loess country of Galicia. One group brought a seminomadic hoe-farming technique, brought emmer, barley, oats, small herds of cattle, sheep, and pigs, built villages of pit dwellings and wattle, daub barns rectangular in shape; the group made brown or grey pottery, bowls often hemispherical in shape, decorated with incised meandering ribbons or zigzags, or with stabbed or pricked lines. This group of peasants intruded from Moravia, and carried their typical Danubian culture eastward even beyond the upper triangle of the Vistula-San rivers to the border of the southeastern Galician Black Earth region where, some time later, farmers with the more advanced Tripolye culture intruded from the Ukraine.

These farmers of the Tripolye culture grew wheat, barley, millet, raised pigs, sheep and, above all, cattle. They lived in rectangular as well as in oval dwellings, some of which had sunken floors. They painted polychrome pottery with swirling bands of brilliant color, and they began to use both copper and silver. Their introduction of wheat, large herds of cattle, and an agricultural system whose inferred use of manure and fallowing allowed permanent settlement in one place was a striking advance, though it may not have replaced at once the simpler Danubian economy. At the end of the third millennium the Tripolye people, in turn, were replaced by other more aggressive and pastoral southeastern invaders. Meanwhile, probably before the middle of the third millennium, the Danubians had pushed northward from Sandomierz down the Vistula. This broke up the south-north zoning of peasants, Mesolithic hunters, and remnants of Paleolithic fishermen, and by the time the Danubians reached the Baltic coast and the rich Pomeranian soil, they were actively absorbing the Tardenoisian hunters, whereas their relatives on the Oder were passing on the essentials of farming to the Paleolithic survivors of southern Scandinavia.

By this time, also, the forest hunters of central Russia not only had begun to use domestic animals and polished stone tools, but also were making pottery—innovations probably brought from a north Caucasian source. These hunters, who were known by their use of a distinctive type of round-bottomed pot decorated with pits and impressions of comb teeth, had pushed down into eastern Poland as far as the northern Bug and even the Vistula, and they were not the least important of the four ethnic elements in Mesolithic Poland: Tardenoisian hunters, Comb-pottery hunters, Tripolye farmers, and unifying Danubian peasants.

By the end of the Atlantic period a new group of invaders had spread rapidly across Poland from south Russia and the north Caucasus to Denmark and later to Thuringia. Many separate groups brought individual versions of a culture which crystallized differently in various regions of northern Europe; this difference is found in the pottery marked with cord impressions on pots of globular amphora, beaker, and flask shapes. But battle-axes of stone (derived from antler axes as well as from Mesopotamian copper prototypes), mound burial, and the use of flint substitutes for copper daggers and axes also characterized the Corded-ware people who appear to have been beef-eaters rather than peasants.

Before the end of the third millennium, groups of invaders from the Scandinavian northern (Megalithic) cultures were pushing south and mixing with and transforming the Danubian peasantry of central Europe and western Poland (sometimes called Danordic cultures). And the Corded-ware invasion modified the culture of these northern tribes even before their movement south was completed. Some time after the start of the second millennium B.C. (sub-Boreal climate) a scattering of the Bell-Beaker people, traders, archers, copper-users, and perhaps prospectors for copper, entered Galicia from Bohemia. And from then on an immense ethnic complexity characterized Poland which had been made more habitable because of climatic reduction of the forests.

In west Poland various versions of the northern and Danordic cultures developed. In Pomerania the stone-outlined Kujavian graves, mounded and rich in amber, seem to mark a movement from the stone-cist grave region of Jutland where Corded, Megalithic, and Mesolithic traditions were fusing. In Poland, a stone-cist mode of burial marked a northern culture stretching from the upper Bug down to east Galicia, and from the Sandomierz-Kielce region the battle-ax users of the great Polish Złota culture spread their unifying influence. This was the chief focus of development of the Corded-ware invaders of Poland, and after the Mesolithic survivals and the Danubian peasants, the Złota people made the greatest ethnic contribution to the population of later Poland.

Out of this welter of ethnic complexity, after 1800 B.C., the Aunjetitz Bronze Age developed in Bohemia and Moravia, crystallizing diverse cultural traditions into the first effective unity in Europe, inspired by an indirect Near-Eastern influence and by the Slovakian-Bohemian metal trade. It is marked by the use of pins with pierced heads, triangular daggers, and flanged celts of bronze; the mining operations and trade which were carried out under its aegis indicate increased population and coöperation between villages and tribes. Partly through the nascent amber trade, Saxo-Thuringia and Silesia were included in the Aunjetitz culture; and the Early Bronze culture of west Poland, extending only from the Warta to Danzig, is a branch of the Aunjetitz.

Not earlier than the middle of the second millennium the new Lausitz culture was developed locally in the area between the Elbe and Vistula (though centered on Lusatia), and developed through three major phases in Poland: (1) a pre-Lausitz phase limited to southwest Poland, with the beginning of cremation, and scattered exports to east Poland Corded-ware peoples; (2) an Early-Lausitz phase more widely spread northward and eastward, marked by a polished dark pottery with angular profile and wart decoration, urnfields of biconical-shaped urns containing ashes of the dead, more bronze, and with several local inhuming groups in the Warta-Vistula region, in Galicia, the Ukraine, and Volhynia; (3) a Late-Lausitz phase with six local groups outside the typical one in southwest Poland and Galicia, with a richer material culture, with socketed celts, swords, local survivals in east Poland, and a date in the first half of the first millennium B.C. The long-continuing Lausitz Bronze Age in west and central Poland is a period of prosperous peasants living in villages of gabled houses built sometimes of the megaron type, of itinerant peddlers, and of gradual assimilation of the pastoralists and battle-ax people of east Poland. The careful rite of cremation is new; and it is possible that at the end the scratch-plough period may have been introduced, starting an agricultural revolution. But neither of these practices indicates an immigrant people, and this is a period of relatively peaceful development until the changes of the Late-Lausitz phase as indicated by an introduction of the slashing sword and the earth ramparts around the villages.

The "revolution" just suggested continued throughout the Iron Age, and was linked with change to a wetter climate, population pressure, improved metallurgical methods and knowledge, and the secondary expansions of the various major Indo-European-speaking groups, a millennium or more after their primary settlement in Europe. The Early Iron Age of Poland was divided into three major provinces: a southern and western Hallstatt-derived culture, northern and western local cultures, and an east Galician variant. The first of these is a slightly modified continuation of Lausitz with more inhumations than cremations (Ivanovič culture), with a west-Polish pottery decorated with polychrome painting, incrustation, and graphite polishing of Bohemian-Silesian-Hallstatt origin. The second includes the face-urn complex of the Baltic coastland and the Vistula, in which long-necked ash urns with modeled faces are crowded together in a stone cist of northern derivation, and with ornaments of northern type, sometimes covered with a tumulus; the analogous bell-grave complex of northwest Poland, in which a bell urn covers the single ash urn inside a stone covering, may also be included here.

The third culture is that of southeast Poland where inhumation graves sometimes with a stone covering, continued the local Lausitz culture, modified by strong Scythian Iron-Age influence. The Scythian tumulus graves themselves are concentrated around Tarnopol, and the two groups show a certain amount of blending. All of these cultures began not long before 500 B.C., and they all reflect LaTène influences in the scattered use of LaTène fibulae, and the increased use of iron for tools and weapons. Then, just before 100 B.C., Late LaTène metalwork, Celtic long swords, and pottery were imported in large quantity, coming from the west in order to avoid the backwater of Upper Silesia-West Galicia. Iron was used for fibulae, neckrings and torques, beltplates, and ploughshares, as well as for lanceheads, shieldbosses, and swords. Burial is by cremation, with the unsegregated ashes and pyre waste swept into the pit together. All this is particularly true for north Poland where one culture group is sometimes linked with the Burgundians. In the south and east older Lausitz rites continue and the LaTène influence is less Germanized. Later, during the Roman Empire period, LaTène imports are replaced by Roman coins, glassware, bronze vessels, fibulae, jewelry, and *terra sigillata* provincial Roman pottery.

During the last half of the second century A.D. the Goths moved in two groups southeast from the lower Vistula region, where they had replaced the Burgundians, into Dacia and into southern Russia, coming into close contact with civilizing Byzantine Greek influences; during the third and fourth centuries the Goths included the Slavs in their empire. Efficient plough agriculture was usual by now, as was also petty warfare; horse riding and wheeled vehicles had been introduced plausibly just before the Iron Age began. Peasants and peddlers continue, and under the tutelage of the "Byzantine" Goths to the southeast, the aristocracy of Poland (perhaps traceable from the battle-ax people) was militarized, stock raising was improved, and a medieval level of culture was reached by the fifth century A.D., immediately before the Slavic expansion.

Peoples.—The ethnic elements in any nation are ordinarily defined by language rather than by other cultural criteria, probably because language comes nearer to expressing the common attitudes and conventions of a people than do pottery types, for instance. On linguistic and historical evidence, L. Niederle has defined the territory controlled by the Slavs shortly before the time of Christ as including: the middle Dnieper, Pripet River and southern marshes, upper valleys of Black Sea rivers west of this, upper and middle Vistula north from the West Beskids with extensions to the upper Warta. Presumably the ancestral Poles would be in the western part of this range. Linguistic paleontology hints that relations of Slavic speakers with Baltic, Scythian, Celtic, and Germanic speakers are ancient. Tacitus places the Veneti (Wends) [Jordanes in the sixth century identifies these as Slavs], in approximately the area described above, though he places Fenni (Finns ?) as well as Aestii (Balts ?) in contact with them in the north, and Bastarni or Peucini (Germanized Celts ?) between them and the Carpathians. The Cotini, a Celtic group, were also in the Carpathian region, as were, of course, German tribes to the west of the Vistula. Earlier, in the fifth century B.C., the Slavs had been equated with the Neuri of Herodotus, in contact with farming Scythians, and plausibly placed between the Vistula and Bug rivers. Earlier identifications are mere speculation, resting on assumed continuity of language with culture.

It is plausible to identify with ancestral Germans the northern LaTène cultures of Poland, the northern stone-cist cultures (face urns, etc.) and the late Neolithic intruders from north Germany. Scythian cultures in southeast Poland cannot be traced earlier than 600 B.C., and though the earlier Cimmerians may be identified with either Corded-ware or Tripolye cultures or both, this is on the basis of geography only. It is tempting to use the evidence of river names to connect ancestral Celts with eastern as well as with western appearances of the Lausitz culture, but though the LaTène influences on Poland are Celtic in origin, it is not clear how large a group of Celts remained in touch with the Slavs during the Iron Age when Germans were pushing southward and Celts were scattering into Spain, Britain, and Asia Minor. The inhuming tendencies in south Poland in Late-Lausitz and Iron-Age Ivanovič cultures have been linked with Illyrians from Moravia or farther south, but this is highly uncertain. Thus, to some extent, the archaeological record of Polish cultures suits the hypothesis of Germanic-Celtic-Scythian contact already arrived at on linguistic grounds. Furthermore, Indo-European speakers as a group entered Europe from the southeast or east, and no invasion which would suit the linguistic fact can be identified either culturally or racially after the movement of the Corded-ware people and the Danubians at the end and beginning of the Neolithic period.

Differentiation of Indo-European languages and traces of earlier languages in Europe both show that a still earlier introduction, as with the hunting Gravettians, is highly unlikely. One is therefore led to look to the blending of Danubian peasants and Corded-ware cattle people for the formation of the proto-Slavs, but it must not be forgotten that non-Indo-European Tardenoisian and Swiderian hunters, as well as Comb-pottery forest peoples, also contributed toward this ethnic amalgam in Neolithic Poland. Although one may be led further to speculate on the possibility that the Złota culture and its Bronze- and Iron-Age descendants in the area from the Vistula to Volhynia might have been products of Slavic speakers, it must be remembered the great effect which Northern (German ?), Lausitz (Celtic ?), and Scythian cultures had upon eastern Poland, not to mention Bell-Beaker and Aunjetitz peoples, and Illyrian and Roman influence. Influence from the northeast (Balts ?) is assumed, but that of the period after the Neolithic is not clear, and it seems unlikely that the forest people, as a whole, were other than Finno-Ugrians.

The ethnic bases of the Polish people are therefore both highly complex and highly composite, the product of interaction of a number of diverse peoples and cultural influences, a product which appears more a checkered mixture than a unified blend. North-south stratification of peoples in the Paleolithic and Mesolithic gave way to an east-west differentiation, with an irregular Vistula boundary during the late Neolithic and Bronze ages; north-south contrast dominated during the Iron Age, and following the Slavic expansion a partial return to the Bronze-Age condition is evident. At all periods Poland was a transitional area between cultures to the southeast, northeast, west, and southwest, which were the main gateways for prehistoric migrations. And because of this reason the periods of Poland's success or unity have been human creations made in spite of geography.

Race.—Though less important historically than language, economy, or other aspects of culture, human heredity is a basic factor in the development of any people. It is quite impossible at present to connect objectively the measurable and observable characteristics which physical anthropologists arbitrarily use in order to describe race with any definite mental-emotional characters or trends. But it is clear that the character and achievements of a people are a product of interaction of individuals often of different hereditary (racial) background, a great deal more than the average derived from the sum characters and actions of all these individuals. And on this basis it is perfectly certain that a stimulating degree of racial interaction and mixture is a prerequisite of the historic achievements of any people. Investigations of the process of race mixture are only beginning, but they confirm this generalization, and suggest that knowledge of its processes are of basic importance to a rapidly changing and crowded world.

Neanderthal remains from the Subalyuk cave in the Hungarian Bükk Mountains near Eger, as well as the Šipka jaw from Moravia, suggest that Neanderthal man inhabited south Poland as the user of the Mousterian culture. In Gravettian times the Brünn-Předmost tall, large, and excessively rugged dolichocephalic and deep-jawed variety of *Homo sapiens* may plausibly have intruded as the dominant type in Galicia as in Moravia, and a certain amount of Neanderthal genes were probably perpetuated through mixture. The American anthropologist, C. S. Coon, tentatively postulates that mixture between the gerontomorphic and broad-brained Neanderthal type and more paedomorphic and long-brained *Homo sapiens* produced also the rugged, large, but brachycephalic Borreby type and the more infantilized ("reduced") rounded, and brachycephalic Alpinoid and Lappish types. Whether or not this happened in Europe, brachycephals formed part of the racial composition of central Europe by Late Gravettian and Mesolithic times, and some prototype of both Alpines and east European Ladogans may well have existed in Poland by the Mesolithic period. Another major element linked elsewhere with the Tardenoisian culture is the Mediterranean race, and inasmuch as the Neolithic and later invaders introduced varieties of the Mediterranean type, in its broadest sense, the major racial interaction of Europe since the Mesolithic has been the clash between Mediterraneans of various types and Alpinoid and other types already present.

The post-Mesolithic racial history of Poland is most easily explained in terms of ten racial types which are used to symbolize the tendencies for certain groups of traits to occur together as a result of genetic linkage and selection. The following list gives the types recognized by Professor Coon; each type is followed by a Greek letter which indicates the corresponding type recognized by Jan Czekanowski, the leader of the Lwów school of anthropology in Poland.

Linear, relatively long-legged, and long-headed Mediterranean subtypes are the following:

Mediterranean proper (ϵ, ρ) is a relatively short and gracile type, with steep forehead, medium-narrow face and nose, shallow and pinched jaws, dark brunet hair and eyes. Rare, except among Polish Jews.

Atlanto-Mediterranean (ι) is a more rugged and relatively tall type, with sloping forehead, a face as long and narrow as the angular head, a straight narrow nose, long jaws, and brunet or disharmonic pigmentation (as dark hair and light eyes). Rare.

The Nordic type (α), almost exclusively tall and blond by definition, is clearly a blend of two skeletally disparate types: the Danubian, which is a slightly higher-headed version of the Mediterranean proper with blondism typical perhaps partly from environmental selection; and the Corded, notably tall and rugged, with exceedingly long, narrow, high, and smooth skull, long, deep-jawed and rectangular face with salient nose, set back behind the sloping forehead. Skulls show similarities both with Upper Paleolithic long-heads, and with the Iranian type of the Near East from which it may be ultimately derived. Pigmentation is by no means invariably blond. Both these types are important in Poland.

Laterally-built, relatively long-bodied, somewhat infantile, and chiefly short-headed types, of eventual Paleolithic derivation appear in the list below:

Alpine (λ) is a short, stocky, round-headed and broad- and moon-faced type, with short, low, infantile nose, fleshy face, and brunet pigmentation.

Ladogan (λ, β) is a similar but less round-headed type, with low and angular face showing a trace of prognathism, with weak chin, prominent cheekbones, low orbits, broad nose with flaring wings and markedly snub tip of "shoebutton" form, and generally brunet pigmentation. It is rare in unmixed form in modern Poland.

East Baltic (γ) is a relatively tall and large-bodied brachy-mesocephalic type, bigger and more rugged than the Ladogan, notably blond, and intermediate between the Ladogan and rugged Borreby brachycephals of Paleolithic origin, with noticeable Nordic influence. Not common inside political frontiers of Poland.

Neo-Danubian (β) is a parallel compound of Ladogan and Danubian, short-statured, mesocephalic, relatively short-faced, snub-nosed, and strong-cheeked type of mixed blond pigmentation. It is an important type in Poland.

Intermediate blends, with disharmonies in body and skull form, round heads, long faces are the following:

Dinaric (δ, ω) is a tall, linear, long-legged type with large hands and feet. A short and high head is combined with a narrow, drooping face, having a thin and beaky nose, and of brunet or mixed pigmentation. An analogous blond type is called Noric.

Armenoid (χ) is a somewhat shorter-legged and heavier-bodied version of the Dinaric, with steeper back of the head, much fleshier face, with fleshy convex nose with depressed tip. It is hairy, and has dark pigmentation. Although rare in Poland, it is common in the Near East as an Iranian-Alpine combination. Among later Turkish-speaking invaders of western Eurasia it is sometimes changed by addition of mongoloid blood to a type called Turanid.

In the Neolithic period the Danubian type was brought into Poland from Moravia and began its long period of blending with the Ladogan type present among the Comb-pottery people and probably also among the Mesolithic hunters. Mediterranean and Alpine minorities were probably also present. But it is the Corded (Nordic) type, brought in by the makers of the cord-marked pottery, which constitutes the third major racial element in the early racial mixture. And during the Bronze Age this is the dominant element found in inhumation graves, though minorities of Dinarics partly brought into Galicia by the Bell-Beaker people, and mixture with Danubians or Mediterraneans are also obvious. Thus by the Iron Age a group of Nordic types may be distinguished, ranging from a more or less intermediate compromise of Danubian and Corded, dominant among the Völkerwanderung Germans, to a lower-vaulted, more cylindrical, and fuller skull, with prominent nose, common among Celts and Scythians.

All these Nordic types are typical of the cemeteries which are definitely Slavic and, until the Middle Ages, the dominant Slavic racial complex is this Nordic one (among the Poles very close to the Corded type); although the Nordic type is broadened and modified very slightly by Alpine or Ladogan admixture, these early population elements of central and eastern Europe do not really make themselves felt until after the eleventh century A.D. And even during the Middle Ages, Poland was never so strongly brachycephalized as was Germany, central Europe, or Russia. In fact, typical Alpine and Dinaric brachycephals never seem to have left the loess region of the Carpathian foothills in large numbers, and it is the Ladogan element of the Neo-Danubian mixture which is important as the pre-agricultural survival which transformed Poland racially.

The average modern Pole is of short-medium stature, is strongly built, with long body and broad shoulders and hips. The brachycephalic head is of medium size, with a fairly broad forehead appropriate to a relatively broad and slightly squared face of medium height with generally narrow and straight nose, with slightly snubbed nasal tip. Poles are as blond as Scandinavians, with brown eyes frequent only in the Carpathian foothill region and dark hair common only in the southeast and east.

Blood groups show the following distribution: A—41.4 per cent, B—17.3 per cent, AB—8.1 per cent, and O—33.1 per cent. Nordic and Dinaric types are said to show more A, Alpine, Ladogan, and Neo-Danubian more B, with Poland as a whole in its expected intermediate position between west and east blood-group frequencies of the North European plain. Blood groups change from west to east rather than from north to south, except along the Sudeten-Carpathian line. Cephalic index is zoned diagonally from north to south, with the greatest brachycephaly in southwest and southeast in the Beskid and Carpathian regions respectively. Facial index shows an irregular belt of relatively narrow faces reaching from southeast to northwest, but though broad noses correspond with broad faces in the northeast and southwest corners, really narrow noses are limited to the west and northwest; narrow faces in the southeast are not consistently accompanied by narrow noses. Stature is tallest in the northwest of Poland, shortest in the Kielce region just west of Lublin-Sandomierz. This distribution is explained adequately by comparatively clearcut differences in geographical concentration of the major types.

The Nordic type is dominant in the northwest and along the German borders, and extends southeast along the Vistula-Bug migration route to persist with some clarity into Volhynia where it is replaced by a Pontic Mediterranean minor type and by the Neo-Danubian type, with a Noric type just south of Volhynia. The more numerous Neo-Danubian element is strongly represented in eastern Poland as a whole, among both White Russians and Volhynians, but it also extends through central Poland and is well represented west of the bend of the Vistula south of Warsaw, where it may partly preserve the Danubian peasant type, and Danubian blends with Dinaric-Alpine type occur in the Tatra foothills in west Galicia. Alpine and Dinaric types are dominant only along the loess and Carpathian belt, the Alpines possibly in excess at the west end, and Dinarics dominant among the mountaineers of southeastern Galicia. The east Baltic type occurs only in the north along the Baltic coast, and blends into the Borreby type dominant in West Prussia. The Armenoid type is rare, and its scattered occurrence may possibly reflect the effect of Khazar intrusions or those of other Turkish-speaking groups, inasmuch as skulls of Kumans or Petchenegs in the Ukraine are of Armenoid-Turanid form. This picture of racial distribution in Poland may be simplified: a south-north zoning ranging from Alpine Dinaric to Nordic east Baltic, crossed by a west-east zoning ranging from Nordic to Neo-Danubian, resulting in the diagonal checkerboard complexity outlined.

Social distinctions are reflected racially in the taller, slightly blonder, more hawk-nosed (Nordic-Noric) trends among the nobility, as contrasted with shorter, more Ladogan-Danubian peasantry. The racial segregation of Polish Jews is even more marked, with a predominant Dinaric or "Armenoid" combination of short head with otherwise Mediterranean features, including the convex "Iranian" nose in a definite minority of cases. The Jews are as variable as the Poles themselves, or any modern European ethnic group, and tend to show parallel regional differences. The Armenoid element among them is not sufficiently strong to indicate dominance of Karaites or Crimean Jews, who might be expected to reflect racial trends of the Khazars, and Polish Jews are clearly of German and west European origin as far as Alpine and other non-Mediterranean tendencies are concerned, though they have absorbed a certain amount of Neo-Danubian and show a small minority of blonds. Polish Jews are concentrated in city ghettos, especially in Galicia, and the reduction in total body size resulting from this environment is very noticeable in contrast with the children of Polish Jew emigrants in the United States. Polish immigrants to the United States are also taller than non-migrants, apparently because of selection.

Summary.—The prehistory of Poland is one of conflicting cross influences and irregularly alternating phases of sweeping change and stagnation. At almost all periods the country held an uneven checkerboard of differently oriented cultures, brought together by the geography of the Polish plains, but so dependent for any measure of unity on purely human bonds that Poland was always a transitional region. Because of the work of anthropologists, Poland is now one of the best-known regions in the world from a racial standpoint, and is an admirable example of clearly marked racial contours. Its long continuous history, and particularly the survival in mixed form of early elements like the Ladogan type, give it perhaps more racial than cultural unity. But this is a result more of complexity of mixture of varying racial tendencies than of dominance by Ladogan or Danubian alone. And in the future one may look to further race mixture and assimilation of both regional and social subtypes as forces to aid in the country's recovery from its present decimation. Like the past, the future of Poland's racial and ethnic development will be dynamic, not static, in pattern.

Part Two

HISTORICAL BACKGROUND

CHAPTER III

The Formation of the Polish State

BY FRANK T. NOWAK

THE ORIGINAL HOMELAND of all the Slavs was the territory located north of the Carpathian Mountains and extending northeastward to the swamplands of the Pripet River basin. From this center the Slavs migrated in all directions until they had made contact with other peoples and cultures and had become differentiated into the various Slavic nations of the present day. Those who, in ancient times, migrated to the Dnieper River and beyond came into contact with Iranian, Turco-Tartar, and Mongoloid invaders from Asia and founded the eastern group of Slavs known today as White Russians, Ukrainians, and Great Russians. Other Slavic tribes moved southward to and beyond the Danube where, in the fifth century, they came into contact with Greco-Roman civilization. Later they established the Bulgarian, Serbian, and Croatian states. Still other Slavs moved directly westward until they were stopped by the Germanic peoples. These western Slavs founded Poland and Bohemia.

In the time of Charlemagne (800), this ever-expanding mass of Slavs overflowed almost all of central Europe, with a western boundary extending approximately along the Elbe River and the Saale southward to the Adriatic Sea. From this line in the west the loosely organized Slavic tribes extended their rule over nearly all the lands of central Europe eastward as far as the Dnieper River. Although reputed to be peaceful by nature and primitive in political and social organization, the Slavs proved to be so tenacious of the soil which they occupied that they could not be dislodged easily by the counterpressure of militarily stronger and more civilized peoples who pressed inward upon the Slavic mass on all frontiers. When conquered by superior force, they often absorbed their conquerors without losing their own identity. Only in the tenth century did the Slavs suffer a major disaster at the hands of the Hungarians who drove a wedge into their very midst and there founded the Hungarian State.

The southern Slavs who crossed the Danube River in the sixth century were the first to come under the influence of Greco-Roman civilization. Compelled to fight hard for their very existence, they were the first to organize effectively for self-defense into larger units which soon emerged as Serbian and Bulgarian states.

Among the last tribes to unite and to organize politically were those of the north which occupied the territory between the Oder and Vistula rivers and lived in comparative isolation and security untroubled by frontier wars and Greco-Roman civilizing influences. The first mention of their ruler is found in the record of the German chronicler, Widukind, who relates that in the year 963 a Slavic ruler named Mieszko was defeated in a frontier skirmish by the German, Count Wichman.

Perhaps it is symbolic that this first mention of the existence of the Polish State should begin with an account of a frontier struggle between Poles and Germans. That there had been earlier contacts between the two peoples seems certain. Indeed, some historians are of the opinion that this eastward German pressure was an important factor in welding together the scattered Slavic tribes of the Oder and Vistula basins, since Mieszko, by 963, already was ruling over a well-organized Polish State.

Absence of written records of the period prior to the appearance of Mieszko compels the historian to resort to conjecture based on tradition, legend, archaeological discoveries, and analogous development of other Slav states. Many picturesque legends connect the origin of the Polish State with both the Warta and Vistula rivers and the tradition of Mieszko's day furnishes the names of three earlier rulers from the time of Charlemagne.

Of the many tribes which united to form the Polish nation, the Polanie lived on the banks of the Warta River, the Ślęzanie in the valley of the Ślęza River in Silesia, the Vislanie on the upper Vistula, the Mazovians on the lower Vistula, the Pomeranians on the shores of the Baltic Sea, and the Kuyavians near the historic town of Kruszwica. These tribes, with others of less importance, were united after much intertribal warfare by the strongest of them all, the Polanie or "dwellers of the plains" from which originated the name Poland. This tribe imposed its name upon all the other tribal entities and gave to the country an able national dynasty of the Piast family which governed the country until 1370.

The exact date when Mieszko, the fourth Piast ruler, began his reign at Gniezno, the first capital of Poland, is not a matter of record although he was already in his thirtieth year when he emerged as a historical figure in the year 963. That date was a landmark not only in the history of Poland but of Europe as a whole with its two powerful institutions—the Papacy and the Holy Roman Empire of the German nation. The latter had been established by Otto I in 962 as a universal secular organization for all Europe, although its very title belied its universal character, for its rulers could never completely overlook the interests and desires of the German people. The Papacy, too, claimed universal authority and came into conflict not only with the Holy Roman Empire but also with the conflicting claims of Eastern bishops who soon were to divide Europe into rival camps and separate cultural units, the Byzantine-Greek Orthodox tradition and the Roman-Latin culture of the west.

At this critical juncture in European affairs, Mieszko made far-reaching decisions that affected the destiny of both Poland and the Polish people. He realized that a pagan country could not long survive the combined pressure of the German eastward expansion when supported by the ambitious projects of Otto I for Christianizing the heathen. The fate of the Slavs living on the lands between the Elbe and Oder rivers and the experience of Bohemia with the German counts of the marches were object lessons of what must be avoided at all costs. Therefore, the Polish ruler sought to divide his enemies by concluding a pact of friendship with the Holy Roman Emperor in 963 or 965 (the date is uncertain). By the terms of this agreement he commended himself to the protection of Emperor Otto I, agreed to pay a nominal tribute for certain lands held west of the Warta River and, in return, received the designation "friend of the Emperor." This clever diplomatic device deprived the counts of the marches of open imperial sanction and support for their border raids into Poland and enabled Mieszko to take part in the internal political contests of the Holy Roman Empire.

In 965 Mieszko made a still more vital decision. He married a Christian princess of Bohemia named Dubravka and, in the next year, accepted Christian baptism for himself and for the entire Polish nation. It is a matter of no small import that he accepted the new faith from the neighboring Slav state of Bohemia, rather than from the German clergy who sought to extend their ecclesiastical authority over all Poland. By this shrewd policy he greatly strengthened Polish ties with Bohemia and simultaneously deprived his German enemies of their chief pretext for waging war against his country. Thus Poland was definitely drawn into the orbit of western civilization. Its reward was a Polish bishopric at Poznań. Later, the ties with Rome were further strengthened by a declaration that Poland belonged to the Patrimony of St. Peter and was entitled to the protection of the Holy See.

Having established secure relations with the Empire and the Papacy, Mieszko turned on his immediate enemies, defeated Wichman in 967 and the formidable Margrave Odo in 972. Seven years later he even repelled the attack of Emperor Otto II and announced his independence. With Emperor Otto III, after several preliminary skirmishes, he managed to keep on friendly terms until his death in 992. His diplomacy averted catastrophe for Poland, his statesmanship brought Christianity and western civilization to his people, and his military skill enabled him to extend his rule over Pomerania in 988 and over Moravia in 990. His only losses were Przemyśl, and certain territories along the Bug River which were seized by Vladimir of Kiev.

Bolesław the Brave (992–1025), succeeded his illustrious father and was the first Polish duke to bear the title of king. His remarkable talents enabled him to continue the policies of his predecessor and even to surpass those achievements by raising the power and prestige of Poland to hitherto undreamed-of heights. Thoroughly informed regarding the German menace by reason of his long residence as a hostage at the court of the Emperor, he proposed to Christianize and unite under the leadership of Poland all the neighboring smaller communities for common defense against the German *Drang nach Osten.* In pursuance of this plan he sent the distinguished religious leader and exiled bishop of Prague, Adalbert, among the heathen Prussians, where the famous missionary suffered a martyr's death in 997.

The martyrdom of Bishop Adalbert, who was a personal friend of both Emperor Otto III and Pope Sylvester II, created a sensation in religious circles throughout Europe. The recovery and transfer of his remains to the church at Gniezno at once raised this church to the rank of a sacred shrine visited by numerous distinguished pilgrims. In the year 1000 when all Christendom, in anticipation of the millennium, was in a mood of expectation and of religious exaltation, the Emperor Otto III made a pilgrimage to Poland. Accompanied by a retinue of great dignitaries, including representatives of the Pope, he visited the shrine of Adalbert at Gniezno. As he approached the shrine, he descended from his mount and walked barefoot to the church where he devoutly prayed and listened to the reading of the papal bull of canonization of St. Adalbert.

"How Bolesław received the emperor at the frontier and how he conducted him through his country as far as Gniezno cannot be related and frankly is beyond belief," reported the German chronicler, Thietmar. After this incredible reception the two rulers feasted sumptuously, exchanged gifts, and pledged themselves to further the cause of Christianity in accordance with the Emperor's mystical conceptions of a universal Christian empire. From the nature of the gifts exchanged and the honors bestowed on Bolesław, as the sovereign of so wealthy a country, it appears that Otto III encouraged his collaborator in Christian endeavors to seek appointment from the Holy See as king of Poland. It is not surprising therefore that Poland not only gained a patron saint at this first international conference on Polish soil, but also achieved an ecclesiastical province with an archbishop resident at Gniezno.

Unfortunately, the sudden death of Otto III in 1002 brought to an abrupt end the collaboration and friendship pledged so dramatically at the Gniezno conference. The new Emperor Henry II repudiated the mystical universal ideals of his predecessor and bent all his energies toward furthering specifically German interests. He saw no advantage for Germans in collaborating with Poland or in supporting its ruler in his endeavor to gain a crown with the consent of the Holy See. Instead, he began his reign by an attack on Poland. This invasion started a war that was to last with brief intermissions for sixteen years, ending finally in a decisive Polish victory in 1018. Bolesław retained possession of both Lusatia and Moravia, definitely stopped German expansion, and even forced the emperor to send military contingents to aid the Poles in regaining their lost territories in the east.

Meanwhile Bolesław did not neglect his Slavic neighbors. In order to prevent German control over Bohemia, he intervened in the dynastic controversy raging there and, for a brief time in 1003, ruled the country from Gniezno. In 1018 he led his armies against Kiev, expelled his enemies, and restored his son-in-law to power as the Grand Prince of Kiev. At the same time Bolesław restored to Poland territories that had been lost in the time of Mieszko.

For his military prowess in extending his authority from the Elbe River in the west to the Dnieper in the east, Bolesław earned the title of "brave." It was equally fitting that this ruler who had established the military power and secured the ecclesiastical and administrative integrity of his country should finally be rewarded with a royal crown in 1025—this honor occurring shortly before his death.

The impetus given by King Bolesław I toward national and political unity was never destroyed but found fitting champions in other outstanding members of the dynasty, especially among those who bore his magic name, such as Bolesław II (1058–1079), and Bolesław III (1102–1138). Even in the tragic thirteenth century, when internal strife brought political decentralization, when continuous division between branches of the Piast dynasty disrupted unity, and foreign invasions overwhelmed a goodly part of the country, the tradition of kingship and the memory of national unity were never lost. Indeed, the disruptive forces of the century seemed at the same time to intensify the national consciousness of the people who sought escape from chaos and longed for the restoration of law, order, and unity.

Two events of that remote period demand particular emphasis because of their great influence on the whole course of Polish history. In the year 1225 Conrad, Duke of Mazovia, seeking to safeguard his lands from the nuisance raids of the heathen Baltic Prussians, unwisely invited the Teutonic Knights to settle on the border of Poland. The land-hungry German knights, who recently had been driven from Hungary for their rapacity, attacked the Baltic Prussians, seized their lands, and established a German colony which became a formidable advance post of the *Drang nach Osten* in that entire region. In 1308 the Teutonic Knights did not hesitate to seize Polish territories in eastern Pomerania with the hope of choking off all access for Poland to the Baltic Sea by way of Danzig. Poland thus inherited a problem that was to tax the ingenuity of her ablest rulers and eventually was to threaten the very existence of the State.

The second event occurred in 1241. In that year the Mongol Batu Khan, grandson of the terrible Genghis Khan, after the conquest of Russia, invaded and devastated southern Poland as far as Silesia. Although the barbarian horde halted its victorious march at the battle of Lignica in Silesia, and Poland was spared the fate of conquered Russia, the Polish nation henceforth had to assume the burden of guarding western civilization from the devastating inroads of the Mongol hordes. This onerous responsibility resulted in a constant and heavy drain on the resources of the nation and gave rise to new problems of a military, social, and political nature.

The ever-present need for military defense of the eastern borders enormously increased the importance of the class of Polish knights or nobles on whom the responsibility for defending the country chiefly rested. This numerous class of nobles, unlike the chivalry of western Europe, was organized on a clan basis which did not permit the development of a feudal hierarchy. All members of the nobility, whatever their economic status, who carefully guarded their individual rights from invasion by royal authority, were equals. As a class they abhorred royal absolutism and administrative interference with their "golden liberty." Like the *barnagium Angliae* at Runnymede, they paved the way for constitutional government, guarantees of individual liberty, and laws of toleration which became the glory of Polish constitutional development.

Another consequence of the Mongol invasion and devastation of territories was the influx of German settlers who came to Poland as colonists to repopulate the devastated regions. They came in large numbers, bringing with them their own laws and customs under the protection of the Polish landowning nobility. The complete assimilation of these foreign elements without recourse to pressure was further striking evidence of the vitality and cultural solidarity of the Polish nation.

The next century, the fourteenth, witnessed the triumph of cultural and political unity in the person and reign of Poland's greatest ruler, King Casimir the Great (1333–1370). Casimir consolidated the nation once more, raised the royal dignity and prestige of the crown to unprecedented heights, and made Poland a European power of the first rank. The domestic reforms of this "king of the peasants" were so far-reaching in character that he has been regarded as Poland's first modern statesman. He strengthened the central government, reformed the administration, restored the prestige of the courts, and guaranteed justice for all. Like his English counterpart, Henry II, he determined to codify the laws that there might be "one law for the whole kingdom," for he perceived the importance of the common law as a powerful integrating influence in national life. Nor did he fail to appreciate the constructive influence of the Church and the achievements of the clergy in maintaining ecclesiastical unity throughout the realm during the darkest periods of national weakness.

For the improvement of general prosperity, Casimir drained marshes, cleared forests, and fostered agriculture. Along the main trade routes he built improved roads, bridges, and trading posts where, under his special protection, Polish merchants were encouraged to take an active part in the growing transit trade throughout Poland. For all classes of people he guaranteed law and order, giving his protection to all who needed it, whether they were Christians or Jews. These enlightened social and economic policies made possible great cultural advancement symbolized by the founding of the first Polish university at Cracow in the year 1364.

In the domain of foreign relations, Casimir gave a new orientation to Polish policy. In the west, he sacrificed Pomerania to the Teutonic Knights and Silesia to the supremacy of Bohemia, for he hestitated to involve his newly reorganized kingdom in a war of doubtful issue, preferring to rely on diplomacy for the achievement of his program. In the east, however, he campaigned vigorously to regain for Poland the disputed region today known as Eastern Galicia and to prepare the way for closer relations with his eastern neighbors, the Lithuanians, White Russians, and Ukrainians.

This eastward orientation of Poland's policy bore fruit shortly after the death of the great king, when one of his descendants, Queen Jadwiga of Poland, brought about a union between Poland and Lithuania by marrying the Grand Duke of Lithuania, Władysław Jagiełło, in the year 1386. This event proved to be of outstanding importance in the history of Europe. Lithuania received Christianity from Poland and entered the circle of western civilized nations, and Polish influence and culture penetrated far to the east, affecting the destiny of the Slavic peoples of eastern Europe.

CHAPTER IV

Poland as a European Power

BY OSCAR HALECKI

THE KINGDOM OF POLAND, which had been a European power for a short time as early as the eleventh century, reoccupied that place under Casimir the Great after a long period of division. Casimir's successful reign was, however, only a preparation for the leading role in East Central Europe which Poland was to play under the next dynasty—the Jagiellonian.

The last of the Piasts was fully aware that Poland could reach such a position only through a federal union with one of the neighboring countries. The personal union with Hungary, under the rule of his nephew, Louis of Anjou, whom Casimir designated as his heir, was only a temporary, and rather disappointing solution of the problem. Louis, too, had no sons, and it was not without difficulty that he persuaded the Polish nobles, granting them in 1374 a first charter of liberties, to accept as his successor one of his daughters. When he died in 1382, the Poles did not want to continue the union with Hungary under Mary who became the ruler of that country, and chose her younger sister, Jadwiga. But neither did the Poles want to be governed by Jadwiga's prospective husband, William of Austria. They changed the matrimonial plans made by her father, and arranged her marriage with Jagiełło, Grand Duke of Lithuania, who promised to be baptized, together with his people, and to add forever to the Kingdom of Poland (*Coronae Regni Poloniae perpetuo applicare*) his Lithuanian and Ruthenian lands. The latter included all of what now is called White Russia and the Ukraine, and then was a conglomerate of principalities which, after a period of Tartar overlordship, had been united with Lithuania proper in the course of the last century.

The Polish-Lithuanian union concluded in 1386 was much more

than a dynastic combination. It was the decisive turn in Polish history and an outstanding landmark in European history. In an entirely peaceful way, a federation came into being which after the disintegrating Holy Roman Empire was the largest monarchy of the later Middle Ages. Under Polish leadership, but under a Lithuanian dynasty, two nations, hitherto hostile, joined in a political system guaranteeing their security and attracting smaller neighbor countries. The federal constitution, discussed at a series of conventions, eventually recognized the equal status of the kingdom and the grand duchy, as well as the autonomy of the Ruthenian provinces of both. The pagan Lithuanians spontaneously adopted the Catholic faith, and western culture influenced also the orthodox Ruthenians.

The founder of the Jagiellonian dynasty, acting in close coöperation with his cousin Vitold who governed Lithuania under his control, defeated the Teutonic Order at Tannenberg in 1410, supported the Czechs against the Emperor Sigismund, checked the Tartars of the Crimea and the growing power of Muscovy; and when his delegates appeared at the Councils of Constance and Basel, Poland proved ready to participate in the settlement of all the European problems, entered into relations with both France and England during the Hundred Years' War, contributed to the appeasement of the Occidental Schism, and was considered one of the decisive factors in the relations with the Greek and Turkish East.

Jagiełło's eldest son and successor, called Władysław III, like his father after his conversion, was soon elected also King of Hungary; Władysław heroically died in the battle of Varna, 1444, when conducting the last crusade for liberating the Balkans and saving Constantinople from the Ottoman onslaught. His younger brother, Casimir, ruling over Poland and Lithuania until his death in 1492, regained Polish Pomerania with Danzig in 1466, and made East Prussia, which had to be left to the Teutonic Order, a fief of Poland. Casimir lived to see one of his sons on the thrones of both Bohemia and Hungary, and, despite increasing difficulties in the relations with Muscovy, the Tartars and the Turks, he maintained a powerful and respected position in the East.

Under Casimir's successors this position suffered from defeat in

1497, when an expedition toward the Black Sea ended in a total failure, thus loosening the ties with Moldavia, and in 1500 when the Russians invaded the borderlands beyond the Dnieper. But in the same year an alliance concluded by the Jagiełło brothers with France and Venice, and a little later negotiations with Henry VII of England gave evidence of the role of a dynasty which had federated the entire part of Europe extending between Germany, Turkey, and Russia, with the view toward securing peace and independence to all the nations living on that territory.

Their political system proved strong enough to meet the concerted hostility not only of Basil III of Moscow who took Smolensk in 1514 and was defeated a few weeks later, but also of the last Grand Master of the Teutonic Order, Albert, who was a prince of the Hohenzollern family, and of the Habsburgs who claimed the crown of Bohemia and Hungary. The Vienna Congress of 1515 when the Jagiellonian and Habsburg dynasties concluded a double matrimonial alliance, and the recognition of Albert of Hohenzollern ten years later, as secular duke in East Prussia, although he remained a vassal of the Polish Crown, certainly were attempts at appeasement. After the battle of Mohács, in 1526, when their Jagiellonian king was killed in the defense of Christianity, Bohemia and Hungary were lost for the dynasty. But its last representatives, Sigismund I and his son, Sigismund Augustus, both great Renaissance monarchs, so successfully governed Poland and Lithuania from 1506 to 1572 that the end of the Jagiellonian period was scarcely less brilliant than the beginning.

In addition to a settlement of Poland's relations with its German neighbors, which seemed to be final, and to closer contacts with France and even with Elizabethan England, three great achievements were accomplished by a peaceful and well-balanced policy. The permanent defense of the long eastern frontier was better organized than ever before. To check the conquests of Tsar Ivan the Terrible, and at the request of the dissolving German Order of Livonia, the territory of Latvia and Estonia was received into the federation. And eight years later, in 1569, after a patient and careful preparation, the Diet of Lublin replaced the hitherto chiefly dynastic link between Poland and Lithuania by an organic and permanent union. According to the wishes of a large majority in both nations, it was decided that even after the extinction of the Jagiełłos, they would always elect a common ruler and have a common parliament. Chiefly for reasons of defense, all the Ukrainian provinces now went to the Polish part of the Commonwealth receiving a substantial autonomy; Lithuania proper with the White-Russian lands remained a grand duchy on a footing of full equality, with its own administration, army, and treasury.

Because of that timely agreement, the "Common Republic," as the federation was now called officially, safely went through the unavoidable troubles of three successive interregna: after the childless death of Sigismund Augustus; after the unexpected return to France in 1574 of his successor, Henri of Valois; and after the premature and also childless death of Stephen Báthory, Prince of Transylvania, whose short but glorious reign (1576–1586), with its victories in three campaigns against Ivan the Terrible, confirmed and completed the accomplishments of the last Jagiełłos. When in 1587 Prince Sigismund of Sweden was elected in Báthory's place, Poland hoped to have again a dynasty which would extend its sphere of influence by an intimate coöperation with the Scandinavian kingdom of the Vasas, especially on the Baltic, and follow the Jagiellonian tradition of Sigismund's mother.

Favorable future prospects were the more justified because not only Poland's foreign policy, but also its internal development seemed extremely hopeful. Such a statement is incontestable, as far as cultural progress is concerned. If the sixteenth century is frequently called Poland's "golden age," it is not so much because of political victories as the promising evolution of its civilization. Prepared throughout the fifteenth century, since the renovation of the University of Cracow (1400), which by the end of the century was to become an international center of humanism and the "alma mater" of Nikolaus Copernicus, that cultural evolution reached a real climax under the Sigismunds, when first in Latin and then in the Polish language a brilliant literature was created, artistic life was developed by the influence of the Italian Renaissance, and all the stimulating religious trends of the Reformation period met in Poland in an atmosphere of unusual tolerance, favorable to exciting discussions. New universities were formed, and Latin civilization, already inseparable from Polish nationality, spread over the

Lithuanian and Ruthenian lands, where near the end of the century, when Catholicism regained its predominant position in the Republic, the leaders of the Greek Orthodox Church concluded a union with Rome.

The most distinguished representatives of Polish Renaissance culture, writers well known in Europe like Andrzej Frycz Modrzewski, and well-educated statesmen like John Zamoyski, were at the same time genuinely interested in constitutional and social reforms. Such reforms were undoubtedly needed and insufficiently executed, but Polish institutions had not deteriorated irremediably. If they differed from those of practically all the other countries, it mainly was because of an extreme devotion to ideas of liberty, in opposition to the progress of absolute government west and east of Poland. A long series of privileges granted to the gentry since the end of the fourteenth century had considerably reduced royal authority, and at a time when even in England the Parliament had lost some of its importance, the Polish Diet as developed in the fifteenth century, depending on the local Dietines of all the provinces, was steadily increasing its competence. There was, indeed, a serious danger involved in such a limitation of the central executive, but just these features of the Polish Constitution had attracted the other constituent parts of the Commonwealth, especially the Grand Duchy of Lithuania, which long had been ruled by a feudal oligarchy but on the eve of the Lublin Union reformed its own institutions on the model of Polish democracy.

It was much more regrettable that all the democratic liberties remained limited to only one class of society—to the nobles; for the influence of the towns, never very considerable, now was disappearing almost entirely, and the position of the peasants, rather satisfactory in the later Middle Ages, instead of improving, was gradually being reduced to serfdom. The gentry was so numerous, however—approaching one-tenth of all the inhabitants—that nowhere in Europe did a higher percentage of people enjoy full political rights; and class distinctions, detrimental to the lower orders, especially to the rural population, were then a general rule, hardly more shocking in Poland than elsewhere.

In spite of the shortcomings of its Constitution, even the Poland of the first two Vasa kings, Sigismund III and his much more popular son, Władysław IV (1632–1648), still was a great European power, able to interfere in the Russian troubles and thus recover lost territories in the east, and to enjoy real prosperity while the Thirty Years' War was raging beyond its western frontier. And in spite of all the foreign invasions during the reign of the last Vasa, John Casimir, who abdicated in 1668, and of the weakness of his immediate successor, Michał Wiśniowiecki, the new king elected in 1674 out of the ranks of the gentry, John III Sobieski, the famous liberator of Vienna from the Turks in 1683, played a most conspicuous part in the general policy of Europe, although sometimes he did hesitate between coöperation with France or with Austria.

The real decline of Poland, which started after Sobieski's death in 1696, had of course deeper causes which had developed throughout the seventeenth century. One of them certainly was the most harmful cessation of the constitutional evolution, any idea of reforms having been abandoned, whereas on the other hand degenerate forms of parliamentary life, chiefly the well-known *Liberum veto,* the unanimity rule, rigidly practiced since the middle of the century, came to be considered intangible guarantees of freedom. Unskillful attempts at strengthening the royal power twice resulted in open rebellions which, although crushed, succeeded only in discrediting the reform party.

Much more dangerous, however, was the great Cossack insurrection in 1648 which, following earlier movements of a similar character, grew into a true civil war. Having been originally a social group which found no adequate place in the Polish system, the Cossacks of the Ukraine, an undisciplined, warlike population of the steppes on both sides of the lower Dnieper, eventually turned leaders of the Orthodox Ruthenian peasantry, and in 1654 submitted with the whole of the Ukraine to the Russian Tsar. This decision, which the Cossacks themselves soon wanted to change, planning in 1659 another union with Poland or looking for Turkish protection, resulted in the devastation of the Ukraine after long years of cruel fighting and led in 1667 to its division between Poland and Russia, with no effective autonomy on either side of the Dnieper.

In addition to these troubles, Poland, from the beginning of the century, had to suffer from Swedish and Turkish aggressions. The

Swedes who under Gustavus Adolphus conquered most of Polish Livonia, occupied under Charles X Gustavus, in 1654, almost the whole of western and central Poland where only the famous monastery of Częstochowa succeeded in resisting the invader. During the next years, known as the "Deluge," Poland was simultaneously attacked by the Russians, the Prussians, and even the Transylvanians. At the same time, the Tartar incursions, a permanent plague from the thirteenth century to the end of the seventeenth, now closely connected with the Cossack insurrection were, as usual, backed by Turkey which had already threatened Poland during the reign of Sigismund III and remained a continuous danger until Sobieski's great victories.

It therefore was a proof of Poland's vitality, even more than in the thirteenth century, that it emerged from all these ordeals, if not without territorial losses, at least without any breakup of its unity, as one of the largest countries in Europe. But it is hardly necessary to emphasize the terrible economic consequences of all these wars conducted almost exclusively on Polish territory, or their disastrous influence on a national culture the normal progress of which had been so violently interrupted. There was, however, still another, and probably a decisive reason for the protracted crisis which was to lead to the catastrophe of the partitions. At the very moment when Poland, exhausted and weakened, needed to recover in peace and security, both of its chief neighbors, in the east and in the west, after having benefited from its entanglements, achieved the rank of great military powers and soon started an aggressive policy directed against the very existence of Poland as an independent country.

The relations with Muscovite Russia seemed to improve under Sobieski when, in 1686, a "permanent" peace replaced the truce of 1667 and Poland definitely renounced Kiev. But very soon the new Russian Empire created by Peter the Great, aiming not only at an outlet to the Baltic and the Black seas but also at a direct contact with western Europe and the role of a leading power in European policy, found it necessary to bring all or most of Poland under its control. Simultaneously, the Hohenzollern dynasty whose possessions in East Prussia had been freed in 1657 from Polish sovereignty, made this province the very basis of a new Prussian kingdom (1701) and wanted to unite it with Brandenburg, from which it was separated by the northwestern part of Poland. Russia and Prussia now had a common interest in destroying Poland by partition, a plan which had appeared again and again since the first coöperation of the two Powers had succeeded in imposing on the Poles, after Sobieski's death, their worst king—Augustus II of Saxony.

The reign of Augustus II and that of his son (1697–1763) proved indeed most unfortunate. Augustus II entered the Northern War against Charles XII of Sweden in close alliance with Peter the Great who, after having defeated the Swedes as well as their Polish and Ukrainian partisans, became the real master of Poland by forcing upon it a strong limitation of its already insufficient armaments. At the death of the first Saxon king in 1733, the great majority of the nation elected a Polish nobleman, Stanisław Leszczyński, who already had been put forward by Charles XII during his invasion and was now the father-in-law and ally of Louis XV. Inadequately supported by France, this most suitable candidate had to yield to Augustus III, who was imposed, like his father, by Poland's enemies. Augustus proved to be a most indolent king who condemned Poland to an entirely passive role, while the Prussian conquest of Silesia completed Poland's encirclement by Frederick the Great. When the latter agreed with Catherine II of Russia in 1764 to make the weak and unpopular Stanisław Augustus Poniatowski king of Poland, the next step in their coöperation could only be a dismemberment of the country.

Their plan, however, met with a resistance which after Poland's decline under the Saxon kings and after the long-lasting stagnation of its cultural and social life, was rather unexpected. Once more Polish vitality manifested itself in a national revival which made the reign of its last king, deplorable as it was in the political field, not only a brilliant stage of Polish civilization, especially in art and literature, but also a landmark in the progressive development of constitutional government. Even the conservative elements, participating in the rebirth of patriotic feeling, had organized a heroic resistance against Russian encroachments—the so-called Confederation of Bar, under the leadership of the Pułaskis. Quarreling with the king, they did not succeed in preventing the First Partition in 1772, which gave a large border region in the northeast to Russia,

Polish Pomerania—but still without Danzig—to Prussia, and the south of the country—now called Galicia—to Austria, which country without any serious reason joined in the spoliation of a friendly neighbor. But the national reform movement, after years of effort, resulted with the participation of the King, in the famous Constitution of May Third (1791). The Great Diet, in session from 1788, abolished the *Liberum veto* and the "free" election of the king, making Poland a parliamentary but hereditary monarchy with a strengthened executive; it opened to the townsmen access to the privileges of the gentry; and granted to the peasants the protection of the government. Without a bloody revolution or even without disorder, the nation succeeded in reforming its public life and in eradicating all the internal causes of decline.

There remained, however, a mortal danger from both Russia and Prussia. Hoping to appease at least one of them, the Great Diet concluded in 1790 a defensive alliance with Prussia, apparently a first step toward joining the "federal system" then being built up by British policy. But when in 1792 Russia invaded Poland, under the pretext of supporting a handful of oligarchic opponents of the new constitution, Prussia, disregarding its recent engagements, claimed its share in the Second Partition which reduced Poland to a rump state under Russian hegemony. Kościuszko's insurrection, in 1794, had important initial successes including the temporary liberation of Warsaw and Wilno (Vilna), supported not only by a large part of the gentry, but also by the townsmen and the peasants to whom the recognized leader of the nation promised full freedom. The struggle proved hopeless, however, since again the Prussians joined the Russians, and after Suvorov's final victory there followed in the next year, 1795, a third and total dismemberment, again with the participation of Austria. That country now annexed the territory between the Bug and Pilica rivers, including the old capital, Cracow. Warsaw was taken by the Prussians whose share, comprising all of Great Poland and Mazovia, reached the Niemen River, opposite Kowno (Kaunas) and Grodno. All the territory east of a line drawn from that city to Brest-Litovsk and to the new Austrian border, went to Russia. These new, artificial frontiers were to last "forever" and even the name of Poland was to disappear entirely.

CHAPTER V

Partitioned Poland, 1795-1914

BY JULIA SWIFT ORVIS

THE PERIOD covered by this chapter is known in Polish history as "the captivity." During these hundred and twenty years there was no united Polish state, and no free life for the Poles who lived, divided, under three separate alien governments, animated by a common purpose—to destroy Polish nationalism and to make the new generations of Polish youth into Russians, Prussians, or Austrians unaware of their Polish heritage.

The Polish response to this policy was opposition, unceasing, uncompromising opposition, active or passive as circumstances dictated, to every form of foreign domination. The Russian Poles made two armed risings against the Tsar's government—in 1830 and 1863. The Austrian and Prussian Poles both made revolutionary risings in that year of revolutions, 1848. Outside their own homelands, also, in every movement for freedom Polish leaders and Polish soldiers played a part, hoping against hope that some turn of the wheel of international politics would work to the deliverance and reunion of Poland.

It did not happen. Yet Polish activity won the most important victory. It kept the Polish question alive as an international issue much to the distaste of the Partitioning Powers, who wanted Poland forgotten by Europe as well as by the Poles themselves.

It is this continuing struggle in which, with all the odds seemingly against them, the Poles finally won out, that gives meaning and vital interest to the period. Why and how they were able to do it, what effects this century of struggle had upon the people themselves, how the different conditions under which Russian, Prussian, and Austrian Poles lived out their captivity altered their outlook and determined the character of the contribution each group was to make to the resurrected state—these, and other related questions, make the period a truly formative one and of vital importance.

In January, 1795, the Austro-Russian convention arranging the Third Partition of Poland was signed and the last vestige of an independent Polish state wiped off the map. In June, 1796, Napoleon Bonaparte led the French army into Lombardy and began his campaigns to expel the Austrians from Italy—to "liberate the Italians" from the Austrian yoke. Several thousand Poles formed part of that army of "liberation."

In his boyhood Napoleon was an enthusiastic disciple of Rousseau and, like all friends of liberty of that day, deeply sympathetic with the Poles. In September, 1796, at Verona Napoleon said, "I like the Poles. The Partition of Poland was an iniquitous deed that cannot stand. When I have finished the war in Italy I will lead the French myself and force the Russians to reëstablish Poland."[1]

Thousands more Polish volunteers flocked to Napoleon's army, and for the next twenty years there were always Poles fighting for him, believing, in spite of repeated disappointments and false promises, that the reconstituted Polish State was just " 'round the corner." Some leading Poles, notably Tadeusz Kościuszko, early lost faith in Napoleon, realizing that military considerations, not enthusiasm for liberty, had become the basis of his Polish policy. As long as Napoleon needed soldiers, however, he renewed the promises and made the gestures which kept alive in the rank and file of the Polish people the faith that he would be, ultimately, their liberator.

In 1807 military considerations were favorable to Poland. By his great campaigns of Austerlitz, Jena, and Friedland, Napoleon had defeated Austria, Prussia, and Russia in succession, and for a brief period all three Partitioning Powers were at his mercy. He had destroyed the Prussian army and had occupied most of Prussia's territory. The Tsar Alexander was ready not only to sign a peace but to make an alliance with him, with the result that at Tilsit in a famous interview on a raft moored in the middle of the river Niemen, the Tsar agreed to recognize a small independent Polish state, the Duchy of Warsaw, created by Napoleon from Prussia's Polish territories.

[1] Quoted in *Cambridge History of Poland,* p. 210.

The joy and hope of the Poles knew no bounds. After the defeat of the Prussians at Jena the Poles in all the Prussian-Polish territories had risen *en masse* and driven the Prussian garrisons from the country. They also raised an enormous army which they put at Napoleon's disposal.

The Duchy of Warsaw, as finally organized, seemed to many observers scarcely to merit so much enthusiasm. It contained only Prussian Poland, and not all of that as Napoleon had at first proposed. In making his bargain with the Tsar he had been obliged to lop off several substantial slices of territory. For the Tsar the district of Białystok (Byelostok) on the east, for the Tsar's defeated friend, the King of Prussia, a most important section lying along the lower Vistula connecting East Prussia with the Brandenburg territories and giving the Prussians access to the port of Danzig but cutting that port off from the rest of Poland. Danzig itself, finally, was made into a Free City and free navigation of the Vistula was guaranteed to Poland.

In 1809, after his defeat of Austria at Wagram, Napoleon added to the Duchy Austria's share in the Third Partition, including Cracow. This was only about half of Austrian Poland instead of the whole, for which the Poles had hoped. Napoleon had now, however, arranged an alliance with Austria to be sealed by his marriage with the Archduchess Marie-Louise, and Austrian feelings had to be considered.

This little state, comprising some 45,000 square miles and about four and a half millions of population, was given the King of Saxony,[2] Napoleon's ally and friend, as its duke. He ruled under a constitution prepared by Napoleon and imposed quite arbitrarily on the country. It was not, however, a bad constitution. It provided: (1) a Diet or legislative body (*Sejm*) composed of two houses, the lower house elected by the nobles and townspeople; (2) a system of independent courts operating under the *Code Napoléon;* and (3) a strongly centralized system of administration of the French type. The abolition of serfdom and the introduction of civil equality, though decreed theoretically by the Constitution, were objected to by the Polish nobles and were never put into practice. The French

[2] The Polish Constitution of May 3, 1791, had designated the Elector of Saxony and his line as heirs to the Polish throne. Perhaps this influenced Napoleon's choice.

Minister at Warsaw, Napoleon's personal representative, however, was the real ruler, and Marshal Davout, very pro-Polish but nonetheless French, was in command of the army.

In spite of French political control the Poles nevertheless felt that the Duchy was an independent Polish state. The government was not oppressive and along many extraconstitutional lines the Poles were able to work freely and to accomplish much, notably in education.

It was, however, through its army that the Duchy of Warsaw made its most important contribution to national development. The introduction of conscription and the organization of the army on the new French instead of the older Prussian pattern completely transformed it. Conscription, as in France, equalized all classes and pulled the nation together. Sons of peasants served side by side with the sons of nobles and burghers, and in this way many peasants became conscious for the first time of their Polish nationality. The quality of the Polish soldier was uniformly high. He fought with bravery, verve, and endurance, and proved himself a match for the best armies of the world. The old fame of the Poles as one of the great military nations had been lost during the disasters of the eighteenth century. During the Napoleonic Wars the Poles of the Duchy of Warsaw won it back.

After the failure of Napoleon's invasion of Russia, and his retreat from Moscow, Russia took possession of the Duchy. This was not regarded as a disaster by all Poles. During the whole life of the Duchy opinion had been sharply divided as to whether Napoleon was, after all, the best hope for Poland's future. A considerable party, conservative landowners and supporters of vested privilege for the most part, favored union with the Conservative party in Russian Poland whose program was peace with the Russian Government, submission for the moment, for the sake of ultimate union of all Poles in an independent state with the Tsar as King. They counted in this upon the well-known liberal sentiments of the Tsar Alexander I, and his deep sympathy, since boyhood, with the cause of Polish freedom.

Alexander I was brought up at the court of his grandmother, the Empress Catherine II, who was, intellectually, a disciple of the eighteenth-century "enlightenment" and filled her court with members of that movement. She chose as tutor for her grandsons a French revolutionary and republican, La Harpe, under whose guidance the future Tsar, when still a boy, became a pronounced Liberal. His particular interest in the liberation of the Poles was traceable largely to the influence of a young Polish noble, Prince Adam Czartoryski, who had lived at the court of Catherine II for several years. He acted as aide-de-camp to the Grand Duke Alexander and became one of his closest friends. Prince Adam had been sent to Russia to beg for the restoration of his family estates confiscated by the Empress after the Third Partition, and had been kept there by Catherine as a hostage for the good behavior of the Polish landowners. Like all Poles, Prince Adam was a flaming patriot. He imparted to Alexander some of his resentment over his country's grievous wrongs and won from Alexander a promise that when he became Tsar, Poland should be given its freedom.

After he became Tsar, however, Alexander was made to realize the practical difficulties in the way of his plan. There was no popular sympathy in Russia for the Poles, who were, indeed, disliked by most Russians. Even the Russian Liberals, though theoretically in sympathy with the Tsar's ideals, thought that practical reform should begin at home, with Russia itself. The Tsar's ministers and responsible advisors had no interest in a free Poland, and systematically gave it a cold shoulder. And even the Tsar himself soon realized the impossibility of risking a break with Austria and Prussia when their coöperation against Napoleon was essential to him. The possibility of the restoration of the Polish state at some future time, by international agreement, was, however, never lost sight of by the Tsar. On the contrary, as the years passed and he became increasingly interested in foreign relations, the enormous value of a Polish state as a factor in European affairs became increasingly patent to him. By 1815 he wanted to control not simply Polish *territory* but a Polish *state*.

Alexander regarded Napoleon's creation of the Duchy of Warsaw as a definite encroachment upon his preserves, and his constantly growing suspicion of Napoleon's Polish aims and plans was certainly a considerable factor in his ultimate break with France.

When Alexander took possession of the Duchy of Warsaw after his defeat of Napoleon he treated the Poles well, but refused to discuss their future until the Congress of Vienna met in 1814–1815 to rearrange Europe after Napoleon's disruptions. He had, indeed, determined to continue the independent existence of the Duchy of Warsaw with himself as King, as a nucleus for a restored Polish state. But Austria and Prussia, which were fighting with him against Napoleon and expected to get back their Polish territories after Napoleon's defeat, could not be told of that plan in 1812. On the contrary, the Tsar signed a treaty with the King of Prussia in 1813 guaranteeing the restoration of the Prussian Kingdom. The King interpreted this to mean that the Polish territories taken from him by Napoleon would be returned, but the Tsar's plan was to give him Saxony instead.

At the Congress of Vienna the Tsar's plan met with serious opposition not only from Prussia but also from Austria, Great Britain and, finally, from France, whose ruler, the restored Louis XVIII, had a Saxon mother and refused categorically to countenance the destruction of the Kingdom of Saxony. The Tsar's threat to go to war against his allies in support of his position very nearly broke up the Congress, but a compromise was finally arranged. The Tsar agreed to reduce the size of his new kingdom by ceding to Prussia the province of Posen, comprising about a quarter of the Duchy of Warsaw, and the King of Prussia agreed to take part of Saxony in lieu of the rest of his Polish lands. This left a much reduced but still independent Kingdom of Poland. Finally the town of Cracow with some surrounding territory was made by the Congress into a free city, the Republic of Cracow, because neither Austria nor Russia would let the other have it.

What was left of the Duchy—a scant three-quarters of it—was then turned over to the Tsar who made of it the new Kingdom or "Tsardom" of Poland, the "Congress Kingdom."

The Polish problem was perhaps the most difficult and delicate of all those with which the Congress of Vienna had to deal. The partitions had outraged the moral sense of most European peoples, and when the Napoleonic conquests made necessary the reopening of the Polish question at the Congress of Vienna, it was felt that this opportunity to right, at least in some measure, the wrongs done to the Poles should not be neglected. On the other hand the partitioned territories were in the possession of the three strongest powers of continental Europe which regarded the retention of such territories as essential to the future safety and well-being of their respective states.

British public opinion was strongly sympathetic to the Poles, and Lord Castlereagh, Britain's chief representative at the Congress, interested himself particularly in the Polish problem. He did not like the Tsar's Congress Kingdom but was obliged to accept it. It was under his influence, however, that the Congress did two things which greatly benefited the Polish cause: (1) at the demand of the Congress the Partitioning Powers agreed to give to their Polish subjects separate special administrations, recognizing their Polish nationality and treating them as a people distinct from their conquerors; (2) they also agreed to maintain freedom of transit and communications throughout the territories of the old Poland, irrespective of political lines of control, thus maintaining the economic unity of the politically divided Poland.

Although these promises were not kept they were, nevertheless, of great importance to the Poles, since they gave official international recognition to the national historic rights of Poland. The Powers, moreover, which made these promises were the very ones which, after the partitions, had agreed to banish the name of Poland forever from political use and to keep the three sections of the partitioned country rigidly separate in every way. The Congress of Vienna left the territories of the old Poland divided into five separate parts: (1) Austrian Poland; (2) Prussian Poland; (3) the western provinces of Russia acquired by it in the partitions of the eighteenth century; (4) the Congress Kingdom of Poland; and (5) the Republic of Cracow. Russia controlled, in one way or another, about three-quarters of this territory. This accounts for the fact that for the following fifty years it was Russia toward whom the enmity of the Poles was almost entirely directed.

The constitution which the Tsar Alexander gave to the Kingdom was based on that of the Duchy of Warsaw. In some ways it was even more liberal, but in practice it was not a success. No constitutional safeguards were provided against Russian encroachment on the rights granted to the Poles, and such encroachments were constantly made.

The Poles deeply resented the Tsar's appointment of his brother, the Grand Duke Constantine, as commander in chief of the army of the Kingdom. Constantine was stupid, brutal, tyrannical, and entirely unsympathetic to the constitution, which, in fact, he ignored altogether, pursuing his own autocratic way as though it did not exist. He increased both the size of the army and its equipment without regard to expense or to the constitutional budget, and thus nearly ruined the country.

Although the constitution made no provision for it, the Tsar created the office of Russian Imperial Commissioner to watch over Russian interests in Poland and appointed Nicholas Novosiltsov to fill it. Novosiltsov, like Constantine, was opposed to the constitution and constantly usurped authority for himself as well as encouraged Constantine to do so. Novosiltsov was, indeed, the evil genius of the Poles, hated by them as perhaps few men have been. Clever, astute, and thoroughly informed, he concealed under an outward profession of the most liberal opinions and enlightened aims the characteristics of the most arbitrary and evil of Russian bureaucrats. As one of the early friends of Alexander I, a confidant and, supposedly, a sharer of his liberal views, Novosiltsov had great influence with the Tsar and was probably one of those largely responsible for the fact that after 1818 Alexander gradually but surely abandoned his liberal ideas. This continual violation of the constitution profoundly disillusioned the Polish people. Many of them lost faith in the Tsar's intention to create a greater Poland and began to form secret societies and to prepare for revolution.

The death of Tsar Alexander in 1825 ended all hopes of a greater Poland. Nicholas I, who succeeded him, was an extreme reactionary and autocrat, opposed on principle to constitutions and to nationalist aspirations. He wanted only an excuse to destroy the Kingdom altogether. From the moment of his accession revolution was inevitable. It was precipitated in November, 1830, by the students of a military school in Warsaw when the report reached them that Polish troops were to form part of the forces Russia was sending against the revolutionists in France and Belgium. The movement thus started soon became general. In December the Diet issued a proclamation declaring the insurrection national—that the Poles would not lay down their arms until they had won their independence and united Russia's western provinces with the Kingdom.

Unfortunately, the parties of the Right and Left could not agree upon a war policy. This meant that there was no capable and efficient leadership and in spite of brave and well-trained soliders, and good battle plans, no decisive victories were won.

In January, 1931, the Diet declared Nicholas I dethroned and made Prince Adam Czartoryski head of the government in the hope that his prestige and wide foreïgn connections would enable him to unite the Poles at home and win help from abroad—which was now Poland's only hope. He was unable to do either, and defeat was inevitable. In October, 1831, Warsaw surrendered to the Tsar's General Ivan Paskievich and the revolution was over.

In February, 1832, the Tsar issued an *Organic Statute* declaring the Kingdom an integral part of the Russian Empire, and providing for its government by a Council of State, composed of both Poles and Russians, appointed by himself. That he consented to set up this form of separate administration was due to the influence of France and England, which reminded him of those terms of the Treaties of Vienna providing for special treatment of Polish subjects.[3] It was, however, only a gesture. The government was actually in the hands of a new department of the Russian Government—the Department of the Affairs of the Tsardom of Poland—created for this purpose. The head of this department and the real ruler of Poland for twenty-four years was General Paskievich, the leader of the Russian army which had crushed the revolution.

During these years Poland was treated as part of Russia. Education was discouraged, Russification pushed, the use of the Polish language in the schools prohibited; the publication and circulation of the works of the great Polish poets and historians were forbidden, and contact with the outside world reduced to a minimum by a rigid passport system. Under this stifling pall of ignorance and frustration the Russian Government believed Polish nationalism must die of suffocation.

Fortunately the issue had not to be decided here. Another group of Poles under freer circumstances took up the task and not only saved the Polish cause from extinction but gave it a prestige and a quality it had never had before. They made of it a religion.

This was the group of exiles who, after the defeat of 1831, had

[3] See above, p. 54.

fled abroad, chiefly to France and especially to Paris, which became the center of the movement known as "the Great Emigration." These exiles had not left the Kingdom simply to escape destruction and persecution, but particularly to find a spot where they could form a new Polish legion with which to return to renew the struggle for freedom. The French people were very sympathetic with the Polish cause, and the Poles believed that the French Government, itself a revolutionary one, would aid them. In this they were disappointed. The French Government not only did not aid, but forbade the formation of a Polish legion on French soil. Nor were other governments more accommodating. General Bem and other Polish leaders tried successively Portugal, Belgium, Spain, Italy, and even Egypt, but everywhere without success. No government was willing to risk a war with Russia, which made it plain everywhere that such might be the price of assistance to the Poles.

Blocked in regard to the legion, the Emigration turned to other means of keeping alive Poland's cause and preparing for a new struggle. Unfortunately, within the Emigration there were, as always among Poles, two political groups—the aristocratic Right and the democratic Left. They were never able to act together and their enmity made any practical achievement impossible. The Left set up a National Committee immediately on arrival in Paris which issued a proclamation declaring that the Conservatives were responsible for the failure of the uprising of 1830, and calling upon liberals to refuse to accept their further leadership.

The Democrats wanted immediate revolution and to this end made contacts with opposition groups wherever in Europe revolution was preparing—which was nearly everywhere. Their idea was that the cause of liberty was universal and would be won for all peoples by common action. So they not only conspired but fought constantly in every European uprising from 1830 to 1863.

The Aristocratic party, the Right, believed that this activity without the support of governments was useless. They saw the Polish question as one of international politics which could be solved only by diplomatic action. They conceived their special task to be through diplomatic means to keep the Polish question ever in the minds of the rulers of Europe, not for one moment to allow them to think that the problem of Poland was solved or shelved.

Prince Adam Czartoryski was the leader of this group. He worked from London, from 1831 to 1833, by which time the Democrats had lost their best leaders, and thousands of their members had died in foreign revolts which had failed utterly. Most of the Democrats by this time had accepted Prince Adam's leadership, and in 1834 he set up a "government" in Paris which worked constantly, widely, and by all available means for nearly twenty years to promote the Polish cause, but without success.

It was not the politicians or the diplomats but the poets of the Emigration who saved Poland from extinction by reminding its sons and daughters that the greatest influence in human history is the human spirit, and that as long as the spirit lives, though states may perish, peoples do not die. Listening to them, Poles found new faith in their future destiny and new courage to live and to die for it.

The greatest of the poets of the Emigration were Mickiewicz, Słowacki, and Krasiński—and they are great names indeed in Polish history as well as literature. The movement of which they were the leaders was in its beginnings simply the Polish expression of the European movement of Romanticism and followed its usual lines. But under the influence of the Emigration it was transformed into a nationalist movement unique in literary history. The poets of the Emigration revived the failing faith and hope of the Polish people by giving them a reason for believing in their ultimate national resurrection. They taught that the Poles were a chosen people called upon to suffer crucifixion, even as Christ had suffered, because they had stood for and fought for a great universal Cause, the cause of Human Freedom; that even as Christ rose from the dead, so, inevitably, must Poland rise, and that the day of its resurrection would usher in the day when justice, liberty, and love would rule the whole world—the Kingdom of God on earth. Upon that faith in Poland's resurrection was founded the mystic nationalism of the Emigration known as Messianism, which gave to the poetry of the era its peculiar beauty, character, and importance.

The idea of Poland as the Messiah of the nations was not wholly new in Polish thought but it was Mickiewicz who gave it the force and form of a doctrine in his *Books of the Polish Nation and of the Polish Pilgrimage* written to the exiles in 1832. Here Poland appears as a sinless sacrifice crucified to expiate the sins of the nations. Part of that expiation was the sufferings of the nation under partition and during the revolution of 1830. But the poet saw expiation as a continuing process. The poet's pictures of life in old Poland idealized by suffering and exile, inspired his homesick compatriots to continue the struggle and die for its revival.

Juliusz Słowacki and Zygmunt Krasiński writing a little later than Mickiewicz and for another generation expressed the same Messianic interpretation of Poland's history and were scarcely less influential than he. In Krasiński's poem "Dawn" appears what many Polish critics consider the most perfect expression of Poland's Messianic ideal.

> "... and I heard
> A voice that called in the eternal sky:
> As to the world I gave a Son
> So to it, Poland, thee I give.
> My only son he was—and shall be,
> But in thee my purpose for Him lives.
> Be thou the truth, as He is, everywhere
> Thee I make my daughter!
> When thou didst descend into the grave
> Thou wert, like Him a part of human kind.
> But now, this day of Victory
> Thy name is: All Humanity."[4]

From the inspiration of these three great poets, supplemented by a host of their contemporaries only less great, sprang all the revolts and attempts at revolts of the years from 1832 to 1863.

Not all the Poles of the Emigration era, it must be said, accepted in full the highly mystic doctrine of Messianism, but for all of them it held a meaning and a message. This was because the doctrine was based on two fundamental ideas, the solidarity of peoples and the Christian idea of sacrifice, both of which were familiar and congenial to Polish thought and hence easily accepted. Even to the nonmystics the insurrections were regarded as necessary, chiefly for two reasons. To them Poland was not the sinless victim of the Messianists but had itself sinned and the insurrections were expiation for those sins of class or individual so disastrous to the old Polish State, and were to make Poland worthy of its role of Messiah.

[4] Quoted in *Cambridge History of Poland*, p. 323.

Also, the insurrections gave proof to the world that the words of the poets were not mere words but expressed the ideals of the whole nation, and that the whole nation was ready to accept their practical consequences.

The failure of the insurrection of 1830 did not discourage these idealists, nor those other Poles who for different reasons saw in military revolt Poland's only hope for freedom. But it was thirty years before their next rising took place in 1863. By that time the Democratic wing of the Emigration, always militant, had been reinforced by the masses of Polish students, welded by underground activities into a compact political force, and by the Conservatives or "Whites" disillusioned at last as to any hope of freedom for Poland through coöperation with Russia. But the majority of the peasants were quiescent, there was no Polish army worthy of the name, and intervention by the European Powers, upon which the "Whites" had counted, did not materialize. The result was the complete failure of the uprising, and the punishment of the vanquished with a severity not before shown to the Poles.

The revolution of 1863 was the final expression of the Romantic movement of the Emigration, and the last attempt at armed opposition to the Partitioning Powers until 1914. This was due not only to the extreme severity with which the revolt was crushed but more, perhaps to a change in the thinking of the Poles themselves. The generation growing up after 1863 had never known the old free Poland which their fathers venerated and their poets glorified. Their era was a very different one, also, from that of the Emigration. The lofty idealism of the Romantic period had given way everywhere to a more realistic attitude under the influence of the great economic forces whose operation was transforming the European world. Industrial development and the growth of the democratic ideal were bringing about fundamental changes in social as well as in economic systems. Young Poles, studying the history of old Poland in the light of their own era, found it a land of serfdom, intolerance, and class privilege. These were not the foundations which they wished to restore, and they set themselves the task of building up a new united nation based on civil equality, freedom of thought, and political democracy. The old landed aristocracy had been greatly reduced in size and wealth by partitions and confiscations. Of those who were left, many accepted the new situation and became leaders and workers in it. Far more numerous were the sons and grandsons of the dispossessed nobles who found themselves obliged to earn their living and turned to business and the scientific development of Poland's resources for it. They became the basis of a new, vigorous, and wealthy middle class, which old Poland had lacked, and which built up and gave new life to the towns. They also formed the new intelligentsia.

Most important of all, however, was the change in the peasantry—72 per cent of the population of the old state. Deprived of their freedom and of their land in the sixteenth century, the condition of the Polish peasantry had deteriorated steadily and by the late eighteenth century was as bad as any in Europe. The persistent opposition of the powerful and unenlightened Polish landlords had prevented any amelioration of their lot. It was, finally, the Partitioning Powers and not the Polish lords—to their shame be it said—who freed the serf in all three parts of Poland[5] and thus provided the solid foundation for a modern democratic state. This was done not from any altruistic or humanitarian motive but in the hope of winning the support of the peasants against their old masters and thus dividing the nation. It was a clever move fraught with grave danger to Poland's future and it achieved, for a time, a measure of success. But only for a time.

Another powerful factor in the new orientation of the Poles was the great economic opportunity opened to them by the industrial movement just then spreading to eastern Europe. The building of railroads in Prussia and Russia and the opening to the Poles of the vast new markets of these states accelerated the development, already started, of Poland's rich natural resources, created great cities and an urban proletariat whose necessities, in turn, stimulated agriculture—and, also, created a new social problem. As in other countries under similar conditions, rapid growth led to long hours of work, low wages, and bad housing conditions. This in turn was followed, as in other countries, by the rise of socialism among the workers. Repressed with severity, the socialist movement was driven underground but its work went on, and in the hands of able leaders it became the means of educating the Polish worker in nationalism.

[5] This was done by Prussia in 1823, by Austria in 1849, and by Russia in 1864.

Through its propaganda many of them became conscious for the first time that they were Poles with a share in a rich national heritage.

During these years when for the first time all classes worked and worked together, the old chasms between social classes were bridged. The growth of a wealthy and influential middle class, also, and the division of a large part of the lands of the aristocracy among preasant proprietors did away with the most glaring economic contrasts of the old state.

This period when Poles under the three governments were building themselves, through concentration on day by day work, into a modern, economically prosperous and democratically minded people, is known as the period of "Organic Work." It was not a happy period, but it was fruitful. The knowledge, experience, discipline, and wealth necessary for the construction and maintenance of their resurrected state of 1918, were acquired during that half-century before the First World War.

In spite of the fact that during these years the Poles abandoned all direct political activity, they were harshly treated by Russia and Prussia. Of the two, Prussia's policy was more severe and more persistent. This was partly because of the greater efficiency of the Prussians but chiefly because the destruction of Polish nationalism was regarded by Prussian rulers as essential to the future of their state. That state owes its existence and its greatness to eastward expansion. The Mark of Brandenburg was created to fight and conquer the Slavs on the eastern frontier of the Empire and to colonize their lands. The Knights of the Sword and the Teutonic Order carried on the struggle for three hundred years, and when the Brandenburg Hohenzollerns succeeded to the Duchy of Prussia they inherited a policy already hallowed by age and tradition. The process was always the same. First the "peaceful penetration" of German traders and subsidized German settlers prepared the way for military conquest. After conquest, through steady administrative pressure and continued colonization, the conquered peoples became completely German. When applied to the Poles, however, the system did not work. The peaceful penetrators and German colonists instead of Germanizing the Poles were, in many cases, themselves Polonized. They married Polish women, adopted Roman Catholicism, and their children were Poles resentful of the obligation to use German instead of their "mother tongue" in public affairs!

In Prussian Poland the policy of Germanization was carried out only intermittently between 1815 and 1873. It was with the coming of Bismarck to the head of the Prussian government that pressure on the Poles became steady and relentless with all the power and wealth of the new German Empire behind it. The Polish question was always a matter of grave concern to Bismarck. He feared the revival of the Polish state (which, he said, it would be "suicide" for Prussia to permit), and he framed his policies, both internal and foreign, to prevent it.

In 1873 he began his war against the Poles with an attack on the Church. Until 1873 Polish education had been largely in the hands of the Polish Roman Catholic clergy, who had been leaders in the Polish national movement since 1815 and who saw to it that Polish children were instructed in Polish. Bismarck took it out of their hands and put it under the exclusive control of the state. He made German the only language permitted in the schools as well as in the public administration. For protesting against these acts and preaching passive resistance to them, many priests were fined and imprisoned, including even the archbishop, who was finally deposed, his see being left vacant for twelve years.

It was this war against the church which brought the Polish peasants into the struggle on the side of their own nation. They had been freed from serfdom and given land by the Prussian government and had been far better off than they had ever been under their Polish masters. They had, therefore, been slow to respond to the efforts of the Poles to draw them to the Polish side. But religious persecution struck home to their ardent Catholic souls and henceforth the war against Germanism was their war.

In 1886 Bismarck returned to the policy of colonization. By the Settlement Act of 1886 a Commission was set up to buy land from Poles and resettle it with German farmers. The Poles responded to this by forming societies of their own to buy up all the land on the market and thus keep it out of the hands of the Commission. Faced with failure, the Germans finally resorted to the Expropriation Act of 1908 by which Poles were compelled to sell their land when the

Commission demanded it. This law was enforced in 1912. In spite of it, however, by 1914 Polish holdings had gained while those of Germans had decreased.

Culturally a secret underground system of education in Polish homes kept alive the Polish language and traditions. Even the children took part in the national movement as the famous school strikes of 1906, when the children refused to answer questions in German, bore witness.

In this struggle against extermination the Polish people were ably led. The two outstanding leaders in Poznań were Maximilian Jackowski, a landowner, and Father Piotr Wawrzyniak, a Roman Catholic priest, known as the "uncrowned King of Poznań." Both of them saw clearly that to preserve Polish nationalism it was essential to raise the level of the economic life of the Poles and especially to free their business from dependence on German capital and German management. For ten years before 1873 Jackowski had been working among the peasants, urging and directing the formation of "agricultural circles," local organizations for the education of the peasants in agriculture. Progress was slow before 1873, but after that period it moved rapidly. The peasants, once awakened, learned from the higher German development which was all about them, adopted German methods, and were soon competing on nearly equal terms. In the towns the urgent need of Polish artisans and traders for capital was slowly met by coöperative credit associations.

From these beginnings Father Wawrzyniak during forty years as worker in, and then as leader or Patron of the Union of Coöperative Societies, built Prussian Poland into a strong financial and economic organization independent of the Germans and able to hold its own against them. He did not live to see the resurrection of the Polish state but his work contributed greatly to its prosperity. Father Wawrzyniak was a great man, a genius in finance and organization, but also a father to his people whose trust in him alone made his work possible and enduring.

This fierce economic struggle for national existence made Poznań the richest and economically the most highly developed of all the Polish lands, but it left little time for the other sides of life. Art, literature, and politics took second place and played minor parts.

In Russian Poland the policy of "Organic Work" was adopted immediately after the revolution of 1863 and brought about, in spite of repression and persecution, a real transformation in industry and agriculture in the following twenty years. The level achieved was not so high as in Poznań but the progress made was great.

"Organic Work" made necessary an attitude of conciliation toward Russia, but it was not necessity alone which dictated it. Under the leadership of Roman Dmowski a group of Poles worked for coöperation with Russia because they believed it was the most direct way to Polish unity and independence. Long before most of his countrymen, Dmowski recognized the fact that Germany, not Russia, was the real enemy of the Poles, and the common enemy of Poles and Russians. In spite of all their differences, Poles and Russians were both Slavs and both lay in the path of Germany's *Drang nach Osten*. Dmowski foresaw that ultimately Russia would have to fight Germany and its satellite Austria, and that a Russian victory would unite all the old Polish lands under Russia. He did not think complete separation from Russia necessary for Polish freedom but envisaged independence within the framework of the Russian Empire, which he believed Russia would see it was to its own interest to grant, as it would establish a common Slav front against Germany. Dmowski's book, *La question polonaise,* explains his policy and foretells with amazing accuracy the course of international events before the First World War. Dmowski's group carried on wide activities in all three parts of Poland under the name of the Polish League. After 1897 it became the National Democratic party and in the elections to the First Duma carried all the Polish seats.

Great as was its influence, however, other political currents were running strongly in Russian Poland by the turn of the century. The strongest was the Polish Socialist party of which Józef Piłsudski was the leader and one of the founders. By 1890 the policy of "Organic Work" had achieved substantial results and the rising generation demanded something more. As a schoolboy in Lithuania, Piłsudski had come to know Russian tyranny and dedicated his life to fighting it. With Dmowski's National Democracy he had no sympathy. He rejected both its aims and its methods. Not by playing one tyrant off against another but by fighting all tyrants, beginning with Russia, was his idea of the path to freedom. And freedom to him meant not autonomy but complete independence of all non-Polish control. The industrial workers of Russian Poland, a numerous and growing group, already somewhat socialistic, were the class through which he believed he could work. He made himself a leader in the socialist movement and in 1893 took part in the foundation of the Polish Socialist party (P. P. S.)—exclusively a *Polish* party with all ties to Russian socialists severed—in order to use it in the cause of Polish nationalism. Its policy was freedom first, reforms later, since only under a free government could reforms be real and lasting. Through the party newspaper, *The Workman* (*Robotnik*), which he published and circulated illegally for nearly six years, he built up a following ready to seize opportunity when it came.

In 1900 his printing press was discovered by the Russian police. He was arrested and imprisoned but escaped after two years to Austrian Poland, the only part of Poland where he was safe from arrest and free to carry on his work. There he started the shooting clubs or associations of riflemen which were to become the army—his private army—upon which as a foundation the new Polish army of 1918 was to be built. For ten years before 1914 he had foreseen the war and had resolved to use it as Poland's path to freedom, but he saw too that it could be so used only if the Poles had an army of their own and were prepared to use it. The Austrian Government also believed that war with Russia was imminent and made no objections to his activities. So his little band was ready and marched out from Cracow early one August morning in 1914 to begin the struggle for a free Polish state.

Austrian Poland, or Galicia, was and is the most backward of the Polish lands. In 1863 it was also the least patriotic in feeling. The greater part had been under foreign rule since 1773 and had had no part in the national revival of the late eighteenth century. Almost entirely an agricultural region, without railways or schools, the peasants were poor and ignorant and were ruthlessly exploited by their Polish landlords as well as by the Austrian Government. Revolts in 1846 and 1848 ended in failure, and after 1846 Austria annexed the little Republic of Cracow, thus destroying the last vestige of free Poland.

After 1863 there came a change. Excluded from Germany by Prussia, Austria felt obliged to become a constitutional state, and to rely upon its Slav subjects for the support of its Empire. This made the Poles valuable to Austria. Not only were they one of the largest Slav groups, but they were also the only ones definitely opposed to Pan-Slavism, which was a very real menace to the continued control by Austria of its subject peoples. The Pan-Slavism of this period sought the preservation and development of a Slav civilization through the union of all Slav peoples in a strongly centralized, autocratic and orthodox state, ruled by the Russian Tsar as the head of the most important of Slav peoples. The Poles had always opposed Pan-Slavism as it would have meant giving up their nationalism and their Catholicism, which was unthinkable.

As the Galician Poles since 1850 had abandoned the policy of insurrection and applied themselves to "Organic Work," Austria had nothing to fear from them, and they were able to make a bargain with Vienna. In return for a large measure of autonomy and self-government, including a separate school system and exclusive use of the Polish language in schools and public administration, the Poles agreed to support the imperial policies in the Reichsrat where they were often the controlling factor in giving the government its majority.

Under the able leadership of Count Agenor Goluchowski, skillful use was made of these advantages. Galicia roused itself from the lethargy produced by many years of neglect (or worse) and began the development of its very considerable natural resources, and the modernization of its agriculture. By the turn of the century, economic and social reforms had brought about an appreciable increase in wealth and culture, particularly among upper class Poles in Western Galicia. In comparison with the economic prosperity of Russian and Prussian Poland, however, Galicia remained poor and backward right up to 1914. Peasant conditions especially in Eastern Galicia were even at that date distinctly bad. Politically and governmentally, on the contrary, circumstances permitted Galicia a development impossible elsewhere. Poles carried on the administration of Galicia and in considerable numbers entered the Austrian Government service. They thus acquired training and experience in the work of government which was of the greatest value to the resurrected state. This freedom which Austrian Poles alone enjoyed made Galicia the artistic and intellectual center for all Poland and provided a refuge for the victims of oppression elsewhere.

The gravest problem which the Galician Poles had to face was the Ruthenian or Ukrainian question of Eastern Galicia, the old principality of Halich which belongs racially with the Russian Ukraine and where the Ukrainians or Little Russians formed the majority of the inhabitants. Largely a peasant population and Uniate by religion, they were ruled by a Polish Roman Catholic land-owning class, whose interests were favored by the Austrian Government until the early years of the twentieth century, when changes in Austria's European alliances obliged it to conciliate its Ukrainian subjects. Ukrainian nationalism grew rapidly in the twenty-five years before 1914 and became not only a Polish problem but one of the troublesome factors in European diplomacy. Although opposed by a number of Poles in influential positions, a policy of no compromise with Ukrainian nationalism was followed steadily until 1914. At that time no solution to the problem of the relations of the two peoples in Galicia had been found.[6]

[6] See Chapter X, "Minorities," by Joseph S. Roucek.

CHAPTER VI

Rebirth of Poland, 1914-1923

BY BERNADOTTE E. SCHMITT

THE OUTBREAK of a European war in August, 1914, caught the Polish nation unprepared. Prussia and Russia, which had coöperated for a century in keeping Poland in subjection, were now involved in mortal conflict, and it was not easy to predict which would win; moreover, Austria, which had been the most lenient partitioner, was allied with Prussia, which was the most efficient represser. In addition, Poles saw the bitter necessity of fighting each other in the armies of their masters. Perhaps no nation ever faced more cruel decisions.

As it happened, the first decision was made by Józef Piłsudski, the leader of the Polish Socialist party. A bitter opponent of Russian rule and more than once an occupant of Russian prisons, Piłsudski had fled to Austria, where, after the suppression of the revolutionary movement of 1905, with the assistance of the authorities, he had founded Associations of Riflemen throughout Galicia. Piłsudski was convinced that Poland's independence could be restored only if Russian power were broken and, therefore, on August 6, 1914, he invaded Russian Poland with 176 ill-equipped "legionaries" who were required by the Austrian military authorities to take an oath of allegiance to the Emperor Francis Joseph. Because of the objections of Hungary, no official declaration of Austro-Hungarian policy toward Poland was issued, but a Supreme National Committee was formed in Galicia to superintend the organization of 20,000 soldiers who were to be commanded by Austrian generals of Polish lineage.

This Austrian maneuver accomplished little, for Russian Poland did not rise as a result of Piłsudski's attack. Furthermore, the Grand Duke Nicholas, the commander in chief of the Russian army, on

August 8th issued a manifesto promising the Poles the reunion of their land under the scepter of the Tsar. "Under this scepter, Poland will be born again, free in its religion, its language, and its self-government." This pronunciamento aroused tremendous enthusiasm among the Russian Poles, and the leaders of the Realist and National Democrat parties protested against the attitude of the Supreme National Committee in Cracow. In November the Russian Government sanctioned the establishment of a Polish National Committee in Warsaw; this committee hastened to declare that a victory of the Central Powers would only lead to "a new partition of Poland." In consequence of these developments and of the Russian occupation of Eastern Galicia, many members of the Cracow committee seceded, and the "rump" committee was restricted by the Austrian authorities to conducting propaganda in Russian Poland.

Meanwhile Piłsudski's legions fought well in the Austrian army, particularly at Mołotkowo (October), Rafajłowa (November) and Tarnów (December), but they were carried along in the general retreat. They then participated in the great Austro-German drive which began at Gorlice in May, 1915, and pushed forward to the rivers Stochód and Styr, where the Russians were able to make a stand. At the town of Kowel and the village of Kostiuchnówka the Poles proved their first-class fighting qualities.

In June, 1915, the Russian Government made a half-hearted attempt to implement its promises by convening a committee of eight Russians and six Poles, but the statement of the Russian premier, Goremykin, that "self-government" depended on the reunion of the Polish lands reduced the discussions to futility, for on August 5, 1915, the German armies captured Warsaw, and Russian Poland was soon overrun by the Central Powers. The devastation of Poland by the retreating Russian armies began to turn Polish sentiment once more against Russia, even though Goremykin declared in the Duma that Poland might look forward to autonomy after the war.

The German and Austrian armies administered occupied Poland on a strictly military basis, the Austrians employing a few Poles in their sector, the Germans none. The country was despoiled economically, especially by the Germans, and large numbers of unemployed were shipped off to Germany to work in mines and factories. Since Austria and Germany were not agreed on the future of Poland, they saw no necessity of treating the unfortunate Poles in a conciliatory spirit.

The truth was, of course, that not one of the three Partitioning Powers wished to commit itself until the outcome of the war was more assured. In June, 1916, the Russian foreign minister, Sazonov, who wished to make a generous settlement with Poland, urged the Tsar to establish a Polish parliament of two houses which, under a Russian viceroy, would provide autonomy for Poland, but this was blocked by the premier, Stürmer, who, as a reactionary, possibly dreamed of a separate peace with the Central Powers at the expense of Poland. As long as Poland was occupied by Austro-German armies—and the Russian campaign of 1916 did not succeed in expelling them, in spite of some initial successes—this negative attitude of the Russian Government mattered only so far as it showed the Poles how uncertain their future was.

Circumstances gradually forced the Central Powers to adopt a more positive attitude. Disillusioned by the policy of the occupying powers in Russian Poland, Piłsudski resigned the command of the Polish Legions in September, 1916, and many of his officers followed his example. Much more important was the fact that the battles of Verdun and the Somme had put a severe strain on the German army, creating an urgent need for men. Accordingly, General Ludendorff, the first quartermaster general of the German army, conceived the plan of establishing an "independent" Polish state, in return for which the grateful Poles would be invited and expected to enlist in the armies of the Central Powers. On November 5, 1916, the emperors William II and Francis Joseph issued a manifesto declaring that the Polish territories wrested from Russia would become "an independent state under the form of an hereditary and constitutional monarchy," the frontiers of which would be settled later, and that the organization of a Polish army would be undertaken by the Central Powers.

This announcement created an enormous sensation, but it proved to be a bad calculation. Russia protested against so crass a violation of international law, and Tsar Nicholas II, on Christmas Day, 1916, issued a proclamation rejecting the proposals of peace made by the Central Powers on December 12th and reaffirming the will of Russia to victory and the promises made to the Poles.

As for the Poles, they showed no enthusiasm for the plan. A few politicians were willing to accept office in the Council of State and the Diet, but fewer than two thousand men volunteered for the German armies, and a committee of Polish politicians which had been established at Lausanne, Switzerland, asserted that the program of the Central Powers amounted to "a new sanction of the work of partition," for German and Austrian Poland were not included in the new state.

Even more awkward for the Central Powers was intervention of the United States. Ignacy Jan Paderewski, the famous Polish pianist, had gained the ear of Colonel E. M. House, the adviser and friend of President Wilson. On January 22, 1917, Wilson addressed the Senate of the United States on the problem of peace and, at the suggestion of House, declared that "statesmen everywhere are agreed that there should be a united, independent, and autonomous Poland." Statesmen were certainly not so agreed, more particularly those of the Central Powers, but henceforth there was only one solution of the Polish question that would be acceptable to the Poles—the establishment of a united and independent Poland. On May 28th the Austro-Polish deputies in the Vienna Parliament unanimously passed a resolution calling for the reunion and independence of all Polish lands.

Unquestionably Tsarist Russia hoped to conquer all the Polish lands from Germany and Austria. Whether reunited Poland would have received autonomy is a question that cannot be answered. The provisional government established by the revolution of March, 1917, at once recognized the independence of a Polish state "consisting of all the territory where the Polish people constitute a majority of the population," which was invited to join in a "free military union" with Russia, and appointed a commission presided over by Aleksander Lednicki, a Pole, to liquidate Russo-Polish relations.

From this time the Poles undertook an active propaganda for their cause. As early as November, 1915, Roman Dmowski, the leader of the National Democrats, had left Russia for western Europe. At Lausanne he joined with Marjan Seyda, a journalist from Prussian Poland, to form a Polish press agency for propaganda in the Entente countries and the United States. In the summer of 1917 Stanisław Grabski arrived from Galicia, and Dmowski became president of a Polish National Committee representing all three sections of the country. This committee presently transferred itself to Paris, where it was recognized as the "official Polish organization" by France, Great Britain, Italy, and the United States. Dmowski's program, as set forth in a pamphlet, *Problems of Central and Eastern Europe,* called for the restoration of Poland more or less on the basis of the frontiers of 1772, more in the north in East Prussia and in the west in Upper Silesia and the Duchy of Teschen, considerably less in the east against Russia where the proposed frontier was to run west of that of 1772. Northern East Prussia was to be entirely separated from Germany and converted either into an autonomous province of Poland or a republic in customs union with Poland. In return the Committee undertook to organize a Polish army in France which would fight by the side of British, French, and American soldiers. Ultimately a force of some 50,000 men composed partly of volunteers from the United States and partly of Polish prisoners from the Italian front, was created and placed under the command of General Józef Haller, who had succeeded in reaching France from the eastern front. These troops took part in the final battle on the western front in the autumn of 1918 and thus justified the claim of Poland to be treated as an Allied Power.

In the "kingdom" a Council of State of twenty-five members was constituted by the occupying powers in January, 1917, Piłsudski being one of those appointed. Since he had already determined that Poland must be free of Austro-German as well as of Russian control, he refused to allow his legions to be transformed into a "Polish armed force" and to take an oath committing them to "brotherhood-in-arms" with the Austro-German armies. He had to resign, of course, and he and his chief of staff, Casimir Sosnkowski, were arrested on July 22, 1917, and confined in Magdeburg until the end of the war. The legions were dissolved and the Austrian members sent to the Austro-Hungarian armies. Thereupon the Council of State of twenty-five members resigned in a body.

The next move of the Central Powers was to set up a Council

IGNACY JAN PADEREWSKI

PRIME MINISTER, 1919

of Regency consisting of the mayor of Warsaw, the archbishop of Warsaw, and a landowner, and a cabinet of ministers headed by Jan Kucharzewski. Both Dmowski's National Democrats and Piłsudski's Socialists held aloof, so the prestige of this regime was limited from the start and disappeared entirely when it was unable, despite strong protests from Polish members of parliament in both Vienna and Berlin, to obtain the right to participate in the negotiations at Brest-Litovsk between the Central Powers and the Bolsheviks or to prevent the cession of the province of Chełm to the Ukraine by the treaty of February 9, 1918. In the course of the Russo-German negotiations, Premier Kucharzewski resigned (January 30th), issuing a declaration to the effect that the Polish nation would establish an independent state based on democratic principles and that it would never recognize any decisions taken without the consent of Poland's representatives. General Szeptycki, whom the Austrian Government had appointed Governor of the Austrian occupied part of Russian Poland, also resigned. Even more significant was the action of the Polish troops stationed in Bessarabia. They abandoned their lines and marched eastward into Russia; at Kaniow, on May 11th, they were surrounded by German troops, but some of them managed to escape and finally reached France by way of Murmansk.

For the rest of 1918 the government of the Council of Regency in Warsaw was of little consequence, for the future of Poland was being settled on the battlefields of France. Germany and Austria were never able to decide what should be done with Poland. The German chancellor, Hertling, and the Austrian foreign minister, Czernin, agreed that Austria should receive most of Russian Poland which, with Galicia, would form a third unit within the Dual Monarchy; Germany was to obtain a rectification of her Polish frontier and certain other cessions. But neither the German general staff nor the Hungarian Government had accepted this "Austrian solution," which would have left Poland divided and subject. On the other hand, President Wilson on January 8, 1918, proclaimed his "Fourteen Points," the thirteenth of which read: "An independent Polish state should be erected, which should include the territories inhabited by indisputably Polish populations, which should be assured a free and secure access to the sea, and whose political and economic independence and territorial integrity should be guaranteed by international covenant." This was accepted by the Allied governments on June 3, 1918.

As the military power of Germany and Austria deteriorated in October–November, 1918, the Poles took every advantage of the situation. In Warsaw as early as October 7th the Regency Council proclaimed a united and independent Poland, but it was unable to establish an effective government. At Lublin the Socialist leader, I. Daszyński, formed a government with a radical program which, however, failed to secure general support. In both these governments, Piłsudski, who was still imprisoned in Magdeburg, was named minister of war. In Galicia the Austrian administration was supplanted on October 31st, by a committee formed in Cracow—although Lwów was seized by Ukrainians and remained in their hands until November 22d. The German revolution of November led to the release of Piłsudski, and he arrived in Warsaw on November 10th. He at once assumed command of the army and was universally recognized. The Council of Regency resigned on November 14th, and Daszyński became the first premier of a free and partly united Poland; when Daszyński was unable to form a cabinet, another Socialist, Jędrzej Moraczewski, was made premier. Piłsudski assumed the title of "temporary chief of state" and announced the summoning of a constituent assembly to be elected by both men and women in secret ballot, with proportional representation.

The collapse of the three Partitioning Powers was instrumental in enabling the Poles to reconstitute their country, but unity was not yet complete. Eastern Galicia, from Lwów to the Russian frontier, was held by the Ukrainians. In the north, Wilno was in the hands of the Bolsheviks. In Poznań a local committee had proclaimed itself the "supreme council of the people" on November 10th, but the Germans continued to hold the province until, on December 27th, an armed uprising broke out. Finally, in February, 1919, Marshal Foch, the Allied commander in chief, forced the Germans to withdraw their troops from both Poznań and West Prussia.

The delimitation of Poland's western frontiers was obviously a matter for the general peace conference that opened in Paris on

January 10, 1919, to which Poland was admitted as an Allied Power. The Peace Conference had no title, however, to determine Poland's frontiers with Russia, for the Bolshevik government had not been recognized by the Western Powers and was not represented at Paris. As it happened, the principal Polish statesman in the west, Roman Dmowski, who, as head of the Polish National Committee, enjoyed the confidence of the British and French governments, and the principal Polish leader in Poland, Józef Piłsudski, represented conflicting tendencies in Polish politics, the former being of the Right and (prior to the Bolshevik revolution) friendly to Russia, the latter belonging to the Left and being strongly anti-Russian. To meet this situation the best-known of all Poles, Ignacy Jan Paderewski, who belonged to no political party, was appointed premier and foreign minister in January, 1919. He and Dmowski were chosen as Poland's delegates to the Peace Conference. Through this manifestation of political unity, Poland was formally recognized by the United States on January 30, 1919, and by the other Powers on various dates in February.

The Polish claims were presented to the conference on January 29th by Dmowski, who spoke alternately in French and English for more than five hours. In general terms he claimed the southern strip of East Prussia (Allenstein), West Prussia, including Danzig, Poznań, Upper Silesia, Galicia, Teschen, and small sections of Hungary along the Carpathians; he based his claims primarily on the Polish character of each area. On March 3d, Dmowski handed in a memorandum indicating what Poland would claim in the east; although the line fell short of the frontier of 1772, it included considerable areas where the Poles were in a minority. The Polish claims were referred to a special commission representing the four Great Powers, the American delegate being Professor R. H. Lord, of Harvard University, a specialist in Polish history. On March 12th the commission reported in favor of accepting the greater part of the Polish claims. It awarded Danzig, West Prussia, Poznań, and Upper Silesia to Poland, recommended a plebiscite in East Prussia, gave Teschen to Czechoslovakia, and left the question of Eastern Galicia open. The questions of Danzig with its German majority and of Teschen with its Polish majority were decided on the basis of "economic necessity," one for, one against Poland. Ethnographically, the frontier with Germany on the whole was justified, even according to German statistics.

In general, France was the strongest supporter of Poland, upon which it looked as a possible future ally against Germany and as a buffer against Bolshevik Russia. The United States was also quite friendly to Poland. The British Government, on the other hand, was skeptical of Polish political capacity and fearful of the consequences of including large minorities in Poland. At the instance of the British prime minister, Mr. Lloyd George, the "Big Four" revised the commission's recommendation for Danzig and established it as a Free City which should be politically autonomous but economically part of Poland, with the League of Nations as referee. After the German Government had protested against the draft treaty presented to it on May 7, 1919, and had made counterproposals on May 29th, Mr. Lloyd George insisted on more concessions, with the result that the Polish-German frontier line was modified in a few points and a plebiscite was stipulated for Upper Silesia. The Poles resented these concessions, but on the whole they had good reason to be satisfied, for they obtained access to the sea and practically all territory that was "indisputably Polish." Because the territories awarded to Poland contained a large number of non-Polish citizens, the Allied Powers required Poland to sign, simultaneously with the Treaty of Versailles, a minorities treaty, by which it undertook to assure the minorities complete protection of civil and religious rights.[1]

The plebiscites in the Allenstein and Marienwerder districts were held on July 11, 1920, when the Polish line was cracking before the Bolshevik advance, and the existence of Poland was at stake. Poland had appealed to the Allies for help on the day before. In the Allenstein district the Polish peasantry had not been connected with Poland for centuries, and most of them were Lutherans. Only 7,980 votes were cast for union with Poland, 363,209 for remaining part of East Prussia. In the Marienwerder district, which Poland desired in order to possess the direct railway from Warsaw to Danzig, but where the population was predominantly German, another plebiscite gave only 8,018 votes for Poland, 96,923 for East Prussia. In Upper Silesia the settlement proved much more difficult. In

[1] See Chapter X, "Minorities," by Joseph S. Roucek.

August, 1919, while the area was still under German rule, the Polish population revolted, but the rebellion was suppressed. Even after an Inter-Allied Commission took over the administration, friction between Germans and Poles continued, and in August, 1920, a second Polish uprising occurred. When on March 20, 1921, the plebiscite was finally held, 479,000 votes were cast for Poland, 707,000 for Germany; of the latter, some 200,000 were cast by former residents of Upper Silesia whom the German Government brought back to vote, according to the provisions of the Treaty of Versailles. Germany at once claimed the whole area, but the treaty clearly intended partition. The Inter-Allied Commission and then the Great Powers proved unable to draw a satisfactory line. France desired Poland to receive as large a part of this rich industrial province as possible, so that it would possess mines and factories otherwise lacking in Poland and the loss of which would weaken Germany. Great Britain, impressed by the German argument that without Upper Silesia Germany would be unable to pay reparation, wished to take as little as possible from Germany. The British proposals produced a third uprising among the Polish population (May, 1921), which was demanding the "Korfanty line," so called from the Polish member of the Inter-Allied Commission, which awarded the whole of the industrial section and part of the agricultural to Poland; 420,000 votes in 560 communes had been cast for Poland, as against 400,000 for Germany in 150 communes. Considerable fighting ensued for more than a month. Meanwhile the Italian Government proposed a compromise line which satisfied no one. In August, 1921, all parties agreed to submit the dispute to the League of Nations, whose award was to be unreservedly accepted.

The League's decision, rendered on October 12, 1921, on the basis of recommendations by a committee of disinterested experts from Belgium, China, Brazil, and Spain, was on the whole a victory for Poland, in that it secured a compromise. Poland received by far the larger part of the industrial districts and some of the agricultural areas; 231,000 Germans were included in Polish Upper Silesia, about 200,000 Poles were left in German Upper Silesia. Because the industrial district was closely linked together by water supply, electric power, and railway systems and by the location of the workers' settlements, the League asked Germany and Poland to make arrangements for preserving the economic unity for a period of fifteen years; this was done by a treaty of 606 articles signed on May 15, 1922. The material losses of Germany in Upper Silesia were very great, but they weighed far less in the German mind than the loss of Poznań and West Prussia, the value of which was largely sentimental. In every instance Germany yielded only to force, and Poland had to face the prospect of unrelenting German hostility.

Poland's frontier with Czechoslovakia was settled directly by the Allied Powers. Upon the collapse of Austria, the Poles and the Czechs agreed to divide the Duchy of Teschen (Cieszyn), where the population was a mixture of Pole and Czech. In January, 1919, the Czechs, irritated by the Polish decision to allow representatives from the Polish-occupied districts to send representatives to the Polish constituent assembly, suddenly drove out the small Polish garrison while the main Polish army was stationed in Galicia facing the Ukrainians, but they were driven back by the Polish miners. The Allies then intervened and provisionally divided the duchy between the two claimants. Since no agreement could be reached, the Allies finally consented to a plebiscite, as demanded by Poland, but the continuing excitement of the population, which the Poles claimed was caused by the Czechs, made this solution impracticable. Finally, in July, 1920, the Allies imposed a decision which Poland, then at war with Russia, accepted. Czechoslovakia received more than one-half the area and two-thirds of the population, together with the railway station of Teschen. Poland was awarded the town of Teschen, but lost the coal mines and approximately 140,000 Poles. Farther east were two small districts—Spisz (Spiš) and Orava—belonging before 1918 to Hungary, each being claimed by both Poland and Czechoslovakia. By the award of the Allied Powers, Poland received the smaller share of these territories and lost 40,000 Poles. These decisions of the Allies left Poland with a feeling of considerable bitterness toward Czechoslovakia.

There was no hesitation by the Allies in awarding Western Galicia to Poland, for it was overwhelmingly Polish, but Eastern Galicia was another matter. Although figures differ somewhat, there is no doubt that more than half the population was Ukrainian (or Ruthenian, as the Austrians said) and about 42 per cent Polish, according to Polish sources; there was also a considerable Jewish element. The Poles constituted the upper and professional classes, as well as a large part of the population in general, and it was natural that they should insist on being included in Poland. East of Lwów, the population of which has a Polish majority, the country was in Ukrainian control. Intermittent fighting went on for months, until in June, 1919, the Allies authorized Poland to occupy the region up to the river Zbrucz, after General Haller's army had been transported from France to Poland. The British Government was opposed to recognizing the Polish claim, which was supported by the other Powers. By way of compromise the Allies adopted a plan in November, 1919, whereby Poland was authorized to occupy and administer Eastern Galicia for twenty-five years under the League of Nations, after which its fate was to be settled by a plebiscite; the oil fields of Drohobycz were included in the mandated zone. Poland refused to accept this solution, and the Paderewski government resigned; under French pressure the plan was then quietly dropped. Poland continued to occupy the country, in spite of Ukrainian protests, and on March 15, 1923, the Allies finally recognized the *fait accompli.*

Although the Allies had no right to determine the frontier of Poland with Russia, they inserted in the Treaty of Versailles an article (87) requiring Poland to accept their decisions regarding its future frontiers. As a step in that direction the Polish Commission of the Peace Conference prepared a frontier including in Poland all territory that was "indisputably Polish"; this line was roughly that of "Congress" Poland, except in the northeast. This line, later (1920) known as the Curzon Line from the name of the British foreign secretary, was communicated to the Polish Government in December, 1919—without prejudice, however, to the ultimate disposition of territory farther east—as indicating the limits of the area in which Poland was entitled to establish its administration. Poland, however, was unwilling to accept this line for several reasons. In the first place, the frontier of 1772 lay far to the east and many Poles insisted that Poland was entitled to its old frontier. Secondly, the Poles had long thought of themselves as defenders of the west against the barbarism and tyranny of the east—at the moment represented by the Bolsheviks. Finally, there was the practical consideration that although they were definitely in a minority, there were many Poles—several million—living east of the Curzon Line who constituted the leading political, economic, and intellectual forces over a large area, and it was unthinkable that these Poles should be excluded from reborn Poland.

The Poles themselves were not agreed upon how this problem of the eastern frontier should be solved. Piłsudski and the Socialist party favored a policy of federation with Lithuania and White Russia, which would reconstitute the Poland of 1772, but at the same time would allow the Lithuanians and the White Russians to enjoy both national unity and national autonomy. The difficulty with this plan was that the Lithuanians would have none of it; for various reasons they had come to fear the Poles and they claimed Wilno, the ancient capital of the Grand Duchy of Lithuania, a town with but only a small number of Lithuanians (Wilno being in fact as Polish as Lwów). The National Democrats, on the other hand, recognized that the easternmost provinces of old Poland were White Russian and Orthodox, and they were prepared to compromise by claiming and incorporating in Poland only those regions where the Polish elements, though not a majority, were the dominant race and where the White Russians were Catholic rather than Orthodox; traditionally Russophile, they did not wish to injure Russia unduly when that state was momentarily weak, and were eager to make a compromise which the Bolshevik government would accept.

As the German troops retreated at the end of 1918, the Bolshevik troops advanced into the Polish districts, and then proceeded into Lithuania as far as Wilno and Grodno, from which, however, they were ejected by the Poles in April, 1919. For the next nine months uncertainty reigned all along the front. In January, 1920, the Bolsheviks made overtures for peace; as the suspicious Poles hesitated, the Allies declared that if Poland decided to carry on the conflict with Russia, they would come to its aid only if it were attacked within its ethnographic frontiers. The Poles then decided to negotiate, but their conditions were not acceptable to the Bolsheviks. Piłsudski in April made an alliance with Hetman Petlura, who had been expelled from the Ukraine by the Bolsheviks, by which the

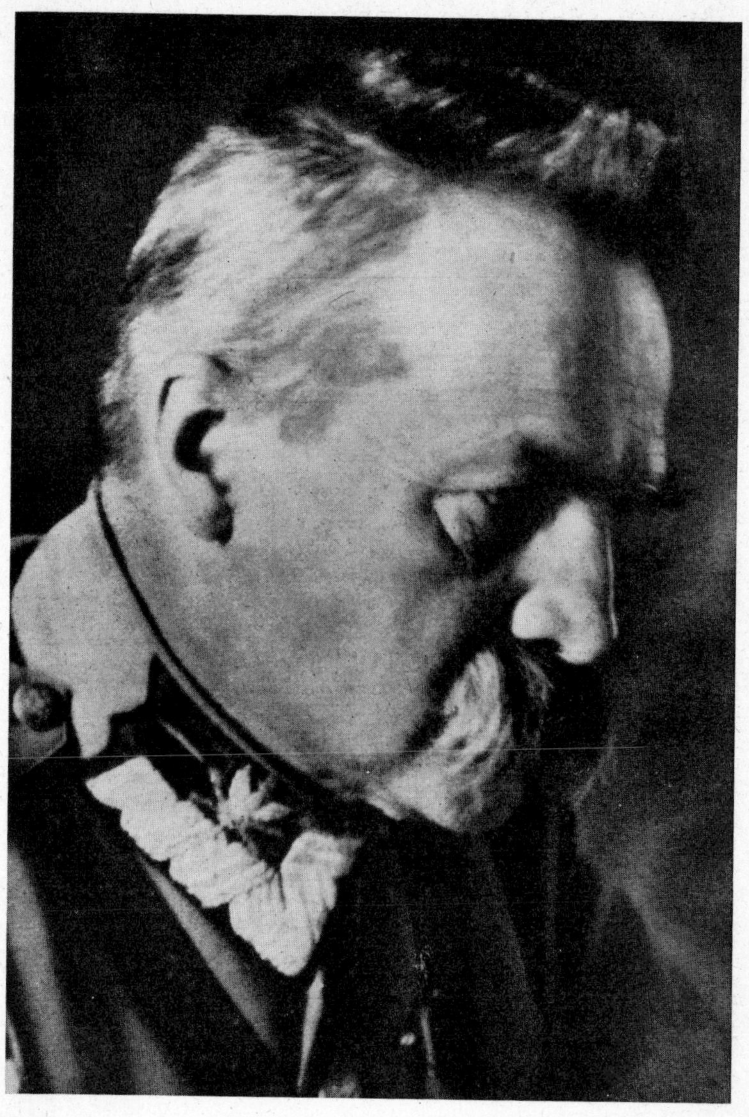

MARSHAL JÓZEF PIŁSUDSKI

Ukraine, with Polish help, would become independent and in return cede Eastern Galicia and Volhynia to Poland. An offensive was started all along the front, and on May 8th the Polish army captured the city of Kiev.

It was soon evident that the Poles had overextended themselves, for the Bolsheviks gathered all their forces and soon began to push the Poles back. By mid-July the Russians had captured Wilno and Grodno and had entered Congress Poland; they made clear their intention of Bolshevizing Poland and actually set up a Soviet government at Białystok under two Polish Communists. In desperation the Poles, who created a Council of National Defense representing all parties, appealed to the Allies under the terms of the statement of February, 1920. France was quite ready to help, but the British Government, reproaching Poland for its "imperialistic tendencies," imposed severe conditions which Poland had of course to accept. At Danzig the German workers refused to unload munitions for Poland, whereas Czechoslovakia, disaffected by the Teschen dispute and always Russophile, remained officially neutral.

The Polish prospect was dark. But General Maxim Weygand, the *alter ego* of Marshal Ferdinand Foch, arrived from France. Piłsudski and Weygand carried out a maneuver which in a few weeks turned the tide and sent the Russian armies fleeing eastward about as rapidly as they had marched westward. All classes in Poland responded magnificently to the call of danger, and the new state acquired much-needed cohesion from this ordeal. After a good deal of haggling, negotiations were opened and successfully concluded at Riga on October 12, 1920. A frontier was agreed to, running from the Russian-Latvian border near Dvinsk to the border of Eastern Galicia. Of the 4,000,000 persons acquired by Poland, nearly one-third were Poles, about one-quarter each White Russians and Ukrainians; the line represented essentially the policy of the National Democrats. Slight modifications to the advantage of Poland were made in the definitive treaty signed at Riga in March, 1921. Russia agreed to return to Polish archives works of art and libraries seized since the partitions, and to free Poland from all obligations resulting from membership in the Russian state; Poland was also promised a large sum in gold rubles in compensation for various losses, but this was never paid. In general, normal relations were established between the two states. Poland, it should be added, had to abandon Petlura to fight the Bolsheviks alone. In some quarters the treaty was strongly condemned for its "imperialistic" tendencies and because it added to Poland's already numerous minorities. The Russians seem to have been indifferent to the territorial losses because they still counted on world revolution, and frontiers would not matter in a sovietized Europe. As for the White Russians and Ukrainians, they may not have relished Polish rule, but it is not certain that they would have preferred Soviet control.

There remained the question of Wilno. As the Bolsheviks were advancing, they not only occupied Wilno but on July 12, 1920, they also concluded a treaty with Lithuania ceding the city to that state, and Lithuania joined the war against Poland. On September 4th Poland appealed to the League of Nations, and on October 7th the League brought about the armistice of Suwalki, which left Wilno in Lithuanian hands. By this time Poland had defeated Russia and the peace negotiations were practically concluded. Acting under the secret orders of Piłsudski who, with most Poles, cherished a strong feeling for Wilno, a Polish army under General Lucjan Żeligowski seized the city and surrounding district on October 9th. The population was preponderantly Polish and the Lithuanians, the least numerous element, but the high-handed Polish move caused great indignation among Lithuanians and aroused loud protests abroad. Żeligowski proceeded to set up the state of Central Lithuania.

The Council of the League of Nations proposed to settle the future of Wilno by a plebiscite under neutral control, but this was declined by Lithuania, which feared that it would lose. In May, 1921, the Belgian foreign minister, Hymans, as president of the League Council, produced an elaborate scheme for a kind of Polish-Lithuanian condominium in the two provinces of Polish Wilno and Lithuanian Kaunas; Lithuania was averse to this project unless the Poles were reduced to the status of a minority. In September, 1921, Hymans produced another plan by which Wilno and its district were to form an autonomous canton within Lithuania—which was rejected by Poland and also by Lithuania, although both the Council and the Assembly of the League accepted it. Poland then tried its own solution by holding a plebiscite on January 8, 1922, from which the Lithuanians, the Jews, and most of the White Russians abstained; 64 per cent of the population voted for union with Poland. In March, 1922, the Polish Diet passed a bill incorporating Wilno in the Polish State, in spite of the protests of Britain and France. On March 15, 1923, the Allied Powers formally recognized the Polish title. Naturally, Lithuania did not recognize it and for years a "state of war" continued between the two countries. Poland's ethnic title to Wilno was good, but the manner in which the claim was applied was questionable.

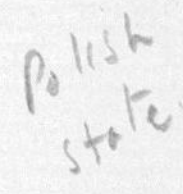

Poland thus emerged from the turmoil of the First World War as a free and united state of 149,359 square miles of territory with a population of 27,192,674 (Polish Census of 1921). Of this number 18,814,000 or 69.2 per cent were Poles, according to the language used at home. The minorities were 3,789,000 Ukranians, 14.3 per cent; 2,121,000 Jews, 7.8 per cent; 1,059,000 White Russians, 3.9 per cent; 1,033,000 Germans, 3.8 per cent; 376,674 miscellaneous, 1 per cent. It lay between Germany and Russia, both much larger and more powerful states, both traditionally hostile to Poland, but it faced the future with confidence and hope.[2]

[2] See Chapter XXV, "Foreign Relations," by S. Harrison Thomson.

Part Three

POLITICAL DEVELOPMENT

CHAPTER VII

Constitutional Development of Poland

BY JOSEPH C. GIDYŃSKI

THE CONSTITUTIONAL development of Poland falls into five distinct periods: (1) November 11, 1918–February 28, 1919: the period when the state was without a constitution. (2) February 28, 1919–June 1, 1921: the period of the so-called "Little Constitution." (3) June 1, 1921–September 4, 1926: the period of the Constitution of March 17, 1921. (4) September 4, 1926–April 24, 1935: the period of the Amended Constitution. (5) Since April 24, 1935: the period of the Constitution of April 23, 1935, still in force.

The preconstitution period.—The Polish State came into being after the world war of 1914–1918, and existed for a short time without any legal basis for its institutions. The actual fact of Poland's independence was traceable to the Polish National Revolution rather than to international treaties. The National Revolution broke out on November 11, 1918, and swept over the central, eastern, and southern provinces of Poland. On December 27, 1918, when Ignacy Jan Paderewski arrived in Poznań, the western provinces also joined the movement. The Polish nation took advantage of the collapse of Germany and Austria, and in a powerful and united struggle for independence disarmed and expelled the German and Austrian forces from Polish territory, thereby liberating Poland from the hated sovereignty of those powers which had partitioned the country in the eighteenth century. Thus it was that the independence of Poland became an accomplished fact.

Poland's independence is closely interwoven with the development of political events. Before the First World War Poland was not a state, but merely a nation with a highly developed national consciousness and a common culture, both of which were reinforced by the tradition of almost nine hundred years of political independence ended by the partitions of the eighteenth century. The First World War gave opportunity for the realization of Poland's undying desire for independence, a desire which had found previous expression in several bloody but unsuccessful revolutions and uprisings. Immediately after the First World War began, Józef Piłsudski created the Polish Legion as the nucleus of a Polish army in that part of Poland which was occupied by Austria. On August 6, 1914, he led his Legion across the Austro-Russian frontier as a symbolic proclamation of the independence of Poland.

Meanwhile Russia on the one hand and Austria and Germany on the other—states which had partitioned Poland in former days, now locked in their own life and death struggle—tried to win the support of Poland for their respective war aims. Thus on August 14, 1914, the Commander in Chief of the Russian troops issued a proclamation promising the autonomy of those Polish territories occupied by Russia. On November 5, 1916, the emperors of Germany and Austria issued a joint proclamation of the creation of a Polish Kingdom out of those Polish territories which had been wrested from Russia by Germany and Austria. On September 12, 1917, the Germans created a temporary Regency of three men, and these three regents appointed the cabinet and state council vested with legislative powers. In reality these agencies were dependent upon Germany, and their freedom of action was strictly limited. The policy of Germany and Austria toward Poland was dictated solely by the political necessities of the moment and the hope of stirring the Poles to fight for the German cause. The insincerity of these proposals was clearly understood by the Poles who remained devoted to the Allied cause. Germany's aims were completely frustrated.

Poland's sincere demand for independence found expression in President Wilson's "Fourteen Points," for which the Polish nation is forever indebted to the United States. It was these principles which were accepted as a basis of peace by the Allies and were imposed on defeated Germany. However, even before these principles could be enforced through incorporation into the peace treaty, the independence of Poland had become an accomplished fact through spontaneous national revolution. On November 11, 1918, during the German revolution, Piłsudski was liberated from a German prison in Magdeburg and came to Warsaw. The German-appointed Polish Regency then dissolved itself, and handed over all powers to him.[1] Piłsudski assumed supreme power as Chief of the Polish State "until the convening of the first Polish Parliament."[2] He then appointed the first Polish Government headed by Jędrzej Moraczewski, the well-known socialist leader. This was the restitution of the truly independent Polish State.

Although the war against the Bolsheviks was raging on Poland's eastern frontier, the Chief of State immediately issued the two decrees of November 28, 1918, which ordered general elections for a Constituent Diet (*Sejm Ustawodawcy*) to take place in accordance with the most democratic principles, and fixed the election day for January 26, 1919. It was the task of this Constituent Diet to formulate the legal and constitutional structure of the new state.

The Little Constitution, February 28, 1919–June 1, 1921.—The Constituent Diet convened in solemn session on February 9, 1919. On February 20th, immediately after the election of its officers, Piłsudski handed over the assumed supreme power to the Constituent Diet as the true and freely elected representative body of the Polish nation. On the same day the Constituent Diet voted a declaration as follows:

"The Constituent Diet acknowledges the declaration of Józef Piłsudski by virtue of which he has handed over his authority as Chief of State to the Diet. The Diet also expresses its gratitude to him for the fulfillment of difficult functions in the service of his Fatherland. The Diet entrusts Józef Piłsudski with the further execution of the functions of Chief of State until the Constitutional Charter shall be enacted in accordance with the following principles: (1) the Diet embodies the sovereign and legislative authority of the State of Poland. The President of the Diet shall publish all laws which shall be signed by the Prime Minister and the appropriate minister; (2) the Chief of State shall represent the State; he

[1] The message of Regency of November 14, 1918, published in the *Official Journal of the Laws of the Polish State,* item 14.

[2] *Ibid,* items 46 and 47.

shall be the Supreme Executor of the decisions of the Diet in all civil and military matters; (3) the Chief of State shall appoint the government as a whole with the previous consent of the Diet; (4) the Chief of State as well as the government shall be responsible to the Diet for the fulfillment of their functions; (5) acts which shall be passed by the Chief of State in the name of the State shall be countersigned by the appropriate minister.

This declaration laid down the first constitutional structure of the new independent Polish State. It was based upon the assumption that a constitutional charter very shortly would be enacted. For many reasons, however, such as the war with Russia and preoccupation with many problems of domestic and foreign policy, this Declaration, or "Little Constitution," as it was called, remained in force for almost two and a half years. The Constitution was not voted until March 17, 1921,[3] and did not become effective until June 1, 1921.

The Constitution of March 17, 1921.—The Constitution of March 17, 1921, was one of the most democratic instruments in postwar Europe. It created the Polish Republic and adopted the fundamental principle of the division of executive, legislative, and judicial powers as the basis of state organization. It safeguarded all democratic civil liberties for the citizens and residents of Poland.

Executive power.—The supreme executive power was vested in the President of the Republic, elected for seven years by the Diet (*Sejm*) and Senate united in a National Assembly (*Zgromadzenie Narodowe*) or Parliament. In contrast to the United States, the executive power appertained only nominally to the President, for he could exercise it only through ministers appointed by him but responsible to the Parliament. The Government (Council of Ministers) as a whole and each minister individually had to resign should the Parliament so desire. Also, the Government must appear before the Parliament and submit its policies to the Diet's approval. In practice, therefore, the President could appoint a government supported only by a parliamentary majority. Thus, the principle of parliamentary government was clearly established. The Prime Minister and his ministerial colleagues, each within his respective department, were required to countersign the acts of the

[3] *Official Journal of the Laws of the Polish State,* No. 44, item 267.

President and were responsible for them to the Parliament. Besides this they were responsible to the Parliament for their entire political and official activity, for the Cabinet's conformity with the Constitution, and for the activities of all their subordinate officers. In that way the constitutional role of the President was reduced to the role of the highest representative of the State and the actual executive power was in the hands of a Council of Ministers which was directly dependent on a majority in the Parliament. Because the number of political parties represented in the Parliament was large—about ten in all—the parliamentary majority was unstable and changes of government were frequent. Hence the control of the legislative power over the executive led to the overwhelming preponderance of the legislative over the latter.

Legislative power.—The dual-chamber system of legislature was adopted in Poland. The legislative power was vested in the Diet and Senate together, but not on equal terms. Initiative in legislation belonged only to the Diet. A bill passed by the Diet became law if the Senate did not raise any objections within thirty days after receiving the bill voted by the Diet; or if the Senate raised objections but did not vote any amendments within the next thirty days; or if the amendments voted by the Senate were adopted by the Diet or voted down by a majority of eleven-twentieths of the voting members of the Diet.

It appertained to the powers of the legislature to: (1) issue all legal rules which involved legal obligations or privileges, each executive order to be based on a legal provision; (2) vote on the state budget for the ensuing year; (3) fix the number of armed forces and to authorize the annual recruitment; (4) authorize the borrowing of money, the alienation and exchange of real property belonging to the state, and the raising of mortgages upon it; (5) establish the monetary system and issue state guarantees for any debt.

Besides its control over the Government in the matter of the budget the Diet was empowered to control other activities of the Government by special commissions, with the right to subpoena witnesses and experts. Each individual member of the Parliament was given the right to interpellate any minister of state, who was obliged to answer within six months. The Diet also had the right to demand a discussion of such answers rendered by ministers of the Government, and a vote of "no confidence" was sufficient to entail the resignation of the minister in question.

The Diet consisted of 444 deputies elected for a period of five years by universal, secret, direct, and equal ballot in conformity with the principle of proportional representation. The right to vote appertained to every Polish citizen of either sex provided he or she was at least twenty-one years of age, enjoyed full civil rights, and had been domiciled at least since the eve of the proclamation of the election. Any citizen twenty-five years of age could be elected as a deputy.

The Senate consisted of 111 senators elected in the same way, save that the age limit, as compared with that of the Diet, was respectively twenty-five and forty, and constituencies for the Senate were considerably larger. All deputies and senators enjoyed full parliamentary immunity; they were not legally responsible for their actions save to the Diet or the Senate, and any kind of judicial inquiry or warrant for arrest required the consent of the Diet or the Senate, or the consent of the President of the Diet or Senate in event of emergency.

Power of the judiciary.—The judicial power was vested in the courts, with the Supreme Court of Poland as the court of final appeal. The judges were appointed for life by the President of the Republic. In the exercise of their judicial duties they were independent. Their decisions could not be modified by either the legislative or the executive powers. A judge might not be dismissed, forced to resign, suspended in his duties, transferred to another position, or placed in retirement against his wish, unless it were by judicial decision, or in special cases provided by law. Unless a judge were apprehended in the perpetration of a crime he might not be made criminally responsible, or deprived of his liberty without an express authorization of a tribunal designated by statute. The courts of law had not the right, however, to challenge the validity of statutes duly promulgated.

Rights of citizens.—In regard to the legal relationship between the State and its citizens the Polish Constitution proclaimed principles and introduced positive guarantees to safeguard the freedom and equality of all citizens and to protect their safety, property, and labor. All these guarantees applied also to foreigners domiciled in Polish territory; however, foreigners naturally had no political privileges such as the parliamentary franchise, or participation in the military or civil services.

Thus "the Republic of Poland guaranteed to everyone within its territory whatever their origin, nationality, language or religion, absolute protection of life, liberty, and property." The principle of the equality of all citizens was proclaimed—all citizens were equal before the law, and all public appointments were open to every citizen. Every citizen had the right to maintain his nationality and to cultivate his language and his national customs. Freedom of conscience and religion also were safeguarded.

The Constitution also contained guarantees of personal immunity, of due process of law and judicial inquiry, of inviolability of domicile, of freedom of speech and of the press, of freedom of petition and organization. Private property was preserved and safeguarded as "forming the basis of social and legal order." The value of labor was specifically emphasized and it was afforded special protection by the state and by state aid in instances of unemployment and disablement.

The Constitution of March 17, 1921, laid the legal basis of the fully modern and democratic Republic of Poland.

The period of the Amended Constitution.—On May 12, 1926, a military *coup d'état* was executed by Marshal Józef Piłsudski. The President of the Republic and the Government resigned. An overawed Parliament elected Marshal Piłsudski as the new President of the Republic, an office which Piłsudski refused to accept because of the limited authority vested by the Constitution in the presidency. On his suggestion, however, the Parliament elected the well-known scientist, Professor Ignacy Mościcki, to the presidency. On August 2, 1926, the Diet and Senate voted an amendment to the Constitution on the initiative of the Government.[4] The essence of this amendment consisted in an extension of the presidential powers, coupled with a curtailment of those of the Parliament.

Thus the President of the Republic was given the power to: (1) dissolve the Diet and the Senate on the motion of the Government, to be followed by a new election within ninety days; (2) issue de-

[4] Constitutional law of August 2, 1926, amending and complementing the Constitution of March 17, 1921. *Official Journal of the Laws of the Polish State,* No. 78, item 472.

crees with the force of law in event of emergency when the Diet and Senate were not in session (this power, however, did not cover the assessment of the annual budget and the annual recruitment, nor the amendment of the Constitution or the declaration of war); (3) issue decrees with force of law at such times and in regard to such matters as shall be expressly delegated to him by the Parliament.

Not only did these provisions considerably increase the power of the President, but the powers of the Parliament were still further curtailed by the forfeiture of their right to vote on the motion requesting the resignation of the Council of Ministers or of an individual minister in the same meeting in which such a motion was proposed. This measure provided for a "cooling off" period and, moreover, gave the President the opportunity to exercise his legal power to dissolve the Diet and the Senate. Then, too, the voting of the annual budget and the yearly recruitment were speeded by special provisions. On that very same day—August 2, 1926—the Diet and the Senate passed a law empowering the President to issue decrees with the force of law for a limited term, in accordance with the provisions of the new amendment to the Constitution.

The *coup d'état* of May 12, 1926, together with the change in the presidency and the passing of the amendment to the Constitution, inaugurated a new regime in Poland. It was characterized by a preponderance of the executive power so far as was consonant with constitutional forms, and also by the overwhelming personal authority of Marshal Piłsudski. A new political group, a nonpartisan party in favor of coöperation with the Government, was created. The old political parties split on the question of the support of Marshal Piłsudski's regime. A number of deputies and senators belonging to the old parties joined the new nonpartisan group, and a bitter fight ensued between the supporters of the new regime, and the former political parties which formed the opposition and held a majority in the Diet.

Consequently the Parliament was dissolved and in the election that followed, the new nonpartisan group gained the majority in both Diet and Senate. In the midst of bitter controversy in the Diet, a new constitution was adopted by both Diet and Senate and became law on April 24, 1935.[5]

The Constitution of April 23, 1935.—The Constitution of April 23, 1935 (still in force), was marked by the enormously increased power of the President of the Republic, together with a great limitation of the principle of parliamentary government; in brief, the overwhelming power in the State was vested in the President of the Republic. This delegation of the power of the State to the President was very different from the situation that obtained under the Constitution of March 17, 1921.

The following is a brief summary of the Constitution of April 23, 1935.

The President of the Republic.—The President holds the highest position in the State and coördinates the activities of all government departments. Many personal prerogatives pertain to him. Thus, the President of the Republic: (1) nominates one of two candidates for the presidential elections; (2) appoints his successor in time of war for its duration; (3) appoints and dismisses the Prime Minister, the Chief Justice of the Supreme Court, and the President of the Supreme Court of Control; (4) appoints the commander in chief of the armed forces; (5) appoints the members of the Tribunal of the State which is empowered to try ministers for willful violations of the constitution; (6) elects one-third of the members of the Senate; (7) can dissolve the Diet and Senate before their terms expire; (8) can impeach ministers; (9) can exercise the right of pardon and respite.

All other acts of the President are required to be countersigned by the Prime Minister and the appropriate departmental minister. Moreover, the President cannot be held legally responsible for his official acts, nor can he be impeached during his term of office.

The President is elected for a term of seven years. One candidate for the Presidency is nominated by an Electoral Body composed of seventy-five members, two-thirds of whom are elected by the Diet and one-third by the Senate. The retiring President has the right to nominate a second candidate. Should the President nominate the same candidate as the Electoral College, or should he refrain from the exercise of his right of nomination, the candidate nomi-

---

[5] *Official Journal of the Laws of the Polish State,* No. 30, item 227.

nated by the Electoral College is automatically elected. If the retiring President should nominate a second (different) candidate, a general election must be held between the two candidates. In event of war the presidential term is extended for the duration of the war and for three months after the conclusion of peace.

The Government.—The Government (Council of Ministers), is responsible to the President of the Republic and to the Diet. The responsibility to the latter is very limited. The Diet has power to vote for the resignation of the Council of Ministers or of an individual minister. If, then, the President of the Republic does not dismiss the said council or minister within three days, the question can be voted upon by the Senate. Only if the decision of the Diet is supported by the majority of the Senate does it become the constitutional duty of the President to dismiss the Council of Ministers or the individual minister in question.

All functions which do not pertain to other agencies of state pertain to the Government (Council of Ministers) and to the cabinet ministers. Power is vested in them to issue executive orders consonant with the statutes defining their powers.

Legislative power.—The dual-chamber system is maintained but the power of the Senate is increased. The legislative power pertains to both chambers on more or less equal terms, except for the legislative initiative which pertains to the Diet alone. The Diet has also the right to overrule the Senate's amendments by a majority of three-fifths. Legislative control over the Government is reduced; a decision of nonconfidence is to be voted by the Diet and the Senate to entail the President's duty of dismissing the Council of Ministers or a minister.

The membership in both Diet and Senate was left to be settled by an electoral law. Deputies are to be elected by universal, secret, direct, and equal ballot. The principle of proportional representation is dropped. The right to vote in elections for the Diet pertains to all citizens enjoying full civil rights who are twenty-four years of age. The right to be elected, however, is confined to citizens over thirty years of age. The requirements for voting in elections to the Senate were left to be settled by an electoral law. This law ordained that the right to vote should pertain to citizens over thirty years of age, and the right to be elected to citizens forty years of age.

The deputies and senators are granted the privilege of parliamentary immunity only in respect of their parliamentary activities. Thus they are not legally responsible for their parliamentary actions except to both Diet and Senate. But in event of treason or of violation of the criminal code, a deputy or senator could be liable for trial by the Tribunal of the State and, if found guilty, deprived of his seat by the Tribunal.

Deputies and senators are legally responsible for all actions not connected with their parliamentary duties in the same manner as ordinary citizens. Both Diet and Senate, however, are empowered to request the suspension of all judicial inquiries in connection with deputies or senators for the duration of their terms.

In conclusion, it should be noted that the President is granted vast powers in the field of legislation. He has the right to veto all bills passed by both Diet and Senate within thirty days after he has received them. This veto can be overruled only by a new vote in the next session of both Diet and Senate with an absolute majority of all members.

The President of the Republic is granted power to issue decrees with the force of law in event of emergency during the dissolution of the legislative bodies. This power, however, does not extend to changes in the Constitution or the electoral law, the fixing of the annual budget, the imposition of taxes and establishment of monopolies, nor in the altering of the monetary system.

Power of the judiciary.—The power of the judiciary is organized on the same principles as in the Constitution of March 17, 1921.

Rights of citizens.—The rights of citizens remain in general almost unchanged as compared with the Constitution of March 17, 1921. Many of the former civil liberties are guaranteed in identical terms; several others are reformulated without any essential change of principle. The new Constitution, however, emphasized "the general good" as the effective limitation of all individual freedom. Moreover, the principle was introduced that individual effort for the common good should be the criterion in terms of which the right of individual citizens to influence public affairs should be determined. In this connection race, sex, religion, and nationality are to be disregarded.

This principle was embodied in the new electoral law, which

reserved the right to nominate candidates for the Diet and Senate to specially limited bodies of members designated by social groups supporting the new regime. This law constituted the crux of the political controversy. The opposition parties refused to participate in the elections held on the basis of the new electoral law. For that reason supporters of the Government were almost the only representatives in the last Parliament.

Poland and Second World War.—In September, 1939, when German troops overran Polish territory and overpowered the stubborn resistance of the Polish Army, the President of the Republic, Ignacy Mościcki, and his Government, left Poland and sought refuge in Rumania, where they were interned. Before leaving Poland, President Mościcki appointed Władysław Raczkiewicz as his successor, according to the explicit constitutional provision, and himself resigned. The new President took the oath of office in Paris, and assumed his constitutional duties. He dismissed those members of the Government interned in Rumania and appointed a new Government under Prime Minister General Władysław Sikorski, who was also appointed Commander in Chief of all Polish troops organized abroad in Allied countries. The President, on the motion of the new Government, dissolved both Diet and Senate on the ground that they did not represent the real public opinion of Poland.

In that manner the regime inaugurated in Poland by the *coup d'état* of 1926 came to an end. The new Government, headed by General Władysław Sikorski, made an official declaration outlining its principles concerning the future organization of the Polish Republic. Its main points are as follows: (1) all forms of government by a single individual or by an oligarchic group shall be prohibited; (2) the Polish State shall be based upon Christian principles; (3) the future structure of the Polish Republic shall be democratic, based on legal equality of all citizens, regardless of race, nationality or creed; and on the preservation of civil liberties, and respect for the rights of Slavic, Lithuanian, and Jewish minorities; (4) the Government shall uphold the law of the Constitution, and be responsible to, and controlled by, the National Representatives; (5) elections shall be held by universal, secret, equal and direct ballot; (6) the social and economic structure shall be in accordance with the principle of justice and the right of all people to work.

Land shall be divided fairly among the peasants. Manual and non-manual workers shall have a share in the control of production and the right to participate fairly in its output. Labor shall be protected from exploitation.

Needless to say, Poland's future constitutional structure will be decided by the people of Poland themselves when they are freed from barbarian invaders.

Territorial administration.—The government fulfills its function through two channels: subordinate local governments and autonomous local governments. The legal organization of these local governmental units and their methods of functioning, together with the rights and privileges of citizens, are defined by statute. Poland inherited four distinct and independent legal systems which were in force before it achieved its independence. Therefore the Poles were confronted with the enormous task of welding them into a coherent whole to serve the needs of the new Polish state. In addition, many new legislative problems were awaiting solution, among which labor and agrarian reforms were the most important. After several years of prolific activity on the part of both executive and legislative bodies, a coördinated organization of state and local governmental agencies was created, together with new labor and agrarian legal codes and other necessary legal reforms. The foreign statutes of the former Partitioning Powers were abrogated and gave place to native statutes. The full account of these legal changes is contained in the forty-odd volumes of the *Official Journal of Laws of the Polish State.*

The general scheme of territorial administration agencies is as follows:

State agencies of territorial administration.—The Republic of Poland is divided into sixteen provinces (*województwa*), each of which is subdivided into several smaller administrative units, or districts (*starostwa*). Local administration in the provinces and districts is centralized as much as possible. Naturally this concentration of authority does not include the judicial administration, military affairs, or public education which are handled separately by special offices.

The office of the province is administered by a Governor (*Wojewoda*) appointed by the President of the Republic on the motion of the Council of Ministers. He is the representative of the Government in his province, subordinate and responsible to the appropriate ministers of the central government. His authority is great and is defined by statutes.

Each district office is headed by a District Executive Officer, (*Starosta*), appointed by the Minister of the Interior and subordinate and responsible to him as well as to the governor. He is the representative of the Government in his district and has administrative authority defined by statute.

The decision of each state official, governor, executive officer, or special officer must be based upon statutory provision. Persons concerned have the right of appeal first to the immediately superior authority, and then to the Supreme Administrative Tribunal which is an independent court capable of passing judgment on the decisions of government officials and of controlling their actions.

This new territorial administration is built upon the principle of the unitary, homogeneous state. There is no trace of federalism as Americans understand it.

The state agencies mentioned above deal with questions concerning the State as a whole. The vast province of purely local problems is left to the following autonomous self-governing agencies: (a) rural self-government, (b) urban self-government, and (c) district self-government.

(a) *Rural self-government.*—The unit of rural self-government is the commune. It consists of one, or, more often, of several villages or small towns, bound together by common local interests. Each commune has a local legislative body, or council, and an executive body, or board, the latter headed by the Sheriff. These bodies handle only local matters. If the commune consists of several villages, each village has its own executive officer. All members of these legislative and executive bodies are elected by universal, equal and direct ballot.

(b) *Urban self-government.*—Urban affairs are administered, or managed, by legislative councils and executive boards, the executive officers of the latter having the title of President in the larger cities and Burgomaster in the smaller ones. The city councils consist of from twelve to one hundred members, depending upon the size of the city. These members are elected by universal, secret,

WŁADYSŁAW RACZKIEWICZ

PRESIDENT OF THE REPUBLIC OF POLAND, 1939–

direct and equal ballot in accordance with the principle of proportional representation. Members of boards are elected by city councils.

(c) *District self-government.*—With the exception of the largest cities in the country which were exempted from district supervision, all units of rural and urban self-government unite to form a unit of district self-government. This district unit comprises a district council and a district board. Members of the former are elected by a special electoral body composed of members of the councils and boards of the smaller administrative units comprising the district. Members of the district board are elected by the district council, save the chairman of the board. The District Executive Officer is ex-officio chairman of the board.

State supervision.—All agencies of self-government are subject to state supervision as to the conformity of their activities with statutory law. In addition, their most important decisions require the approval of the appropriate government officials.

CHAPTER VIII

Polish Political Parties

BY MALBONE W. GRAHAM

BETWEEN THE DISAPPEARANCE of the ancient Polish State and the establishment of the Republic of Poland at the close of the First World War, there was no common forum for the meeting and merging of Polish political opinion. In default of an institutional medium through which the currents of political life could normally flow, public opinion in the partitioned lands became, in the course of more than a century, extraordinarily divided. This was in part attributable to the different regimes to which the Polish people were subjected—regimes which, all too frequently, laid their hands heavily upon the press; the progressive segmentation of opinion was further traceable to the divisive force of both religious and revolutionary ideologies. In consequence, Polish public life, already stagnating for want of political outlets, suffered from the legacy of a stubborn individualism. Thus atomized, Polish public opinion in prewar days was handicapped as a cohesive force.

In Prussian Poland, under the incessant pressure of German masters, the national character of the Poles hardened, lost its romantic and Messianic exuberance, and, although becoming sternly realistic, remained politically implacable. To a limited degree Poles and Germans, though generally intransigent, found common ground in effecting public improvements and in advancing the general well-being. But neither in the Prussian Landtag, where the Poles were an impotent minority, nor in the German Reichstag, where they were less obviously in evidence, was there at any time the slightest *rapprochement*. In Prussian Poland all Polish opinion was oppositional but, keeping well within the bounds of legal obstructionism, never assumed revolutionary forms. In the years between the formation of the Hohenzollern Reich and the outbreak of the First World War, public opinion among the Prussian Poles was consistently anti-German. Although united in general hostility toward their German masters, the Poles were not basically in agreement upon any chartered course to bring them national deliverance.

In Russian Poland, and among the Poles in Russia the situation, between 1864 and 1905, looked even more hopeless. Without any forum for institutionalized expression of their wishes, the unhappy Poles were denied even the scant leeway for articulate expression vouchsafed their brethren under German rule in the Reichstag, the Landtag, and in local government. Their press and language alike were pitilessly dragooned, and every type of administrative barrier to the achievement of national purposes was imposed by an obnoxious bureaucracy which was wholly Russian. To an extent, however, the Poles received solace from the fact that the Russians themselves lived under comparable political difficulties. In default of licit channels, open and aboveboard, for the play of political forces, many Poles were led to make common cause with the Russian revolutionaries of both socialist and agrarian persuasions and so to join forces in the hope of a common liberation when the pillars of autocracy fell. Down to the Revolution of 1905, therefore, formally organized Polish political activity was scarcely distinguishable below ground from that of Russian groups, although there were separate Polish groupings at work in the common subterranean cause.

The first Russian revolution gained for the Poles of Russia both an altered political climate, with the consequent opportunity for work aboveground, and a tribune in the Duma where Polish opinion could make itself articulate. Out of this crisis there emerged the National Democratic party, itself the outgrowth of an earlier National League (*Liga Narodowa*) under the brilliant leadership of Roman Dmowski, who was hailed by his colleagues in the Duma as "the unofficial Polish Foreign Minister." Without here entering into the domestic program of a party whose democracy was much less in evidence than its nationalism, let it suffice to say that of all the parties in the Polish lands Dmowski's group was most genuinely all-Polish in its outlook on the world scene. Because personally he was so completely convinced that Germany, not Russia, was the real enemy of Poland, Dmowski took an undeviating line of policy, second only to that of Masaryk in its consistency and anti-Teutonic character. It is worth recording, after a lapse of nearly two score years, that the ebullient chauvinism and romantic nationalism of Dmowski were historically accurate in their analysis and depiction of the hereditary enemy (*Erbfeind*), of the Polish nation, and that they furnished a far sounder basis of statesmanship than the anti-Russian policy in which Poland indulged at times after recovering its independence. With this initial orientation, the National Democrats formed the first political party in Russian Poland to take effective form and display discipline in constructive parliamentary life.

The second main current in the political life of Russian Poland was socialist. Polish socialism, however, though internally divided on tactics, was only lightly impregnated with the doctrines of internationalism pervading Russian socialism, and remained from its inception staunchly nationalist, and, as was true of almost all other European socialist parties, bitterly anti-Russian, i.e., antiautocratic, antimonarchical, and antidynastic. It was from this camp, as yet ill-defined and ill-organized, that there emerged in the 'nineties the significant figure of Józef Piłsudski. But down to the collapse of Tsarist Russia, the Polish Socialist party (*Polska Partja Socjalistyczna*) was totally impotent as a partisan force. Only as it crossed its influence with that which came from the Socialists of Austrian Poland did it become a significant factor in the hour of the resurgence of the Polish State.

Under the milder administration of Austria, the Poles of the Dual Monarchy fared exceptionally well. Because they formed the ruling upper class of gentry in Galicia, they continuously possessed a political status which their kinsmen in Prussia and Russia lacked; because they were the possessors of the soil, they were, from the standpoint of the monarchy, a conservative, stabilizing force; because they were overwhelmingly Catholic, they found in their religion an additional bond to the dynasty that governed polyglot Austria. All these factors, however, would not have given the Austrian Poles a favored position had they assumed an intransigent attitude toward Vienna. In and under Austria, instead, they discovered their utility to the regime—for a price. That price, to the dynasty and the government in Vienna, was one of continuous concessions and a free hand in Galicia; to the Poles it meant a parliamentary support of the Germans in the imperial capital. Hence, there developed, between the hour of the dynasty's desperation in 1867 and the death of Francis Joseph in 1916, three generations of astute bargainers, clever political manipulators who obtained many advantages in Vienna. In consequence of the tactics employed for half a century, there was built up in Galicia another Piedmont—a vantage point from which to work for the eventual reconstitution of a unified Polish State.

There were many additional rewards. The basic compromise of 1867 served almost without interruption to give the Poles entree to the whole Austrian administration and thousands of political careers and many more bureaucratic positions were opened to the men from Galicia. In consequence the imperial administration, even the Austrian diplomatic service, came to contain key men, trained to the business of governing even though only in the easy-going manner of Austria-Hungary. In the Galician Diet, and in the Imperial Reichsrat, the Austrian Poles found effective and continuous representation. Small wonder, then, that in time political parties came into being in Galicia, to subserve, at both Lwów and Vienna, the interests of Polish nationality. Cracow, the oldest and most historic city of Austrian Poland, became the center of conservative activity, but other political groupings, largely particularist in outlook, also rose to work, within the territorial and administrative limitations imposed by Austrian suzerainty, for the well-being and advancement of the Poles. Thus it was that the Polish Socialist party established its strongest center in Galicia; it was here, too, that Polish agrarian radicalism first found its political expression in the Polish Populist party (*Polskie Stronnictwo Ludowe*) which further appropriated to itself the name of the ancient Piast dynasty. Though all these groupings viewed their kinsmen outside Galicia with sympathy and interest, the political parties in Austrian Poland were, and remained, down to 1916, wholly provincial and regional in character, except for a limited group of the National Democratic party formed on Galician soil after 1907.

One further word must be said regarding the Austrian Poles. Because of the restricted franchise and the curial organization of voting before the great reform of 1907, what parties took shape were not drawn from wide segments of the populace. Only after the adoption of universal suffrage for elections to the Austrian Reichsrat did it become possible to organize vote-getting parties in the western European and American sense. These parties functioned for two parliamentary elections, those of 1907 and 1911, before the war came, and thus possessed the organization and the facilities for making articulate and effective the political claims of the various segments of the Galician populace. Austrian Poland thus stood in an entirely different category from Russian and Prussian Poland in the degree of political expression it enjoyed, and in the weapons it devised for political combat.

From the foregoing survey it becomes apparent that in each of the three parts of partitioned Poland before 1914 powerful forces were at work to organize the force of public opinion among the Poles of each area with a view to safeguarding the interests of the Polish population, holding it together, preventing hostile governmental pressures, and utilizing, wherever possible, every shred of vantage given by the regime dominating the particular land. But it was chiefly the National Democrats of the Congress Kingdom who dared envisage a unification of Poland, or its resurgence as an independent state. In consequence, the advent of war in 1914 found the Poles, though romantically patriotic, without an agreed program.

The Austro-German conquest of Russian Poland in 1915 created a new, fundamentally changed situation. Not for a century had the Polish lands been united under a single administration. Now, within a twelvemonth after the outbreak of war, all the Polish-inhabited lands were within the control of the Central Powers, and the hope of uniting the country passed from the domain of reverie to the hard, cold terrain of military administration. It was a brutal geopolitical fact of the first magnitude, with a series of far-reaching political and psychological consequences. The dazed populace of Russian Poland, seeing deliverance from Russia come with unexpected suddenness, once more saw the possibility of an independent political organization—a Polish state—loom large, and oriented itself accordingly. Likewise, the Polish population in Austria and Prussia, many of whose sons were in the "liberating" armies, watched with strange fascination the developing drama on the eastern front and concluded that the historic occasion for the renascence of an independent Poland was in the making. Under these circumstances there occurred, with the beginning of this new period, as dramatic a welling up of opinion, and its crystallization into new groupings, as has ever been seen in modern times. With the prospect of new life for Poland, the living forms which political vitality employs began to take visible shape.

This dynamic process of party formation began almost simultaneously in all parts of Poland. "At every point in Polish territory," wrote a French observer of the rapidly changing scene, after the withdrawal of the Russian armies, "there at once appeared numerous groups, many of which, however, were only clubs having merely a few dozen adherents. Little by little a crystallization took place, and from city to city kindred elements united." In the presence of elemental forces such as war and revolution, the fusion process accelerated and secondary groupings tended to disappear. In season "there were created great federations representing rather clearly, on the whole, the three principal trends of the Right, Center, and Left." These were given new stimulus by two major events: the decision of the Central Powers in 1916 to accord a limited "independence" to Russian Poland, and the Russian revolution early in March, 1917, which for all practical purposes temporarily eliminated Russia as a factor in determining the future status of Poland.

The parties which thus took national shape crystallized at an extraordinary moment in world history—one in which Russia was almost wholly without influence as a political factor, and in which the military fortunes of the Austro-German coalition temporarily hung high. The conjuncture of these two circumstances predetermined that the newly formed political parties were to have virtually no opportunity to exercise power until the golden hour of Austro-German success had passed and the coalition of the Central Powers lay in pieces. The transition from party formation to the formulation of policy therefore occurred in Poland when the momentary weakness of its immediate Great Power neighbors left it under a double illusion of power. The historic legacy of discrete opinion and the unusual setting of world history at the moment when Poland was reborn therefore operated to an unwonted degree in shaping the attitude and the outlook of the parties whose genesis is presented in this volume.

In the formation of genuinely national parties in Poland, four major ideologies converged. First and foremost was the powerful dynamic of nationalism which ran, in varying degrees, through all the party groups which eventually entered the political scene. The second was that of the Christian tradition, represented in Polish political life exclusively by the Roman Catholic Church as an organized political force. The third element was that of democracy, variously interpreted by differing social classes as a political, or economic, or social philosophy isolatedly or in combination with other ideologies. Lastly, socialism offered itself as a programmatic solvent of most of the ills of a war-wracked world. But precisely because none of these dynamic forces was monopolized by any one faction, the peculiar combinations which emerged from these four constituent philosophies were predestined to make Poland's political life a continuously changing, kaleidoscopic picture.

Though nationalist ideology permeated every group in the Polish lands, as the common denominator and common bond, its very pervasiveness, however, kept it from being per se an active, successful, partisan force. On a program of support of national aims, such as the reconstitution of the Polish State, it was possible quickly to organize fanatically nationalist groupings, but unless a further factor of cohesion in terms of common religious belief, common economic interests, or social aspirations shared in common reinforced the nationalist ideology, exclusively nationalist party groupings tended to prove extremely unstable and short-lived. Only in combination with other ideologies did they exhibit the capacity for survival over any extended period of time. It may therefore be set down in the record that the enthusiastic nationalist groups emerging as the moment of Poland's renascence approached were fated to flourish but briefly, and, ultimately, were to find their appointed place in a more enduring combination of political forces. Once this fundamental fact of emergence and fusion is thoroughly appreciated, it markedly decomplicates and clarifies the general party situation; it then becomes possible, in any computation of the mortality of political groupings, accurately and scientifically to account for the reappearance of the same dynamic political energies in some new and altogether understandable combination. However necessary, however useful as instrumentalities in the reconstituting of an independent Polish state the partisan groupings having as their primary or major objective the fusion into one living entity of the divided lands and peoples making up Poland fully subserved their purpose when a united Poland became a *fait accompli*. They thereupon quickly passed from the scene into different groupings organized about new foci.

The same cannot be said of the remaining dynamic forces entering into the makeup of the Polish party constellation. Neither clerical nor democratic nor socialist objectives could be attained overnight; hence, apart from the upholders of extreme socialism, whose attitude was likely to be stigmatized as antinational or antipatriotic, all other partisan groups tended to combine two or more of the dynamic factors in political life in order to secure a wider basis for action and to gain a greater following. The forms assumed by the successive fusions occurring in the Polish lands may now be reviewed.

The direct crossing of the nationalist ideology and tradition with its principal competitors was destined to produce (1) Christian nationalism, (2) national democracy, and (3) national socialism. Of these, national democracy was already regionally in existence, but had not, as yet, developed on a countrywide scale; in the religiously linked parties of the three Polish lands were found, as will presently be seen, all the ingredients of Christian nationalism; but national socialism, in any form even roughly analogous to that in Germany completely failed to materialize, largely because of the impossibility of polarizing public opinion around such foci. When these binary combinations of political ideas are viewed more closely, it is interesting to note that the combination of the religious motif with the other prevailing ideologies produced Christian nationalism, Christian democracy, and Christian socialism—all of which presently found actual concrete political expression.

The democratic ideology, initially embodied almost wholly in the populist program directly connected with the democratic ownership of land, in part was ultimately diverted to the National Democratic, Christian Democratic, and Social Democratic parties, and dissipated throughout the one-sided struggle for land reform in the factionalism which subsequently developed within the populist ranks. Finally, politically articulate socialism, as it exfoliated in Poland, tended to be an exotic luxury in a peasant land, finding itself violently at odds with the nationalist parties, pilloried by the partisans of the clerical tradition—and so destined to impotence, opposed by the conservative Populists and aided only grudgingly by the more radical Populists, the minorities and, as in many other countries, by splinter groups of bourgeois Liberals.

The catalogue of political combinations and permutations is, unhappily, not exhausted by the foregoing groupings. There remained the possibility of combining the nationalist outlook with either Christian democracy or Christian socialism—a fusion which the National Workers party (*Narodowa Partja Robotnicza*), forged with clerical assistance from recruits gathered from the National Democratic party, most vigorously embodied, and which also appeared at the elections for the First Parliament in the loosely federated bloc calling itself the Christian League of National Union (*Chrześcijański Związek Jednośći Narodowej*). Of any attempt at creating a party with democratic orientations, yet pledged to a national socialist program, there is not a trace. On the contrary, in the last half dozen years of the Republic, after successive cabinets had espoused a course of feebly initiative *rapprochement* with the Third Reich, certain new groupings, such as the National Radicals, or the NARAS, came into being which ironically attempted to fuse—not altogether successfully—the Christian nationalist tradition with some of the procedures and organizational forms of national socialism. With this initial bird's-eye view of the whole political scene, it is now possible briefly to characterize the more important parties noted on the accompanying chart.

In the Constituent Diet the nationalist tradition was represented first and foremost by the National People's Union (*Związek Ludowo Narodowy*), formed by the electoral fusion, in the hour of recovered independence, of the National Democratic party and a number of kindred groups. With the motto "Poland for the Poles" as its major objective and the force of the Prussian Poles added to those of the Kingdom and of Galicia behind it, the party was the backbone of every governmental coalition from Paderewski's first all-national ministry, backed by the Diet in February, 1919, to the fall of the first Witos cabinet in September, 1921, when Poland, as is noted elsewhere, passed under the control of a succession of minority ministries.

Strongly Catholic, pro-French, and bitterly anti-German, the party epitomized in its makeup and orientations the dominant trends in the world politics of the period. Possessing a strong press and commanding such powerful papers as the *Poznań Courier* (*Kurjer Poznański*), the *Polish Word* (*Słowo Polskie*) at Lwów, the *Voice of Lublin* (*Głos Lubelski*), the *Wilno Daily* (*Dziennik Wileński*), and the *Warsaw Gazette* (*Gazeta Warszawska*), and the *Morning Gazette* (*Gazeta Poranna*), in the capital city, it had abundant opportunity to mold public opinion and manipulate its responses in the early postwar years. In its ranks were found Paderewski, Dmowski, Marjan Seyda (today Minister of State in the Polish Government-in-Exile), Erasmus Piltz, Konstanty Skirmunt, and Count Maurycy Zamoyski—the whole galaxy of early diplomats and foreign ministers, not to mention numerous prelates. Because the party was in the closest possible touch with Allied circles and free of all taint of pro-Germanism, it undoubtedly had a higher prestige, nationally and internationally, than any other party in 1919.

In consequence of the party's composition, its insistence on the union of church and state and church and school, on a strong army, on the integrity and security of the nation's frontiers, on strong, centralized government in many matters was to be expected. The industrialist element in the party stressed the need of repression of all strikes, the solution of labor controversies solely by peaceful means, the rapid commercial and industrial development of the country and, very reluctantly, the undertaking of moderate land reform. Viewed in the large, the nationalist program looked to the creation of a strong, militant, armed Poland, industrially developed, vigilantly alert against both foreign foes and domestic dissenters, particularly among the minority groups. In the presence of large non-Polish populations, it manufactured and propagated the myth of a solidly national state. A more perfect epitome of Christian nationalism could hardly be found. By the time of the elections to the First Parliament, the nationalists had gathered into one fold not only the National People's Union but also the Christian Nationalist Labor Club (*Narodowe Chrześcijańskie Stronnictwo*

Pracy), the Catholic People's party and the Christian Democrats to form the large bloc calling itself the Christian League of National Union (*Chrześcijański Związek Jedności Narodowej*), commanding approximately 170 seats in the Parliament and representing 2,500,000 electors.

The second major grouping in Polish politics was made up of the cluster of parties espousing, in varying degrees, populist doctrines. In its broadest sense, populism may be regarded as an amorphous, mass democratic movement growing out of the failure of the revolutionary upheaval in the Russia of 1905 to bring about economic change. In consequence, land-hungry groups of Polish nationality, both in the Kingdom and in Galicia, continuing their sullen opposition to the existing societal pattern of both Austria-Hungary and Tsarist Russia and to the maldistribution of landed property which this entailed, found articulate expression in political party form.

The first embryonic manifestation of populism took the form in Russian Poland of the National Peasant Union (*Narodowy Związek Chłopski*), which separated in 1905 from the National Democrats of the Kingdom on account of intransigent opposition to any dealings with the Tsarist regime. Reorganized in 1913 as merely the Peasant Union (*Związek Chłopski*), it indicated by its more realistic caption the priority in urgency of land reform over amorphous plans for national independence. That this sense of primacy of social reform over political independence was shared by the Poles in Galicia is evident from the organization simultaneously at Cracow of the Piast, or Polish People's party (*Polskie Stronnictwo Ludowe*)—also known from the initials of the latter as the P.S.L.—under the leadership of Wincenty Witos. With its nuclear core already made up of Reichsrat deputies or those from the Galician Diet, the party obtained a head start over its Russian Polish rival, and had a defined program, an electoral mechanism, a formal leadership to its credit when the First World War began. It emerged from the conflict in an hour when radical agrarian reform was taking place all over Europe, and pushed forward, along with its more radical associates, toward a comprehensive system of land reform. Entering into power, however, it became progressively less radical in its outlook during 1919 and 1920, and its leadership, particularly under Witos, drifted rapidly in the direction of the nationalist and Christian nationalist groups. After the promise of agrarian reform in 1919 and its formal enactment in 1920, the party felt freed from its original reform program and became quite opportunist in tactics. Down to 1926 it remained the mainstay of successive coalitions of the Right parties and even of non-parliamentary cabinets. Only for a brief moment, however, between October, 1919, and March, 1920, could the party claim to be thoroughly representative of peasant wishes in agricultural or social questions; thereafter the party suffered successive secessions and ultimately entered the camp of the nationalist opposition, particularly after the *coup d'état* of Piłsudski of May, 1926. In the story of Polish parliamentarism the populist leadership must be held to a certain extent responsible for the instability of governmental coalitions and the rapid deterioration of the system of ministerial government. In the schism produced by the struggles for leadership within the party, populism lost much of its force and its historic opportunity to remold Poland from a feudal to a democratic state.

The history of the other main branch of populism is much shorter. It represents the Left Wing of the movement which utilized the Peasant Union of the Kingdom and the Dawn of the People group (*Ludowcy Zaraniarze*) in the hours of national renascence to found the Liberation (*Wyzwolenie*) branch of the Polish People's party in 1918. Once the elections to the Constituent Parliament had demonstrated it to be the weaker partner, negotiations for the formation of a common bloc were undertaken and the formal fusion of the *Wyzwolenie* and Piast groups was announced in October, 1919. However, differences in fundamental attitudes between the Populists of the Kingdom and those of Galicia, accentuated by the clash of personalities between Witos and Stanisław Thugutt, the leader of the Liberation movement, proved too strong to hold both parties in a common bond, and the *Wyzwolenie* faction separated, in March, 1920, to go its way toward meeting the real wishes of the people in agrarian reform matters. Vigorously triumphant in coalition with various minority groups in the elections to the first Parliament in 1922, it returned 48 deputies to the Parliament and polled nearly a million votes, largely at the expense of the Piast group. Because its objectives were broadly social, the party did not hesitate to make common cause in the Parliament with the representatives of minority groups, thereby incurring the odium of strictly nationalist parties. Eventually, Thugutt was displaced by a secret poll of the party, on the grounds that he was evolving far too much to the Left.

From this point on, the efforts to hold the populist forces in line were rather futile. During the long period between 1920 and 1925, when agrarian reform became a political reality, a subsidiary grouping, known as the Union of the People (*Jednośći Ludowa*) broke away from the *Wyzwolenie* in May, 1923, hoping to lure the Piast party from its evolution to the Right, since too great a gulf between the factions of the Right and Left threatened the unity of the country. But the gesture was futile and the effort to find common ground on a platform of genuine democracy and republicanism—in reality a sort of Popular Front program—foundered. Thereafter the populist movement stumbled along in the Parliament, and with the enactment of the final land reform law in 1925 lost its last material reason for cohesion. Thenceforth doomed to play an increasingly subordinate role in the Parliament, the Radical Populists became the backbone of the Center-Left combination which twice attempted, disorganizedly in 1928 and with close-knit ranks which were broken only by police violence in 1930, to oppose the government bloc of Marshal Piłsudski in parliamentary elections.

The third persistent and continuously operating force in Polish party politics was socialism. Mention has already been made of the peculiar background role played by the socialist movement in the days preceding the Russian Revolution of 1905, particularly in furnishing to the ranks of the underground movement Józef Piłsudski and Stanisław Wojciechowski, both of whom were destined to mold Polish politics in the 'twenties and in the early 'thirties. After 1907, when the movement was once more forced under cover by the reaction in Russia, Austria became the Piedmont of Polish socialist activity, inasmuch as the Galician Diet and the Imperial Reichsrat each offered a forum for the dissemination of ideas which were officially untenable in Russia. Here, matters rested until the hour of unification, when the possibility of coöperative action was vouchsafed to the Socialists of the Kingdom and those of Galicia.

After its abortive effort to govern Poland in the late fall of 1918,

Polish socialism settled back, with the exception of the months at the height of the Russo-Polish War, into the role of a constitutional opposition party, in general abstaining from power, but from time to time giving its parliamentary confidence to the nonparliamentary ministries of the pre-Piłsudski period, and, after the Marshal's march on Warsaw, they supported the transitional regime of Casimir Bartel. With Piłsudski's personal assumption of power, however, the Polish Socialist party corporately passed into open opposition, and eventually incurred the cold, distilled wrath of the Marshal. It is nevertheless quite apparent that a certain segment of the party eventually allowed personal loyalty to the aging Marshal to transcend the convictions accruing to a party program. In consequence, they followed him, both as individual electors and as personal retainers in Parliament, into the Government. After the elections of 1930, which were vindictively directed against the Socialist party in particular, the group, as such, ceased to be a formidable influence in Polish political life.

A closer glimpse at the composition of the party and its program reveals additional reasons for its swift decline. In the first place, the membership was strictly national, thus sharply differentiating it from the Jewish, Ukrainian, White-Russian, and German socialist groups which, tactically at least, and on one tragic electoral occasion, were content to coöperate with one another. Socialism of this variety, in a polyglot state, could never be more than skin deep. In the second place, socialism was, in its organized form, urban. Its program could not hope to find a wide appeal in a prevailingly agricultural country; hence, its main strength was confined to the large industrial centers such as Warsaw and Łódź, with a sprinkling of support from lesser centers. A third reason for the weakness of Polish socialism was its similarity to Austrian and German socialism. In consequence, it was more friendly to pre-Nazi Germany than to Russia. Finally, Polish socialism was profoundly circumscribed by the fact that it had to flourish in an officially Catholic country, whose national and Christian traditions flowed through the single portal of the Church. Small wonder that, with the Church thundering against socialism in the interval between the two world wars, the Polish Socialist party, albeit half its membership was nominally Catholic, could hardly prosper. "The purely rural population," wrote an embittered German critic in 1926, "sees in the Socialists enemies of the faith, and this characterization suffices to keep the deeply pietistic populace from such sympathies." Only as the Polish Socialist party, along with the Populists, drew the fire of the Piłsudski dictatorship did it become a focal point for the rallying of contrarient opinion.

No discussion of political parties in Poland would be complete without mention of the minority parties, i.e., political groups representing the non-Polish nationalities. Four principal groups merit attention: Ukrainian, White-Russian, Jewish, and German. Although practically unrepresented in the Constituent Diet, the minority groups, ironically under German leadership and electoral manipulation, were first brought together as a bloc at the Parliament elections of 1922 and, notwithstanding their internal differences, both between and within nationality groupings, succeeded in winning a very sizable representation—66 deputies.

In the Ukrainian camp were found almost as many tendencies as those exhibited by the Polish groups, so that the impact of events in Russia was more palpable, the memory of coöperation in a short-lived Ukrainian state still vivid. Moreover, the divisions between pro- and anti-Soviet factions were far sharper. On the extreme Right was found the following: (1) The Ukrainian National Labor League (*Ukraińska Konfederacja Pracy Narodowej*) a conservative nationalist grouping with fascist tendencies. Strongly antisocialist, anti-Soviet, antimonarchist, it stood, above all else, for private initiative and the sanctity of private property and tended, with the other parties grouped into the Ukrainian Club (*Klub Ukraiński*) in the Parliament, to flirt with Germany both under the Republic and under the Hitler regime. (2) The Ukrainian Christian Socialist party (*Ukraińska Partja Chrześcijańsko-Społeczna*), strongly supported by Cardinal Sembratowicz, believing in the union of Ukraine with Poland, and so incurring the opposition of all the other Ukrainian groups. In consequence, it was only slightly influential. (3) Last among the "constitutional" parties, i.e., parties accepting the legal position of Ukrainians in the Polish State, came the Parliamentary Club of the Ukrainian Peasant party (*Klub Sejmowy Ukrainskiej Włościańskiej Partji*), generally called the *Chliboroby*, a "collaborationist" group, sharply opposed by the nationalist factions for its tendency to work along with the Polish parties. The *Chliboroby* group found the center of its strength in Eastern Galicia. (4) Of the irreconcilable Ukrainian groups the first, and most conservative, was the Ukrainian National Labor party (*Ukraińska Narodowa Trudowa Partja*), like the Polish group of the same name, an offshoot of the National Democratic movement and with very much the same societal perspectives. Not recognizing the legality of the incorporation of western Ukraine into Poland, the party took its stand with all the other remaining Ukrainian groups as "irreconcilable" and conducted a wholly oppositional, provocative policy.

Because of the absence of any buffering, middle-class parties, the political pendulum swiftly swung to the Left and found: (5) The Ukrainian National party (*Ukraińska Narodowa Partja*), the oldest among Ukrainian political groupings, sponsored a radical liberal program, particularly in matters of land reform, though by no means as far-reaching as that of its nearest competitor the Ukrainian Radical party. (6) The Ukrainian Radical party (*Ukraińska Radykalna Partja*) a Left Wing offshoot, was militantly anti-Tsarist, anticlerical in character; it heartily welcomed the Russian revolution in 1917, and actively supported the short-lived Ukrainian Republic. Mildly socialist in its outlook, the party favored a radical solution of the land problem by the expropriation and partition of large estates without compensation to the owners. In other respects it was largely at one with the program of the Ukrainian National party.

Finally, there existed four Socialist party groupings: (7) The Ukrainian Social Revolutionary party (*Ukraińska Partja Socjalistów-Rewolucjonistów*), known for short, as their Russian namesakes, as the *"Es-erzy."* Constituting the largest political force in the Russian Ukraine of 1917, and with considerable strength in Galicia, also, the party stood for a parliamentary republic, opposing the dictatorship of the proletariat. However, because its membership boycotted the Parliament elections, it was not represented in that body. (8) The grouping of seven Ukrainian Socialist deputies (*Ukraińskie Socjalistyczne Zjednoczenie "Selanskyj Sojusz"*), in the Parliament between 1922 and 1925, distinguished itself both by the extremely radical character of its land-reform program and by its bitter and savage attacks on communism. Meanwhile it demanded that all governing power pass into the hands of the workers and peasants of the Ukraine. (9) The Ukrainian Socialist party (*Ukraińska Socjalistyczna Partja*) which in January, 1925, broke its communist affiliations and returned, chastened, to the socialist camp, hoping somehow, in collaboration with other socialist parties, to "liberate the Ukrainian proletariat from capitalism." (10) And, finally, there was the Ukrainian Social Democratic party (*Ukraińska Socjal-Demokratyczna Partja*), the main embodiment of Ukrainian socialism after 1890. Tremendously influential in 1917 and 1918 in backing the short-lived Ukrainian Republic, it adopted, after 1918, an "opportunistic attitude" scarcely distinguishable from communism, with the avowed objective of bringing about the annexation of the Polish Ukrainian lands to the Ukrainian Soviet Socialist Republic.

All told, it can be seen that with two exceptions—the Christian Socialists and the Peasant party—all the remaining political parties among the Ukrainians were overtly or covertly working, if not for the complete overthrow of the Polish State, then certainly for the separation of the Ukrainian-inhabited regions into an independent Ukraine. The danger to the Polish State from so large a group of irreconcilables is manifest.

In the early years of the Polish Republic, there existed as important elements of the social situation, whether articulate or not, the following groups among the White Russians: (1) The Christian Democratic Union of White Russians (*Chrześcijańsko Demokratyczny Związek Białorusinów*), led by Father Adam Stankiewicz. This grouping, of solidly Roman Catholic character, early enunciated a vigorous program of rustic religious equalitarianism much more akin to that of the Christian Democrats of Lithuania or of the Kingdom than to either populist or Christian nationalist doctrine. (2) The White-Russian Populist party (*Białoruska Partja Ludowa*), the analogue in the White-Russian inhabited regions of the Populist party in the Polish regions. (3) The White-Russian Democratic Council (*Białoruska Rada Demokratyczna*) a somewhat radical democratic group, more to the Left than either the socialist or social revolutionary groups. In a sense these two parties were the outspoken advocates of land reform through democratic processes. In any event, they are almost indistinguishable ideologically from the Socialist-Populist party in Lithuania, with which the White-Russian parties coöperated during 1918 and 1919. (4) The White-Russian Social Democratic party (*Białoruska Socjalno-Demokratyczna Partja*) first was formed as a revolutionary grouping in 1903, but received new baptism in the revolutionary hours of 1918. It espoused a far-reaching program of nationalization and socialization. (5) The White-Russian Independent Socialist party (*Białoruska Partja Niezależnych Socjalistów*), separating from the parent social democratic group in 1924, evolved steadily in the direction of communism. (6) The White- Russian Party of Social Revolutionaries (*Partja Białoruskich Socjalistów-Rewolucjonistów*), which took its stand on openly communist principles. Although electing two deputies to the Parliament, one was forced to flee the country and the other was made a political prisoner early in the republican regime.

Owing to the fact that the Jews in Poland constituted the nuclear core of the Zionist movement, most of the parties formed on Polish territory cannot properly be said to have had political objectives concerned with Poland itself. Apart from their general insistence on the maintenance of their cultural, religious, and linguistic rights, some of the Jewish groups were concerned with preparations for return to their new homeland, and divided principally on religious, educational, or economic issues. In this they mirrored politically the inner currents of Jewish life. Any survey quickly reveals the split between the Assimilators, seeking to make Polish citizens out of the Jewish residents of Poland, and the non-Assimilators, seeking to maintain and perpetuate a distinct, even anti-Polish nationality. The principal trait held in common by most of the Jewish party groups was an almost Messianic belief in the future of socialism, along with an unwillingness to follow internationally the course laid down by either the Second, the Second-and-a-half, or the Third International! Notwithstanding these main trends, three small party groups stand out as indicating the carry-over, across lines of nationality and religious confession, of the main ideologies actuating adjacent groups: (1) The Jewish People's party (*Żydowska Partja Ludowa*), closest in its program to that of the democratic Populist parties in Poland; (2) the Jewish Democratic party (*Żydowska Demokratyczna Partja*), both strong in the Wilno region, and analogues of the Christian Democrats and populist-socialist groups of Lithuania.

The German elements in Poland constituted a single bloc for electoral purposes, in an effort to maintain their rights and privileges against the Poles. In this endeavor all party lines were obliterated and the traditional lines of division in Germany itself were not recognized. The German party press, however, revealed a weak sprinkling of socialist papers, primarily in Upper Silesia, amid an otherwise uniformly nationalist phalanx.

With this analysis of the forces at work in Poland at the time of its liberation and the establishment of its republican institutions, it is possible to turn to their actual operation in the period between the two wars. It is worthy of note that, just as the groups advocating independence found their program exhausted when Poland was once more united, so, in the subsequent period, the role of the Socialists, who played their uneasy hour upon the stage, was soon over, as was that of the liberal intelligentsia which adopted more the form of French institutions, than their spirit in renascent Poland. It was only after the socialist, national democratic, and populist movements had almost spent themselves, or lost their dynamic momentum, that new forces entered the scene to give to Poland a distinctive regime. That evolution is presented in the following chapter.

CHAPTER IX

Polish Politics, 1918-1939

BY MALBONE W. GRAHAM

THE POLITICAL HISTORY of the Republic of Poland after its proclamation in November, 1918, is broadly divisible into four periods of uneven length but clearly differentiated policies. These embrace the brief inning of the Socialist parties at the inception of national life; the "critical period" of the definition of Poland's international status under the basic leadership of conservative elements; the era of populist leadership, embracing the long struggle for land reform, and lastly, the thirteen years of pretorian government by the forces surrounding Józef Piłsudski and continuing in office after his death down to the Fifth Partition of the Polish State in September, 1939. In a broad sense they coincide with the trial and exhaustion of successive political forces within Poland; they also demonstrate the basic interdependence of domestic and foreign affairs and the fact that at every stage the policies adopted constitute the nation's response to the total internal and external situation with which it is confronted.

The socialist interlude, 1918–1919.—It is well initially to recall that resurrected Poland came into being at a critical moment in world history when, in the wake of the Tsarist Empire, the Hohenzollern Reich and the Habsburg Dual Monarchy were in complete collapse under the double impact of military defeat and internal disruption. As the backwash of the reverses suffered on the Western Front reached the occupied areas in the east and the Central Powers were compelled to sue for peace, all the pent-up forces of suppressed nationality were released into a situation of military, political, and economic chaos. The victories of the Allies on the Salonica front and in the Argonne suddenly swept away the moorings of the hollow ship of state which the Central Powers had launched at Warsaw, and all norms of recognized legality swiftly disappeared. There was thus created, in Austrian Poland by the Imperial Manifesto of October 16, 1918, in Russian Poland by the Central Powers' acceptance of the "Fourteen Points," a double vacancy of power, national and international, and a political vacuum which successive combinations of political elements vainly tried to fill. It is useless even to catalogue the futile combinations of ministerial lists which the Regency Council at Warsaw put forth in an effort to fill that political void.

It is small wonder, then, that in this critical hour of upheaval and revolution, when all the traditional legalities were lapsing, the forces of the extreme Left in Galicia and the Kingdom, feeling the impact of social revolution elsewhere, were tempted to make their own bid for power. The appeal of the Russian Revolution to a largely landless peasantry, the contagion of its sloganry across regions in which all boundaries had been obliterated by war, the sense of impending alteration of the social order in large areas of Europe were psychological imperatives not only to the representatives of the Populist parties of all shades and factions, but also to the working classes throughout the Polish lands. It is not surprising, therefore, that the Socialists and the Populists of the Kingdom looked to their more experienced kinsmen in Galicia for leadership and acted in concert to assume the political authority that was falling from the feeble hands of the Regency Council and the Council of State.

As early as October 11, 1918, the Left parties of Russian Poland put forward a demand for a government in which they should have a majority and, for the first time in their existence, announced their readiness to assume power. This evoked a favorable response from the Left parties in Austrian Poland, which were already coöperating, across an indiscernible border, with their compeers in the Kingdom. An appeal from the phantom cabinet functioning in Warsaw to the Left parties for support was peremptorily rejected by the Populists and Socialists, who felt themselves equal to governing alone. On November 1st, these two parties in Russian Poland determined to create by themselves a provisional government excluding representatives of all other segments of national opinion, and sent divers emissaries to Galicia to rally the cohorts there. The moment seemed peculiarly auspicious for a seizure of power, as the conservative Prussian Poles were not yet on the scene, and in Warsaw there was complete deadlock between the bourgeois parties.

In consequence, on November 6th several of the Galician Socialist leaders, headed by Ignacy Daszyński, left Cracow for Lublin, and on their arrival proclaimed the "Provisional Government of the People's Republic," took over public authority, and edicted a number of measures having the force of law for the whole Polish nation. The new regime pledged that it would direct affairs pending the convocation of a Polish Diet (*Sejm*), but threatened pitiless suppression of counter-revolutionary resistance to its decrees. Actually only the soldiery in the vicinity of Lublin, including General Edward Śmigły-Rydz, gave their support to this all-Socialist combination, whereas the more conservative Populists of the Kingdom immediately repudiated it, as did all the Center and Right parties. In the face of this solid phalanx of resistance from the nonsocialist groups, the Lublin regime was predestined to be short and its existence insecure. In the words of a hostile critic at the time:

> Born of force, deciding to maintain itself by force, supported by only a narrow democratic base, immediately combatted by all groups theretofore called Activist or Passivist, who came together in a common declaration, the Government of the People's Republic seemed condemned from its appearance to collapse in the convulsions of a civil war. It had engaged in an adventure without issue. By an unexpected chance help came to it, at the end of three days, from Warsaw. On November 10, 1918, it was learned in Lublin that Piłsudski had arrived in the capital. Daszyński telegraphed him immediately that he placed himself at Piłsudski's orders, and twenty-four hours later, Daszyński was in Warsaw.[1]

This severe stricture is not altogether accurate or convincing. In the retrospect of a quarter of a century it can be seen that the so-called *coup d'état* by Daszyński did not materially differ in its techniques from either that of the Social Democrats in Germany or of the revolutionary Hungarian National Council at Budapest. Rather is it the clearest evidence of the impact of revolutionary ideology at the moment, coupled with the firm expectation that, by mass action elsewhere, the yoke of the Regency Council, so uneasily borne by the Left parties, would quickly be shaken off. And in this expectation the Galician Socialists were not mistaken. The

[1] *Bulletin périodique de la presse polonaise*, No. 57, Dec. 12, 1918, pp. 3–4.

whole revolutionary movement in Poland at the time of the collapse of the Central Powers in the main was a replica of what took place in the Dual Monarchy. What occurred at Lublin in a sense marked the extension to the territories of the Kingdom of the policy which the other political parties in the Austrian Reichsrat had already obediently followed, of organizing their own national institutions within Austrian territory. For with Austria already extinct and her armies no longer in the field, there existed no barrier, in fact or in law, to keep the Austrian and Russian Polish lands apart, or under different regimes. Indeed, it was the first attempt to proclaim a government for a really independent Poland, and to move freely where the power of the defunct Monarchy had already lapsed. And like many other movements in adjacent lands, the first nuclei of independent governments swiftly merged to attain a unified government for the whole country. Years later, Marshal Piłsudski gave his validation of this initial enterprise:

> All the acts of the Government of Lublin have a sound conveyed by no other. This fact is due to the existence there not of a government which "collaborated," but of a government which *governed;* moreover, its efforts were the most powerful and the most far-reaching yet made with a view to constituting one Polish government. The Government of Lublin went so far as to call itself the sole government and to ask all other governments in the process of appearing to submit to it. This shows that one must acknowledge its efforts as historically the first to found a single government for the whole Republic.[2]

Once Piłsudski was established in Warsaw, and was joined by Daszyński, long his coadjutor in revolutionary efforts, both men sought to expand the efforts made at Lublin in order to give the whole of Poland a single government that should resolutely break with a discredited past—the difficult era of enforced collaboration with the hated Occupying Powers. To that end, after offering Daszyński the premiership and finding the latter not in favor with the party leaders who had flocked to Warsaw, Piłsudski, on November 18, 1918, gave the reins of the government over into the hands of Jędrzej Moraczewski, another Galician Socialist, who created the first national cabinet.

It was characteristic of Piłsudski, as an old revolutionary, to in-

[2] Józef Piłsudski, *Du revolutionnaire au chef d'État, 1893–1935.* (Paris, Société Française d'Editions Litteraires et Techniques, 1935) p. 242. (Address at Cracow, November 15, 1924.)

trust the governance of the country to men who had grown up in the revolutionary movement. Nevertheless, the men who came into power with Moraczewski were not Bolsheviks. A third were Socialists, a third were Populists, and the other third of the group was comprised of independent Radicals and Right Wing Socialists. They represented the powerful currents of moderate socialization, agrarian reform, and democratic renovation, which were then overwhelming feudal regimes all over central and eastern Europe. Far less radical than the groups in control in Germany and Austria, they resembled more closely the political groupings which soberly took power in Lithuania, Latvia, and Estonia than the chauvinist groups in western European capitals. The program enunciated by the Moraczewski cabinet was undoubtedly radical, seeking to achieve at a stroke, in an hour of revolution, the progress laboriously attained in other countries in an evolutionary way, but it was in keeping with the tempo of the times. In a manifesto to the nation the Premier declared:

> We have issued from the people. The Polish peasants and workers have placed in our hands the governmental authority over the hitherto enslaved portions of Poland. Thus we desire to be a popular government, defender of the interests of millions of workers; we wish to point out new ways for their expansion, to accomplish their will. . . . We are preparing draft bills looking to the compulsory expropriation of large landed properties which, under the control of the State, will be handed over to the working people. Other bills concern the nationalization of mines, salt works, petroleum industries, ways of communication, etc., the participation of the workers in the administration of the nationalized industries, the protection of labor, insurance against unemployment, sickness and old age, the confiscation of fortunes made by speculation during the course of the war, the introduction of the eight-hour day in all branches of industry, commerce, and trades, the abolition of entailed estates, the creation of free, secular and public schools accessible to all. We are suppressing all titles with the exception of scientific degrees. We ask the country to aid us in our work by relegating to the background all partisan interests and those of secondary importance.[3]

The Moraczewski program was destined to remain programmatic. Not only did Piłsudski put a moratorium on the translation of the wishes of the governing coalition into law until the Constituent Diet should have been elected, but the pressures of the other political parties combined to strangle the program, without afford-

[3] *Kurjer Polski,* November 21, 1918.

ing it even the mildest opportunity for application. With an empty treasury and the country bare of taxable materials, Moraczewski was forced to resort to loans as expedients for the renovation of Poland, and the citizenry of bourgeois stripe, particularly the Poles from Poznań, boycotted the loans, leaving the Socialist-Populist coalition resourceless. When direct taxes were levied, the bourgeois citizenry refused to pay. No regime, however well-intentioned, could subsist on so exiguous a diet; hence, long before the elections to the Constituent Diet, the government was impotent and discredited in the eyes of its own people.

In this impasse, and with the specter of exclusion from the Peace Conference staring Poland in the face if it pursued too radical a domestic policy, the extreme conservative elements, wishing to be rid of socialism integrally, conspired under the leadership of Prince Eustache Sapieha, who subsequently became Foreign Minister, to overthrow the Moraczewski regime on the night of January 4–5, 1919, and to replace it by a ministry of extremely reactionary character.[4] Moraczewski himself was arrested, along with a number of his ministers, but the conspirators failed to bag Piłsudski, and so the plot failed of execution. Piłsudski released the ministers, caused the arrest of the conspirators, but did not change the regime. It was obvious, however, that the international situation, the skepticism of the Allied Powers as to Poland's future, the lack of foodstuffs which only Allied credits could purchase, were determining factors. For ten days the situation hung in suspense, then Piłsudski gave in. On January 16, 1919, the colorless socialist regime was replaced by a new cabinet under Ignacy Jan Paderewski, and the socialist interlude was brought to a close. This change was destined to bar throughout the duration of the Republic the kind of program which the Socialist-Populist coalition espoused. Power now passed to the Nationalists, to whom, in the last analysis, Poland was responsible for the definition of her place among the nations and the carving out of her political frontiers.

The nationalist phase, 1919–1922.—In this new phase, covering

[4] *Bulletin périodique de la presse polonaise,* No. 63, March 3, 1919, p. 2. According to Robert Machray, "Paderewski was privy" to the plot of Prince Sapieha. *Cf. Poland, 1914–1931,* p. 110; cf. also H. H. Fisher, *America and the New Poland,* p. 122. It is worthy of note that the Sapieha conspiracy coincided with the arrival in Warsaw of the American Relief Administration.

four decisive years, Poland took the first steps in defining its foreign and domestic policy. These were moves of momentous consequence and were destined to have long-range repercussions on relations with all of the neighboring countries for the duration of the Republic. Because of the different patterns of policy which they offered to the Polish nation, the ideological foundations of the courses supported by various party groups deserve brief consideration.

The first policy proffered to the Polish people was that of a return to the Poland of medieval grandeur, stretching from the Baltic to the Black Sea. Whether it stressed the frontiers of 1772 or a grandiose federation of Slavic states embracing Poland, Lithuania, White Russia, and the Ukraine, this conception of foreign policy involved the conquest, without regard to cost or consequences, of all these areas in the hour of Russia's greatest weakness. To the Poles, there was strange irony, historic justice, in seeing the partitioner partitioned, in thrusting back to a "purely Asiatic" position the Power whose greatest westward reach was made over the body of prostrate Poland. The promulgators of this "federalist" conception in foreign policy were joined in large part by the Galician Poles whose earliest memories ran back to deep-rooted fear and hatred of Russia. In their view, the Russian Revolution, by weakening the greatest of Slavic states, gave to renascent Poland the unparalleled opportunity to replace Russia in the councils of the nations as a Great Power.

By applying to the internal administration of these territories, when "liberated" from Russian rule, the same federal principle as was involved in the organization of Soviet power, Poland would emerge with an enormous domain, vast, untapped or slightly exploited natural resources, a population more than that of Germany, and an outstanding place in the world's economy. Small wonder, then, that the Left parties, with visions of what socialist production might accomplish in those areas, lent themselves to the policy and became champions of the federalist principle. Both Piłsudski and Leon Wasilewski, who was foreign minister in the short-lived Moraczewski administration, were among the earliest and most persistent advocates of this policy. The legitimate implications of a federalist policy, if successful, would, under a republican regime, have been to guarantee a wide degree of self-government for the constituent republics, with a consequent marked reduction, by reason of the contemplated federal structure, of the racial, religious, and linguistic minorities in any one of the republics. This should have conduced to a rapid reconciliation of the distraught populations of the war-ravaged regions to their political fate.

The principal alternative to the federalist solution was that of "incorporation"—a policy designed to extinguish the corporate entity of non-Polish populations and to subject them to centralized control in a Poland with a much smaller area, but a relatively large Polish majority. Although useful as a policy intended to break the dominance of the Germans over the administration of Poznań, and to permit the will of Warsaw to prevail in the regions with clearly defined Polish majorities, it could only operate, when applied to Poland's immediate neighbors, none of whom was strongly entrenched, as a policy of denationalization, scarcely concealed behind the formulas of administrative centralization.

It is a matter of historic record that the Polish people were never vouchsafed a real choice between these two alternatives. In the formative year, 1919, when Dmowski and Paderewski represented Poland at Paris, the keynote of Polish policy was to incorporate into a unified state all the Polish lands, particularly Pomorze, Poznań, and Silesia, all at the expense of Germany. So long as the Peace Conference of Paris was the arbiter, the argument of an anti-German policy prevailed and the tailoring of the map was entrusted to hands fully sympathetic with Polish aspirations. The same argument applied to Teschen (Cieszyn), this time at the expense of Czechoslovakia. When the argument was stretched to cover Eastern Galicia, in the closing months of 1919, the Polish thesis encountered stiff opposition from the British, and was an important factor in causing Paderewski's downfall. The end of the phase of Allied tolerance was reached in December, 1919. Thereafter the definition of Poland's frontiers was made with an eye to Russia rather than to Germany. The consequence was that in the historic year of 1920 Marshal Piłsudski undertook to carry out militarily the other policy, that of expansion to include large buffering areas on the east. But the conception of according autonomy to the eastern confines had died stillborn in Warsaw, and the controls which Poland exerted over the areas east of the so-called Curzon Line were strongly centralized. When, in the end, the frontiers were drawn in terms of military stalemate, every conception of self-determination had vanished, and all thoughts of autonomy for the non-Polish populations were dissipated. It is not without significance that the legalization of the appropriated areas was made to synchronize, through the signing of the final Peace of Riga, with the adoption of an inflexible and rigorously centralist constitution. All this occurred in March, 1921, but action to implement the Constitution was postponed, and the election of the regular Diet and Senate, and the choice by both of a President of the Republic did not occur until the end of 1922.[5]

What, may be asked, was the peculiar combination of political forces that permitted this amazing evolution from the peaceful promise of democratic federation in support of the principle of nationality to a unitary state holding large blocs of hostile minorities under central political control? The answer is to be found in the tactics of the party groups in the Constituent Diet. That body, elected within a few days after Paderewski took office, produced an array of political forces which was overwhelmingly Polish—there were only a score of minority representatives in a body of some 420 members—but strongly divided by differences in social outlook and religious orientation. In the presence of the strong forces of the National Democrats and the National People's Union, no combination of the Left parties could command a majority; it was therefore the task of the Right parties, under National Democratic leadership, to wean away as many Populists from the ranks of agrarian democracy as were needed to maintain continuity of general policy and to frustrate radical experimentation. By a pact between the leaders of the Nationalist parties and Wincenty Witos, the Galician Populist leader, the essential controls were lifted from the hands of Moraczewski and his socialist following and, with the support of the Piast, or moderate Populist party, placed in solidly conservative and Christian Nationalist hands.

From January, 1919, until December, 1922, that combination of political forces controlling more than two-thirds of the membership of the Constituent Diet determined national policy. It was this grouping which passed the Little Constitution and converted the commanding role of Józef Piłsudski into the high magistracy of the

[5] See Chapter VI, "Rebirth of Poland, 1914–1923," by Bernadotte E. Schmitt.

Chief of State. To this body fell the tasks of waging war and making peace, the arduous but necessary duty of creating the very institutions of government, the thankless job of keeping an unfamiliar currency afloat on the world market, and the all-important responsibility for undertaking land reform. Added to these was the basic function of constitution making. Surely few constituent bodies in history have faced more difficult tasks.

During the existence of the Constituent Diet, Poland's parliamentary life embraced nine successive ministries—those of Paderewski, Skulski, Grabski, Witos, Ponikowski (whose cabinet was twice reconstructed), Śliwiński and Nowak. Of these only the first, second, and fourth can appropriately be called "parliamentary," i.e., clearly commanding more than half of the Diet. From February, 1919, to September, 1921, the parliamentary system operated tolerably well, with Grabski's transitory thirty-day ministry, at the height of the Russo-Polish war, as the only exception; from September, 1921, until the meeting of the First Parliament in December, 1922, and beyond it to the second Witos ministry late in May, 1923, not a single ministry except the short-lived Śliwiński combination, which was in office little more than a fortnight, claimed a parliamentary majority. In default of long traditions, such as those of Britain, and burdened from the outset with a multiple-party system, the functioning of responsible government in Poland was unhappily destined to be similar to the less enviable practices of the French Chamber of Deputies and to perpetuate a tradition of ministerial instability. The succession of nonparliamentary ministries was, however, proof of the existence of certain elemental democratic controls, for no ministry could long remain in power without reckoning with the Diet. When, added to this, the Constituent Diet further adopted a constitution giving the Chief of State no power of dissolution, except with the approval of three-fifths of the Senate, it was clear that the self-perpetuating tyranny of a capricious party system, and the constitutional dominance of an essentially irresponsible assembly were saddled upon a country left virtually impotent to change the system without forcibly changing the regime.

In actual experience, save for the hectic six months' period between July, 1920, and January, 1921, when socialist representatives were included *pro forma* in the Ministry of National Concentration, the Left parties were virtually excluded from power under parliamentary cabinets and only technically admitted to positions on nonparliamentary cabinets. This marked repression of the social ferment, so widely prevalent at the end of 1918, was therefore predestined to drive the Left parties to intransigent irresponsibility and malignant discontent. At every turn their wishes were overridden by the solid clerical-nationalist groups in the Constituent Diet which, if they could not agree among themselves as to this or that measure, or could not assent to some specific leadership, were at one in wishing to check the Left parties, irrespective of the feeling of public opinion outside the Diet. In the last analysis, the bicameral constitution passed by that body imposed serious technical barriers to the return of any considerable body of radical deputies to any future Parliament. By keeping the socialist deputies out of power until the wave of postarmistice revolutionary socialism had spent itself, it was possible to avoid economic experimentation which would have been frowned upon by the Paris Peace Conference. By passing, at the height of the Russo-Polish War, a blanket agrarian reform law dependent for its execution on subsequent enforcement legislation, which was continually deferred, it proved possible to still the strident clamor of the Populist forces without shaking the position of the landed gentry in a largely peasant state. By protracting the period of making the constitution until frontier wars were over and boundaries were fully determined, it was possible to avoid, for more than three years, the entry into the political arena of the Parliament of the representatives of any save the German and Jewish minorities, and of these only a handful.

All told, the period of the Constituent Diet, coinciding with the rule of the Right parties, was significant for the way in which it brought into relief the cross currents in Polish politics, the divergent objectives of the chief political groups, the unyielding character of the landed conservatives, and the uncompromising nationalism of a nation heady with the new wine of renascence. The political achievements of this period were largely confined to the fields of military and foreign policy. Many routine matters relating to the reorganization of the country occupied the attention of the Diet, but Poland eschewed social reform at a time when the need for it was greatest, and consciously deferred it to a period when its territorial position was secure, its survival was assured and the new possessions had received international recognition. It remained for the first elections to the new Diet and Senate, which together would constitute Poland's First Parliament, held on November 5 and 12, 1922, to reveal the changes which four years of a common national experience had wrought in the mentality of the Polish people and the effects of the conquest of allogeneous territory on the parliamentary representation of minorities.

Careful comparison of the political forces represented in the Constituent Assembly with those in the First Parliament shows that little change took place at the opposite ends of the political spectrum, since neither the out-and-out Christian Nationalists nor the members of the Polish Socialist party showed appreciable alterations in strength. Because of the prevailing system of proportional representation, the two parties gave evidence of a consistent and uniform backing among the electorate. Here were "core" parties, granitic, unyielding and intractable, parties that either would have to be crushed and driven into exile before their ranks could be depleted, or taken into power to give support to the existing regime. Between these two extremes were found the various shades of Populists, already disintegrating, as has been shown elsewhere, owing to the delays in the realization of their fundamental program of land reform. The only new factor in evidence, apart from some relabeled splinter parties, was the bloc of minority parties, skillfully mobilized by astute German political manipulation into a political cartel for electoral purposes, but possessing little coherence beyond that point. The election's major significance lay in the golden moment of opportunity which it afforded the Left parties to accomplish, through their coöperation with the bloc of minority representatives, what had been absolutely beyond their grasp in the Constituent Assembly.

The initial trial of forces came in the election of the first president of Poland, Gabriel Narutowicz, who was put into office by the combined votes of the minorities and the Left parties, to the utter chagrin of the Right. His assassination followed immediately, setting a baleful pattern. Actually, no chief executive of Poland served out the term of office for which he was last chosen. Viewed against the backdrop of a century and a quarter of partition and oppression, the reaction was psychologically understandable, but it augured ill for the future. For a love of Poland so intense that it would not let the procedures of legality operate was certainly not destined to create the conditions for institutional or political stability.

The choice of Stanisław Wojciechowski, one of the early friends and close co-workers of Piłsudski, to fill the place of Narutowicz proved more widely acceptable, and succession to the premiership of General Władysław Sikorski introduced a temporary calm into public life. It opened the way for a succession of cabinets, especially the one under Władysław Grabski, to which, among many other tasks, fell the unenviable one of undertaking financial reforms, stopping the printing presses and stabilizing the currency—a sharply deflationary program. The ministry of Count Aleksander Józef Skrzyński, an internationally known Liberal, was supported by all parties. In this period, which sharply terminated in May, 1926, Wincenty Witos, the versatile moderate Populist leader, strengthened his alliance with the conservative elements in the Chamber to prevent the adoption of policies widely at variance with the interests of the Right parties—of which the watering down of land reform by dilatory tactics was the most eloquent witness. A Parliament with a preponderantly Left grouping was maneuvered by parliamentary finessing into invertebrate conservatism.

Throughout this period the lone, silent figure of Józef Piłsudski always remained in the background or in the wings of the political stage. Poland's great military hero grew increasingly dissatisfied with the turn which events were taking, as he witnessed the steady dilution of executive power by a quarrelsome Parliament, reminiscent of the 1770's. The otherwise inexplicable Piłsudski is understandable in the light of two factors dominating his personality. The first was his inherent revolutionary psychology, which utterly scorned the formal trammels of legality, yet was occasionally radical to the point of sentimentality, as the Daszyński episode of 1918 clearly reveals. The second was his formal conviction that politics was peacetime war, to be fought by stratagem and careful timing—probably little more than the other, tactical, side of his revolutionary personality, but sufficient to explain a large part of his political behavior. To a man of such temperament power comes by a *coup d'état,* which establishes for the time being a new pragmatic correlation of political forces which may at will be destroyed by a new political coup, hence there is little veneration at any given moment for the legal edicts of an existing regime. One searches the writings of Piłsudski in vain for an organic philosophy of the social order; in fact there is none. The early anti-Russian socialism of Piłsudski's youth was in fact overlaid long before 1918 by a truculent militarist nationalism, but the Marshal's followers tended to remember only the earlier episodes of revolutionary effervescence, and to follow him with an impetuous and unrestrained fanaticism long after his political outlook had fundamentally changed.

In the light of this analysis, Piłsudski's actions assume a discernible pattern: the bold assumption of power in the midst of the political vacuum following the armistice of 1918; the dictating of the exiguous constitution of 1919; the impetuous dismissal of Ponikowski in 1922 and the attempt—then unsuccessful—to impose a minority ministry upon a reluctant Parliament. Piłsudski learned much from the episode. Successful imposition of a regime depended upon force, and he, and not the government of the day, would command it. Hence the continued alliance with the Legionaries, hence the close contact with the Army, hence the cultivation of Śmigły-Rydz to succeed him, hence, finally, the march on Warsaw in May of 1926 and the forcible ousting of both Wojciechowski and Witos. Force was on the side of Piłsudski and he commanded it. To his dying day he never again let the ultimate controls pass out of his hands.

The Piłsudski era, 1926–1939.—From May, 1926, to September, 1939, Poland lived under a succession of relatively short-lived "pragmatic correlations of political forces" which drove it ever more sharply away from the democratic institutions it had adopted after 1919. These thirteen vital years find their link of continuity in the person of Ignacy Mościcki, their differentia in the persons actually holding power. When broken down into assimilable form, the years of the Piłsudski era reveal several distinct phases of the evolution of the dictatorial regime.

Phase I. The Period of Reinforced Presidential Authority: From the March on Warsaw, May 12, 1926, to the End of Piłsudski's First Premiership, May 12, 1928.

The essential problem confronting Piłsudski at the outset of his personalized rule was that of increasing executive authority beyond the scope allowed by the Constitution of 1921, and of ending the overwhelming dominance of the legislative branch of the government with its congeries of diverse and dissident parties. This was effected constitutionally, i.e., in keeping with the formal requirements of the legal system then in force, by a series of statutes, sometimes spoken of as the August Laws, which gave to President Mościcki an extensive ordinance power, thus narrowing, by incremental delegation, the general scope of legislative authority without formally changing either the party system or the principle of parliamentary responsibility. Under Premier Casimir Bartel, who engineered the reforms while the Right parties were paralyzed after Piłsudski's coup, the foundations were laid, between May and October, 1926, for Piłsudski's assumption of power as premier. With a gifted and renowned scientist in the presidential chair, with a plenitude of constitutional authority at his disposal, Piłsudski undertook to rule in a way which would have been altogether impossible under the unamended Constitution of 1921. This period of office-holding as premier, though irksome to Piłsudski, lasted approximately two years, during which the endeavor was made by Piłsudski's lieutenants to organize a "Government bloc" of personal supporters of the Marshal and so to create, after the debacle of the Witos Center-Right coalition, a substitute basis for parliamentary support.

While this work of political merchandising went on, not without appreciable success, Roman Dmowski, renewing the feud with his political adversary, organized at Poznań on December 4, 1926, the Camp of Great Poland (*Obóz Wielkiej Polski*) as the first of the "camp" structures into which the country was later organized. Dmowski appears to have intended this organization to be not a political party in the traditional sense, but rather "a nationalist militia, uniting but not eliminating parties." Endeavoring to organize the Conservatives opposed to Piłsudski, the "camp" divided the country into five regional commands and numerous sub-commands, with a grand council above all. "The organization shows Fascist influence," promptly declared a restrained contemporary commentator. Such influences were not, however, confined to the Opposition. After the elections to the Second Parliament in January, 1928, the regime emerged with only a compact bloc of 125 deputies in the new Government Bloc—barely half of what it needed to control the body. The election returns permanently ruined the populist cause, some of its leaders going over to the Right Opposition, rump of the once powerful National People's Union, now reduced to 38 deputies, or moving far over to the Left, close to the Socialist camp. It was clear that free elections, even with official government pressure would never suffice, given the existing system of proportional representation, to give the regime the majority it desired, hence other alternatives were progressively canvassed. By the middle of 1928 a number of anti-democratic movements were fully under way, some seeking to "Americanize the Constitution" by vastly extending presidential power, some seeking various and devious ways of restricting voting—also *à l'Americaine*. Moving in an entirely different direction, obviously in imitation of contemporary Italy, Austria, and Spain, was the demand for a corporative chamber with advisory powers, on the theory that Poland needed "syndicalist democracy to complete the individualistic democracy of today."[5] Only under such a strengthened regime, it was alleged, would Piłsudski be content.

Phase II. The Period of Military Intimidation of the Parliament: From the Third Bartel Ministry, June 27, 1928, to the Defeat of the Centro-Lew Coalition, November 16, 1930.

In this second stage of development the Marshal of Poland once more retired from the political foreground, largely leaving to his principal aides, Colonels Casimir Świtalski and Walery Sławek, the invidious task of intimidating the Parliament into passing their plan of constitutional reform. Beginning with a stern warning to the Parliament from Piłsudski in late June, 1928, there began a period of interminable deadlock, as the Parliament steadfastly refused to abandon its powers under the successive projects laid before it. By the beginning of 1929 it was obvious that the more radically nationalist among Piłsudski's supporters were dividing into one camp, while the civilian element, originally represented by Bartel, was rapidly being frozen out of the Government Bloc's

[5] Jean Allary, "La fausse sortie du Maréchal Pilsudski," *L'Europe Nouvelle*, 11e année, No. 553, pp. 1249–1251.

deliberations. Under the first of the famous "Cabinets of Colonels," formed in April, 1929, by Colonel Świtalski, Piłsudski's following carried the process of coercing the Parliament one step farther, including an invasion of the parliament building on October 31, 1929, in a final effort by a show of force to dragoon the deliberative bodies into acceptance of their constitution. The Parliament stood its ground and demanded the withdrawal of the military, only to find repeated adjournments and prorogations by Mościcki utilized to break, by attrition, its remaining power of resistance.

The culmination was the actual invasion of the parliament buildings and the roundup of the principal opposition deputies, which occurred shortly before the elections of 1930. There was no longer even the pretense of reform of democracy, only the forcible establishment of a new "pragmatic co-relation of forces" permitting the pretorian element an almost unlimited sway. In fact the fifth Bartel Cabinet, early in 1930, may legitimately be regarded as Poland's last civilian cabinet. From the end of August, 1930, to the end of the regime in September, 1939, the heavy hand of the military was at the helm of the ship of state. In the elections to the Third Parliament, held November 16, 1930, the "colonels" turned with fury on the coalition of political forces of the Center and Left parties, the so-called Centro-Lew coalition, in the hope of destroying it and the minority groups throughout the republic. And they very largely succeeded. While the Right Opposition absorbed into its ranks many more dissidents from the Center and the Left, until it was almost as strong as in the Constituent Assembly, the Government Bloc, by large-scale use of intimidation and violence, procured for itself a clean-cut majority in the Third Parliament. The end of the parliamentary republic was clearly in sight. Thenceforth only a policy of obstruction was constitutionally open to the combined Right and Left Oppositions.

Phase III. The Period of Pure Pretorianism: From the Defeat of the Centro-Lew Coalition to the Death of Piłsudski, May 12, 1935.

With a majority of the lower chamber under the control of the Government Bloc and the major opposition parties smashed beyond hope of regaining power, Marshal Piłsudski turned over the reins of government to three generals and six colonels, comprising the key figures at the head of the various government departments.

In so doing Piłsudski affirmed his possession of the power to crush the legislative body, declaring "It is impossible to admit that victory can be assured anew, under any circumstances whatsoever, to the supremacy of the Parliament. . . . The answer to the question I have raised is no longer conditioned on the possibility of failure on my side."[6] Power now lay unquestionably in the hands of the leaders of the Polish Legions, the cohort around Piłsudski, headed by Colonel Sławek. The issue was now clearly between the pretorians and the Parliament to determine whether the legislative body would consent, not merely to a reduction of its powers and a minimizing of its control but to a permanent, legalized subordination to an all-powerful executive. The defenders of parliamentarism soon discovered that although the artificially gained majority backing the government could enact ordinary legislation, it was not sufficiently strong to put through a basic constitutional reform. It was therefore possible, by measures fully within the rules of procedure of the two chambers, to prevent the legal consummation of the desires of the Government Bloc.

For the ensuing four years, from the beginning of December, 1930, to the final vote of the new constitution by a rump Parliament in 1935, Polish politics, under the successive premierships of Sławek, Prystor, Jędrzejewicz and Kozłowski, involved a protracted parliamentary duel, a continuous cat-and-mouse game, in which each side watched the other, waiting for the unguarded moment when even the slightest break in the ranks would afford an opportunity for either side to win a decisive victory on the major issue of constitutional revision. The record of 1931, 1932, and 1933 is politically sterile, punctuated by the efforts of the Government to curb the flow of oratory in the chambers, while the Parliament, in turn, rejected such measures as the bill for Galician autonomy. At a half-way stage during this period, on March 15, 1932, the Parliament passed a new measure appreciably widening President Mościcki's ordinance power—in fact making it possible for him to legislate during the period of parliamentary recesses for a three-year period, which in fact ended only a month before the definitive

[6] Casimir Smogorzewski, "La Quatrième Diète en Pologne restaurée," *La Pologne politique, économique, litteraire et artistique*, 11ème année, No. 12, 1er Décembre 1930, p. 980, citing the *Gazeta Polska* of October 25, 1930.

adoption of the new constitution. From that point on, the ordinary business of legislation could be taken care of during the long recesses, and the problem of constitutional revision could be solved by attrition. In the circumstances the renewal of Mościcki's presidential mandate for an additional seven years[7]—to 1940—became almost automatic, and there was no break in the continuity of administrations. The occasion of Mościcki's reassumption of office for a new term coincided with the end of Colonel Prystor's regime and inaugurated the ministry of Jędrzejewicz, who had earlier been Minister of Education.

Although long rumored, and preceded by a very considerable press campaign, the constitutional reform bill was not actually presented to the Parliament until the end of 1933, and then only as a series of general principles. The definitive measure was passed by the lower house on January 26, 1934, but delayed in the Senate for well over a year. It was only as the illness of Marshal Piłsudski grew grave that Premier Kozłowski pressed for the enactment of the reform in such a manner that the framework of government operative during the Piłsudski regime should survive the failing Marshal. The Constitution was accordingly rushed to enactment and officially signed by Mościcki on April 24, 1935. Three weeks later Piłsudski passed from the political scene, with the authoritarian Constitution and the pretorian tradition anchored as firmly as humanly possible in the Polish political system. Almost the last act of the Government, before the Marshal's death was to introduce a new electoral law looking to the virtual abolition of parties.

Phase IV. The Period of Presidential Government: From the Death of Piłsudski to the Fifth Partition of Poland, September, 1939.

The final phase of internal political life in Poland before the Fifth Partition opened with the endeavor of the veteran friend of Piłsudski, Colonel Sławek, once again premier, to establish a law

[7] The two chambers were convoked as a National Assembly on May 8, 1933. President Mościcki received 332 out of 343 votes cast. When it is remembered that the membership of the lower house was 444 and that of the upper chamber 111, or a total of 555, it is obvious that 212 members of the National Assembly were either absent or failed to vote. With 278 votes required to elect, it is clear that Mościcki had only 54 votes above the minimum required for election, and that he received slightly less than 60 per cent of the vote of the National Assembly. In 1926 Mościcki received 281 votes to 200 for Count Bniński, candidate of the Right parties.

with the help of the new constitutional instrument a new "pragmatic correlation of political forces" supporting the pretorian regime. This entailed the passage, and proclamation, on July 8, 1935, of three major electoral laws, whose entry into force was immediately followed, on July 10, 1935, by the dissolution of the legislative chambers. This marked the end of the parliamentary regime, inasmuch as the nomination of candidates for office was no longer a function of political parties, but of a complex series of electoral bodies, aided by the President of the Republic. In consequence during the two months of the electoral campaign preceding the elections of September 8 and 15, 1935, virtually none of the Opposition parties made any effort to acquire votes or enlist candidates, as they had pledged themselves, during the last days of the Third Parliament, to abstain from voting and to boycott elections which they could not help regarding as illegal. Only a group of dissident Populists, assured of government support in fifteen constituencies, and, oddly enough, the Ukrainian National Democrats, who were promised 19 seats by the Government Bloc, broke ranks. According to official figures, only 46.51 per cent of those eligible to vote cast their ballots. Of these, the Government Bloc collected about 86 per cent. In the view of the Opposition journals, which regarded the elections as "a plebiscite of silence," and as "a rejection of the Constitution by the country on the fourth reading[8] only 25 to 30 per cent of the electorate took part. Sixteen Ukrainians and four Jews were elected to the Fourth Parliament, but no German succeeded in obtaining a seat.

Once its electoral victory was gained, the Sławek cabinet resigned to make way, on October 14, 1935, for a new ministry headed by Marjan Zyndram Kościałkowski, Minister of the Interior in the outgoing cabinet. The change involved the entry on the scene of new men, primarily those coming to maturity since the period of political independence. It was, therefore, something more than a "changing of the guard" or a "swapping of pilots" characteristic of preceding cabinets. It augured a new phase of political development. The new pragmatic correlation of political forces was destined to be such that, with the support of Mościcki's personal prestige, the military caste would remain in power, irrespective of

[8] *Warszawski Dziennik Narodowy*, September 10, October 15, 1935.

whether the new Parliament accorded it support, or whether public opinion was favorable or adverse. With an almost childlike naiveté, they believed the instrument drawn up to perpetuate their power to be intangible and self-operating. That is why Colonel Sławek forthwith officially liquidated the carefully built Government Bloc as having outlived its usefulness. Brought into being to give the Government support in a hopelessly divided Parliament, it could now be discarded as an outworn survival of an age of parliamentarism. "The role of the bloc," he declared, "is terminated."[9] The dream of the military that Poland would function as a martial state accepting their orders and discarding all other organizational forms, was soon destined to be rudely shattered, for, bereft of their usual forms of political expression, partisan tendencies in the country presently took on a new and unenviable anti-Semitic form.

It is a tribute to Piłsudski's sense of realities that, although he dragooned the political parties, he did not dissolve them, and that, although the censorship was heavy, the partisan press continued to exist. Under the Constitution of 1935, however, the parties, without being dissolved, were deprived of their *raison d'être*. During 1936 and 1937, therefore, a part of the effervescence of partisanship turned against the hapless Jews in Poland. Beginning with provocative municipal ordinances directed against ritual slaughtering of animals, the manifestations of anti-Semitism promptly extended to the universities and other institutions of higher learning, seeking the physical segregation of Jewish and Polish students, proceeded from there to the bar, the learned professions, the trade unions, and almost every group in the national life. This movement, which the Government appears to have been powerless to check, was seized upon by the Right parties as a means of enhancing their popularity, with the result that anti-Semitism became far more strident in the Nationalist and Christian Democratic camps than among the Government's own supporters. Presently the movement took the form of demands for the more effective migration of rural populations into the great cities, to break the hold of Jews on municipal commerce; it took the shape of proposals for the nationalization of some types of industry; it culminated in a program carried even to Geneva by Colonel Józef Beck, the Polish Foreign Minister, to

[9] *Gazeta Polska,* October 31, 1935.

bring about a mass migration of Jews from Poland to other parts of the world. The high tide of the movement was reached when, in 1938, after the annexation of Austria, Poland, by special laws, edicted the withdrawal of Polish citizenship from persons of the Jewish race, resident abroad, previously acknowledged as Poles and holding Polish passports. Needless to say, this entire line of development shocked the Left parties, which were utterly powerless to prevent it, and quickly saw how inexorably the policy played into Germany's hands, carrying with it the persons chiefly responsible for the propagation of anti-Semitism. Such was the situation down to within a few weeks of the end of the Republic.

For a half year after taking office, Kościałkowski endeavored to hold together the cohort of which he was the spokesman, and to carry out a constructive program. But neither time nor the temper of opinion were in his favor. The guiding principle of the military was political immobility, and immobility meant disintegration. By May, 1936, the first efforts to free Poland from the rigidity of the Piłsudski regime were acknowledged to be a failure, and Kościałkowski went into the discard. He was succeeded on May 15, 1936, by General Felicjan Sławoj-Składkowski, who remained thereupon continuously in office until after the Fifth Partition. The change marked a new rigor in the regime. "The Premier's uniform is the symbol," declared a governmental paper, "of the program of the new government. The uniform announces the reinforcement of discipline in the face of turbulent elements and political agitators."[10] Nevertheless, it soon became apparent even to Składkowski that a government without partisan organization behind it, was destined to hang in mid-air, while its competitors organized and reorganized at will.[11]

The answer to the needs of Składkowski's ministry was found in the organization, early in 1937, of the so-called *OZON*,[12] or Camp of National Union, fostered by Colonel Adam Koc, and given increasing degrees of support by the Składkowski regime. The emergence of miscellaneous groups demanding action finally forced the Government to undertake the establishment of the *OZON*. This organ-

[10] *Kurjer Poranny*, May 16, 1936.

[11] *Warszawski Dziennik Narodowy*, January 31, 1936; *Czas*, May 16, 1936; also *Kurjer Warszawski*, June 5, 1936.

[12] *Obóz Zjednocenia Narodowej*.

ization, which was brought into being by the increasing jeopardy of the country's well-being, alike by internal disunity and the rise of new enemies across the political frontiers, was put forward in a great mass movement of spontaneous character. Assured of the sponsorship of General Śmigły-Rydz, who, on November 11, 1936, was elevated to the position of Marshal of Poland and "second personage in the Republic," the *OZON* received his personal benediction and proceeded, during 1937, to spread its organization throughout the length and breadth of Poland, obtaining both individual and collective adherence to its program. "Our aim," declared Colonel Koc on June 1, 1937, "is to create in Poland a new democracy working for the good of the Nation and of the State and in which the interest of the individual and the interest of the State are indissolubly united."[13] This was a formula broad enough to mean all things to all men, and by the use of such devices the Camp of National Union grew numerically with great rapidity without, however, reconciling the innumerable divergences of opinion between those who entered into its ranks, or operating to dissolve or reduce the opposing political parties.[14] In the end, the numerous rifts in the ranks of the Camp of National Union led to the resignation of Colonel Koc and the rapid rise to power and prominence of General Stanisław Skwarszyński, who became its nominal head.

Meanwhile the Opposition was not idle. At the beginning of 1938, the Populist party, convening in Cracow, adopted a new program frontally challenging the pretorian leadership and rejecting *OZON* and all its works. Putting foremost in its program a demand for electoral reform and the holding of democratic elections, it declared its readiness "to collaborate with all the political parties and all the organizations which take their stand on the grounds of the public welfare and democracy." Finally, it announced an entente with the Polish Socialist party to act in common, while maintaining the internal autonomy of their respective organizations. This, in the opinion of the principal socialist daily, marked "a great day in the evolution of Polish political life." The arch-conservative Cracow *Times*[15] unreservedly acknowledged that "at the present

[13] *Gazeta Polska,* June 1, 1937.

[14] *Kurjer Warszawski,* October 11, December 13, 1937; *Kurjer Poranny,* December 20, 1937.

[15] *Robotnik,* March 2, 1938; also *Czas,* March 3, 1938.

time the Populist party is the most powerful political representative of the rural elements in Poland and in consequence is called upon, sooner or later, to play an important role." The success of this organizational venture led the vice-premier, Eugeniusz Kwiatkowski to tender the olive branch to the Opposition in the hope of bridging, in part, the gap between the Government and the Populists. But there was no hope of finding common ground. Instead, there were continued defections from the Camp of National Union, beginning with a solid bloc of Christian nationalists. It was beginning to be obvious that the Government was fast losing support. A new pragmatic correlation of forces was necessary.

The answer of President Mościcki was to prepare the way for new elections by extending legislatively to municipal elections the same scheme of nominative choice which, after 1935, had operated in the national elections. Then, at the auspicious moment after Munich, when Czechoslovakia was partitioned, and Poland, by ultimata, regained possession of Teschen (Cieszyn), Mościcki dissolved the Fourth Parliament and ordered new elections. In this move he was extraordinarily successful, as an aroused electorate turned out, under repeated governmental exhortations, to register approval of what the outside world construed as a territorial aggrandizement. In the elections of November 6, 1938, 64.5 per cent of the voters, or 11,844,704 out of 17,585,385 electors, cast their ballots. Under threat of penalties for nonvoting or incitement to nonvoting, the Camp of National Union thus managed to secure 161 deputies out of the 208 in the lower house and an approximately similar result in the senatorial elections. The new Parliament was free of industrialists, its clerical representation was sharply reduced, the Ukrainians succeeded in augmenting their representation, and only five Jews were returned. The Government press was jubilant. By this plebiscitary procedure, a new working correlation of forces was attained.

The communal elections held at the end of 1938 revealed, notwithstanding, the hollow character of the legislative victory, obtained, as it was, through a merciless dragooning of the Opposition press and a governmental monopoly of radio broadcasting. Whatever the effect of such tactics in national affairs, the local communities could not be so easily suborned. In fact, the municipal elections showed the national party to be overwhelmingly in strength in Pomorze, Poznań, and strongly represented in Cracow and in sixty other municipalities. They also revealed the Populist-Socialist strength to be greater in Łódź than that of all other Polish parties combined; in Cracow, the Socialist-Populist coalition topped both the *OZON* and the Party of Work. In short, as Poland entered its last year of independent existence, the antigovernmental forces more than balanced the apparent show of the Government's strength.

On the eve of the war that temporarily entombed Polish independence, it was possible to see behind the façade of strident and oppressive militarism, behind the marshal, generals, colonels, and legionaires that held Poland in the iron manacles of their own making, something of the shape of a deeply democratic Poland, pious, populist and radical—even socialist—looking across the frontiers to cognate forces in other democratic lands. Even from America, the other Poland could be discovered, the Poland that for nearly a decade and a half had been in the shadow, the Poland of liberal traditions, worshiper of freedom, believer in the equality of all men, copartner in the fraternity of free peoples, the Poland which the mailed fist of German aggression could never really destroy.

CHAPTER X

Minorities

BY JOSEPH S. ROUCEK

THE RESTORATION in 1919 of the independence of the Polish State, which had not appeared on the European map since 1795, was an act of historic justice. The political leaders of the reborn state endeavored to secure national frontiers which would approximate to the greatest possible degree those of historic Poland. In trying to realize this goal, however, the Polish Government collided with the peoples located between the Polish and the Russian ethnic elements—the Ukrainians, the White Russians, and the Lithuanians—who, while the territory of the former Republic of Poland had been subjected to the influences of Austria, Germany, and Russia, had gained a national and political consciousness, and had endeavored to secure the greatest possible degree of independence.

Hence, Poland's frontiers proved to be a troublesome problem. Discordant claims of natural and historic frontiers, of ethnic and economic boundaries, only served to accentuate the difficulties. Furthermore, at the end of the First World War, the heritage of national strife and the bitterness of four years of warfare did not contribute to a peaceful and rational demarcation of frontiers. Poland became involved with Russia on the east, with Lithuania on the north, and with Czechoslovakia on the southwest; in the meanwhile, the Germans looked on sullenly at what they considered the partition of their fatherland.

To increase the seriousness of the problem, the Treaty of Versailles left several of Poland's frontiers quite vague, left them for plebiscites or war to decide. Eventually, however, following the defeat of the military forces of the rebellious Ukrainians in eastern Galicia, and after a victory over the Red Army, the Poles secured a large part of the White Russian territory and a small section of Ukrainian territory by the Treaty of Riga in March, 1921. Furthermore, Poland emerged from its postwar diplomatic problems and its other struggles with a German minority in Pomorze (Pomerania), Poznań (Posen), and Upper Silesia. Despite Poland's need for secure access to the sea, the Peace Conference rejected Poland's claim for the annexation of Danzig, and decided that Danzig should become a Free City governed by a local legislative council, subject to the control of the League of Nations; Poland, in return, was given the right to control the customs and to use the port.

But, in order to connect the interior of Poland with the Baltic, the Treaty of Versailles granted to Poland the disputed strip of territory called Pomorze by the Poles, and the "Polish Corridor" by the Germans. This territory, which had formed an integral part of Poland before its partition, with the majority of its inhabitants Polish, in 1918, became one of the most effective propaganda weapons of the Germans in their systematically sustained attacks on the Treaty of Versailles. Berlin's opposition to the arrangement was particularly based on the fact that the so-called Corridor separated East Prussia, one of the strongholds of German patriotism, from Germany proper.

The ill-fated Polish Corridor became one of the most troublesome territories in postwar Europe. Almost all experts agreed that Poland needed an outlet to the Baltic. The narrow neck of territory, Pomorze, peopled primarily by Poles, ran from Poland to the Baltic; but east and west of this were lands which were Prussian. With Prussians to right and left, the tenure of the Corridor by Poland was doomed to increasing controversy and ultimate loss.

There were many reasons why the doctrine of national self-determination was not fully applied to Poland—as well as to all the other states of eastern Europe. Partly it was because the "victors," themselves, especially Italy, demanded such strategic frontiers as the Brenner Pass. In some instances economic considerations prevailed. The principal obstacle, however, was that in many areas the intermingling of various nationalities, and the presence of nationality enclaves and long-established minority settlements, made it utterly impossible to draw a map along purely ethnographic lines. Minorities thus became unavoidable.

In an effort to secure and to safeguard the existence of international protection of Poland's minorities within the new boundaries, the Allied Powers instituted a system of protection under the control of the League of Nations. This system was created by means of minorities treaties which the defeated powers—with the notable exception of Germany—and the "succession" states were compelled to sign. Poland, in particular, protested very bitterly. Prime Minister Ignacy Jan Paderewski was very emphatic in resenting any obligations which did not apply to all members of the League of Nations. He supported Premier Ion Bratianu of Rumania, who pointed out that all the helpful maxims of good government are of universal application and, therefore, if a protection of minorities indeed was indispensable or desirable, it should not be restricted to the countries of eastern Europe, but without exception should be extended to all.

Notwithstanding the protests which Premier Paderewski had made at an earlier stage, Poland was required to sign the first of the minorities treaties on June 28, 1919, which served as the model for other pacts of this kind. Under this agreement, Poland granted "full and complete protection of life and liberty to all inhabitants of Poland without distinction of birth, nationality, language, race, or religion," assured to all nationals belonging to a minority the free exercise of their religion and the use of their language, and guaranteed to nationals of non-Polish speech "adequate facilities . . . for the use of their language, either orally or in writing before the courts." It not only gave minorities protection against affirmative acts of discrimination, but also attempted to assure them the means of preserving their national character, culture, and religion. In addition to other detailed protection, it was provided that "Jews shall not be compelled to perform any act which constitutes a violation of their Sabbath, nor shall they be placed under any disability by reason of their refusal to attend courts of law or to perform any legal business on their Sabbath."

It should be noted that, although the German Republic was not bound by a minorities treaty, non-Germans in Upper Silesia were protected by a German-Polish convention under the control of the League of Nations. This agreement, concluded in 1922 and effective for fifteen years, not only gave minorities in that area substantially the same legal assurance as the treaties, but operated under special local machinery which resulted in much more effective League control. The Upper Silesia Convention was in force, despite the advent of Hitler, until its expiration in 1937. Furthermore, Nazi Germany concluded a bilateral pact with Poland for the reciprocal protection of their co-nationals on November 5, 1937. This agreement was not subject to League control and, unlike the Upper Silesia Convention, gave no protection to other minorities. Its value might be construed from the fact that Germany concluded a similar agreement with Czechoslovakia shortly after Munich (November 20, 1938).

There was also the treaty between Danzig and Poland (of November 9, 1920), whereby Danzig agreed to apply provisions contained in the Polish Minorities Treaty, as well as provisions in the treaty of October 24, 1921,[1] regulating language and school questions. In addition there was the Treaty of Riga with Russia of March 18, 1921.

The hope of the Peace Conference that it could solve the problem of Poland's minorities by the Treaty of June 28, 1919, proved to be, as may be seen from a historical perspective, quite illusory. Unfortunately, the proponents of the system for the international protection of minorities, headed by President Wilson, could not foresee two aspects of this dynamite-laden problem of Europe's minorities—and, thus, also of Poland's which, as the subsequent events disclosed, not only doomed to failure the whole elaborate minorities system under the League of Nations, but also eventually proved to be one of the major causes leading to the Second World War.

In the first place, the majority-minority group relationships are power relationships, based on the assumption that either can force

[1] Note: the Polish Constitution provided for minorities as follows: Art. 109. Every citizen shall have the right to preserve his nationality and to cultivate his language and national qualities. Special state laws shall guarantee to minorities within the Polish State the full and free development of their national qualities with the assistance of autonomous minority associations of a public-juridical character within the limits of general self-government associations. The State shall have the right of controlling their activities, and in case of need, the duty of supplementing their financial means.

Art 110. Polish citizens belonging to national, confessional or lingual minorities shall have equal rights with other citizens to establish, supervise and administer at their own expense, philanthropic, confessional, and social institutions, schools and other educational establishments, as also freely therein to use their language and to carry out the precepts of their religion.

the other to act in a certain way even against its own will—an approach which has been largely ignored by the legalistically minded treaty makers enticed by the working of the constitutional law in this respect in the United States. It is the dominance-submission relationship. Thus, the failure of the League of Nations to protect Europe's minorities may be traced, in part at least, to the fundamental mistake in the notion that the dynamics of the majority-minority relationships can be frozen into legalistic forms, the so-called "minorities treaties." Furthermore, when the minorities treaties were put into operation, it did not occur to anyone that the majorities might need to be protected against the minorities. In the second decade after the signing of the minorities treaties, Hitler, quite aware that central and eastern Europe was "freckled" with minorities on the wrong side of frontiers, utilized the principle of self-determination for his aggressive international policies as an explosive doctrine which was applied to the planned and ever-growing irredentism of German minorities in Poland (particularly in Danzig) as a means of helping to bring about the Second World War and thus the defeat of Poland.

Without analyzing in detail the operation of the international guarantee by the League of Nations, it is sufficient to say that the states with minorities, headed by Poland and Czechoslovakia and supported more or less openly by their ally, France, vigorously resisted in the first postwar decade attempts to increase the degree of outside interference and, hence, opposed the movement to improve the procedure of the League in regard to the minorities complaints and repeatedly endeavored to render more difficult any effective appeal to the League. Such course met with keen opposition from the states defeated in the war which sought to increase the effectiveness of the League's guarantee.

The efforts of Poland and Czechoslovakia generally succeeded until Germany entered the League in 1926. With Germany's entrance into the League and the Council in 1926, the minorities acquired a vigorous champion. Germany was insistent in demanding an effective discharge of the League's obligation as guarantor. For instance, during the Council's session held on December 15, 1928, Stresemann, the German Foreign Minister, at the conclusion of an exchange of heated words with Zaleski, the Polish delegate, on the right of the minorities to petition the League, expressed his intention of raising the whole question of procedure at the next session of the Council. In general, however, the desire not to offend states with minorities made the minorities committees of the League extremely reluctant to employ their acknowledged power in order to draw information from every available source. But, according to one appraisal of the effectiveness with which the League executed its guarantee of the rights of minorities, covering the period from 1920 to January, 1931, of 525 petitions addressed to the League, 155 (the largest number) had been addressed to the League from Poland's minorities. Among the cases originating in Poland affecting minorities and dealt with by the Council may be mentioned the expropriation of settlers of German lineage in Poland, the question of the acquisition of Polish nationality by certain categories of former German nationals, and the question of German schools in Polish Upper Silesia. It was largely because of the vigorous demands of Germany that the Council acted on the complaints of organized violence against the German minority in the Polish elections of November, 1930.

The persistent policy of Germany, as a member of the League's Council since 1926, of intervening on behalf of its minorities in Poland was bitterly resented by Warsaw. The Poles were not slow in pointing out that no other government abused this privilege so often as Berlin in order to promote revisionist propaganda and to keep the "Corridor" question before world opinion. Warsaw became quite disturbed over this situation, fearing that German minorities were fast becoming docile instruments of German propaganda (now called "fifth columnists"), and was particularly bitter because Germany was under no obligation to protect the Polish minorities in Germany.

A definite step against the whole system of the protection of minorities by the League was taken by the Polish Government in 1934. Russia became a League member and Poland, remembering Catherine II's intervention on behalf of her Orthodox minorities in the eighteenth century, feared that the Soviets might intervene even more often than Germany in the internal affairs of Poland. This led to Foreign Minister Beck's declaration in Geneva in the fall of 1934 that, until a general system of minority protection was adopted, Poland was "compelled to refuse all coöperation with the international organization in the matter of the supervision of the application by Poland of the system of minority protection" under the Minorities Treaty of June 28, 1919. According to a Polish version, Poland had "no reservations to make against the principle of minority protection as such, but that she will no longer agree to remain one of the countries which as regards the application of the principles of equal rights for all her citizens is controlled by other countries which have accepted no obligations of a like nature." Hence, in actual practice thereafter with the lapse of the 1919 agreement, Poland was bound only by the provisions regarding minorities of the Treaty of Riga and the Upper Silesia Convention of 1922, each of which, signed by both parties to the agreement, met Poland's demand for equality.

In the actual execution of the Minorities Treaty by Poland the general political position of the national minorities, offered to them by the democratic system of general franchise rights, was substantially narrowed by the Electoral Law of June, 1935, which limited the free choice of candidates. The results showed in the elections of August, 1935, at which time the national minorities, which should have had a third of the total seats according to their numbers (that is, sixty-six seats out of a total of two hundred), obtained only twenty-four, of which the Ukrainians had nineteen, and the Jews five. The White Russians, the Lithuanians, the Czechs, and the Germans were without representation. In the Senate, which was composed of ninety-six members, the minorities, instead of obtaining thirty-two seats, obtained only ten (six went to the Ukrainians, two to the Germans, and two to the Jews).

The official language in Poland, of course, was Polish. But the Ukrainians in the provinces of Lwów, Tarnopol, Stanisławów, Wilno, and Polesie, the White Russians in the provinces of Polesie, Nowogródek, and Wilno and also in two parishes in the province of Białystok, and the Lithuanians in several parts of the administrative district of Wilno, could use their language in the state and administrative offices as well as before the courts. Language rights for the German minority were granted for Upper Silesia by the stipulations of the Polish-German Treaty, for the administrative area of the Poznań and Toruń (Thorn) Appeal Courts by a special law of March, 1925. Educational facilities were granted by the Polish School Statute of 1924 for the Ukrainian minority in the provinces of Lwów, Stanisławów, Tarnopol, Volhynia, and Polesie, for the White Russians in Polesie, Nowogródek and Wilno, and for the Lithuanians in the province of Wilno—in districts where the minorities formed more than 25 per cent of the population and where parents of at least forty minority children demanded the provision of a school. In the Polish part of Upper Silesia the question was adjusted in a very similar manner by the Polish-German treaty already referred to.

In the matter of schools for Poland's minorities, private schools could be founded on the same footing as the Polish schools. "The Ukrainian language," writes S. J. Paprocki, "was used in the elementary schools in three fashions: (a) as the sole language of instruction; (b) jointly with Polish as a language of instruction; and (c) as one of the subjects taught. In this connection it is possible to classify the elementary schools into three groups: Ukrainian schools, Polish-Ukrainian schools (bilingual), and Polish schools having Ukrainian as one of the subjects of instruction. Of these three categories, periodical school statistics are kept only for the first two; the third class is embraced only by the detailed Census of Schools taken every five years." Since the only available data of this type was procured in 1930–1931 there are no later data available as to Polish schools where Ukrainian was taught as a subject. "Data is on hand for Ukrainian and bilingual schools, however, for the school year 1933–1934. In that year there were 2,682 bilingual (Polish and Ukrainian) schools of which only one was privately owned, and 494 schools having Ukrainian as the language of instruction, this figure including 34 which were privately owned."

In the territory of the three southeastern provinces of the Republic, there were 2,138 bilingual schools and 487 Ukrainian, and in the eastern provinces of Poland there were 544 bilingual and seven Ukrainian schools, or a total of 3,176 elementary schools, including 35 private schools in which Ukrainian was the sole language of instruction used or was used parallel with Polish. In addition to this total there were over 2,000 elementary schools in Poland where Ukrainian was taught as a subject. "In all," according to Paprocki, "there were in 1933–1934 about 5,200 elementary schools in Poland which had the Ukrainian language in their curricula."[2]

Other accounts show that the Germans had 490 elementary schools, the White Russians, 16, the Jews 87 Jewish and 172 Hebrew schools, the Lithuanians 72, the Czechs 18, and the Russians eight. The Ukrainians had 26 secondary schools, besides two bilingual schools, the White Russians one, the Germans 20, the Jews 11, the Lithuanians two, and the Russians five. The Ukrainians had seven teachers' colleges, as well as one bilingual training center, the Germans four, the Jews three. The other minorities had no institutions for the training of teachers.

Poland was indeed a state with large national minorities totaling almost one-third of the whole population. But, contrary to a widespread idea that Poland was, after Czechoslovakia, the most minority-laden state in Europe, it must be noted that actually the Soviet Union (Europe and Asia) had a higher percentage of minorities (47.2 per cent) than Poland (31.1 per cent). According to the Census of 1931, out of 31,915,800 people in Poland, 21,993,400 (68.9 per cent) spoke Polish as their mother tongue. The statistics for the other "mother tongues" as well as religious distribution are shown in the tables on facing page.

The Polish census figures must be accepted with reservations, since all the majority-minority relationships are relationships of power, for the Polish Government made the census; the minorities, in turn, exaggerated their claims. There are additional difficulties also. The Ukrainian minority was artificially divided by the census into Ukrainians and Ruthenians. There is included in the figures under the designation "others," a group of people known by the title of "tutejsi" (people of local origin, indicating no marked national consciousness). Most of them should be considered as White Ruthenians. The Census of 1921 divided the population according to nationality, but in the Census of 1931 mother tongue replaced nationality as a standard by which minorities might be distinguished.

The Ukrainian minority.—The largest Polish national minority people were the Ukrainians, living near the eastern border of Poland and predominating in the territories of eastern Galicia and

[2] S. J. Paprocki, *Minority Affairs and Poland.* Warsaw: Nationality Institute, 1935, pp. 72–73. See also chapter XVII, "Education," by Wojciech Świętosławski.

Volhynia (Wołyń). In eastern Galicia (in its three provinces of Stanisławów, Tarnopol, and Lwów) the Ukrainians numbered more than 2,750,000, and comprised more than one-half the local population. In Volhynia the Ukrainians numbered about 1,000,000, nearly 70 per cent of the population. The eminent Polish statistician, Dr.

NATIVE TONGUES

Native tongue	Number	Per cent
Total population	31,915,800	....
Ukrainian	3,222,000	10.1
Ruthenian	1,219,600	3.8
White Ruthenian	989,900	3.1
Russian	138,700	0.4
German	741,000	2.3
Yiddish and Hebrew	2,737,600	8.6
Others	878,600	2.8

RELIGIOUS DISTRIBUTION

Religion	Number	Per cent
Roman Catholic:		
Latin rite	20,670,100	64.8
Greek rite	3,336,200	10.4
Greek Orthodox	3,762,500	11.8
Protestant	835,200	2.6
Other Christian	145,400	0.5
Hebrew	3,113,900	9.8
Other non-Christian	6,800	0.0
Unknown and not given	45,700	0.1

A. Krysiński, came to the conclusion that in 1931 the Ukrainians made up 51.9 per cent of the population in eastern Galicia, with about 4,870,000 Ukrainians in Poland as a whole.[3] The Ukrainians, on the other hand, put the figure as high as 7,000,000.

The Ukrainians live in the territory extending from the northern shore of the Black Sea to the Carpathian Mountains, which includes the basin of the Dnieper and a large part of that of the Dniester. Ethnically, they belong to the eastern branch of the Slavic people, and are closer to the Russians proper than to the western or south-

[3] S. J. Paprocki, *Minority Affairs and Poland,* pp. 52–54.

ern Slavs. Hence, they are also known as the Little Russians, and claim to have a single language, varied only by local dialects and a district culture represented by folk poetry. American and English writers and encyclopedias use the names Ukrainians, Little Russians, and Ruthenians, but chiefly the name Ukrainian. Ukrainians have been listed by the immigration authorities of the United States as Ruthenians and Russniaks; the United States Census listed them first as Ruthenians and, in 1930, as Ukrainians and Ruthenians.

For the purpose of this chapter, it is necessary to note that the cultural leadership of the Ukrainians passed, as a result of the oppression in Russia, to Lwów (Lviv in Ukrainian) in the nineteenth century, where it was encouraged by the Austrians as a check against both the Russians and the Poles. A definite development of Ukrainian nationalism in eastern Galicia resulted. The majority of Galician Ukrainians are Uniate, i.e., they observe the Greek rite in the Roman Catholic Church (whereas those in Russia are Orthodox).

The difficult situation of the Ukrainians was further complicated by the fact that the territory they occupied was contiguous with the Soviet Ukraine. Hostile to Polish domination, the Ukrainians by characteristics and sympathies were Russian rather than Polish. This did not mean, as a consequence, that they favored Russian rule rather than Polish rule. But for four centuries before its partition, Poland had possessed this section of the Ukraine. Hence, despite the obstacles set by the hostile intrigues of Germany, Russia, or the Ukrainians themselves, by armed opposition, or by the League of Nations, Poland stubbornly demanded and held the Polish Ukraine.

After 1919 the Polish authorities did their best to oppose the Ukrainian national movement, and Polish colonists were settled on Ukrainian territory. The resulting terrorist activities reached a feverish pitch in 1930 at which time the Government used the army in a policy of "pacification," punishing entire villages in which terroristic acts had occurred. The Council of the League of Nations considered the matter in January, 1932, and a turn for the better came when the new Minister of the Interior, M. Pieracki (subsequently assassinated by a Ukrainian revolutionist) adopted a more conciliatory attitude. A compromise with the Cabinet was reached before the 1935 elections, and the "normalization" policy gave the Ukrainians eighteen seats in Parliament in addition to other national privileges.

When, after Munich, Czechoslovakia granted autonomy to Sub-Carpathian Ruthenia, the Polish Ukrainians were electrified in their desire for self-government and bitterly resented the efforts of Poland to turn over Sub-Carpathian Ruthenia to Hungary, not only in order to reach a common frontier with Hungary, but also with the hope that Budapest would soon liquidate its newly won liberties. New tensions cropped up, in evidence until Poland's collapse.

The Jews.—The Jews constituted the second largest minority of Poland, as they comprised one-tenth of the population. Poland developed a small native middle class and, thus, the Jews and Germans chiefly came to form that class in Poland down into the nineteenth century. They built and populated the towns and cities and formed a stratum of society as far above the peasants as it was below the elite. The nineteenth and twentieth centuries produced a revulsion against the dominant position of the Jews. With the growth of nationalism, the Poles felt increasingly bothered about the important part played by Jews in trades, industries, and professions. Unquestionably, the Jewish minority of one-tenth exercised upon the majority of nine-tenths an influence out of proportion to its numbers.

The Jews were scattered throughout Poland. According to the figures in the Census of 1921, they numbered 2,110,448 (7.8 per cent of the total population) and by 1931 increased to at least 2,753,000, whereas by 1936 they were counted at 2,916,000 (Yiddish- or Hebrew-speaking) or 3,351,000 (Jewish religion).

From whatever angle their difficulties are viewed, they were a serious problem to themselves, and to Poland as well. In the last two decades about one-third of the total urban population of Poland was Jewish; this fact created grave economic problems. The occupational distribution of gainfully employed Jews and non-Jews (as revealed in the Polish Census of 1931) is presented in the table on the following page.

Thus, every Jew engaged in agriculture was outnumbered by

eight non-Jews. But the percentage of Jews engaged in trade and finance was twenty-three times as great as among non-Jews. In addition, the employment of nearly one-third of Polish Jewry in industry and handicrafts indicated an unhealthy economic tendency because the vast majority of Jews listed in this category were artisans. Only 18 per cent of the non-Jewish industrial workers were occupied with the handicrafts (200,000 against 900,000); but 80 per cent of the Jewish workers were artisans (200,000 out of a total of 250,000). Furthermore, the Jewish workingmen of Poland were

Occupational distribution	Per cent	
	Jews	Non-Jews
Agriculture	9.8	80.7
Industry and handicrafts	32.2	7.7
Trade and finance	35.1	1.5
Communications and transportation	2.7	1.7
Liberal professions	3.8	.7
Public service	.6	1.6
Other occupations	15.7	6.1

concentrated in an antiquated branch of production, a domestic system which was disintegrating in the face of a new industrialization being actively promoted by the strongest elements of the Polish middle class and by the Government. The nationalization of nearly a quarter of Poland's industry and trade also affected Jews adversely in far greater measure than non-Jews, for between two-thirds and three-quarters of them were concentrated in these callings, whereas 80 per cent of the non-Jews were in agriculture.

The situation of the Jews in Poland was complicated by other factors. Similar to the fate of the Poles themselves, thousands of houses belonging to Jews were reduced to ruins during the First World War, and several hundred thousand occupants rendered homeless and destitute. But the Poles felt no special sympathy for the terrible economic situation of the Polish Jews because many Jews had been accused of supporting Germany during the war. Pogroms took place in the Ukraine in 1919. In addition, the Polish Government and intellectuals held the Jews responsible for the

Minorities Treaty—a point which, in fact, is supported by historical evidence.[4]

These attitudes were reflected in the policies of Poland. The language law of 1924 did not apply to the Jews, inasmuch as no provisions were made for Jewish minority schools. As a result, the Jewish school system included only a few primary and secondary schools with Hebrew and Yiddish as the languages of instruction.

The great importance of the Jewish religious communities, the Cahals, in Poland must be noted. As a community organization the Cahals survived the period of the partitions and were continued in the new, independent Poland. By a regulation of the President of the Republic, issued on October 14, 1927, on the ordering of the legal status of Jewish religious communities, the legal force of this law was also extended to former Austrian Poland. This law also provided for the creation of a Jewish religious council as the chief organ of Polish Jewry. But, down to 1939, the prescriptions providing for a religious council had not been put into effect.

In March, 1931, the Polish Parliament finally abolished legislative discrimination against the Jews who had survived from prewar days. But after the death of Piłsudski, anti-Semitism again increased in Poland. The former tacit acquiescence of the regime in the anti-Jewish activities of certain political parties gave way to more open participation. In 1938 the Government declared that Jewish emigration was the only solution of the Jewish problem and started agitating world opinion for international plans to be worked out on behalf of Polish Jews. Meanwhile, the economic boycott was carried on, together with other devices, particularly an unofficial *numerus clausus*.[5] The Government's efforts to bring about more Jewish emigration continued throughout the critical months following the dismemberment of Czechoslovakia.

---

[4] Joseph S. Roucek, *The Working of the Minorities System under the League of Nations* (Prague: Orbis, 1928), pp. 28–42; see also his "The Problem of Minorities and the League of Nations," *Journal of Comparative Legislation and International Law*, XV (February, 1933), pp. 67–71; L. Luzzatti, *God in Freedom* (New York: Macmillan, 1930), and particularly "American Supplementary Chapters" by Louis Marshall; Research Institute on Peace and Postwar Problems of The American Jewish Committee, *Jewish Postwar Problems*, Unit IV, *Europe between the Two World Wars, 1919–1939* (New York: The American Jewish Committee, 1943), p. 8.

[5] All details may be found in the *American Jewish Year Book* (Philadelphia: The Jewish Publication Society of America, 1938).

The excesses against Jews were organized and perpetrated primarily by members of the National Democratic party (*N.D.*) and by the even more violently anti-Jewish National Radical Camp (*Nara*), an offshoot of the *N.D.* These political elements were in opposition to the Government which made sporadic efforts to suppress rioting.

The progressive limitation of the number of Jewish students in the higher institutions was designed to prevent the preponderance of Jews in some of the professions like medicine and law. Although the number of non-Jewish students in higher education rose from 29,656 to 40,954 between 1923 and 1936, the number of Jewish students fell from 9,579 to 6,207, and the number of Jewish medical students fell from 1,469 to 588.

The Germans.—The German minority was not so numerous as it was influential. The Census of 1921 ascertained that there were 1,059,194 (3.9 per cent) Germans in Poland, of whom the greater portion, or 318,786, lived in Upper Silesia, forming 28.3 per cent of the local population; in addition there were 327,846 Germans who represented 16.7 per cent of the population in the province of Poznań and 175,771 Germans who represented 18.8 per cent of the local population in Pomorze. Smaller numbers lived in the provinces of Łódź (Łódź alone containing about one-fifth of all the Germans in Poland), Warsaw, and Volhynia. According to the Census of 1931, there was a substantial decrease in the numbers of the German minority who now included only 715,000; on the other hand, the Germans themselves claimed that there were at least 1,700,000 Germans in Poland.

A goodly proportion of the Germans were large landholders and were exempt from agrarian reforms. Hence, they added to the economic burdens of the State and, at the same time, were groomed—as subsequent events were to show—as Hitler's "fifth columnists" who helped to betray Poland. Nevertheless, unlike the Germans along the German frontier, those of Łódź at first opposed Hitler and the Nazi regime.

In many respects the Polish Germans were better off than any other minority group of Poland. Although the German representatives made repeated complaints to the League of Nations about the use of agrarian reforms as a means of depriving the German landowners of their possessions, the fact remained that the German-owned part of cultivated land had a much higher yield per hectare than the average Polish farms. Furthermore, their social and occupational structure was better balanced than that of the Poles or that of other national minorities. Whereas the Ukrainians and White Russians lived overwhelmingly in rural districts and the Jews for the most part in cities, the Germans were artisans, workers, manufacturers, landowners, farmers, professionals, and technicians. Also, the majority of the German farmers, unlike Poles, Ukrainians, and White Russians, lived on medium-sized, independent holdings.

The chief German complaints concerned the policy of nationalizing the economic life of the country and of Polonizing cultural and educational institutions. The Poles used their power especially to reduce German influence in Upper Silesia and in other former German provinces—convinced that the German minority was but an advanced guard of German imperialism—a conviction sustained by subsequent political events.

Upper Silesia formed another basis for a series of controversies between Poland and Germany. The first draft of the Treaty of Versailles planned to hand over nearly all of Upper Silesia to Poland. The German counterarguments persuaded the Allies to hold a plebiscite on March 20, 1921, which gave 59.6 per cent of the votes for Germany, although only 54 per cent of the communes had a German majority. After a long period of tension, the League of Nations gave to Germany about 75 per cent of the area and 57 per cent of the inhabitants; and Germany and Poland signed the elaborate Upper Silesia Convention of May 15, 1922, providing for the mutual protection of minorities within this area.

After the nonaggression pact of January 26, 1934, between Germany and Poland, the Government in Warsaw more emphatically pursued its Polonization policy, especially along its western frontiers. This led to recurrent disputes between Berlin and Warsaw, especially after the expiration of the Upper Silesia Convention in July, 1937. A declaration promising protection of minorities was promulgated by Berlin and Warsaw on November 5, 1937, an international act which for the first time accorded protection to the Polish minority in Germany outside Upper Silesia. But the solemn agreements of the declaration were but empty promises, and both governments continued their traditional policies. The situation actually became worse. The minority problems arising from the Polish-German frontier, and particularly in Danzig, eventually led to the Second World War.

The White Russians.—The Russo-Polish Treaty of Riga (1921) gave Poland, roughly speaking, the boundary of 1793, and about 1,500,000 White Russians (also called White Ruthenians by the Poles), which meant that almost one-half of the population of the two eastern provinces, Wilno and Polesie, was made up of this minority, which also formed 40 per cent of the population in the province of Nowogródek. The White Russians themselves estimated that there were at least 2,000,000 of them living in Poland; after 1921 more than 300,000 repatriated White Russians returned to Poland. The White Russians formed the least disturbing minority, but their low economic and cultural status served as a drag upon the Polish state.

The Lithuanians.—The Lithuanian minority which, in 1921, counted only 68,667 people, had grown, according to Polish sources, in 1931 to 84,000 (the Lithuanians themselves claiming the figure of 300,000). They were chiefly concentrated in the provinces of Wilno and Nowogródek. The situation of the Lithuanian minority also was adversely affected by considerations of foreign policy, in particular by the strained relations between Poland and Lithuania regarding the Wilno question.

In addition there was the Russian minority numbering only 56,239, according to the data of 1921, who lived on the frontiers of the eastern provinces, and a Czech minority concentrated primarily in Volhynia (30,628), to whose number ought to be added several thousand Spisz Slovaks whom the Poles simply counted as Poles.

The complex picture of Poland's minorities would be incomplete without noting that on the morrow of Munich, Warsaw sent an ultimatum to Prague, demanding the evacuation of the western part of Teschen (Cieszyn) and the sections west from Ropice to Darkow. Despite an appeal from Secretary Hull not to use force, Warsaw applied pressure on Prague to yield and occupied this area, together with the district of Bohumín. Warsaw acquired, according to Czech figures, more Czechs than Poles by this action.

Historical perspective.—The difficult problem faced by Poland in regard to its minorities received little impartial consideration during the two decades of Poland's independent existence. The liberals of Britain and the United States frequently cited Poland as an example of the "terrible" Treaty of Versailles. Others assailed Poland as a chauvinistic state which was unable to solve its minorities problem because the Government, as well as the masses, would not adopt the policy of "toleration" and "appeasement." Many of these students of the Polish question came under the spell of German propaganda which, even under the Weimar Republic, maintained a steady barrage of attacks against the postwar eastern frontiers, particularly the Corridor.

Little has been said about the other side of the picture: the dilemma confronting the successive Polish cabinets which were trying to represent the social forces of their nation, resentful of the foreign and nonassimilated minorities as well as of foreign interventions on behalf of these minorities; the need for promoting the assimilative forces against the minorities who were only too anxious to prevent such policies; and the fear that the minorities question was but another technique of giving blows to Poland's foreign policy. That this Polish viewpoint was not unfounded was proved by subsequent events. Today one wonders at the objections raised by the German representatives before the League of Nations over the treatment of minorities; after all, Germany was not required to sign a minorities treaty, but it was Germany which, as a Nazified nation, was to treat all its minorities, including the Poles, in a manner which in its ferocity, brutality, and inhumanity cannot even be compared to the minorities policies tried by Poland.

To be sure, Poland made its mistakes in the treatment of minorities, just as Poland's minorities made their mistakes in their policies toward the state in which they lived. Especially in eastern Poland were the minorities much intermingled. To a certain extent the groundwork for all the difficuties was laid as early as 1918 when the Polish leaders attempted to acquire for Poland its "historic" boundaries. This "historicism," this universal European tendency to work for the restoration of the "ancient" boundaries and thus bring about "justice" to the newly restored state, is a problem which plagued the statesmen of Versailles and which will plague the statesmen who will determine the fate of the states at the end of the present war.

The vital importance of securing equal rights for all men, regardless of their religion or their ancestry, is recognized by all scholars and statesmen who are giving thought to the foundations on which a just and durable world peace can be established. The problem of harmonious fraternity by persons belonging to different ethnic, linguistic, and religious groups is far along the way to solution in the democratic countries of western Europe and of the American Continent. Indeed, one of the most precious principles of the democratic form of government is that of investing persons belonging to minority elements in the population with the same rights and duties as those of the majority.

But no solution will be found in eastern Europe as long as national minorities can be exploited by their so-called fatherlands for political purposes—as shown by Hitler's game of power politics. A flagrant example of such exploitation was the arousal by Nazi Germany of Germans in Danzig to revolt against the legally constituted government of this State, in order that a "peaceful" conquest of the territory might be achieved.

Furthermore, it is not only essential to secure the necessary guarantees for all minorities, but also to establish the position that the rule of the majority is no crime in a democracy or in any other form of government. It will be necessary to prevent a minority within a minority from exercising a veto power over the destiny of the majority.

This also implies that the reconstructed Poland (and thus also Europe) will put a definite limit on the concept of self-determination. How, indeed, can the establishment of a stable international order be anticipated if at any given moment particularistic aspirations may break the territorial unity of states by invoking an unlimited right of minority existence and thus also of secession? Self-determination and the rights of minorities must find their limits in the conditions of existence of the established state and the vital interests of society.

Part Four

ECONOMIC AND SOCIAL DEVELOPMENT

CHAPTER XI

Poland's Economy between Two World Wars

BY HENRYK ZIELIŃSKI

IT IS POLAND of 1918, torn into three parts—Poland as it was when history called it back to life after one hundred and twenty-three years of bondage. The totally different political and economic regimes exercised by Russia, Prussia, and Austria-Hungary created cleavages between the provinces which were to handicap social and economic integration for decades to come. In speaking of the economic progress of Europe between the two great wars, one must realize that the situation of Poland was unique, and a comparison, therefore, with any of the states already established or with those created in 1918 can be only inaccurate.

The dismemberment of Poland, as shown on the map, resulted in a situation, after the collapse of the Partitioning Powers, wherein no sovereign Polish territory existed which could serve as a core around which to crystallize the restored Polish State. In contrast to Poland, Czechoslovakia has never lost its national unity and Jugoslavia was formed around the nucleus of the old Serbian kingdom. All three parts of Poland were in a deplorable state of economic backwardness, for it had been the policy of the Partitioning Powers to keep Polish lands from participating in the tremendous economic and technical progress of the nineteenth century.

For obvious political, national, and strategic reasons, the Partitioning Powers organized the Polish lands as border territories which, in the event of an armed conflict, would be in constant danger. Russia constructed no communication lines in the territories it occupied; Prussia denied Polish areas any participation in the industrial development of the Reich; Austria paralyzed all efforts at economic improvement in the southern part of Poland over which it ruled. At the same time, however, the three Partitioning Powers exploited their Polish holdings, abstracting from

DISMEMBERMENT OF POLAND PRIOR TO 1918

them—by means of taxation—a large share of their national income. The exclusion of Polish territories from the epoch-making progress of industrialization which had raised the majority of European nations to a high level of prosperity in sixty years, had serious effects on the economy of renascent Poland.

For the same strategic reasons, Poland took no part in the tremendous industrial development achieved in most countries during the First World War. Whereas on the strategically safe territories of the three Partitioning Powers a host of new plants was springing up to meet the demands of war, Poland was the battlefront throughout which destruction raged. Whereas, because of the exigencies of war, new industries were absorbing masses of unqualified labor in the secure hinterland of the three Powers and turning them into an army of skilled workers, Poland became the scene of mass deportations. About three million people were deported to Germany and Russia and, in addition to manpower, the occupation authorities confiscated and evacuated stocks of raw materials, machinery, technical installations, and tools. Thus Polish lands were largely stripped of the means of production. This evacuation of industrial facilities added to the destruction wrought by war activities, dealt a heavy blow to Poland's economy, and especially devastated the metal, textile, chemical, and lumber industries, as well as communication and transportation facilities.

Beside this, Versailles did not symbolize the end of war for Poland, and Poland did not, therefore, participate in the immediate postwar boom in Europe. In 1919 and 1920, the two years when hunger for consumer goods, capital goods, and services was at its height in continental Europe, as is demonstrated by imports of approximately $17,400,000,000 in gold (the highest level ever reached), Poland was at war with Russia. It was busy with cementing together the torn sections of its patrimony, with plebiscites, with the repatriation of millions of its citizens, and with the cleaning up of the ruins and debris of war, and thus took practically no part in this process of rehabilitation and reconstruction. What is more, the German Reich, which had persistently claimed that it could not exist without its Polish lands, paradoxically enough closed its frontiers to the import of Polish food products on the assumption that Poland's economy could be "smothered" by lack of German markets.

It took five arduous years to cement together the torn sections of Poland. It was necessary, during that time, not only to liquidate six kinds of currencies of the occupation period, to create a unified administration, and to restore efficiency to the communication system, but also to evolve a plan, at least temporarily, for the adjustment of the dissimilar standards of living in the three provinces and of the different costs of production resulting therefrom. There was such a marked divergence as to the standards and the nature of needs that the market planning was bound to meet with well-nigh insurmountable difficulties. Beside these difficulties, Poland in the eastern districts inherited from Russia an appalling percentage of illiteracy; in 1921—shortly after the Polish-Russian peace treaty—this percentage for persons above ten years of age was 64.7; for school children (ten to fourteen years old) it was as high as 71. Not until ten years later (Census of 1931) did the percentage of illiteracy of the group over ten years old drop to 41 per cent and for the children ten to fourteen years old to 17 per cent as compared with the old figure of 71 per cent. In an effort to raise the economic level of these territories, Poland had to struggle for twenty years with this legacy of Russian civilization.

Only in 1925 did Poland finally emerge from currency chaos. After stabilizing its currency and overcoming the devastating effects which the existence of the several media of exchange left by the occupation period had exercised on its savings and capitalization processes, Poland had to proceed with the final task of organizing its national budget.

It is more evident today than it was in 1925 that the primary objective in achieving a budgetary equilibrium does not consist in a purely technical balance, but in the change from an administrative budget to an investment budget. In a country where years of political bondage under foreign occupation, where destruction caused by war, and economic backwardness intentionally and methodically fostered by the Partitioning Powers had stopped processes of capitalization and investment, the question of raising the standard of living of the masses had to head the list of the national problems to be solved. In the once-ruined, now newly created Poland, with its insignificant capital resources, the bulk of investments had to be financed from funds provided for by national budgets. This is best illustrated by the fact that whereas from 1924 to 1936 the sum total of budgetary expenditures amounted to 30,000,000,000 złotys net, the sum total of investments was 6,000,000,000 złotys, or 20 per cent of budgetary expenditures. Under the Polish four-year plan the investments provided for by the budget for 1937 constituted an even higher item, which corresponded to 27.5 per cent of the total of budgetary expenditures. This was relatively a greater effort than that made by other European countries (France—19 per cent, Belgium—20 per cent, Czechoslovakia—19 per cent, and Italy—15 per cent).[1]

As in other countries in the throes of an economic crisis, not all capital investment in Poland could, nor for that matter should have been considered profitable from the point of view of productivity. In many instances, capital investment served social rather than economic ends, inasmuch as the chief objective of the struggle against the crisis was to achieve optimum employment and to combat unemployment. If the problem of unemployment is regarded as a structural process, rather than a phenomenon accompanying the changing business cycles, then unemployment in Poland has a particular significance for two reasons. First, because of a century of economic backwardness and destruction by wars the country neither could supply sufficient capital to develop production facilities on an adequate scale nor absorb all its potential labor supply; and second, the ratio of increase in Poland's population was one of the largest in Europe. Each year a new generation of approximately 350,000 reached the working age of fifteen years and pressed upon the labor market. If the American measuring stick for calculating the investment cost required for each newly employed worker were applied, the total yearly outlay for the employment of the yearly increment of the productive age classes alone would amount to approximately $1,250,000,000.

Because of the slow formation of capital in Poland, this capital requirement, without substantial assistance in the form of loans from the big creditor nations, was beyond the realm of feasibility. But Poland had to limit itself to its own capital resources while watching with apprehension the flow of international capital to neighboring Germany. The orthodox policy of international capi-

[1] This effort should be illustrated by a few examples. In 1919 the railway rolling stock numbered in round figures, 1,930 engines, and 39,700 cars, whereas in 1938 there were 5,100 engines and 163,200 cars. Upon the rebirth of Poland there were four universities, whereas in 1939 Poland had twenty-seven universities and academic institutions of learning. In 1919 there were 6,000 school buildings in Poland; in 1938 this number rose to 28,000.

tal considered investments in the German Reich as being infinitely safer and more secure than those in the countries which through the misfortunes of their history were retarded in their economic development. For instance, so far as the foreign investments of the United States were concerned (both direct loans and portfolio securities) they amounted in Germany to $1,421,000,000, a per capita average of $21.60, whereas in Poland they were only $177,-000,000, a per capita average of $5.63. The absurdity of this situation becomes even more evident when it is realized that in the period between the two world wars, the natural growth of the population in the Reich in absolute figures was only slightly higher than in Poland and in percentages almost one-half lower.

To no lesser degree was Poland's economic development hampered by the protectionist trends in international trade. Whereas the investment movements of international capital did not provide sufficient means for the development of Poland's economy, the world-wide evolution of the policy of economic self-sufficiency inevitably hampered any attempt at raising the standard of living of the population. Poland's foreign trade for the most part was European, although during the ten years before the Second World War overseas markets had become increasingly important. Poland's total export trade for a number of years was divided as follows:

Markets	Per cent			
	1928	1935	1936	1937
European	97.3	85.0	84.7	80.0
Overseas	2.7	15.0	15.3	20.0

Because of the economic structure of the country, foodstuffs, lumber, and semimanufactured articles played a decisive part in Polish export trade. An analysis of the customs tariffs of Poland's chief European markets gives an eloquent picture of the difficulties with which its foreign trade had to contend. In percentages of prices, the rise in tariffs is presented in the following table.

Agrarian protectionism, especially in recent Germany, where it was instrumental in bringing about the costly reagrarianization of the most highly industrialized country in Europe, impeded immensely the transformation of the occupational structure of the Polish population. German markets were always of great impor-

CUSTOMS TARIFFS INDICATED IN PERCENTAGES OF PRICES FOR THE YEARS 1913, 1927, AND 1931 AS MAINTAINED BY POLAND'S CHIEF EUROPEAN MARKETS

European markets	Customs tariffs in percentage of prices					
	Foodstuffs			Semimanufactured articles		
	1913	1927	1931	1913	1927	1931
Germany	21.8	27.4	82.5	15.3	14.5	23.4
France	29.2	19.1	53.0	25.3	24.3	31.8
Italy	22.0	24.5	66.0	25.0	28.6	49.5
Switzerland	14.7	21.5	42.2	7.3	11.5	15.2
Czechoslovakia	....	36.3	84.0	....	21.7	29.5

tance to the economy of Poland. Paradoxically, however, both the Weimar Republic and the National Socialist State surrounded German territory with a wall of unbelievably high tariffs, simultaneously attempting to convince the world of the intolerable lack of "living space" in Germany. The evolution of German tariff prohibitionism, which has been a vital factor in Poland's economic situation, is clearly shown in the table below. Taking the German tariff rates of 1913 as 100, they amounted to:

GERMAN TARIFF RATE INDEX OF 1927 AND 1931 FOR SELECTED POLISH PRODUCTS*

Selected Polish products	Tariff rate index	
	1927	1931
Foodstuffs	156	350
Semimanufactured articles	89	125
Textiles	132	206
Lumber	122	138

* 1913 = 100

Because of the pressing need for consumer products and capital goods, Poland could not and would not retaliate by similar measures in the field of tariffs. In contrast to the German policy, the Polish tariff level was lower than in 1913 in the group of semi-manufactured articles as well as in the group of manufactured goods. (Figures for 1913 are for erstwhile Russian-held Poland):

TARIFF RATES FOR 1913, 1927, AND 1931 ON POLISH IMPORTS*

Products	Tariff rates		
	1913	1927	1931
Semimanufactured articles	63.5	33.2	40.0
Manufactured goods	85.0	55.6	52.0

* In percentages of prices.

The comparatively bright, though unfortunately brief period from 1927 to 1931, when it seemed as though the world would be capable of returning to the international principles of free trade and the movement of capital, was for Poland a period of rapid progress. The national income grew substantially; in 1929 it reached $3,175,000,000 in gold; incentives to private investment were greatly stimulated and, most essential of all, a shift of wage earners from agricultural pursuits to more highly paid employment in industry began. It must be remembered that this happy turn of events took place within ten years of the cessation of hostilities. Yet this period of prosperity, far too short in which to provide the country with the necessary reserves, was shattered under the impact of the World Depression to an extent which was as great as in any other country.

Following in the footsteps of German prohibitionism, the great trading powers proceeded to set up systems of protective tariffs. The United States, in passing the Hawley-Smoot Tariff Act of 1930, hoped to create conditions for optimum employment by protecting the market for the American producer. Great Britain tried to solve the problem by the Ottawa Imperial Preference Agreement of 1932, and France, following Britain's example, tightened the economic ties between the various units of her colonial empire. A wave of disinclination to invest and give credits swept the world. The general level of prices dropped so low that, according to the report of the League of Nations, the annual service on external loans in 1932 required from countries of central and eastern Europe from 40 per cent to 50 per cent more goods to secure repayments.

It is small wonder, therefore, that in the wave of depression the Polish national income in 1933 dropped to 55 per cent of the 1929 level. It is true that in the same period the income of the United States fell even lower, to 49 per cent; yet, the lack of reserves in Poland and the withdrawal of foreign credits made the situation much more difficult for that country.

Poland's balance of payments, modest as it perforce had been, changed most unfavorably in the depression period. According to the calculations of the Polish Ministry of Finance, the per capita payment of revenues and expenditures presented the following picture:

POLAND'S PER CAPITA BALANCE OF PAYMENTS FOR THE YEARS 1927–1931 AND 1934–1937*

Revenues and expenditures	Per capita	
	1927–1931	1934–1937
Accounts receivable for goods exported	7.96	3.30
Accounts receivable from interest and dividends	0.08	0.02
Accounts receivable for services	2.50	1.08
Accounts payable for goods imported	9.03	3.14
Accounts payable for interest and dividends	1.20	0.53
Accounts payable for services	1.72	0.60

* In gold dollars.

Rightly or wrongly, Poland, in spite of the serious crisis, remained faithful to the tenets of free trade as compared with what was taking place in some countries in Europe. By maintaining the principle of keeping its economy dependent on the fluctuations of world prices, it allowed the international movements of gold to determine the life of each individual in the country. Within a few years, Poland was surrounded by a number of states which, through the manipulation of their currencies, the control of their trade, and the application of restrictive and discriminatory measures, endeavored to protect their economic systems from the convulsions of the crisis. And again, wisely or unwisely (Polish opinion varied on this point), Poland tried to remain faithful to the principles of world trade solidarity within the limits of its power. This is eloquently shown by the following figures, compiled by the International Chamber of Commerce and illustrating the status of controlled trade in specifically selected countries. The figures for 1937 read as follows:

CONTROLLED TRADE AS A PERCENTAGE OF TOTAL TRADE IN SELECTED EUROPEAN COUNTRIES

Country	Percentage of total	
	Imports	Exports
Germany	52.60	57.10
Bulgaria	87.60	70.20
Hungary	60.10	66.70
Rumania	74.90	66.70
Jugoslavia	61.00	49.00
Czechoslovakia	21.70	30.30
Poland	20.70	23.00

In the eyes of many observers, Poland's policy of budgetary equilibrium, of currency stabilization, and of free external trade, seemed out of proportion to the expansion which European economy was undergoing as a result of the German rearmament program. Perhaps an optimistic faith in the permanence of peace also contributed to the fact that the transition from depression to prosperity proceeded in Poland at a slower pace than in the rest of Europe. Not until 1938 did the index of industrial production in Poland exceed the index for Europe as a whole. Taking the 1928 index as 100, the indexes of industrial production for Europe (without Soviet Russia) and Poland developed as follows:

	1928	1932	1933	1934	1935	1936	1937	1938
Europe	100	75	80	89	96	105	115	113
Poland	100	64	70	79	85	94	111	119

This slow process of revival of production in Poland from 1934 to 1937 was traceable to still another factor—perhaps the most fundamental one—that Poland was compelled to work her way out of the acute world-wide crisis without the capital reserves that stood at the disposal of the great industrial powers. Beside this, the withdrawal of short-term and medium-term credits as well as of gold continued throughout the crisis. The movement of gold and of capital is illustrated by the following table:

	1928	1929	1930	1931	1932	1935	1936	1937
Gold	−107	− 81	+141	− 61	− 13	+ 22	+ 18	−124
Capital	+109	+593	−416	− 4	− 32	−108	−147	− 39

(in 1000 złotys. +, income; −, expenditure)

In a normally functioning economic organism, the outflow of gold and capital can have no other result than deflationary market fluctuations. In such instances, deflation is the only means by which the debtor nations can uphold their competitive position on the world markets. The dependence of the domestic market and of the standard of living of each individual in Poland on international fluctuations of gold and international credit markets is illustrated in the following table of wholesale prices, cost of living, and workers' wages which prevailed in Poland during the depression period. With 1928 representing 100, indexes for the years 1933 and 1937 are as follows:

INDEX OF PRICES, WAGES, AND COST OF LIVING IN POLAND, 1933 AND 1937*

Item	Indexes	
	1933	1937
Wholesale prices:		
Total	59	59
Industry	61	61
Agriculture	52	54
Workers' wages:		
Nominal	46	66
Real	68	106
Cost of living	71	63

* 1928 = 100.

Although the fact that the real wage rate of workers was not only maintained but was even raised above the 1928 parity may be hailed as a great success, nevertheless the effects of the World Depression must be considered as devastating (evident by the fall in wholesale prices), especially in view of the occupational composition of the Polish population, 63.7 per cent of which was engaged in independent occupations.

So far as the occupational structure of the population is concerned, Poland is predominantly agricultural, and although the percentage of the agricultural population was reduced in the last decade from 72.30 per cent to 60.90 per cent, even at that ratio the economic strength of the nation depends decidedly on the purchasing power of that very stratum of the population.

Because of the need of providing a livelihood for the farming population, paramount importance was attached in Poland to agrarian reform. Contrary to some opinions, this problem did not arouse doubts or questions in a social, political, or legal sense; the difficulty in carrying it out to its fullest extent and with great speed was entirely financial in nature. In spite of these difficulties, in the course of twenty years the agrarian reform yielded the following practical results: 6,500,000 acres were parceled into 734,000 farmsteads, 13,000,000 acres were consolidated and 1.3 million acres were reclaimed. The percentage of larger estates (of 123.6 acres or more) was reduced from 36.5 per cent of total farm land in 1921 to 15.2 per cent in 1939.

When the Polish Parliament for ethical reasons and on the basis of the constitutional guarantee of private ownership (corresponding with the Fourteenth Amendment to the Constitution of the United States) rejected the proposal of land expropriation without compensation, it became clear that the division of land would take much longer than the Polish people wished and expected. It must not be thought, however, that agrarian reform—vitally necessary as it was—constituted the final solution of Poland's structural difficulties; in the race between the natural growth of population and the process of parceling the land, the latter must be the loser in the course of one generation. Within twenty-five to thirty years after the planned completion of the agrarian reform (from 1948 onwards) the population pressure per unit of arable land would have reverted to the level of 1921.

The basic issue of Poland's economic problem consists in the radical transformation of the occupational structure of the population. The overcrowding per unit of arable land keeps at a high level the consumption of the farm produce by the land population, lowers its money income and investment capacity, and, as a result, slows the pace of domestic capital formation. All these processes do not accelerate but rather retard any programs for shifting the excess of land population to other occupations and employment. The creation of new productive activities for the natural increase of population, as well as for the "superfluous" farming population, was and is one of the chief issues of Poland's economy.

The theories about improving the intensity of cultivation and efficiency of agricultural production, popular as they have been recently, do not seem to take into account the consequences of population pressure on the arable land. The curve of Poland's economic evolution between the two wars clearly proves that in view of the strong agrarian overpopulation a radical transition from grain and potato farming to advanced farming cannot be considered. In this respect, Poland exemplifies the condition of a number of central and south European nations. Although the Germans constantly complain of the alleged overpopulation of their area, Poland and some other nations of that part of Europe could rightly envy the functional relation between population pressure and the standard of agricultural efficiency in the Reich. The table which indicates the relation of the population pressure as well as of the ratio of livestock and of production of butter and meat, per unit of arable land, also illustrates the difficulties resulting from agrarian overpopulation in Poland and in other countries as compared with Germany.

This analysis shows conclusively that the lower the pressure of the rural population per unit of farm land, the higher the per capita ratio of livestock and the higher the level of advanced and high-value production. Poland, whose situation in 1920 was still similar to that of Rumania and Jugoslavia, with about 73 per cent of its population living on and from the land, toward the end of the peace period stood half way between the highly industrialized countries and the classically agricultural ones.

Among the many symptoms of Poland's economic progress—such as the stabilization of currency and of the budget, development of overseas trade, construction of the Central Industrial District, the steadily advancing electrification of the country, and the maintenance of labor's purchasing power—the progressive relief from rural overcrowding per unit of arable land may be regarded

RATIOS BETWEEN RURAL POPULATION, FARM LAND, AND FOOD PRODUCTS IN POLAND, GERMANY, AND COUNTRIES OF SOUTHEASTERN EUROPE

(Average for the last five years)

Countries	Percentage of rural population	Per 1,000 hectares of farm land (excluding forests)		Per 1 hectare production of	
		Rural population	Heads of horned cattle and pigs	Milk (kg.)	Meat (kg.)
Germany	20.9	515	1,587	911	128.2
Czechoslovakia	34.5	602	920	...	44.9
Poland	60.9	878	706	341	29.6
Jugoslavia	80.0	960	536	318	....
Rumania	83.0	904	409	158	12.6

as the most characteristic change in the structure of Poland's economy. The shifting of the "surplus" rural population to non-agricultural occupations not only offers to this category a prospect of higher wage levels, but also gives the small farmer a chance to change from the traditional form of family farming to a higher grade of agriculture such as the production of protective foods and animal husbandry. This process is a proof of the principle that the higher the degree of industrialization of the country, the higher the efficiency of agricultural production and the higher the national standard of living.

In the twenty years of its independence, Poland made great efforts to provide new fields of profitable productive activity for her population. It worked under conditions handicapped by a world-wide economic chaos and in an atmosphere surcharged with the political unrest that swept over all the continents after the "unfinished" First World War. Poland, with the other nations, hopes that this time after victory has been won, the principles of a world-wide economic solidarity and an effectively functioning organization of collective security will lay the foundations for a better economic progress of free communities, without fear of unemployment, depressions, or political uncertainty.

CHAPTER XII

Industry, Foreign Trade, and Communications

BY LEOPOLD WELLISZ

BEFORE THE First World War there existed in Polish lands numerous industrial plants which had an adequate technical level. Industry as a whole, however, was not adapted to the modern requirements of the nation, and a homogeneous Polish industry as such did not exist, although the worker was Polish, the employee and the manager usually Polish, and the capital frequently Polish.

The origins of Polish industries date back many centuries. The real development of the large manufacturing industries of the European Continent took place, however, during the hundred years when Poland had no government of its own, and when the territories were divided among the Partitioning Powers—Austria, Russia, and Germany. Their different systems of economic policies, embracing such aspects as currencies, customs tariffs, fiscal policies, legal codes, and social legislation, were found to make a distinctive mark on the regions of partitioned Poland.

After the restoration of Poland's independence, it became apparent that some of its industries had been overdeveloped, whereas others showed serious deficiencies. In the largest territory of Poland, which had been under *Russian* domination, the number of industrial enterprises was greatest. These industries, however, were adapted to the needs of the Russian markets which had become the export territory for goods produced on Polish soil after the abolition of the customs frontiers between Russian Poland and Russia in the first half of the nineteenth century. After the rebirth of independent Poland, these industries therefore had to readapt themselves to the needs of the national economy.

The population of Poland was one-fourth as large as that of Russia, but its cultural level was incomparably higher. Thus Polish industries faced a double problem: to limit their production to a smaller market, and to improve the quality of many consumer goods. To find new export markets quickly was an impossibility, especially in the years immediately following the war, not only because of the chaotic conditions prevailing in Europe, but also because of import prohibitions by the majority of foreign countries.

When independence was restored in Poland, adjustment to the new conditions was made particularly difficult by the deplorable state of almost all Polish industrial enterprises in the territory formerly occupied by Russia. This condition had been caused by the compulsory removal of part of the industrial equipment to Russia at the beginning of the First World War, and by the ruthless requisitioning by the Germans of machines, raw materials, and products. Damages suffered at that time by Polish industries amounted to approximately $2,000,000,000.

The creation of new industries was no less difficult a task than the reconstruction of war ruins. Many industries essential to state and to national economy did not exist on Polish territory at that time.

Fear of Polish insurrections and of a conflict with its plundering partner, Germany, had prompted Russia to treat the part of Poland under its control as a strategic vanguard. Foreseeing the necessity of evacuating that area in event of war, Russia made no attempt to develop it. The Russian Government not only paralyzed private initiative, but also prevented the building of railroads, and the accomplishment of municipal improvements. It hindered the expansion of certain factories, for fear that some day these factories might supply the Poles with armaments.

The *Germans* considered the annexed provinces of Poznań and Pomorze to be the granary of the Reich and made great efforts to maintain their exclusively agricultural character. Assuming it would be much easier to restrain Polish peasants living in small settlements than it would Polish industrial workers inhabiting larger centers, the Germans prevented the industrialization of Poznań and Pomorze, even though these provinces possessed natural advantages for the development of various types of industry.

Inasmuch as agricultural progress in these provinces made unavoidable the establishment of factories connected with agricultural production, such as distilleries, breweries, and sugar and starch factories, the German administration which controlled the financial circles in Berlin limited to a minimum Polish participation in such enterprises. Only a few Polish factories therefore could survive.

The Upper Silesian industries, as far as their management and financing were concerned, were even more German in character. The natural riches of that province (coal, iron, and zinc ores) were especially favorable to the expansion of heavy industries. Underestimating the national consciousness of the local Polish population, the Germans did not hinder this expansion, although they always favored their western Westphalian basin. The powerful, yet one-sided Upper Silesian industry was instrumental chiefly in satisfying the demands of the other provinces of the Reich. The reintegration of a part of Upper Silesia into Poland two years after the unification of the other Polish provinces made more difficult the amalgamation of Poland's industrial enterprises into one organism. Yet German hopes that Poland would be unable to surmount these difficulties proved as ill-founded as their earlier belief that the Upper Silesians had lost their Polish national consciousness.

In *Austria,* where policies toward a number of the nationalities of the Dual Monarchy were somewhat liberal, those elements which considered the Polish provinces primarily as consumers of the industrial products of the central provinces kept the upper hand almost to the outbreak of the First World War. These policies were very injurious to the inhabitants of Galicia, which was overpopulated and was rich in such raw materials as coal, salt, oil, natural gas, potassium salts, lumber, and water power. Although conditions improved in the years immediately preceding the First World War, and in spite of a series of laws facilitating the expansion of industries, passed by the autonomous Galician Diet, the industries of former Austrian Poland were somewhat undeveloped. Thus, in 1919 the new Poland faced the problem of industrializing this province which had suffered as a result of the war almost as much as had former Russian Poland.

PROGRESS BETWEEN THE TWO WORLD WARS

Poland's industry was built on the sound foundation of the natural riches of the country, the inborn ability and skill of the Polish worker and technician, and the potentialities of its internal market. Through the patriotic efforts of all social strata, Poland succeeded rapidly in its task of reconstruction and in the adaptation of its industries and commerce to the needs of the reborn state. The sense of historical responsibility of the generation which witnessed the realization of the ideal of independence was powerful. The understanding of the social importance of having the workshops set in motion as rapidly as possible was almost universal; it was to be found among manufacturers, employees, and workers alike. During the twenty years of freedom, the majority of disputes between the employers and workers were settled by means of arbitration. The sense of solidarity was generally stronger than the divergence of interests. The establishment of the State Institute of Weights and Measures, of the Geological Institute, of the Patent Office, of the Export Institute, of new technical and business high schools and colleges, and the development of the means of communication as well as many other governmental measures largely contributed to economic progress.

It is superfluous to dwell any longer upon the difficulties which resulted from the deficiencies of the state administration in the first years of its existence, from the lack of financial and currency stabilization, from general autarchic tendencies, from the consequences of the economic crisis of 1929, and last but not least, from the almost universal political unrest. In spite of a series of obstacles delaying economic progress, Poland had achieved the rational organization of its industries within the first twenty years of independence, and was able to supply the most important needs of its population. The number of industrial workers increased during the 1919–1939 period from 130,000 to 900,000.[1]

Polish industry, to be sure, constituted only a small fraction of

---

[1] The growth of Poland's industrial production, between the peak years of prosperity, 1929 = 100, and the spring of 1939 is best illustrated by the index of industrial activity which in Poland amounted to 127.6 per cent; in Great Britain to 124.2 per cent; in the United States to 92.7 per cent; and in France to 91.9 per cent.

world industries; yet it revealed an efficiency and a heterogeneity of production to be found only in highly industrialized countries. The following review will give an idea of the typical obstacles which had to be surmounted by the most important Polish industries, and of the results which were achieved.

Coal mining.—It was fortunate for Poland that the equipment of its coal mines had not been seriously damaged during the First World War, and that the country had not been deprived of its chief sources of heat, light, and power. Because of these fortunate circumstances, the principal task of the coal-mining industry was limited to maintaining, developing, and distributing its production under new conditions.

The Polish coal basin, one of the greatest in the world, and formerly divided among Russia, Austria, and Germany was almost entirely restored to reborn Poland. It occupies an area of 2,100 square miles and abounds in rich strata of all kinds of easily mined coal of high caloric value. The coal reserves of Poland are estimated at 100,000,000,000 to 160,000,000,000 tons. This figure is larger than that of any other country of the European Continent, and approximates that of Great Britain.

The total amount of coal mined on Polish territory before the First World War was 41,000,000 tons yearly, of which 32,000,000 tons were mined in Upper Silesia. During the war, coal production decreased by 20 per cent in Russian Poland and by 34 per cent in Austrian Poland. This was caused chiefly by defective conservation methods, by the diminishing number of skilled miners, and by a lack of proper auxiliary materials.

After the Armistice, the mines of these two districts were in critical condition because of the disorganization of transport facilities, the almost catastrophic lack of food and currency, and the stoppage of deliveries of materials. Simultaneously, the country suffered greatly from lack of coal.

Because of the combined action of the Government, of the association of coal-mine owners, and of labor, transportation was rapidly restored, miners returned to work, and the mining of coal gradually increased. However, the supply could not meet the demand which was growing in proportion to the revival of the economic life of the country, and for a long time the rationing of coal was necessary.

The situation changed radically in 1922, when a part of Upper Silesia was united with Poland. Having been a "deficit country," Poland now had much more coal than was needed for internal consumption. Hence, new foreign markets had to be found for the coal which hitherto had been almost exclusively consumed by Germany. Poland proved equal to the task, in spite of the fact that before the war Russian and Austrian Poland had imported annually only some 2,000,000 tons from Upper Silesia.

The absorption of Polish coal until 1925 was facilitated by the obligation imposed upon Germany to permit the entry of approximately 6,500,000 tons yearly, duty free. In 1926, after the closing of the German frontier, the lack of coal on the world markets, caused by the strike of English coal miners, was of benefit to Poland. Yet the solution of the coal problem was achieved principally through the rapid increase in Poland's internal consumption, as well as through the skill of Polish industrialists and coal dealers in introducing the coal to new export markets.

The real causes of the expansion of Polish coal exports were the high quality of the coal and the low cost of production, traceable to advantageous natural conditions, liberal investments in mine equipment, and the increased efficiency of the miners, of transportation, and of the organization of the industry. All these features made it possible for the industry to overcome the only serious handicap in the export of Polish coal—the great distance of three hundred miles from the mines to the Baltic ports.

As a matter of fact, only about 10 per cent of those exports went by rail to neighboring countries. The greater part, approximately 40 per cent, went by sea to the Scandinavian countries which heretofore had never imported Polish coal, 25 per cent went to western European countries, and the rest to various other nations.

In 1928 Poland's coal production reached its prewar level, and in 1929 it exceeded this by 15 per cent. In the following years it decreased temporarily as a result of the international economic depression, but had again risen and attained its maximum before the outbreak of the war in 1939. The average output per manshift was 1.4 tons for all miners in 1913. In 1925 it dropped to 0.94 ton. In 1938 it increased to 1.82 tons—the highest in Europe. In 1939 Poland ranked seventh in the coal output of the world, and fourth in coal exports.

Iron and steel industry.—The iron and steel industry, which is linked the closest with the coal-mining industry, may serve as an example of another type of difficulty that had to be surmounted by Poland. The Polish iron and steel industry worked under much less favorable conditions than the coal industry—to mention only poor iron ore and coke of mediocre quality—for the best metallurgical coke was produced in that part of the coal basin which, though possessing a large Polish population, had been awarded to Czechoslovakia.

Unlike the coal industry, the steel and iron industry in the parts of Poland formerly occupied by the Russians had been thoroughly looted by the Germans during the First World War, and its production had sunk to the level of almost total extinction. The Germans had stolen everything of use to them, from electric motors to floor slabs. The number of workers had decreased from 20,000 in 1913 to 2,000 in 1915. Energetic leadership in the industry was responsible for the production of iron again within a few months after the evacuation of the Germans; within a few years all these foundries had been rebuilt and were producing.

The Upper Silesian foundries, which had not suffered the ravages of the war and had a much greater production capacity, were united with Poland two years after the liberation of the other parts of the country. Their production found new markets when the term of tariff-free imports to Germany had elapsed.

There has been a market for iron and steel in other parts of Poland which, before the war, imported great quantities from the distant Donets Basin. Moreover, Poland's consumption of iron and steel increased rapidly after the restoration of Polish independence. Progress in the organization of industry and in the modernization of equipment gained for Poland's foundries a steady place in the markets of the world, and satisfied all the demands of the Polish market.

In 1937 an era of great progress for the metallurgical industry began with the creation of the new Polish Central Industrial District. The prewar level of production would easily have been surpassed by 1939 had it not been for the outbreak of war.

Metalworking industry.—The Polish metalworking industry serves as a model for the reconstruction of a branch of industry which was totally ruined by the war. Its structure was entirely different from that of the coal-mining and the steel and iron industries which comprised a few large enterprises with a limited number of products. The metal industry, by its very nature consisting of numerous enterprises of manifold production, had expanded chiefly in the Polish provinces under Russian rule before the First World War. There were about 1,500 factories employing approximately 60,000 workers. All of these factories were robbed of their raw materials, machine tools, and equipment by the German occupants. The only railroad car factory in southeastern Poland had its equipment totally destroyed. The number of factories in former Upper Silesia, Poznań, and Pomorze was insignificant.

Immediately after the Armistice, Polish industrialists began the reëquipment of their factories. A part of the machines and tools were recovered from Germany; others were constructed in Poland. Some enterprises obtained capital from abroad, partly through their former relations with foreign firms, for the purchase of machines. Within two years, all enterprises were operating again.

Many branches of the metal industry could not easily attain their prewar output. In steam-boiler factories, bridge construction plants, and enamelware factories, for instance, prewar production had been so great that it nearly satisfied the demand of the whole Russian Empire. Clearly, the output of these factories had to be temporarily reduced until new export markets could be found. At the same time, there was a scarcity of many facilities for the production of equipment essential to the security of the nation.

As early as 1919, Polish industrialists began to build factories for the manufacture of ammunition, airplanes, locomotives, railroad cars, and machine tools. The Government assisted the establishment of these factories, guaranteeing the purchase of their output for a number of years at prices which assured a proper profit as well as the appropriate amortization of the investments.

Several years later, when the World Depression limited private initiative, the Government constructed its own armament factories. In the years preceding the outbreak of the Second World War, private initiative was stimulated again by the reduction of taxes on new enterprises and the granting of credit facilities. The establishment of new factories in a domain of production heretofore nonexistent in Poland was inevitably dependent upon the coöperation and experience of foreign technologists and foreign capital. After a few years, however, Polish industries were able to rely exclusively upon their own technicians.

Having attained a high degree of technical perfection with low production costs, some of the new industries began to export their products. Polish locomotives were exported to Bulgaria, French Morocco, China, Latvia, and the U.S.S.R.; guns were sold to Holland; air planes and rails to Brazil; ammunition to Greece; spinning-mill equipment, enamelware, pipelines for hydroelectric plants, and other products to many foreign countries. The extent of the effort in this field may be estimated best when one considers that the investments of the metal industry, in the period of 1919–1939, amounted to 2,000,000,000 złotys, i.e., the equivalent of the yearly expenditure of the Polish State. In the same period the number of workers in the metal industries increased threefold.

The situation in nearly all other branches of Polish industry was similar to one or another of these three examples.

Textile industry.—Before the First World War, the textile industry had employed 150,000 workers, but during the war only 30,000 workers. The industry had been infamously looted by the Germans who had requisitioned in the cotton and wool center of Łódź alone, eight hundred miles of driving belts. By 1928, however, the number of workers in the field had increased considerably over the number of prewar workers. The manufacturers not only succeeded in reconstructing their industry, but also quickly adapted themselves to new conditions; they raised the standards of their products and produced many kinds of new goods. Special attention was given to increasing the manufacture of linen products. Poland was one of the largest flax-growing countries in the world and gradually expanded its exports of linen fabrics to the United States and to other countries.

Paper industry.—This industry, which had decreased by 75 per cent during the war, increased its prewar production by 100 per cent in the period of 1919–1939. The expansion of the industry clearly demonstrates the stimulating effect of independence upon industrial progress. The publication of periodicals and books increased enormously. Instruction in the native language, as well as the introduction of compulsory education in large territories which heretofore had been deprived of public schools, resulted in a heavy production of Polish schoolbooks. Shortly before the outbreak of the Second World War, two additional cellulose mills and two paper mills were constructed in vast forest areas within easy access of navigable rivers, this location assuring cheap raw material and good communications.

Chemical industry.—The chemical industry in Poland had excellent natural resources; it had at its disposal the most essential of raw materials: coal, salt, oil, natural gas, pyrite, zinc, clay, and gypsum. Its other valuable assets were a well-trained, technical management, thoroughly schooled chemical engineers, clever workmen, a solid industrial trade organization and, equally necessary, an understanding of the importance of this industry by state authorities.

In the fields of artificial nitrous fertilizers, of artificial silk, powder and other explosive materials, pharmaceutical products, soda (tenfold increase in production), and dyes, new production was started, new factories were built, and investments in the twenty-year period amounted to several hundred million dollars. The turnover of the chemical industry was much larger than in prewar days, amounting annually to 1,000,000,000 złotys, a figure which was rather imposing under the conditions prevailing in Poland.

Electrical-equipment and machinery industry.—This industry deserves special mention as another example of Polish industrial achievement. It was almost nonexistent in Poland before the war. Electrification throughout the country was still in an embryonic state. The small quantities of equipment and appliances which were then necessary were produced almost exclusively by German factories. The modernization and reconstruction of Polish industries, as well as the increased consumption of electric light and power after the war, required a considerable increase in all kinds of electrical equipment, machinery, and apparatus.

Unable to find Polish experts for all branches of industry, the industrialists established their new factories or enlarged the old ones in coöperation with the specialized Swedish, Swiss, French, and Dutch factories which were willing to make investments in Poland. By the end of the twenty-year period, Poland was manufacturing its own electric motors, transformers, accumulators, batteries, cables, telegraph and telephone equipment, radio apparatus, bulbs, isolation materials, and electric meters.

In 1939 there existed in Poland over two hundred plants in the electrical equipment and machinery industry, employing approximately twenty thousand workers. These plants produced about 200,000,000 złotys' worth of goods, whereas foreign imports decreased to one-fourth that sum.

Meat-products industry.—The Polish meat-products industry was also created in the years of independence. In collaboration with the Government, the Union of Bacon and Meat-Products Exporters, the farmers' organizations, and enterprising merchants and industrialists built modern plants for the production of new varieties of meat products. The industry succeeded in exporting bacon, ham, and other meat products to some fifty countries, in spite of ever-increasing trade barriers. The total export equalled one-fifth the normal yearly increase of hogs in Poland. Their success in the United States was so great, indeed, that the produce from export sale sufficed to cover a large part of Poland's purchases of American cotton.

Potassium-salts industry.—Another example of Polish efficiency is to be found in the production of potassium salts. This industry, although a state monopoly, was operated on an organizational plan similar to that of a commercial company. Within twenty years, production increased from 14,000 to 567,000 tons, giving Poland a rank of third in the world.

Miscellaneous industries.—In the reconstruction of plants and the adaptation to new conditions, the beet-sugar, leather, cement, glass, building, and lumber industries were analogous to the textile industry. Poland became the fifth largest beet-sugar producer in the world; it produced twice as much cement as before the war; and it ranked first in the field of alder-plywood production.

Throughout Poland, despite the difficulties resulting from the unsettled political and economic situation, reconstruction and adaptation to new economic conditions were accomplished within a few years after the restoration of Polish independence. The expansion of industry was checked during the period of the World

Depression; but the following years showed a gradual yet marked increase in production, and on the eve of the German invasion, with few exceptions, it had attained or exceeded the prewar level.

Although these advances were indisputable, the level of industrialization in Poland even in 1939 was still much lower than that of western European countries. The chief hindrance to its development was the slow accumulation of the nation's capital and the inadequate influx of foreign capital. The importance of a strong Poland, situated between the imperialistic totalitarianism of Germany and the communistic imperialism of Russia, was realized too late for the peace of the world. The mistakes committed by Polish economic policies of deflation during the third decade of this century and, above all, the chaotic political and economic conditions prevailing throughout the world in this period, arrested the development of Polish industries which had not kept pace with the needs of the nation. Unfortunately, the far-reaching program of industrialization and electrification which had been initiated only a few years before the war and too late for its full realization, was paralyzed by the invasion.

Yet, whatever was restored or created during the short period of independence—even though it was destroyed in the present war—was proof of the prevailing spirit of enterprise, as well as the skill and energy of Polish industries. This will ensure the progress of Poland's industrialization when the hour of liberation strikes. There is no doubt that after the victorious conclusion of the war, Poland will redouble its efforts to rebuild and enlarge its production apparatus in order to ensure the fullest employment of its population and, simultaneously, to raise its standard of living.

The tragedy of the Second World War has taught all countries of Europe two lessons: First, modern technique and organization methods make it possible for all well-organized nations to give employment to all their citizens and to produce enough goods to assure a decent standard of living to all. Clearly, the very consciousness of that fact will stimulate the industrialization of all backward countries, especially of those like Poland where the rise of industrialization was hampered only by lack of capital. Second, even the most obdurate of skeptics are convinced that there are no zones of diverse safety in the world, and the political risk of investments in Poland is the same as that in Norway, Belgium, or on the island of Java; that the risk proved lesser in Australia or in Egypt was by mere chance only.

The writer feels certain that after this war, because of the progress of financial techniques, the accumulation of capital within the country will be rationally utilized for the realization of the far-reaching industrialization plan which has been elaborated in broad outlines under the auspices of the Polish Government. It is no less certain that the influx of foreign investment capital would greatly facilitate the purchase of raw materials and machinery which are indispensable for the speedy execution of this great plan.

FOREIGN TRADE

The progress of Polish international trade paralleled an improvement of the country's economic situation. Poland's working capital was almost entirely lost during the war; inasmuch as there were neither gold mines nor a steady influx of large capital from abroad, Poland had to devote special care to the development of its international trade. The obstacles which Poland met were far more serious than those of other countries. The two largest and nearest export and import markets were closed to it. Soviet Russia had isolated itself at once, and Germany, having regained its freedom of action in 1924, cut itself off from Poland by high trade barriers. These markets were later opened by both countries but only occasionally and for purely political reasons, not according to real economic needs.

Not only because of economic reasons but also to emancipate itself from political pressure by its neighbors, Poland was compelled to make a sudden and organic transformation of its international trade channels, a unique phenomenon in world economics. The prewar experience of Polish exporters was of limited value, inasmuch as Polish goods before the war were seldom seen on foreign markets other than Russia, Austria, and Germany.

For this purpose an independent Polish port was established in Gdynia, and the port of Danzig extended and modernized. In 1938, 77.7 per cent of Polish trade in weight and 62.7 per cent in value passed through these two Polish ports. Imports into Polish territories before the First World War, 90 per cent of which came by land from Germany, Russia, and Austria, in 1939 amounted to only 0.8 per cent from the U.S.S.R., and only 23 per cent in value from Germany and Austria, although Poland, in order to recover German debts, was compelled to import from Germany goods at even higher prices. Exports from Poland to Germany and Austria in 1938 amounted to only 24 per cent, to the U.S.S.R., 0.1 per cent.

Poland found new markets all over the world for 75 per cent of its trade, although it was compelled to change not only its import and export markets, but also the nature of its import and export goods. Polish exports originally had consisted almost exclusively of raw materials and agricultural products, but gradually had come to include more and more manufactured goods.

The largest export item in 1938 was coal which amounted to about 18.4 per cent. The second largest exports were lumber and wood products, the latter steadily increasing in proportion with the decrease of raw-timber exports. Polish alder plywood, bent furniture, and similar products became known on all important world markets. The export of cured ham and meat preserves steadily increased in spite of fixed quotas and other difficulties which Poland had to meet in the chief purchaser countries—the United Kingdom and the United States. In the years immediately preceding the Second World War, when the consequences of the international crisis had subsided, Poland intensively developed exports of a great variety of metal, textile, and chemical products.

At the same time, gradual but steady changes in Poland's import trade took place. The import of consumer goods decreased in proportion with the expansion of Poland's industrialization and was replaced by an increase in the import of raw materials and of capital equipment for its industry. The chief imports of raw materials consisted of cotton, wool, iron ores, scrap, copper, and raw hides. Approximately 15 per cent of the total import value were machine tools and apparatus not produced in Poland.

Poland's participation in international trade barely exceeded 1 per cent of the world's trade turnover. This resulted chiefly from the enactment of autarchic measures in all countries in the third decade of the twentieth century, at the moment when Poland had succeeded in adapting itself to novel conditions of overseas trade. It must be mentioned, however, that Poland's part in international trade almost equalled that of the U.S.S.R.

The international trade turnover per capita in Poland was approximately one-third less than in the United States, but fourteen times larger than the corresponding figure in China, and five times greater than that of the U.S.S.R. After the depression years, Poland's international trade steadily improved, justifying the most optimistic predictions of Poland's future share in the exchange of goods between nations. The German invasion of 1939 put a sudden end to this development.

COMMUNICATIONS AND PUBLIC UTILITIES

One of the most serious handicaps to Polish economic development was the policy of destruction or retardation which had been carried on by the occupying powers. Russia especially opposed any important modernization of the general equipment of the country. The communication system in Poland was poor, the production of electricity low, most cities were neglected, and a large part of the equipment of public utilities was destroyed. A similar problem of reconstruction after the Second World War will face Poland.

The reconstruction of ruins, as well as the establishment of the most essential public utilities that had been neglected during a century of foreign rule, absorbed the best efforts of Poland during the period separating the two world wars. Only the economically most important aspects of general equipment, namely communications, electrification, auxiliary economic investments, and housing problems will be discussed in this chapter.

Communications and transportation evidently are a *sine qua non* of the proper functioning of any economic organism. The transportation system of Poland in 1919 consisted of fragments of the road systems of the three Partitioning Powers. Because of the strategic reasons of these mutually distrustful enemies of Poland, the road systems were poorly connected with one another, and were entirely unadapted to the needs of a homogeneous Polish state.

Highways.—In 1919 there were in Poland only about 26,000 miles of hard-surfaced roads. This figure corresponds to 19 miles per 100 square miles, a ratio far below the average prevailing in western Europe. In the twenty years from 1919 to 1939, all these highways were improved and approximately 50 per cent more were constructed. The quality of the new roads also was better adapted to the country's climatic condition than was that of the old roads. Many new bridges were built. The efforts made by Poland to repair damaged and worn roads, and to build new ones have been great. But the work still to be done is considerable. In order to attain a density of highways similar to that in Germany, for example, it would be necessary to construct about 1,875 miles of roads annually for twenty years.

Railroads.—From the Partitioning Powers, Poland inherited only about 10,000 miles of railroad lines, mostly in poor condition, and a quite insufficient and antiquated rolling stock. On the average, there were in Poland 8.5 miles of track per 100 square miles, whereas in Germany there were 18.7 miles per 100 square miles. During the war, 40 per cent of Poland's bridges, 65 per cent of the station buildings, and 80 per cent of the water towers had been destroyed. Within twenty years these were reconstructed, the rolling stock was modernized, all new locomotives were constructed in new Polish factories, except for the 150 purchased from the Baldwin Locomotive Works. About 1,500 miles of new railroad lines were built, the longest among them being the Silesia-Baltic line, built by private French capital. Constructed to facilitate and increase Polish coal exports, it proved profitable, although its tariffs were low. The Polish Government planned a further construction of 2,500 miles of railroads, principally to improve communications between the Baltic and the Black Sea, as well as with the new Central Industrial District.

Waterways.—The waterways in Poland were neglected even more than the railroads and highways, although before the partitions in the eighteenth century, Poland had had a considerable network of canals and a river traffic by no means negligible. Poland possesses a number of rivers which constitute a network of waterways covering almost the whole country. After the necessary regulation work has been carried out and a few new connecting canals (of moderate length) have been constructed, these rivers will be excellent arteries for the transportation of goods between the primary centers of economic activity in Poland. There are a number of products, among them coal, timber, and cement, which are more suitable for mass transportation and, therefore, should be shipped by water rather than by the more expensive railways.

In the years 1919–1939, the existing principal natural and artificial waterways which had been partially destroyed or damaged by long neglect and military operations, were repaired and made navigable. A large-scale plan of regulating the waterways was undertaken, but was only partially realized. The minimum program of hydraulic works in Poland demands the regulation of approximately 1,250 miles of navigable waterways, a drainage of an area of about 1,250,000 acres, and the construction of dike works for protecting against floods an area of about 175,000 acres.

The construction of great reservoirs on the Carpathian tributaries of the Vistula at Porembka and Roznow, which had been partly accomplished before the war, was the first step in the complete regulation of the Vistula River and created a large source of electric power. In this domain after the war, Poland will have to achieve a task of great importance not only for its own sake, but also for the prosperity of its immediate neighbors, and for the benefit of the whole European economy (Baltic-Black Sea waterways, an east-west waterways net, and the Baltic-Vistula-Czechoslovakia waterway).

Maritime transport.—Although the work accomplished in the period of 1919–1939 in the realm of land and river communication consisted chiefly in reconstruction of war damages and in the adaptation of existing investments to the needs of the reborn nation, the necessity of maritime transport resulted in two fundamentally creative enterprises: the development of the Baltic Coast, with the construction of the port of Gdynia, and the establishment of the Polish merchant marine.

No other territorial change in Europe has brought about such important and far-reaching economic results as the union of Poland's territory with Pomorze and Danzig. In that brief period the short Polish seacoast and the Free City of Danzig underwent a radical change. Once a neglected area, with its somnolent, small, stagnant, provincial seaport, it became one of the busiest regions in Europe, expanding with incomparable speed.

In 1920 the Polish Government realized that the security of access to the sea, dependent on the whims of the Free City of Danzig which remained under German influence, was highly problematical. This was the reason why Poland decided to establish its own independent seaport as early as 1921. Thus it came to pass within a decade that the little fishing port of Gdynia became one of the largest and best-equipped ports of the world. In 1939 the total area of the port embraced 2,126 acres, of which 554 acres represented the water area. The greatest depth of the port was 45.6 feet, the total length of the shore 8 miles, with 138 miles of railway tracks, 35 storage yards, 57 port warehouses, 87 mechanical transloading installations, with cranes having a lifting capacity of 350.7 tons. The port also had many corn silos, mineral-oil reservoirs, and other structures necessary to industry and commerce. It was as though in a trice a small village had been transformed into a seaport having the most modern of equipment, and into a city of 100,000 inhabitants.

At the same time, and notwithstanding the hostile attitude of the Danzig municipality toward Poland, a systematic development and modernization of the Danzig port, which had been badly neglected by Germany in prewar days, was begun, primarily with Polish funds. Having ranked under German domination as the seventh Baltic port, under Polish protection Danzig became the second in importance after Gdynia. The number of its cranes increased from 13 to 70 odd. The shoreline, 10 yards or more deep, increased from 507 yards to several miles.

Antiquated, narrow warehouses were replaced by modern and spacious ones. Large, well-lighted and excellently equipped transshipping halls were built; the entire port was dredged; three new basins were constructed; new machines were installed for the quick transshipping of coal, ore, and timber; and large grain silos were erected. The loading of ships was accelerated and the cost of transshipping reduced. Convenient equipment, low cost of operation, efficiency of the newly created customs, insurance, arbitration, and supply apparatus, construction of new railroads, and rational transportation tariffs—all these were steadily attracting increasing cargoes to both of Poland's home ports.

The entrance of the first freighter into the port of Gdynia in 1923 marked for Poland the beginning of a new era. By 1938, a total of 6,498 ships had entered the port. Their tonnage amounted to 6,500,000, of which 876,000 were under the Polish flag. The corresponding figures for the port of Danzig were 2,983 ships in 1913, and 6,601 in 1939. Danzig's turnover increased from 2,500,000 tons in 1924 to over 7,000,000 in 1938. Yet, the Free City complained that it was being wronged by Poland.

The short period between the two world wars demonstrated the great importance of this access to the sea, not only for the economic development of Poland, but also for that of other central and eastern European countries. This success was accomplished in spite of the narrowness of the Polish seacoast, of impediments placed in the way by German policy and, finally, in spite of the distance of both Polish ports from certain of the provinces of Poland. Real prosperity for this region will be possible only when Poland obtains a wider access to the sea.

Merchant marine.—Before independence was restored to Poland, no Polish ships sailed the seas, nor were there many Polish seamen. Among the exceptions was Joseph Conrad, sailor and world-famous novelist who proved that Poland did have a "sense of the sea" and that its sons did have qualifications and a fondness for navigation. The expansion of the Polish merchant marine could be only comparatively slow, for it required a thorough study of all its complicated problems, and a careful preparation for entrance into its service. Polish seamen have demonstrated the high qualities of their seamanship in the present war by having saved most of their ships from the Germans. They fulfill their task heroically while coöperating with the fleets of the other United Nations.

The number of ships increased in proportion to the completion of the training of ships' crews and officers. In the first months of 1939 Poland had 135 ships, with a tonnage amounting to about 100,000 B.R.T. In comparison with the merchant marine of other countries, the figure was not imposing. Yet it was an important step in the expansion of Polish overseas trade. Poland had two modern motor ships of 16,000 tons each, and two of 11,000 tons each which plied regularly between Gdynia and American ports. It also had a number of coal carriers, special herring fishing boats, and other craft.

Air communications.—Though disposing of slender financial means, Poland within twenty years developed a rather extensive system of air communication not only between its own larger cities, but also with neighboring countries. The airlines reached northward as far as Finland, and southward as far as Bagdad. In 1938

Polish commercial planes made 10,000 flights, covering almost 2,500,000 kilometers. The exceptional qualifications of numerous Polish pilots contributed largely to the expansion of aviation, and these pilots, in 1941, were to give a brilliant account of themselves in the defense of Great Britain. Actually they are now fighting for freedom in the van of the United Nations airfleets.

Electrification.—Before the restoration, electrification in Poland was undeveloped. Polish resources of rich coal deposits in the southwest, of oil in the southeast, and of great reserves of hydraulic power in various provinces, had been exploited to only a small extent. Fully realizing the importance of electrification for the country, the Polish Government as early as 1922 passed a law concerning the granting of concessions for the production, transformation, transmission, and distribution of electric current. This law was completed in the following years by granting important privileges to capital investors. As a consequence, with the participation of English, Belgian, and Swedish capital, the number of electricity plants increased rapidly.

During the period of 1919–1939 the number of plants increased from 835 to 3,198, and their production (in millions of kw-hr from 1,800 to 3,977). However, even in 1939 Poland occupied one of the lowest places among the nations of Europe as a consumer of electric energy; its consumption per head was only one-sixth of that in France, one-tenth the per capita consumption of the United States, and was less than half that in Czechoslovakia.

The principal reason for this backwardness was an insufficient influx of foreign capital, inasmuch as electrification required purchases made abroad. The manufacture of electric equipment would mean heavy imports of copper, machines, and special equipment, none of which could be produced in Poland. The program of economic postwar reconstruction for Poland's electrification will be of foremost importance as the basic factor of economic progress and a general rise in standards of living.

To keep abreast of the anticipated general economic progress of the country, in the years to come, the consumption of electric energy will have to rise to the level of 300 kw-hr per capita annually, thus approaching that of Czechoslovakia and Italy. In order to execute this plan, in the first years following the cessation of present hostilities, it is proposed to install generators for at least a further 2,000,000 kw-hr, both by expansion of existing power stations and by construction of new ones, based chiefly on coal power and also on water power, so that the aggregate power would reach a figure of 4,000,000 kw-hr. Simultaneously, a national grid several thousand miles in length will have to be set up for high-tension transmission, linking the more important power stations. As a natural corollary of this plan, projects dealing with local distribution and with domestic and factory installations will have to be developed on a large scale.

Auxiliary economic investments.—After the basic equipment indispensable to the economic life of the country (communications, electric-power plants, etc.), various auxiliary installations of public service are of the utmost importance for the expansion of trade. This was well understood in Poland, especially in the field of agriculture where great advance was made within the 1919–1939 period. With the assistance of the central government and of autonomous bodies, considerable progress was made, including the construction of a number of modern grain elevators, cold-storage and seed-cleaning plants, mechanical dairies (mostly coöperatives), and oil mills in various regions of the country. In this field, also, the twenty-year period was too short a time in which to repair all the equipment that had been neglected during the century of oppression.

Housing investments.—Sanitary requirements and reasonable comfort in living quarters were badly neglected in Polish cities and towns, especially in former Russian Poland, where the population was deprived of autonomous rights. During the twenty years of its independence, Poland had made considerable progress. Conditions prevailing in the largest Polish cities had changed to such an extent that appearance and comfort were almost comparable with that of western Europe. Progress was also noticeable in the countryside. The fact that the average death rate of 22.4 per 1,000 inhabitants in 1909–1911 had dropped to 13.9 in 1938 is the best proof of general improvement in sanitary conditions.

Credits granted by Polish banks, as well as French, American, and English investments, made it possible to construct modern sewerage systems, electric-power plants, and gas works in a number of cities, as well as to organize motorbus and suburban railway lines. It is evident that the modernization of cities which, for one hundred years, had been deprived of autonomy, could not be achieved within the short space of twenty years. In 1939 the major part of the country still lacked electricity, telephone service, and other modern improvements. After peace is restored, in collaboration with the United Nations for the benefit of all, much will need to be done in Poland, not only in the reconstruction of Warsaw—savagely destroyed—but also in many other cities and in rural districts as well.

And this reconstruction will take place. The work which was accomplished by the Poles during the twenty-year period of political insecurity and of autarchic tendencies throughout the world, should be an assurance of great economic and social development in Poland when, after victory, an era of lasting peace and of peaceful collaboration of all the United Nations will ensue.

CHAPTER XIII

Poland's Monetary and Financial Policy, 1919-1939

BY ZYGMUNT KARPIŃSKI

"All countries in Europe were suffering at the end of the war from a lack of working capital and from a loss through wear and tear or physical destruction of fixed capital." These words, with which one of the latest publications of the Economic Department of the League of Nations[1] characterizes the European situation during the years 1919–1920, are especially applicable to Poland. In addition to sharing the unfavorable conditions to which almost all European countries were exposed after the First World War, Poland had to combat a series of very important difficulties, with which other countries were not faced, while building her economy and finances.

The war with Russia, fought principally on Polish soil, brought forth new destruction of large areas of the country which had already served as battlefields on many occasions during the World War; the reconstruction of the country was hampered for a further two-year period, during which time other European countries were already profiting from the benefits of peace. The establishment of a uniform administration for the entire country was a difficult problem, inasmuch as the country was comprised of three parts which had belonged to separate administrative and economic units. This task was further complicated by the fact that it had to be accomplished by young and technically unprepared executives.

The aid rendered to Poland by other countries was relatively small and was limited to the most essential foodstuffs sent for the

[1] *Europe's Overseas Needs, 1919–1920,* Geneva, Economic Department of the League of Nations, 1943.

BANK OF NATIONAL ECONOMY, WARSAW

DESIGNED BY ARCHITECT RUDOLF ŚWIERCZYŃSKI

starving population. However, there was a total lack of international coöperation in the economic or financial field.

At the end of 1918, throughout the territories of the new Republic of Poland, there were in circulation no less than five various paper currencies which had been left by the authorities of occupation. The unification of the currency in circulation was the first task of the Government; it was accomplished in a relatively short time. During 1919 all other currencies were exchanged for Polish marks which were issued by the temporary Central Bank (*Polska Krajowa Kasa Pożyczkowa*), and from January, 1920, they became the only medium of payment throughout Poland.

During the first period there was a lack of suitable political, economic, and technical-financial conditions for the settlement of the next problem, i.e., stabilization of the value of the currency. Poland did not acquire reserves of the central banks of the three powers which had partitioned her. When, on November 11, 1918, the Polish authorities took possession of the temporary bank of issue, which had been established in Warsaw in 1916 by the German occupational authorities, that institution showed a note circulation of 880,000,000 Polish marks. The corresponding item among its assets was an amount of 800,000,000 German marks (constituting the equivalent of approximately 200,000,000 dollars) due from German banks. This amount, however, was not repaid to Poland. Also the financial provisions of the Treaty of Riga, which provided for financial contributions from Russia, were never carried out. From the liquidation of assets of the Austro-Hungarian Bank, only a small amount of barely several million crowns in gold was awarded to Poland. It must be stressed further that Poland was not granted a share in the Reparation Payments from Germany.

The idea of international action toward universal monetary stabilization, to which so much attention is being given during the Second World War, was not ripe after the First World War. The International Financial Conference of Brussels in 1920 limited itself to formulating numerous recommendations, aimed at returning to the principles of the prewar era, but did not create any concrete plan or machinery for the reconstruction of the destroyed European economy, or for international monetary coöperation.

In view of such conditions existing in Europe, and because of the lack of capital from abroad, with an unstabilized currency and, as yet, unorganized financial apparatus, the Polish Treasury had to perform numerous tasks resulting from the war and from the necessity of reconstructing the destroyed country. The budget deficits during the first years were, of necessity, covered by the printing press with the value of money constantly decreasing. In 1923 the situation entered a stage of hyperinflation, and the exchange rate of the dollar rose to 6,400,000 Polish marks at the end of the year.

In the first quarter of 1924, conditions finally matured for a general financial and monetary reform. Parliament granted far-reaching authorizations to the Government which proceeded to introduce reforms, to balance the budget, and to stabilize the currency. In April, 1924, the Bank Polski (Bank of Poland) was created, as a corporation, with a capital of 100,000,000 złotys. The entire population—weary of the cares and losses suffered during the inflation period—participated in the subscription to this capital and readily assigned gold and foreign currencies, formerly hoarded by it, for the founding of an institution which was to become the mainstay of monetary order.[2] Foreign capital did not participate in the creation of the Bank Polski. The Polish mark was exchanged for a new monetary unit, "złoty," at the rate of 1,800,000 marks = 1 złoty, and the exchange rate of the dollar was fixed at 5.18 złotys.

This first attempt at monetary stabilization became the basis for a well-organized financial system, which, however, did not give completely satisfactory results at once. The balancing of the budget was not attained immediately, and the bad harvest of agricultural products caused a deficit in the balance of trade and the outflow from the Bank Polski of gold reserves which had been accumulated with such difficulty. The rate of exchange of the złoty suffered a decrease in the middle of 1925. However, the economic organism, established on basically sound principles, succeeded in finding a new stability within a year. The rate of the dollar became stabilized in fact at the end of 1926, at approximately 9 złotys. During the following months the Government, in agreement with foreign

---

[2] Immediately upon the stabilization of its internal monetary position, Poland took steps to consolidate its external indebtedness. In November, 1924, the most important part of this indebtedness was covered by an agreement with the United States, which consolidated—in an amount of $178,000,000—Poland's obligations for foodstuffs and military equipment imported in the demobilization period.

financial advisers, established a new stabilization plan and obtained a stabilization loan, issued in New York and in other foreign markets, for a total amount of $62,000,000 and £2,000,000, which supplied a strong foundation for the currency, stabilized at the new rate of 8.90 złotys per $1.00.

The second period in the history of Polish financial policy began from 1926 and lasted until 1936. A characteristic trait of this period was the tendency to establish the policy on classic principles of the prewar area, which were being recommended in the 'twenties almost universally by economic authorities. The maintaining of a stabilized currency and a balanced budget became unshattered dogmas, taking first place in the hierarchy of economic aims; in the defense of these principles all other problems became secondary.

The carrying on of a cautious financial policy, based on a stable value of the currency and avoiding all financial experiments, had two aims: to inspire a feeling of security and confidence in the population, which remembered still strongly the evils of the recent instability; and to solidify and expand the coöperation of Poland with the outside financial world, which had been established with such difficulty, and which was regarded as a basic condition for economic development.

During the first three years—the period of world-wide prosperity—this policy did not present any major difficulties. The reserves of gold and foreign assets in the Bank Polski, strengthened by the Stabilization Loan, enabled the deficit on the balance of trade, which reached the maximum amount of 850,000,000 złotys in 1928, to be covered. Expanded foreign trade enabled the internal economy to be maintained on a relatively high level, guaranteeing to the Treasury not only an equilibrium, but also certain surpluses in the budget. Bank deposits showed a large increase.

Not all elements, however, completely conformed to the optimistic horoscopes. The hopes that the Stabilization Loan would be a "key loan," that, as a consequence of it, numerous other credits and loans would be extended to Poland, as they were to other continental countries, were realized only to a small degree. There were obtained two minor long-term loans, one for the city of Warsaw and the other for the province of Silesia, and the Polish balance of payments in 1928 and 1929 showed a surplus of capital imports.

These were small amounts, however, in comparison with the sums flowing into other countries situated west of Poland, and they were granted principally in the form of short-term credits, which—as it later appeared—were withdrawn from Poland in rapid tempo after the crisis of 1931.

When, after 1930, the world economic situation became worse, Poland was also faced with major difficulties. The world banking crisis, begun in Austria in 1931, accentuated by the suspension of the gold standard in Great Britain, and in the beginning of 1933 by the collapse of the American banking and monetary systems, produced a severe shock also to the Polish financial situation. A crisis in public confidence caused a large outflow of foreign credits, a flight of domestic capital, and a withdrawal of deposits from banks. In view of the growing difficulties, there rose in Poland—as in other countries—the problem of whether to save the solvency of the banks, or the monetary system. Whereas other countries, in selecting one of these alternatives, took recourse to different remedies (exchange controls, exchange depreciation, bank moratoriums), Poland succeeded in surviving this difficult period without introducing any basic changes into its monetary policies. The banks retained full solvency, exchange control was not introduced, completely free movement of capital and an unchanged rate of exchange were maintained.

This policy affected the entire economic system of Poland which suffered in an especially grave manner from the effects of the World Depression. The Polish banks had to meet the difficult task of paying domestic deposits which were being withdrawn simultaneously with the hasty withdrawal of foreign credits. These credits, amounting at the end of 1929 to 673,000,0000 złotys, shrank at the end of 1933 to 247,000,000 złotys, i.e., to almost one-third of their previous amount. The credits from the United States which, during the 1929–1933 period, decreased from 65,000,000 to the minimal amount of 4,000,000 złotys were withdrawn in the greatest proportions.

During this same period foreign-trade credits, granted previously to Polish importers, suffered a considerable decline and shrank by the large amount of 800,000,000 złotys. Concurrently, Polish exports—principally of agricultural products directed to England or billed in sterling—found themselves in difficult competitive conditions and lost their previous rentability because of the depreciation of the exchange rate of the pound. Poland did not follow Great Britain's policy in contrast to numerous other countries which created the so-called "sterling bloc" and thus caused a depreciation in their currencies, which in certain countries at that time was called a necessary "adjustment," and later was criticized by other countries as an unjustified, harmful "competitive" devaluation.

Poland withheld itself also from an "adjustment" of its currency in 1933, when the dollar depreciated. The fall in the exchange rate of the dollar, along with an unchanged relation of the Polish złoty to gold, decreased the amount of Polish debts, expressed in dollars, but also decreased the value of Polish assets, expressed in American currency. And these assets were considerable at that time, inasmuch as Polish citizens, in order to profit from the absence of exchange control, hoarded a part of their savings in dollars—and also in dollar banknotes—to a rather large extent. When, because of the fall in the dollar exchange rate, the losses from these investments were made known, there ensued a mass "dumping" of dollar banknotes—in the years 1932–1937 over $40,000,000 in banknotes were sent back from Poland to America, not including shipments to other countries.

When in 1933 the International Economic Conference in London failed to reach an agreement on monetary matters and, under France's leadership, there was created a "gold bloc," Poland entered it as the only debtor country, again displaying its intention of carrying on an unchanged monetary policy. During the next three years Poland maintained its policy of retaining the old gold parity of the złoty, of a full service on her foreign loans, and of not restricting the export of capital.

The economic life of the country suffered gravely as a result of the World Depression and the steady outflow of capital. Industrial production dropped (1928 = 100) to 64 per cent, wholesale prices to 53 per cent, cost of living to 58 per cent, Treasury income from taxes, duties, and monopolies to 60 per cent. The most serious shrinkages were felt in foreign trade, which—with decreased quantities and lowered prices—fell to 25 per cent in imports and to 38 per cent in exports.

The reserves of gold and foreign balances in the Bank Polski, from their highest level, amounting to 1,400,000,000 złotys, at the end of 1927, at the end of 1935 fell to 470,000,000 złotys, and upon deduction of credits, of which the Bank took advantage at that time at foreign financial institutions, to an even lower amount. The weakened economic organs of Poland gradually began to feel the increasingly unfavorable symptoms, arising from the exchange restrictions of other countries. Its own foreign assets were frozen in many countries; large amounts due from railroad transit, which previously had constituted an important position in the Polish balance of payments, were blocked by Germany.

Because of the devaluation introduced in other countries, the fears that Poland also would be unable to avoid similar remedies became widespread, indeed, prompted an increased flight of capital. When the development of the world-wide political situation became worse, and the hope of renewing international credit transactions clearly began to perish, Poland was finally faced with the problem of discontinuing the policy it had practiced up to that time and of following the example of many other countries. The considerations regarding necessary changes revolved about the question of whether a system of exchange control should be introduced or whether it was advisable to endeavor to regain the strained equilibrium of the balance of payments through a devaluation of the złoty.

The first alternative was chosen although, on proper analysis with the passing of time, both remedies had become necessary. Exchange control was the appropriate and only means of counteracting flight of capital; and devaluation of the złoty would have removed its overvaluation, caused by the fall of the exchange rate of the pound, the dollar, and practically all other currencies.

In April, 1936, five years after the majority of European countries, Poland introduced foreign-exchange control. Even then, however, the gold parity of the złoty was retained and remained on an unchanged level up to the outbreak of the Second World War. The third period of Poland's financial history began then. At that time the economic life showed an improvement in almost all fields and had the earmarks of prosperity until the political events in the latter months of 1938 and in 1939, heralding the oncoming storm, caused disturbances on the money market and created numerous undesirable consequences in the general economic situation.

The development of industrial production, which was already marked in 1936, showed a further noticeable improvement in 1937, aggregating 18 per cent in comparison to the preceding year and leading—in some branches of industry—to a complete utilization of the existing production capacity. Investment activities improved. The budget of 1936–1937, after a few years of deficits, was balanced. Turnovers increased in domestic, as well as in foreign trade.

The foreign-exchange control provoked also a strict control of imports. Neither of these controls, however, unfavorably influenced the volume of Poland's foreign trade. The foreign trade turnovers, upon having attained the former highest level in 1928 and 1929, had decreased in the following five years of depression, simultaneously with the world foreign trade, and had reached the lowest level in 1934 and 1935. However, from 1936 there began a new period of improvement. Imports increased during 1935–1938 from 860,000,000 to 1,300,000,000 złotys, and exports from 925,000,000 to 1,185,000,000 złotys. Deserving of special mention is the fact that the increase in Poland's foreign trade did not suffer a reversal in 1938, despite the fact that during this year as a result of a temporary economic depression (principally in the United States), there was a reduction in world trade turnover by approximately 14 per cent. Poland's share in the world trade, although still very small, rose from 0.9 to over 1 per cent.

Polish relations with countries which had based their policy on a system of foreign-trade control became the subject of bilateral payment and clearing agreements. To enable their execution a Polish Clearing Institute was created which, at the end of 1938, controlled turnovers with eleven countries aggregating approximately 35 per cent of Poland's foreign trade. Two-thirds of the turnover was still carried on in free currencies and the tendency to keep turnovers with overseas countries on a possibly high level was maintained. An example of the efforts exerted in this direction is the steadily increasing trade carried on by sea.

An improvement characterizing the period under discussion became especially notable in the money market. The stoppage in the flight of capital and the protection of the domestic money market assured a liquidity in the market, expressed by an accentuated increase of deposits in banks and a rise in quotations of shares and bonds. These facts enabled the Polish Government to carry out a far-reaching reduction of the disproportionately high interest rates. The inflow of deposits in savings and current accounts during 1936 and 1937, contributed to a substantial improvement in the situation of Polish banks. As indicated at the very beginning of this survey, in the period of the First World War, and in the four-year period of inflation, the working capital had been destroyed almost completely in all forms, particularly in the form of deposits in banks. When the stabilization reforms made savings in money possible, deposits in Polish credit institutions began to increase in rapid tempo and in 1929 reached 3,000,000,000 złotys. This increase, expressed in percentage relation, was very notable at that time. If, however, the amount of deposits in Poland are compared with corresponding figures in other countries, they will be found to be on a very low level. A comparatively low national income, resulting principally from an overpopulation in the agricultural districts and the structural unemployment of a part of the peasant population, was the chief cause of this unfavorable symptom.

During the banking crisis in 1931, deposits in Polish banks fell by about 350,000,000 złotys and only after a five-year period—at the end of 1934—did the amount of deposits again reach the 1929 level of 3,000,000,000 złotys. In 1937 the amount of deposits reached its peak of 3,800,000,000 złotys. This was the last year of favorable development, however; in the following year political events every few months provoked a wave of growing unrest in the entire international financial world, as well as in Poland. In March, 1938 (occupation of Austria), the banks noted the first wave of outflowing deposits which became very marked in September, 1938 (Conference of Munich), when the Polish banks lost deposits amounting to 340,000,000 złotys. The third run on Polish banks occurred in March, 1939. As in previous instances, it was successfully counteracted without any serious disturbance of the economic life. The fourth run took place in August, 1939, immediately before the war.

The withdrawal of deposits from banks had a direct reaction on the volume of money in circulation. During the five-year period, from 1932 to 1937, the money in circulation in Poland became almost completely stabilized, undergoing only minor, seasonal fluctuations, and amounted to approximately 1,500,000,000 złotys, representing the circulation of banknotes of the Bank Polski, together with the circulation of silver and small coins. Only as a result of the political events of September, 1938, did the money circulation increase to 2,000,000,000 złotys, and in the middle of 1939 reached 2,300,000,000 złotys.

The above-mentioned loss of working capital during the period of inflation, as well as the slow tempo of its reconstruction, were factors which contributed to a high level of the interest rate. After the Stabilization Loan of 1927, the discount rate of the Bank Polski was fixed at 8 per cent; it was gradually decreased to 4½ per cent in 1937. The high interest rates tended to retard the development of enterprises and became particularly burdensome for the debtors when, during the depression period, world-wide, as well as domestic prices suffered a drastic fall, which event increased the weight of the debts and the interest rates expressed by the volume of production.

In view of the fact that Poland avoided a depreciation of its currency, the burden of the debtors had not been lightened as it had for debtors in other countries, i.e., in the United States, where the problem of indebtedness became a principal motive in the decision to devaluate the dollar and to cancel the gold clause in all private loans and government bonds.

As the depression grew more marked, the necessity of lessening the burdens of the debtors became all the more apparent. After having rejected other means which could lead to a solution of this problem, the Government decided to introduce the necessary changes, by way of decrees, which enacted adjustments in three directions: the reduction of interest rates on long-term private, as well as on national loans; the extension, in many instances, of the amortization periods of long-term loans and bonds; and finally, the conversion of short-term loans, with which farmers were encumbered, into medium or long-term loans through the intermediary of a special bank created for this purpose.

As a result of these measures, the interest rates on mortgage loans and securities issued on their basis were reduced from 8 and 7 per cent to 5½ and 4½ per cent. Internal government bonds, bearing a higher interest rate, were converted into 4 per cent bonds. Bonds, issued on foreign markets and/or in foreign currencies, were included in this policy. Such a measure was found necessary, especially because the high interest rates of foreign loans were extremely burdensome. For example, the service of the Stabilization Loan, bearing a nominal interest rate of 7 per cent, in fact resulted in a burden of approximately 8 per cent, if the former price of issue is to be taken into consideration. Other loans had an even higher interest rate. If such bonds were in the possession of Polish citizens, they were converted into bonds of a new 4½ per cent internal loan, issued in złotys. Finally, the interest rates on bonds in the hands of foreign creditors were also reduced, through negotiations with representatives of the bondholders who acknowledged and approved the necessity of such change. Thus, the former interest rate on foreign bonds was reduced from 8 and 6 per cent to 4½ and 4¼ per cent. The amount of Polish external bonds to which this conversion pertained, was relatively small, inasmuch as a large part of the bonds issued abroad were repurchased by Polish citizens before the foreign exchange control was introduced.

A characteristic trait in the 'thirties was the steady and considerable decrease in Poland's private and national foreign debt. Such debt continued to decrease also after the introduction of the foreign-exchange control. For example, foreign participation in the capital stock of Polish enterprises was reduced, during the period 1935 to 1937, from 2,000,000,000 to 1,800,000,000 złotys, and the foreign cash debts of Polish enterprises decreased during this period from 1,800,000,000 to 1,500,000,000 złotys.

The reduction of the national foreign debt was particularly noticeable. Poland's national debt had reached the total amount of 5,200,000,000 złotys at the end of 1931, and in the following years it showed comparatively small changes, fluctuating within the range of from 4,300,000,000 to 5,000,000,000 złotys, which amount was again reached in 1938. However, within this total amount there occurred the following important change. The internal debt rose during this period from 500,000,000 to 2,500,000,000 złotys, whereas the foreign debts decreased from 4,500,000,000 to 2,500,000,000 złotys. The percentage of foreign debts in the total amount of Poland's indebtedness decreased, therefore, from 90 per cent to below 50 per cent.

The decrease in the total amount of foreign debts—although in 1937 and 1938 the Treasury incurred some new, relatively small, foreign loans—was caused by three factors: decrease of the nominal amount of the debts, as a result of the devaluation of the currencies in which the credits were obtained, i.e., dollar and pound; large amortization of the debt; and finally, repatriation through purchases of bonds on foreign markets by nationals.

As a result, the status of Poland's foreign debts, according to a statement of October 1, 1938, was as follows (in millions of złotys):

Loans issued in the United States	253		
Loans issued in other countries	217	470	
Debts toward governments—			
United States	1,098		
Other countries	526	1,624	
Other debts		421	
Total			2,515

The total national debt corresponded to a burden of about $27.00 per capita of the population, of which approximately $13.00 constituted the external indebtedness, and $14.00 the internal indebtedness. This burden was much smaller than in most other European countries. (In 1939 the national debt in the United States exceeded the amount of $300.00 per capita.)

As a debtor country, Poland strongly endeavored faithfully to fulfill its obligations. It must be admitted—as mentioned above—that in 1937 the interest rates on Poland's outstanding loans had to be reduced. After the outbreak of the war, when the Government of Poland found itself in exile and was deprived of all sources of income, the service on loans was temporarily suspended. Both these facts, however, found complete justification in the opinion of foreign creditors, whose chief representative in the United States, the Foreign Bondholders Protective Council, in their declaration of January 3, 1940, stated:

> The Council would point out that the Polish Government did not take unilateral action in cutting down service on their bonds. That Government throughout has shown the will to pay which is a very essential factor in the credit of a nation. Poland offered the bondholders a temporary plan for reduced interest, in the first instance, after setting forth to the Council its financial difficulties and the imperious necessity under which the Government found itself, surrounded by neighbors who were rapidly increasing their armaments,

to take steps for the protection of the country. To do this the exchange position of Poland did not permit full service on the bonds. Of her own accord, Poland bettered that offer a few months later, when she found herself in a position to do so, and, after further negotiations with the Council, this was followed shortly by an offer of a fair and equitable permanent settlement.

"... the Council has no hesitation in saying that in its negotiations in the past regarding service on the Polish bonds, it has invariably found the Polish Government taking a highly moral and honorable position and that it has throughout shown sedulous care for its credit.

CHAPTER XIV

Agricultural Reconstruction in Poland

BY JERZY RADWAN

THE AGRICULTURAL structure of Poland in the second half of the eighteenth century resembled that of western European countries. In those days land was owned almost exclusively by members of the nobility of Poland.

The nobility of Poland socially and economically was somewhat differentiated. It was composed of a small group of large landowners, of a more numerous group of proprietors of medium-sized estates, and of a very large group who owned small farmsteads which were of practically the same size as socage lands of the serfs. This last class of the nobility constituted around 15 per cent of the total population. It was thus a predominating group among the nobility who, in those days, enjoyed a fullness of political rights and great political influence. The existence of a comparatively large number of these small-sized farmsteads which were the unlimited property of their owners, to a large extent contributed to the shaping of the country's agricultural structure, above all to an early appearance of the so-called strip system.

In the second half of the eighteenth century, social and political trends toward granting the serfs personal liberty and equality of rights quickly penetrated Poland. Such trends found their partial expression in the Constitution of May Third (1791) as well as in Kościuszko's proclamation of May 7, 1794. Kościuszko not only granted the peasants personal liberty, but he also eased their socage duties and announced the granting to them of the propriety of the land by legislative action. But political events delayed the realization of those promises for a long time. The three Partitioning Powers deferred such important social reform for many years. The enfranchisement of the peasants was completed on the territory of the former Polish State only in the second half of the nineteenth century and was then accomplished from the viewpoint of the political interests of the Partitioning Powers.

The enfranchisement was first effected in the early half of the nineteenth century in the Polish provinces annexed by Prussia. From an economic viewpoint it was accomplished most efficiently in these provinces inasmuch as it abolished usufructs, the strip system, and the land communities—all primitive forms of agriculture which make a rational exploitation of the soil difficult. The quick expansion of German industries, as well as emigration backed by the Prussian Government to facilitate Germanization, resulted in a large decrease in the Polish rural population.

About 1850, enfranchisement in the Polish provinces annexed by Austria was effected somewhat quickly and carelessly. The size of the farms was comparatively small. Usufructs, common property of certain land, and the strip system were left to stay. The Austro-Hungarian Monarchy did not permit industrial expansion on its annexed Polish territories. Nor did Polish territories profit by the industrial development in Austria and Bohemia where industries had absorbed all the urban population. Overseas emigration, though somewhat intensive before the First World War, did not counteract the economic results of the large increase in rural population. These factors caused a rapid overpopulation of the countryside, as well as a growth of the strip system and a shrinking in the size of individual farms.

Conditions in the provinces annexed by Russia were analogous. There the enfranchisement was effected in the seventh decade of the nineteenth century, approximately twenty years later than in the provinces annexed by Prussia. Enfranchisement was accomplished under the pressure of the Polish people only after the Central National Committee of the Insurrection had proclaimed the enfranchisement of the peasants; it was done quickly and by simplified methods. As a result, usufructs, the common use of some fields, and the strip system remained.

Industries in the so-called Congress Kingdom, assigned to Russia in 1815, expanded rapidly at first. But by the end of the nineteenth century the pace of that expansion was slowed by the growth of industries in Russia and in the Ukraine. Hence, here too, the natural increase in the rural population did not find openings in nonrural trades, nor was there a sufficient counterbalance in overseas emigration. The result was rural overpopulation and its natural drawbacks in the realm of agricultural structure. Rural overpopulation also occurred in Poland's eastern provinces; here it was still more detrimental not only because of the poorer quality of the soil and worse climatic conditions, but also because an inferior type of farming culture was practiced.

Rural overpopulation and its accompanying phenomenon—the shrinking of peasant farms—produced what was known as land hunger which, in turn, resulted in an increase in the price of land far above its productive value. This lack of proportion between the price of land and its economic value caused the parceling of large landed estates.

In the Polish provinces annexed by Prussia there were no economic reasons for such parceling. The Prussian Government, in conformity with its policy of Germanization created in 1886 the so-called Colonization Committee and placed large financial means at its disposal. The task of the Committee was to buy and expropriate Polish landed property and by means of parceling to create out of it farms for German colonists. In spite of the fact that the Committee, during the period of its activity, had settled in those Polish provinces about 20,000 colonists, the total number of farms decreased there between 1907 and 1921 by about 11 per cent. This was caused by the fact that the outflow of the Polish rural population was larger than its natural increase.

In the other Polish lands the process of partitioning the land holdings progressed quickly. The increase in the number of farms, to a large extent, was caused by the division of existing farms and, to a much lesser degree, by parceling, inasmuch as a rather large area of the parceled land was used for increasing the size of existing farms. The division of small farms was especially disadvantageous because it resulted in a great expansion of the strip system, which was manifest principally in the eastern provinces, though it occured also in western Poland.

The rural structure of Poland in 1918.—The Census of 1921 made it evident that the Polish State had inherited from the Partitioning Powers a very unsound rural structure which, in many instances, greatly hampered the development of agriculture. This is corroborated by the following table:

NUMBER OF FARMS*
(in thousands)

Polish provinces (województwa)	Farm area, in hectares (one hectare equals 2.471 acres)				
	Total	Up to 5	5 to 20	20 to 50	Over 50
Total	3,262	2,111	1,045	76	30
Central	1,224	635	550	29	10 Russian annexation
Eastern	585	290	268	20	7 Russian annexation
Western	279	164	85	22	8 Prussian annexation
Southern	1,174	1,022	142	5	5 Austrian annexation

* The Census of 1921 did not include Upper Silesia nor a part of Wilno Province. Were these areas included, the total number of farms would probably exceed 3,300,000.

The striking feature in the table shown above is the preponderance of farms up to 5 hectares in size. In view of climatic conditions, quality of soil, rural culture, and general economic conditions, the farms of that size usually did not suffice to keep the farmer and his family busy, and often did not even produce enough for their sustenance. Husbandry conditions were rendered worse by the irrational structure of plots which were excessively elongated, very narrow, and often scattered. All these flaws of structure are known as the strip system. The system was not uniform in the various provinces in Poland. It appeared at its worst in farmsteads belonging to the small nobility, where sometimes several hundred scattered plots belonged to one farmer. There were even villages where individual farmers had over one thousand such scattered strip plots.

Most frequent were hamlets where the strip system did not exceed more than 30 to 90 scattered plots per farm. As the area of the entire farm on the average amounted to 6.3 hectares, of which 4.3 hectares consisted of arable land, the average area of the strip plot was less than 10 ares (1,000 sq. meters). When such a plot was approximately one kilometer (five-eighths of a mile) in length, its width did not exceed one meter (39.38 inches). A mechanical tillage of such strips was possible only when all owners agreed to it and, at the same time, agreed to cultivate the same plants; otherwise crops on neighboring lands would have been imperiled.

To arrive at such an agreement was practically impossible. And that is why the method of three-year crop rotation was maintained in Poland's eastern provinces, a method which had been given up long ago in provinces free of the strip system. In conforming to the data of the Census of 1921 it seemed necessary to adjust the land holdings on some 10,000,000 hectares in approximately 2,000,000 farms in order to abrogate the nuisance of the strip structure. The number of peasant farms entitled to usufructs on land belonging to the manor in 1921 amounted to approximately 500,000. Common ownership of land used most frequently as pasturage embraced about 2,000,000 hectares.

A direct comparison of figures pertaining to the rural structure of Poland with those characterizing the rural structure of western European countries may lead to many a misunderstanding. These misunderstandings result chiefly from the fact that the farm area which, for easily comprehensible reasons is being used as a unit in statistics, is but one of the many factors characterizing its vitality. Of far greater actuality is the sum of natural factors, like soil and climate, as well as economic factors of the individual provinces. In Poland a farm of 5 hectares is considered, in theory as well as in practice, too small to keep a farmer busy and sometimes even too small to give sustenance to the family of the farmer. In Denmark a farm of the same size belongs rather to the class of middle-sized farms.

Changes in rural structure, 1918–1939.—The years of 1918–1925 in Poland were a period of crystallization of agrarian legislation, an era during which working methods were elaborated, organization was built up, and the executive and administrative apparatus trained. The period was rather long. But one must take into consideration the fact that the new Polish State was composed of territories, formerly annexed by the Partitioning Powers, having distinct codes of law and different economic conditions. Under such circumstances it was not an easy matter to find a solution to the multifarious problems or to find ways and means of unifying and consolidating the nation.

Differences in the program of the individual political parties made themselves felt especially in the evolution of the agrarian reform legislation, as the parceling of land was generally called. The agrarian reform acts, passed by Parliament in the years 1920–1925, ordered a gradual voluntary or compulsory parceling of landed estates having an area of over 180 hectares. In suburban districts that minimum had been reduced to 60 hectares whereas in the eastern border provinces it could be raised to 300 hectares.

From 1918 to 1938, there were parceled 2,655,000 hectares, out of which number 160,500 new farms were formed, and the area of existing dwarf farms increased. For the establishment of new farms 1,522,000 hectares were used or an average area of about 9 hectares each, whereas out of 1,004,000 hectares, 503,000 existing dwarf farms obtained an average increase of about two hectares each. The parceling process was of different intensity in the individual provinces. Its pace depended on the size of the territory. The table shown below gives a precise idea of the territories of the various provinces as well as of the areas which had been parceled:

PARCELING, 1918–1938

Provinces, area in thousand square kilometers, per cent of total area, and thousand hectares and per cent of total in parceled areas

Provinces (Województwa)	Area in thousand square kilometers	Per cent of total area	Parceled areas	
			In thousand hectares	Per cent of total
Central	127	33	868	33
Eastern	125	32	1,025	39
Western	59	15	360	13
Southern	79	20	402	15
Total	390	100	2,655	100

Comparatively speaking, the figures given above indicate that the parceling embraced the largest area in the eastern provinces and the smallest in the western group. The slow pace of action in the west resulted first from the fact that there was no overpopulation in the rural districts, and second, from the stubborn resistance of German landowners who, according to the Census of 1921, owned

36.2 per cent of landed estates above 50 hectares in the Poznań Province, 43.7 per cent in Pomorze, and 90 per cent in Silesia. In opposing the agrarian reform, the Germans availed themselves of international agreements concerning the protection of national minorities. In submitting their claims to the League of Nations the Germans succeeded in defending the property rights, which they had acquired after Poland's partitions, by means of the policies of extermination and Germanization pursued by the Prussian Government.

The "commassation" of land.—The so-called "commassation" (redistribution) of land began in the last years of the nineteenth century on the territories annexed by Russia. Owners of small farms, whose land was scattered in plots, began to abandon the strip system without any assistance by the Russian administration which showed little interest in the problem. This was accomplished by means of voluntary exchange confirmed by private notarial documents. Such a spontaneous commassation could not embrace larger areas because the process was rather expensive and also because it required an agreement of all interested parties.

On the territory annexed by Austria a few commassation procedures were started before the First World War. The formalities took many years because of well-known Austrian legal red tape.

Polish legislation pertaining to commassation was accomplished by tests and experiments within a comparatively short period. It succeeded in avoiding the flaws of Russian as well as of Austrian laws, and in meeting the needs of the Polish farmers.

The owners of small farms were fully aware of the advantage resulting for them from commassation, and they willingly collaborated wherever the strip system was a hindrance to the introduction of modern farming methods.

The annual commassation (temporarily reduced in scope during the years of the economic crisis), embraced on the average 90,000 farms which represented an area of over 400,000 hectares. By September 1, 1939, the work was accomplished on 930,000 farms with an area of 5,750,000 hectares. It was still to be done on an area of 4,250,000 to 6,350,000 hectares.

The abolition of usufructs.—Usufructs, which had been established at the time of the enfranchisement of the serfs, consisted in giving peasant farmers the right to pasturages, the right to gather wood in the forests, to dig clay, to fish, and similar privileges. From an economic viewpoint usufructs were very harmful. Yet, they had been established or left by the Russian Government to maintain contentions and misunderstanding between the manor and the peasants; the Government, to be sure, had permitted their abolition by private agreements, yet it had rendered such agreements purposely difficult in order to facilitate its influence over both classes of the population. Under such circumstances, the abolition of usufructs on a larger scale before the First World War was not feasible. And this is why obsolete farming methods remained in use, and why the destruction of forests continued until, in 1920, the Polish Parliament passed a law concerning the abolition of usufructs.

After a few years of experience the law was amended in a spirit favoring voluntary agreements. And, indeed, it proved very successful, inasmuch as 65 per cent of usufruct abolitions were achieved in that way. Whenever the transaction was done by administrative channels the valuation was based upon the net annual profits derived from said usufructs by the individual farmers. Within two decades (1919–1939) about 600,000 hectares of land were transferred and 3,900,000 złotys paid in cash as the equivalent of losses and profits resulting therefrom.

During that period, 95 per cent of usufructs were abolished in the central provinces, 80 odd per cent in the eastern ones. The finishing of the task in the east depended upon such basic improvements as river regulations, the building of canals, and similar accomplishments. In the southern provinces, embracing for the most part mountainous regions where farming is based chiefly on livestock breeding and usufructs on pasturage rights, the raising of the productiveness of the pasturage had to precede the abolition of usufructs; otherwise economic harm was done. This is the reason why the reform was inaugurated in that part of the country only one year before the outbreak of the present war.

Division of common property lands.—Common property of land was of a nature similar to that of usufructs. It appeared in instances where enfranchisement of the serfs had been effected, but where small peasant farmers of one or several hamlets, with the estate owner, possessed common property and fruition rights. There existed also common property of land whose partners consisted exclusively of peasant farmers from one or several hamlets. The same common ownership existed also in hamlets whose inhabitants belonged to the small nobility. Lacking precise statistical figures, one may nevertheless state that these common properties (mostly pasturage grounds) in 1918 had an area not exceeding 2,000,000 hectares. The division of land communities among individual farmers was accomplished in most instances simultaneously with the commassation. It is probable that about 70 per cent of such properties have been divided. Farmers were always in favor of such divisions which, in numerous instances, were voluntarily brought about by them through agreements. The trend was sound from an economic viewpoint, too, for those grounds used chiefly as pasturage grounds could also be more advantageously exploited as arable land than as pastures, not only because of the quality of the soil but also because the average rainfall in Poland often is insufficient for pasturable farming.

Liquidation of small tenancies.—Tenancies were never numerous nor popular in Poland, because of the desire of the farmer to own his own soil. According to the Census of 1921, less than 6.5 per cent of farming land was tenanted. Out of 1,900,000 hectares of tenanted land 1,100,000 hectares (or 60 per cent) represented tenancies of farms having an area of over 100 hectares. Not more than 2.5 per cent of farmers were tenants. In spite of this, Polish legislation favored a complete liquidation of small tenancies by means of land grants, especially in cases of long-term tenancies.

Land improvements in rebuilding the agrarian structure.—It is very hard to establish the facts and the figures of the need for improvement. Not only does the matter require a detailed investigation of the irrigation conditions and the qualities and peculiarities of the soil, but also a determination as to whether each individual improvement will pay. Hence, there are huge divergencies in calculating the size of area needing improvements, divergencies going into millions of hectares.

Improvements in connection with the rebuilding of the agrarian structure in most instances were accomplished simultaneously with the commassation. They consisted of draining the land, of regulating rivers, digging canals and ditches, and of building general irrigation works. The work was comparatively inexpensive inasmuch as its most costly part, the earthworks, was done by the small farmers themselves in seasons when they were least busy in their fields. The Government supplied the plans, professional management, and technical supervision. The work began in 1927. Up to the outbreak of the war about 600,000 hectares were thus improved.

Division of small farms.—The increase in the rural population from 17,400,000 in 1921 to 20,300,000 in 1939 resulted in an increase in the number of farms. In 1939 there were more than four million farms, among which approximately 50 per cent were dwarf farms. In 1921 dwarf farms amounted to 2,200,000 or 64 per cent of the total number of farms. The above figures make it evident that the agrarian reform had seriously contributed to the decrease in the percentage of dwarf farms. In the last two decades the number of farms increased by more than 700,000, of which 160,000 were independent farms created by parceling, and 540,000 were formed in the partitioning of existing farms. From a social and economic viewpoint this partitioning of small farms was undesirable. Fully aware of the harmfulness and inefficiency of mechanical prohibitions in that realm, the Polish Government did not issue any rules regarding the indivisibility of small farms. Restrictions of that kind were aimed rather at ensuring government credits granted to purchasers of land for the construction of farm buildings and for general husbandry purposes. The tempo in the growth of the number of farms slowed down steadily in proportion with the decrease in the percentage of the rural population. The increase in the number of farms in the period 1921–1931 amounted to 13 per cent, whereas in the years 1931–1939 it was only 5 per cent. One may infer therefrom that the expansion of nonagricultural occupations, and partly also the decline in the natural population increase had reduced the partitioning of small farms. The hope seemed justified that a complete realization of the great economic industrialization program would stop entirely the partitioning process within the coming decade.

Financing of the agrarian reconstruction.—A special working fund administered by the State Agricultural Bank was established to meet all expenses connected with the measures necessary for improving the agrarian structure of the country. In the beginning it amounted to 900,000,000 złotys. After a cancellation of part of its obligations due on small farms, the balance by December 31, 1938, was more than 667,000,000 złotys. Besides the interest from the capital, the fund was receiving subsidies from the Treasury's budget.

The fund was used for the purchase of land for parceling purposes from the landowners who had not parceled on time areas exceeding the allowed maximum. Also there were paid the general husbandry expenses of the new farms established by the State by means of parceling, the expenses of commassation and abolition of usufructs, and the costs of improvements connected with agrarian reconstruction. Furthermore, the fund granted loans to the purchasers of the land parceled either by the State or by individuals, to the owners of commassated farms for the transfer of buildings and for general husbandry on the improved lands. The above loans were at an annual interest rate of 3 per cent, and were to be repaid within fifteen or more years according to the amount of indebtedness. Landowners received compensation for their parceled land and for their buildings in 3 per cent state land bonds; these bonds had different privileges, like other Treasury bonds, and could be used for the payment of taxes.

Private parceling was financed chiefly by the State Agricultural Bank which granted loans for land purchases in debentures. These credits had a higher interest rate—lowered to 4.5 per cent in 1934. Besides credits for the purchase of land the State Agricultural Bank also granted loans for general husbandry: the buying of livestock, artificial fertilizers, the improvement of drainage, the paying off to members of the family in event of heritage, and similar needs. These credits granted to farmers, and resulting from agrarian reconstruction, exceeded 650,000,000 złotys.

Conclusions.—Rural overpopulation, and "land-hunger" logically connected therewith resulted in a rather quick passing of land ownership from the big landholders to the small farmers. From the days of enfranchisement to 1939, the area of large landed estates has decreased as a result of parceling by more than 6,200,000 hectares and, if one includes land ceded as equivalent of the abolished usufructs, by more than 6,800,000 hectares. Over 50 per cent of that decrease occurred within the two decades preceding the present war.

Poland, whose agrarian structure in the middle of the nineteenth century was still based upon large landed estates, later became a country of small farmers. In 1939 not less than 61.6 per cent of land belonged to farms having an area of less than 50 hectares each. Only 23.6 per cent came into the category of land holdings of over 50 hectares each, whereas 14.8 per cent were the property of the State, of autonomous bodies, churches, and similar organizations. Taking into consideration land utilizable only for agriculture, which in this instance appears more correct, the figures will be as follows: small farms comprised 81.9 per cent of the land, large estates 15.1 per cent, and public institutions 3 per cent. In spite of such a rapid concentration of the land ownership in the hands of small farmers, peasant farms continued to show a tendency to shrink by further subdivisions below a level indispensable for the maintenance of full employment or even the growing of sufficient food for the peasant family.

During the period 1921–1939 the number of such dwarf farms increased by 180,000, which seems to indicate that the pace of parceling was not in proportion to the growth of the rural population. One may infer from the above that, after this war, parceling must be accelerated to avert a further deterioration of the agrarian structure and to make possible an increase in the size of dwarf farms.

It must be stressed that, as a consequence of parceling, the agricultural output was increasing. This resulted from the fact that the Polish farmer, greatly attached to the soil, was able, because of a larger number of working hands on his land, to exploit with greater efficiency every piece of land, and to produce, per land unit, more plant crops and more livestock than the larger estates. This increased output—according to Professor W. Grabski, one of the greatest Polish authorities on agricultural matters—amounted to 14 per cent in the production of the four chief cereals (rye, wheat, barley, and oats) and 44 per cent in the production of potatoes.

As far as livestock breeding was concerned the increased production was still more imposing. Agricultural statistics for 1930–1931 give the following figures for each 100 hectares unit of usable land:

a) Cattle—on large estates 17.3 head
on small farms 41.4 head, or 139 per cent more

b) Pigs—on large estates 12 head
on small farms 31 head, or 158 per cent more

The increase in the agricultural production of small farms, as a result of other land improvements, and particularly of commassation, was indubitable though as yet there are no precise statistical tables on the subject. Some inferences may be made, however, from available production figures. Thus, in the eastern provinces where farming had been greatly intensified, the potato-planting area in the years 1930–1934 on the average amounted to 513,000 hectares. In the years 1935–1937 the average was 721,000 hectares, or 40 per cent more. The crop increase per unit of area amounted to 18 per cent.

Agrarian reconstruction to which Poland has devoted her best efforts, is, evidently, only one of the means of solving the basic social and economic problem of rural overpopulation, estimated roughly at 5,000,000 people. This problem can be solved only by using at the same time three means: a more radical agricultural reform, intensified systems of rural culture, and a general increase in Poland's industrialization. In conformity with the general agreement of all Polish parties, the upper limit of the rural property will be settled after the war at 50 hectares. This will free around 3,500,000 hectares more for redistribution among peasants in addition to the 800,000 hectares already acquired before the war and not yet distributed.

Inasmuch as this area is small in comparison with the number of unemployed, the size of the new family farms after the war will be as before—only 7 to 12 hectares. Size will affect considerably the kind of agriculture; the production of root plants, vegetables, and fruits will predominate. Cattle, dairy, and meat products also will be of greatest importance for the Polish export trade.

The completion of agricultural reform and progress in production methods probably will increase the number of people gainfully employed and also increase the welfare of the peasant. However, only an increased industrialization of the country can solve radically the unemployment problem.

CHAPTER XV

Social Progress in Poland, 1918-1939

BY JAN K. KASPRZAK

IN SPITE of more than one hundred years of political terror and economic exploitation by the three Partitioning Powers, Poland entered the international arena in 1918 with a clearly homogeneous cultural tradition. The economic reality and social organization which was imposed on Poland was quite contrary to its culture and the interests of its people. The situation was complicated by the fact that Poland in the era of political enslavement, went through a phase of enormous population growth. This tremendous expansion occurred despite economic and social conditions which disregarded the real needs of the population.

The spirit of initiative and the great efforts of the Poles, as well as their national consciousness, enabled them to surmount, at least to a certain extent, the limits imposed upon them and the deficiencies in all aspects of life. Their task in the field of social work was facilitated by their ancient tradition of social reforms and social ideals. Even under foreign domination, that tradition had served them well as a protection against the reactionary conservatism imposed by the enemy.

Although the Poles were subjected to a despotic regime and to the surveillance of police states, they did not forget that in the Middle Ages they had been the pioneers of social ideals in central and eastern Europe. In the sixteenth century Poland had outstanding social thinkers, among them Frycz Modrzewski who had advocated many modern social reforms, including protection for prisoners and homeless people. Shortly thereafter, Father Skarga established institutions to assist the poor which have endured up to the present. In the seventeenth century many hospitals, homes for the aged, and orphan asylums were founded. At the end of the eighteenth century Poland was also one of the more advanced countries. Its Diet enacted the memorable Constitution of May Third (1791), introducing many advanced social and political reforms. This century also had seen important educational and social reforms. Special mention must be made here of Stanisław Konarski, the creator of the most modern educational system existing in Europe in those days, and of Stanisław Staszyc, who was the first to introduce labor insurance in Poland.

The Poles also remembered that all the struggles for political independence were, at the same time, struggles for social reform. This is true as far back as the time of Kościuszko, who not only was a political and military leader of the Poles but also a social leader. The same conditions prevailed during the insurrections of 1831 and 1863, up to 1905 and during the years following when the Polish Socialists fighting for the country's independence worked simultaneously for social reforms.

The First World War aroused new hopes of freedom as the Partitioning Powers fought each other. In expectation of the defeat of their enemies, the Poles openly as well as secretly began energetic preparations for the political, economic, and social organization of the free Poland to come. Because of the growing difficulties of Germany, however, and the outbreak of the Russian Revolution, it was not until 1917 that active social measures could be taken. In that year, at the initiative of the Polish Socialist party, the first central office of labor and social affairs was established as the Department of Labor which, in 1918, was converted into the Ministry of Labor and Social Welfare.[1]

After the Armistice of 1918, questions of labor and social security quickly took precedence over other national problems because of the growing unemployment which resulted from the destruction of workshops and capital, as well as from the mass return of refugees and prisoners of war. Within six weeks after the Armistice, 650,000 refugees and prisoners of war returned from Russia alone. Soon after, that number exceeded one and a half million.

---

[1] After the occupation by Germany in 1939, it was transferred to France and then to London from whence it protects Polish refugees throughout the world and continues its preparatory work for postwar Poland.

The problem of aid for the needy and the unemployed had to be solved in the first weeks of independence under conditions that one may call actual legal, administrative, and economic chaos. In the field of social insurance alone, there were in force not less than six divergent laws, namely the Austrian, the Hungarian, two German, and two Russian laws. Germany had one law for the provinces of Poznań and Pomorze, and another for Upper Silesia. Russia had a special law for Poland's eastern provinces, and another for so-called "Congress Poland." This situation was complicated still further by the fact that matters of social insurance were regulated by more than a thousand institutions of various types. If, in addition, one takes into consideration the fact that the funds and reserves of insurance companies had, in great part, disappeared in consequence of the war, it is easy to understand the tremendous difficulties which reborn Poland had to face without a trained administrative staff of her own.

Yet, despite all these difficulties, it became Poland's chief ambition to organize institutions corresponding to modern western European standards, and in accord with that social ideal which had ever been for Poland synonymous with true liberty. The very first decisions taken by Poland demonstrate the outlook and tendencies prevailing in the field of social policies. Legislative acts were passed concerning working hours, labor inspection, collective bargaining, employment offices, protection of refugees, social insurance, and labor unions. The social trend was also shown in the electoral law elaborated by the Government, a law abolishing all racial, denominational, and class differences and conferring equal political rights upon women.

Twelve days after the restoration of independence, the Poles realized an aim which the labor leaders had tried for years to achieve, that of an eight-hour working day and a forty-eight hour working week. Shortly thereafter (in January, 1919), the Institution of Labor Inspectors was created by governmental decree. These government officials were to play an increasingly important part in matters of arbitration, investigation, and the stabilizing of relations between employers and employees.

This decree also created the entirely modern Institution of Delegates of Labor, which was to represent the workman before the state authorities. At the same time Rural Arbitration commissions were established which contributed to averting disturbances in agriculture. The problem of subsidies to the unemployed was regulated by the law of November 24, 1919, which granted to unemployed aliens the same rights as to unemployed Polish citizens, thus going even further than international regulations demanded.

As a result of the efforts of the trade unions, they were now given full freedom of organization; the settlement of disputes by collective agreement was initiated, a practice as yet unknown in many countries. The trade unions established the standards of wages, working hours, overtime work, assistance in illness or death, resting hours, retirement limits, hygiene regulations, and educational contributions.

At the same time that laws for the protection of labor were being passed, original and basic research was being conducted in the field of social insurance. Within one year after the rebirth of independent Poland, a law was passed settling the problem of insurance in event of illness. It was based upon the premises of universality, and included compulsory features, as well as the regional and autonomous character of administration. The law required the employer to pay three-fifths and the employee two-fifths of the insurance premium, which amounted to 6.5 per cent of the wages fixed by law. Free medical assistance in event of illness extended for a period of twenty-six weeks and could be prolonged to a limit of thirty-nine weeks.

Women took a prominent part in public life, especially in the protection of maternity and children as well as in that of working women and minors. Because of their efforts, courts of minors (below seventeen years of age) were established in November, 1919, and began to function in the cities of Warsaw, Łódź, and Lublin.

In considering the work done by the Parliament and by the young administration of Poland, one cannot overlook the spontaneous initiative and continuous generosity of the people themselves, especially in the domain of public assistance. This coöperation made it possible to feed millions of children and unemployed during the first years of Poland's independent existence and to take care of the sick and homeless. Unheard of difficulties were overcome through the efforts of the population. The United States in those days gave great succor to Poland by sending food and by helping to introduce methods of sanitation.

In 1921, as soon as the Treaty of Riga had put an end to the period of struggle for Poland's political independence, the era of state building under conditions of political stabilization began. Peasant and labor leaders were fully aware of the flaws and deficiencies in Poland's social structure, as well as of the need for quick reforms. With military operations continuing, peasant and labor leaders succeeded in having passed by Parliament the bill for agricultural reform to establish a better balance in social conditions.

The first Constitution of Poland of March 17, 1921, ensured the future evolution of the country on democratic lines, based upon the principles now called the "Four Freedoms." In this Constitution, social problems were given broad consideration, and in the introductory part the principle was formulated that the rights and special protection of labor should be guaranteed by the State.

Article 102 stressed once more that labor should be protected by the State and that every citizen was entitled to the protection of his work; the article foresaw the organization of social insurance, declaring that every citizen "was entitled to social insurance in cases of unemployment, of illness, accidents and incapacity to work." Article 103 stated: "Labor of children below the age of fifteen, as well as night work of women and minors in industries imperiling their health is forbidden," and "Continuous employment of minor children and minors of school age is forbidden. . . . ," "Children lacking sufficient parental protection and proper education are entitled to protection and assistance on the part of the State . . . ," "Special laws are to regulate the problem of protection of motherhood. . . ." The ideas expressed in the Constitution of 1921 continued to be the guiding principles of legislation dealing with labor and social security, during the entire period of independence up to 1939.

On May 22, 1922, the Parliament passed a law introducing eight days of vacation annually with pay, which period increased to fifteen days after three years of continuous employment. Intellectual workers were entitled annually to one month's holiday with pay. Young workers, including apprentices, without distinction of age, were given fourteen days with pay after a year of work.

The work of minors and women was also regulated in accordance with the spirit of the Constitution. The act of July 2, 1924, prohibited the employment of minors under fifteen years of age. Preventive medical care and medical treatment, as well as periodical examinations, were carried out in quarters specially organized for that purpose. It was compulsory for young workers to attend trade schools, and for this they were to be released from their work six hours weekly. Overtime work was not allowed.

The same act regulated the problem of the work of pregnant women who were entitled to rest periods six weeks before and six weeks after childbirth. All factories and workshops employing more than ninety-nine women had to possess a crèche for infants and to give all nursing mothers two half-hour breaks in the working day in order to feed their children. Women were forbidden to work underground or to work at night. In 1925 a list of types of employment forbidden to minors and women was promulgated. This was followed by the establishment of an organization of inspectors of women's work. Finally, the physical training of working women and minors was initiated as was the establishment of special rest institutions.

Unfortunately, this progress in labor protection occurred at the time of the international economic depression when the procuring of new capital for production facilities was becoming more and more difficult. This circumstance had a serious effect on employment conditions in a country where the average annual increase of population surpassed the figure of 400,000. The emigration which the Poles were compelled to adopt as a way out did not remedy the increasingly difficult situation.

The Parliament, wishing to attenuate the morally and socially fatal consequences of unemployment, in July, 1924, passed an act relating to unemployment insurance for manual workers. An unemployment fund was established, based upon a 2 per cent deduction from wages and salaries, one-fourth of which was paid by the worker, and three-fourths by the employer. The unemployed were entitled to the dole for a period of thirteen weeks. In addition, 5 to 10 per cent of the dole was granted to men having families to support. Alien workers enjoyed the same rights as Polish citizens. The Unemployment Fund also assisted unemployed workers who were not receiving unemployment insurance. Independently of the dole, the Government financed public works and granted loans to autonomous institutions and private concerns.

During this period, the activities of the various institutions of public assistance underwent a process of coördination by the act of August 16, 1923, in conformity with the principles enunciated in the Constitution. It defined public assistance as "the satisfying, by public means, of the indispensable necessities of life for the people who, permanently or temporarily, are unable to do it themselves for lack of personal means or earning capacity."

Public assistance consequently was a substitute for insurance which, for economic reasons, could not be applied to all people in need of help. It embraced protection of mothers and children as well as of minors under the age of eighteen. Its task was to supply them with food, clothing, homes, working tools, sanitation, and medical aid.

Labor and social-security legislation in Poland after 1926 was primarily concerned with questions of organization, consolidation, and revision based on previous experience. Such matters as public hygiene and safety, labor inspection, labor contracts, and labor courts (and securities given by employers) were regulated during that period. At the same time a series of decrees was enacted amending obsolete insurance systems still existing in former Austrian Poland and Upper Silesia. In Upper Silesia, insurance rates based until then upon German standards were raised.

Among the important acts of social legislation in these years was that of insurance for intellectual workers, passed on November 24, 1927, which included unemployment insurance as well as retirement pensions. Up to that date intellectual workers were included in the general workers' insurance system.

As a result of the economic situation and the transformation which the regime had undergone, the influence of the administration in the field of social problems was steadily increasing. The activities of trade unions and labor organizations after this time concentrated upon problems of public assistance, educational work, the training of skilled workers, and hygiene. Nevertheless, social policies continued to be based upon the interests of the working masses. Certain limitations which had been placed on social initiative were, to a large extent, counterbalanced by the work of experts which had been lacking in the past.

The struggle against unemployment was reorganized and its scope broadened. For this purpose there was created a special organization called the Labor Fund which, in 1934, took over the functions of the Unemployment Fund. The Labor Fund dealt with the financing of public works, employment offices, unemployment insurance and first aid for the unemployed, providing occupation for minors, vocational training and educational work among the unemployed. The Labor Fund had its offices in every province (*województwo*) and also in some districts (*starostwa*). Special councils composed of local citizens coöperated with the Fund. The sources of income of the Labor Fund were regular as well as special dues, voluntary contributions, and Treasury subsidies.

Similar progress was made in the domain of labor protection. The law of April 14, 1937, limited the work in mines to seven hours daily and forty-two hours per week, including portal-to-portal journeying, while work done in a temperature higher than 82 degrees Fahrenheit was shortened to six hours daily and thirty-six weekly, without any wage reduction.

On April 14, 1937, there was introduced an important reform concerning collective agreements, making them obligatory, ordering their registration and entrusting labor inspectors with their supervision. Collective agreements could be concluded only between registered trade unions on the one hand and employers, or their organizations, on the other. The arbitrators in the collective agreements were either nominated or appointed *ad hoc,* but in event of serious disputes the Minister of Labor was empowered to set up an arbitration board. Analogous disputes in agriculture were dealt with primarily by the labor inspector. If he failed to bring the parties to an agreement a special arbitration board was set up. Individual disputes between employers and employees were subject to the jurisdiction of labor courts, composed of a judge and two lay members, selected by the Minister of Justice from the panel submitted by the trade unions and by employers' organizations.

Of importance were the unification and improvement of insurance legislation accomplished by the law of March 26, 1933, and by later amendments. Thus the first Polish codification of social insurance was effected. In 1935 the Social Insurance Institute was organized. Under the supervision of the Ministry of Social Welfare it directed sixty-seven social-insurance offices, and administered the insurance laws of the Social Insurance Institute to regulate the following risks: old age, invalidity, cases of death, trade sickness as well as common, and motherhood. Unemployment insurance, as stated above, formed a special organization.

In cases of illness the insured obtained medical aid and, for a period of not more than twenty-six weeks, financial assistance which amounted to 60 per cent of his average earnings in the preceding thirteen weeks. In event of death, funeral expenses were paid to an amount equaling three weeks' earnings of the deceased. Motherhood insurance included medical aid, one childbirth allowance for eight weeks, and another for a period of twelve weeks for nursing mothers. Members of the families of insured persons were entitled to medical aid for a period of thirteen weeks.

Comparatively insignificant changes were made in accident insurance which also embraced agricultural workers. The principal benefits in this instance included a pension, plus supplement for family; medical aid and the cost of any eventually needed prosthesis; pensions for widows and orphans; and posthumous aid. In instances of total disability the insured individual received two-thirds of his earnings, plus 10 per cent supplementary aid for children.

The law granted pensions to individuals who had lost two-thirds of their working capacity, and to persons having attained the age limit of sixty-five (widows and widowers, sixty). Miners and foundry workers were entitled to a pension on reaching the age of sixty years (widows, fifty years). Orphans received assistance to the age of seventeen for boys, and to eighteen years of age for girls. The revenues of insurance institutions consisted of dues paid by employers and employees and of an additional payment by the Treasury to cover invalids' pensions and accident insurance for rural workers.

The following figures illustrate the activities of all kinds of social insurance in Poland before and after their amalgamation:

1. Number of persons subject to social insurance in 1938:

a) health	2,254,000
b) accident	2,273,000
c) pensions	2,407,000
d) unemployment	1,531,000

2. Receipts of social insurance institutions for the period of 1925–1937: 6,495,700,000 złotys.

3. Expenditures for the period of 1925–1937: 5,433,100,000 złotys.

4. Receipts in 1937: 566,000,000 złotys.

5. Expenditures in 1937: 430,300,000 złotys.

Among the activities of public-assistance organizations, special mention must be made of the following: social-protection stations for immediate aid; social-protection stations for mothers and children; so-called "cradles" and kindergartens; reading rooms; summer colonies (450,000 children in 1937); and night lodging. Special care was given to children and minors. At the initiative of the Ministry of Social Welfare, committees of aid for children and minors were organized throughout Poland, which, in 1936–1937, supplied food to no fewer than 659,000 undernourished children.

Of great importance were private foundations for social and medical aid, the origins of which went back in some instances to the Middle Ages. One such foundation was the Holy Spirit Insurance in the city of Sandomierz, founded in the year 1222, which maintained a hospital, a home for the aged, and an orphan asylum. In 1937 there existed in Poland 1,516 foundations of this kind. Subsidies of the Ministry of Social Welfare for public assistance in the period of 1927–1939 amounted to 416,200,000 złotys. In the same period, the expenditures of local government boards and of the Treasury of Silesia Province amounted to 736,200,000 złotys. In 1936–1937, there were 1,040 organizations of public assistance, the receipts of which amounted to 29,735,000 złotys, and the expenditures to 28,364,000 złotys, of which 10,875,000 złotys were spent for the feeding of undernourished children and minors alone. Mention should also be made of the results achieved in the domain of hygiene and sanitation. General health conditions were greatly improved, as is shown by the decline in the death rate, which was 20.9 per 1,000 in 1921, and 13.8 per 1,000 in 1939. In this field the following government offices and social organizations were active: the State Health Service, the health service of autonomous boards; the social-insurance organizations; the Polish Red Cross; the Polish Anti-tuberculosis Society; the Polish Hygienic Association; the Polish Eugenic Society; the Women's Union for Civic Work, and many others.

The number of physicians rose from 6,408 in 1921 to 16,088 in 1935, and the increase in the number of pharmacists and nurses was analogous. The number of guest patients in health resorts rose from 47,744 in 1919 to 189,810 in 1931. The Union of Social Insurance made it increasingly easy for poor people, as well as for members of self-aid associations and trade unions to visit these spas.

As soon as Poland had regained its political independence, it made every effort to be an active, useful, and creative member of the international community. The young State was ambitious to overtake other nations and to adapt itself in the realm of social work to the requirements of international collaboration. In some instances, Poland even became a leader in the international arena and proposed a number of universal reforms. Unknown before because of its loss of independence, Poland, in its new political status, soon acquired the reputation of a country striving earnestly to collaborate with the nations which had the social progress of the world at heart.

The Polish representatives in the Commission for International Labor Legislation (established in 1919 by the Peace Conference), distinguished themselves by their serious work. The Polish delegate in that Commission, consisting of representatives of nine countries, could indeed point with pride to the fact that the trend of the Commission's work and the guiding principles of Poland's social legislation since 1918 were analogous.

Poland ratified altogether twenty international conventions: six concerning the age of working minors (in agreement with earlier Polish legislation and with the Constitution of 1921); a convention regarding the compulsory medical examination of minors employed in shipping; another concerning the regulation of weekly rest in industrial undertakings (also enacted earlier by Polish legislation); three conventions regarding unemployment; one concerning the right of association of agricultural workers (the principles of which were embodied in the aforementioned Polish Constitution); four conventions concerning the payment of damages for accidents and occupational diseases (also anticipated in Polish legislation); a convention regulating the use of white lead in paint; one covering agreements with seamen and their repatriation; one about the marking of weight on heavy packages transported by ships; and, finally, one establishing a scheme for the maintenance of rights under invalidity, old age, and widow and orphan insurance. Poland refrained from ratifying only those conventions which could not be applied in the conditions prevailing in Poland, or of which the rules had already been applied in their entirety by Polish legislation and decrees.

Poland strictly followed the recommendations of the International Labor Office, and its delegates always attended the annual sessions. In the League of Nations, Poland's representatives took an important part in the studies concerning public health and hygiene, and in 1921 a Polish citizen was appointed director of the Section on Health in the Secretariat of the League. The Polish Health Service closely collaborated with nine international societies devoted to questions of hygiene and public health.

In the field of social welfare, Poland concluded a series of agreements with various nations. The most important of these were the agreements regarding reciprocity in matters of social insurance and public assistance. In 1936, Polish experts to a large extent were instrumental in the passing of the international agreement concerning protection of aliens. From 1925 Polish delegates were members of the advisory committee of the League of Nations for the protection of children and minors, as well as of anti-white-slave-trade committees. In the domain of intellectual collaboration, the participation of the Polish Association for Social Policies in the work of the International Association for Social Progress, as well as the contributions of Polish scientists to the work of international institutions, must be specially mentioned.

In this brief survey of social evolution in Poland during the period of 1918–1939, the writer has been able to show only in part the magnitude of the effort of the Poles who have always identified the idea of political liberty with that of social justice. The result of these efforts was social and labor legislation which could be compared favorably with that of the most advanced countries of Europe.

Because of economic difficulties, Poland's social organization was still unable to satisfy all the needs of its population. Yet, through continuous improvement, it attained a high degree of efficiency and elasticity, which made it broad and adaptable to the economic evolution of the country.

For this reason, once the war is won and Poland's independence is reëstablished, the nation will be able to benefit from the experiences and achievements of the period from 1918 to 1939. Equally useful will be the social progress of the United States and Great Britain, which is being diligently watched by the Polish Ministry of Social Welfare in London. All these factors will enable Poland to obliterate quickly the traces of Hitler's barbaric "new order," and to realize still more closely than in the past the ideal of social justice based upon international collaboration.

Part Five

CULTURAL DEVELOPMENT

CHAPTER XVI

Religious Life

BY OSCAR HALECKI

FOR A GENUINE understanding of Poland, the study of its religious life is as important as the study of its history. Both problems are closely connected. The Polish mind always was, as it is today, deeply religious. In the Middle Ages the unreserved devotion to the Roman Catholic Church was a distinctive feature which Poland had in common with all the nations of western Europe, and for that very reason it undoubtedly belonged to the west, at least culturally if not geographically. Moreover, for medieval Poland the Church was also a permanent political ally: the ecclesiastical organization was an element of unity in times of internal divisions; the Holy See was the protector of Poland's independence against the encroachments of the empire in the west; and the Popes considered Poland's self-defense against pagan or schismatic neighbors in the east another crusade, and supported it accordingly.

Poland's union with Lithuania secured the conversion of the last European heathens, and the inclusion of Ruthenian populations within Polish boundaries seemed an opportunity to promote a union between the Greek Church and the Roman Church, at least on Polish territory. Even the Renaissance appeared in Poland mostly in its Christian expression, having as leading representatives distinguished members of the Catholic hierarchy. And Poland's interest in the Reformation movement was much less determined by economic and social reasons than by a serious religious concern, by a passionate desire to discover the ultimate truth.

It may be wondered how in a country so attached to the Catholic Church the Reformation, in its Protestant and even in its anti-Trinitarian form, could exercise such a strong influence that in the 'fifties of the sixteenth century Poland seemed to be lost for the

Papacy. The main reason was an already old tradition of tolerance in a country where for two hundred years Catholics and Orthodox had lived together, where Jews had been received in a friendly way, and where Armenians and even Tartars had settled in many places. But for the same reason, combined with an unlimited curiosity in religious matters, the great number of quarreling sects, representing the new doctrines, proved unable to create in Poland a united Reformed Church which could have replaced Catholicism. When in 1573 the Warsaw Confederation guaranteed religious peace to everybody, the traditional faith, strengthened by the decisions of the Council of Trent, was already regaining its leading position, not by way of compulsion, but by the spontaneous return of the overwhelming majority of the dissidents. There remained, it is true, a small group of Protestants—chiefly Calvinists, but also some Lutherans and Czech Brethren—as well as a much larger Orthodox minority; and even the anti-Trinitarians were allowed to stay in Poland until the middle of the seventeenth century. But from the beginning of that century Poles and Catholics were identified more and more, especially because all foreign invaders were of different religions; Protestant Swedes and Prussians, Orthodox Russians, and Mohammedan Turks and Tartars.

Such a situation could not but threaten the traditional principles of religious tolerance. In spite of riots against the "heretics," which sometimes occurred among the masses almost untouched by the Reformation, the legal position of the non-Catholics who continued to occupy high official dignities, was not changed, however, before the first half of the eighteenth century; at that time the decline of Polish culture also brought about a deterioration of its religious life, and a formalistic bigotry often replaced the lofty spirit of the past. But even then the limitation of the political rights of Protestants and Orthodox in Poland could not be compared with religious persecutions in other countries; such limitations only served as a pretext for Prussian and Russian intervention which necessarily provoked a Catholic and national reaction. On the other hand, the sound reaction against the moral and intellectual crisis in eighteenth-century Poland was largely initiated by members of the Catholic clergy, one of whom was the great reformer of education, Father Stanisław Konarski, whose reorganization of the schools of his own order, the Piarists, influenced also the numerous schools of the Jesuits. After the temporary abolition of the Jesuit order, whose allegedly pernicious role in Poland to a large extent has been misrepresented, its funds were used for educational purposes and many of its former members contributed to the cultural revival of the country.

The contemporary trends of the Enlightenment were of course not favorable to religious life, but the Romanticism of the early nineteenth century in Poland, more than elsewhere, had a marked religious character, just because it was strongly patriotic and was inspired by national suffering. In seeking an explanation of these ordeals, Polish Romanticism produced a Messianistic conception which in its extreme statements approached heresy. But profoundly religious though it was and never separated from Catholic tradition, it contributed to the development of the decisively Christian spirit of Polish literature where again and again the idea was expressed that Christian principles should govern not only private life, but also international relations. At the same time the hardships of the Roman Church under Orthodox Russian and Protestant Prussian rule created another tie between Polish nationalism and religion, particularly impressing the popular masses where devotion to Catholicism was sometimes stronger than national consciousness.

In the last decades before the First World War the general European trends of positivism and religious skepticism also influenced Poland, especially its intellectuals. But even the most radical movements had to reckon with the traditional connection of religious and patriotic ideals, and when the latter were realized in the reborn Republic, there started almost immediately a remarkable progress in religious life. The new Polish Constitution officially recognized the "leading position" of the Catholic Church "among all the denominations enjoying equal rights." A close contact was established with the Holy See which even during the war had sent to Poland an Apostolic Delegate, Monsignor Achille Ratti. Deeply interested in the reconstruction of independent Poland, he was appointed Papal Nuncio at Warsaw, in 1919, and when elected Pope, as Pius XI, in 1922, he continued to show to the Poles a particular sympathy. The Concordat concluded in 1925 easily settled the problems concerning the relations between Church and State which in Poland, old and new, were much less controversial than in other, even Catholic, countries, and adapted the ecclesiastical organization to the new political conditions. In accordance with an old tradition, the Archbishop of Gniezno and Poznań again became Primate of Poland; other archbishoprics, in addition to those which already existed in Warsaw and Lwów, now were erected also in Cracow and in Wilno; and the frontiers of all the twenty archdioceses and dioceses, including those of Silesia and Pomorze, were brought into conformity with the boundaries of the Republic.

In practically all of them the contemporary Polish Church had highly distinguished leaders, two of whom, the archbishops of Gniezno-Poznań and of Warsaw, were made cardinals. The See of Warsaw had been occupied since before the war by Monsignor Aleksander Kakowski who enjoyed such great authority that under the German occupation he was placed at the head of the Council of Regency; until his death, at the eve of the Second World War, he exercised, in spite of his age, a restless activity equaled only by Cardinal Augustus Hlond who in 1926 succeeded Cardinal Dalbor in Gniezno-Poznań. The new Primate of Poland proved to be a really outstanding personality whose pastoral letters most thoroughly discussed all the big contemporary problems, and whose relations with the Catholics of foreign countries were successfully developed. Both cardinals did their best to promote in Poland the organization of the Catholic Action in which Pius XI, their personal friend, was particularly interested. With its central headquarters in Poznań, the Catholic Action had special "institutes" in all the Polish dioceses. In Warsaw a magnificent building was constructed to house all the numerous associations connected with the Catholic Action, including an institution of higher education in the religious field, inaugurated in 1938.

The Catholic Action was exceedingly important for the progress of religious life in Poland, because, faithful to its program and character, the Action remained truly unpolitical, independent of any party or political group. There was indeed a serious, twofold danger resulting just from the intimate connection between Catholicism and Polish tradition. On the one hand, there were good Catholics in almost all the political parties, and for that very reason

NATIVITY AT ŁOWICZ

BY BOLESLAW CYBIS

(Shown in 1934 at International Exhibition of Paintings in Carnegie Institute in Pittsburgh. Owned by Dr. Andrey Avinoff of Pittsburgh.)

their rivalries sometimes had a fatal repercussion on purely religious matters, creating divisions between those devoted to the same faith. On the other hand, only too many people were inclined almost to identify Catholicism and nationalism, a tendency which proved particularly harmful when the extremists of the latter attempted to utilize the religious fervor of most of the Poles as a tool for achieving their own political aims. For those hostile to the Church, similar cases were of course an opportunity to challenge Catholicism as being reactionary or "fascist," and to hold it responsible for movements, as for instance, anti-Semitism, where religion at best was an additional pretext. Fortunately, however, in the really religious sphere, controlled by the hierarchy and consequently concentrated around the Catholic Action, entirely different trends were contributing to a spiritual revival of the nation; one of them was social, the other was intellectual.

Even before and during the First World War some of the most eminent Polish bishops had been deeply concerned with social problems and with a modern, efficient organization of charitable activities. The war relief work of Bishop Adam Sapieha of Cracow had been particularly remarkable. Later, as Archbishop, Sapieha remained one of the leaders of the Polish Church in the social field. In the new Republic the dioceses with a large population of miners and factory workers had the good fortune of having bishops especially trained and interested in social progress and welfare, who enjoyed a well-merited popularity: Monsignor Adamski in Silesia, Monsignor Kubina in Częstochowa, the famous place of pilgrimages to the shrine of the Blessed Virgin, and Monsignor Jasiński in the industrial city of Łódź. The teachings of the social encyclicals of the Popes, *Rerum novarum* and *Quadragesimo anno,* were studied and strongly recommended not only by the clergy, but also by lay associations devoted to the principles of Christian democracy. The political party called by that name never was very strong, but the movement was represented by numerous syndicates of Catholic workers and by the *Odrodzenie* [Renaissance] group, chiefly students and alumni of the universities, with their headquarters at Lublin, organizing there and elsewhere "social weeks" for the discussion of contemporary problems.

At the same time Lublin was the seat of a Catholic university, founded in 1918 by private endowment, supported by the episcopate which itself had distinguished scholars among its members [Bishop Szlagowski, one of the most successful presidents of Warsaw University; the historian, Archbishop Nowowiejski, in Płock], and eventually recognized by the State as an institution of academic standard. It was the only Catholic university in the whole of central and eastern Europe, connected with a learned society, whose publishing activity was steadily increasing, as well as the number of its professors and students, chiefly in religious and social sciences. Moreover, the growing influence of Catholicism among the Polish intellectuals was notable also in the state universities all of which, except Poznań, had faculties of theology and in the field of literature. The Catholic writers of Poland in 1933 formed an association with leading novelists, poets, and journalists as active members. Among the numerous Catholic periodicals the old monthly magazine *General Review* (*Przegląd Powszechny*) edited, with many other publications, by the Jesuits, had the highest standard; a new weekly, *Kultura,* was published by the Catholic Action.

The future of this promising development seemed to be assured by the fact that Catholicism, based upon deep convictions, serious religious education, and regular practices, was in rapid progress among the younger generation, including the university students. Here again the movement had started before and during the war, chiefly because of the Marianic Congregations. During the last decade, religious associations were playing a prominent part in academic life, organizing social and cultural activities and joint pilgrimages to Częstochowa where, in 1935, the whole academic youth of Poland was placed under the patronage of the Blessed Virgin, an example followed the next year by a pilgrimage of professors and teachers. It ought to be emphasized that this powerful trend of religious thought and culture had nothing to do with superficial bigotry, and although political influence succeeded in distorting it occasionally and in exciting political differences between various groups, the movement itself was undoubtedly sound and was inspired by the ideal of making Poland a truly Christian nation, faithful to the teaching of the Gospel both in private and in public life.

Roman Catholicism is the religion of 95 per cent of the Poles, but of only 65 per cent of all the citizens of the Republic of Poland, because racial minorities, except the few Lithuanians, were almost all religious minorities. It is inaccurate, however, to apply that term to those who, as Catholics, differed from the majority only by their non-Latin rite. Lwów is the only city in the world having three Catholic archbishops, two of them of Eastern or Uniate rites. The Armenian Catholics whose archbishop during almost the whole period of Poland's independence was the outstanding writer and preacher, Monsignor Józef Teodorowicz, are a very small group, chiefly landowners and merchants, descending from immigrants who had been settled in Poland since the Middle Ages, and had been Polonized long ago. The problem of the Greek Catholics, 3,600,000 in number and forming 10.3 per cent of the whole population, is entirely different and much more intricate.

Since its eastern expansion, in the fourteenth century, Poland has had a considerable Orthodox population. In contradistinction to Muscovite Great Russia, there had been, however, among these Ruthenians, even before their political union with Poland, a notable trend toward a religious union with Rome. The Florentine Union of 1439 was accepted there only temporarily, but in 1596 the Ruthenian hierarchy of Poland, gathered at Brest-Litovsk, concluded a similar union which, before the Partitions, had gained the overwhelming majority of all the Ukrainians and White Russians. In the nineteenth century this so-called Uniate Church was cruelly persecuted and eventually suppressed by the Tsarist Government. Only in Austrian Galicia was it left undisturbed, and its local organization with an archbishop at Lwów and two other dioceses was, of course, maintained in the new republic of Poland; after some initial difficulties with the Polish authorities, Archbishop Andrzej Count Szeptycki, descending from an old, Polonized family, remained not only the spiritual, but to a large extent, also, the political leader of the Ukrainian movement. In the former Russian territories attempts were being made to restore the Union, chiefly on the initiative of the Holy See. Polish opinion was rather skeptical. Some progress was obtained through the propaganda of monastic orders, and an increasing number of the former Uniates were returning to Catholicism of an Eastern rite somewhat different from the one used in Galicia. The form of their ecclesiastical organization had not been finally decided when the Soviet invasion of 1939 put an end to these achievements.

One and a half million of the Ukrainians and most of the White Russians, with the exception of a Roman Catholic group of about 80,000 had remained Orthodox as they had been obliged to be under Tsarist rule. Numbering, together with a small Russian group, about 4,250,000, or 12 per cent of the inhabitants of the Republic, they formed its largest religious minority, with an archbishop in Warsaw and four dioceses in the eastern provinces. In 1922, not without having been influenced by the desperate situation of their Church under the Soviets, they decided at a synod—the first held since 1791—to separate from the Patriarchate of Moscow. Two years later the autocephaly of the Orthodox Church in Poland was officially recognized by the Patriarchate of Constantinople. Its metropolitan, Archbishop Dionysius, was placed at the head of a School of Orthodox Theology in the University of Warsaw, which opened in 1925 and greatly contributed to the cultural standard of the Eastern clergy. The attitude of the Polish Government toward the Orthodox Church was very friendly; in agreement with the Constitution, the mutual relations were fixed, as in the cases of other religious minorities, by a direct agreement with the representatives of that Church, which settled all legal and financial problems, including delicate questions of property resulting from the situation in the partition period. In the last year before the present war these relations of normal coöperation were unfortunately disturbed by the retaking from the Oxthodox Church of a certain number of church buildings which, before the Russian rule, had belonged to Catholics, Roman or Uniate. Even when legally justified, such untimely decisions, occasionally carried out by military force, were in striking contrast with both the tradition and the practice of religious tolerance in Poland.

There were no similar troubles with the Protestant minority, or rather with the various Protestant communities which had existed in Poland since the Reformation, with a membership considerably reduced after the Catholic restoration, but augmented later on by the afflux of German colonists. Whereas in eastern Poland difference of religion and even of ritual usually coincided with difference of nationality—at least among the peasant population it was more distinctly realized—just the contrary must be noted in the west. The Protestant Poles, few as they were—less than 300,000—either descendants of Polish families which had embraced Protestantism in the sixteenth century, or immigrants from Germany who had become Polonized during many generations, were not less patriotic than the Catholics nor separated from them in any way. Three-quarters of all the Protestants in the Republic [almost 1,000,000, or 2.7 per cent of the total population] belonged to the German minority. The relations between them and the Poles, Catholic or not, were scarcely more difficult than in the case of the Catholic Germans. Having to consider in the present chapter the religious situation only, it will suffice to observe that all the Protestant denominations, whether Lutheran or Calvinist or representing the Union of both, were, of course, recognized by the State and enjoyed not only toleration, but also a full equality of civic rights. The Protestants were not only particularly numerous in Poznań, but also in Silesia, where they included a great many Poles. In Wilno there was an old Calvinist community of purely Polish character. In general, there were seven Protestant groups in Poland, the most important of which were the Evangelical Augsburg (Lutheran) Church of Poland and the United Evangelical Church in both Poznań and Silesia. In 1928 a Council of the Evangelical Churches in Poland was definitely established which united the various groups within the political limits of the Republic. The first president of the Council was Superintendent Dr. Juliusz Bursche, who belonged to a Polonized family. The Council had its seat in Warsaw, where the university also created a Faculty of Protestant Theology. The tension between the German and the Polish Protestants of the Republic increased, however, after 1937.

Among non-Christians, the Jews, counting more than 3,000,000, or 9.5 per cent of the population, were by far the largest and most important section. But although most people of Jewish origin kept at the same time the Mosaic faith, the Jewish problem in the Republic of Poland was not at all a religious problem and, therefore, must be discussed elsewhere. The religious life of the Polish Jews was of a greatly varying intensity. But a majority of those who officially professed Mosaism could be considered as truly orthodox as were, among others, the adherents of the *Agudas*

Israel and *Mizrachi* (Orthodox Zionist) movement. Their religious communities, more than eight hundred in number, having kept throughout the ages their full autonomy were scattered over the entire country, chiefly in the central and the eastern parts, especially in the cities and towns. The Jewish Community Law of 1927 created a legal basis for all their activities which it tried to coördinate. The Great Rabbi had his headquarters in Warsaw; the most important Rabbinistic school was in Lublin, and in addition to two institutions of Jewish studies in Warsaw, several other well-known schools existed in the eastern provinces, in Mir, Kleck, Kamieniec, etc.

Finally, there were in Poland not only a thousand Karaites, a racial and religious group connected with the Jews, although strictly separated from them, with their chief communities at Wilno, Troki, Halicz, and Łuck, but also, as a remnant of Tartar settlements in medieval Lithuania, about six thousand Mohammedans. These Mohammedans, who were attached to their faith, had been culturally Polonized for centuries; they had at their head a Chief Mufti at Wilno. These minor religious groups of far remote origin, being another outcome of historical toleration, were all living in most friendly relations with their Christian fellow citizens.

CHAPTER XVII

Education

BY WOJCIECH ŚWIĘTOSŁAWSKI

IT WOULD BE impossible to find in the history of education another example that would reflect, even in part, the difficulties faced by Poland at the time of its rebirth. Of the three hostile governments that had ruled Polish territories before the First World War, only one, namely the Austrian, had maintained a system of compulsory Polish schools, but with the required attendance in a four-year curriculum only. The other two occupants, Germany and Russia, had prohibited the functioning of Polish schools. Germany had maintained for Poles an eight-year compulsory schooling—solely in the German language. Before 1905, Russia stubbornly blocked any kind of education for Poles, even in the Russian language, spending in Russia proper seven times as much on each child in school as it did on a Polish child. Private teaching was also persecuted under Russian rule. This was changed, at least in part, after the Russian revolution of 1905, when a private Polish educational organization, known as Alma Mater (*Macierz Szkolna*), was permitted to establish Polish private schools. These schools were not allowed in the eastern part of Russian-occupied Poland, however, and as a consequence, the percentage of illiterates in that section was exceptionally high.

Such was the situation in 1918, when the Poles occupied the seat of government in their own country. The task of introducing throughout the entire country a compulsory and unified system of education for a population of 25,000,000 seemed more than difficult. There was no code of school legislation; there were only a few school buildings in the country; and the trained teaching personnel was far from sufficient to meet the educational needs.

Not one of the three occupants of Poland had spent much money on school buildings. In agricultural Poland the one-room type of school building predominated. Everywhere the primitive buildings were overcrowded, and in eastern Poland there were large areas of land where few school buildings could be found. War darkened the picture, too; in eastern, southern, and also in parts of central Poland almost half the school buildings had been destroyed. The restored Poland had to begin practically anew in the field of school building. Many of the newly created schools had to be located provisionally in private houses.

Even worse was the problem of teachers. In a country like Poland, where the population was increasing rapidly, a seven-year compulsory system of education affected one-seventh to one-sixth the entire population. In Poland, at the time of its rebirth, there were some four million children to be considered. Allowing, on the average, thirty to thirty-five children for each teacher, approximately one hundred and twenty thousand teachers were needed, whereas only twenty-five thousand had passed through normal-school training. If, nevertheless, the problem was solved, it was because there had been mobilized among the population many amateur teachers whose lack of professional training had been compensated in part by their great enthusiasm. Both the teachers and the youth were conscious of the fact that after long years of foreign domination they were now attending their own Polish institutions.

Elementary public-school system.—The basic difficulties which Poland faced, after its rebirth, in the field of education—the variety of school systems left by the occupants and the lack of teachers and school facilities—were felt most keenly in elementary public education, where there was a "mass production" problem.

It was in 1919 that compulsory education was introduced for the first time throughout Poland. This was to consist of seven years of schooling under the unified control of the State, for in Poland it was the State and not the municipalities that maintained the public schools. The municipalities furnished only fuel and certain other school facilities for the schoolrooms in winter. The educational work for the whole country was centralized in the offices of the Ministry of Education in Warsaw.

The large fluctuation in the numbers of children of school age presented a handicap. There was not only a normal, considerable

PUBLIC SCHOOL IN KRÓLEWSKA HUTA

DESIGNED BY ARCHITECT WOJCIECH SOBOŃ

increase in population—a Polish tendency well known both in Poland and abroad—but there was another phenomenon in Poland which usually follows great wars. When the First World War ended in 1918 and the Polish-Russian War in 1920, there occurred in Poland an increase in marriages and, subsequently, in births. The number of children of school age steadily increased until there were at this time 3,900,000 children from seven to fourteen years of age. By 1937 this number had increased to 5,324,000, or by 33 per cent.

Another difficulty in building up the new school system grew out of the exceptionally large migration of people inside the country. As soon as the old internal frontiers ceased to exist, people moved from one place to another seeking better jobs. New cities like Gdynia were built, new industries were created. The general direction of this migration was from country to city.

The problem of teachers, however, was the most acute of all. Here was a problem of migration, too, since in former Austrian Poland only had there been a sizable number of trained teachers. By now more than 17,000 of them had migrated to other parts of Poland. The big gaps still existing in trained personnel were temporarily filled with amateur teachers. Those amateurs, however, were relatively well prepared for their jobs, as they had been recruited mostly from the ranks of prewar underground teachers. Under both the Russians and the Germans, nearly every intelligent and patriotic Polish citizen secretly had helped to teach the youth the forbidden Polish language and Polish history.

But even this supply of teachers was not sufficient; the regular yearly increase in the number of children required a reservoir of at least five thousand new teachers annually. This difficulty was not overcome until 1930, at which time another obstacle was confronted. The World Depression created an exceptionally critical financial situation for the Polish Government, which was obliged to curtail the budget. As a result, there rose the paradoxical situation of unemployed teachers who actually were badly needed in the schools to relieve the employed teachers who were still greatly overburdened. Between 1936 and 1938, this obstacle had been overcome to some extent by the employment of ten thousand young teachers.

The systematic and adequate training of teachers was perhaps a more important and more difficult problem in Poland than elsewhere. In Poland, as in numerous other countries, the teachers constituted one-third of the total number of professional intellectuals. Large numbers of teachers had to be prepared for their duties in a very short time. It should be emphasized that the Government was assisted by the teachers themselves. Over fifty thousand of them were organized in the powerful Professional Teachers Association. This association established a special kind of institute by which a teacher, while residing in a rural community, would learn through correspondence.

In agricultural Poland there was a tendency to enroll the highest possible contingent of teachers from among the rural populations. The Polish Government granted numerous privileges to those who devoted themselves to the teaching profession. There was a carefully planned system of schools for teachers. Poland had two types, one for those who had graduated from primary schools, the other for students who had completed the entire secondary-school course, including what is equivalent to that of an American junior college. The first group of candidates had to attend five years, the other for only two years. Besides these normal schools for teacher training there were established institutes for teachers who, aften ten years of teaching, wished to prepare themselves for more responsible positions in the educational system.

The problem of a proper school network was more complicated in Poland than in many other countries, because of the many sparsely populated areas where it was sometimes practically impossible to maintain a complete six- or seven-room school, and where the old type of one-teacher school was often the only solution. And it might be emphasized that the rural population in Poland had a tendency to insist that its youth enjoy the benefit of the best type of elementary school. It was difficult to meet the requirements of the population, as there were no proper buildings, no adequate transportation facilities and, of primary importance, no funds with which to build the schools. Poland inherited from its occupants only a few good school buildings. The rest were either primitive or had been destroyed. In 1919 Poland needed at least 100,000 units of school space. In 1936 it still needed 45,000 classrooms. At that time 3,000 class units were annually completed, so that the entire building program was capable of being achieved within some fifteen years, or, according to more optimistic prognosticators, within nine years. When the Second World War opened, many schools in Poland still were located in private homes which had been converted for school use. The school authorities assisted themselves in different ways. For example, they successfully established the so-called "consolidated schools" which were attended by children from different school districts.

Public-school education was given free of charge. The elementary public-school system was uniform throughout the entire country, so that, after completing the sixth grade, all graduates enjoyed identical rights of admission to the gymnasium. This was a sound democratic principle, for it assured to the whole population a uniform basic education. In addition to many other advantages this system made it possible for a student, who had changed his residence, to find in the new location a school which did not differ from the one he had been attending.

The fundamentals of a teaching program in an elementary school in Poland were almost a counterpart of the primary school in the United States. Compulsory elementary schooling in America begins one year earlier than in Poland and ends one year later. But the general idea of both school systems is the same—that the youth of fourteen years should first acquire the fundamentals of a general education rather than study certain special subjects.

It may be said that the Polish school, like the spirit of Polish youth, was entirely devoid of stiffness and routine. After the First World War, the life of resurrected Poland developed in such a feverish fashion, there was such an intense spirit of animation throughout the country that the atmosphere of the school life was likewise influenced. Lessons were often in the form of discussions. The prevailing spirit of animation in Poland enabled teachers to secure adequate results within a period of seven years. Among the teachers, however, an eight-year compulsory schooling was largely favored.

In contrast to the American system, the Polish school was charged with the duty of training its children in a religious spirit which included also the principles of ethics and morality. It is interesting to note that in Poland the Minister of Education was officially called "Minister of Religious Denominations and Public Education."

In the teaching program in the Polish public schools there were also special difficulties. Outside Poland it is not realized what obstacles and dangers resulted in every field of public life from the mere fact of Poland's location between Nazi Germany and Soviet Russia. This was true also of the Polish school, where neither the parents of the children nor the teachers were immune from influences created by the special geographical position of Poland. Under these conditions, children in Polish schools were given a special training in nationalism and citizenship. But sometimes this training offered problems. Because of the minorities living in Poland, it was difficult to find a definition for the word "national" which would not offend the minorities. The school authorities also were very careful. Any subject that might wound the sensibilities of certain individuals, even certain masterpieces of Polish literature, were eliminated from the public schools, and Polish youth was trained to understand the kind of sacrifices Polish citizens would have to make in order to defend Poland against aggression. Of course, according to Polish traditions, the general trend of national training was to transform a child into a patriotic citizen, ready to give his very life to the defense of Poland.

Other nationalities that lived in Poland had the right to maintain their own public schools where the children could be taught in their native language. If a group of nationals applied for such a school, it was maintained by government funds exactly as a regular Polish school was maintained. This was a type of burden unknown in America. This liberal law created difficulties because efforts were made, especially by Germany, to organize the strongest possible opposition among the minorities against the Polish Government and the Polish people. In numerous schools in which there were teachers of nationalities other than Polish, friction resulted because of the ultranationalistic tendencies inculcated by foreign propaganda. This factor aroused strong opposition by the Poles, especially by those residing in districts where the population was mixed. Because of these undesirable phenomena there was a tendency to decrease the number of minority schools, especially those conducted by minority teachers. In connection with this, it should be emphasized that the real protection against foreign propaganda especially among the teachers is one of the most essential and, at the same time, one of the most difficult problems to be solved in the postwar peaceful collaboration of the nations of the whole world.

Secondary schools.—"Gymnasium" is the official name of the Polish secondary standard school which corresponds to the high school in America. Until 1932 secondary schooling in Poland, as in many other European countries, extended over a period of eight years. The school reform of 1932 brought important changes. The two lowest grades were transferred to the elementary school, and the two upper were transformed into a separate unit called "lyceum," which was, however, still attached to the gymnasium, forming with it a common combined unit. Students were not obliged to go through the lyceum, but could be graduated from the gymnasium only, receiving after four years of study in the gymnasium the so-called "little matura." They could then be enrolled in any kind of vocational school. If, however, they wished to attend a university, it was necessary that they be graduated from the lyceum. In principle, the two-year lyceum corresponds to the junior college in America.

In general, the organization and the curricula for the gymnasium were similar to that of the American high school, although there were more required subjects in the Polish high school than in the American. The chief task of the Polish high school was to furnish a general education, whereas the lyceum prepared pupils for university studies.

The gymnasium offered a broad general program of education but did not provide an exhaustive treatment of any specific subject. This was true also of the lyceum, which was divided into the four departments of classics, humanism, physico-mathematics, and natural science. Consequently the student who passed through the physico-mathematical department of the lyceum and who decided to study history or literature at the university had to pass only a supplementary examination.

In Poland, the desire to be graduated from a university or at least from secondary school was so universal that the annual increase in the number of students attending four-year high schools (gymnasiums) and two-year junior colleges (lyceums) was relatively greater than in many other European countries. In addition a high percentage of these students graduated from both the gymnasium and the lyceum. Sixty out of one hundred who graduated from the lyceum attended university courses. The annual matriculations reached ten thousand in the period from 1929 to 1939.

The following comparative data for Poland and three other European countries show the total number of graduates from secondary schools for each one million inhabitants.

Country	*1933–1934*	*1934–1935*	*1935–1936*	*1936–1937*	*1937–1938*
Poland	449.6	411.1	395.4	443.4	536.1
France	.....	.....	284.9	.....	.....
Germany	.....	.....	389.7	.....	.....
Sweden	414.2	471.8	537.5	.....	.....

The ratios between the number of students in elementary and secondary schools varied in different parts of Poland. In southern Poland this ratio was seven to eight per cent, whereas in western Poland it dropped to four per cent. The average was five per cent. These differences resulted from the fact that in western Poland a larger number of students attended the vocational schools than in other parts of Poland.

The steady increase in the number of students attending secondary schools is characteristic of the entire civilized world. The university graduate spent seventeen years, or nearly one-third of his life in different kinds of schools; a man who completed both primary and secondary schools (including junior college) spent twenty-five per cent and one who completed one primary school spent twelve per cent of his life in different kinds of schools. These figures are based on the assumption that the average span of life is fifty-eight years and that seven years of childhood should not be taken into consideration. The expenditures in the state and family budgets are very high, especially if the percentage of children in the country is also high. This was typical of Poland.

Vocational schools.—Vocational schools have developed in Europe only in comparatively recent times. In an earlier period an apprentice learned handicrafts from his master. When Poland regained independence in 1918, besides commercial schools there were only a few vocational schools of other types. This was not only because Poland was somewhat of an agricultural country. All three oppressors of Poland—Russia, Germany, and Austria—had purposely neglected the economic development of Polish territories, and this also paralyzed the growth of vocational schools in Poland. After the First World War ended there followed throughout Europe a feverish trend toward the development of various vocational schools. In Poland this necessity was felt even more keenly than in many other countries, but it took time for the war wound to heal, for the demolished factories to be rebuilt and for new industries to be created, before graduates from the vocational schools could be employed. Therefore, it was only a few years prior to the present war that vocational schools in Poland began to train at full speed. The general rearmament in Europe also contributed to this quickened development of trade and industrial schools. In rough figures, in 1938–1939 in Poland the schools numbered 1,000, with some 100,000 students in attendance.

Vocational schools in Poland, like the standard secondary schools, were divided into gymnasiums and lyceums. There were also "junior" schools, with two-year and even one-year courses of study, belonging to the group of elementary schools. The vocational schools were mostly organized by local municipal authorities, by factories and, to a small extent, by private associations and industry. Some schools were maintained by the Government, but in most instances the contribution of the Government consisted in paying the salaries of teachers.

There were many types of vocational schools in Poland. The agricultural schools were established by a large majority of provinces, a few of them being sustained by the State, and they corresponded to the junior colleges in the United States. Numerous technical schools of different kinds were located throughout the country, some of them conducted by the management of industrial establishments. In these schools learning in a most effective way was combined with practical manufacturing or drawing exercises under the supervision of highly skilled technical personnel. Some of the numerous business schools were organized by professional associations of business men. Vocational schools especially for girls, which taught nursing, housekeeping, horticulture, hotel management, and art decoration were especially attended. The development of vocational schools was closely related with the progress made by Polish industry and by the modernization of cities. The following comparison with other countries may be of interest.

NUMBER OF PUPILS PER MILLION INHABITANTS

Country	1933–1934	1934–1935	1935–1936	1936–1937	1937–1938
Poland	1,989	2,118	2,364	2,656	3,021
France	.....	.....	1,838	.....	.....
England	805	.....	1,132	.....	.....
Germany	2,063*	.....	.....	.....	.....
Finland	4,998	.....	5,709	.....	.....
Estonia	5,241	5,933	.....	7,493	.....

* Since 1934 no statistical data have been available.

Continuation schools.—In Poland the continuation schools developed later than other types of schools. Two chief factors made it impossible to develop them in the early stage of Polish reconstruction—financial difficulties and lack of teaching personnel. The belief prevailed that under existing conditions the basic educational system, consisting of elementary schools, should be organized first.

This fact was especially regrettable because Poland needed this type of school probably much more specifically than any other country in Europe. If the chief purpose of continuation schools is to raise the general cultural level of the entire population, there was a special need for supplementary education in Poland. In fact, because of the policy of Russia, of Germany, and to some extent of Austria, there were many gaps in education to be filled. Both youths and adults needed supplementary schooling and training.

The law of 1937 which regulated the financial bases of the continuation schools promoted the realization of the idea that everybody who needs supplementary education should be able to get it. Uniformity for the entire country was achieved with the Government paying two-thirds the expenses for teaching personnel, and the municipalities bearing the remainder of the cost. Since this time urban continuation schools have developed rapidly, especially in large cities. In 1937–1938 there were 110,104 students in urban continuation schools. Because of the lack of teachers, most of these schools were held in the evening in order to use the teaching personnel of the standard public schools.

In rural communities the number of continuation schools was limited. Consequently the Minister of Education sent to every inspectorate a specialist in organizing extrascholastic education.

In order to assist those who required supplementary schooling, he organized popular lectures and provided for traveling or permanent libraries in the county. In addition, he promoted choral ensembles and meetings in order to propagate popular knowledge.

LANGUAGE OF INSTRUCTION IN THE SCHOOLS FOR POLISH MINORITIES
SCHOOL YEAR 1937–1938*

Language of instruction	Number of schools							
	Nursery schools	Primary		General education		Teacher training	Vocational	Higher education
		Total	Private	Gymnasium	Lyceum			
Total	1,659	28,723	1,488	769	691	74	764	28
Polish	1,524	24,047	720	671	604	72	733	28
Polish and Ruthenian-Ukrainian	....	3,064	4	2	2	..	..	..
Polish and German	5	203	4	..	..	..	1	..
Polish and Yiddish or Hebrew	20	226	226	38	34	..	5	..
Polish and other	4	56	2	1	1	..	..	..
Ruthenian-Ukrainian	16	461	41	24	21	1	5	..
White Ruthenian	....	...	...	1	1	..	..	..
German	49	394	234	15	13	..	6	..
Yiddish or Hebrew	40	226	226	12	10	1	14	..
Lithuanian	....	23	14	1	1	..	..	..
Czech	....	18	13	..	..	..	..	..
Russian	....	5	4	4	4	..	..	..
French	1	...	....	..	..	..	..	..

* See p. 138 of Year Book. See also Chapter X, "Minorities," by Joseph S. Roucek.

Radio was largely used to bring different educational and cultural activities to the whole country.

Minority schools.—There were two kinds of schools for children of other than Polish nationalities. Some of them were maintained by the Polish Government, the others by private sources. In order to furnish a more exact idea about the schools for minorities in Poland two tables are taken from the *Concise Statistical Year Book of Poland* (1941), published in English by the Polish Ministry of

Information. In both tables the terms "trade" and "academic schools" have been replaced by "vocational" and "schools of higher education."

University education.—Before the First World War, when Polish territories were ruled by three foreign empires, only the Austrian

LANGUAGE OF INSTRUCTION IN THE SCHOOLS FOR POLISH MINORITIES
SCHOOL YEAR 1937–1938*
(Number of students in thousands)

Language of instruction	Schools							
	Nursery schools	Primary		General education		Teacher training	Voca- tional	Higher educa- tion
		Total	Private	Gym- nasium	Lyceum			
Total	83.3	4851.5	150.3	181.3	40.1	4.8	106.4	48.0
Polish	79.0	4174.5	61.7	163.3	36.2	4.6	103.0	48.0
Polish and Ruthenian-Ukrainian	....	473.4	0.6	0.9	0.3	....	....	....
Polish and German	0.2	36.5	0.1	....	....	....	0.1	....
Polish and Yiddish or Hebrew	0.8	28.5	28.5	6.8	1.5	....	0.6	....
Polish and other	0.1	4.5	0.2	0.1	....	....	....	....
Ruthenian-Ukrainian	0.5	58.8	6.4	4.7	1.0	0.1	....	....
White Ruthenian	....	....	....	0.2	....	....	....	....
German	1.6	36.3	15.1	2.5	0.4	....	0.3	....
Yiddish or Hebrew	1.1	36.4	36.4	2.2	0.4	0.1	1.8	....
Lithuanian	....	1.1	0.4	0.2	0.1	....	....	....
Czech	....	0.9	0.6	....	....	....	....	....
Russian	....	0.6	0.3	0.4	0.2	....	....	....

* Year Book, p. 139.

Government permitted universities to give instruction in the Polish language. Those schools were the University of Cracow, one of the oldest universities in Europe whose history started as far back as the fourteenth century, the University of Lwów, and finally the Institute of Technology of Lwów. Besides these, there were only two more schools of higher learning in Polish territories: the University of Warsaw and the Institute of Technology, also in Warsaw.

But these were Russian institutions, boycotted by the Poles. When Poland regained its independence in 1918 this was the system of higher education.

In independent Poland the first step in the field of university education was the Polonization of both the University of Warsaw and the Institute of Technology.[1] Shortly afterward two new state universities were established, one in Poznań and another in Wilno; the latter university which was a resurrection of an ancient Polish university of 1579, was closed by the Russians in 1831. In addition, certain professional schools of higher education were established: Academy of Mines at Cracow, Principal School of Rural Economy at Warsaw, Academy of Veterinary Medicine at Lwów, Stomatological Academy at Warsaw, Central Institute of Physical Education at Warsaw, and the academies of fine arts at Warsaw and Cracow. All these were state schools. In addition, the following private schools of higher education were founded: the Catholic University at Lublin, the Free University at Warsaw, the Principal School of Commerce at Warsaw, at Poznań, and at Cracow, and the Higher School of Foreign Trade at Lwów. A thousand professors taught approximately fifty thousand students in all these schools. According to S. K. Turosienski's *Poland's Institutions of Higher Education,* in 1933–1934 there were 55,980 students, and according to the *Concise Statistical Year Book of Poland* (1941), there were 48,000 students in 1937–1938.

At the start of Polish independence, in 1918, it was difficult to find an adequate number of university professors. They were found chiefly in the two old universities at Cracow and Lwów. Later, however, the return to Poland of many men of learning among the Poles who before the war had taught in Russia, Switzerland, Austria, and even in Germany tended to overcome the lack of teaching personnel. Some years later the home "production" of young men of learning began and was continuously maintained by the policy of sending thirty to forty capable young men abroad to complete their studies and to examine certain new laboratory techniques, new methods of investigation, or to broaden their horizon of thoughts and ideas. The Piłsudski Foundation for National Culture helped these students financially. The results were satisfactory.

[1] They became Polish schools in 1916, when Poland was under military occupation by Germany and Austria.

The average level of professional education was the same as that in other countries and in some branches was even higher than the average European level.

In Poland, as in other European countries, the enrollment of students was large immediately after the war; then, because of the economic crisis and financial depression, the number was slightly decreased. The following statistical data give some idea as to the numbers of university students per million population in Poland and in several typical countries. In 1936–1937 there were 1,409 students per million inhabitants in Poland, 1,903 in Germany, and 1,383 in Great Britain; in 1935–1936 there were 1,975 in Sweden, and 3,817 in Latvia.

In many European countries there were discussions of the problem of restricting the enrollment of university students in order to avoid an overproduction of professionally trained people and a consequent dangerous increase of unemployed intellectuals. Germany and Italy limited the number of students; numerous other countries maintained a liberal policy and did not introduce a restriction. In Poland opinion favored permitting people to continue freely with their studies. It was assumed that, if some were unemployed, they would be forced to take the initiative in order to create new enterprises and therefore, indirectly to develop the economic life of the country. Poland was convinced that an increase in the number of university graduates was in reality a gain for the country. Therefore, if certain restrictions in enrollment did occur, they were brought about by a lack of space in laboratories or in similar school facilities.

Another problem was the sociological structure of the "white-collar" group. In fact, the majority of university graduates was from the cities. The group of state, municipal, and private employees furnished the highest percentage of university students. Not more than 30 per cent of the university students were children or grandchildren of peasants, and most of these not only had been born in the cities, but constituted the second generation living in cities. There still was a small percentage of those who came directly from the country. In the last prewar period this group of students had increased but not rapidly enough. Inasmuch as some 650,000 students graduated annually from primary schools, and 6,300 from the universities, only one out of one hundred had an opportunity to complete the full sixteen- to seventeen-year course of education. Similar phenomena existed in the prewar period in many other European countries. It is obvious that this problem must be solved in a more radical manner in the near future.

The average level of university graduates was relatively high when compared with that of other countries. In some fields of professional training, as a result of specialized curricula, it was very high. In general, the young generation of professionally trained specialists was adequately prepared to serve their country and to develop not only Polish culture but also to promote the industrial and economic life. Hundreds and thousands of these youths died on the battlefield, in concentration camps, and in Siberia. The survivors have the tremendous task of regaining all that has been lost in this most cruel and barbarous war.

Ideological and political trends in teacher and student organizations.—In the description of the educational system and the statistical data given in previous paragraphs nothing has been said concerning teacher and student organizations participating in political activities. The four teachers associations in Poland were the Professional Teachers Association, which was the largest and most powerful, the Christian Teachers Association composed also of a large majority of the elementary-school teachers, the Association of High School and Lyceum Professors, and the Association of University Professors. The three latter associations were inspired by a political ideology which can be compared, to some extent, with the ideology of the American Republican party.

Generally speaking, European associations of teachers and university students are much more politically active than those in America. From time to time controversies developed between the Government and the teachers associations. For instance, both the university professors and the high-school and lyceum teachers were against the governmental proposal of the school reform of 1932 and also the university regulations. The greatest controversy, however, took place in 1938 when the Polish Government suspended the activities of the largest of the professional associations of teachers. This step was motivated by the strong radicalism that prevailed among the leaders of the association. Several months passed before the controversy was settled and normal activities were resumed.

The largest university student association, the Student Brotherhood (*Bratnia Pomoc*), was under the powerful influence of several hundred ultranationalists who were very active in politics. This movement was a direct result of the ideological influence of the ultranationalistic tendencies prevailing at that time in many European countries, especially in Germany and Italy.

The strong and cruel anti-Jewish policy in Nazi Germany created among a part of the Polish youth the belief that the so-called Jewish problem could easily be solved in Poland. As a result of this conviction anti-Semitism spread among university students. There were riots in several of the largest universities where the gentile students demanded that they be separated from the Jewish students. In order to solve this difficult psychological and juridical problem, the university presidents (rectors) were authorized by the Minister of Education to make regulations designing special benches for those gentile students who did not want to sit with the Jewish students. All other benches were designated for those who did not want to be separated from the Jews. The student unrest was accompanied by acts of violence in which three Jewish students and one Pole died of wounds. This is an example of what can happen if youth is submitted to the influence of ultranationalism when dominated by a small number of very active leaders. What has happened in Germany and Italy is the result of a long-lasting campaign of ultranationalistic propaganda which had been spread throughout the country by the systematic activities of the dictatorial governments themselves.

All was changed, however, with the invasion of Poland first by Germany and then by Russia. Thousands of students died on the battlefield or in Warsaw while defending their country. Then began the underground battle for the liberation of Poland. Many participants of the underground have given all possible assistance to the Jews who have been isolated in the ghettos.

Those Polish youths who were interned in Rumania or Hungary found miraculous ways in which to escape from the camps in their attempt to reach France. In France no Pole fled from the battlefield, no Pole surrendered. The majority of youths who reached

France, however, crossed the channel and joined the Polish army, navy, or air force now organized once more in Great Britain. A few weeks later they showed how the Polish youth could fight.

After the collapse of France still others left, many months later. In spite of incredible difficulties they succeeded in crossing the Russo-German military zone, traveled thousands of miles through Soviet Russia and joined the British army in India. One of these boys wrote to a friend in the United States, saying that half his way to the Polish army was then behind him. These young men have shown that they are to be found wherever the fight for freedom and for the liberation of Poland is being waged.

CHAPTER XVIII

Science and Scientific Institutions

BY WOJCIECH ŚWIĘTOSŁAWSKI

BEFORE THE OUTBREAK of the war in 1939 some European countries were large enough to support an adequate number of universities and professors in order to participate in the development of all or nearly all branches of human knowledge; other countries were too small in population to organize all faculties and departments. In the latter countries a percentage of the youth had to go abroad for specialized studies. Poland belongs to the first group of nations, inasmuch as it was the home of some one thousand professors who represented all specialties in pure and applied sciences and certain specialties in other sources of human knowledge. Poland was one of the first countries in the world where studies were made to determine the number of men of learning required to provide, to some extent, an adequate number of specialists.[1]

In the early period after the rebirth of Poland, conventions were organized and papers were published on the subject of how many men of learning were required for a normal development of the culture of the nation. It was found that there existed practically a constant relation between the number of specialists graduated from universities and the number of men of learning. Of one hundred university graduates, five are men of learning. Twenty to forty per cent of them devote their entire lifetime to creative work and scientific investigation. The remaining group contributes to the development of knowledge for a limited period of time and then is replaced by a younger generation. It was found that some kind of equilib-

[1] *Nauka Polska,* Warsaw (1937), *Przegląd Akademicki* 157 (1932), *Nauka Polska* 8, 6 (1927).

rium should exist between the number of specialists working in the field of pure science and the number contributing to the development of applied science.

According to university regulations in Poland it was the duty of the departments and of the professors themselves to be responsible for the continuity of the scientific activities of each chair by preparing young people for academic careers. The special Foundation of National Culture was created by Marshal Józef Piłsudski to give all assistance possible to the development of Polish culture and fine arts. A journal, *Polish Science* (*Nauka Polska*), was published in which were examined all problems relating to the development of human knowledge and sciences in Poland. As a result, the program could be elaborated for many years ahead, establishing the number of young men and women who should be prepared for the continuation of creative work in all branches of human knowledge. A survey was made to show the lack of specialists in some branches of pure and applied sciences.

In spite of certain criticism directed against the functioning of Piłsudski's National Foundation, the system worked quite well and, in 1939, Poland had a relatively large number of young people adequately prepared to replace retiring professors or other men of learning. The rate of death or retirement of professors was twenty-eight to thirty-two persons a year. Because of the abnormal conditions which existed in 1919 there was a lack of middle-aged men of learning and the percentage of older highly qualified specialists was abnormally high. It was believed that within five to ten years a normal balance between old, middle-aged, and young people would be established in the group of men of learning.

It is certain that similar problems will reappear after this war and that Poland again will need to exert every possible effort to find young people to replace the highly qualified scholars who died either in German concentration camps or in the camps in Siberia to which they had been sent by the Russians for hard physical labor.

When summarizing the activities of the scholars in Poland, the following figures may be given. The total number of scholars was about 6,000; the number of papers published yearly in the last period before the outbreak of the war was approximately 3,300—actually 3,292 in 1936. When expressed in relative numbers with respect to one million inhabitants, the figures are: the number of graduates annually—180; university students—1,430; university graduates employed in the country—3,571; men of learning—178. The absolute figures may be obtained by multiplying the given figures by 35, which corresponds to the number of millions of inhabitants in Poland. From these data it appears that the productivity of a man of learning, who is in charge of the research work of younger men, is two papers annually.

Among Polish scholars it was the custom to publish papers that summarized the research work continuing over a period of years. The readers preferred articles containing the results of a series of investigations rather than a description of a single new observation, a new apparatus, or a new method. This attitude of Polish scholars was unfavorable when compared with that of the scholars of other countries. In fact, the international abstracts which furnish a summary of the results published in a paper do not give more space to the description of a large and extensive work than to one less extensive. As a result, the reader of an abstract does not have any idea of the new results given in the longer paper.

The role of a man of learning consists not only in doing research work and publishing monographs and papers, or in teaching in universities, but also in giving all possible assistance to the country or the community that needs his help. Men of learning constitute a certain social group which, as an entity, should be concerned with the progress of human knowledge and the culture of the nation. It is among the duties of a scholar to furnish exhaustive information on the state of contemporary knowledge and to express an opinion on the basis of professional knowledge. The scholar, who recognizes his duties, should see that the nation has adequate publications dealing with his specialty by presenting the achievements, statistical data, and other useful information of this kind.

In order to assure to the nation a fulfillment of this need, many efforts have been made to promote close collaboration between the state authorities and the communities. The National Research Council was created for the purpose of offering the assistance of experts. Numerous advisory committees, such as those for synthetic rubber, defense problems, highway construction, railroad exploitation, and many others were organized.

In spite of the fact that a series of research institutes was created in which the full time of the men was devoted to research work, the universities, the institutes of technology, and the other schools of higher education remained as the chief centers of the development of knowledge. It often happened that professors on active duty, or in retirement, became directors of research institutes. This was characteristic not only of Poland, but also of many other countries. It can be explained by the fact that university teachers are skilled in conducting the research work of young men, and that they are in a position to select among the graduate students the best possible candidates for collaborators in the research institutes.

Other factors favored the development of science and knowledge in the schools of higher education. In accordance with official regulations, university professors in Poland were charged with the duty not only of teaching but also of conducting their own research work. In addition to these duties, professors often edited scientific publications, presided over scientific societies, participated on special committees and advised, as experts, on many questions associated with their specialty.

The efforts made by the men of learning will not be forgotten in the history of the development of Polish independence. Even greater efforts will have to be made after the present war is over. The Polish nation is facing a cultural catastrophe never experienced before in the darkest days of Poland's history. It is now more evident than ever how effective the scholars were in the period from 1919 to 1939. Overburdened with teaching, social activities, and advisory work, they nevertheless found time for their own research, and succeeded in preparing hundreds of young men and women who now are the only hope of the Polish people in the period of postwar independence.

The research institutes did their best to develop pure and applied science. The feeling remains, however, that they could not have been so effective without the help of the university professors. The universities and other schools of higher education still were the chief centers of maturing cultural strength, because they were filled, almost beyond capacity, with young men and women who were learning how to be useful to the nation as creative intellectual forces.

In 1917 numerous Polish scholars were outside the limits of the newly created Republic of Poland. In regions ruled by Russia and Germany there were no Polish universities. The few existing Polish societies of scholars made every endeavor to keep alive the culture of the nation in spite of the absence of schools of higher education—the natural centers of classical, humanistic, and scientific activities. Thus, the only existing Polish Academy of Arts and Sciences in Cracow, founded in 1873, was recognized by the nation as the highest authority on matters affecting knowledge, and protecting the development of Polish culture. For this reason Polish scholars who had scattered throughout the world usually forwarded to the Polish Academy of Arts and Sciences their papers, monographs, and other documents of importance for the cultural development of the nation.

The Polish people held in high esteem the Academy of Arts and Sciences, the highest seat of knowledge, which was associated with two other institutions—the famous Jagiellonian University and Jagiellonian Library, both symbolic of Polish culture and spiritual tradition. For that reason, since its founding and throughout the period between the two world wars, the Academy was the beneficiary of many liberal bequests and gifts, in the form of lands and forests, as well as of buildings, funds, and valuable securities. The holdings increased steadily as the years passed and the institution itself became independent and was able to extend its arm of protection and financial assistance to numerous men of learning who were engaged in creative work, particularly in those subjects associated with historical research, Polish literature, language, and even music and the fine arts. Also, there were numerous legacies and bequests earmarked for the benefit of young students who were beginning their academic careers.

In reborn Poland, the Academy was the subject of a legislative act and was given the privilege of representing Poland abroad at international unions, congresses, research councils, and at other conventions. It developed later that this recognition was of great importance. Often, different cabinet ministers received invitations to attend congresses convened for special scientific, as well as utilitarian purposes. In these instances the government officials wished to organize their own delegations. An understanding between them and the Academy was always reached, with the result that the delegation was headed by the appointee of the Academy of Arts and Sciences. According to the same legislative act, the Government paid into the treasury of the Academy sums of money designated as Poland's contribution to various international unions and to other scientific organizations.

It is impossible to describe in a short sketch the activities of the Polish Academy of Arts and Sciences. Numerous publications were issued, not in terms of material profits, but as priceless contributions toward Polish national culture. Monographs, encyclopedias, bibliographies, textbooks for use in universities, treatises on important geological and archaeological excavations, together with numerous other contributions constituted that essential work which made the Polish Academy famous at home and abroad. In addition, the Academy maintained its normal activities by publishing in Polish and in foreign languages current papers and articles presented by the members or by any other scholar to one of the sections of the Academy. Posthumous works of famous Polish scholars also were edited, as, for instance, the work of the eminent Polish physicist, Marjan Smoluchowski.

Independently of the Polish Academy of Arts and Sciences there existed other academic societies. For years they played an important role in the struggle against the anti-Polish policy of Germany and Russia. Such societies existed at Warsaw, Poznań, Wilno, Torum, and Lwów. After the rebirth of Poland two of them, one at Warsaw and the other at Lwów, changed in character and in structure, became similar to the Academy of Arts and Sciences at Cracow. Thus the membership became restricted in each of their sections and the members could be elected only after their activities as scholars were examined thoroughly.

The existence of academic societies in different Polish cultural centers did not change the policy of the Academy of Arts and Sciences of electing all eminent scholars independently of where they lived and worked. It frequently happened that a member of the Academy of Arts and Sciences was a member of one or two other academic societies at the same time. Before 1918, however, there was no institution similar to the Academy of Arts and Sciences whose activity was devoted to the development of applied sciences.

This need, therefore, was met after the rebirth of Poland by the founding of the Warsaw Academy of Technical Sciences.

For a number of years the Academy of Technical Sciences functioned on the basis of a temporary charter. Only a short time before the outbreak of the war in 1939 the legislative authority, at the insistence of the Government, granted a charter investing this institution with certain rights, privileges, and financial support. This Academy published the journal *Mémoires de l'Académie des Sciences Techniques,* as well as monographs in Polish and in foreign languages. Among its notable services the publishing of a Polish dictionary of pure and applied sciences was very important. Each word in this dictionary contained the definition given in the Polish language and its translation in English, French, German, and Russian. Several volumes of such vocabularies covering different branches of pure and applied sciences were published, and practically all the chief branches of pure science and engineering, of technology, architecture, etc., were in course of preparation.

When discussing the activities of Polish academic organizations one fact must be mentioned which at first caused friction among Polish scholars, but in time became a reconciling and coördinating factor. Some scholars living in Warsaw were under the misapprehension that there should be created in the nation's capital another academy of arts and sciences. It was proposed to consolidate the Warsaw Society of Scholars and the Academy of Technical Sciences into one body—the Warsaw Academy of Arts and Sciences. Although preliminary steps were undertaken, the proposal was voted down because it was thought that the establishment of a new national academy would create a certain discord among the scholars whose duty it was to guard the spiritual unity of the nation.

The repercussions of this decision in the years which followed were beneficial. It became necessary to coördinate the efforts of all scholars and their associations. A committee was formed from among representatives of the various academic organizations. Moreover, there was established a council similar to the National Research Council in the United States.

To understand how Poland in so short a time could organize numerous schools of higher education, how it could organize its centers of development of pure and applied sciences, or how it could create a series of new industries unknown in partitioned Poland, it is necessary to know the historical background of the development of Polish science. With this background, it also can be understood how Poland could build a new well-organized port, Gdynia, in a period of several years. This port became one of the largest ports on the Baltic Sea. Knowing the history of Poland, one can understand how, in a very short period of time, the nation could raise considerably the standard of living in many cities, or increase crops, or improve the architecture in the towns and cities.

First of all, it should be stressed that there was no paucity of intellectual life when Poland was reborn. Hundreds of intellectuals, sometimes highly specialized inventors, scientists, and skilled engineers, were living in Russia, Austria, Germany, Switzerland, and far beyond Europe. Numerous Poles had become professors in Switzerland, Austria, and even in Russia and Germany. There were thousands of engineers and industrialists in many European countries. Some of them crossed the ocean and became well known as specialists in North and South America. In Poland itself, there is a long story of the development of Polish science and culture, starting from Copernicus, whose work in astronomy is considered by all as the turning point in the history of pure and natural sciences. Two eminent scholars, J. and V. Sniadeckis, contributed much to the development of natural sciences in Wilno as well as in other cities; K. Olszewski and Z. Wroblewski experimented with liquified air, nitrogen, and oxygen for the first time in 1883 and thus created a new branch of human knowledge—low-temperature technique. Warsaw was the city in which Mme Curie's scientific genius matured, in which I. Mościcki, in the period from 1905 to 1912, demonstrated the application of high voltage current in chemical plants and the building of electrical condensers which could resist high tension. G. Narutowicz was an eminent hydraulic engineer who was recognized in Switzerland as an outstanding specialist in hydraulic technique. Several branches of industry developed in Russia in the period from 1880 to 1917 under Polish engineers and industrialists. Metallurgy, the manufacturing of engines, tools, and agricultural machines, as well as the sugar industry, developed in Russia in part because the Poles had to leave their country and find outlet for their abilities elsewhere.

All these facts are of great importance to an understanding of how Poland could develop its industry and its centers of higher technical education in the first years of its independence. In the second decade there were numerous young specialists already prepared to continue the work started by the older generation. Now thousands of these young men have died on the battlefield, in concentration camps, or before German firing squads. When this war is over, Poland will have to face the enormous task of preparing a new generation of specialists in a very short time to replace those who have lost their lives in this greatest tragedy of the nation.

It is not the purpose of this chapter to give the names of all the outstanding Polish scholars and scientists who contributed to the development of science in the period of the last two decades. The list is given below of the most outstanding Polish scholars who not only devoted themselves to the creation of a new and better Poland, but who gave also their lives in the defense of their country and its culture.

MEMBERS OF THE POLISH ACADEMY OF ARTS AND SCIENCES

Władysław Abraham, died in Lwów during the Russian occupation
Ignacy Chrzanowski, died in the concentration camp in Oranienburg, Germany
Ludwik Cwikliński, died during the German occupation
Bronisław Dembiński, died during the German occupation
Stanisław Estreicher, died in the concentration camp in Oranienburg
Tadeusz Grabowski, died in the concentration camp in Oranienburg
Kazimierz Kostanecki, former president of the Polish Academy of Arts and Sciences, died in the concentration camp in Oranienburg
Stefan Kreutz, died during the German occupation
Józef Morawski, died in the concentration camp in Oswiecim
Jan Nowak, died after his return from the concentration camp in Oranienburg
Józef Trzebiński, died during the German occupation
Zygmunt Woycicki, died during the German occupation

MEMBERS OF THE ACADEMY OF TECHNICAL SCIENCES

Kazimierz Bartel, former Prime Minister of the Polish Government, Minister of Education, Minister of Communication, killed by German firing squad at Lwów
Wiesław Chrzanowski, former Minister of Industry and Commerce, died during the German occupation
Andrzej Pszenicki, died during the German occupation
Stanisław Pilat, former Director of the State Petroleum Refinery at Drohobycz, killed by German firing squad at Lwów

FORMER MEMBERS OF THE POLISH GOVERNMENT

Bolesław Miklaszewski, former Minister of Education, died during the German occupation

Antoni Sujkowski, former Minister of Education, died during the German occupation

In addition to this list, the names of sixty-five other Polish scholars have been furnished by the Polish Institute of Arts and Sciences.[2] The latter list cannot be considered as complete because there still are numerous scholars who are listed as missing or who have died under "unknown circumstances."

Great effort should be made in the future to rebuild and to replace all these men of learning, these scientists and inventors who were vitally useful in the building of Polish culture and in the developing of Polish knowledge in the two decades of Polish independence.

[2] *Bulletin of the Polish Institute of Arts and Sciences in America,* 1, 159–165 (1942).

CHAPTER XIX

Polish Literature

BY MANFRED KRIDL

As is true of any period of a nation's literature, that in Poland between 1919 and 1939 was not distinguished by uniformity of character. In addition to new tendencies, old trends manifested themselves for brief or for prolonged periods. At times the new and old trends intersected, conflicting with each other more or less intensely; at other times they influenced each other. Young authors were not infrequently the spiritual successors to older colleagues, whereas the latter, consciously or unconsciously, succumbed to the influence of the rising generation. Among the new groups, or schools, as well, there was not only friction, but also a mutual influence. Accordingly, when the period of the Republic was reviewed in its totality, it was not found to be revolutionary in character, although it did have a literary complexion of its own and it did enrich Polish literature by a sizable number of new values. The very fact that in speaking of the span of years between 1919 and 1939, one may designate it as a definite period of literature, and not just a continuation of the prewar literature, has a peculiar significance. This meaning will be still further enhanced if one realizes that the period from 1919 to 1939 followed immediately upon the era of "Young Poland," at the close of the nineteenth century, which had abounded in literary talents of the first magnitude. Thus, the young literary generation did not find it easy to strike its own note or to produce a gallery of new and outstanding writers.

Poetry.—It is a characteristic phenomenon that as early as the first few years of the Republic there was an unusually abundant crop of lyric poets. Lyricism dominated the literary production of almost the entire decade, took by storm the general public—until then not overly partial to the reading of poetry—and was represented by a number of outstanding poetical talents. In the front rank the style was set by a group of poets called "Scamander," an appellation derived from the title of a poetical monthly published by the group. In order to understand the relationship of this group to poetry in general, one must consider the fact that during the enslavement of Poland from the end of the eighteenth century to the time of the Republic Polish poetry, as well as fiction and drama, voluntarily took upon itself the task of serving the nation's interests and of keeping alive the flame of national spirit which was in danger of being quenched by the policy of extermination of the three Partitioning Powers—Russia, Prussia, and Austria.

Inasmuch as there was no Polish state, no normal political or community life, no division of social functions among ordinarily existing institutions, the poets and writers became the chief spiritual leaders of the nation. They gave moral succor, advice, counsel, direction, warning. The greatness of their works was measured by the standard of these elements. The poets and the writers not only accepted the nation's claim upon their creative powers, but also considered such service the loftiest possible vocation. Although the artistic value of the works of the really great poets was not diminished thereby, the international scope of those works perforce became narrowed, and the creative freedom of the poets labored under limitations. The lesser poets frequently fell prey to the illusion that merely to deal with national issues and act as prophets and moralists was sufficient to secure for them a niche in literature's hall of fame.

By and large, such encroachment by the public upon the field of art could not possibly be viewed as a normal phenomenon. This the young poets of the Scamander group perceived and understood. Their literary debuts and slogans were bred of freedom to create without restrictions imposed from above. When Poland had regained its independence, and the direction of its public affairs had passed into hands which normally would have been called upon to control it, these young poets realized that their first task was to create as good poetry as possible. "We wish to be the poets of today. This is our credo and our program in its entirety. We do not care for high-sounding words [meaning lofty slogans or programs]. What we want is great poetry. Then each of our words shall become important." Such was the point of view as set forth in the Scamander group. One of the young poets, Lechoń, expressed similar sentiment in a somewhat more poignant manner: "Now the spring has come over the world, let me look at the spring and not at Poland."

This, to be certain, did not mean severance from the realities of life, nor an ensconcing of oneself in the proverbial ivory tower. The members of the Scamander group wanted to be, and in fact were, the poets of today, the poets of contemporary life. All they wanted was to rid themselves of fetters which in Poland had been traditional and had impeded creative freedom. They wanted to "see the spring," but not a spring obscured by any veil of duty imposed from above. They were simply reverting to a normal poetical outlook on the world. They felt and understood the age-old problems of poetry as well as the problems of contemporary life; but they wanted to present those problems in a manner appropriate to the art of poetry and not to moral philosophy.

With the relationship to the task of poetry so changed or, rather, with a reversion to the normal tasks of poetry, went the modernization of the media of poetic expression. The themes of poetry changed accordingly. Instead of themes drawn from nature and from country life, prevalent in older Polish poetry of both the romantic school and the commonly called "Young Poland" group, a new element came to the fore, not exclusively, to be sure, but to a considerable degree—the urban theme drawn from the landscape or from a large modern city, its life, its population, its beauty, but also its ugliness and its squalor. That urban element gave to the poetry produced by the Scamander group a distinct and specific brand, and linked to it the battle cries of Italian futurism and the "revolutionary" poetry of Russia.

A change in the language used by the young poets also came about. To say that the language became more realistic falls short of adequately explaining the change. What really happened was that the language used by the Scamanders—their similies and metaphors—was gradually enriched by urban elements, the vernacular of the intellectual class and of plain city folk. A number of words and phrases hitherto unused began to appear in Polish poetry. Because of this new usage, the metaphors coined by the young poets operated with new juxtapositions, became more daring, more poignant, unusual and startling. It would, however, be erroneous to deduct that the language had become prosaic or vulgar. It remained poetical to a very high degree, not merely serving to describe some phenomenon, but in itself possessing artistic value. Ordinary, commonplace words gain poetic power through their proper use in proximity to other words, by appropriate accentuation and rhythm.

Versification underwent changes as well. Metrical compositions grew more complicated but, at the same time, became freer, without sacrificing rhythm or becoming a sort of "poetic prose" devoid of distinct metric composition. Traditional syllabic verse also is to be found frequently. Accordingly, there was no revolution in this field, although there was a great variety of forms, and there were interesting although not-too-daring experiments. In the fields of stanzaic structure and rhythm, this same conservatism existed. The stanza—either the traditional, or the modernized which was cast in a rigid frame, or the free stanza which was uneven but was a stanza, nevertheless—in the main was preserved. In a study of rhyming, however, all the acquisitions of more recent poetry are met, such as complicated, unusual, and unexpected end rhymes and assonances of varying degrees of harmonizing vowels with consonants. However, traditionally easy and simple rhyming frequently may be found in the works of even outstanding poets. These few general traits may be said to be somewhat characteristic of the leading poets of the Scamander group. Aside from such traits, however, the individualities of the poets are greatly divergent.

Juljan Tuwim (born 1894) forged to the front rank of the Scamander group rather early. His works are distinguished by an unusual eruptive force of lyricism. The emotional tension of this force is such that almost every one of Tuwim's verses is like the bursting of a volcano, in a series of sudden explosions, out of which cascade metaphors, visions, poetic phrases, abbreviations of thinking emotional processes, symbols of racial thoughts and acts, drawn from commonplace and quasi-casual occurrences, wholly unexpected juxtapositions and combinations, all of which seem to reek with freshly spilled blood. Significantly, one of the most outstanding collections of Tuwim's poems bears the caption, "Słowa we krwi" ("words bathed in blood, dripping blood"). To Tuwim the word "blood" is an element, a metaphysical symbol which has become flesh, on which he lives as on meat, which he drinks as though it were cool water, which he breathes as though it were pure air. "I have no occupation. I am a catcher of words," he said in his poem, "Word and Flesh," "my speech is my blood, the core of the earth."

It must be added that Tuwim's keen feeling and mastery of the Polish tongue is coupled with a probing study of the language in its old-Polish form, including its Slavic roots. Tuwim himself once admitted that his favorite volume was Alexander Brueckner's *Etymological Dictionary of the Polish Language*. His erudition and his philological sense enabled him to take full advantage of the treasure-trove of the language as an expert, yet with an artist's moderation.

The characteristic tendency of poets to make all phenomena unique and startling, in Tuwim attains so high a degree of the explicit that his work at times actually assumes the form of an eerie phantasmagoria. But he is capable, also, of striking tones so simple as to be almost hackneyed yet imparting to them a new sound and a new meaning. "A nightingale, a garden and trees mean a great deal in my speech," says Tuwim, referring to certain elementary, enduring poetic themes. There is none of the romantic in him, nor of the young Polish nebulosity, breeziness, or, so to speak, moodiness. On the contrary, his use of metaphors is explicit, poignant, at times stinging to the point of harshness, without the "modernistic" tendency to rhythmic deformation, far-split rhyming, oddities, or artificial linguistic neologisms.

The lyric poetry of Antoni Słonimski (born 1895), the next in importance in the Scamander group, is considerably less eruptive than Tuwim's, and his versification is less "melodious." Instead, it is characterized by a tendency toward concentration, self-possession, toward operating with "intellectual," discursive, and rhetorical elements. Słonimski does not hesitate to use Communism or the importance of science in setting up a new and better world. Now and then, however, there comes to the fore the temperament which made him a columnist and author of brilliant articles published for years by the Warsaw *Literary News*—articles bearing the imprint of forthright courage, of daring in the discussion of delicate issues, of exquisite wit, of biting sarcasm. It would be wrong, however, to assume that his poetry was of a journalistic or propagandizing nature. On the contrary, he treats the various problems poetically and with pathos. Not only these elements, but others also of Słonimski's poetry are permeated with pathos, mystery, and tragedy. Too, there may be noticed an undercurrent of loneliness. From behind the trend toward self-possession there emerges time after time a suffering, sorrowful, lonely "lyrical ego," which continually quivers under the blows dealt by the world. But it is the ego not of a warrior, but rather of a martyr who, however, possesses enough strength to thunder, to hurl flashes of lightning, to challenge the world, to alarm his fellow men.

Among the poets of the Scamander group, Słonimski perhaps shows the most pronounced tendency toward breaking down some of the old-established poetical canons. Especially is this true in the composition of lyrical poems. Freedom in composition not infrequently leads to the loss of structural uniformity, to an obliteration of lines, particularly in longer poems. Słonimski's language, however, has a force, a weight, an expressiveness, and frequently a simplicity, like that of Mickiewicz, whom he reveres and holds to be the "world's greatest poet." In the field of versification (metrical and stanzaic composition) Słonimski experiments with forms both simple and conventional, involved and complicated. In experimenting with complicated forms, he emerges in most instances as a perfect master. In the field of rhyming, however, he does not display a commensurate degree of inventiveness.

The youngest of the group, Jan Lechoń (born 1899) who, at the early age of nineteen recited his poems at public literary reunions, is the least prolific. Thus far he has published only a few small collections of poems. In the beginning, as is known from his previously quoted words, he took an attitude of sharp opposition to "national duty" when applied to the art of poetry, and demanded a break with the past. Gradually, however, he reverted to that very past and to a simple, traditional patriotism. He used to dedicate his works to historical and contemporary personages, for instance, to Piłsudski; he also wrote about Norwid, a Polish poet, about Byron, Conrad, Proust, Mann. Such historical and literary themes give to Lechoń's poetry a more intellectual character than is found in the discursive works of Słonimski. But even when he turned from the fields of literature and history and probed the age-old problems of love and death, of flesh and soul, Lechoń did not divest himself of a specific "academism" in expressing his almost absolute pessimism. In every thematic field, however, he is capable of attaining a high level of poetic crystallization which, to quote Coleridge, consists of using "the best words in the best order," and in formulating by means of these words the given problem in a clear-cut, crystal-like shape. Each and every element of his verse is thoroughly thought over and worked out with an etcher's precision. Among the poets of the Scamander group, Lechoń is the most "classical" so far as his vocabulary and his traditional versification are concerned. The essence of his creativeness shows more clearly in his traditionalism than in the characteristics of his specific "literary program."

Kazimierz Wierzyński (born 1894), though older in point of years than Słonimski and Lechoń, in spirit is unquestionably the youngest of the entire group. His first works, "Springtime and Wine," and "Sparrows on the Roof," especially showed a joy of living, an almost childlike carelessness and happiness at being alive, and an intoxication with the world as had not been evidenced in Polish literature for some time. Almost every line of his poems breathes and overflows with this eagerness, and one finds time and again such phrases as, "How happy I am, I could not possibly say"; or, "How well I feel, how refreshed, how joyful, how light"; "Its green in my head and violets bloom therein"; "I flirt with the entire world and smile at the sky."

It required no mean degree of artistry to play on that single chord different and ever new melodies without becoming monotonous. The one tone, however, could not last forever. Wierzyński was forced to turn to other problems. At first he touched kindred chords, for instance in "Love's Diary," and "Olympic Laurel." The latter collection is a paean, unique of its kind, to the healthy and athletic human body, a hymn in honor of athletes, football players, high jumpers, runners. Wierzyński's talent gives to these pursuits both importance and dignity and, what is more, a certain metaphysical interpretation. The translation of "Olympic Laurel" into German must have preserved some of the original pathos and the fervid ideology of "sport for sport's sake," inasmuch as Wierzyński was awarded the first international prize at the Ninth Olympic Games at Amsterdam in 1928.

Later, Wierzyński turned to other problems. He touched on the metaphysical in "Discourse with the Wilderness"; on social questions in an entire collection of poems under the title of *Fanatical Songs*. Political and national themes prompted the poem, "Tragic Liberty." Although Wierzyński produced at times interesting poems in the problem fields, his specific style is to be found in his earlier creations which displayed a pronounced eagerness for life.

Somewhat more loosely affiliated with the trend exemplified by the Scamander group is Kazimiera Iłłakowicz (born 1892), a woman poet both prolific and erratic. In the wealth of her imagination and her leaning toward the fantastic she resembles Tuwim, but her sense of the fantastic is principally with spirits, ghosts, and witches. Characteristic of her work is an entire cycle of poems, *The Death of the Phoenix,* devoted to weird adventures with a lion which the author is supposed to have kept in her home as a pet and with which she took walks through the streets of her town. In another collection of her works, *Prophetic Images of Names,* are imaginary, phantasmagorical pen portraits of sundry psychological types, composed on foundations so frail as the mere sound of a given name.

Often, however, Miss Iłłakowicz can speak in a vein quite different, without in any way surrendering her preference for making normal phenomena unusual. She does so without roguishness or exaggeration and produces accordingly very powerful effects. Poems of this kind may be found scattered throughout her collections—including the cycle about the lion—whether they are devoted to general problems, to matters national or political, or to the purely "inner personal." In these poems the author achieves astounding hypostases by identifying her lyrical ego with a "weeping bird" caught somewhere along the highway, with a "weeping fiddle casually put for a moment against the cheek," with "a blind, fluffy moth dashing itself against the window pane." Elsewhere, a stone described in a seemingly epic fashion becomes, through an abrupt transition, a symbolic stone which "lies heavy on my heart"; dead, frozen leaves of a mutilated birch tree lie "under the very heart like spilled blood." The poem, "Mother Country" begins with the words, "The country as a whole took possession of my heart"; the nature of the mother country becomes symbolic of love and replaces erotic love. A similar sentiment is expressed in a simpler manner, but with great force in the cycle, "Our Home."

Speaking generally, Miss Iłłakowicz's verse is not simple. In her most original works she uses a "free," nonsyllabic verse, of greatly varying length, whose rhythm consists of an approximate, although loosely observed, equality of the accents. Moreover, the bold, often widely separated assonances of her rhyming and occasional verses without rhyme have very little in common with traditional rhyming forms.

Maria Pawlikowska (born 1895) presents a totally different, though nonetheless original female talent. Polish literary criticism had much to say about the "femininity" of Miss Pawlikowska's poetry, but to define exactly, without commonplace phrases, the quality of this femininity has proved to be difficult. Indeed, the best of her verses are distinguished by great concentration of expression, by control of the lyrical element, and by an objectification of emotions. Maria Pawlikowska expresses herself in brief, epigrammatic forms, many of her poems consisting of four lines only. It is also true that some of her small collections, particularly among her early works, are saturated with the drawing-room atmosphere of a fashionable, super-refined life. This atmosphere caused the author's writings to be classified as "precious," to be called "filigree baubles." Nevertheless, in this filigree quality there is a specific style; it possesses a compactness of expression, it knows how to encompass extensive problems in concise and purposeful forms. This ability secures for Miss Pawlikowska a prominent place in contemporary Polish lyric poetry.

The poet, Władysław Broniewski (born 1898), had to face violent attacks. Harassed by the Polish Government for being a Communist, he was deported to Russia and imprisoned by the Soviet authorities of occupation, most likely on a charge of Polish patriotism (social patriotism). This is proof positive that neither the official Patriots nor the official Communists were capable of understanding his intellectual world. Studying his history from the literary point of view, one must say that Broniewski is a brilliant poet who espouses the cause of the proletariat. It would be a mistake, however, to classify his work, as a matter of course, with proletarian poetry. The latter poetry, defined as works containing strong social accents especially concerned with the urban proletariat, had had its exponents in former times as well, but it gained in popularity because of the young Russian poets of the post-Revolutionary era. Although Broniewski is linked to them by the same abstract theme, his artistic treatment of that theme is different. The Russian poets were revolutionaries not only in the slogans they proclaimed but, first and foremost, in their artistic media. In poetic technique, Broniewski is rather a Conservative; for this reason, he is classified in this review with the Scamander group rather than with the Vanguard. He likes best to employ standard metrics and language devoid of radical innovations. This traditionalism notwithstanding, he is capable of great inventive power, of unusual, really overwhelming force of tone, of a "white, glowing fire" of lyrical emotion, of splendid outbursts of wrath and love. There is no trace in him of commonplace, cheap propaganda, of official public-meeting pathos, of shallow slogan-slinging or, still less, of any desire to be impressive. His proletarian poetry is real poetry of a high order.

Simultaneously with the trends of the Scamander group and poets more or less kindred, other trends much more given to innovations were making their appearance. Their exponents sharply attacked the Scamandrites as lyrical "organ grinders" who played old tunes on worn-out chords, who lacked feeling for modern spiritual needs, and who had no poetic program of any kind. These trends, however, had no clearly defined common character beyond the intention of bringing about a radical reform in lyric poetry. Influenced by sundry movements which agitated western Europe and, to some extent, eastern Europe—futurism, expressionism, and super-realism—these poets endeavored to interpret such movements individually and to adapt them to their own needs. The foremost theorist among them was Tadeusz Peiper (born 1891), a poet. He advocated breaking away from romantically impressionistic volubility and emotional directness and, instead, supporting lyrical objectivism as a conscious construction of lyric poems. "Poetry means creating beautiful sentences. . . . Not the word but the sentence should constitute the primary objective of poetic creativeness." The metaphor remains, as of old, one of the most essential poetic media, but such metaphor is to be new, based on remote associations and constituting combinations of notions "to which nothing in the world of the reality corresponds." Peiper did not scrap rhyme, not even a regular one, but demanded that rhymes be remote from one another and separated by a number of verses. In this way he wanted to emphasize the rhyme's structural importance to the poem as a whole. So far as the rhythm was concerned, its function was "to serve the emerging sentence and the sentences to follow."

The theory, as presented, contained a number of justified demands together, however, with demands of a doubtful or not sufficiently specified nature. Needless to say, all this caused polemics and protests not only from the "youngest" poets, but also from the older generation of critics who, on the whole, were not kindly disposed toward the new trend. Some among the Vanguardists wanted to have the social element represented more strongly in poetry although Peiper spoke explicitly of the beauty of "the city, of the masses and of the machine," as well as of "sewing the nerve of up-to-dateness into human beings." Others again turned back to the theory of pure form (formism).

The poetic accomplishments of the Vanguard were of varying value. The several coteries into which the Vanguard split were linked together, to be sure, by one tie common to them all, a more or less radical destruction of the traditional forms of poetry, a discarding of the regular rhythms to such an extent that frequently the difference between verse and "poetic prose" was entirely obliterated. Another common characteristic was the endeavor to create a poetic language so new and so different from the prevalent literary language that frequently it is impossible to understand. This is a result of a liking for neologisms, as well as an inclination to impart to plain words some far-fetched meaning, or to use abbreviations and changes of syntax. It goes without saying that the traditional strophes disappeared from poetry produced by the Vanguard.

Within the framework of such general tendencies there was room for sundry individualities, thus proving that the movement had vitality and met the intellectual needs of the new generation. Another proof of its vitality was its spread to various literary centers, chiefly Cracow, Warsaw, and Wilno. In addition to Peiper, the most outstanding exponents of poetic accomplishment in the Vanguard were Juljan Przybos, Jalu Kurek, Czesław Miłosz, Marjan Czuchnowski, and Józef Czechowicz.

Active concurrently with the Scamander and Vangard groups were also the poets of the bygone era. The most outstanding among them was Jan Kasprowicz (1860–1926). His rich poetic production, which covered many years, went through various evolutions, all of which, however, were within the general frame of the literary currents of symbolism and aestheticism at the close of the nineteenth century. A radical change in Kasprowicz's poetic productivity came only at the time of the First World War, a change independent of the prevailing literary currents, a turn toward an almost monastic simplicity in both language and verse, a philosophical resignation, a reconciliation with God, and a forbearance with his own erstwhile Promethean struggles. This new attitude found its best expression in *The Book of the Poor,* published in 1916, and reached the height of artistic abnegation in the collection, *My World,* published in 1920, wherein the poet intentionally descends to the level of a village fiddler and plays his melodies on one chord, choosing the simplest possible words and avoiding, as though intentionally, not only artistry but any and all poesy. This style stood in radical opposition to all Kasprowicz had created previously, but it had very little in common with the trend of the era.

The story of the youngest poet of the previous generation, Leopold Staff (born 1878), was entirely different. Staff influenced the latest era of Polish poetry more than any other poet. This is evidenced both by the statements of the young poets themselves, who admitted having learned from him, and by the verses they wrote. Staff passed into the new era with a matured and fully developed creative mind, and produced even more than in the bygone period. Even as Staff influenced the creativeness of the young poets, he was partially under their influence. He did not loose contact with modern times and was considered the most outstanding of the living poets—an opinion not concurred in by the Vanguard which, on principle, could not possibly give him any recognition. Among the many collections of Staff's poems, published in the last twenty years, two merit special attention: *The Needle's Eye,* published in 1927, an expression of boundless, ecstatic, pure and unselfish veneration for the Creator, and *Tall Trees* published in 1932, which clearly shows a formal link between him and the younger generation.

Tadeusz Boy-Zeleński (born 1879), though in point of age a member of the previous generation, is one of the youngest, most lively and progressive of Polish writers. He began as early as the close of the last century with light verses and songs in which he showed a high type of poetic talent. A number of his gay songs have a greater poetic and intellectual value than many a philosophically inspired poem of pathos. Boy's great and abundant talent also appeared in his translations of French literary works, both in verse and in prose. An enthusiastic admirer of French literature and culture, a consummate connoisseur of their various periods, Boy accomplished the most unusual task of translating over one hundred volumes of works by various French authors and succeeded in interesting the Polish public in reading translations to such an extent that some of his books went through several editions. Among the French authors he translated were Villon, Rabelais, Montaigne, Pascal, Descartes, Molière (complete works), Racine, Brantôme, Laclos, Montesquieu, Voltaire, Diderot, Le Sage, Rousseau, Beaumarchais, Mlle de l'Espinasse, Marivaux, Musset, Chateaubriand, Mérimée, Stendhal; in addition, he translated a score or more of the bulky volumes of Balzac. The scope of Boy's talent was immense. Even more astounding was his ability to penetrate the language and style of both verse and prose of such heterogeneous periods; his translations of Rabelais are in the best Polish language used by the sixteenth-century writers; in translations from Molière and Racine, the classical style of Polish eighteenth-century poets was used, whereas his translations of Balzac are in the realistic prose of Poland's best novelists.

For his translations, Boy prepared exhaustive forewords and commentaries in which he summarized not only the period in which the given author lived but also that author's entire literary output. If collected into one volume, those forewords would constitute a unique history of the principal currents of French literature written by one of its best connoisseurs in Poland. In general, Boy's relationship to literature bears many earmarks reminiscent of French tradition. He is interested not so much in literary as in biographical, psychological, and moral problems. He is passionately interested in finding a connection between an author's private life and his works, and he loves to reveal the various *dessous* of recognized celebrities. Boy's "debunking" of the lives and activities of certain Polish idols made quite a stir at one time. Such activities constituted a wholesome reaction against official and, for the most part, false historical and literary standards and patterns. Nevertheless, it was a misleading transgression against the principle, now almost universally accepted, that a literary work constitutes no "memoirs of the author's soul" and that to reconstruct the author's psyche on the basis of his works is impossible.

For years, Boy also had been a theatrical critic, and his reviews came to fill nearly a score of volumes. The reviews, too, were characterized by his highly cultivated taste, keen judgment, original and courageous approach. However, they dealt with the literary side of drama and disregarded its theatrical aspects. His interest in moral and social issues, his passion for exposing any and all hypocrisy and sham soon carried him beyond the field of literary criticism into journalism. Here, too, he exercised a constructive influence with his sharp pen, but he plunged into controversies which kept him away from his real domain of literature.

The novel.—Whereas in the first decade of the Republic lyric poetry reigned in Polish literature, in the second decade the novel gradually moved to the foreground. It goes without saying that neither date is to be taken literally, nor does the predominance of one branch of literature mean that the other branch ceased to exist. It is rather a question of the interest of the reading public in the novel being aroused at the same time that new talents appeared in the field of the novel. During the first decade, it was the novelists of an older vintage—authors who had come into the new period of literature with definite literary complexions and who adhered to patterns evolved by themselves—who were the chief, though not the only novelists.

Foremost among these authors was Stefan Żeromski (died 1925) who had been the most oustanding novelist of the preceding generation. He continued to write novels strongly saturated with a lyricism which frequently rent asunder the framework of the composition. He continued to touch fundamental social problems in a sharp, uncompromising and moving manner, a trait which already, at an earlier date, had made of him the nation's social conscience, a writer "who tore at the vitals" of his generation, who endeavored to open its eyes to the evils of social wrongs and degradation. In the years following the First World War, Żeromski published two long novels. One book, *Wind from Seaward,* contained tales of old Polish Pomorze; the other, entitled *Early Spring,* was a contemporary novel in which the contrast between the carefree life of the Polish landowning gentry and the threatening social problems clamoring for solution by the reborn Polish State was presented in Żeromski's customarily forceful manner.

Of similar character was the literary production of Andrzej Strug (pseudonym, Tadeusz Gałecki, 1873–1935). In the stories he wrote before the First World War he perpetuated for posterity the personages and lifework of the Polish socialist fighters who had struggled for liberty against tsardom. After the First World War, he expanded the scope of his themes, one of which was a touching story about Piłsudski's legions under the caption *A Badge for Faithful Service* (published, 1920); in *Yellow Cross* (published, 1932), he attempted to present an epic story in the form of a panoramic cycle of novels of the life of Europe before the war. Less talented than Żeromski and other leading contemporary Polish novelists, Gałecki nevertheless possessed one valuable quality as an author; he carefully planned his stories, gave strict attention to composition, and diligently adopted all the new methods of novel technique.

One would hardly say the same of Włodzimierz Perzyński (1878–1930). This greatly talented novelist and playwright was astonishingly careless in his "literary business," in the composition of his writings, in developing and climaxing the action of his stories. He possessed, however, a gift of keen observation, a narrative style both simple and clear, and a very subtle sense of humor and irony. Two of his novels, *Once in a Life Time* (1925), and *Two People* (1928), as well as certain others, resembled a documentation of Warsaw's contemporary life. At times Perzyński succeeded in producing real masterpieces of the short story, as in "Stigma" (1927).

Wacław Berent (1873–1940), was author of a novel, *Rotten Wood,* characteristic of the preceding literary period, which sharply portrayed European "decadence" at the close of the nineteenth century. In 1918, at the very beginning of the new literary period, Berent published a typically symbolic and modernistic fictional study under the caption, *Living Stones,* which portrayed the cultural life of the Middle Ages in a language stilted and artificial in the extreme; this study could hardly be called a novel. However, Berent had fallen under the spell of the new period. His last work was *The Current,* published in 1934, a biographical romance of prominent Polish personages at the end of the eighteenth century and at the beginning of the nineteenth. It was a new genre, originated in France and quickly transplanted to other countries of Europe, which expressed the predilection of both authors and reading public for anecdotal and "novelized" history based on facts and documents about real persons—that is, actual characters from history.

Zofja Nałkowska (born 1885) one of the most prominent of the Polish women novelists, also went through a long process of evolution. The first period of her literary activity was characterized as one of "preciousness," a classification which fails to describe the essence of her writing. Far more important was Miss Nałkowska's endeavor to portray in her novels and short stories a new world, or at least a world new to Poland, a world of female psychology, one might say, in its specific, age-old manifestations. Joseph Conrad once wrote of the inborn, ageless instincts of woman, of woman's inborn wisdom manifested in the simplest young girl. These qualities are to be found in Miss Nałkowska's characters and in her interesting plots. It needs to be added that all these types of women are drawn from a certain strictly defined milieu—the intellectual class in the period at the end of the nineteenth century—women who are beautiful and refined, products of a bourgeoise culture, who want their lives to unfold aesthetically. From her very first novels, of which there is space to name only *Women* (1906), *The Prince* (1907), and *Narcissa* (1911), an original, matured talent was manifest, a talent well aware of its resources and its objectives, an unusual knowledge of penetrating analysis and well-planned composition, and a style fully harmonizing with the hothouse world which she interpreted.

That world changed considerably after the First World War. New problems were interpreted by Miss Nałkowska. War as a "terrible evil regardless of what it is waged for" was presented in *Count Emil* (1920); "changes in people and among people which had occurred in Poland" in *Theresa Hennert's Romance* (1923). Next came a gloomy book on prison people, *Walls of the World,* treating with human beings "who took the evil upon themselves, who took evil up as their duty as it were, since its necessary quota in the world must be somehow apportioned among the people." At the same time. Nałkowska's style also underwent a thorough change. It became simpler, more austere, more streamlined, and more concentrated. The change undoubtedly went hand in hand with her striving for authenticity in grasping and elaborating her themes. The hunger for authenticity and truth which engrossed the minds of all postwar Europe made itself felt in Polish novel writing as well. The slogan of "new objectivism," as it was called, was modified by Miss Nałkowska to "written reality." This meant consciously foregoing many traditional means of arousing the reader's interest and of keeping him in suspense; it meant foregoing at times even the traditional novel form for the sake of an exact, dispassionate description of a seemingly simple and commonplace reality which, however, contained profound problems. Many of Miss Nałkowska's novels, which date from that period, are not in the traditional form with absorbing plots and conflicts; nevertheless, they are original and well-constructed works of art, for instance, *House by the Meadows* (1925), and *Choucas* (1927). Miss Nałkowska, however, did not enclose herself within the shell of this form. The force of the novel tradition is evidently so powerful that a true novelist must write novels in the fullest sense of that term. Miss Nałkowska's last work, *The Border,* is just that kind of novel in which a fascinating plot and a style of written reality combine to make an original literary entity.

The younger among the novelists of this period sought new means of expression either within the broadest possible province of realism or beyond it. In both instances the evolution was in composition and style. Generally speaking, the majority of these attempts had no revolutionary character. In only a few instances did a novelist go beyond the sphere of realism. Most authors were satisfied to change the realistic technique by employing new methods for development of the plot. Chronological sequence of events was abandoned and, instead, subsequent events were put first, followed by a turning back to earlier occurrences. Parallel narration of several actions was used, with commentaries and mixed points of view presented by the author, or the pseudo authors scattered throughout the story. Synthetic shortcuts in the characterization of the types, as well as dramatization of the dialogues are relatively frequent innovations. Among the younger crop of novelists, however, there have been attempts to revert to the traditional and simple novel technique. The artistic results depended, of course, not so much upon the type of the technique, as upon the method of its application and upon the author's sense of having reached his objective.

Ferdinand Goetel (born 1890), first wrote a series of stories entitled *Karapeta the Pilgrim,* based on his own experiences during four years in Turkestan, to which country he had been deported at the time of the First World War. The stories are simple, both in style and composition, but show considerable narrative talent and an unspoiled outlook on life. The same characteristics are found in his first novel, *Kar Chat,* translated into English with a foreword by G. K. Chesterton; the action of this novel is also laid in Turkestan. Several years later, Goetel wrote another novel under the title, *From Day to Day,* also translated into English, in which he used the technique of entwining two parallel stories. One plot deals with the hero's erotic adventure in Turkestan and the other with his normal, civilized life in Cracow. Among the original effects resulting from such composition is the equally vivid and realistic portrayal of the past and the present, as well as the analyzing of each period from the point of view of the other period. Unfortunately, the book ends with the breaking off of the story rather than with a solution of the novel's problem. It must be regretfully added that Goetel's subsequent novels are inferior to his earlier ones.

As an innovator in the field of composition, though still within the limits of realistic probability, Michał Choromański (born 1904), went farther in his novel, *Jealousy and Medicine* (1932). The real plot and problem of the book is not the history of the love and jealousy of a small-town physician, but the method by which the theme is composed. As in Miss Nałkowska's *The Border,* wherein the action jumps backward, Choromański's story begins at the end. In relating what had occurred during the preceding week, the author presents the beginning of the story and, as the tale proceeds, intersperses it with more reversions to past months or even to past years. This technique produces an atmosphere of unrest, strangeness, and mystery which harmonizes with the spiritual life of the characters. For the sake of intensifying the atmosphere thus created, the author employs various methods of presentation, such as indirect narrative by himself and direct narration by the several characters, dramatic dialogues, ruminations, and confessions in a diary. Moreover, its great heterogeneousness, notwithstanding, the novel does not by any means fall apart into unrelated fragments but, on the contrary, constitutes an artistically organic entity.

On a somewhat more modest scale were the experiments of Jarosław Iwaszkiewicz (born 1894), a poet of multifarious talents who was one of the original members of the Scamander group, a short-story writer, a novelist, and an author of essays. He began his career with lyric poetry which had a style of its own, and later turned toward prose. His numerous short stories and novels are of varying value. He tried many different methods and styles, favoring, however, realistic patterns which he attempted to imbue with new life. Therein he succeeded best in his novel, *The Moon Rises* (1925); and in a volume of short stories, *Girls from Wilk* (1933), which shows considerable skill in handling literary material in true short-story fashion. The vivid, succinct, truly personal language of the author also deserves mention.

In his novel *Kordjan and Plebeian* (1932), Leon Kruczkowski (born 1900), chose the traditional novel pattern for his analysis of the Polish insurrection against Russia in 1830 from the point of view of the laboring masses. He pointed out, in his book, the actual sore spot of the Polish cause, namely the oppression of the peasants, but did not succeed always in documenting his arguments artistically.

The art of novel writing owes much of its development, in the second decade of the Republic, to a number of talented young women novelists. They, too, either traveled over the beaten path or else sought new roads, but, regardless of the structures adopted, these women writers often produced interesting and valuable works. Thus in Helen Boguszewska's novel, *Sabina's Entire Life* (1934), is found an interpretation of the reminiscences of an average and unlucky person during a fatal illness, presented in a structurally interesting frame. Helen Boguszewska wrote jointly with George

Kornacki a social novel of the unanimistic type under the title, *The Brick Carts Are Rolling* (1935). Maria Kuncewicz (born 1897), produced in her *Foreign Woman* a novel almost classical in character. Maria Gojawiczyńska, in a series of parallel stories filling two volumes about *Girls from Nowolipki* (1935), presented a gallery of vivid and original types of girls from a Warsaw suburb. Eva Szelburg-Zarembina (born 1899), combines realistic elements with visionary and fantastic ones in a novel, *The Wanderings of Joanna.* Zofja Kossak-Szczucka (born 1890), revived the historical novel, limiting herself at first to Polish history—*Golden Freedom* and others—but later conceived the ambitious plan of depicting the story of the first crusade in *Crusaders.* That novel is impressive through the wealth of historical material which Kossak-Szczucka assembled and studied, and through the language, modeled on the best Polish historical novels, but shows defects in the artistic treatment of the material and in the structure. Aniela Gruszecka, writing under the pseudonym of Jan Powalski, displayed considerable intuition and historical flair in her novel, *By the Lake.*

Maria Dąbrowska (born 1892) went in an entirely different direction in her novel, *Nights and Days,* consisting of several volumes. The first volume, which appeared in 1932, met with enthusiastic reception by certain critics, and by a part of the intellectual public. The work was hailed as the beginning of a new era in the evolution of the Polish novel. Such opinion was the outcome of psychic moods rather than of careful analysis of the initial volume; few readers thought of waiting for the later volumes. The public—and probably some critics as well—already were somewhat tired of the sundry experiments in the field of novel structure. Accordingly, with a sense of relief and with joy the reading public greeted the book whose basic characteristic was simplicity—simplicity in all its component elements of structure, language, characters, and the type of life portrayed.

In the structure of *Nights and Days,* Maria Dąbrowska reverted to the old novel form, a form which might be called a chronicle. Similar to a chronicle, a novel of this type usually opens "at the beginning," with the genealogy of the leading characters and the various incidents narrated in chronological sequence. This form continues for a shorter or a longer period of time and could, for that matter, continue indefinitely, portraying the history of one, two, three, or more generations. Such method brings the novel structure nearer to the course of normal human life, and endows it with the charm of authenticity. The latter characteristic becomes even more pronounced in the author's work because of the types she portrays, the manner in which she treats them, and the novel's language. The characters of the novel are simple and average. In addition to the two leading characters, there are a host of secondary characters which are frequently brought into the picture, "just as in life," without any artistic necessity, especially in the later volumes. The author's narrative is also of the very simplest kind. It flows slowly, in a broad stream, in true epic fashion. Description and narrative are frequently interrupted by the author's interesting observations and aphorisms which also harmonize with the traditional character of the novel. Miss Dąbrowska's style possesses the epic breadth of Tolstoy's work. Her linguistic material is equally plain, colloquial; her manipulation of it is on a high artistic level and produces a style of great originality, plasticity, and vivacity.

It should be specifically pointed out that Miss Dąbrowska's simplicity is not the result of her being an average writer but, on the contrary, because she has strong talent and produces art of a high quality. Her novel, although not constituting an epochal event, is, nevertheless, a crowning of the traditional novel form which it imbues with new life. Furthermore, because of its historical authenticity and artistic truthfulness, it is a document of no mean value, eloquently portraying the life of plain, commonplace folk during the period beginning in the 'sixties of the nineteenth century and continuing to the outbreak of the First World War.

Józef Wittlin (born 1896), presented another type of simplicity in his novel, *Salt of the Earth*. Here the author, previously known for his poetry—for instance, the impressive post-World-War "Hymns" in which he had depicted the stark horror of war, and his brilliant translation of the "Odyssey"—produced a war novel totally different from other books of this kind which thus far had been common in Poland and in western Europe. Several factors are responsible for the originality of *Salt of the Earth*. To begin with, the war (Volume I, the only volume to have appeared thus far, covers the opening months of the First World War) is seen through the eyes of a plain Huzul peasant of Ukrainian-Polish descent. This man lives in a state of never-ending bewilderment. Mobilization, militarization of railways, medical examinations, evacuation—everything confronting him is puzzling, mysterious, paradoxical. That oddness of the world, as it is reflected in the soul of Piotr Niewiadomski, becomes an extremely potent medium of artistic expression. Facts and phenomena become symbolic of weighty and profound problems; the experiences of a plain human soul become the universal experiences of all souls oppressed by the monstrous conditions of life during wartimes. A deep truth emanates from this plain, epic novel and enriches the knowledge of human life. The novel is not altogether placid and dispassionate narration, however. A distinct though discreet lyrical element shines through the story, manifesting itself in emotion, subtle irony, comments and aphorisms by the author, in generalizations and symbolical pictures. The combination of the lyrical element with a considerable degree of solicitude for the tangible, realistic details of the picture produces a unique epico-lyrical entity decidedly more impressive than the topically kindred writings of Remarque or Barbusse. Wittlin's novel has already been translated into several foreign languages, among them English, and has met everywhere with great appreciation.

As a conclusion to a review of those novelists who sought new means of expression within the scope of a broadly conceived realism, the literary activity of Juliusz Kaden-Bandrowski (born 1885) must be considered. The beginnings of his literary career extend back to prewar days, but he wrote his most characteristic works during the period under discussion. His novels stand on the border line, as it were, between experimental realism and antirealism. They are voluminous novels, one entitled *Black Wings* (1928), the other, *Mateusz Bigda* (1933). One of the Polish critics, Wacław Borowy, very aptly and picturesquely described the style of the novels as follows: "... His characters are painted not with a brush but with a broom, yet the ferocity alone with which he handles it makes them startling. And what still enhances the impression is his method of amalgamating processes of the body.... He has shown us, indeed, people who apprehend with their noses, feel with their stomachs, and make decisions with their legs...." This is neither realism nor consistent antirealism. In addition to the care for probability and for logical motivation may also be found certain weird visionary elements, distortion of shapes, sounds, and colors of the real world, gaudy, blatant expressiveness—one might say expressiveness for its own sake. It is needless to add that this mannerism at times produces powerful effects, but eventually becomes monotonous. The problems dealt with by Kaden—for instance, the life of the various strata of society in the mining region as well as the sundry aspects of parliamentary life—assume, through the application of his technique, correspondingly weird dimensions which are still more enhanced by the truly Juvenalian fury with which he tears away the veil from the sundry festering wounds of community life.

In his earlier works, Kaden was able to apply a different, more moderate technique. Noteworthy among his works of that period is *My Mother's Town* (1925), a series of reminiscing tales from his childhood, replete with lofty and tender emotions.

In spite of the fact that the transcendence of realism in the novels of that period was unusual, this trend did have some rather interesting exponents. One exponent in drama, and to some extent in novels as well, was Stanisław Ignacy Witkiewicz (born 1885), the son of a well-known painter and art critic and himself a talented painter and theorist of pure form. Unfortunately, however, his theory is not clear, and constitutes a collection of views and opinions, often just and new, rather than a compact system of ideas. Witkiewicz applies the principles of pure form primarily to painting and to drama. To quote his own words, "... essential is the possibility of freely deforming life or the world of fantasy for the purpose of creating an entity, the meaning of which would be defined only by an internal, purely scenic construction and not by the requirement of a consistent psychology and action according to some premises of life. . . ." Witkiewicz wrote many dramas of this character, only a few of which were presented on the stage. His dramas are interesting experiments, disclosing considerable dramatic talent, but they do not constitute an organic entity such as must, in the last analysis, be demanded from every work of art, no matter how greatly it may distort life. This is more or less true with Witkiewicz's novels. Having arbitrarily excluded the novel from the realm of art and reduced it to the level of a "bag" into which he may stuff whatever he pleases, Witkiewicz wrote novels in which, as in his dramas, the element of distortion manifests itself strongly, combined from necessity not only with realistic but also with hypernaturalistic elements.

More consistent in his antirealism, as well as more mature, is Bruno Schulz. In his *Cinnamon Shops* (1934), he presented a picture of the oddness and mystery of existence far more expressively than Witkiewicz could have done.

The drama.—The drama always has been a weak spot in Polish literature. In the course of several centuries of its existence, there were only three epoch-making authors in the field of drama: Aleksander Fredro, the father of the Polish comedy in the first half of the nineteenth century; Juliusz Słowacki, a brilliant romantic poet who, particularly during his mystic period, strove to create a new form of drama; and Stanisław Wyspiański, at the turn of the nineteenth century, who not only revived, in truly artistic fashion, the popular forms of folk drama, but also modernized the classical theater through his powerful and original imagination.

In the last score years no startling developments have occurred in the realm of drama. Depicted as the most outstanding dramatic playwright was Karol Hubert Rostworowski (born 1877). Prior to the First World War, his drama *Judas* was presented on the stage. The very theme of the work was proof of the author's far-reaching ambitions; his treatment of the subject disclosed considerable talent, not only for the handling of great conflicts and the following of great dramatic lines, but also for moral problems and for the pathos of the classical theater. His subsequent works of a similar nature failed to produce the expected results. Neither did endeavors to continue Wyspiański's type of stage productions prove successful. A series of dramas, however, in which moral and social themes were treated against a contemporaneous background—*Surprise* (1929), for instance—again disclosed Rostworowski's dramatic powers in portraying the problems of crime, its origin and consequences.

A literary and theatrical event of moment was the production, in 1925, of Żeromski's *The Little Quail.* That great novelist had written and produced plays before, but they were all rather indifferent works from the dramatic point of view. Their shortcomings were charged to his lyricism which was the dominating element in his novels. But here he displayed—and in the last year of his life—surprising stage flair, a consummate ability for stating his conflicts dramatically with great conciseness and concentration. The problem underlying *The Little Quail* was reminiscent of that of the most impressive of his earlier novels and short stories, that is, a conflict between personal feelings and duty resulting from serving a cherished ideal. A conflict of this type was more difficult to solve in a stage play than in a novel where there is more time and room in which to prepare the ground and the motivation. Accordingly, the weakest spot of Żeromski's drama is in the motivation of the leading character's heroic decision to renounce his love.

It was less surprising to see Nałkowska invading the field of drama, because her mastery of the literary material, her objectivity, and her understanding of dramatic conflicts were already evident in her novels. The two plays she has written thus far, *The House of Women* (1930), and *The Day of His Return* (1931), constitute an important item in the Polish dramatic literature of that period. The first of the two plays is noteworthy because of its dramatic tension. It is devoid of action, in the sense of events which occur, develop, and become entangled—an element considered to be the cornerstone of every drama—but it is remarkable, nevertheless, for its high degree of dramatic tension. That tension is attained by a most subtle introduction of reminiscing among women of various ages who live together in one house. These reminiscences are of men and of erotic experiences, but beneath the theme lies a much deeper problem, that of human loneliness, of one's limited knowledge of fellow human beings, of the relativity of everything, including the truth of reminiscences. The purpose of *The Day of His Return* is, in the author's own words, the portrayal of a crime and its ramifications in the moral and emotional life of people connected with the criminal. These ramifications lead to a number of highly dramatic conflicts intensified and gradually laid bare with consummate skill. The entire story is overshadowed by the ominous theme, the "imperative of evil," already noted in one of Nałkowska's works in prose, which theme must in some way be apportioned among people, and is combined with the problem of the potentiality for crime lurking in every human being.

Klemens Szaniawski (born 1887), centered his attention on a revival of the symbolical and Stimmung drama. In a series of well-written and sometimes even intriguing plays, the most noteworthy of which are *The Bird* (1923), and *Attorney-at-Law and Roses* (1929), Szaniawski portrayed the conflict between reality and fancy by means of somewhat cheap pseudo-poetical moods and effects attained through significant silences and half words.

Another writer who turned to the revival of the drama, in the form of historical comedies, was Adolf Nowaczyński. This author, born in 1876, belonged to an older generation. His comedies were historical chronicles in dialogue, written with considerable dash and stage flair. Nowaczyński earned for himself the reputation of a Polish Léon Daudet—a literary talent who had surrendered to the darkest forces of reaction.

Contemporary comedy had its contributor in the person of Włodzimierz Perzyński, the novelist. This writer, though possessing a great dramatic talent, unfortunately used it in a still more careless way than he had in the field of the novel. It was a frequent and painful experience to see a play by Perzyński, admirably set up in the first act, disintegrate and break down in the later acts, thus presenting in the end a picture of the ruin of frequently brilliant ideas, characters, and scenes.

In point of structure the comedies written by the poet Słonimski stand on a higher level. Their atmosphere is somewhat similar to that in the dramas of Bernard Shaw; the plays indicate a splendid talent for creating action by and from dialogue. That dialogue is so scintillating and so intelligent, it contains so much wit, irony, and sarcasm, it so completely bares the inside of paltry souls, that the events, the entanglements, and the conflicts are contained in the dialogue itself and do not need to resort to outside action. Among the best of Słonimski's comedies are *The Warsaw Negro* (1928), an extremely witty caricature of snobbery in certain Polish-Jewish circles, and *The Family* (1928), a brilliant satire on Hitlerism, Bolshevism, and on the Polish landed gentry as well.

Bruno Winawer's comedies, one of which, *The Book of Job,* was translated into English by Joseph Conrad, although written in a vein somewhat similar to Słonimski's, are really more forced.

The structure of Antoni Cwojdziński's comedies is also in the spirit of Shaw. The novelty of the comedies consists in the dramatizing or, to be more explicit, in the staging of actual scientific problems. The author is a physicist and his profession has influenced his choice of themes. One of his comedies is called *Theory of Relativity,* and another *Freud's Dream Theory*. In presenting themes of this type which rarely, if ever, had been presented on the stage, the author assigned to himself the difficult task of making them understandable for the general public. The fact of his ability to make these dramas clear, even though in an overpopular and amusing manner, is proof positive of his consummate knowledge of stage technique and of the psychology of the public. On the contrary, inasmuch as Cwojdziński wanted to be amusing, he was forced to resort to caricature, which is unusually apparent in *Freud's Dream Theory,* and to leaven all with even an insignificant plot in order to comply with the basic requirements of the theatrical code. Such a combination of theory with comedy action is very ingenuous; it brought great success to Cwojdziński.

Speaking generally, the contemporary Polish drama remained within the bounds of realism, just as the Polish novel had, by experimenting with both modernization and a revision of realistic stage effects. The sole noteworthy deviation from this course was in Witkiewicz's pure-form dramas.

It may be stated impartially that Polish literature in the last two decades performed its task well. It was not epochal in character, but then no literature was epochal in the period under review. However, it was represented by a number of outstanding talents in the various fields, particularly in that of lyric poetry and the novel, and moved at a lively pace, often keeping step with the literatures of western Europe. Had the other fields of Polish public life, particularly the political and social, been maintained at the same high level as Polish literature, Poland today might not be the devastated country it is. Alas, what had been true of other periods of Polish history, again took place, namely, the intensity of effort in the realm of art and intellectual life was not equaled in other fields of endeavor. It is hoped that in the new Poland there will be a harmonizing of effort in all fields of endeavor.

CHAPTER XX

The Fine Arts

BY IRENA PIOTROWSKA

IN POLAND before the Second World War, art had become a field of paramount importance, not only as a reflector of national culture, but also as an archive of social research. Inasmuch as the facets of Polish art had always caught the reflections of eastern Europe and of western Asia, as well as of western Europe, the two elements of East and West have constantly crossed and recrossed; "now they exist side by side on a separate and even hostile footing, now they intertwine and, mingling, create a new and entirely different entity."[1]

Architecture.—In partitioned Poland, architecture suffered more than any other branch of art. Architecture had no opportunity to bloom in a subdued country. All the architectural designs of Stanisław Wyspiański (1869–1907), a most original and talented poet, dramatist, painter, interior decorator, and architectural designer, have remained on paper. During a period of international eclecticism in architecture, Wyspiański turned his attention, and that of his generation, to the beauty of the wooden homesteads and churches built by the Polish peasants; in foreseeing that these forms of peasant architecture would be applied to monumental buildings, Wyspiański helped to create a national style in modern Polish architecture. His views were supported by a number of other artists of his time and by the studies and publications of eminent writers who were enamored of the art of the Polish mountaineers of the Podhale Valley, with the village of Zakopane, on the northern slopes of the Tatras, as its artistic center.

As soon as Poland had regained its freedom, great opportunities

[1] Irena Piotrowska, "Polish Painting—Historical Influences, Present Tendencies, and Future Possibilities," in *Polish Science and Learning,* No. 2 (1943). (Printed in Great Britain.)

opened for Polish architects. During the twenty years of national independence, architecture was the only field in which Polish art could prove best its innate possibilities and its power. For more than one hundred years, art had been forced to remain, to a large extent, in a latent state.

After the devastation left by the First World War, when the reborn Republic began to build anew its villages, towns, and cities, to erect new homes, schools, railroad stations, post offices, workers' settlements, apartment houses, churches, hospitals, banks, and imposing government buildings, Warsaw, the capital of the country, became the center of modern Polish architecture. All the best Polish architects, young and old, were called upon to teach at the reorganized Faculty of Architecture at the Warsaw Polytechnic Institute. Some of the older architects still adhered to the conservative school of eclecticism. They did advocate, however, the imitation of national relics rather than those of foreign countries. They tried to recreate and continue the old tradition of Polish architecture as it had flourished during the Renaissance and Baroque periods.

However, in keeping with the spirit of the time, other Polish architects introduced greater simplicity into the construction of their buildings. Among these, Karol Jankowski (1868–1928), and Czesław Przybylski (1880–1936), both of the new Faculty of Architecture at Warsaw Polytechnic Institute, achieved the best results. Przybylski based his style primarily on classic work of the late eighteenth and early nineteenth centuries. The accent which he placed on beautiful proportions and tectonics was easily understood by the younger generation of architects whose chief concern was to stress with honesty the construction of the building.

These younger architects fully realized that both the demands of modern business and sanitation, and the new materials used—such as steel and concrete—necessitated the creation of a new type of building. They rejected all conservative forms of architecture, all ornamentation copied from historical styles, and went to the extremes of rationalism and simplicity.

In this modernistic style, two tendencies soon became apparent, one marked by strict adherence to the so-called "international style," widely adopted in France and in the Netherlands, the other characterized by an effort to combine rational modern forms with architectural and decorative elements peculiar to Polish peasant art. This new individual Polish style, instead of conflicting with the uprightness of the buildings, endowed them with decorations which created a richer aspect. Here, the Polish style contrasted with modern "international" architecture which lacks all decorations and relies exclusively on proportion and on rational character.

The Polish national style, to a large extent inspired by native peasant huts and churches of wood, has one of its sources in the unrealized architectural designs of Wyspiański. Thus, this great artist's effort was not wasted but bore ample fruit, although not until almost two decades after his premature death. The modern national architectural style found its purest expression in the Polish Pavilion, built from the plans of Józef Czajkowski (b. 1872) for the International Exhibition of Decorative Arts in Paris, 1925.

The adherents of the international style, meanwhile, did not remain inactive. The vogue of the radical movement in modern Polish architecture reached its crest in the various pavilions at the Polish National Exposition in Poznań in 1929. Szymon Syrkus (born 1893), Bohdan Lachert (born 1900), and Józef Szanajca (born 1902), were the leading architects working for the Poznań fair. This style is evident in many villas, sanatoria, workers' settlements, and in other buildings scattered throughout the country.

As time passed, there evolved a tendency toward a reconciliation of the two opposing movements in modern Polish architecture, a tendency adhered to both by the older and the younger architects. On the whole, the new style was so all-pervading that even when certain architects turned again to old Polish monuments for inspiration, their style remained modern. When the Germans suddenly invaded Poland in September, 1939, Polish cities and towns, as well as the countryside, had many beautiful public buildings, parks and playgrounds, and homes built to admit air and sunlight.

Examples of the more recently erected buildings of Warsaw are the Bank of National Economy and the Ministry of Communication, both designed by Rudolf Świerczyński (born 1883); the Ministry of Education, designed by Zdzisław Mączeński (born 1878); and the Annex to the Ministry of Foreign Affairs, built after the plans of Bohdan Pniewski. The simplicity of all these buildings and their monumental character, combined with a moderate decorativeness, rightly merit the name of neoclassicism. Outside Warsaw, among many other buildings, the Country House in Wisła, designed by Adolf Szyszko-Bohusz (born 1883), for the President of the Polish Republic, is worthy of special attention because of the Polish national elements which seem to predominate.

An instructive illustration of the blending of the modernistic tendencies with old Polish traditions was provided with impressive results by the Polish Pavilion at the New York World's Fair in 1939–1940, designed by two young representatives of the rising generation of Polish architects, Jan Cybulski and Jan Galinowski. The tower that rose above the entrance to the Pavilion had the same proportions as the old towers built in Poland during the Middle Ages which served as lookout posts against invaders. Yet, its steel-frame construction covered from top to bottom with gilt shields gave it an entirely modern character. A monumental equestrian statue of the Polish king, Władysław Jagiełło, stood in front of the tower. This statue was created by the eminent Polish sculptor, Stanisław Ostrowski.

Sculpture.–Stanisław Ostrowski (born 1878), in contrast to the two young designers of the Pavilion, was an adherent of the impressionistic movement which had reached its apogee toward the close of the last century. In the Polish sculpture of the independent Republic, however, new artistic tendencies were well represented already by Ostrowski's generation, through the strong personality of Ksawery Dunikowski (born 1876), who had begun an artistic career as an impressionist. As time went on, Dunikowski simplified his sculptures to a greater extent, but did not allow them to become abstract or inorganic. His work acquired a distinctly monumental character. He created sculptures in stone for architectural decoration, and he also carved in wood, as exemplified in the expressive heads executed for a ceiling of the Wawel Castle in Cracow, which Poland was restoring to its former splendor. These carved heads show the influence of both Polish late Gothic and Polish peasant art.

However, the chief exponent of the national style in Polish sculpture was not Dunikowski but Jan Szczepkowski (born 1878), who also was an impressionist at first but who, like many others, afterward revised his style under the pressure of new art movements. Although he became well acquainted with French cubism, his greatest inspiration came from the wood carvings of the Polish highlanders of Podhale. His wooden sculptures, true in style to the medium used, are flat and are predominantly decorative in character. The *chef d'oeuvre* of Szczepkowski is the wooden chapel carved for the Paris International Exhibition. The artistic beauty and genuinely Polish style of the chapel made more desirable its acquisition by the French Government to adorn one of France's old churches.

In strong contrast to Szczepkowski, Edward Wittig (born 1877), who died from malnutrition in Warsaw in 1940, represented international tendencies in modern sculpture. He was a pupil of Emile-Antoine Bourdelle. Wittig, chiefly working in stone, was master of well-balanced masses and of tranquil contour. Neoclassical tendencies, clearly discernible in Wittig's art, appear still more distinctly in the work of Henryk Kuna (born 1883), whose chief concern was an even rhythm of soft and waving lines.

These, the leading masters of modern Polish sculpture, were followed by a number of younger artists no less talented. Like most sculptors of their generation, they were influenced during their artistic gropings by certain phases of art which were more or less archaic. The effect of such early sources of inspiration is evident at times even in the work of their maturer years. Thus, August Zamoyski (born 1893), a sculptor in hard stone—granite, diorite, or basalt that he himself hews—reminds one forcefully of the best in Egyptian art. Maryla Lednicka (born 1895), has attained her best results in religious statues which breathe the calm atmosphere of the early French Gothic. On the contrary, Stanisław Szukalski (born 1895), has created monumental sculptures, decorative and symbolic, restless and tense, vividly reminiscent of pre-Columbian Maya and Aztec art.

First of the youngest generation of sculptors educated in the art schools of liberated Poland was Alfons Karny (born 1901). He and his colleagues, like the Polish painters of the same generation, directed all their attention to the solution of technical and formal problems. They chose the best material obtainable for their sculptures and worked in it directly; they did not restrain themselves solely to clay models, as did most of the nineteenth-century sculptors, and as do many sculptors today. As a result of such working methods, these youthful Polish artists attained a very high standard of workmanship. Furthermore, honesty toward the medium used, simplicity of outline, and sincerity of expression may be named as common characteristics of the younger Polish sculptors.

Painting.—The fluctuations of style in Polish art during the last twenty years may best be followed in painting. It is painting, not sculpture nor architecture, that was the leading fine art in Poland. Although architects, and to a lesser degree sculptors, are often dependent for their existence upon official commissions—which were lacking in subdued Poland—for buildings and monuments, the painter's art is a much less expensive one and may develop under even less prosperous conditions. The Poles have a deep appreciation of colors, a characteristic which is very apparent in the gaily decorative arts of the peasants. It is in painting that the Polish artists had the best opportunity in which to express their innate feeling for vivid yet harmonious color arrangement. These reasons, and perhaps still others, contributed to the fact that when Poland regained its independence after the First World War, Polish painting was in full development. The painters themselves were absorbed in aesthetic controversies which tended to heighten their perfection.

In the realm of Polish painting, in the early days of Poland's regained independence, a cleavage existed between the two styles prevalent at that time in the modern art of the Western World. Conservative naturalism and impressionism were ardently opposed by a number of antinaturalistic and ultramodern art movements including cubism, futurism, and expressionism. In Poland, most of these antinaturalistic trends were grouped under the name of formism. As a matter of fact, two generations were fighting for their ideals—the older generation of realists and impressionists, who had gained recognition already before the last war, and the younger generation of formists who, by the end of the war, were only beginning to realize their aims.

Among the oldest Polish painters who still were producing works of art in the independent Republic, Leon Wyczółkowski (1852–1937), and Juljan Fałat (1853–1929), especially should be mentioned as the major creators of the Polish variation of impressionism. These painters were followed by a number of eminent colorists who based their art on an observation of nature and its varied phenomena. To the most prominent of these artists who, as professors at art academies, had a great influence on the younger generation, belonged Wojciech Weiss (born 1875), Fryderyk Pautsch (born 1877), Kazimierz Sichulski (born 1879), as well as Władysław Jarocki (born 1879), who in 1929 came to the United States to serve on the jury of the Carnegie International Exhibition of Painting in Pittsburgh. Jacek Malczewski (1854–1929), was the symbolist of this group, and Stanisław Noakowski (1867–1928), Professor in the Faculty of Architecture at the Warsaw Polytechnic Institute, was an inspired creator of phantasies on the theme of old Polish architecture.

These artists, and many others professing the same art ideals, belonged to a society known as Art (*Sztuka*), which, founded in 1897, was active until the last days of the Republic. These artists differed from the conservative painters of other countries in their choice of brighter colors, their somewhat melancholic outlook, often lyric in quality and, last but not least, their choice of Polish themes.

On the contrary, Olga Boznańska (born 1865), an outstanding portrait painter of that same generation—well known in this country by her works which have been displayed at the Carnegie Institute in Pittsburgh, in the Brooklyn Museum in New York, and in other American museums—and Józef Pankiewicz (1866–1940), were ardent admirers of Parisian art. Both painters were residents of France for many years. Of the two, Pankiewicz was the most important in his influence on the younger generation of Polish artists. From 1925 to his death, Pankiewicz was head of the Parisian Branch of the Academy of Fine Arts in Cracow, and in this capacity introduced a great number of young Polish art students to the problems of French painting, helping them to understand its real and permanent values in order to distinguish them from the transient, ever-changing art "fashions" of Paris.

The second generation of painters in independent Poland consisted principally of champions of Polish antinaturalistic art, that is, the formists and their adherents. Here, by way of example, Tytus Czyzewski (born 1884), Stanisław Ignacy Witkiewicz (1886–1939), Wacław Wąsowicz (born 1891), and Henryk Gotlib (born 1892), should be mentioned. Of the sculptors, the previously mentioned August Zamoyski also belonged to the formists. Although not members of this group, many other Polish artists of that day were formists through their style. One, for instance, was the unusually expressive Tadeusz Makowski (1883–1932), for many years a resident of Paris.

However, by the middle of the third decade of this century the majority of the followers of extremely leftist currents returned to nature, having experienced a yearning for this inexhaustible treasure house of inspiration. But the conflicts that preceded this period of reinvigorated art endowed it with new elements of color and composition, and introduced new problems. French cubism, an application derived from the word "cube," and Polish formism, from "form," had taught artists to respect the rules of a carefully planned composition, and to combine its different parts in order to produce a harmonious whole. It also taught them to stress the essential elements of a picture and to omit the incidental ones. This new tendency in Polish painting has often been termed "neoclassic."

Those from among the formists who, consciously or unconsciously, had begun to follow the path leading toward neoclassicism were encouraged by a number of other eminent Polish painters who had not gone through a decidedly antinaturalistic period, but whose style, more or less approaching neoclassicism, evolved directly from impressionism and its different variations. In 1922, a group of these artists already had formed a society called Rhythm (*Rytm*). Although a rhythmically arranged composition of painting was their common artistic aim, most of them, because of the contributions of impressionism, were outstanding colorists. Among these, Tadeusz Pruszkowski (born 1888), shot by the Germans in 1942, was the most popular. His unusual pedagogical talents had given him predominating influence over that generation of artists whose artistic training dated from the rebirth of the Republic. Wacław Borowski (born 1886), was the master of *chiaroscuro* and lyricism; in style his work was closely related to Eugeniusz Żak (1884–1926), who lived in France and took a prominent part in the evolution of the modern Parisian school.

This varied group of the founders of the *Rytm* society, among whom should be included the sculptors, Henryk Kuna and Edward

Wittig, and the wood engraver, Władysław Skoczylas, dominated the horizon of artistic Poland for many years, together with a number of somewhat younger artists who followed in their footsteps. Internationally, the most famous among these was Zofia Stryjeńska (born 1894), who concentrated on decorative painting, such as murals and book illustrations. Her works form a counterpart to Jan Szczepkowski's decorative reliefs. They are Polish in line, color, composition, in spirited vigor, and in their interpretation of the scene represented. At the same time Stryjeńska's manner of stylization, her strong simplification of form, stamps her work with those qualities which characterize all art of the postformist period approaching neoclassicism in its style. Rafał Malczewski (born 1892), was a landscapist of neoclassical tendency; Felicjan Kowarski (1890–1942), a mural painter of monumental style. Special attention should be given to Ludomir Slendziński (born 1889), of Wilno, the most decided Polish neoclassicist, linearist, and faithful follower of the Florentine *quattrocento.*

The last generation of artists to reach maturity in free Poland embraced pupils of the erstwhile antinaturalists and of the neoclassicists. These younger artists, trained from the beginning in independent Poland, remained true to the ideals of their masters. In sharp contrast to the preceding generation, they wasted no time on controversy, but concentrated all their efforts on perfecting their painting, on analyzing the methods of the great masters, old and new, in order to discover the technique responsible for the creation of masterpieces that have endured for centuries. Small wonder, then, that one of the group of younger artists took the old-fashioned name of "Brotherhood of St. Luke," which proclaimed: "The organization is bound by ties of comradeship and long collaboration. Its object is to paint as well as possible, of course within the limits of our possibilities." This group was founded in 1925 by the first pupils of Tadeusz Pruszkowski as soon as they had finished their studies at the Academy of Fine Arts in Warsaw. Bolesław Cybis (born 1899), was among the foremost representatives of this group.

Aside from membership in the Brotherhood of St. Luke, many of the younger Polish artists were grouped in other societies. Among these was a group formed by the younger pupils of Pruszkowski. This group became well known in Poland and abroad as the "School of Warsaw," with Eugeniusz Arct as their leader. Members of the group differed from those of the Brotherhood in that they preferred to study the modern painters rather than the masters of bygone ages. Too, this group produced many fervent admirers of Parisian art; these particular artists were headed, among others, by Zygmunt Waliszewski (1897–1936), Józef Czapski, Józef Jarema, and Tadeusz Potworowski.

However it may be, national influences were so strong that, in recent Polish painting, Polish elements of design and color were apparent in the work even of those artists who were not consciously preoccupied with national style. All in all, even though some Polish painters of the last twenty years succumbed to foreign influences and others to national traditions, even though some showed clear traces of antinaturalistic trends and others patterned their art more directly upon nature, all sought the same goal, albeit by different paths. All served the same ideal—perfect form combined with clarity and logic of composition. Besides, most of them were splendid colorists.

Graphic arts.—During the twenty years of Poland's independence, the older generation of Polish artists who worked in the domain of the graphic arts primarily made use of lithography, etching, and those related techniques which were the most suitable to rendering the pictorial and impressionistic elements of their creative work. The foremost Polish graphic artists of that generation were the painters Leon Wyczółkowski and Józef Pankiewicz. The former artist chiefly created lithographs, the latter etchings.

However, the Polish graphic artists of the last twenty years produced their most daring and, stylistically, their most singularly native works of art in the field of wood engraving by applying the features of the folk woodcut which had been cultivated by the peasants for centuries. Although copper and steel engravings, as well as etchings, had forced the woodcut from the world market in the seventeenth century, the Polish peasant, dwelling at a distance from artistic centers, had remained faithful to the woodcut technique. Up to a very recent time, the peasant reproduced in this medium pictures of the saints which he had seen in the churches. The figures of the saints, as represented by the peasant, are in truth primitive, but they are faithfully executed in the woodcut style and, most important, they are full of expression. Small wonder, then, that these woodcuts became a source of inspiration for that generation of Polish artists which, at the close of the second decade of this century, began to take a stand against conservative realism and against impressionism.

The initiator of this trend toward folk expression in Polish graphic art was Władysław Skoczylas (1883–1934), painter in water colors, best known as a wood engraver. Skoczylas not only studied the peasant woodcut, but also peasant art in general. Like so many other Polish artists, he was chiefly inspired by the art of the mountaineers of Podhale. Through his choice of folk themes and folk-art motifs, his work is native in character, as well as in its execution and its technique. Contemporaneously with Skoczylas, Edmund Bartłomiejczyk (born 1885), who died in a German concentration camp in 1940, played an important part in the renascence of the Polish woodcut. But Skoczylas was the more influential artist. In 1926, he founded a society of Polish graphic artists called Engraving (*Ryt*), in which he grouped such of his colleagues as Bartłomiejczyk, and his pupils of the Warsaw Academy of Fine Arts, where he was professor. The coöperation of artists, under the leadership of Skoczylas, soon brought about an unprecedented development of the Polish woodcut.

The artists grouped in the *Ryt* were able to unite, in a most masterful manner, the native qualities of the Polish peasant woodcut with the international, so-called modernistic principles of composition and drawing. The most outstanding among the artists were Stefan Mrozewski (born 1894), Tadeusz Cieślewski, Jr. (born 1895), Stanisław Ostoja-Chrostowski (born 1897), Bogna Krasnodębska (born 1900), Tadeusz Kulisiewicz (born 1901), and Janina Konarska (born 1902).

The cartoons by Zdzisław Czermański (born 1896), and the drawings by Felix Topolski (born 1907), are on the borderline of graphic art and painting. Both artists, excelling in draughtsmanship, are illustrators of international renown. The miniatures created by Artur Szyk (born 1894) constitute an interesting part of Polish art by itself. Inspired by medieval and Persian art, Artur Szyk is recognized throughout the world as the foremost living exponent of the long-forgotten art of illumination.

Besides the fine arts, interior decoration and various kinds of crafts achieved a high degree of perfection during the twenty years of Poland's independence. Especially do modern Polish stained-glass windows, textiles, bookbindings, posters, toys, metalwork, furniture, and all woodwork deserve attention. They bespeak a genuinely national style, a style combining traditional Polish art forms, as inspired by the arts and crafts of the Polish peasant, with the most advanced tendencies of inter-European art. It must be emphasized that in contrast to all other branches of Polish art, in applied arts no cleavage has ever existed between the imported foreign elements and the native ones. In this field of Polish art, of 1919–1939, the Polish style was triumphant and had no rival. It subordinated the incoming alien influences quickly and without struggle.

A few of the artists mentioned in this survey of Polish art have escaped the deluge of invasion of Poland and will carry on in allied countries the traditions of Polish art; a few are with the Polish fighting forces. In Poland itself, all expression of art has ceased—to be resumed, however, when the sun of freedom shines once again.

CHAPTER XXI

Music

BY FELIX RODERICK LABUŃSKI

POLISH MUSIC has always played a very prominent part in the cultural life of Poland and, since its origin in the fourteenth century, it has made a notable contribution to the evolution of European music. When the political resurrection of Poland as a nation engendered in a freed people a fresh impulse for artistic expression, it followed naturally that music assumed an important place in the general renascence of the arts. This impetus was beneficial not only to the development of music in general, but also to the fostering of native performing and creative talents.

For the first time in many years, a Polish composer could receive an adequate musical education in his own country. He could acquaint himself with the masterworks of Polish and foreign music in his own city, could receive from his government both encouragement and financial help for his studies and work, and could have his music performed and published in his homeland. It is not surprising that these favorable conditions not only stimulated the work of established composers, but also contributed to the growth of new generations—the first to be educated in their liberated country.

The first years after 1919 witnessed the return to Warsaw and to other Polish cities of many prominent composers, scattered heretofore in different parts of Europe. Henryk Opieński came from Switzerland to Poznań, where he became the first director of the new Poznań Conservatory; Ludomir Rogowski, Adam Wieniawski, and Eugeniusz Morawski left the hospitable banks of the Seine, in Paris, and came to establish themselves in Warsaw. The new capital also became the goal of Karol Szymanowski, Emil Młynarski, Grzegorz Fitelberg, and Witold Maliszewski, all of whom had spent the years of the First World War in Russia. Here they joined a few composers who had remained in Warsaw, the most outstanding of whom were: Ludomir Rożycki, Felicjan Szopski, Roman Statkowski, and Juliusz Wertheim. Władysław Zeleński, the Nestor of Polish composers, still was living in Cracow, whereas Henryk Jarecki and Stanisław Niewiadomski were in Lwów, and Felix Nowowiejski in Poznań. The creative talent of all these composers received fresh inspiration; as a consequence, many works of the highest merit were produced.

Limited space does not permit a description of these works, nor an analysis of the influence which the new conditions brought upon the character and style of the music, but one striking example may give an idea of the process which so many of these composers underwent. This process can be seen in the development of Szymanowski's creative art after his return to Poland in 1920.

In 1922, Szymanowski composed "Slopiewnie"—five songs to the text of Tuwim, in an imaginary archaic Polish language. It was the first time, since his early "Variations Op. 10," that Szymanowski had turned again to the roots of Polish music, but from that time on his compositions bore the influence of his homeland and were basically influenced by native folk music. He was especially attracted to the songs and dances of the mountaineers of the Polish Tatras, whose culture, as a result of their isolation from the rest of the country, had conserved its racial purity and originality. To Szymanowski, the mountain music offered ways of solving new musical problems, as it was free from the influence of established systems. The mazurkas for piano which followed, and the "Stabat Mater" (for soli, chorus, and orchestra), written in 1928, were inspired by the music of the mountaineers, and made Szymanowski the leading national composer. Szymanowski was fully aware of the change that had taken place in himself and his music since his arrival in Poland. He wrote, "Each man must go back to the earth from which he comes. Today I have developed into a national composer, not only subconsciously, but with thorough conviction, using the melodic treasures of the Polish music."

Another masterpiece, the ballet "Harnasie," based on the life of the mountaineers, and "Kurpian Songs," "Symphonie Concertante," and "Second Violin Concerto" were the outstanding works of this period, and were considered the most important works in the composer's creative development. During this time, Karol Szymanowski succeeded in liberating himself from German and French influences and in creating his own style, drawn from the roots of his native folk music.

Other composers, mentioned already, underwent a similar evolution in their creative processes. The new conditions not only favorably affected mature composers, but also fostered the appearance of new composers heretofore unknown. This generation followed the example of its elders, also turning for inspiration to folk music.

It should be emphasized that it was not for the sake of patriotism that their music was closely related to the sources of native music, but rather for purely artistic reasons. The modal character of this music, its unusual scales, its fresh and vigorous rhythms, were well in keeping with the reaction of this new generation against the romantic school to which belonged the majority of their predecessors. The treatment of folk material by the modern composers was quite different from that of the older school. They also escaped romanticism by giving to their music more gaiety and humor, more healthy objectivism; in other words, their music corresponded better to the spirit of the new Poland, the spirit of self-reliance, action, and optimism. There was no longer the dreamy melancholy, nor the tragic despair so often found in the earlier Polish music.

Among the composers of this generation, two distinct groups may be discerned. One group, most of whom were pupils of Szymanowski, was at first strongly influenced by him; only later did the group grow away from his influence and gradually became neoclassic. The group included Michał Kondracki, Jan Maklakiewicz, Kazimierz Sikorski, Piotr Perkowski, and Stanisław Wiechowicz. The second group, from the very beginning of its creative work, took a decided stand against romanticism and its later derivation, impressionism, and also against the artistic credo and methods of Szymanowski. These were the first Polish neoclassicists. To this group belong Roman Palester, Antoni Szalowski, Tadeusz Szeligowski, and Bolesław Woytowicz. Several of these young composers, after graduating from music schools and conservatories in Poland, in order to perfect their education or to acquaint themselves with modern trends, went to Paris, at that time the center of European music.

A group of composers comprising Perkowski, Wiechowicz, Czapski, and Labuński in 1927 founded the Association of Young Polish Musicians which became a nucleus for all Polish musicians who went abroad, and which, during the following twelve years, played an important role in the development of new generations of composers and performers. Although, in many European countries, neoclassicism often produced music almost totally devoid of emotion, sometimes partaking not only of the spirit of classical composers but also of their style and melodic material, emotionalism did not disappear from the music of the Polish neoclassicists. Instead, it always has been a major characteristic of Polish music.

The music of this generation began to be known to the public around the year 1930, and since that time Polish composers have contributed many works of importance, several of which frequently have been performed in Europe and in the United States, and have been acclaimed as the new artistic expression of liberated Poland. Among the most successful of these works are: "Chmiel," a symphonic dance by Wiechowicz; "Dance of Osmoloda," by Palester; "Overture," by Szalowski; "Suite," by Woytowicz; "Soldiers," by Kondracki; string quartets by Sikorski and Szalowski; and songs and instrumental music by Perkowski and Szeligowski.

To the composers whose education or creative activity during the years 1919–1939 were carried on in Poland, there must be added a few who spent these years abroad, but who, nevertheless, belong to the Polish school. First among them is Aleksander Tansman, who, though educated in Poland, established himself after 1920 in Paris. He was one of the first Polish composers to join the neoclassical movement, and by the year 1930 acquired high recognition in France and in other countries. Tansman is one of the most prolific of present-day composers, and since 1919 has composed some sixty opuses, among which are one opera, four ballets, a symphony, several symphonic works, and chamber music. One of his most acclaimed works is the "Triptyque" for string orchestra.

Two other composers began their musical education in their homeland and completed it abroad. The eldest of them, Tadeusz Jarecki, started under the influence of Russian music, but in 1920 he made a definite break with this school and oriented himself toward the radical trends of the postwar era. His "Second String

WOODEN HEADS

BY KSAWERY DUNIKOWSKI

(Carved for Ambassadors' Hall in Royal Castle, Cracow.)

Quartet" received the Coolidge Prize in 1918 and was successfully performed in the United States. The younger composer, Czesław Marek, settled in Switzerland, where he has remained since 1916. He acquired world-wide reputation, after having won the Second Prize for a symphony entered in the Schubert Memorial Contest which was offered by the Columbia Phonograph Company in 1928.

The musical education of two other composers, Grzegorz Fitelberg and Karol Rathaus took place in Germany. Both lived there until approximately 1933, and later established themselves respectively in France and England. The development of their creative work took a different course from that of other Polish composers. The maturing of their art naturally was more closely related to the evolution of music in Germany than in Poland.

These influences did not prevent Fitelberg and Rathaus from emerging as strong creative personalities, composers with their own style and technique. Several of their works display elements characteristic of Polish music. These elements are found to a greater extent in the music of Fitelberg, the younger of the two musicians, than in that of Rathaus. Fitelberg's "Fourth String Quartet" was awarded the Coolidge Prize in 1936. He has written a great amount of orchestral, chamber, and instrumental music, as well as ballets. Among his most successful works, the "Second Violin Concerto" and the "Second String Quartet" should be mentioned. The medium of composition of Rathaus is extremely varied, and his scale of expression very broad, including one opera, two ballets, two symphonies, other orchestral works, and chamber music. He also wrote incidental music for the theater and for the movies. The overture "Uriel Acosta" belongs to his most frequently performed orchestral works.

CHAPTER XXII

The Polish National Spirit

BY EDMUND ZAWACKI

STRUGGLE FOR freedom leaves its mark on the spirit of a people. The mark on the Polish spirit is patriotism. He who has never known slavery will hardly understand and cherish his freedom with the patriotic fervor of a Pole. For five generations, the Polish people have struggled for freedom; and when a nation, with a noble, thousand-year record of civilized achievement has lived on, despite a century and a half of existence as a disembodied soul apart from the flesh of statehood, with its spiritual and physical strength manifest in desperate, recurring revolts, the patriotism of that nation's sons must needs have become a dogma of national faith. Otherwise the nation would have perished. Inasmuch as Poland did not perish, it is imperative to search for the secret vitality of its national spirit.

Patriotism, to be sure, is a cardinal element in almost any national spirit. But the patriotism of the Poles has a specific character. Perhaps no nation has lived so close to the thoughts of its greatest poets, so intimately with the visions and music of its greatest artists, and so faithfully with the noblest traditions of its freedom-loving past as the Polish people throughout the nineteenth century when they were a nation without a country. No other avenues of self-expression were open to them. Consequently, the most powerful themes in Polish literature, painting, and music are patriotic; and the noblest words ever written in the Polish language are the opening words of the Polish national anthem: "Poland is not lost forever, while our lives remain." It was from this song that the Pole learned to regard patriotism as a dogma, and to foster it in his children as a categorically imperative article of national faith.

The anthem was written in 1797, within two years after Poland had ceased to exist as a separate power among the nations of Europe, but no words of despair nor of empty threat to the oppressors mar its simple and sincere patriotic dignity. Its exaltation lies not in florid words, but in the simplest possible statement of a spiritual conviction—that Poland cannot die so long as there remains a single Pole alive to sustain its meaning in his heart.

How firmly this conviction took root in succeeding generations may be seen in another Polish dictum attributed to Józef Piłsudski a hundred years later: "To be defeated but unconquered, that is a victory." Three desperate but unsuccessful revolts for Polish national freedom, with long and ruthless periods of repression afterward, had intervened between these two statements of Polish patriotic convictions, yet the second statement is even more positive than the first.

What is conveyed in both the anthem and Piłsudski's paraphrase of it is not only an assertion of the ultimate triumph of spirit over matter and right over might, but an outline of the actual progress of this triumph in Poland. The anthem is a promise to fight to the death to regain Poland's ancient freedom. Piłsudski's dictum is a bold intuitive assertion of the moral and spiritual gains won by three heroic but politically sterile insurrections which broke out in fulfillment of that patriotic promise.

When in 1922, after three years in free and reunited Poland, Stefan Żeromski, the great Polish writer and spiritual leader of his generation, looked back upon the five generations of Poles who had fought and died in vain for Polish freedom, he acclaimed the final victory of their patriotic spirit. "It now turns out," he wrote, "that the policy of craft trying to outwit the foe was a false course, while that of struggle against hopeless odds was perfect."

For five generations, the Pole singing his national anthem had not counted the odds against him when fighting for his country. It was therefore inconceivable to anyone at all acquainted with the Polish national spirit that in September, 1939, the sixth generation would have reckoned with the odds either. When the whole Polish nation stood up as one man in that terrible September, and alone faced the overwhelming might of the Nazi war machine, it was not haughty conceit in the strength of Polish arms but steadfastness in the Polish national spirit which fought to the bitter end and asked no quarter. And when from Poland today is heard the crackling flames of a hundred Lidices and the muffled volleys of countless firing squads, yet there is seen no compromise with the dogma of Polish patriotism and no Polish Quisling bargaining away his birthright, even though pressed both by ally and enemy, it can be understood dimly how the Pole translates his dogma of patriotism into the thoughts and actions of his daily life. To see it clearly, one should call to mind an oath composed in 1845 for all true Poles by the philosopher, Bronisław Trentowski. It is as timely and binding today as it was a hundred years ago.

"I swear to God that so long as I have breath I will live only to lift my Fatherland up out of the grave; that I will devote to my country my abilities, my time, my property, my blood, and all the spiritual and moral treasures I have; that for her independence and ancient luster I will be ready to suffer the most shameful tortures from her oppressors; that by no treasures of the earth will her enemies purchase my friendship; that I hate the Prussian and Austrian oppressors no less than the Muscovite oppressor and will never debase myself by seeking or accepting their favors; that I will spread this patriotic conviction to the utmost of my power; that it is my will to kindle to new life those of my countrymen who may have died in spirit, embolden the fearful, and inflame with my own fire those who are apathetic and cold. I swear that even should I be the only one to think and feel as I do, even should all my countrymen forget their duty to the last jot, I shall still remain a true, even if the last, Pole. So help me God."

To those who have never known what it is to yearn and suffer for freedom and still not be free, this oath may perhaps seem excessively nationalistic and exalted. Spiritual values count for little to short-sighted and sheltered political theorists who place great weight on economic and social determinism, spheres of influence, and similar insidiously imperialistic concepts. But to crushed and tyrannized nations—and Poland at this writing is not alone among them—the very last rampart of national and human dignity is the spiritual rampart of patriotism. If that rampart is unbreached, five generations of Polish experience prove that the nation seeking refuge behind it will not perish. It is for this reason that the cardinal element in the Polish national spirit is the dogma of patriotism.

Around such a core are grouped other more outward characteristics of the Polish national spirit—the Pole's pride in his ancient cultural heritage, his chivalrous and romantic temperament, his fondness for rural life and the out-of-doors, and his proverbial hospitality. Closer to the inner core of patriotism than any of these, however, are the soaring idealism and the individualism of the Pole. The one marks his entire thousand years of national history, the other, particularly in political thinking, has made him tolerant and friendly across class lines, an unfaltering believer in democratic government. To be sure, not at all times and not in all Poles have these qualities been more prominent than their accompanying extravagances. But the main course of Polish national aspirations was never more compactly described than in one of the lyric outbursts of Poland's greatest poet, Adam Mickiewicz:

> I shall beat one wing against the past,
> The other against the future,
> And steering by the dictates of the heart,
> Strive toward the feet of God.

The high moral purpose, the consciousness of a great historical and cultural past, and the sublime faith in its unbroken continuity into the future, which are here compressed by poetic genius into a few simple words, have all been fused by the intense heat of Polish patriotism into one spiritual heritage common to every Pole. From this spiritual heritage comes the Polish consciousness of fulfilling a mission in the world family of nations. That the world, in the past, has been loathe to attribute morally important missions to numerically and militarily weaker nations detracts nothing from their essential moral importance. This is a lesson which the great and powerful nations must eventually learn, if a workable peace on this planet is not to be forever an illusion.

The Polish past, which Mickiewicz had in mind, was marked with numerous blunders and extravagances, but in its spiritual substance it was a noble record of idealism and high moral purpose, brightened with magnificent cultural and political achievements. In the struggle of right against brute force, which is the criterion of civilized progress in any community of people, the Polish sense of right was not only a moral and spiritual guide but a political principle as well.

Perhaps the noblest illustration of this truth is the peaceful union between Poland and the Grand Duchy of Lithuania. Begun as a defensive alliance, and sealed by a dynastic marriage in 1386, this agreement between states was steadily developed by successive accords in 1413, 1434, and 1501 into an alliance of nations, until, in 1569, these countries became a republican brotherhood of nations with a common parliament and a commonly elected king. A multitude of problems had been involved—religious, economic, social, and political—but the methods employed for their solution were methods based on the premise of voluntary union of equals with equals, free with the free. This attitude of the Poles, who possessed far greater natural resources, incomparably greater military power, and who represented a much higher level of cultural attainment than the Lithuanians and Ruthenians of the Grand Duchy, is a testimonial not only of the essential harmony between political idealism and realistic political acumen, but also of the fundamental processes of Polish moral thinking.

Nor can the Poles point only to this single instance, amazingly ahead of the times as it is, of the translation of high moral purpose into concrete acts. When a Polish delegate to the League of Nations in our own times cast the slogan of moral disarmament among nations as a necessary step preceding actual military disarmament, he was only echoing another Pole who, at the Great Council of Constance in 1414, had proclaimed the ringing thesis that small, weak, pagan nations have the same rights as Christian nations so long as they live in peace with their neighbors. At the time, Poland had been Christian for five hundred years, and it was not a small nation seeking to enlist allies against an aggressor; it was a great Christian power which had just smashed the terror of eastern Europe, the Teutonic Order, at Grünewald (Tannenberg) in 1410, and was striving to introduce a new departure in international relations compatible with its own fundamental philosophy. That philosophy, as can be deduced from the history of the Polish-Lithuanian-Ruthenian union, was that morality among nations is no different in kind from the morality required in relations among individuals.

It may be stated that in these early centuries of modern European history, national feelings did not run high; the growth of nationalism was something which followed in the wake of the Protestant

Reformation, and, consequently, the limitations of national sovereignty, which were inherent in a brotherhood of national groups like the Polish-Lithuanian-Ruthenian Commonwealth, were relatively easy concessions for the strongest partner, Poland, to make. This is true. But, although in those centuries nationalisms were relatively mild, religious convictions, on the contrary, were fanatical. Was the idealism of the Polish spirit strong enough to prevail over the emotional extravagance of religious fanaticism?

The page of Polish history which treats of religion is the brightest record of Poland's thousand-year chronicle. In 1413, the Poles, who were uniformly Catholic, accepted into their family coats of arms only Catholic Lithuanian and Ruthenian clans. Twenty-one years later this privilege, with all its rights and liberties, was extended also to the Orthodox Lithuanian and Ruthenian clans, and from then on there were no distinctions among them, religious or political, in the incipient Polish-Lithuanian-Ruthenian Commonwealth. In 1573, at the very height of the religious wars in Europe, almost in the very year of the massacre of St. Bartholomew's Eve in France, the Polish-Lithuanian-Ruthenian Parliament decreed:

"Although in our Commonwealth there are considerable differences of conviction with regard to the Christian religion, nevertheless being desirous of avoiding harmful conflicts among our people on that account, such as we clearly see in other countries, we hereby jointly pledge ourselves and our successors under solemn oath, with our honesty, our honor, and our conscience, that even though we may have different religious convictions, we shall maintain peaceful relationships and shall not shed blood for differences in faith or in church practices."

In resurrected Poland the tradition of religious tolerance continued unabated. In fact, the Pole's respect and tolerance for any religion other than his own is perhaps even stronger than his piety in his own faith. The Pole is attached to his Catholicism, and he values it as a stable cohesive element in his national spirit; but he is not a fanatic, and his individualism is too well developed either to make him a conformist, or to make him insist that others conform in any matter so personal as one's religion.

In looking back over these great civilized achievements of ancient Poland, at a time when all of Europe was laying the sound foundations of royal absolutism, one cannot but admire this noble historical and cultural tradition. Brotherhood of national groups, and freedom of person and conscience under law in these instances cannot be ascribed to Polish political expediency only, or to economic and social advantage. These considerations entered, of course. That they did enter, however, is a further proof that social and economic advantages are attainable and perfectly compatible with freedom of person and conscience, and that the national pride and prestige of Great Powers is enhanced only by brotherhood on equal terms with the small. These concrete political attainments flowed naturally out of the Polish spiritual concept of right, out of high moral purpose, idealism, and a truly classical sense of proportion. They were, therefore, noble reflections of the Polish national spirit of that epoch.

One might ask why this magnificent spiritual and political maturity of the Polish nation in its Golden Age did not develop the capacity for further bold and decisive development. The answer would be that the capacity was not exerted to produce results comparable with those already attained. Seeds of decay had been sown even during this splendid period of development. In time, the Polish sense of proportion was lost under a rococo ornamentation of republican catchwords, and the great and promising institutions of true personal and spiritual freedom deteriorated into anarchical license for one large and powerful class—the landed gentry. The fact that this class was extremely numerous and comprised nearly 12 per cent of the total population mitigates, perhaps to some extent, the moral evil of its republican extravagances, but not the evil done to Poland. Election of ill-suited kings, concentration of wealth in the hands of a few, isolation from the rest of Europe and the resultant unawareness of Poland's national peril—such factors tended to create an apathy among the Poles toward the moral principles underlying Poland's great institutions of free, law-abiding living.

The First Partition of 1772, however, was a sobering shock to the Poles. The nation awakened to its danger, and by 1791, in the famous Constitution of May Third, it had effected an astounding spiritual and political regeneration. Certainly the deliberations on the articles of this great document were heated and long. Ingrained prejudices, vested interests, anarchical habits (the notorious *Libe-*

rum veto), indeed, more than a century of the rankest sort of privilege and license could not be overthrown without a struggle. After four years of debate, however, they were overthrown and, unlike France of that period, without bloodshed. In what other national history is there recorded a similar evidence of spiritual regeneration, when the very class which held and enjoyed all privileges met in parliament and proceeded to vote privileges away in favor of a broad-based, truly democratic system?

What had happened is relatively simple to explain. The Polish national spirit had sloughed off the accumulated ornamentations of specious catchwords, had reappeared in the classically balanced proportions of political idealism and realistic political acumen of the great past, and had reasserted and reëxerted its capacity for further bold and decisive development. But it was too late to save the Polish State. Enclosed in a fierce triangle of rising Russian, Prussian, and Austrian imperialism, Poland was attacked with overwhelming force, and it fell. Its body was destined to remain prostrate under the heels of three empires for five generations.

Then it was that the present Polish national anthem was written, and the Polish nation took refuge behind its last rampart, patriotism. Under these circumstances, it is naturally impossible to seek manifestations of the Polish national spirit throughout the nineteenth century in concrete, political implementations by the nation of new and noble principles of democratic government, religious toleration, or international morality. The Poles, in their new condition, could not express themselves in self-government. The national spirit could find expression only in literature, painting, and music.

All the civilized world knows the ethereal melodies and powerful, virile rhythms of Chopin's polonaises. Only the Poles, however, know the heroic canvases of Matejko and Grottgier and the great spiritual teachings of the exiled Polish nineteenth-century poets. They know them well, for only in the realm of the spirit were five generations of Poles free to develop.

A Poland spiritually regenerated, but physically crushed and shattered, was the background against which the three great Polish poets, Mickiewicz, Słowacki, and Krasiński matured. With the new national anthem ringing in their ears, they proceeded to fight for Polish freedom with the sharpest weapon they had—the pen—and it was with a sense of patriotic duty that they assumed the burden of sustaining and cultivating the Polish national spirit manifested in the anthem and in the Constitution of May Third, the last great concrete achievement and the political testament of the former Republic of Poland.

To Mickiewicz in particular, chronologically standing so near to the events which had precipitated Poland's downfall at the very moment of its spiritual and political regeneration, the physical destruction of his country was a tragic enigma. He saw all the political institutions so nobly established being abolished or emasculated; he saw the Catholic church being persecuted, a church which he identified with the Polish national spirit as against the Byzantine Christianity of the Russians or the Lutheranism of the Germans. The schools, the law, customs, traditions were forcibly being warped to fit the *raison d'état* of the oppressors. Yet, in his deepest convictions, the mark of the national anthem was on Mickiewicz. He could not believe that Poland had perished. Even in its enslavement he believed it remained a living, spiritual force and a creative factor in civilized progress toward a better world. He simply could not understand how God had allowed his country to succumb before mere brute force.

To find the answer to this tragic enigma, he soared to the highest summits of inspiration and peered into the mysteries of God's will. In his mind there took shape a political gospel which to men of pedestrian temperament cannot but appear absurd or even blasphemous. In his search for spiritual anchorage, by which to give his countrymen his own conviction in the inevitability of Poland's resurrection as a free and sovereign state, he exalted the sufferings of his prostrate nation into a Christlike martyrdom.

In Mickiewicz's *Books of Polish Pilgrimage,* which the poet wrote in sonorous Biblical prose as a political and spiritual guide for his countrymen, Poland was a Christ among nations, crucified for the redemption of corrupt European peoples who had reverted to idol worship. "... And the nations forgot," wrote Mickiewicz, "that they all stem from one Father. And the Englishman said: my Father is the *Ship,* and my Mother, *Steam.* The Frenchman said: my Father is the *Land,* and my Mother, the *Bourse.* And the German said: my Father is the *Workshop,* and my Mother, the *Beerhall* ..."

To the poet, there was nothing immorally proud or blasphemous in the concept of Poland as a Christ among nations which his poetic imagination was creating. It was the only philosophic explanation he could find which afforded a spiritual anchorage indestructible by any new storms. Indeed, had not Polish political and cultural history in previous centuries proved to him, by astounding acts of moral greatness, that Poland alone among the great nations of Europe had not bowed before idols, but in actual political deeds had implemented the Christian principle of love and brotherhood among men and nations? He looked back to the Polish-Lithuanian-Ruthenian brotherhood of equals with equals, free with the free; he followed Polish history in its forward march to the great religious proclamation of 1573; and in 1683, he had seen King John Sobieski, at the head of a Polish army of relief, hurl the Turk back from the very gates of Vienna to save Europe for Christendom and to rescue Austria, a country which was in no way Poland's friend. To Mickiewicz's poetic and patriotically exalted imagination, therefore, there could be nothing fantastically absurd or blasphemous in this Messianic concept of Poland. To his countrymen, oppressed and insulted at home, ridiculed abroad as "*condottieri* of freedom," touched to the quick by the slanderous interpretations of their history, as expounded not only abroad but even to Polish children in school by the Russian and Prussian despoilers, this new Messianic historiosophy had tremendous appeal. The sufferings of the Polish people now began to make moral sense, for Mickiewicz was unfolding to them what seemed to be a divinely ordained scheme of circumstances on earth in which their sufferings were necessary. Without sacrifice, there could be no redemption. Poland had to endure a holocaust in order to be redeemed together with all mankind.

The soaring poetic inspiration, and the utter sincerity of Mickiewicz's historiosophic vision made it sublime to his countrymen. Its sublimity, in turn, made this Polish national Messianism a source of spiritual strength for the Polish will to freedom, a strength which exists to this day. From their history, the Poles could confirm their positive contributions in the past to the progress of civilized living. From the teachings of their greatest poet they now acquired both a sense of the unbroken continuity of that past into the future and a consciousness of martyrdom in the cause of a better world. The result of martyrdom is always spiritual strength.

"In proportion as you enlarge and perfect your souls," wrote Mickiewicz in his *Books of Polish Pilgrimage,* "by so much will you improve your laws and enlarge your frontiers." In other words, he put the moral responsibility for the redemption and future greatness of Poland squarely upon each individual Pole, for the morality of a nation, to his mind, was only the sum of the moral perfections and imperfections of the individuals comprising it. This may be recognized as an old Polish concept, a further development of the Polish attitude at Constance, in 1414, when the Polish spokesman insisted that morality among nations is no different in kind from the morality required among individuals.

Consequently, Mickiewicz did not place much importance on material considerations: "Do not, therefore, excessively admire the nations which grow fat in prosperity," he taught his countrymen, "or which concern themselves mainly with efficient husbandry, or with disciplined organization.

"For if a nation which eats and drinks well is most to be respected, then respect those people among you who are fattest and healthiest. Behold, even animals have these virtues, but for a human being this is not enough.

"And if nations which are efficient in husbandry are to be regarded as most perfect, then even ants surpass them all in husbandry; but for a human being this is not enough.

"And if nations with disciplined organization are most perfect, then who is better organized and disciplined than the bees; but for man this is not enough.

"For a civilization truly worthy of man must be Christian."

Mickiewicz translated this civilized Christian attitude into the familiar dogma of Polish patriotism, but he conceived it as self-sacrifice not only for country, but also for all humanity. He cast the watchword not of "liberty or death," but "liberty through death"—the liberty of future generations through the sacrificial death of his own in the cause of human freedom. "For," he teaches his countrymen, "Christ said: 'Whoso would follow me, let him leave his father and his mother and hazard his soul.'

"The Polish Pilgrim says: 'Whoso would follow Freedom, let him leave his country and hazard his life.'

"For whoso remains in his country and suffers slavery in order to save his life, he will lose both country and life; but whoso leaves his country in order to defend Freedom at the hazard of his life, he will save his country and will live forever...."

It is with the spiritual conviction born of these great teachings that the Polish armed forces fight in the ranks of the United Nations today; it is, therefore, not surprising that the number of Poles engaged surpasses the number in the forces of all the other occupied nations taken together. Even to a non-Pole these teachings of Mickiewicz, by their very nobility and sincerity, carry no little conviction. To the Polish people, exiles and prisoners in their own native land, these words were and still are a faith and a law. From the ethereal summits of Mickiewicz's poetic inspiration, spiritual sustenance has never ceased to flow.

Mickiewicz closed his *Books of Polish Pilgrimage* with a prayer for freedom.

"O Lord God Almighty! from the far corners of the earth the children of a fighting nation raise their hands to Thee. They cry out to Thee from the depths of Siberian mines, from the snows of Kamchatka, from the deserts of Algeria, and from France, a foreign land. And in our native land, Poland faithful to Thee, it is forbidden to call upon Thee, and our old men, and women, and children pray to Thee in secret, in their thoughts, and with their tears. God of the Jagiełłos! God of the Sobieskis! God of the Kościuszkos have mercy on our country and on us. Permit us once more to pray to Thee as our fathers did, on the field of battle with a weapon in our hand, before an altar of drums and cannon, under a canopy of our Polish eagles and banners; and permit our families to pray in the churches of our cities and villages, and our children to pray over our graves. But, indeed, may not our will but Thy will be done, Amen."

No other nation in Europe has a literature so intensely patriotic and sublime as Poland's, nor one which has had such great influence on the national spirit. To the splendid balance of high moral purpose, idealism, and political acumen which had characterized the Polish national spirit in the greatest days of the old Republic, and which had reasserted its presence in the Constitution of May Third, Polish romantic literature had added tremendous intensity of feeling. The contemporaries of Mickiewicz–Słowacki and Krasiński–soared as high as he, and spun the philosophical thread of Polish national Messianism so fine that it soon snapped.

But, although Polish literature shortly abandoned its attempt to transfigure Poland into a Christ among nations, it had already reached and reinforced the last fortress of the people–their hearts. All the more earnestly, therefore, have the Poles followed the spiritual leadership of their poets. Of patriotism the poets had made a dogma; of the inevitable resurrection of the Polish State they had made a faith and a law; for they preached and still preach a sublime nationalism purified by suffering, imbedded in Christian morality, and leading to freedom. If the teachings of Polish literature soared too high for pedestrian logic to follow, if poetic fervor at times blinded the poets to the difference in levels between the bitter facts of Polish life and the idealistic plane on which their visions could come true, their only fault was that they had placed too much emphasis on "Thy will be done on Earth as it is in Heaven" and too little on "Give us this day our daily bread."

Their great and lasting virtue was that they had reached the hearts and souls of the Polish people with a soaring Christian political gospel. They had taught their countrymen the meaning of freedom and greatness, not in terms of economic determinism or material benefits, but in terms of the dignity of the human spirit, in terms of honor, and honesty, and moral and civic duty. "Measure your strength by your aims," sang Mickiewicz, in romantic fervor, "not your aims by your strength." When Poland faced the tenfold greater power of Germany in 1939, because it had rejected the base expedient of joining in an attack upon Russia, it was the voice of the Polish national spirit which spoke through the words of Józef Beck, when he said: "Peace . . . has its price, high but definable. . . . There is only one thing . . . without price, and that is honor."

This, in brief outline, is the substance of the Polish national spirit as it has manifested itself in the past. Modern Poland, from its rebirth in 1918 to the present, has not faltered in its expression of the national spirit nor has it discarded any of its commandments. If anything, modern Poland has even toughened the fiber of the ancient spiritual heritage. The Pole in reborn Poland has been schooled in the greatness of spirit of his nation's past, and he has accepted the obligations to his nation and to humanity which the continuity of that past has imposed on him. Amid the ideological hysteria and political turmoil of Europe, in the twenty-five years between two world wars, Poland may have erred at times in political judgment, but the buoyant idealism, dogmatic patriotism, and the deep Christian concept of the right, which characterized the Polish national spirit in the past, remained the guide of Polish actions. When this war is over, and the world has recovered its sense of proportion in judging the material attainments and the spiritual qualities of nations, two facts about Poland in the twenty-year armistice will stand out in their true perspective.

The first is that, with little advertising and no boasting, Poland reconstructed its cities, villages, communications, factories, and farms which were ravaged more fiercely than in any other theater of the First World War. Despite this devastation, Poland built a firmly knit, compact state, in which material and social progress made no less rapid strides and at less cost to individual freedom than in many more widely propagandized countries. That these achievements were not publicized is an omission for which Poland is now paying dearly in world opinion. As early as 1918, however, the great Polish patriot and writer, Stefan Żeromski, had set the lofty material and spiritual goals of Poland's re-won freedom:

> Free Poland must work out and will work out a higher and more perfect ideal of social life than Communist Russia, and must create a higher material civilization than efficient Germany, for only in this way can she ensure her independence for ages. All we who in the days of our enslaved youth bent down without hesitation to the feet of laboring and suffering man, to the workman oppressed by tyranny,—are we to drop our hands idly now that fate has put into them the great fortune of freedom?

The comparisons in this passage are not haughty assertions of Polish social and technical excellence, but contemporary admissions rather that Poland is far behind and must catch up before it can lead in the material benefits of modern civilized living.

It is worth noting that in this modern reflection of the Polish national spirit, freedom is a "great fortune," i.e., it is the spiritual capital with which to build a just and perfect social system, and an elevated standard of living. These technical and material attainments, however, are not ends in themselves, but only the means by which to perpetuate and enlarge that freedom. The major tone is idealism, and the heaviest emphasis falls on spiritual values. This is characteristic of the Polish national spirit, for it is the result of a long historical and cultural tradition.

That the execution of the ideal fell short of the ideal itself in Poland, is not a sign of failure; it is a sign of "Measure your strength by your aims, and not your aims by your strength." The job to be done was tremendous and the stumbling blocks were many, for the ideal was high. The perspective of time, however, will eventually place the actual social and material attainments of Poland in their proper relation to the attainments of Europe as a whole. When all the known facts of the last twenty-five years are brought together, the true measure of Poland's achievement will be seen.

Pulling itself up economically by its own bootstraps, Poland transformed an obscure fishing village into a modern wonder city of over 100,000 population, and developed it into the largest and finest port on the Baltic. By tightening its belt in the depression, Poland held its currency stable when the currencies of rich and powerful states were crumbling. Having inherited a railroad system in which more than half the bridges, water pumps, stations, and repair shops were destroyed in the First World War, with the rolling stock the refuse of Austria and Germany, in the twenty years of its freedom Poland repaired all the war damage and built up its roads and rolling stock to stand without peer in Europe. (In 1939 in Warsaw alone, 550 trains a days entered its stations.)

In the fields of education, coöperative movements, and social legislation, the record is one of amazing progress. In 1918, there were three institutions of university standing in Poland; in 1939, there were twenty. With the completion of nearly 15,000 new primary and secondary schools in Poland, by 1939 some 33,000 schools were teaching nearly 5,000,000 pupils a year. In other words, every seventh person in Poland was in school. Coöperative societies numbered nearly 14,000 and embraced over 3,000,000 members. Social legislation protecting workmen and the rights of organized labor as early as 1925 had outstripped the guarantees which American and British workmen have only most recently acquired. The irony of it all is that this was accomplished by a nation which has never ceased to bear the stigma of backwardness in the eyes of the world.

HEAD OF OLD MOUNTAINEER

WOODCUT BY WLADYSLAW SKOCZYLAS

The second fact is that, after twenty years of peaceful and creative coöperation with all nations of good will, it was Poland which did not shrink from setting a price on peace with states motivated by ill will and cynicism. Poland's achievements in beautifying its cities, in cultivating the material benefits of newly won freedom, and in distributing these benefits among all its people were doubly precious to it, for these achievements had been hard of attainment in a country which had to repair the devastation of the First World War before it could even begin to build anew.

In spite of these difficulties, it was Poland which first, among the nations of Europe, set a price upon peace. Cherishing peace no less than any other nation, Poland was the first which dared to cherish national honor more. It refused to weigh its national dignity and honor in the same scales with material safety and political expediency. It unequivocally asserted that its freedom and honor as an independent state were worth the lifeblood of its people, and it was the first to stand prepared to pay this price. Before this mark and proof of greatness, other virtues pale and shortcomings shrink. Never, in all the thousand-year history of Poland, did its spirit shine with higher luster than in the ominous period preceding the Second World War, nor in the martyrdom it has suffered since. Sustained by the Polish dogma of patriotism, the Polish people still hold to their noble Christian political gospel; their pride in their great historical and cultural past only strengthens their conviction in the continuity of that heritage into the future. By their conduct, the Poles have shown that national spirit today, as in the past, demands no reward for virtue and no pity for martyrdom, but only justice and honor among men and nations.

Part Six

POLISH-AMERICAN RELATIONS

CHAPTER XXIII

Polish-American Cultural Relationships

BY STEPHEN P. MIZWA

AMERICA HAS BEEN KNOWN to the Poles from the very beginning of its discovery. Sometimes it has appeared as a heroic land, but more often it has been thought of as a land of bliss to which many Poles longed to go and, indeed, to which many did go.

Happy Isles—heroic land of bliss
Known to our country long ere this....

Thus did a Polish poet, Sebastian Klonowicz, allude to America in the sixteenth century.

The first, although somewhat confused reference to the New World (*Novum Mundum*), is found in a book printed in Cracow in 1506, *A Brief Introduction on the Treatise on the Earth* (*Introductorium Compendiosum in Tractatum Sp[h]ere Materialis*), by Joannes Sacrobosco, with commentaries by Joannes Głogoviensis (Jan z Głogowa), both professors at the University of Cracow. On the Jagiellonia Golden Globe, constructed in Cracow about 1510–1512, America was placed as "newly discovered land" (*Terra noviter reperta*). Copernicus, in his epoch-making treatise of 1543 *On the Revolutions of the Heavenly Bodies* (*De Revolutionibus Orbium Coelestium*)—the quadricentennial of which the American educational and scientific world celebrated on May 24, 1943—uses the discovery of America as one of the important arguments—the sphericity of the earth—in building up his heliocentric system. Marcin Bielski, a Polish geographer, in his *Chronicles of the Entire World* (*Kroniki Wszystkiego Świata*), published in Cracow in 1551, speaks of America as being "so large that it may be considered as the fourth grand division of the earth." Thus, from the beginning of the sixteenth century, America finds its way with increasing frequency into Polish literature and, in time, assumes growing importance in the lives of the Poles.

In retrospect, four factors seem to stand out, with their interplay and mutual reinforcement, as cornerstones of spiritual and cultural relationships between Poland and America—the "Polish Americans," the exchange of heroes between Poland and America, President Wilson's "Thirteenth Point," and American relief in Poland after the First World War.

In the course of time and for various reasons—spiritual, political, but primarily economic—there have come to the United States considerable numbers of Poles. These Poles now constitute a relatively large component part of the American population, some four to five million Americans of Polish blood, with Polish temperament and Polish sympathies, and not entirely devoid of Polish cultural traditions. At first, even among themselves, they were called "Poles in America," then "American Poles," then "Polish-Americans," and, finally, "Polish Americans" without the hyphen (using the term "Polish" not necessarily coequally, but rather in a sense of derivative adjective). Finally, during the period under discussion in this volume, 1919–1939, they "came of age," and more recently began to call themselves "Americans," or "Americans of Polish descent or extraction." Even a new term has come into use—"Polish Yankees."

But by whatever name the American Poles have been known, either as individuals, as a group, or as disjointed groups, they have made their contributions to America, economically and culturally, and have played an important part in Polish-American relationships. Physically, they are lost to Poland; but, at the same time, they are the best national investment Poland has ever made. The capital is gone, never to be paid back more than a cent on a dollar, if that much; but these Polish Americans continue to bring moral dividends to Poland. They serve as one of the solid buttresses in the structure of Polish-American relationships. They are cobuilders and cobenefactors of American civilization. They helped to build America, helped to make it strong, and now, when America speaks in behalf of oppressed European nations, its voice carries weight and Poland benefits. And because there are so many Polish Americans here, Poland is a little better known—and perhaps a little better understood. To their cousins in Poland, once or twice removed, they are a source of pride; they are relatives who have gone into the world and made good. Here, on the free soil of America, they send their sons to Congress and to state legislatures; they possess thousands of relatively large farms and own thousands of businesses and manufacturing concerns—most of them relatively small, but all their own. They have fraternal benefit organizations with over a half million members and tens of millions of dollars in resources. They publish about sixty newspapers—dailies, weeklies, and other periodicals—and although the number of their readers is growing ever smaller, they freely write in the language of their forefathers without any governmental interference. They have erected about nine hundred churches (approximately 90 per cent Roman Catholic and about 10 per cent of the Polish National Church) where they have freedom of worship. They have also built some four hundred schools—mostly primary, the remainder secondary, with a few higher institutions of learning of college grade—where their children enjoy freedom of instruction. They have hundreds of singing societies, art clubs, and amateur theatrical associations. Thousands of their children and grandchildren attend American colleges, universities, and music schools, and over one hundred thousand are in American secondary schools. These children are a source of hope and inspiration to their cousins in Poland.

The second cornerstone on which Polish-American relationships have been based, and which has become a spiritual heritage of both nations, is the fact that in critical periods of struggle for the liberty of both nations, Poland and America have exchanged not goods but heroes. The terms "heroes" and "liberty" may have become hackneyed, but time has not dimmed their historic significance. There were Americans who championed and fought for the Polish cause, and there were Poles who nobly served under George Washington in the army of the Revolution, as they have in every war in which America since has been engaged.

Kościuszko and Pułaski, who have often been mentioned, have caught the popular imagination. Although there were many other Poles, even in the Revolutionary Army, those two names serve as symbols of Polish-American relationship. Kościuszko was the first foreign soldier of distinction to land on American soil—in the late summer of 1776; and Pułaski was the first, if not the only foreign soldier of his rank and distinction, to give his life for the American cause. In Paris, before his departure for America, Benjamin Franklin was told by Pułaski, "Wherever on the globe men are fighting for liberty, it is as if it were our own affair." During the Civil War there was General Józef Karge, born in Poland under Prussian occupation, who became one of the most skilful Union cavalry leaders. And there was General Vladimir Krzyżanowski, first cousin of Frederick Chopin, who volunteered as private and finished as brigadier general, even though there was a delay in confirming his nomination by President Lincoln because the senators could not pronounce the name "Krzyżanowski." His men knew better right along; they called him "Kriz" for short.

Less known is the fact that, among the younger if not the youngest soldiers in actual combat, were Polish lads who volunteered at the age of sixteen—Edmund L. Zaliński of Syracuse, New York, and Stanisław Rydzewski of New York; among the older ones, if not the eldest, was another Polish "lad," Józef Krokowski of Jones County, Iowa, who enlisted at the age of sixty-one. Incidentally, Captain Edmund Louis (Gray) Zaliński (1845–1909) later became professor of military science in the Massachusetts Institute of Technology, at which institution he developed several military devices. Among the first, if not actually the first, Union officers to die on the field of battle was a Polish exile, Captain Constantine Blandowski of the Third Missouri Infantry, who was mortally wounded on May 10, 1861, and died on May 25th. Captain Blandowski had formerly taken part in the Hungarian insurrection of 1848 and had served under Garibaldi in Italy. Tytus Filipowicz, the Polish Ambassador at Washington in 1929, when America commemorated the sesquicentennial of the death of Pułaski, apparently had the first two "cornerstones" in mind when he said: "Poland is proud that in the glorious edifice of the American Republic there are stones laid by Polish hands and cemented with Polish blood."

Whereas during the first World War the Central Powers and Tsarist Russia were making promises to the Poles which they did not intend to keep, there came a clear voice from the President of the United States demanding unequivocally a free and independent Poland. What Lincoln's Gettysburg address is to Americans, Woodrow Wilson's "Thirteenth Point" is to the Poles: "An independent Polish State should be erected which should include the territories inhabited by indisputably Polish populations, which should be assured a free and secure access to the sea, and whose political and economic independence and territorial integrity should be guaranteed by international covenant."

The moral influence, direct or indirect, of Polish Americans was not altogether absent in the championship of the Polish cause by Woodrow Wilson. The roles which Ignacy Jan Paderewski and his friend, Colonel Edward M. House, played in securing President Wilson's interest are well known to both Poles and Americans. The Poles in Poland, as well as those scattered all over the world, did not wait for their independence to be handed to them on a silver platter. They labored, fought, and bled to regain their freedom. Yet, the entire Polish nation has been grateful to the American people for the moral stand their President took with respect to the "Polish question," and has regarded Woodrow Wilson as a symbol of America's good will toward Poland.

When, after the war, the Poles were despoiled, hungry, and sick, and their children were dying from starvation, there came to Poland an American Food Mission, a part of the American Relief Administration, to administer first aid and to feed the hungry. There were other American agencies in Poland: the American Friends (Quakers), the American Red Cross, the Jewish Joint Distribution Committee, and the Y.M.C.A. The Students' Relief of the Y.M.C.A., for example, from April, 1921, to June, 1922, at times fed as many as 11,000 of the 33,000 Polish university students. Within the critical period of fifteen months, a total of 2,337,165 meals were served at student kitchens. Herbert Hoover, as chairman of the American Relief Administration, became a symbol of American generosity and philanthropy to the Poles.

Thus, the historical and the contemporary relationship of the four cornerstones, the ideal and the sentimental, the material and the practical, have become intertwined to constitute a sound basis for mutual friendship and cultural relationships between the two countries. Among many evidences in both countries of this mutual respect and friendship are the monuments. The Corps of Cadets at West Point, as early as 1828, erected a statue in honor of Pułaski. The nation also erected a beautiful equestrian statue of Pułaski in the capital of the United States. The New Jersey Skyway, a magnificent modern highway, also was named in honor of Pułaski. There are Kościuszko and Pułaski streets, squares, even towns and counties throughout the country. In Poland, also, streets and squares have been named in honor of America, of Woodrow Wilson and Herbert Hoover, of Washington and Lincoln. In Lwów there is a monument in honor of those American aviators who died in the war of 1920. Paderewski, at his own expense, erected a monument to Woodrow Wilson in Poznań and one to Colonel House in Warsaw. Also, in Warsaw, on October 29, 1922, there was unveiled a Monument of Gratitude "in commemoration of the material, moral, and political aid given Poland by the United States."

In Poland, throughout the period from 1919 to 1939, certain American national holidays were celebrated with no less fervor than in America—especially Memorial Day and Independence Day, and also Lincoln's and Washington's birthdays. On each Memorial Day at Lwów, at the American Aviators' Monument, there was always an impressive ceremony with pilgrimages; delegations arrived from many parts of the country and an official representative of the American Embassy in Warsaw, usually the military attaché, attended.

Two American anniversaries that fell within the twenty-year period were celebrated in Poland on a truly nation-wide scale—the sesquicentennial of the Declaration of Independence on July 4, 1926, and the bicentennial of Washington's birthday in 1932. On the occasion of the latter anniversary a postage stamp was issued and a popular story of Washington was published and distributed to all elementary and secondary schools throughout the country. The celebration of the sesquicentennial of the Declaration of Independence reached every hamlet and village, in fact every remote corner of the nation. On that occasion, messages of tribute and gratitude to America were collected from all sections of the country, signed by all the officials from the President down to the mayor of the smallest village and by over 5,000,000 school children. These messages were bound in one hundred and twelve large volumes, in leathers of variegated colors and in the woven cloths of the Polish peasant craft, each volume having a distinctive artistic decoration. They were later presented to President Calvin Coolidge, who accepted them in behalf of the American nation. An introductory message of tribute, signed by the President of Poland in behalf of the Polish nation, reads in part:

> We, the people of Poland, send to you, Citizens of the great American Union, fraternal greetings, together with the assurance of our deepest admiration and esteem for the institutions which have been created by you. In them liberty, equality and justice have found their highest expression, and have become guiding stars for all modern democracies.
>
> Noble Americans, Your National Holiday is sacred not for you alone.
>
> It finds a warm reverberation over the whole world, and especially in our Motherland Poland, which is proud of the fact that in that momentous hour of your history when George Washington raised the banner of liberty, there stood also beside him our champions of national liberty, Thaddeus Kościuszko and Casimir Pułaski.
>
> The blood then mutually shed has forever united us by bonds of common feelings for the same ideal of the Free Man and the Free Nation.

As though in response to this Polish national sentiment, although quite independently, on October 18, 1926—marking the One Hundred and Fiftieth Anniversary of Kościuszko's enrollment in the Revolutionary Army as Colonel of Engineers—there was observed in America a Kościuszko Recognition Day. Many governors of the thirteen original states issued public proclamations calling upon their respective citizens to pay fitting tribute to the memory of this Polish national hero and Revolutionary War patriot. On that day, under the auspices of a national committee headed by Charles Evans Hughes, and including governors of the thirteen original states and heads of leading American patriotic societies and higher institutions of learning, commemorative exercises were held in Memorial Continental Hall, in Washington, D.C., with the Secretary of War presiding. Addresses were made by members of the Cabinet, and by prominent educators and representatives of patriotic societies.

There were various factors, individuals, agencies and, as a rule, uncoördinated activities that promoted, tended to promote, or contributed to the cultural relationships between Poland and America within the twenty-year period, 1919–1939. Some twelve American universities and thirty American high schools—the latter mostly in and around Chicago, Milwaukee, and Detroit—offered courses in the Polish language and in Polish literature, either throughout or during a considerable part of that period. No statistical data are available, but through personal contacts the present writer knows that many American students at their own expense went to Poland for special studies, and that some Polish students came to America in quest of special knowledge. These numbers were not large and, because of self-selection, there was a considerable difference in ability and academic preparation between individual students, but in sum total they exerted some influence in their subsequent work.

The World Alliance of Poles, with headquarters in Warsaw, granted scores of scholarships to young Americans of Polish extraction for supplementary studies in Poland. The American Polish Chamber of Commerce in New York City, from 1920 to 1931 inclusively, published an illustrated monthly magazine, *Poland,* which contained articles on various phases of Polish art, literature, history, biography, reviews of books on Polish topics—education, music, dances, costumes, customs, and folklore. The Polish-American Chamber of Commerce in Warsaw for a while published a similar monthly in the Polish language, *America-Poland* (*Ameryka-Polska*), with leading articles on American life. That chamber, jointly with the Polish-American Society, furnished guidance and counsel to prominent American tourists in Poland; it also held monthly luncheons, in which the American colony in Warsaw participated, with some prominent visitor from America almost always a guest of honor. The Polish-American Chamber of Commerce also sponsored various pro-American manifestations in Poland; it prepared and distributed articles for the Polish press on American topics; distributed American books and periodicals of special interest to Polish organizations, institutions, and various chambers of commerce; coöperated with the Kościuszko Foundation in New York in the selection of candidates as business and industrial apprentices for further practical training in America.

The Carnegie Endowment for International Peace also made an incidental contribution within that period. Under its auspices, an American scholar spent a few months in Poland and a Polish scholar gave a series of lectures in America; a group of American economists, who were in central Europe, visited Poland; one student from Poland was granted a Fellowship in International Law for study in America; two Polish scholars were invited to deliver a series of lectures, each in connection with the *Chaire Carnegie* established by the Endowment at Paris; nine Polish publicists, diplomats, scholars, and professors of international law were invited to deliver a course of lectures, each on some phase of international law at the Academy of International Law at The Hague; six Polish university libraries and three special libraries were designated as depository libraries to receive all publications of the Endowment; an original work in two volumes, *Poland's Economic and Social Life During the War (La Pologne, sa vie économique et sociale pendant la guerre*), was financed by the Endowment.

The contribution of Mr. Miecislaus Haiman must also be noted. Although Mr. Haiman is the organizer and custodian of the Archives and Museum of the Polish Roman Catholic Union of America, with headquarters in Chicago, he is a Polish-American institution by himself. Starting as a newspaperman, in an inconspicuous position, he labored ceaselessly at dusty shelves and through inaccessible manuscripts for the records of a Polish past in America. As the result of his toil he has published, in English and in Polish, more than a dozen monographic contributions—ranging from pamphlets to fairly large-sized books. Jointly, within the twenty-year period, these books constitute the greatest contribution of a single author to a better understanding and an appreciation of the Polish past in America. Mr. Haiman is a pioneer in the true sense of the word; he has plowed the long-neglected field and shown that it can yield rich harvests. He himself modestly maintains that he has only scratched the surface, yet no author on the history of Poles in America can possibly afford not to consult the works of Mr. Haiman. The Archives and Museum which came into being through Mr. Haiman's efforts, also is a most useful institution. It collects and preserves letters, documents, pamphlets, books, pictures, and works of art pertaining to Poles in America in the past, to Americans of Polish extraction in the present, and to Polish-American cultural relationships.

One of the most important factors in the promotion of Polish-American cultural relationships has been the almost steady stream of Polish intellectuals, writers, and artists who have been coming to America since the days of Dr. Curtius in 1659. In 1783 a poet, Tomasz Kajetan Wengierski, toured nearly all of the states of the Union, met most of the Revolutionary leaders, including George Washington, and wrote a diary of his travels which was the first description of the United States by a Polish author. In his footsteps followed Juljan Ursyn Niemcewicz, statesman, poet, and historian, companion and friend of Kościuszko. Niemcewicz spent two weeks at Mount Vernon as guest of George Washington. He married Elizabeth Kean in Elizabeth, New Jersey, in which state he settled for a while. Upon his return to Poland he wrote what appears to be the first original biography of George Washington, *A Short Sketch of the Life and Deeds of George Washington (Krotka Wiadomóść o Życiu i Sprawach Generała Washingtona).*

In the first group of Polish priests that came at the beginning of the nineteenth century, one of them, Father Francis Dzierożyński, became vice-president and treasurer of Georgetown University. Excluding the three waves of Polish intellectuals who came to the United States after the Uprising of 1830–1831, the Revolution of 1848, and the Insurrection of 1863, from the middle of the second half of the nineteenth century there have come some of the greatest men and women of Poland—among numerous others who also made some impression.

For several decades Helena Modjeska (Modrzejewska) delighted American audiences throughout the country with her appearances in Shakespearean roles. In addition to Modjeska, for a few years, there was Henryk Sienkiewicz, the first Polish Nobel Prize laureate whose *Quo Vadis* has traveled over the entire world and has become cosmopolitan property. Sienkiewicz's sojourn in America played a decisive part in maturing his genius. While here, he wrote *Letters from a Journey in America* and the tale, *Sketches in Charcoal.* Also, while here, he found prototypes for two of his immortal characters in Polish literature, "Old Captain" Rudolf Korwin Pietrowski for *Zagloba,* and Captain Francis Wojciechowski for *Longinus* (*Podbipienta*). Already within the period under discussion there were two other Nobel Prize laureates: Władysław Reymont and Maria Skłodowska Curie. There was also the great Paderewski. Among numerous others were the De Reszke brothers, Jean and Edouard, Marcella Sembrich-Kochanska, and Adam

Didur, all of the Metropolitan Opera of New York; more recently Jan Kiepura, baritone; Józef Hofmann and Artur Rubinstein, pianists; Paul Kochański and Bronisław Huberman, violinists; and Wanda Landowska, undoubtedly the greatest living harpsichordist, now a resident of New York. Leopold Stokowski is of Polish extraction, as is Dr. Artur Rodziński from Lwów.

All these people have made their contributions to American-Polish relationships. And, because of their unique place in this sphere of activity, one organization and two foundations merit special attention, namely, the American Y.M.C.A. in Poland, the Rockefeller Foundation, and the Kościuszko Foundation. The American Y.M.C.A., which was adapted to Polish conditions and became a Polish Y.M.C.A., is a unique institution and a unique contribution. An institution which had its roots deep in the Protestant tradition and way of life was adopted by a Catholic nation. No less unique also is the fact that Protestant leaders of the American Y.M.C.A. were willing to feed, clothe, and finance the education of this strange offspring for the enjoyment, so to speak, of a strange family.

The American Y.M.C.A. came to Poland in 1919 with the Polish Army in France, known as "General Haller's Polish Army." Amply supplied with American funds and trained personnel, the services of the Y.M.C.A. soon extended to all parts of Poland. The entire range of army Y.M.C.A. work was made available to all Polish soldiers; it did everything that the present highly streamlined U.S.O. is doing for men in service in the current war. It also helped Polish students with cheap and decent dormitories, feeding stations, recreation and social centers, and supplementary courses of study.

When the war of 1920 ended and the country was gradually returning to relatively peaceful conditions, an urgent request to the American Y.M.C.A. came from a group of Polish leaders in every walk of life to organize a Polish Y.M.C.A., one which would permanently do for Polish young men what the American Y.M.C.A. had done as a temporary service. The task was not easy. This Catholic Y.M.C.A. had to be financed, to a large extent, by its Protestant constituents. When the war came in September, 1939, the Polish Y.M.C.A. was one of the strongest and also one of the richest in Europe. It had considerably over $2,000,000 worth of property, of which about $1,000,000 came from America. The new building of the Warsaw Y.M.C.A., with the most modern of American conveniences, was the largest Y.M.C.A. plant in Europe. The Cracow Y.M.C.A. building, with the first indoor swimming pool in that ancient capital of Poland, was donated by the late Sereno P. Fenn of Cleveland, Ohio. Mr. Fenn gave $150,000 for the building in Cracow, and contributed $300,000 toward the building in Warsaw. There were five Polish Y.M.C.A. buildings in all; the large ones were in Warsaw, Cracow, and Łódź and the smaller ones in Poznań and Gdynia.

Starting with no money at all the Polish Y.M.C.A. was entirely independent of American financial subsidies for several years prior to the outbreak of the present war. The staff of eight American secretaries was gradually reduced to one, Paul Super, who, for almost the entire period, was technical specialist of the Polish Y.M.C.A. He learned the language of the country and himself became a national institution. As the American personnel was gradually reduced to one, the Polish personnel grew into forty-one permanent secretaries whose work was not so much directed as guided by the American technical specialist. This proved to be a very successful arrangement.

The American Y.M.C.A. contributed to Poland the Polish Y.M.C.A., and through that medium introduced certain features of permanent social and educational value. They may be summarized under the following four heads: (1) Social—the idea of a club combining character-building activities with the features of wholesome and cultural implications; methods of social work and social work as a permanent profession for men of higher education; one large social organization serving all classes of the population. (2) Educational—practical vocational education through private initiative—the first radio school and the first automobile courses; the Y.M.C.A. type of summer camp for boys on an educational as well as a recreational basis. (3) Physical education and sport—the scientifically trained physical director, basketball, volleyball, recreative gymnastic work, the modern swimming pool, and its program of training, amateur boxing as a popular sport, scientific training for track athletics, the large modern gymnasium hall. (4) Financial methods—modern efficiency methods of social-work financing, including the finance campaign; new ideas and methods in social-work budgeting and administration.

Paul Super, whom the Poles call "Superski," writes:

> Tens of thousands of people used these five Polish Y.M.C.A. buildings and three camps, serving, quite literally, all classes from the poorest to the richest and most prominent.
>
> Notwithstanding the difficulties involved in adapting the Y.M.C.A. idea to a Catholic society, no people in postwar Europe more heartily accepted this movement than did the Poles, none put more of their own money into it, none valued its American coöperative relation more highly. Nowhere in Europe did Americans work in happier fraternity than did the American Y.M.C.A. secretaries in Poland, even though they worked under Polish authority. The Polish Y.M.C.A. has been, since December 8, 1923, a completely independent and autonomous organization. On that day the American Y.M.C.A. turned over to the Polish movement all its authority, property, money, and personnel, and the Polish Association was then really born.

How completely it was adapted to Polish conditions and Polish needs, and how thoroughly it has become Polish, is revealed in the fact that the Polish Y.M.C.A. has survived the war, is now operating in twelve different countries on three continents at several hundred points, with an annual budget of about $3,000,000. Of this amount only 10 per cent comes from America—including Polish-American contributions—and 90 per cent comes from Polish sources. There is no other Y.M.C.A. movement that serves its own people in so many different countries.

The contributions of the Rockefeller Foundation to the Polish-American cultural relationships were restricted, after rather sporadic attempts at relief, to a few definite channels within the Foundation's comprehensive scheme of general European policy; and within those restricted channels these contributions have been most substantial and of permanent value. If the American Y.M.C.A. applied scientific methods to social work in Poland, the Rockefeller Foundation applied science to philanthropy and constructive educational work.

The most substantive and constructive work of the Rockefeller Foundation in Poland began when Poland became independent, was continued to the outbreak of the present war, and even during the present war is being carried on, for the most part, in the form of fellowship grants to a few Polish refugee scholars. The coöperation of Thomas B. Appleget, Vice-President of the Rockefeller

Foundation, and H. B. van Wesep, its Chief of Information Service, has made possible the construction of two tables in terms of expenditures for work in Poland and the corollary expenditures for fellowships. Jointly, these tables summarize the scope of the Foundation's contributions to Poland and Polish-American cultural relationships.

EXPENDITURES FOR WORK IN POLAND

Public Health—including control of communicable diseases, nursing, sanitary engineering, School of Hygiene and Public Health in Warsaw	$568,304.37
Medical Sciences—including schools of nursing in Cracow and Warsaw, salaries, grants in aid	233,502.92
Natural Sciences—mostly equipment of the Institute of Physics at the University of Warsaw, partly grants in aid to the University of Warsaw, partly grants in aid to the University of Cracow	47,585.31
Social Sciences—grants in aid to the Polish Academy and the University of Lwów	28,000.00
Humanities—grants in aid to the University of Cracow	3,100.00
War Relief—1914–1924	86,781.37
	$967,273.97

EXPENDITURES FOR FELLOWSHIPS
(as of July 30, 1941)

Public Health:			
Regular Fellowships	50	$135,900.00	
Nursing Fellowships	31	84,258.00	$220,158.00
Medical Sciences	26		70,668.00
Natural Sciences	53		144,054.00
Social Sciences	38		103,284.00
Total number of fellowships	198	Total grants	$538,164.00

And last, though perhaps not least, is the Kościuszko Foundation, the only institution in existence organized for the sole purpose of promoting cultural and intellectual relationships between Poland and America. Established in December, 1925, as a living memorial to General Kościuszko, on the eve of the one hundred and fiftieth anniversary of his enrollment in the American Revolutionary Army, the Foundation's primary purpose has been to do for Polish-American cultural relationships what so many other foundations, institutes, and scholarship funds were doing for the exchange of students and professors and the interchange of spiritual goods, so to speak, between the United States and practically all other civilized countries of the world. Organized, jointly with other Americans, by Dr. Henry Noble MacCracken, President of Vassar College and President of the Foundation from the very beginning, the late Samuel M. Vauclain, President of Baldwin Locomotive Works, and Stephen P. Mizwa, the Foundation stated its aims and purposes in the charter as follows:

1. To grant voluntary financial aid to deserving Polish students desiring to study at higher institutions of learning in the United States of America; and to deserving American students desiring to study in Poland.

2. To encourage and aid the exchange of professors, scholars, and lecturers between Poland and the United States of America.

3. To cultivate closer intellectual and cultural relations between Poland and the United States in such ways and by such means as may from time to time seem wise, in the judgment of the Board of Directors [Trustees] of the Corporation.

"Ways and means" have differed from time to time, but the "judgment" of the Board of Trustees has always been "wise" in this respect, so that through times of prosperity and of depression, through peace and war, the Foundation has followed strictly its self-prescribed policy; it has never meddled in such controversial questions as religion or politics in either country and, although its capital fund has not as yet reached even a quarter of a million dollars, it has never lost a penny of its endowment through default or speculation. The activities of the Kościuszko Foundation may be summarized under the following heads:

Exchange of students and professors.—The backbone of its work has been the exchange of students and professors. From the time it was organized, it "exchanged" between Poland and America 170 students, research scholars, industrial apprentices, and professors; 101 Americans went to Poland and 69 Poles to the United States, with total scholarship grants of $125,000. The fields of study, both in Poland and in the United States, included art, economics, education, English and Polish, banking and business administration, chemistry and physics, drama and theater, history and political science, various branches of engineering—including wood technology—philology, sociology, and studies in other fields. Polish students came to America, generally speaking, for practical and applied courses; Americans went to Poland for the most part for cultural courses. As the Rockefeller Foundation emphasized public health and medical sciences, and was superbly equipped with adequate funds and a technical staff, the Kościuszko Foundation did not grant scholarships in these fields.

Clearinghouse of information.—The Kościuszko Foundation has been the only institution of its type to serve as a clearinghouse of information pertaining to all phases of Polish-American cultural relationships. Since 1925 thousands of inquiries—by mail, by cable and telegram, by telephone and by personal calls—have been answered on an endless variety of topics. The most frequent requests for information had to do with educational opportunities either in Poland or America, with and without scholarship aid; requests from American authors, teachers, lecturers, and social workers for information available in printed form, preferably in English, on certain aspects of Polish culture (art, history, biography, music, folklore, costumes, and customs) and from Poles on cultural aspects of America; requests for information from prospective visitors to Poland as to what to see within the limited time and whom to meet, with a speaking knowledge of English, in order to get assistance and guidance in a foreign country, and vice versa. For these purposes the Foundation has gradually collected a working reference library.

Publications.—Through the direct and indirect influence of the Foundation, including the output of its former exchange students and professors, about twenty books have been published in America in the English language, on Polish topics, and in Poland in the Polish language on American topics; nearly a hundred monographs and pamphlets—scientific, historical, or of a descriptive nature in both languages, treating some aspects of both countries, have been printed, as have several hundred articles in periodicals in America about Poland and vice versa. The majority of the more serious publications of basic informational value and of mutually interpretative character that have appeared in both countries about each other since 1925, have been the direct or indirect result of the Foundation's activities. The first American exchange professor's story of medieval Cracow, Eric P. Kelly's *The Trumpeter of Kraków,* won the Newbury Medal as the most distinguished contribution to the American literature for school children in 1928 and is now in its twentieth printing.

Publicity of educational character.—The Foundation has always eschewed all forms of propaganda, especially of a political nature, but, as occasions rose, it has liberally contributed to a better popular understanding of the cultural aspects of Poland. For example, the one hundred and fiftieth anniversay of Kościuszko's enrollment in the Revolutionary Army, a tribute to Paderewski on the tenth anniversary of Poland's independence, the two hundred and fiftieth anniversary of the defense of Vienna, and Jan Sobieski's part therein, and lately the quadricentennial of the death of Copernicus and of the publication of his great book that gave birth to modern science—all have been given nation-wide publicity through the press and other media. In lighter form, through the Foundation's annual "Night in Poland" Ball in New York and in other cities, Polish folk songs and folk dances, costumes, and customs have been popularized.

Aid to Polish refugee scholars.—When the present war broke out in September, 1939, the Foundation concentrated its efforts—until such time as other agencies with more ample funds could aid—upon preserving the intellect of Poland by helping Polish refugee scholars to survive. It has helped, materially and otherwise but mostly materially, in the bringing of twelve Polish refugee professors to America; it has rendered assistance in a great many other instances of Polish intellectuals of nonacademic standing; it has extended material aid, whenever direct contacts were possible, to over two hundred Polish professors and younger scholars in distress scattered in many countries on several continents. About 10 per cent of the total number of Polish professors and younger instructors of prewar days have received aid from the Foundation. In addition, until such time as other agencies saw their way clear to assume the task, the Foundation supplied the necessary extra funds to make it possible for eight hundred Polish students in Swiss internment camps to continue their studies in special camp university centers. For this first aid to Polish professors and students the Foundation spent directly and secured from other sources for this purpose the total amount of approximately $75,000.

One of the problems which the Foundation is preparing to face in the postwar period is assistance in the educational reconstruction of Poland—more specifically, of Polish university libraries, by establishing nuclei of working libraries with basic books, in various scientific fields, which had been published in the United States. The Foundation has already taken definite steps in this direction by starting, on a smaller scale, to supply medical books and journals to the Polish Medical Faculty in Edinburgh, Scotland. After the war, this Faculty will take all such books and journals to help reëstablish medical-school libraries in the new free Poland.

CHAPTER XXIV

Polish-American Political and Economic Relations

BY ELDON R. BURKE

It has been well said that the First World War began as a war between governments but ended as a struggle between peoples. As this transition took place, the rights of subject nationalities received additional emphasis in the war statements of the belligerents. In America the renowned pianist, Ignacy Jan Paderewski was prophet and evangelist of the movement for Polish freedom. The conversion of President Wilson gave a powerful impetus to the campaign, and in the pronouncement of the Fourteen Points the United States pledged its support to the Polish cause.

In Europe, at the same time, Polish aspirations were assiduously cultivated by Józef Piłsudski and Roman Dmowski. Piłsudski, a leader of the Polish Socialist party, had propounded and exemplified a policy of "active struggle" within the domain of the Central Powers. Toward the end of the war he was incarcerated in a German prison, but his followers continued an underground movement against the occupation authorities. Roman Dmowski, on the other hand, leader of the National Democratic party, opposed the violence of Piłsudski and insisted on a "realist" solution of the Polish problem. This meant reliance upon the Allies; at first Dmowski was "Russophile," later "Ententephile" in his policy. Through his efforts, the Polish National Committee was organized in 1917. It established its headquarters in Paris and soon won the recognition of the Allies as the official organization of the Polish people. Under its auspices, a Polish army was recruited for service on the western front. But, as Dmowski could not obtain recognition from Piłsudski, schism again appeared to threaten the future of the Poles.

So long as Germany dominated Polish territory, the problem of unity among the Poles was easily handled. The withdrawal of German contingents from Poland with the assumption of authority by Piłsudski and his associates gave rise to the apprehension that the Allies had erred in granting recognition to the Paris Committee. At this juncture Paderewski played an important role. Previously, he had aligned himself with the Paris Committe; yet, at the invitation of Piłsudski, he became Premier and Foreign Minister of Poland. Roman Dmowski was selected by him to represent the Polish Republic at the Peace Conference. Under such circumstances, even though the Western Powers were suspicious, recognition could not be withheld from the Piłsudski government. On January 22, 1919, the United States led the way, and thus antedated by over a month the action of France, Great Britain, and the other powers which had delayed, awaiting the report of a special fact-finding mission which had been sent to Poland. On May 2, 1919, the United States representative, Hugh Gibson, presented his credentials to the Polish Government.

The tangled story of Polish interests at the Peace Conference has been narrated elsewhere. Much credit is doubtless to be given to Woodrow Wilson and his advisers for their efforts to secure for Poland its proper ethnic frontiers, as well as the territory necessary for economic self-sufficiency. Dmowski seems to have persuaded Wilson that an outlet to the sea by way of the Vistula was not sufficient, but that part of the Baltic littoral should be included in Polish territory, especially as this might also be supported on ethnic grounds. But, although generous in the settlement of the western frontier, the United States and the Allies were not willing to countenance much expansion to the east at the expense of Russia. When the Polish Government launched its attack against the Soviets in 1920, it did so against the advice of the Supreme Council. In June came the counterattack, with the Polish retreat and the advance of the Russians on Warsaw. Lloyd George urged the Poles to retire to the so-called Curzon Line, but promised aid if the Bolshevists crossed the line. The Bolshevist army advanced beyond it at Nowy Dvor on July 24, 1920. The next day an inter-Allied commission, composed of British and French representatives, arrived in Warsaw and military supplies were rushed to Danzig.

American policy in this crisis can be gathered from a few incidents. The United States Liquidation Commission had sold the Polish Government various supplies, including almost four million dollars worth of ordnance and gas equipment. Some of this material probably was used during the struggle. Much more had been sold to the French Government and these items may have been sent to Poland. On August 31, 1920, the U.S.S. "Pittsburgh" entered the port of Danzig. This event "pacified the Danzig population" and facilitated the unloading of the munitions which had arrived in French and British ships but which, prior to this, could not be unloaded because of the opposition of the Danzigers. Moreover, it should be remembered that General Haller's contingents, composed at first largely of Americans, were there to give actual aid in the struggle. Likewise in New York a group of American fliers organized themselves under the Polish flag and, with the slogan "For Our Liberty and Yours," became famous on the battlefront as the Kościuszko Squadron. But against Polish pressure as well as American, the United States Government remained adamant to the demands for direct intervention; on the contrary, it urged the Powers to limit Polish expansion when the Russian advance had been reversed.

The people of the United States had quickly turned from active participation to nonintervention. In fact, by the summer of 1920 American revulsion to the war policy was complete. The Wilsonian peace had been repudiated and the Franco-American treaty of guarantees was not ratified by the United States Senate. This action had encouraged the British to allow the lapse of their parallel agreement with the French, and had forced the latter into a policy of active alliance with the Poles and the other *status quo* powers of Europe. France helped Poland because "the existence of a strong Poland, as a counterweight to Germany, has always been considered one of the indispensable factors of the European balance of power," a continental equilibrium in which the preponderance of power would be directed by France. Thus, as the United States withdrew from direct participation in European affairs, French influence on the Continent became dominant; and Poland was perforce bound to the military-alliance system of which France was the creator.

Two reasons may be advanced for the failure of the British and American peoples to continue their support of the small national states, whose creation had been so loudly championed by them during the war. One explanation was the lack of imagination which failed to appreciate the problems involved in the creation of a new state, but a less worthy motive was the fear that such commitments would incur for Britain and America fresh continental obligations. Like the British, the relations of the United States henceforth were concerned chiefly with relief and business. Sometimes relief became business and sometimes business became relief; seldom were they entirely disentangled. Relief as such lasted only a few years; business and finance were major interests throughout the period from 1919 to 1939.[1]

Woodrow Wilson, the schoolmaster, was the first great American friend of Poland; Herbert Hoover, the business man, was the second. At the cessation of hostilities of the First World War, Herbert Hoover became the relief administrator of Europe. It is true that the Allies had other plans, but inasmuch as the food supplies had to come from America, and inasmuch as Mr. Hoover was most active in its operation, the relief program became known as the American Relief Administration rather than by the name of the parent agency, the Supreme Council of Supply and Relief. Hoover arrived in Europe on November 23, 1918. Within two months, the basic structure of the relief organization had been established. By mid-February of the new year, ships carrying flour arrived in Danzig, and a month later American recognition was granted to the Polish Republic and American food was distributed in Warsaw. In the seven months which followed, because of the appropriation by the United States Congress of $100,000,000 for relief purposes, a total of 260,202 tons of foodstuffs was delivered to Poland. During the same period the United States Liquidation Board sold large quantities of supplies to Europeans rather than return them to the United States.

Of the "liberated nations," Poland was the largest purchaser and probably the most needy one. Judge Edwin B. Parker of the Liquidation Commission admitted that it was not bad business to deal

---

[1] See Chapter XIII, "Poland's Monetary and Financial Policy, 1919–1939," by Zygmunt Karpiński.

with Poland. "On the whole," he says in his report, "the prices were rather higher than could have been procured at wholesale from any other purchaser." The most important commodities purchased included clothing, foodstuffs, machinery, locomotives and cars, hospital supplies, ordnance, 5,900 animals, and various other items. Thus, in a very short period of time Poland received great quantities of food and supplies, which did much to prevent the spread of disorder and aided greatly in the establishment of the new state. Additional credits increased the amount of Polish indebtedness and when funded in November, 1924, it was calculated to be $178,560,000. The New York Federal Reserve Bank also loaned the Polish Government the sum of $10,000,000, and in the same year, 1919, the first bonds of the Polish Republic were offered on the New York market.

From the foregoing statements it will be observed that Polish relief was not American charity, but rested in a large measure on credits advanced by the American Government or by American individuals. Some of the supplies were of inferior quality, some of the prices charged were too high even in a period of high prices; yet it must be admitted, as one commentator expressed it, even low grades of flour will save human lives. One phase of relief, not handled directly by the Polish Ministry of Approvisation but retained under the direct control of the American Relief Administration, was the Children's Relief. This work extending from April, 1919, to July, 1922, received its maximum in the spring of 1920 when over 1,300,000 children received one meal a day from this source. Other relief came from private sources in America. Of these nonofficial agencies, the Jewish Joint Distribution Committee, the American Red Cross, the Friends, and various Polish-American agencies did notable work during the first years of the Polish Republic. It has been estimated that from these sources an additional sum of $28,000,000 was expended on Polish relief, so that in spite of the American tendency to "help our friends and help ourselves," the Poles retained a friendly memory of what had been done.

Herbert Hoover laid the basis for American economic interests in the new Poland by a policy of economic first aid to the Polish Republic. The most critical problem of the Succession States was the restoration of production and the reallocation of trade so that some degree of self-sufficiency might be achieved. The recovery of Poland was especially difficult because of the differing trade relations which each section had had before the war, the problem of integrating the economy of a nation which for more than a century had not lived as a territorial unit, and the necessity of completely reversing the flow of trade in most areas. In 1919 at Mr. Hoover's suggestion the European Technical Advisers Mission came into being. In a memorandum to Premier Paderewski, Mr. Hoover urged the selection of three experts—a technical adviser, a food adviser, and a financial adviser. The Polish leader empowered Mr. Hoover to make the selections for one year, and Dr. E. D. Durand and Mr. A. B. Barber were chosen as food and technical advisers respectively. The position of financial adviser was not filled. The mission of the technical adviser was extended by succeeding governments, and with the aid of a number of assistants such matters as transportation, coal, oil and gas production were handled by the commission. Although their function was primarily advisory in character, on occasion they actively participated in the management of Polish enterprises. Indeed, the efforts of the commission resulted in the expansion of railroad facilities by the purchase of 150 Baldwin locomotives and 4,600 cars from America. Facilities for the production of coal and oil were also improved and the output of their commodities increased. The mission returned to America in 1922.

Thus initiated, American businessmen rapidly expanded their interests in the new Poland. Of their enterprises the more important were those directly concerned with the financing of the government itself. The first loan to be launched on the New York market was the Dollar loan of 1920, which has already been mentioned. The suggestion of the Dawes Committee for the stabilization of the German mark by means of loans supported by the resources of a nation was seized upon by the Poles. In 1924 they attempted to obtain a loan supported by the state-owned Tobacco Monopoly, but American financiers failed in competition with the Italians. The Poles were more successful the next year in negotiating a $35,000,000 loan on the basis of railway receipts and the sugar excise.

This loan of the year 1925 may be cited as a typical example of American finance during the period. The issue was floated by

Dillon, Read and Company of New York. The rate of interest was to be 8 per cent, but the bonds were offered at 95 with a redemption of 105 in twenty-five years. A sinking fund was established and one-fiftieth of the total was to be retired semiannually. It was announced that the earnings of the first loan redeemed would be 29.46 per cent which would be gradually diminished to 8.53 per cent for those called in 1950. In spite of the objection to the high rate, the Polish Parliament approved a total bond sale of $35,000,000 for America, and $15,000,000 for Paris and London.

But the fault lay not only in the hard terms of American bankers; it was rooted also in the failure of the Polish Government to balance its budget, and in the shifting value of Polish currency. A British financial mission in 1924 had urged the Poles to inaugurate currency reform. The Polish mark, hopelessly inflated, was replaced by the złoty at the rate of five to the dollar. A change in name, however, could not sanctify the new currency in order to keep it from sliding downward. In 1926, when the New York bankers were sounded on further loans, the Polish Government was advised to try an American expert on finance. The Poles agreed and the Kemmerer Financial Mission was born. Dr. Edwin W. Kemmerer had won fame in South America for his curative powers in prescribing for the financial maladies of struggling governments. His first visit to Warsaw was made in the Christmas season of 1925. The following year he formed a Mission for more detailed study, and after ten weeks of effort he and his associates submitted an extensive report. The Mission urged the stabilization of the currency by means of the resumption of gold payments and the maintenance of an adequate gold reserve. Improvements were suggested in the taxation program of the Republic as well as in the expenditures in order that the budget might be balanced. The Mission also urged the expansion of the capitalization of the Bank Polski to meet the growing needs of the country and in many other ways suggested reform or revision of the financial arrangements of the state.

Not all of the recommendations were accepted, but under Marshal Piłsudski's direction the Parliament adopted many of the more important principles. In 1927 a stabilization loan of $70,000,000 was requested of a number of international bankers. Connected with the loan as agreed upon by the bankers were arrangements for the balancing of the budget, the stabilization of the złoty at the gold value of 11.22 cents, the expansion of the facilities of the Bank Polski and the appointment of an adviser who was to have control of the treasury reserve as well as to sit on the board of the bank. On October 15, 1927, Mr. Charles S. Dewey, Assistant Secretary of the United States Treasury, was chosen for the position; and on October 18, the bonds were offered for sale in New York and elsewhere. The financial stability of the Polish State was now assured.

Polish public finance was not entirely limited to the manipulations of the Government of the Republic. Americans were also interested in loans to municipalities and to other local governments. The City of Warsaw loan of 1928 and the Silesia Province loan of the same year were the largest handled in the United States. The size of these loans, amounting to $21,200,000, easily made Americans the heaviest investors in such Polish securities in the world.

The detailed history of each of the foregoing issues would be difficult to relate, but the principal outlines may be told briefly. On November 22, 1932, the Polish Government proposed the postponement of payments on the United States Government loan funded in 1924. The United States Treasury announced that the amount of the principal in default, according to the terms of the original agreement, would "bear interest at the rate of 3½ per cent, payable semiannually." Americans have contended that this debt was a relief credit and therefore, should not be considered as a "war debt" and in the same category with the loans advanced to the Allies in the war. The Polish Government, on the contrary, insisted that this was a war debt and subject to the same arrangements that the United States would make with any of the other powers. The act of Congress prohibiting loans to those who thus refused to pay, in consequence, applied to Poland.

The loans by private investors in the United States, although declining in value during the World Depression, retained their validity until 1937 when the Polish Government undertook their conversion. Bondholders were offered the right to convert the bonds of the five issues previously discussed into bonds for an Internal Government issue with interest at 4½ per cent. The Foreign

Bondholders Protective Council of New York urged the acceptance of this plan. A total of $45,987,200 was offered by May 1, 1937. In October, the Polish Ministry of Finance announced that henceforth all outstanding, unconverted bonds would carry the uniform rate of 4½ per cent. This action resulted in a significant reduction of the total valuation of American holdings.

A second important phase of American-Polish relations during the twenty years of the Republic is to be found in the history of American private industrial and commercial interests in Poland. Trade relations during the period were always favorably balanced toward the United States, a situation which was emphasized by the American policy of protectionism. In January, 1939, the Export-Import Bank in Washington granted a $6,000,000 credit to the National Economic Bank for the financing of cotton purchases in the United States. But no real amelioration of the commercial relationship between the powers was accomplished before the occupation of Poland in 1939. Otherwise, official policy was devoted chiefly to furthering the interests of private individual Americans or American enterprises in Poland. Thus, the American State Department issued various protests against what were alleged to be discriminatory practices by the Polish Government against Americans and even, on occasion, gave active support against British and French competitors.

Most Americans, however, engaged in Polish business without official blessing and succeeded frequently against their foreign competitors who had official support. Authoritative estimates indicate that such enterprises had a total investment of American capital of around 371,000,000 złotys. This included such enterprises as the exploitation of zinc deposits by the Anaconda Company, the development of oil resources by a Polish subsidiary of Standard Oil, and some investments in textile and in other manufacturing establishments. Other interests included American investments in the International Match Company, which, in 1925, was given the right to exploit the Polish match monopoly, and Messrs. Ulen and Company, which constructed sewerage systems in eleven Polish cities. Indeed, if all the various enterprises are totaled, American public and private investments exceeded, by a billion złotys, those of any other country.

To conclude by rendering sentence on either Americans or Poles is impossible. Many of the detailed facts on which a general judgment must be based are not obtainable. It may be argued that the citizens of the United States took unfair advantage of Polish needs for the sake of their own private profit. Yet, it must be admitted that, at best, investment in Poland during the period proved to be somewhat speculative, although after the depression a greater stability was achieved. Had the war not intervened, Poland probably would have obtained the degree of national self-sufficiency required for it to assume the relative position in the family of nations to which its size entitled it. For this, in the future as in the past, American aid would be indispensable.

Part Seven

FOREIGN RELATIONS

CHAPTER XXV

Foreign Relations

BY S. HARRISON THOMSON

THE RELATIONS of Poland with its neighbors are and always have been peculiarly conditioned by its geographical location. A segment of a flat and somewhat marshy coastal plain, Poland has no natural physical boundaries to the east or to the west. To the north its natural boundary, the Baltic littoral, was almost entirely taken over in the thirteenth century by the crusading Teutonic Knights, and the hold of their heirs on this area is still maintained, although weakened from time to time. The only natural frontier the state has known has been on the south, the northern line of the Carpathian range. Its boundaries have been in flux for centuries, as Germans to the west and Russians to the east have advanced or receded. Poland was cut up and partitioned between Prussia, Russia, and Austria three times in the eighteenth century, rearranged by Napoleon, and later, in the early nineteenth, by the Congress of Vienna. Such a fluid and checkered territorial and political history could hardly be favorable to a smooth course of a restored Polish state.

The fixing of its frontiers after the First World War, related in an earlier chapter,[1] was both a legacy of its complex past and an indication that many of its features would inevitably be projected into the future. Even the most sanguine Pole must have realized, in the early years of *Polonia restituta* that it would take time, patience, outside support, and no little good fortune to solve the acute problems of its relations with its neighbors. No objective study of Poland's policies by an outsider can afford to disregard its geography or its treatment, in recent times, at the hands of the powerful states that have surrounded it. The Poles did not forget

[1] See Chapter VI, "Rebirth of Poland, 1914–1923," by Bernadotte E. Schmitt.

this history, and out of their memories grew their cautions and their fears, in the same degree that out of the absence of memory on the part of western statesmen grew their heedlessness and ultimate disaster.

I

The new Poland had seven neighbors: Germany, Czechoslovakia, Rumania, Soviet Russia, Latvia, Lithuania, and the Free City of Danzig. With only two of these were relations friendly in the early years—Rumania and Latvia.

The conditions of Poland's reconstitution by the victorious Allied Powers and the tangible military support of the most powerful of these western states, France, during the war against Russia, eventuated in a Franco-Polish alliance on February 19, 1921. It was only natural that both Powers, each bordering on Germany whose good faith both distrusted, should make common cause. The preamble of the agreement is, for a diplomatic document, clear and succinct. It reads:

> The Polish Government and the French Government, being equally anxious to safeguard, by the maintenance of the Treaties which have been signed in common, the state of peace in Europe and the security and defense of their territory as well as their mutual political and economic interests, have agreed (1) . . . to consult each other on all questions of foreign policy which concern both States. . . . (3) If, notwithstanding the sincerely pacific views and intentions of the two contracting States, either or both of them should be attacked without giving provocation, the two Governments shall take concerted measures for the defense of their territory and the protection of their legitimate interests.

This treaty only formalized a previously existing actuality and, so far as France lived up to the spirit of it, was one of the cornerstones of Polish foreign policy during the entire period from Versailles to 1939. The whole story of Polish relations with all its neighbors must be read in the light of this alliance and the Polish esteem for the League of Nations. Every Polish Foreign Minister had to guide his policies to satisfy the demand of the Polish people for security against possible threats to the territorial integrity of the country from both the east and the west. The French alliance was an absolute necessity. There was not, nor indeed could there be, any choice of policies so long as this alliance was a political and military reality. There were changes in ministries for reasons of internal politics, but there was no modification of the basic Polish quest for security. Whether or not this security was always sought in the wisest fashion is another question.

Rumania.—Rumania, like Poland, was a beneficiary of the Allied victory. That country, also, like Poland, gained territory at the expense of the Austro-Hungarian Empire (Transylvania), and Russia (Bessarabia). It had, therefore, at least two potential enemies: Russia on its northeastern boundary, and the successor state, Trianon Hungary, on the west. From the first months after the armistice of November, 1918, Rumanian sympathy for Poland was open. At a critical period in Poland's struggle with the Soviet armies, in the spring of 1920, the only arms and munitions of war to reach Piłsudski's legions came through Rumania. It was obviously to Rumania's interest to make common cause with Poland and thereby fortify itself against Russian irredentist claims on Bessarabia.

Take Jonescu, the Rumanian Foreign Minister, in Warsaw in November, 1920, discussed in detail an alliance. A five-year mutual assistance pact was signed on March 3, 1921. This alliance was defensive, specifically directed against "unprovoked attack on their present eastern frontiers," and Poland's alliance with France, signed only six weeks previously, was regarded by both parties as an integral part of Poland's alliance system. As a matter of course, its indirect effects were favorable to Rumania. The two states were bound to consult each other before making alliances with any third party, excepting agreements intended to maintain treaties already signed by both parties. As a matter of political fact, Poland's obligation was greater than that of Rumania, as Russia was more likely to take military action to recover Bessarabia, loss of which it had never accepted, than to take action over the Russo-Polish frontier. Poland was not unaware of this discrepancy in obligation, but felt that French support in the west would counterbalance the likelihood of military action in fulfillment of its engagements to Rumania. During an official visit of Piłsudski to King Ferdinand at Sinaia, in late September, 1922, the Marshal assured the King: "Nothing divides us. . . . From the Baltic to the Black Sea there is but one people, under two flags." Following this visit, the military alliance was extended to include economic collaboration between the two states. King Ferdinand returned the visit during the summer of 1923, and cordial relations between the two states were further confirmed. The alliance was renewed at its expiration in March, 1926, for another five-year period. At that time, as a consequence of the Locarno treaties, it became a treaty of mutual territorial guarantee. All shades of Polish public opinion were unanimous in approval of the treaty and in cordiality toward Rumania.

Baltic states.—Latvia, as a state but recently a part of Imperial Russia and whose independence was not completely assured, had good reason to draw near to Poland. Both states faced Russia on their east. Their own common frontier was not long, less than sixty miles, and commerce between the two countries of little consequence. There was no ground for friction, and good reason for collaboration. Polish policy from 1919 planned to effect some sort of organization of the Baltic states which might offer a solid front against Russia. Poland gladly participated in several Baltic conferences in 1921 and 1922, and acted as host to a conference which met in Warsaw on March 13 to 17, 1922, attended by representatives of Finland, Estonia, Latvia, and Poland. Konstanty Skirmunt, the Polish Foreign Minister, was elected president. Poland, as the largest of the states, may be forgiven for hoping to lead some kind of Baltic league and, in some quarters outside of Poland, such a development was anticipated. Of the four states Latvia was, after Poland, the most desirous of the formation of such a formal organization, and at a later conference of the states (February, 1924), Meierowics, the Latvian Foreign Minister, openly advocated the formation of a Baltic league. It was, however, at the Warsaw conference that a suggestion for the four states to act jointly at the next meeting of the League was opposed by Poland itself.

Friction between Poland and Lithuania continued to be a source of embarrassment for Lithuania's northern neighbors, as Polish opinion would have taken offence at any *rapprochement* between the three northern Baltic states and Lithuania. For a considerable period in 1924 Latvian opinion favored Lithuania in its dispute with Poland. At the same time, the northern Baltic states were inclined to be friendly with Germany, for a large proportion of the foreign trade of all of them was with Germany. The delicate relations existing between Germany and Poland made their acceptance of Polish political leadership doubly inadvisable. Thus, any conversations looking toward closer coördination between the eastern Baltic states and Poland could have no successful outcome. It was, however, possible for Poland to gain a diplomatic victory and to increase its prestige at the twice-postponed Helsinki conference of January 16 to 17, 1925, at which treaties of conciliation and arbitration were signed by all four states and the machinery set up for interstate commissions of conciliation. Poland's success lay in the acceptance of its leadership at a time when Soviet foreign policy was aggressive toward the smaller Baltic states.

It was to the interest of Poland to encourage, by all means at its disposal, unity and collaboration among the Baltic states. It was an open secret that both Germany and Russia were making definite efforts to induce friction among them. If either Russia or Germany were to become too friendly with any of these small states, Poland's international position might be seriously menaced. Poland regarded it as imperative that the Baltic should be an open sea. That country could ill afford to have it become either a German or a Russian lake. It thus participated for over ten years in a three-cornered diplomatic tug-of-war. During this decade it was a close, if indecisive struggle. At times, as in 1927, Soviet obstruction of Polish aims for some sort of Baltic league seemed victorious, at other times German diplomacy was apparently winning, and at still other times, as in 1925 and 1929, Polish foreign policy achieved some measure of success. But, so far as it was a cardinal principle of Polish foreign policy that the Baltic states should continue to maintain their independence from either Germany or Russia, Poland could regard the results of its diplomacy with satisfaction.

With its other neighbors, Czechoslovakia, Soviet Russia, Germany, and the Free City of Danzig, relations in the early years after the war were never completely happy, and at times embittered by sharp disagreements.

Czechoslovakia and the Little Entente.—By all the laws of reasonable expectations Poland and Czechoslovakia should have been firm and loyal friends from the first days of their regained independence. They were both western Slav states, with closely related languages and cultures. Both had suffered for generations from foreign oppression, had had parallel and, at times, intermingled history, and both had won their independence with Allied—mostly

French—aid. But, conflicting boundary claims, prolonged for some years after the Paris Peace Conference, left their impression on opinion in both countries.

The story of the early dispute between Poland and Czechoslovakia over the boundary line in the Duchy of Teschen (Cieszyn) and in Orava and Spisz, in Slovakia, has been presented in an earlier chapter. Neither Polish nor Czechoslovak opinion was ever satisfied with the handling of the dispute by the Supreme Council of the Allies, which seemed to have favored Czechoslovakia, though leaders in both countries—Paderewski, Dmowski, Skirmunt, Masaryk, and Beneš—made sincere efforts to guide the disagreement along just if not amicable lines, and mutual friends of the two parties, particularly Jonescu of Rumania, intervened to effect a friendly and acceptable arrangement of the difference of views.

The dispute over Teschen, Orava, and Spisz was settled at the end of July, 1920, and after sufficient time had elapsed for feeling on both sides to subside, Skirmunt and Beneš, in the summer of 1921, began negotiations looking to a closer relationship between the two states. A number of commercial and transportation conventions of limited scope were concluded. The friendly offices of France were proffered toward the concluding of a broader political treaty. It was to French interest to have its two Slav allies on terms of mutual cordiality. The other French Central European ally, Rumania, was also anxious to cement the friendly relationship between Poland and Czechoslovakia. These outside pressures coincided with the hopes and desires of both the Polish and the Czechoslovak foreign ministers. Skirmunt visited Prague in the fall of 1921 and, on November 6th, a defensive treaty, providing for benevolent neutrality in case either was attacked by a third party, and a guarantee of mutual respect for each other's territorial integrity was signed. Poland did not finally ratify the treaty, but a step in the right direction had been attempted.

It was during the time that Polish ratification was being awaited, and relations with Czechoslovakia were cordial, that advantage was taken of a nondiplomatic gathering of diplomatic representatives of all members of the Little Entente as well as of Poland in Belgrade, during February, 1922. The occasion was the engagement of King Alexander of Jugoslavia and Princess Marie of Rumania.

The diplomats discussed the possibility of common procedure at the coming Genoa Conference. A common economic policy was agreed on at a meeting of experts at Belgrade in March, and European opinion awoke to the fact that a formidable bloc of states, Poland and the Little Entente, would inevitably exercise considerable influence at the conference.

By working in close collaboration, the four states gained quick recognition at the conference (April 10 to May 19, 1922), as essentially a single large power. Skirmunt's participation in the discussions of the conference was second only to that of Beneš in the favorable impression it created among observers. Though the conference itself was a failure, one important result was the clear demonstration that Poland and Czechoslovakia, given circumstances and mutual leadership at all favorable, could effectively and profitably collaborate.

In the meantime, the territorial dispute over Jaworzyna had been tossed from one jurisdiction to another. The importance of the dispute could not be measured by the extent of the territory in question—14,000 acres of mountain woodland on the northern slopes of the High Tatras. Finally, on July 27, 1923, the Conference of Ambassadors referred the dispute to the Council of the League, which, in turn, asked the Permanent Court at The Hague for a judgment. A decision was handed down on November 13, 1923, and a new frontier line was proposed (March 12, 1924), and accepted by the two parties in a protocol of May 6, 1924, definitely ending the dispute. This last phase of the disagreement witnessed increasing tension between the two countries, and further *rapprochement* along the lines followed by Skirmunt and Beneš in 1921 and 1922 was out of the question. Once the Jaworzyna question was settled, however, it was possible for the earlier course to be resumed.

After friendly conversations at Geneva in March, 1925, between Aleksander Skrzyński, Skirmunt's successor as Polish Foreign Minister, and Beneš, the latter went to Warsaw in April and a comprehensive commercial and political treaty was signed, providing for most favored nation treatment in trade and substantial tariff reductions, and conciliation and arbitration on all differences that might arise. France, in particular, welcomed a decisive *rapprochement* between its two allies. Its effect would be to solidify the position of France at a time when the problem of security was the leading question in its policy. The treaty was warmly welcomed in Poland, and it was ratified, April 14, 1926, without further incident. It would not be true to say that there were not, in either country, scars remaining from the ill feeling aroused over the Teschen and Jaworzyna disputes. Even at the height of enthusiasm in both countries over the *rapprochement* of 1925, many Czechs and many Poles had their serious reservations about the good will of the other party. The feelings of Piłsudski, who seized power in 1926, for example, were known to be more or less anti-Czech and pro-Magyar. It was also known that August Zaleski, the new Polish Foreign Minister, was frequently obliged to use all his powers of persuasion to keep Piłsudski from disturbing the smooth course of Polish-Czechoslovak relations. But, while Poland was engaged in an economic war with Germany on one hand, and a tense and continuing frontier "war" with Lithuania on the other, and while, furthermore, the alliance with France had sensibly decreased in value, the sympathy and support of Czechoslovakia was most welcome.

The period of cordiality lasted from 1925 until toward the end of 1933, when Polish foreign policy was oriented in another direction and Czechoslovak political friendship was no longer so useful. During these eight years the two states uniformly and loyally supported the League, Poland's insistence on a permanent seat on the Council of the League (1926–1927), was effectively supported by Czechoslovakia, and in the various phases of their dispute with Germany, the Poles were able to depend on the sympathy of their southern neighbor, who, nevertheless, had no quarrel with Germany. During the delicate and long-drawn-out discussions at Geneva concerning its German minority, Poland had undivided Czechoslovak support. Zaleski frequently and generously expressed to Beneš deep appreciation for his help. Poland's opposition to the German-Austrian customs union of 1931, on the other hand, followed the lines taken by the Little Entente, and Czechoslovak opinion was appreciative.

In view of Poland's frequent and cordial collaboration, particularly at the time of the Genoa Conference in 1922 and again from 1925 on, when relations with each one of the three Little Entente states were friendly, it has often been asked why Poland did not follow obvious suggestions to join this group of succession states. The answer is not far to seek. The aims of the Little Entente, as expressed in the foundation treaties, were specifically anti-Hungarian. Poland, far from having any quarrel with Hungary, had a rather pro-Hungarian feeling, based partly on a similar social and economic structure, partly on a long tradition of friendship. The regional interests of the Entente were Danubian; Poland's interests lay in the Baltic area. Another weighty factor was psychological. Once in such a group, Poland would have been only one of four, and would have been bound by decisions which it could not have outvoted. Polish opinion in the middle and late 'twenties, and even more so in the 'thirties, was convinced that Poland should play the role of a great power, independent of any single state or group of states, relying on its own strength. If Poland was irked by the thought of being a satellite of France, it would have been unlikely that it could have its actions dictated by the grouping of three states, no one of which had even half its population.

On the other hand, it must not be thought that the Little Entente was feverishly anxious to have Poland make a fourth at their table. It was generally reported that they feared that Poland might upset the delicate balance among the three Danubian states, and that they (particularly Jugoslavia and Czechoslovakia) might be drawn into Poland's disputes with Russia, Lithuania, and Germany. As it developed, it was fortunate for all parties that Poland and the Little Entente collaborated sincerely on the numerous issues on which their interests coincided, and acted separately when their respective interests lay in different areas.

Lithuania.—The bitter and apparently irreconcilable dispute between Poland and Lithuania began with the occupation of the city of Wilno, the ancient capital of the Grand Duchy of Lithuania, and of most of the surrounding province by 20,000 Polish troops under General Żeligowski on October 9, 1920, as related in a previous chapter.[1] For two and a half years the Council of the League tried unsuccessfully to bring Poland and Lithuania together for a solution. Lithuania reiterated its legal rights, and international law was certainly in its favor. Poland kept the territory which it wanted. The Conference of Ambassadors, out of patience, frus-

[1] See Chapter VI, "Rebirth of Poland, 1914–1923," by Bernadotte E. Schmitt.

trated and powerless, finally, on March 15, 1923, accepted as legal the Polish military occupation of this district.

But, if the League of Nations thought that by accepting a *fait accompli* Geneva would hear no more of the question of Wilno, the subsequent years were to bring disillusionment. Lithuania formally refused to accept a decision which, it contended, went beyond the legal competence of the Conference of Ambassadors, and had been made without Lithuania's consultation or participation. Relations between the two states were those of a nonmilitary conflict. The frontier between them was closed by Lithuania, and all commercial and diplomatic communication was forbidden.

The Vatican entered the dispute by including Wilno within the ecclesiastical jurisdiction of Poland in a Concordat of February 10, 1925, thus recognizing Polish sovereignty over the district. Lithuanian opinion, normally almost as Roman Catholic as Poland, was outraged. The other Baltic states, uneasy at Soviet propaganda among their populations and anxious for Baltic unity, urged both sides to make concessions, and, under this pressure, agreements providing for the opening of the Niemen for timber flotage, postal communications, and some travel were reached at Copenhagen and Lugano in the fall of 1925. But a definitive resumption of diplomatic relations was found impossible. Whatever augury of a further *rapprochement* these initial steps might have been was nullified by a series of events: the conclusion of a nonagression pact between Lithuania and Soviet Russia early in 1926, the assumption of power by Piłsudski in May, 1926, at Warsaw and a similar coup on the part of Professor Augustine Voldemaras in Kaunas in December, 1926.

Negotiations to end the tension between the two states, at the urgent insistence of the Western Powers early in 1927, proved abortive, and tension was even heightened in the fall of that year by a series of irritating frontier incidents. The Poles arrested a number of Lithuanians in the Wilno district and closed some Lithuanian schools, as reprisals for alleged repressive action against Polish individuals and schools in Lithuania. The charges against Lithuania, in this case, were felt by neutral observers to be not well founded. Lithuania's appeal to the League against these Polish "reprisals" was pigeonholed. But Soviet Russia was not so gentle, and warned Poland that its responsibility for preserving the peace was much greater than that of Lithuania. The situation by December looked most dangerous. On December 7th, at the meeting of the Council of the League, Voldemaras and Zaleski presented their respective cases. Three days later Piłsudski, having suddenly appeared in Geneva, bluntly asked Voldemaras whether he wanted peace or war. There was little for Voldemaras, representing a state of two million, to say to such an ultimatum from the head of a state of thirty million except "peace." The Council was pleased to note in its resolution that the "state of war" had come to an end. But the basic ground for friction was not so easily exorcised. Poland still held Wilno, and Lithuania still claimed that Wilno should be Lithuanian.

The issue was again raised at Geneva in September, 1928, in perhaps less acute form, with no perceptible change in the situation. After the resignation of Voldemaras in September, 1929, however, there was some slight lessening of tension, though there was no fundamental modification of policy on either side. For some years little was heard of the dispute, as both parties were well occupied in other directions, Lithuania by its quarrel with Germany over Memel, and Poland with the thorny Danzig-German problem. Yet the embers were still smoldering, and were to break into flame on very slight provocation.

Soviet Russia.—The Treaty of Riga of March 15, 1921, ended the Polish-Russian War and fixed the boundaries between the two states, later (March 14, 1923), to be confirmed by the Council of Ambassadors. But cordial relations did not immediately ensue. Soviet Russia, though anxious for peace, was not readily reconciled to the loss of large numbers of White Russians now included in Poland's eastern provinces. The presence of many anti-Bolshevik Russians in Poland was a source of irritation to the Soviets, who were concerned lest Poland become the seat of counterrevolutionary activity. The fact that there was a large Polish minority left in Russia with few, if any, minority rights did not ease the tension.

Mutual suspicion between the two neighbors was increased by the German-Russian *rapprochement* of the Treaty of Rapallo, April 19, 1922. The serious character of border incidents seemed, to Polish opinion, to accord with their information about the employment of German staff officers to train the Red Army. As Poland lay between the two greater states, and as revisionism at its expense was openly preached in many quarters in both countries, Polish concern can be understood. In the next few years, on frequent occasions, Russia raised the question of the treatment of White-Russian and Ukrainian minorities in Poland. An improvement in their linguistic and cultural autonomy began to be noticeable after 1925.

There were clear indications that Russian policy looked toward some sort of *rapprochement* with Poland as early as 1924, and the Soviet Foreign Commissar, Chicherin, was accorded a cordial welcome on a visit to Warsaw in September, 1925. At that time nothing came of the visit, and, in the succeeding months, Polish opinion felt renewed suspicions of Soviet intentions when the Treaty of Rapallo was virtually extended for another five years by the Treaty of Berlin on April 24, 1926. Two weeks later, Piłsudski took over direction of the affairs of the Polish State. He was known to be anti-Russian. Yet, in spite of this fact and the uneasiness at the evident friendship between Russia and Germany, relations with Russia were generally viable for the next few years—a condition attributable, in large measure, to the wisdom of the Polish Foreign Minister Zaleski.

Late in 1926, Polish-Soviet discussions of a possible nonaggression pact were begun, and though these discussions did not immediately lead to definitive agreements, there was reason to believe that a *modus convivendi* was not impossible. The untoward incident of the assassination of Voikov, the Russian Minister in Warsaw on June 7, 1927, by a young Russian student disturbed only for a short time the even course of Polish-Soviet relations.

Soviet policy was hopeful of weaning the Baltic states from any Baltic league of which Poland would have been the leading member, and negotiations for nonaggression treaties were carried on separately and collectively with the Baltic states during 1926 and 1927. Lithuania, without a common frontier with Russia, was most willing to conclude a nonaggression pact (September 28, 1926). A Soviet-Latvian nonaggression pact was initialed (March 9, 1927), but not signed.

These preliminary successes led Russia to try to consolidate its gains in the west by a more inclusive regional agreement. While the Kellogg-Briand Pact for the Renunciation of War was awaiting ratification Maxim Litvinov, the Soviet Foreign Commissar, invited Poland, in December, 1928, to join Russia in putting the terms of the Paris Pact into immediate effect as between the two states. Lithuania had just previously been invited to sign such a protocol. Zaleski insisted that the other Baltic states and its ally Rumania should also be brought into the agreement. Somewhat to general surprise, Russia seemed pleased to extend the terms of its engagements under the Paris Pact to all its western neighbors, and the so-called Litvinov Protocol was signed at Moscow by Estonia, Latvia, Poland, Rumania, and the Soviet Union on February 9, 1929. Lithuania came into this multilateral agreement somewhat later, on April 1, 1929. The terms of the Paris Pact did not of themselves constitute a nonaggression treaty and were thus not so comprehensive as Soviet diplomacy would have liked to see in effect.

Immediately before and after 1930, French political and military morale and potential were low. The value of the French alliance to Poland, however its text may have read, was correspondingly low. Indeed, as early as 1928 Briand had, with tragic shortsightedness for French morale, virtually repudiated the Polish alliance, declaring in the French Chamber that "alliances are in contradiction to the Covenant of the League." It was a little late for France to make this discovery. In the face of the German menace, Poland needed added support to maintain its independence, while France, whether it realized it or not, needed any outside help it could muster.

On its part, Russia approached Poland in October, 1930, with a request for the resumption of negotiations begun in 1926 for a definitive nonaggression pact. It was known that Germany endeavored to induce Russia to break off these negotiations early in 1930 and repeated the maneuver in 1931. Poland felt safer to have the diplomatic collaboration of France, and with the rise of aggressive National Socialism in Germany, France found its interests again parallel with those of Poland, and the diplomatic machinery began to move. By the summer of 1931 conversations had gone sufficiently far for the semiofficial Paris *Temps* to remark that France would sign no nonaggression pact with Russia unless both its eastern allies, Poland and Rumania, were also given similar guarantees. Obviously Russia had demurred at giving such broad guarantees.

The international situation, however, was too delicate for France to stand on the whole of this refusal, and when Poland and Russia came to terms, both by a nonaggression pact, July 25, 1932, and a convention providing for procedures of conciliation, November 27, 1932, France signed a treaty of nonaggression with Russia, November 29, 1932. This nexus of treaty arrangements was generally welcomed—outside of Germany—with a sigh of relief.

France had not hesitated to lend its support to Poland in its dealings with Russia. Russia was far from France's borders. In the west, however, France seemed in these years to be playing another game. During the long Disarmament Conference at Geneva, while France was dealing directly with Germany, the Poles, who represented the country most likely to be the object of German rearmament, were not even consulted by their ally. It was precisely in the latter half of the same year in which the Polish-Soviet nonaggression and conciliation pacts were signed (1932), that relations between France and its ally, in other respects, were at their coolest. The initiative for the lowering of the diplomatic temperature must be assigned to France. Thereafter, Poland can hardly be blamed for attaching commensurably greater importance to the *rapprochement* with Russia.

II

After six years of notable success in the office of Foreign Minister, Zaleski asked to be relieved of his trying duties on November 2, 1932, and Colonel Józef Beck, a confidant of Marshal Piłsudski, took over the post, announcing that he would try to carry out the policies his predecessor had so ably initiated. A thoughtful and candid Pole, surveying the international situation of his country at the end of 1932, would probably have concluded that the ledger was about balanced. Poland had proved its right to an important place among European powers; it had consolidated its position on the Baltic and on its eastern borders. On the other hand, it would have been clear that Soviet diplomacy, realistic and frequently inscrutable, had taken the leadership among the Baltic powers which Poland had been unable to hold, and its latent power would, in the sequel, prove to be even more decisive. There were, of course, some Polish leaders, and Beck should probably be listed among them, who felt that Poland's position was stronger than this balance would indicate.

Poland took part in the Disarmament Conference of 1932–1933, at first with great hope for its success, later with realistic doubts because of the belligerency of National Socialist Germany. Count Edward Raczyński, the chief of the Polish delegation in 1933, remarked that there was no reason for anyone to have any "illusions . . . concerning the possibilities of improving the present situation as regards international security." But Russia was not so easily discouraged. Litvinov took advantage of the urgency of the situation to invite all signatories of the Moscow Protocol of April, 1929, for which he had been responsible, to sign a convention defining aggression in the terms of the Geneva draft of May 21, 1933. Seven countries bordering on Soviet Russia, including Poland and Rumania, signed this convention on July 3, 1933. Lithuania made a separate agreement with Russia two days later, and Finland signed the original multilateral convention on July 23d. By reason of the cordial atmosphere surrounding the negotiations, the signing of this convention marked the completion of a long process of normalization of relations between Poland and Russia. The significance of the Polish-Soviet pacts was not lost on Germany, and relations between Poland and Germany immediately took a gentler tone. Tension between Poland and Danzig, which was at times more Prussian than Prussia, was relaxed for a short period.

Germany and Danzig.—Once Poland's western boundaries were fixed by the Paris Peace Conference and the juridical aspects of Polish relations with Germany and Danzig were, if not settled, at least incorporated into a number of agreements and conventions approved by the League of Nations, the story of Polish-German relations ceases to be local and becomes part of a much more comprehensive drama. Security, disarmament, arbitration, the restoration of international confidence—these were the world-wide urges of the middle and late 'twenties. In their connection with the events leading to the present war Polish-German relations are fundamentally much more important in these earlier years than is generally realized.

The mid-twenties, between France and England at least, were a sort of reconciliation honeymoon after a period of estrangement. MacDonald in England and Herriot in France were so oversuffused with affection, generosity, and confidence that they wanted to bring

Germany into the happy family circle. This is the period of the Geneva Protocol, the Locarno Pact, and the Kellogg-Briand Pact to Outlaw War. It was the period of pactomania. But Poland remained unconvinced that these pacts would bring peace or security to anybody. In the autumn of 1924, Poland saw very suggestive full-dress German Reichswehr maneuvers on its northwestern frontier. Poland knew that the German military organization was virtually unchanged from 1918, and that, taking advantage of the Rapallo Treaty of 1922 with Soviet Russia and its renewal in 1926, Germany had an immense supply of arms and munitions of war stored up in Russia. As early as in 1924, informed Poles felt quite certain that the League would not have any real power, for the Geneva Protocol, though defining the aggressor, had no satisfactory answer to the case of a state which refused to accept arbitration. Poland knew only too well that the German terms for entering the League, however they might be phrased, were either specific revision of Germany's eastern borders, i.e., Pomerania and Upper Silesia, or more broadly, a completely free hand in the east.

Poland saw many serious obstacles in the way of any assurances of peace. It saw that the League of Nations, one of the two cornerstones of its foreign policy, was unlikely to exercise any real power in Europe. The very existence of these many and feverishly concluded pacts outside the Versailles Treaty had shown that European statesmen realized that the League itself was inadequate to guarantee peace. Poland saw furthermore that England most definitely refused to interest itself in the area east of the Rhine, directly or indirectly. The texts of these accords—Geneva Protocol and Locarno, and Kellogg-Briand pacts nowhere indicated that Germany gave up its revisionism in the east, that is, plans to take back Silesia and western Poland. The arbitration treaty which Poland signed with Germany in connection with the Locarno Pact, under pressure from England and France, was of no real value—indeed, quite the opposite. Poland believed from 1924 onwards, in the event, quite correctly, that if Germany's basic conditions for dealing with France and England on terms of equality were met, Poland would have to defray the expenses of European peace. Chancellor Luther made this quite clear in a speech at Königsberg on February 16, 1925, in which he denounced the Treaty of Versailles, and especially those provisions which had given Poland access to the Baltic. Gustav Stresemann, the German Foreign Minister, emphasized this German position in a speech before the Reichstag on May 18th of the same year.

Polish resentment against the Western Powers ran high. The *Kurjer Warszawski* represented the Polish mind when, in an editorial of October 4, 1925, it remarked that the Polish nation "refused to be the sacrificial lamb on the altar of peace." In sum, Locarno, on paper, looked like an iron-clad guarantee of France's frontiers, but, because it left Germany virtually free in the east, it was no guarantee of peace in Europe at all. It is difficult, in view of later events, to disagree with contemporary Polish opinion which concluded that the Locarno Pact, far from aiding in the securing of peace, actually made war certain in the east. The Poles knew that European peace was indivisible. Neither the French nor the English paid sufficient heed to the Poles when they remarked upon this pregnant fact. The year 1939 was to reveal the measure of its accuracy.

It was specified in Article 10 of the Locarno Pact that it would "enter into force as soon as all the ratifications have been deposited and Germany has become a member of the League of Nations." Germany asked for a permanent seat on the Council of the League. In principle there was no valid objection to the request. But from Poland's point of view Germany's request for a special "interpretation" of Article XVI of the Covenant, by which, obviously, that country might be free to seek revision of its eastern frontiers, made it imperative that Poland should also have a seat on the Council. Without it, the Poles would be at a great disadvantage when discussions of paramount interest to them were taking place before the supreme body of the League. Germany's opposition to such a seat for Poland, determined as it was, was a kind of proof of Poland's contention. Stresemann threatened Germany's resignation from the League if Poland were to be accorded equal status with Germany. But wiser counsels found, after long discussions, a better solution. Poland was given a seat for three years, and was declared reëligible, which amounted to granting it a semipermanent seat.

But Polish fears concerning German intentions were nonetheless immediately realized. As soon as Germany was safely in the

League, relations between Poland and Germany took a serious turn for the worse. The general impression ruled in Germany that the League of Nations had tacitly if not explicitly recognized, by admitting it to the League and the Council, that the Treaty of Versailles, so far as it touched Germany's eastern frontiers, had been either modified or forgotten. Border incidents, precipitated by German civilians or military personnel, were a source of irritation in both countries. The renewal of the Soviet-German Treaty in 1926 was an additional sign to Poland that the jaws of the east-west vise were tightening upon it.

The question of the German minority in Poland was used by Germany as a convenient handle to discredit Polish integrity and capacity to rule. The *Deutscher Volksbund* in Upper Silesia raised its strident voice, protesting against numerous cases of repression and political and cultural discrimination. In reprisal Germany closed its border to shipments of coal from Polish Silesia, beginning a nine-years' tariff war. Under ordinary circumstances the closing of the German market, which took six million tons of Polish coal, would have been disastrous for Polish economy. The general strike in England gave Poland an ample foreign market, however, and Germany's effort to strangle Poland failed of its purpose. At the same time, by heightening tension on both sides of the border, the act led to further incidents, embittered both parties, and the economic war was sharpened and prolonged. As it turned out, the German-Polish tariff war benefited Poland both economically and politically. This was a result that German policy had not anticipated. Poland showed itself resourceful and capable of playing an independent role in world affairs, and German pride was hurt. But the sensitivity of German pride was a fact of which all Germany's neighbors had long been made aware.

In these years—1925 to 1929—the long-drawn-out negotiations over Polish expropriation of the property of German nationals, provided for in the early treaties, were also irritating. After a number of cases had been taken to The Hague Tribunal, and the Council of the League had intervened, a measure of agreement was reached through direct German-Polish negotiations at Paris and Geneva. Much of the difficulty of the settlement rose from the questions of the determination of nationality of Germans resident in

Poland. In retrospect the long dispute would seem to be less significant in itself, on a basis of differences that could have been readily settled by a reasonable formula, than as an indication in its entirety of deeper-rooted political and national disagreements.

Relations between Poland and the Free City of Danzig were regulated between 1920 and 1922 by a number of detailed conventions entered into by the two parties. Their very detail, instead of effecting a rationalization of affairs, seemed unfortunately to offer added points of friction. The population of Danzig was over 90 per cent German and very consciously nationalistic. In the face of continued friction, and in order to be sure of having a sea outlet which would be free from the uncertainties of German control, Poland began the construction of a seaport at Gdynia, on its own coastline, about 15 miles northwest of Danzig. Construction at first was slow. In 1924 only 10,000 tons cleared from the port. The Danzigers ridiculed the project, but made no effort to accommodate themselves to the needs of Polish trade, by which alone their port could live.

The well-known incident of the defacement of the Polish mailboxes set up in Danzig for mail destined for Poland, January, 1925, was typical of the hair-trigger temper of the Danzigers. The fact that The Hague Tribunal upheld the right of Poland to install such boxes made little impression on the Free City.

During the next few years relations between Poland and Danzig varied from bad to fair, according to the political complexion of the party in power in the City. During 1926 a coalition government in Danzig, consisting of Centrists, Liberals, and Social Democrats, did not seek trouble with Poland. A nationalist government followed, lasting to the end of 1927, and incidents as well as ill-feeling were the rule.

Throughout this whole decade Polish opinion resented the large number of Reich Germans who were imported into the Free City, given citizenship quickly and conveniently, and placed in important posts in the government. For example, Heinrich Sahm, President of the Danzig Senate for eight years, was a Prussian who was subsequently named Mayor of Berlin by Hitler. The close correspondence between the Free City's politics and that in the Reich was at times a source of sardonic amusement to the Poles.

From 1928 to 1930 another coalition government eased relations with Poland again. Bartel, the Polish Prime Minister, received a cordial reception on the occasion of his official visit to the City in February, 1929. But this visit marked the high point of friendliness between Poland and Danzig, and within a few months tension again began to mount. With the rise of the Nazi party in the Reich, trouble over Danzig again loomed. From this time until August, 1933, relations between the two governments were at all times precarious, running so parallel with relations between Poland and Germany that there is no necessity to treat them separately.

In the meantime the Polish delegation at Geneva had brought forward on September 7, 1927, a radical proposal for the outlawry of all war as an instrument of policy. The proposal was so simple as to be revolutionary. Its two points were: (1) All recourse to war for the purpose of adjusting international differences is and remains prohibited. (2) All differences, of whatsoever nature they may be, arising between states may not be adjusted by other than pacific means. It was not intended as a general pact, but merely as a solemn declaration of renunciation of war. The simple proposal was roughly handled by amendments and qualifications, revisions and dilution. It reappears, however, in August of the next year in the Kellogg-Briand Pact. The real credit for the later pact should go in large measure to Zaleski, the Polish Foreign Minister, whose bold suggestion directed the pressure of world opinion into a new channel.

In December, 1928, the question of the activity of the *Deutscher Volksbund* in Polish Silesia, supported by the German Government, came before the Council of the League. It was at this meeting that Zaleski told some plain truths—with supporting figures—about the treasonable action of certain leaders of the *Volksbund,* and the source of much of their finances—Berlin. Stresemann interrupted Zaleski's remarks, pounded on the table with his fist, and blurted out that such language could not be tolerated. A few days later Stresemann said in a speech that there were cases where treason and patriotism were hardly distinguishable. The Warsaw press pointedly remarked that the German fist had been used as an argument before.

From 1926 to 1929 Poland sought consistently, with general

French support, to bring about an Eastern Locarno, guaranteeing the Polish-German frontiers, but to no avail. German militarism was now openly in the saddle, and the program of German rearmament was a subject for open boasting. It may be recalled that this was the period of Stresemann's cordial understanding with Briand. Poland saw huge fortifications in East Prussia obviously pointed at it, with France and England only half-heartedly interested in having them reduced. The "pocket battleships" were under construction. The German *Stahlhelm* was engaged in noisy maneuvers and demonstrations within sight and sound of the Polish sentries. The publication in an English periodical in January, 1929, of the memorandum of General Groener, a high German staff officer, detailing the imminent threat of a Polish invasion caused a sensation. It was immediately countered by an open, telegraphed offer from the Polish Foreign Minister to conclude a nonaggression, mutual guarantee pact with Germany at any time, anywhere. There was no reply to the offer.

For the rest of 1929 and the early months of 1930, relations ranged from bitter to favorable. Attempts were made on both sides to improve the situation. But by the time it began to appear that some *modus vivendi* might be worked out and a formula arrived at, it was June 30, 1930, on which date the Allied troops were to evacuate the still occupied parts of Germany. The Poles had prophesied that when Germany was relieved of pressure in the west the Germans would devote themselves single mindedly to Poland and the "rectification" of the eastern frontier. This is precisely what happened. Through July and August a full-throated, anti-Polish campaign was carried on in the German press and over the radio, some of the German ministers of state, particularly the Nationalist Treviranus, setting the tone. In the elections of November, 1930, the National Socialist party made phenomenal gains. Hitler's demands that the provinces that had once been part of the German Empire should "return to the Reich" were well known.

Tension remained high in both countries during 1931 and 1932, kept at a state of irritation by an apparently concerted anti-Polish campaign in the German press, and, at the Disarmament Conference, by German demands for rearmament. As the Poles knew only too well that Germany was already prodigiously rearming, these public demands caused bitter laughter on the Vistula. Poland would be the first object of German armament. Germany slipped easily from an ostensibly republican government into a Hitler government via the Centrist Brüning, the Nationalist Papen, and General von Schleicher. Brüning fled. Papen had worked faithfully for Hitler for twelve years. Schleicher, knowing too much, was murdered. The Poles, confronted with a Germany determined to take Polish territory, yet stood firm.

It was at this point, as told above, that Russia, also in need of peace in the west, because of Japanese aggressiveness in the east and resonant nationalism in Germany, concluded pacts of non-aggression and conciliation with Poland, denouncing "war as an instrument of national policy in their mutual relations."

When Hitler became Chancellor of the German Reich, at the end of January, 1933, the wisdom of the Polish-Soviet *rapprochement* seemed fully justified. To Hitler, apparently, it seemed such a good move that he felt it necessary to circumvent its effects by a similar move from his side of the border. Poland evidently counted no longer on the French alliance. Stresemann had effectually disarmed France by his flirtation with Briand. It remained only for Hitler to disarm Poland, already weaned away from the western half of its diplomatic and military support, France and Great Britain.

The key to subsequent events is to be found in a remark made by Hitler to Goering, after a conversation with General von Schleicher, at the time that Hitler took over the chancellorship. It appears that Schleicher had counseled Hitler that, in order to eliminate Poland from Europe, Germany should come to an understanding with France and Russia. Hitler later remarked to Goering: "And I shall do just the opposite." The only possible interpretation of this remark, under the circumstances and in view of subsequent events, is that Hitler early in 1933 intended to "solve the Polish-German problem," that is, conquer and absorb Poland, by temporarily making friends with Poland, by its diplomatic and political disarmament, while Germany furiously prepared for eastward expansion.

But first Germany would try Poland's temper. A Nazi demonstration in Danzig was staged. In reply Piłsudski, after reinforcing the garrison at Westerplatte, the Polish munitions depot near Danzig, presented Hitler, according to fairly reliable sources, through the

Polish Ambassador in Berlin, with the simple query, Did he want peace or war? He could have either immediately. From this time, March, 1933, is witnessed the strange spectacle of Germany ardently wooing Poland. Polish public opinion was quite aware of the realities of the situation, and made representations to France and Great Britain, warning them to awake to the danger before it was too late. But in neither country did its pleas find even a courteous hearing.

In the meantime, in mid-March, Mussolini had suggested to Ramsay MacDonald a pact between the four Great Powers—Italy, France, Great Britain, and Germany—which would have made of these four the arbiters of European affairs. The possible revision of European boundaries was openly provided for, and the matter of colonial claims was suggested as a proper agendum. Poland and the Little Entente immediately raised categorical objections to this new Directory of Europe, pointing out that any such arrangement completely disregarded the rights of other European states and would virtually eliminate the League from European politics. The slight matter of nullifying the whole structure of the Paris peace treaties had been blandly passed over by Mussolini. Both Paris and London, sensitive to the acute nervousness the plan had aroused all over Europe, immediately disclaimed such broad and revolutionary aims and introduced such considerable modifications into the Four-Power Pact, as Mussolini had broached it, that in the harmless form in which it was finally initialed, on June 17th, *Il Duce* could hardly recognize it.

But Poland's suspicions, as well as those of the Little Entente, were not to be easily quieted. In April Piłsudski had suggested to France that it join with Poland and the Little Entente to bring Germany's rearmament before the League as a violation of Article 213 of the Treaty of Versailles. But the French Government at that time was in no mood to challenge Hitler. The Polish alliance was still of secondary importance to France. It was thus imperative for Poland to make a definite effort to strengthen its own position. Beck's announced visit to the Little Entente capitals early in April to assure their coöperation against both the projected Four-Power Directory and German rearmament was unfortunately postponed. No small part of Poland's objections to the Four-Power Pact, both in its original and in its modified form, rested in a subjective resentment at not having been taken into the select circle of the Great Powers. France, it was felt, should have insisted on Poland's inclusion. To this wounded *amour propre* the Little Entente had little to say. But in Poland it constituted a deep grievance against the ancient ally, and a swing toward a *rapprochement* with Germany may be sensed in the summer months of 1933, though it took no markedly tangible form until the fall of the year. Piłsudski expressed himself, on several occasions, as hopeful that France would realize what was afoot before Germany would be too strong to resist. German diplomacy, seeing an opportunity to drive a wedge between the two traditional allies, brought the pressure of fair words and flattering attention to bear upon Poland. The reports of conversations between Hitler and the Polish ministers to Berlin, Wysocki and Lipski, from May through November, 1933, show this maneuver in a clear light.

It is fair to presume that Poland was sparring for time, hoping for a change in French policy, but the conditions finally offered by Germany were so promising and France was so uncomprehending that Poland chose to accept a ten-year nonaggression pact. The text was signed January 26, 1934, by Baron von Neurath for Germany and Józef Lipski for Poland.

All matters under dispute between the two powers were almost immediately dropped or were henceforth handled in a spirit of sweet reasonableness. As long as he lived, until the Spring of 1935, Piłsudski is known to have had certain reserves about the new and surprising friendship between thousand-year enemies. In spite of polite assurances from diplomatic quarters that the new accord was welcomed sincerely as a gain for the peace of Europe, informed opinion throughout Europe was deeply disturbed. There were not lacking thoughtful Poles who were profoundly distrustful of German good faith, and regretted that Poland had now, by virtually cutting itself off from the traditional French alliance, put itself at the mercy of an aggressively nationalistic Germany. This formal and radical departure from the direction of Polish policy was to effect significant modifications in Poland's relationships with all its neighbors.

Friction between Czechoslovakia and Poland had sensibly declined during 1930 and 1931, and in 1932 gestures of accord were made from both sides of the border. Both states had reason to be concerned at German rearmament. There had been common, if not concerted, action against Mussolini's Four-Power Pact in its earlier stages, though Poland felt aggrieved that the Little Entente signed the final modified and innocuous form of the Pact. From this time, midsummer 1933, a cooling of Polish sentiment toward Czechoslovakia may be noticed. To what extent this change may be traceable to the negotiations then *en train* between Germany and Poland it is not now possible to say, but the chronological correlation at all events is precise. The Polish press, certainly reflecting official opinion, was ostentatiously warm in its attitude toward Hungary, chilly, and at times acid toward Czechoslovakia, Russia, and the traditional ally, France. To those who could read the signs, this told much.

Hardly was the ink dry on the German-Polish Non-Aggression Pact of January 26, 1934, when an anti-Czechoslovak campaign broke out in Teschen, Polish Silesia, and in the Polish press. The Polish minority in the Teschen area that had been awarded to Czechoslovakia by the Council of Ambassadors in 1920 had never been completely reconciled to being citizens of the Czechoslovak State. The Poles in Silesia west of the border had, on numerous occasions in the fifteen years after the territorial delimitation, reminded their brothers to the east of the discriminations and hardships under which they were suffering. One Polish official, Leon Malhomme, Consul at Moravská Ostrava in Moravia, was particularly belligerent and active in anti-Czech agitation, acting as leader of the Poles in Czechoslovakia. The Czechoslovak Government was finally obliged to demand Malhomme's recall in the spring of 1934. He was immediately named Vice-Governor of Silesia and his successor at Moravská Ostrava, Klotz, followed the same line. A strong Polish radio station at Katowice was the means by which the Poles in Czechoslovakia were instructed and informed. The Czechs made recordings of all these broadcasts, so that the whole campaign is a matter of record. In March, tension along the border reached a serious peak. Demonstrations of nationalistic organizations on both sides of the line were growing increasingly disturbing. This regrettable friction, though essentially local, seemed to fit into a larger picture of a basic divergence of view on the fundamental questions of European politics. Poland had abandoned collective security for a policy of bilateral accommodation. Czechoslovakia was still convinced of the efficacy of the principle of collective security, and had categorically refused to make with Germany the kind of bilateral arrangement which Poland had just accepted. The two countries could hardly be expected to see eye to eye on any political question.

The Prague press and informed circles throughout the Little Entente wondered whether the real point of the Polish-German Non-Aggression Pact had been an engagement by Germany to leave Poland's western frontiers intact, in exchange for Poland's complaisance at Germany's expansion to the south and southeast. In that case, Czechoslovakia saw itself, as well as Austria, directly menaced. In Warsaw, the cool reception accorded Barthou, the French Foreign Minister, thus contrasted significantly with the warmth of his reception in Prague, April 26, 1934, only a few days later. Certainly Barthou's efforts in Warsaw to encourage Beck to pursue a more cordial line toward Soviet Russia, looking to the establishment of peace in the east, found much less sympathy than parallel efforts in Prague, already traditionally well disposed toward Russia.

The Locarno treaties of 1925 had always been a sore point with Poland, because that country felt that France and Great Britain had left it defenseless before the might of Germany on its west. But the so-called Eastern Locarno Pact, worked out by Barthou and Litvinov in May and June of 1934, was hardly less satisfactory to Poland, though for different reasons. In its final form the plan was for Russia, Poland, the Baltic states, the Little Entente, and Germany to engage mutually to accept and guarantee each other's boundaries as they then were. France, though not a signatory, was nevertheless involved by its agreements with Russia, Poland, and Czechoslovakia. The British heartily approved the projected treaty, though Great Britain was in no way involved in its execution.

In the light of its plans, as events have revealed them, Nazi Germany's unwillingness to be bound by any such document can be understood. Poland was late in making any public statement about the Pact, then followed the German line, that their relations were adequately and definitively ordered by their nonaggression treaty.

Later, in September, Beck was obliged to admit that Poland's rejection of the Pact was founded in the fact that under its provisions the Poles would have to guarantee the boundaries with Lithuania and Czechoslovakia, which they were unwilling to do. Beck visited Riga and Tallinn in an endeavor to align Estonia and Latvia against the Pact; but his efforts had only momentary success. The Baltic states, now including Lithuania, having conferred with Moscow, shortly thereafter gave their open approval to the Pact. Poland's formal rejection of the Pact was handed to Barthou on September 27th. Yet even then, Barthou's patience was such that, had not his assassination on October 9th removed him from the scene, he might have reopened the whole question. His successor, Pierre Laval, was unable to induce Germany or Poland to modify their opposition. The general demand that some accommodation be reached took Anthony Eden, British Foreign Secretary, to Warsaw, Moscow, and Prague in March and April, 1935. But Germany and Poland maintained their refusal to alter in any essential respect their rejection of any mutual guarantee pact which provided for military obligations. That was the end of the Eastern Locarno project. Throughout the negotiations Poland had stood faithfully at Germany's side. The bitterness of French resentment against the Polish position was matched by Polish umbrage at the Franco-Soviet Pact of Mutual Assistance, signed May 2d, and the interlocking Soviet-Czechoslovak Treaty. The Poles felt justified in viewing the two pacts as aimed at their peace of mind, if not their military security.

The relations between Poland and Czechoslovakia remained irritated through 1934 and 1935. Notes of protest were exchanged and the respective ministers were withdrawn. Beck steadfastly refused to accede to Beneš' request that the various matters in dispute be submitted to the League. The prolongation of the tension was of concern elsewhere. The *Pravda* of May 10, 1935, did not hesitate to ascribe the responsibility for the dispute to German diplomacy, remarking: "It is well known that Hitler's diplomacy is trying to construct a German-Polish-Hungarian bloc," and *Izvestiia* counseled Beneš to protect his country and the peace of Europe by strengthening Czechoslovakia's ties with France and Russia.

Early in 1936, the tension temporarily eased and for some months relations approximated normal. The air, however, was far from clear. High German military and political figures seemed to be everywhere in Poland, and the Polish opposition press had some caustic and sarcastic things to say about the German "invasion." The Hungarian prime minister, General Gömbös, who had, in 1935, declared that there should be a Warsaw-Budapest-Vienna-Rome-Berlin "defensive line" frequently conferred with Polish statesmen. The actual results may or may not have been serious, but from Prague, Belgrade, and Bucharest the outlook was naturally foreboding.

In September, 1936, when Poland obtained a credit of two billion francs from France for rearmament, Marshal Śmigły-Rydz, Piłsudski's successor, assured General Gamelin that Poland would never align itself against Czechoslovakia, and would permit Soviet air power to fly over its territory, adopting a policy of "benevolent neutrality" toward France's ally.

The relations between Poland and Germany, after the signing of the ten-year nonaggression pact of January 26, 1934, were to vary between the extremes of warmest cordiality and war within the short period of five and a half of the projected ten-year term. The period of cordiality lasted less than two years, until the end of 1935. The two countries agreed to stop mutually antagonistic press and radio campaigns, a sort of "moral disarmament." The two governments tacitly agreed to forget their respective minorities in each other's territories. High German officials, including Dr. Goebbels and General Goering, visited Poland, and a few high Polish personages, among them Colonel Beck, accepted invitations to visit Germany. The two governments followed an identical line in their dealings with the Western Powers. The long-standing tariff war was brought to an end on March 7, 1934, by a compromise, and further commercial agreements were negotiated during the ensuing year. But some deep-rooted factors making for irritation were too potent to be thus conjured out of existence. The most serious, though by no means the only one of these irritants, was the Free City of Danzig.

In August and September of 1933, Poland and Danzig had reached satisfactory arrangements intended to ease the tension over the question of the use of the port of Danzig by Poland. Poland agreed that Danzig should handle approximately 45 per cent of

Polish seaborne trade and Gdynia was to have the remaining 55 per cent. The further problem of the rights of Polish nationals in Danzig was settled on terms satisfactory to Poland. Danzig was represented in these negotiations by Dr. Hermann Rauschning, recently elected President of the Danzig Senate. Though a party member, his approach to the Polish question was not always approved of in Berlin, previous to the pact of January, 1934, but no open disavowal of his expressions of hopeful cordiality seemed to be called for. But other and less moderate Danzig Nazis were at the same time talking about the imperative need for Danzig's "return" to the Reich. Rauschning's policy of sincere collaboration with Poland was being sabotaged by members of his own party, even before Germany concluded the ten-year pact. The high point in Danzig-Polish cordiality antedated, by several months, the corresponding point in German-Polish relations, and that friendliness had then quickly begun to deteriorate.

The troubles of Danzig began to appear again with alarming frequency on the agenda of the Council of the League early in 1934. Months before the enforced resignation of Rauschning as President of the Danzig Senate on November 23, 1934, it was clear to Warsaw that the short *détente* in Polish-Danzig relations was over and that the situation was as fraught with danger as it ever had been before the Nazis came to power in Germany. No serious crisis arose until June and July, 1935, when desperate measures taken by Danzig to avoid a currency collapse brought Polish reprisals. Had not both Berlin and Warsaw wished to avoid a major crisis, this contretemps might have had grave consequences. By the end of this year a degree of normalcy had been recovered. But Poland, on the alert, watched the gradual nullification of the Danzig Constitution by the ruling Nazis and noted that the openly flouted election slogan of the latter was "Back to the Reich." There was little comfort for Beck in the realization that these tactics suffered no reproof from Berlin.

On March 7, 1936, Hitler denounced the Locarno Pact, and German troops reoccupied the Rhineland in contravention of both the Treaty of Versailles and the Locarno Pact which Germany had freely signed, and which Hitler had expressly approved. That same day Beck told the French Ambassador in Warsaw, Noël, that if he were the French premier he would regard the reoccupation as a *casus belli,* and, as Polish Minister of Foreign Affairs, he regarded it as a *casus foederis*. Then he added: "Do we march?" France, divided and cowed, would not accept the German defy, alleging England's unwillingness to join it as France's justification. In the face of such shortsighted poltroonery Poland, which had divined German plans, and had warned Paris and London of its certainties, can hardly be held guilty of faithlessness in seeking help from quarters other than the timid western democracies.

Another brief period of peace and quiet in Danzig followed firm action by the Council of the League in January, 1936, when the President of the Danzig Senate, now Greiser, engaged to respect the Constitution in its guarantees to members of the opposition; but early in the summer a proclamation by the Nazi Gauleiter, Forster, that he was responsible only to Berlin gave Polish opinion much concern. Greiser, defending the Nazi line before the Council of the League on July 4, 1936, was defiant and deliberately offensive, giving the Nazi salute as he finished his speech, and adding vulgar gestures to a stupidly rude performance. Poland, charged by the Treaty of Versailles with handling the foreign affairs of the Free City, was deeply involved in the relations of Danzig to the League. There was not a Pole who did not now realize that Danzig's Nazis were speaking for Berlin in demanding independence from the League of Nations and incorporation into the Reich. It was an irrevocable article of Polish political faith that any change in Danzig's status from that of a Free City meant war. It is not surprising, therefore, that almost immediately after the events of July 4th the French alliance, very cool since early 1933, was being warmed up and Czechoslovakia, France's other Central European ally, was again the object of Polish attention.

The tone of the German press in Danzig was such that representations were made by the Polish Ambassador in Berlin. The German reply, expressing sympathy with the aspirations of Danzig to rejoin the Reich, while protesting no intention on the part of Germany to use force to effect these aspirations, could hardly have been reassuring.

On August 12th, Hitler assured the Polish Ambassador in Berlin that "Polish rights in the Free City could not suffer the least detriment." Two days later Ribbentrop asked this same ambassador for Poland's collaboration with Germany in a crusade against the menace of Bolshevism, a request that was to be frequently repeated in the coming years and always categorically refused.

In November, in spite of the earlier specific assurances from Berlin, Nazi anti-Polish agitation in Danzig reached a new height. Polish newspapers in the Free City were suppressed, Polish nationals were arrested and otherwise seriously molested. Beck's efforts to keep the whole Danzig matter as quiet as possible, in order not to disturb Polish-German relations, were generally received with varying degrees of indignation in Poland. But after November the tension between Berlin and Warsaw eased, largely because Beck chose to follow the line of least resistance and be satisfied with some sort of vague "assurances" from Germany and from the Danzig representative that the international status of Danzig would not be disturbed. It must also be remarked that Geneva seemed as glad to accept this solution—which was no solution at all—as Beck.

The conduct of Beck during and after this crisis calls for comment. In his report to the Council of the League of Nations concerning Danzig's repeated violation of its constitution and Poland's negotiations with the Danzig Senate, Beck assured the Council (January 27, 1937), that there would be no further difficulties experienced by the League High Commissioner. But, he specified, this official "should take care to see that the internal administration of the Free City of Danzig is not hampered." Interpreted, this statement meant that the Nazified Danzig Senate should be allowed to run the city as it wanted to, regardless of the Constitution and the League of Nations. It is significant that Beck returned to Geneva from Warsaw by way of Berlin. The tenor of his report gave some of his hearers occasion to suggest that it might have been dictated, or at least materially influenced by what he had been told in the Wilhelmstrasse. After the report was read, Beck was congratulated by Greiser for his "fairness and tact." In itself, this should have warned Geneva that, at the height of its activity the League had approved a report which was in effect a capitulation to the Free City, its own creation. For Beck, in this case, there is no excuse. It is relatively certain that he had come to an understanding with the Danzig Nazis and Berlin by which the Constitution of the Free

City could be cynically flouted. At all events this was the clear result, and Beck was too experienced in politics not to have known exactly what would result if his recommendations were accepted by the Council. He made no protest at the eventualities, even when Polish commercial houses in Danzig were roughly handled and Polish children were obliged to go to German schools in flagrant violation of all agreements and declarations of intention on the part of the Danzig officials. Beck can thus be held responsible in a considerable measure for facilitating the later phases of the German diplomatic preparation for the precipitation of the war which finally broke on Poland. It is not without interest that there was some sharp judgment of Beck in Poland, but the moves on the European chessboard were now too rapid for measured criticism to have any effect.

There were numerous sources of Polish-German friction aside from the events in Danzig. Late in 1936, the Polish Parliament passed a land-reform bill which bore particularly heavily on the large German landholders in western and northwestern Poland. The Lutheran Church in Poland was subjected to restrictions which, in effect, brought it under Polish control, and German minority schools in Poland were finding their continued existence difficult. In Polish Upper Silesia unemployment among the Germans was serious and unrelieved. In all these cases the Polish populace was less anxious to appease Germany than the Government. All anti-German measures taken by the Parliament were enthusiastically received. The widely known fact that the Polish minority in Germany was even less well treated than the German minority in Poland did not make the Poles any less enthusiastic in their course of action and opinion. The Polish-German minority agreement reached on November 5, 1937, looked promising on paper, but its actual effects were negligible.[1]

During these years, the relations between Poland and its traditional friend to the southeast, Rumania, were cordial. After Rumania's turn to the right in 1936, its political leadership welcomed any support which regarded the Soviet Union with any suspicion. Visits were exchanged, King Carol went to Warsaw in June, 1937, and the general staffs of the two countries held long conversations.

[1] See Chapter X, "Minorities," by Joseph S. Roucek.

Beck would have liked to wean Rumania from the collective security camp and its allegiance to the League and the Little Entente. He was an ardent missionary for the gospel of bilateralism. But Rumania, under French influence, would not go so far to please Poland. The French Foreign Minister, Yvon Delbos, on his swing around the Central European capitals in December, 1937, was reassured of Rumanian support of France and the League.

The Polish-Soviet Non-Aggression Pact had been renewed in June, 1934, for eleven years, but Russia was at all times thereafter aware that Beck was closely following the German lead in rejecting the whole Geneva system. Stalin's remark in 1936 that, "those willing to lend it [Germany] a frontier can be found," was a pointed reference to Poland and its German-oriented foreign policy. But relations were correct. It is indicative of this fact that, in the Polish *White Book,* there is a period of over four years, September, 1934, to November, 1938, devoid of any entries save a short memorandum from Beck to "all Polish diplomatic missions abroad," instructing them to deny Polish adhesion to the Anti-Comintern Pact. The closer Soviet policy came to Geneva, the farther Poland withdrew from the capital of collectivism. Poland was especially suspicious of Soviet action in the Baltic, and the diplomatic tug-of-war for the favor of the Baltic states was, for some years, in very delicate balance, with Russia enjoying a slight advantage. The sudden change in German policy from truculence to amity toward Lithuania, over the question of Memel in April, 1936, was a source of some embarrassment to Poland. Both Lithuania and Poland, after sixteen years of a closed frontier and a perpetual state of war, would have been uncomfortable to find themselves in the same camp. Yet, Germany was friendly to Poland and suddenly Lithuania was chosen to be an object of German affection. It was all very confusing. In order to regularize this anomalous situation Poland, after some preliminary diplomatic efforts had failed, presented Lithuania with a forty-eight-hour ultimatum (March 17, 1938), backed by troop concentrations on the frontier, that their relations be regularized within two weeks. Adequate diplomatic, commercial, and transportation relations were established, to the relief of the other Baltic states and the Western Powers. Somewhat against its will, Lithuania was thereafter to be on terms of diplomatic normality with Poland. The Soviet Union, it was generally understood, was sympathetic toward Lithuania, though not to the extent of counseling rejection of the ultimatum.

It is hardly likely that the time chosen by Poland for this radical *démarche* was intended to coincide with Germany's Austrian coup, when world opinion was so taken aback by the forcible *Anschluss* as to disregard the lesser matter of Poland's threat of force against a weaker neighbor. French charges that Beck had hoped to be able to annex Lithuania, as Hitler had annexed Austria, may be disregarded.

Beck was in Rome from March 5th to March 10, 1938, closeted with Mussolini. As later events were to show, it is not improbable that one of the subjects of their conversations was the Polish-Hungarian common frontier to be achieved by the partitioning between them of Sub-Carpathian Ruthenia, the eastern province of Czechoslovakia. This was a project that Germany would certainly not favor, as it would make a cordon against German expansion into the Ukraine. Mussolini, traditionally Hungary's friend and protector, and not anxious to have his Axis partner control the whole Danubian region, could be counted on to see things in a different light from Hitler. In the reports of these conversations circulating within the diplomatic corps there was no suggestion that Beck brought up the question of a partition of Sub-Carpathian Ruthenia.

During the next few months Poland's problems and relations with its neighbors and allies, for the most part, were buried in the storm and furor of the prolonged German-Czechoslovak crisis. Poland was repeatedly assured, in Hitler's speeches and in diplomatic conferences, of Germany's firm intention to maintain friendly relations between the neighbors. These assurances were, if anything, a little too frequently and easily given. Apologetic reference was always made to Germany's noble self-sacrifice in the matter of the "Corridor," and then Lipski, or Beck, or the world in general would be told that Hitler had given his word and nothing could possibly change that. On the other hand, Beck was busy trying to weld the Baltic states into a diplomatic unity, visiting all the Baltic capitals, with the exception of Helsinki, and strengthening the bonds between Poland on the one hand, and Rumania and Hungary on the other.

It is legitimate to inquire here whether Beck had begun to realize, as early as the time of the Austrian coup, that his German policy had been a help to the German *Drang nach Osten,* which would eventually, necessarily, and logically engulf Poland, too, and whether he was now (after March 12, 1938), reversing that policy and turning his diplomatic energies to the construction of an anti-German bloc. No conclusive evidence is yet at hand to answer this question, but the known facts might bear that construction.

Early in April, Polish popular clamor for a colonial outlet came into the open. "Colonial Week" was given considerable attention. The Maritime and Colonial League, led by General Kwaśniewski, was extended every facility for its propaganda. It was doubtless a trial balloon. It was generally known in the capitals of Europe that Poland had colonial aspirations, but no open diplomatic *démarches,* beyond an expression of Poland's interest in the problem on several occasions at Geneva, had ever been made.

In August, 1938, Poland announced its intention not to stand for reëlection to a semipermanent seat on the Council of the League of Nations, a seat that country had been more than anxious to obtain in 1926. Beck had frequently, in the years after 1934, expressed his opinion that the League had outlived its usefulness. The announcement that Poland was going to give up its seat on the Council therefore caused the informed no great surprise. The subsequent announcement that Poland was suppressing its permanent delegation to the League was essentially implicit in the earlier declaration.

As the Sudeten crisis grew more serious, Poland watched the development of events with careful attention. As early as May the opposition press openly discussed the danger for Poland in any further expansion of Germany to the southeast, threatening encirclement. The government press did not broach the subject, but did give prominence to the Slovak "question," particularly on the occasion of the visit to Warsaw of a group of Slovak autonomists led by Karol Sidor.

In the meantime the growing popular feeling against the Germans in Poland, the German Reich, and Poland's pro-German foreign policy brought about a number of diplomatic conversations during the summer. The German Ambassador to Warsaw, Moltke, made representations to Beck, who expressed regret, but could give only vague assurances that the situation would improve. This anti-German feeling in Poland was to continue to grow in intensity throughout the next year, and should be weighed in the balance against Polish official subservience to Germany for the preceding four years.

Knowing well in advance of Hitler's plans for a dismemberment of Czechoslovakia, Beck made his own plans to get for Poland a section of that land to which Poland had laid claim since 1920—the remainder of Silesian Teschen. On September 19th, Polish troops were concentrated on the border. The demand for cession of the territory came into the open, on September 20th, in a leading article in the Warsaw *Kurier Poranny.* On the next day it was officially presented to the foreign offices in London, Paris, Berlin, and Rome; and in Prague the Polish-Czechoslovak treaty of 1925 was denounced and a formal demand made that the same rights granted to Germans in Czechoslovakia as a result of negotiations then under way should be granted to the Polish minority. Two days later, September 23d, the Soviet Government warned Poland that a Polish invasion of Czechoslovakia would bring about a cancellation of the Soviet-Polish Non-Aggression Pact. Beck immediately replied that the troop concentrations were of "an internal character and had no connection with Soviet affairs." He then ostentatiously conferred with the Japanese Ambassador.

Though Poland was not a party to the Munich Agreement, its claims to Czechoslovak territorial adjustments were mentioned in the text of the document. But this was not enough for Beck, and on the night of September 30th, he sent an ultimatum to Prague demanding Czechoslovak cession and evacuation of Silesian Teschen and some neighboring districts by noon the next day, October 1st. As conditions stood after Munich, Prague could only accede to the demand. Poland gained a total population of 227,000, of whom only 76,000 were Polish, according to the Czechoslovak census. One justification advanced for the action—most Poles, it should be pointed out to their credit, are rather shamefaced about the whole matter—was that, by taking the important rail center of Bohumín, Germany was forestalled in its eastward push to that extent.

Soviet Russia, not invited to the festivities at Munich, regarded Poland's action in a grave light. An editorial in *Pravda* of October 1st said: "There can be little doubt that the time is not far off when Fascist Germany, intoxicated by the lack of opposition, will place the question of the partition of Poland on the day's agenda."

Poland next wished to consolidate its southern position by achieving its long-dreamed-of common frontier with Hungary. It was thought that such a juncture would have offered a barrier to further German expansion toward the east. Italy might have been willing, both to please Hungary and to curb the success of her northern Axis partner. But Germany was now giving orders in the Danubian basin, and the Vienna Award of November 2d did not allow Poland and Hungary a common border in Sub-Carpathian Ruthenia which belonged to Czechoslovakia.

III

This rebuff only confirmed a conclusion that, if it may be deduced from his actions, Beck had reached at least some months earlier, namely that Poland would now have to abandon its German-oriented policy for a policy of balance. His trip to Rome in March, 1938, was the first outward sign of this shift; the independent action of Poland in September in Teschen, the second; and the effort to gain a common frontier with Hungary in October, the third. The tempo of Poland's movement in this direction increased in the months after Munich. The Polish Ambassador in Moscow had numerous conversations during November with M. Litvinov, then Soviet Commissar for Foreign Affairs, and cordial communiques were issued (November 26th). Lithuania, knowing of German designs on Memel, and sensing that Poland was no longer following a German line but trying to strengthen its diplomatic and strategic position against Germany, sought more friendly relations with its ancient enemy to the south. Agreements were reached between Poland and Lithuania in November by which unfriendly broadcasting on both sides of the border was stopped.

At Berchtesgaden on October 24th, less than four weeks after the conference of Munich, Ribbentrop, the German Foreign Minister, presented to Lipski, the Polish Ambassador to Germany, the German "suggestions" for a definitive solution of the problem of

Danzig. Danzig was to be returned to the Reich; an extraterritorial double-track and motor road across the "Corridor" were to be built, to be owned by Germany; mutual guarantees of their frontiers were to be given to both parties; extension of the Non-Aggression Pact by ten to twenty-five years would then be arranged. Ribbentrop also suggested that if Poland acceded to these German suggestions, it might be allowed a joint frontier with Hungary in Sub-Carpathian Ruthenia.

Beck's answer, delivered by Lipski to Ribbentrop on November 19th, was diplomatic but firm, reiterating the Polish position that the freedom of Danzig was a cardinal point in Polish policy, and that any violation of that freedom by Germany would "inevitably lead to a conflict." German diplomatic pressure, undeterred by Polish firmness, was maintained along these lines, and there were numerous conversations in Warsaw and Berlin in November and December. The German representatives emphasized the "broad aspects of German-Polish relations," and "high policy," the Poles stressed special and immediate problems, Poland's specific and irrevocable need for a free Danzig and Germany's encircling tactics in Slovakia and in Sub-Carpathian Ruthenia. With such divergence in points of view it was not possible for the two parties to come any closer together. It is likewise obvious and certain that both parties knew they could not find any middle point upon which they could agree.

On January 5, 1939, Beck and Lipski met with Hitler, Ribbentrop, and Moltke, at Berchtesgaden, and the whole Danzig question was again examined. Hitler emphasized that Danzig was German and would certainly return to the Reich. Beck was unable to see how any change in the status of the Free City could be worked out whereby Poland would receive any equivalent for its economic and political loss. The next day Beck told Ribbentrop that, for the first time, he felt pessimistic about the future of Polish-German relations. It is an axiom of practical diplomacy that one does not admit "pessimism" until long after one has given up all hope. The issue was clearly drawn. From this point both sides were simply marking time or were maneuvering for diplomatic position. It was to the interests of both Germany and Poland to give the appearance of carrying on bona fide negotiations, and many qualified observers were deceived by the quiet surface of the relations between the two countries. Poland was even invited to join the Anti-Comintern Pact again, but declined.

On February 19th, Poland signed with Soviet Russia a number of economic agreements, incorporating the most favored nation principle, indicating to the rest of the world a degree of *rapprochement* with Germany's traditional rival. The point was not lost on Germany. It is also reliably asserted that in mid-February the Polish Ambassador in Paris, acting on instructions from Beck, was holding conversations with the Quai d'Orsay with the intention of reactivating the Franco-Polish alliance to fit the present emergency.

The occupation of Prague and the forcible absorption of the rump of Czechoslovakia were then only a few weeks away, and Germany had no time to be concerned with what Poland did. While the world was trying to recover from the shock of the March 15th breach of international decency, the Germans reached for another outpost on their push to the east. On March 22d Lithuania was presented with an ultimatum, and Memel was summarily incorporated into the Reich. The encirclement of Poland on three sides was completed by the assumption of a German "protection of the political independence of the state of Slovakia and the inviolability of its territory," the formalization of a reality since March 16th.

A careful and comparative reading of the published reports of diplomatic conferences between the Polish Ambassador in Berlin and German Foreign Office officials before March 15th and after March 22d tells eloquently that Germany, once in control of all of what used to be Czechoslovakia, that is, Poland's southern frontier, dropped the mask of fair words and conciliatory approach, sharpened its complaints, and increased its demands. The diplomatic atmosphere was frigid. Lipski, reporting to Beck the details of a conversation with Ribbentrop at the Foreign Office on March 26th, remarked: "Herr von Ribbentrop gave me a distinctly cold reception." It would be correct to say that the overt phase of the German-Polish crisis that eventually led to the military attack of September 1, 1939, lasted more than five months, from March 22d to September 1st.

Poland was the next stop on Germany's timetable, and the German pattern of diplomatic behavior was being repeated. After five years of an agreement with Germany that had furthered Germany's plans only, Beck effected the complete reversal of his policy. Various diplomatic *démarches* mentioned above, made since the Austrian coup of the previous spring, prepared for this change. When Beck was finally forced to make an open break with his previous pro-German policy, he must have prayed long and earnestly that it be not too late.

On March 21st, Great Britain made suggestions to Paris, Warsaw, and Moscow for a joint declaration of a united front against further German aggression. The move was welcomed in Warsaw, but it was Beck's conviction that a mere declaration was, under the circumstances, no adequate guarantee of peace. His own attitude toward Germany, once he had decided to reverse his policy, was firm. His firmness, obviously, was not lessened by the assurances he had received that Great Britain and France would support Poland in an independent policy. In the course of a conversation at Warsaw, on March 28th, Moltke, the German Ambassador, expostulated, "You want to negotiate at the point of a bayonet." Beck rejoined, "That is your own method."

On March 30th, Beck was asked by the British Ambassador if Poland would accept a British guarantee of its independence if Poland "considered it vital to resist with its national forces." This unilateral guarantee was gladly accepted by Beck. The British Prime Minister made the formal announcement of the Government's action to Commons the next day, and added that France had taken an identical position. Beck immediately proceeded to London where, after solemn conversations, a joint Polish-British communiqué was issued on April 6th, which converted a unilateral guarantee on the part of Great Britain into a military alliance. It made public Poland's engagement to "render assistance to H. M. Government under the same conditions as those contained in the temporary assurance already given by H. M. Government to Poland." The Franco-Polish alliance was still, by its terms, in full effect.

In reply to a suggestion by the British and French foreign offices on April 15th, that Soviet Russia issue a declaration guaranteeing the territories of Rumania and Poland, Moscow proposed a military alliance of France, Great Britain, and Russia to guarantee the territories of all of Russia's western neighbors. The long-delayed reply from London and Paris (May 9th) only repeated their earlier suggestion. It would appear that strong elements in the British Government objected to any kind of political or military alliance with Russia, and Poland was known to be reluctant to open the way for Russian armies to set foot on its soil. The popular observation to such a possibility would have been uniformly the same in Poland: "Once on Polish soil, they will never leave. They have been here before." On May 10th the Soviet Vice-Commissar for Foreign Affairs, Vladimir Potemkin, was in Warsaw discussing the situation with Beck. At that time Beck was assured that, in event of war between Poland and Germany, Russia would adopt "a benevolent attitude" toward Poland. The benevolence of this attitude was a matter of subsequent substantial interpretation on the part of the Soviet Foreign Office.

In a speech to the Reichstag on April 28th, Hitler had denounced the German-Polish pact of 1934, alleging that the Anglo-Polish mutual assistance treaty had nullified the 1934 pact. Hitler spoke of a "concrete offer" which Poland had refused. This was the veiled demand which Ribbentrop had made for the incorporation of Danzig into the Reich on March 21st. It was generally noticed that his usual diatribes against Soviet Russia were absent from this speech. Did this portend a German approach to Russia? A German trade mission had been in Moscow since February.

Beck's answer to Hitler's speech, a report to the Polish Parliament on May 5th, was by far the best effort of his whole career. It was cool, clear, and courageous and went far to redeem much of the equivocation of his earlier diplomatic action. The speech ended: "We in Poland do not recognize the conception of 'peace at any price.' There is only one thing in the life of men, nations, and states which is without price, and that is honor." Though these noble words might have come with better grace from someone else, the gallantry of the whole Polish people was to seal that honor in blood within a few short months.

The tension over Danzig between Poland and Germany mounted hourly. Polish citizens of the Free City were mishandled, anti-Semitism was rife, Polish property in Danzig was defaced and destroyed. Germany openly took control in the City, in violation of all law and international practice, and the press and radio in both countries were bitter and belligerent. May, June, and July were used by all the Powers to hasten their military and diplomatic preparations. The French and British general staffs held frequent consultations. The Poles placed orders for quantities of matériel—planes and supplies—though it developed that delivery from France and England was almost negligible. The conversations in Moscow between English, French, and Soviet military and economic experts, though noticeably slow, seemed to give some ground for optimism. But the press in the countries most directly concerned was divided between stark pessimism and the hope of desperation.

It seemed to close observers in Berlin that, though the situation was tense, Hitler was being very careful not to make any move which might precipitate a war. His own military preparations were not complete. It was an open secret in the diplomatic corps in Berlin that the German army would not be prepared until late in August. Then Hitler was assured by Ribbentrop that Great Britain would never go to war over Danzig, and that France was demoralized by factionalism. If he kept the tension high enough and still under control, Hitler might split the Western Powers and get all he wanted without war. For every reason, therefore, the German tactics were to keep matters tense, but not to reach the breaking point.

The Polish attitude toward the Anglo-French-Soviet conversations, which never quite reached any stable basis, was neutral. Poland distrusted Soviet Russia only less than Nazi Germany, and there was no mourning in Warsaw when it was announced, during the first week in August, that the political mission of the Western Powers to Moscow was returning home without having concluded an agreement.

On August 4th, the Danzig Senate decreed that the Polish customs inspectors who had theretofore controlled the passage of goods across the Polish-Danzig frontiers could no longer carry out their duties. The Polish Foreign Office forthwith demanded that this order be withdrawn. The Danzig reply was evasive to the point of misstating the facts. The Wilhelmstrasse entered the dispute on August 9th with a threat to intervene. The prompt Polish reply insisted on Poland's rights in the case, and concluded that any "eventual intervention on the part of the German Government to the detriment of these rights and interests [would be considered] an act of aggression."

While the finishing touches were being put to the German military machine, Berlin and other large cities within range of bombing planes were being fitted with antiaircraft defenses. Then, suddenly, on the night of August 21st, it was announced that Germany and Russia had agreed to sign a nonaggression pact. The whole world was confused, not least of whom were the German and Russian peoples. The English and French were deeply chagrined at having been so egregiously deceived by Stalin. It was clear that with Russia's benevolent neutrality secured, Hitler was now ready and war could be expected at any moment. Actually, it was soon generally known, the date of August 27th had been set for the attack some weeks ahead. Heavy troop reinforcements to East Prussia and the western Polish border were being continuously moved up during August.

The Polish Ambassador in Berlin had no effective contact with the Wilhelmstrasse, and the German Ambassador in Warsaw was in a similar position. Communications of any significance at all were made through the British or French ambassadors. On August 23d, Sir Nevile Henderson, the British Ambassador in Berlin, presented to Hitler in Berchtesgaden a letter from the Prime Minister, Mr. Neville Chamberlain, in which England, while firmly adhering to the terms of its treaty with Poland, offered its mediatory services to bring Germany and Poland to discuss their differences. Hitler's reply was a tirade against England for inciting Polish resistance by giving the Poles *carté blanché*. He had not, at that time, the slightest intention of participating in any discussions. Two days later, however, he made proposals to Chamberlain through Henderson for a solution of the German-Polish dispute and a German-British alliance. It seems difficult, at this distance, to treat such a proposal seriously.

On that same day, August 23d, the good offices of the Oslo group of states were offered by King Leopold of Belgium; and on August 24th, President Roosevelt appealed to both parties, suggesting the mediation of some disinterested American republic. But it takes two parties to agree to mediation and, though Poland welcomed the suggestions, Germany either found them unacceptable or disregarded them entirely.

On August 25th, the definitive text of the Anglo-British Pact of Mutual Assistance was published. It was a full military alliance. On that same day, Hitler proposed to the French that they should withdraw their support of Poland, hoping thus to detach France from an alliance against Germany in which France was, by reason of its common frontier, the most important member. But France was not going to "Munich" again.

In the meantime, incidents were occurring on the Polish-German frontier. Bands of Germans, armed with rifles and machine guns, attacked customs houses and Polish government buildings almost every night, leaving some dead and wounded on Polish soil as evidence. A controlled German press was able to use these incidents in its own way, altering the facts to suit the purposes of the Government in order to inflame public opinion.

The pressure of French and British diplomacy on a further attempt to negotiate the matters in dispute between Poland and Germany brought about a delay of several days in German military action. Henderson left Berlin by air for London early on August 26th to communicate Hitler's suggestions to the British Cabinet. Two days were spent in discussion and formulations of a reply. The tone of the reply was firm. England reaffirmed its will to live up to the terms of its treaty with Poland, but urged that direct negotiations between Poland and Germany be undertaken to relieve the tension and to work out a just settlement of all differences. This reply was handed to Hitler by Henderson at 10:30 P.M. on August 28th. Hitler promised to answer the note in writing the next day. In the meantime, Poland had expressed a willingness to negotiate. An order had been issued to the Polish army by Marshal Śmigły-Rydz to make no counteraction to German provocations unless German military units were found on Polish territory. Several cases of the latter sort were encountered. The French and British diplomatic and consular officials unhesitatingly qualified the reports of Polish mistreatment of German nationals in the German press, as well as those listed by Hitler, as pure inventions and calumnies.

Hitler's reply to the British note was handed to Henderson on the evening of August 29th. The return of Danzig and the "Corridor" was assumed, but it was specified that, if any territorial adjustments were necessary, Germany could not participate without consultation with the Soviet Union. Finally, it was stipulated that a Polish representative with full powers to negotiate should be in Berlin the next day. Henderson immediately pointed out the virtual impossibility of such rapid action. The Polish Government had not even been apprised of the nature of the German demands. In the normal course of the mechanics of diplomatic procedure, it takes hours for messages to be coded and sent, decoded and discussed. Henderson received from London his instructions in answer to Hitler's latest demands in time to pass them on to Ribbentrop at midnight of August 30th. It was a stormy session. Ribbentrop was excited and theatrical. After hearing the reply of the British Government he read rapidly, or rather mumbled, a long document containing sixteen articles, which the German text called "concrete proposals." Henderson asked to see the document, but Ribbentrop refused, adding that it was too late, as no Polish plenipotentiary had arrived. Henderson immediately talked with Lipski, and the latter was in touch with Warsaw during much of the next morning. At one o'clock in the afternoon, Lipski asked the German Foreign Office for an interview. At half past six he was received by Ribbentrop, who asked him if he had plenipotentiary powers to negotiate. At Lipski's reply in the negative the interview was terminated. When he returned to the Polish Embassy and tried to telephone Warsaw he found that his telephone was "out of order." Hitler did not want his plans upset by further discussion.

Early that afternoon Mussolini had offered, through the French and British ambassadors at Rome, to invite Hitler to a conference. This is one of the lighter touches of the crisis.

At nine o'clock that evening the German radio carried an official communiqué declaring that the German proposals had been rejected, and giving the text of the sixteen proposals. Inasmuch as they had never been presented in written form to the French, British, or Polish ambassadors, 'rejection' was a quaint word to use. The text of these proposals was presented to Henderson at 9:15 P.M., and to the French Ambassador at 9:25 P.M. The order for the German army to march on Poland had been issued immediately after Ribbentrop's short meeting with Lipski, before seven o'clock, that is, more than two hours before any French or British diplomat had seen the text. The Poles first heard these "proposals" over the radio.

At four o'clock the next morning, September 1st, without any declaration of war, German military forces, infantry, motorized units, and squadrons of bombing planes crossed the Polish frontier into Silesia, Poznań, Pomorze, and from East Prussia in two directions, south toward Mława and west on Grudziądz. Other forces crossed the line from Slovakia north toward Cracow. The Polish munitions depot at Westerplatte was then bombarded by the German cruiser "Schleswig-Holstein." Systematically all the rail centers, airdromes, and main communication and transport lines were bombed from the air with paralyzing effect. At nine o'clock that morning Hitler spoke to a quickly convened meeting of the Reichstag, and declared that Danzig wanted to be united to the Reich. At that hour the swastika was flying from the flagpole of the League High Commissioner's building. The High Commissioner, Karl J. Burckhardt, evicted, fled to Kaunas.

From the beginning the struggle was uneven. The German forces consisted of 70 infantry divisions, 17 motorized divisions, 1 cavalry brigade, and 6,850 combat aircraft. The Polish forces totaled 22 infantry divisions, 8 cavalry brigades, 2 motorized brigades, and 440 aircraft. The disproportion, added to the advantages of sudden attack and the efficiency of the German fifth column in Poland, was too much even for Polish gallantry. It would be possible to point out many respects in which the High Military Command did not do so well as it should have done: communications and supplies were not adequately provided for; collaboration between political leaders and the High Military Command had not been sufficiently close in the months before the outbreak of war; there seemed to be no over-all strategy which the Polish army had been trained to follow; Pomorze (the "Corridor") should immediately have been evacuated, leaving a much shorter line to defend; there were divided councils at military headquarters; the Polish civilian population had not been adequately prepared for its part in the war. But even if all these errors had been avoided, the final collapse of Poland would only have been postponed.

Great Britain and France went through the formalities of delivering ultimata to Germany; President Roosevelt appealed to both parties to the conflict not to bomb the civilian populations; Soviet Russia, having known beforehand that the attack was going to be made, immediately informed Poland that the entry of Great Britain and France into the conflict changed the whole situation with regard to the Polish-Soviet Non-Aggression Pact. England's unilateral guarantee of Poland was published on March 31st. There is no record of a Soviet warning that the implementation of such a guarantee would alter anything as between Russia and Poland. Consequent upon the expiration of an ultimatum previously delivered, Henderson notified Ribbentrop at nine o'clock on September 3d that a state of war would exist between Germany and Great Britain as from eleven o'clock that morning. Coulondre, the French Ambassador in Berlin, conveyed a similar message to Ribbentrop at noon, specifying five o'clock in the afternoon as the hour from which a state of war should exist. The greatest war in human history had begun its tragic course.

As the Polish troops were forced to withdraw in confusion to the east, and the inadequacy of the government's preparations became increasingly evident, Russian troop concentrations on Poland's eastern frontier began to be noted in the news, though Soviet diplomatic sources denied knowledge of any such movements. On the morning of September 17th, more than 100 Soviet divisions moved across the Polish eastern frontier, along the entire line from the Ukraine to the border of Latvia. There was hardly more than token resistance. Molotov explained to the world that the Polish State had "virtually ceased to exist." The Polish Government, taking what documents and staff it could hurriedly collect, and accompanied by many high ranking officers of the army and air force, Marshal Śmigły-Rydz among them, fled across the border into Rumania.

Twelve days after the Soviet attack Germany and Russia signed a treaty of partition of Poland. Russia took 77,606 square miles of the 150,000 square miles of the Republic of Poland, and Germany took the remaining 72,400 square miles. Germany's share was the richer, more populous and more highly industrialized. Almost 90 per cent of Polish industry was in the German area. It is evident that the partition had been agreed upon in principle and in some detail before war even broke out. With all of eastern Poland in its hands, Soviet Russia made a generous gesture of returning the city and district of Wilno to Lithuania. A treaty of mutual assistance with Lithuania (October 10, 1939), sealed the transfer of the former Polish territory.

Military resistance in Poland to the German invader was heroic if hopeless. Warsaw held out for eighteen days against all German attacks by artillery and air bombardment; a few cities resisted until October 1st, and some guerrilla warfare in isolated areas kept on until November 1st. The Poles had been expecting their Western Allies to make a determined attack on the Siegfried Line, and their disappointment was bitter that they had had to bear the brunt of the German attack alone. The German western front was defended by only a half dozen divisions. Hitler must have guessed that the Western Powers would not attack.

Part Eight

SECOND WORLD WAR AND AFTER

CHAPTER XXVI

Poland and the War

BY STANISŁAW STRZETELSKI

On OCTOBER 5, 1939, the three-day battle at Kock came to an end. An iron ring of enemy troops closed in on a unit of the Polish army which, under the command of General Kleeberg, had been successfully holding off the onslaught of overwhelming German forces. The German army pressing in from the west and south joined hands with Soviet armored divisions rolling in from the east. Having fought a hopeless battle, General Kleeberg, like all the Polish commanders, had but one alternative, namely to instruct the troops under his command to attempt to reach the Hungarian frontiers in small groups. The battle of Kock was the last action of the Polish regular army in the campaign of 1939. Politically, the issue had been decided some time previously.

Two totalitarian powers, Hitlerian Germany and Soviet Russia, already linked with each other by the pact of August 23, 1939, concluded on September 23, 1939, a new Treaty of Friendship and Frontiers destined to last almost two years. This Ribbentrop-Molotov pact established a border line dividing Poland into two halves. Polish lands situated to the west of this line went to Germany, whereas those situated to the east of it were to fall to Russia's share.

In his famous speech of October 6, 1939, Adolf Hitler proclaimed to all and sundry the end of Poland and three weeks later, October 31st, Molotov, echoing Hitler, spoke of "one swift blow to Poland, first by the German Army and then by the Red Army, and nothing was left. . . ."

As early as the first days of October, not one square mile of Polish soil was free from invaders. A brown wave submerged the western portion of Poland as a red wave engulfed its eastern part. From that moment began for the Polish nation a tragic hour of darkness which has lasted now for more than five years.

At times of great events, the historical outline of certain phenomena is slow in maturing if for no other reason than because the many and ever-changing phenomena are crowding the mind of the world at large. After the heroic Polish campaign of 1939, a succession of events which shocked the opinion of the world relegated Poland to the background of public interest. What is more, the Western mind is unable to grasp the extent of German bestiality running amuck in Poland, or to understand that German methods applied in countries intended only for economic or political penetration differ from the methods resorted to in Poland which, in Hitler's scheme should become in one part an essentially German land, and in the other part a colony of the Reich. For these very reasons even today, at the end of the war's fifth year, the immense majority of people fail to comprehend the essence of that phenomenon of history which began on the banks of the Vistula in September, 1939, and has continued to this very moment. The present writer has described this phenomenon as an attempt at "the execution of a nation fighting for its life and its liberty." At this writing a more fitting definition has not been found.

In 1939 the Germans undertook the task of destroying, before the eyes of a stunned world, a nation of 35,000,000 inhabitants, of annihilating it politically, culturally, economically, and biologically. How many people realize the ratio of figures showing the losses of human lives suffered by the United Nations? The British Empire's casualties (for the first three years of the war) amounted to 121,228 dead (soldiers and civilians). The losses of the United States (to May 18, 1943), were 17,848 in dead. Soviet Russia gave its figure of losses in dead as 3,300,000 (to November, 1942).

The sum total of the population of these three countries amounts to 850,000,000 people. Assuming that up to 1943 the sum total of losses in dead had reached 4,000,000, it still does not constitute even one-half per cent of the total population. How does this figure compare with the Polish losses?

The population of Poland in 1939 amounted to 35,000,000. According to the statement made by the Polish Minister of the

Interior, Banaczyk, on July 26, 1943, the number of Polish citizens killed by the Germans alone, as ascertained up to then, reached the figure of 3,200,000, which constituted 9.4 per cent of the population. The number of Poles murdered by Germans does not, however, exhaust the problem. In the course of the last five years the Germans have shipped 2,000,000 Poles to Germany for compulsory labor, and have deported over 1,000,000 from western Poland to the General Government, after having despoiled them completely. The Soviet had deported 1,500,000 Poles to Russia. Thus, it may be seen that well over 7,700,000 Polish citizens either have been killed or removed from Poland. These losses exceed 18 per cent of Poland's prewar population, and it is claimed that no other United Nation had suffered to this extent by the summer of 1944.

This fate of the Poles, however, is not all. As may be seen later, one of the foremost expedients of the German policy of extermination in Poland was the planned starving of the population, a procedure the tragic consequences of which cannot possibly be fully visualized at this time.

The extent of losses in human lives demonstrates the exceptional nature of Poland's problem in the present war. Prime Minister Churchill perhaps gave the best characterization of the Polish nation's situation in his speech of May 3, 1941: "Every day Hitler's firing parties are busy in a dozen lands. Monday he shoots Dutchmen, Tuesday, Norwegians, Wednesday, French and Belgians stand against the wall, Thursday it is the Czechs who must suffer, and now there are the Serbs and the Greeks to fill his repulsive bill of executions. But always, all of the days, there are the Poles." More than seventeen hundred days of fighting to the death with the invader, days filled with heart-rending wrongs and torment had been endured by the summer of 1944 in this the most tragic region of the war.

By way of a start, the invaders introduced a new administrative division of Polish lands. Western Poland, i.e., Silesia, Poznań, and Pomorze, with a number of provinces of Congress Poland, totaling 35,714 square miles, with a population of 10,568,000, was incorporated in the Reich by Hitler's decree of October 8, 1939. Out of the central part of Poland, consisting of the considerably reduced Congress Poland and of western Little (Lesser) Poland, together totaling 36,867 square miles, with a population of 11,-542,000, the Germans have made the General Government constituting, to all intents and purposes, a German colony (Hitler's decree of October 12, 1939). All of eastern Poland, however, an area aggregating 51.6 per cent of Poland's territory, with a population of 13,199,000 at first became Russia's share of the spoils. The Soviets ruled over that territory only until the summer of 1941. As a result of the Russo-German war and of Hitler's victories in the east, all of eastern Poland found itself within the sphere of German occupation until the summer of 1944.

GERMAN-OCCUPIED POLAND

In the Polish territories "incorporated" in the Reich, the Germans made the issue very clear from the first day they assumed power. Forster, the Gauleiter of the "Wartheland," made a speech in Bydgoszcz (Bromberg), on September 27, 1939, in which he stated: "Everything that is Polish is going to be cleared out of this region." The same Nazi official, speaking to German "colonists" in Kielce on October 6, 1940, said: "I promise you that by ten years from now there will not be so much as a single sheaf of wheat growing on Polish soil." Devised with precision, the German plan for the incorporated Polish lands foresees the disappearance of even the slightest vestige of Polonism from the territories in question within ten years.

W. Best, a man high in Nazi councils and at the same time an exponent of Nazi ideology, justifies a totalitarian extermination of the Polish element by the argument that "Historical experience has shown that the destruction and elimination of a foreign nationality is not in the least against the laws of life, provided that destruction and elimination are complete."

By way of putting their plan into execution the Germans began with systematically killing the Polish upper class, that is to say, the intelligentsia, and the leading personalities in each field of endeavor. Together with troops of occupation, there came over Poland a tidal wave of Gestapo agents which proceeded to organize bloody purges in each and every locality, no matter how small. Approximately 60,000 prominent Poles—professors, lawyers, clergymen, landowners, peasant and labor leaders—perished on gibbets or before firing squads in the territories "incorporated" in the Reich in October and November of 1939. Those who succeeded in surviving, as well as those who escaped from the first bloody massacres are being systematically exterminated day by day. Participation in the activities of any prewar Polish organization, be it political, or social, or economic, which could in any way be accused of having anti-German tendencies constituted and continues to constitute sufficient ground for the death penalty. Now and then, information is received about mass executions witnessed by local populations who are driven to the scene of execution by whips wielded by Gestapo men. No Pole abused even by a German civilian may dare to raise a hand against his tormentors because, in accordance with Greiser's statement, made on October 25, 1941, "any Pole who should raise his hand against a German shall swiftly meet his doom."

A special penal code issued by the Germans on December 16, 1941, and applying to the Poles and to the Jews, is the only document of its kind in modern history. The slightest offense—nay, the intention of an offense (Art. 4, Item II)—is, under this code, punishable by death. In addition to the death penalty which is being imposed either by court sentence or else by administrative order, pure and simple, there is but one other penalty meted out by the Germans in Poland—the concentration camp. It suffices to cite but two figures to show what the concentration camps in Poland are. In the camp at Rajsk, which was set up in May, 1942, only 140 persons out of the first group of 1,300 prisoners survived after four weeks of detention. In the camp at Oswięcim, 94,000 of the 125,000 prisoners who had been confined in the camp until July, 1942, died.

The chief expedients for clearing out the Poles from the incorporated Polish lands were expropriations and deportations. A "legal" basis for evicting the Poles was obtained by the decree of October 20, 1939, and an executive order of September 17, 1940, which provided that the only criterion for confiscation of Polish property without any compensation whatever was "the interest of the Reich's defense and the strengthening of Germanism." In the course of the first seven months of occupation, the Germans completely expropriated and deported from the territory of western Poland about one million Poles; on the land thus made vacant, they settled

850,000 Germans imported from eastern Europe. In the majority of instances, the Polish deportees were allowed two hours in which to pack, but as frequently as not they were allowed only twenty minutes, or even only ten minutes in which to put their homes and places of business in perfect order. They were permitted to take one suitcase only, this to contain the most essential articles. If the Germans were to execute their plan in full, they would have to clear out from western Polish lands over 93 per cent of the population, because the percentage of Germans (all immigrants) in the territories in question does not reach the level of 6.5 per cent, whereas the Poles number 87 per cent, and the Jews 6.4 per cent.

It is a matter of common knowledge that the Germans justify their crimes by the alleged necessity of securing for their "hungry" nation a more commodious living space. In reality, however, because of the steady decline of the population in Germany, the Germans not only lack people for colonizing purposes, but also for taking care of their own agrarian needs. As a matter of fact, the rural population in Germany declined by 10 per cent in the period between 1934 and 1940. The German authorities settled colonists from the Baltic countries and from Bessarabia, but otherwise their great colonization plan turned out to be a dismal failure; despite credits, tax abatements, and guarantees of preferential treatment, there was a dearth of candidates in the Reich for emigration to Poland. In fact, expropriations and deportations of Poles were effective only as expedients of biological extermination and destruction of the Polish element.

The methods applied by the Germans in the General Government were somewhat different. The General Government, a body whose legal and political character has never been clearly defined, was intended by the Germans to constitute a *Nebenland,* that is a land belonging to the Reich, a reservoir of slave labor, as it were, and a subservient colony situated on the confines of the Reich. Terrorism constituted the chief expedient of the German regime in the General Government as well as in the Polish lands incorporated in the Reich. The number of death sentences passed in the General Government by court-martial in the course of three and a half years reached the figure of 140,000. This figure, however, represented but a fraction of the bloody balance sheet of death, inasmuch as a far greater number of Polish citizens, without the formality of death sentences, were being murdered in concentration camps, gas chambers, or in connection with razzias and punitive forays.

Proceeding on the same theory as in the Polish lands incorporated in the Reich—that a nation deprived of its leading class would be easier to crush and to subjugate—the Germans started their exterminatory activity in the General Government by committing mass murders among the educated and leading classes. At first, deportations were omitted in the General Government, but approximately one million Poles expelled from western Poland were transported by the Germans to the General Government. Thus the population of that region, which possesses a very inferior soil and is already overpopulated, was artificially increased. At present the density of the population in the General Government, a section not self-sufficient in food and cut off from coal-mining and industrial centers, shows a ratio of 130 per square kilometer.

By applying their methods of ruthless exploitation, the Germans condemned the population to undernourishment and starvation. Goering's threat that he would rather let the conquered peoples die from starvation than permit the Germans to go hungry was put into actual effect in Poland. By means of an immense police pressure, the Germans annually squeezed out of Poland huge quantities of grain and potatoes, as well as cattle.

The brutal exploitation of the rural sections in the General Government brought the farming population of that section face to face with starvation. The technique of the methodical starving out of the Poles was based on a specific wage, price, and rationing policy. In keeping with the rigorously applied ordinance issued by Governor-General Frank on January 31, 1941, the maximum rates of wages paid to the Poles ran as follows:

White-collar workers
- Men, up to 515 złotys per month
- Women, up to 463 złotys per month

Manual labor
- Men, up to 1.20 złotys per hour
- Women, up to .70 złotys per hour

By way of comparison, the minimum wage of a German white-collar worker in the General Government began at 1,200 złotys per month, whereas the wage rate of German manual laborers began at the much more favorable rate of three złotys per hour.

With wages at starvation levels the Poles were able to secure, under the all-embracing system of food rationing, only ridiculously small quantities of food. For instance, in September, 1942, the Polish residents of Warsaw received the following food allotments per person for the entire month: 4.8 kilograms of black (rye) bread; 40 dekagrams of meat; 10 dekagrams of ersatz marmalade. That was all on which a working man or woman could subsist. This food allotment yielded 12,510 calories per month or 417 calories per diem, whereas a human being, depending upon the type of work he performs, requires from 2,000 to 4,000 calories per diem. In the United States, in the years 1930 to 1934, daily consumption was 3,310 calories per capita. Accordingly, whoever did not want to die of starvation was compelled to buy articles of primary necessity in what is known as the open market, at prices which in Warsaw, in September, 1942, stood at the following levels:

	Złotys per kilogram
Black (rye) bread	13
White (wheat) bread	22
Beef	42
Veal	55
Pork	70
Wheat flour	30
Rye	16.50
Cereals	20
Butter and lard	160
Potatoes	3.20
Onions	9
Peas and beans	23
Apples	24
Sugar	65
Milk	11–13 per liter
Eggs	4 per egg
Box of matches	1.20 per box
Ton of coal	1,800–2,000 per ton
Ton of peat	500 per ton

This system was devised to bring about the biological doom of the Polish nation. As a criterion of the distress and starvation prevalent in Poland, there is quoted below a fragment of a letter written in December, 1942, which passed through the German censorship and reached one of the neutral countries. The author of the letter is a university graduate. Here is what he wrote:

> Am working at present about 16 hours per day. Nevertheless, my earnings do not exceed the level of a 2 kilogram of lard per month, and I have a wife and child to support. The wages have not been increased since the beginning of the war and the prices of the most essential food products went up fifty—and even hundred fold. Because the prices of fuel are entirely beyond my reach the temperature in my dwelling goes down during the very cold season to 12 degrees below zero (centigrade).
>
> We eat but once a day and not every day at that. We live exclusively on potatoes without any fats and a few slices of black bread, our only beverage being water. We forgot all about the taste of coffee, tea, milk and dairy produce. For the last three years we did not once taste butter, sugar, bakery products (except bread obtainable on ration cards) or fruit, one kilogram of which (and of the worst quality at that) costs the equivalent of my earnings for three days.
>
> Nor did we see one piece of soap in the last three years, because it would require my earnings for ten days of work to purchase one kilogram of the cheapest kind of soap.
>
> Our clothing is in tatters and we wear practically no undergarments.

The physical extermination of the Poles, however, constituted only a part of the German program. Cultural extermination was an equally essential medium in the hands of the Germans. The Polish nation was to be degraded to the level of a reservoir of slave labor and, accordingly, Poland's cultural life must be paralyzed and destroyed at the very source. All over Polish territory under German occupation, all higher and secondary schools had been closed. Prior to the war, there were twenty-eight schools of university level in Poland. None of them is functioning at present. The five years of the occupation and the consequent interruption of scholastic instruction have deprived Poland of approximately thirty thousand university graduates. The majority of university professors either were killed or were confined in concentration camps.

Secondary (high) schools, technical schools excepted, have also been liquidated. The Polish public-school system was entirely abolished in the Polish lands incorporated in the Reich, whereas in the General Government some of the Polish public schools were left to function, but their program of instruction was changed so greatly that they could hardly be considered Polish schools any longer. As early as the first few months of the occupation, the

German authorities closed all Polish theaters, museums, libraries, bookstores, publishing houses, and sundry cultural institutions. Objects of art from museums and private collections were carried off to Germany, and all books which happened to be on the Nazi prohibited list were burned.

At the same time the Germans declared a ruthless war on the church and on religion, Catholic as well as Protestant. In the Polish lands incorporated in the Reich, the Catholic Church was subordinated, in 1942, to Himmler in his capacity of chief of the German police. Many clergymen and bishops were killed—by the Germans, or else were doomed to slow death in concentration camps. By September, 1942, in the camp at Oswięcim alone, fifteen hundred clergymen had died.

In the last five years no books have been printed in Poland except those published by the Germans. Books of the latter category are either German propaganda, or else trash of a salacious nature. It should be kept in mind that the Germans were conducting a planned campaign to demoralize the younger Polish generation. Although all other articles of sale in Poland at present were very expensive, brandy and spirits still were cheap. In Warsaw, and in other Polish cities as well, the German authorities were setting up gambling establishments intended for Poles only.

German atrocities committed against the Jews in Poland assumed well-nigh monstrous proportions. It looked at first as though Hitler was to set up in Poland a sort of gigantic ghetto, a reserved area for Jews from all the countries of Europe when, in 1940, Governor-General Frank issued an ordinance indicating such a policy. During the first two years of German occupation, the moral suffering of the Jews was worse than that endured by the Poles, but no bloody terrorism was being applied by the Germans to the Jews. In 1942, however, the situation underwent a radical change. The Germans had simply decided to wipe out the Jews completely. In February, 1942, the liquidation of the ghettos began. The accepted procedure was for the Gestapo to transport the Jewish population to special camps where mass executions, mostly by gas asphyxiation, were being carried out. The bestial murders of Jews reached a peak in the spring of 1943. According to trustworthy data, of 3,313,000 Jews in Poland the Germans had killed approximately 1,800,000 by

July 1, 1943. Of a half million Jews deported to Poland from other European countries a substantial number have been killed.

From the economic point of view the objective of the German policy in occupied Poland from the beginning was: (1) To exploit both Polish labor and resources in order to further the Reich's war efforts. (2) To deprive Poland of any and all economic independence by linking it in the closest possible manner with the Reich's economic system. (3) To exterminate the Polish nation economically by reducing the property holdings of the Poles to a minimum.

In Polish lands incorporated in the Reich, the Germans were attaining their objective by the eminently simple expedient of confiscating all Polish-owned property. So far as the General Government is concerned, where only larger industrial, commercial, and agricultural establishments had been confiscated, the German authorities put into operation other methods of extermination. To begin with, the Germans introduced an occupation currency, based on internal bonds of the Reich, which the Reichsbank transmitted, on the basis of fictitious clearing accounts, to the bank of issue in Poland. By this procedure the Germans were stripping Poland of capital and were forcing the Poles, against their will, to finance the Reich's war effort. With the occupation currency, the Germans also succeeded in buying up in Poland what had not already been plundered or confiscated.

All larger industrial and commercial establishments in the General Government fell prey to confiscation. Polish agriculture, which had been forced by the Germans into a vise-like control system, operated on the basis of quotas. The quota system took out of Poland not only a substantial portion of the annual crops but also, on occasion, seed grain and potatoes. The delivery of the quotas was based on brutally terroristic methods. In a number of instances the Germans had burned villages to the ground and murdered the entire male population. In 1942, the occupation authorities ordered a compulsory slaughter of 30 per cent of the livestock in Poland. The supply of meat thus obtained was shipped to the Reich.

In 1942 and 1943, the Germans began to apply the system of deportations in the General Government as well. When preparing a line of defense in central Poland they removed the entire Polish population of a substantial part of Lublin Province. The men were driven to compulsory labor, whereas the young girls and the children were carried off to the Reich.

By way of setting up a system of compulsory labor and of carrying off Polish workmen to the Reich, the Germans were attaining at one stroke two objectives—the extermination of the Polish element and the exploitation of Polish labor. In the first month of German occupation, an appeal was issued by the Germans for Poles to volunteer for work in Germany. When this appeal failed, the German authorities began to make razzias and all Poles caught in the net during such razzias were forthwith shipped to the Reich. By June, 1942, the number of people carried off in this manner had reached the figure of 1,500,000.

The conditions under which the Poles in Germany live and work are monstrous. They enjoy no legal protection whatever. They work from ten to twelve hours a day, receive the lowest possible wages, and have no right to vacations. In keeping with instructions emanating from the authorities, the German employers treat them with the utmost brutality. Every once in a while entire trains arrive in Poland bringing back the "labor veterans," the cripples and invalids who, no longer able to work, have been shipped back home.

The Germans have committed in Poland every base act that could possibly be contrived by the demented imagination of fanatics who have at their disposal the most advanced technical means for the perpetration of their crimes. After each wave of terrorism, the ruffianly hangmen examined the degree of their victims' power of resistance and endeavored to discover among the Poles a Quisling. And, as each attempt to seek collaboration failed, the methods of extermination became sharper as though from rage and revenge.

And yet, the resistance of the Polish nation not only did not diminish but, on the contrary, became increasingly hardened in the white heat of struggle with the invader. From the very beginning of the German occupation an underground Polish government had been active throughout Poland. This underground government remains in constant touch with the Polish Government in London. It is not opportune at the moment to write of certain forms of the active struggle going on with the invaders. It is, however, a matter of common knowledge that an underground organization for combating the German occupation applies such means

WOODEN CHAPEL

BY JAN SZCZEPKOWSKI

(Carved for Paris International Exhibition in 1925; acquired by French Government. The kilims were designed by Wanda Kossecka.)

as sabotage, counterterrorism, an underground press, underground schools, and underground tribunals.

Throughout the Polish lands occupied by the Germans, organized sabotage has been occurring for the last five years. The sabotage is directed against any and all war production and against vital lines of communication, particularly those railway lines on which falls the task of supplying the Russian front. In a single month in 1943, Polish saboteurs destroyed one hundred engines and blew up seventeen railway trains. Thousands of hostages lost their lives through reprisals for those acts of vengeance. Over five hundred of the more prominent Nazi functionaries have died as a result of death sentences passed by underground Polish tribunals. Among those executed was Wilhelm Krueger, the "Polish Heydrich." The balance sheet of the acts of sabotage will be published only after the war; to give publicity now to such information would cause an intensification of terroristic methods by the Germans.

An exceedingly effective weapon in the struggle against the Germans is the underground press. Even though the publishing and distributing, as well as the reading or the possession of an issue of an underground newspaper, is punishable by mandatory death sentence, over one hundred underground papers are being published in Poland. Thousands of young boys and girls are active in the distribution of these publications. Not a week passes but what several, or possibly a score of people pay with their lives for activities of this nature. Because of the closing of all Polish universities and secondary schools the Polish underground organization has set up an entire system of underground schooling. Active at present in Poland are two underground universities, and many high schools; what is more important is the fact that almost every Polish home is a secret school in which instructors, mostly women, teach Polish history to the children.

The activities of the Polish underground administration of justice are best illustrated by a notice published in one of the underground newspapers, *Biuletyn Informacyjny*, that in May, 1943, Polish underground tribunals passed and carried out fifty death sentences on Gestapo functionaries.

SOVIET-OCCUPIED POLAND*

After occupying Polish territories, the Soviet authorities began their activities by drawing up "black lists" in which were enumerated all enemies of the people, that is, not only landowners and members of the middle class, but also professors, clergymen, lawyers, leaders of political parties and social organizations. These people either were executed forthwith or were deported to Soviet Russia and there confined in concentration camps. The executions were carried out in two different ways. In certain instances, mock trials were held and death sentences passed because of "activities prejudicial to the interests of the U.S.S.R.," or else the G.P.U. (the secret police) staged manifestations of the "people's wrath."

The number of people arrested was so large that, in the first week of Soviet occupation, the prisons were filled beyond capacity. In the town of Łuck alone, the Soviet authorities were compelled as early as October, 1939, to requisition fourteen buildings for prisons. In the fall of 1939, between four hundred and five hundred people were arrested daily in Lwów. In addition to starving and brutalizing the prisoners systematically, the Soviet authorities applied scientific tortures, which consisted in breaking down the resistance of the prisoners by keeping them awake for days, or by exposing them for hours to the blinding glare of high-powered reflector lights, or by similar means of torture. At the same time the Soviet authorities began to take preliminary steps in the nationalization of private property. Nor did they lose time in setting into motion a systematic destruction of religion.

By the end of October, 1939, the authorities in Moscow decided that after five weeks of terrorism the occupied Polish lands were ripe for unification. Desirous of creating a semblance of legality, the Soviet authorities announced that elections to the "People's Assembly of Western Ukraine" would be held throughout the southern Polish lands. These so-called elections were held on October 22, in accordance with the provisions of the Soviet electoral system. Only committees of peasants and workmen were authorized to draw up the lists of candidates.

* General Editor's note: The following account represents a Polish interpretation drawn chiefly from the Polish underground sources of information.

For three days before the elections, that is on October 19, 20, and 21, the Soviet authorities throughout eastern Poland carried out mass arrests and executions of any and all suspected elements whereas, at the same time, preëlection meetings were being held even in the smallest localities. At these meetings Soviet agents presented the issue briefly and clearly. Refugees who were present on these occasions unanimously report that statements, like the following, were made to them:

"On Sunday there shall be held an election. Directly after the election the Soviet authorities will begin to issue passports. The passports shall be issued on the strength of the voting lists. No one shall be able to secure employment or an allotment of food without a passport. I know you all are going to vote because anyone evading this duty will thereby show himself to be a counter-revolutionary. As you know, Soviet authorities deal drastically with counter-revolutionaries."

On October 22, the Soviet authorities mobilized in each and every town a large number of motor trucks, whereas in the villages horse-drawn carts were held ready. G.P.U. agents, soldiers, and the "people's militia" went from house to house driving out the people and even dragging those abed with serious illness to the conveyances which had been sent to fetch them to the polling place. In these circumstances there could hardly be any doubt as to the results of the "elections," the more so because in the polling places themselves any attempt to keep the act of voting secret was at once qualified as a counter-revolutionary activity, the penalty for which was death.

After the elections, which gave the Soviets a 91 per cent plurality, the authorities at Moscow instructed the delegates to apply to the U.S.S.R. for legal incorporation into the Soviet Union, which petition was favorably acted upon by the Supreme Council of the U.S.S.R. Such was the way the annexation of southeastern Poland, now called the western Ukraine, had been staged. A similar affair was staged by Russia in the northern part of Soviet-occupied Poland in July, 1940, at the time when the Baltic countries were annexed.

The next act after the elections was the social and economic unification of Poland with Soviet Russia. The Soviets started the introduction of the new system by nationalizing all the land. All land became state property as early as the end of November, and on December 20, 1939, in southeastern Poland, industrial and commercial establishments, as well as houses, became nationalized. In the northern part of Soviet-occupied Poland the same operation was performed in the summer of 1940. At that time Polish currency was declared null and void.

The immediate result of this speedily executed socialization was complete chaos in both agriculture and commerce, from which, in turn, sprang hunger. The peasants had but small quantities of produce allotted for their own needs, but this they sold through barter for industrial products of which there were very limited quantities on the market. As early as December, 1940, the urban population in Soviet-occupied Poland suffered from hunger; the first victims, as a matter of course, were the remnants of the intelligentsia.

Late in November, 1939, the Soviet authorities annulled Polish social legislation and the law on the forty-six-hour work week, and introduced, in lieu thereof, a ten-hour work day. A detailed decree introduced penalties for reporting late for work and for leaving the place of employment without permission. Tardiness of from five to twenty minutes in reporting for work was punishable by two years of hard labor, whereas to leave the place of employment without permission meant a sentence of from one to ten years of imprisonment. The workmen had no opportunity to utilize their leisure time as they saw fit. At least four times a week propaganda meetings were held, with attendance obligatory and subject to close scrutiny by political commissars. The erstwhile crew and plant councils were dissolved, and in their place new crew councils were organized. The function of the new councils was to supervise the workmen at their work and to compel them to achieve "Stakhanov" production quotas. All labor organizations were disbanded, and even workmen's benevolent associations were liquidated. The leaders of labor unions, even those who were not politically active, together with the intelligentsia, were declared to be enemies of the revolution.

The Polish school system was made the object of particular solicitude in the direction of unification. The schools were not closed, but all textbooks were entirely suppressed in order to comply with the requirements of communist and atheist propaganda. Extremely high taxes were imposed on churches of all denominations. In the event of tax defaults, the churches were closed and used for clubs, dance halls, and antireligious museums. Up to the end of 1940, the G.P.U. deported four thousand clergymen of various denominations from Poland to Russia.

The most effective method of extermination practiced in German-occupied Poland was mass deportations of the population. The exact number of Polish citizens deported by the Russians cannot possibly be ascertained at the moment, the several estimates varying between 1,500,000 and 2,500,000. That the figure of 1,500,000 is really the minimum is substantiated by the following facts: (1) Upon the conclusion of the Polish-Soviet Pact of July 30, 1941, the Soviet authorities released 348,000 Poles from forced labor camps, admitting, at the same time, that an additional number of 45,000 remained in the several camps. Inasmuch as it was an established fact that to September, 1941, at least 25 per cent of Polish prisoners had died in Soviet prison camps, one may conclude that a minimum figure of 520,000 had been deported from Poland as prisoners. (2) In 1940, the Soviet authorities drafted in the occupied Polish lands for service in the Red army four classes of recruits and in that way deported at least 150,000 additional Polish citizens. (3) In February, March, June, and November, 1940, the Soviet authorities carried out mass deportations of Poles to the interior of Russia. According to highly conservative calculations, the number of people deported in the four months amounted to at least 1,000,000.

For a long time nothing was heard about the approximately half million persons who were in the Soviet forced labor camps. Not only the conditions which prevailed in these camps, but also the very fact of the existence of the camps have been a closely guarded secret of the Soviet Government. Only after the Polish citizens were released, pursuant to the conclusion of the Polish-Soviet pact in July, 1941, did the appalling truth become known. The Soviet concentration camps constituted a huge system of enforced labor. A number of public works in the U.S.S.R., such as the construction of roads and canals, the operation of mines, and the care of forests were being carried out exclusively by prisoners from forced labor camps. The prisoners worked fourteen to twenty hours a day. The food, served once daily, consisted almost always of cabbage soup, or gruel with boiled fish of the worst quality, for the most part decayed and fetid. Twice daily hot water was issued, at times with bread and with a substitute for coffee. The bread ration was not always the same, the quantity depending on the volume of work accomplished on the given day.

The obligatory quota of work represented one kilogram of bread. The physically strongest prisoners never earn more than 450 to 600 grams. The prisoners were being used for the hardest type of labor, under the most trying of climatic conditions.

Scurvy and typhoid fever rage continually in the Soviet isolation camps, and it is doubtful whether the Polish prisoners would have been able to endure the conditions had not at least a part of them been liberated by the pact of July 30, 1941. The weaker among the prisoners were dying off quickly; they just "passed out." The smaller the quotas of work performed, the less food was allowed, which again reduced the output of work. Within a few months, hardly 30 per cent of the prisoners were able to deliver the standard quotas of work.

So far as mass deportations of the Polish population to the interior of Russia for purposes of settlement are concerned, the Soviet authorities applied the same procedure as the Germans. Specially commandeered detachments of N.K.V.D. (G.P.U.) troops and of N.K.V.D. disciplinary battalions surrounded the village or small towns, invaded the homes, and permitted the people only from two to three hours in which to dress and pack for deportation. In the majority of instances, no personal property or food were permitted to be taken along. The property left behind constituted the loot of the escorting troops. Frequently, with a temperature of 30° below zero (Centigrade), entire families were loaded on trucks or carts and were conveyed to railway freight cars, held ready at railroad sidings. Transportation by rail, on the average, lasted two weeks. The cold did its own share of damage and the rate of mortality was very high. No one was permitted to leave the railway cars. No physicians were called in to attend the ill, not even in cases of contagious diseases. Dead bodies were thrown out of the cars at wayside stations and the families were brutally driven away from the remains. The behavior of the escorting guards was brutal and mean.

Once in Russia proper the Polish deportees were split into three large groups. About 200,000 were located in northern Russia along the course of the Northern Dvina and put to work in the forests of that region. The earnings ran from four to eight rubles per diem, whereas the price of a liter of milk was ten rubles, and the price of a pail of potatoes thirty rubles. Within a short time the deportees were decimated by scurvy, malaria, and tuberculosis. Other deportees numbering between 350,000 and 400,000 were settled by the Soviet authorities on the steppes of Kazakhstan. Those deported to Kazakhstan were not compelled to work, but no one took any care of them. Their only means of livelihood was to collect and process *kiziak*—camel and goat manure—which, after being treated with water and straw, constituted the only building material and fuel in those parts. It is to be doubted whether more than 30 per cent of the deportees to Kazakhstan will ever return home. The third section, where approximately 300,000 Polish deportees were settled, was the Siberian tundra. Their lot also was most difficult.

As soon as the Polish-Soviet Pact of July 30, 1941, was concluded and in connection therewith an amnesty declared, the Polish consular offices were overrun by tens of thousands of people, in tatters, often shirtless and barefoot, covered with ulcers and scars caused by scurvy, some emaciated to skeletons, others again bloated from hunger. All of those unfortunates were Polish deportees released either from the forced labor camps or from "settlement" areas.

Of the huge number of at least 1,500,000 deported Polish citizens, the Soviet Government permitted (besides 75,000 soldiers), less than 40,000 people to go abroad.[1] Out of that number, 1,700 died from illness and exhaustion within the first two months after crossing the Russian border.

THE GOVERNMENT AND ARMY IN EXILE

In the great cataclysm of the Second World War, the Poles succeeded in maintaining the constitutional continuity of their government. The Polish Government in Exile originated after the September catastrophe by means of a legal transmission of the supreme authority. Since then this supreme authority, which rests on the fundamental laws of Poland, has been operating without interruption. All the expenditures incidental to its activities are

[1] To 1943.

being defrayed by the Polish Government from credits which have the character of normal international loans. The financing of the Polish army which fights in Allied ranks and each bomb dropped by Polish airmen on Axis countries, constitutes a debit for the Polish treasury.

On September 30, 1939, the then President of the Polish Republic, Ignacy Mościcki, relinquished, in accordance with Article 24 of the Polish Constitution, the presidential power to the present President, Władysław Raczkiewicz. The new president accepted the resignation of the cabinet headed by Sławoj-Składkowski and appointed a new cabinet composed of representatives of all the chief Polish political parties, with General Władysław Sikorski as prime minister. The Government settled in Paris. Prior thereto, President Raczkiewicz had dissolved the former Polish Parliament and inasmuch as new elections were not feasible under the existing circumstances, he appointed a National Council, composed of prominent Poles living in exile, to constitute a consulting body for the Government.

The foundations on which the newly formed Polish Government based its activities were: (1) An undaunted struggle of the entire Polish nation against the invader; (2) A Polish army, organized in France under the command of General Sikorski; (3) An alliance and military agreement with France; (4) An agreement with Great Britain, which, from a unilateral guarantee given to Poland by Great Britain in May, 1939, changed in August of that year into a bilateral treaty of mutual assistance. Immediately after the close of the September campaign, Polish soldiers, in groups or alone, began to make their way to France. Reinforced by volunteers from among Poles living in France and Belgium, they became the foundation of a new Polish army which, within seven months, numbered approximately 100,000 men and consisted of four and one-half infantry divisions, one armored brigade, and one mountain brigade. The latter made for itself a glorious name in the Narvik campaign in May and June of 1940.

The German attack on France in May, 1940, found at the front the first and second Polish divisions, as well as the motorized brigade. The Polish troops continued to wage a heroic fight even after the armistice between France and Germany had been concluded. In this fight the first division was almost completely wiped out, whereas the best part of the second division succeeded in saving itself by retreating to the Swiss frontier in conformance with General Sikorski's order. The Polish armored brigade took part in the struggle to the very end, suffering heavy losses. All detachments of Polish troops in France received the highest recognition from the French High Command. After the fall of France, the Polish Government moved to England and succeeded in evacuating a substantial part of the Polish army to British soil. On August 5, 1940, Prime Minister Sikorski signed a military agreement with Great Britain.

During the Battle of Britain in September, 1940, Polish airmen in England shot down 210 German planes. The English historian, George Saunders, wrote about them as follows: "Conspicuous . . . are the Poles. Their valor is tremendous; their skill bordering on the inhuman. They have done great service. They are still doing it and they will go on doing it until victory, triumphant and complete, lights up their wings. We are beginning to understand the Poles . . ."

The Polish land forces in England in 1941 grew to two motorized divisions and a brigade of parachutists. The brigade of Polish sharpshooters (riflemen), organized in Syria in 1940, joined the British Eighth Army in August, 1941, and constituted a part of the Tobruk garrison while that city was being besieged, and subsequently took a conspicuous part in the Allied offensive in Africa.

After the conclusion of the Polish-Russian agreement in July, 1941, a Polish army was formed on Russian territory from Polish war prisoners released by the Soviets. That army was subsequently shifted to the Near East and there equipped with American and British arms.

In the summer of 1944 it was reported that Polish Armed Forces stood in sixth place as to numerical strength among the armies of all the United Nations. The Underground Home Army consisted of the Operational Units estimated at 250,000 men and the Regular Army, of undisclosed, but greater strength. Polish forces fighting abroad consisted of the Polish Corps in Scotland of some 30,000 (of which an armored division recently fought in France), the Polish Army in the East including about 75,000 (of which the Second

Corps is fighting on the Italian front), the Polish Air Force of 12,000, and the Polish Navy of 3,000. Polish units organized under the sponsorship of the Soviet Union were estimated at 80,000.

Since 1939, Polish pilots have shot down more than 1,000 German planes. In Tunisia, Polish airmen brought down 79 enemy planes as compared with 527 planes downed by the American air forces. The Polish navy has been fighting for five years alongside the British navy. Polish sailors have taken part in many important naval actions, including the evacuation of Dunkirk, the spirited attack on the "Bismarck," the landing at Dieppe, and the operations off the North African coast. They have played their full part in the Battle of the Atlantic, and have carried on an unceasing vigil with the fleets of the United Nations in the Atlantic and the Mediterranean. A Polish corps distinguished itself in May and June, 1944, in the battles which led to the fall of Rome. Other Polish forces took part in the campaign in France.

One of the chief political moves of the Polish Government in London was in taking the initiative for a Polish-Czechoslovak federation. As early as October, 1940, the Polish and Czechoslovak governments issued a joint declaration and on January 23, 1942, they signed an agreement concerning a federation and close co-operation of both countries after the war. In the spring of 1941, Prime Minister Sikorski came to the United States on an official visit, during which he held a number of important conferences, some of them with a view of securing for Poland a share in lend-lease loans.

At the time the first conference of the Allied Nations was held in London, in 1941, Prime Minister Sikorski made a statement in which, referring to "the rights of man and nation" as formulated by President Roosevelt, he declared as follows: "These ideas enrich and strengthen on the inside the camp of embattled democracies, a camp which in contrast to the totalitarian camp can boast of worthy examples of international order based on voluntary co-operation. The British Commonwealth of Nations, the United States of America are those shining examples. The Polish Republic, which five centuries ago brought about a union of Poland with Lithuania and Ruthenia, took up since November, 1939, the idea of striving for a union of nations in central-eastern Europe."

When in June, 1941, German troops attacked Soviet Russia, the Polish Government overlooking the grievous wrongs suffered at the hands of Russia made a peace offering by taking the initiative in negotiations. Russia, finding itself at the moment in an extremely difficult military situation, accepted the proffered hand, and on July 30, 1941, made a pact with Poland by the terms of which it agreed to declare null and void those terms of its agreements with Germany which had been the foundation of the partition of Poland in 1939. A short time later, Soviet Russia, agreeing to the principles embodied in the Atlantic Charter, joined the ranks of the United Nations. It seemed at the time as though the affairs between Poland and Russia had been definitely straightened out, and a Polish army began to be formed in Russia as a consequence of the Polish-Russian military convention.

A Polish-Russian declaration, known as the "Sikorski-Stalin Declaration," was signed in Moscow on December 4, 1941. During Prime Minister Sikorski's visit to Moscow in December, 1941, Stalin agreed to the proposal made by Poland that the Polish army in the U.S.S.R. should number 96,000 men and, furthermore, that 25,000 Polish troops should proceed from Russia to the Near East. At the same time, the Soviet Government agreed to the suggestion that the Polish Embassy in Moscow should organize a welfare action for the million or more Polish citizens deported by the Soviet Government to Russia.

In the meantime, however, the military situation underwent a definite change. First, the Russian resistance on the eastern front stiffened considerably and soon thereafter the German armies started to retreat. Almost on the morrow of Sikorski's departure from Moscow, the Soviet authorities, contrary to the agreement, stopped recruiting for the Polish army and restricted the size of the Polish army by reducing the allotment of food. At the same time the Soviet Government notified the Polish Embassy that it would not recognize as Polish citizens the Jews, Ukrainians, and Ruthenians deported by the Soviet authorities from Polish territories; Russia justified its attitude by an assertion that the people in question came from areas where the population had voluntarily joined the U.S.S.R. through the medium of elections. Because of an ever-increasing chicanery by Soviet authorities, the situation of Poles in

Russia grew steadily worse. In the summer of 1942, the Soviet authorities categorically demanded that the Polish army should leave Russian territory and, at the same time, arrested all Polish Embassy delegates who carried on welfare activities among the Poles in the U.S.S.R., thus vitiating any and all possibility of succoring Polish citizens.

Finally on January 16, 1943, the Soviet Government addressed a note—which has not been made public—to the Polish Government, in which it explicitly stated that Russia not only claimed the eastern half of the Polish State but that it also looked upon this territory as a component part of the U.S.S.R. The official Russian news agency *Tass* launched in the British and American press a series of articles and speeches branding Poland's defense of her just rights and of her territory as "Polish imperialism."

Parallel with these moves went a lively activity of the Third International (Comintern), all through the Polish lands, as reported by the Polish underground. Soviet agents in German-occupied Poland had huge sums of money at their disposal. In their underground publications and propaganda leaflets they endeavored first and foremost to make capital out of the appalling starvation and distress among the Polish population in German-occupied Poland, by asserting that the fault of the slow progress of the war fell upon the imperialistic and capitalistic countries, namely England and America. Moscow's agents dispatched by air tried to undermine the confidence of the Polish population in the Polish patriotic organizations struggling against the Germans. Nor did the Soviet agents operating in Poland make any secret of the endeavor by Soviet Russia to provoke a world-wide revolution once the present war came to an end.

On April 25, 1943, the Soviet Government broke off diplomatic relations with Poland, a step for which it had been preparing consistently for a long time. As the immediate pretext of this step, the Soviet Government used the incident of the missing Polish officers. On April 13, 1943, the Berlin radio reported that German authorities had found mass graves of more than ten thousand Polish officers. On the very same day, the Polish Government in London, eager to ascertain the truth of the matter and to afford Moscow an opportunity to disprove the accusation at the same time, addressed itself to the International Red Cross at Geneva with a request to investigate the finding of the mass graves of the Polish officers.

To this step Russia reacted on April 25 by breaking off diplomatic relations with Poland. Soon after, in reply to an intervention by England and America, Russia hinted its readiness to reëstablish relations with Poland on condition of changes in the membership of the Polish Government in London. At the same time in Moscow, the Soviet Government permitted the setting up of the Committee of Polish Patriots composed chiefly of Polish Communists. To be sure, the Committee in question stood at first by the frontier line set up in the Ribbentrop-Molotov pact, later by the so-called Curzon Line.

In the summer of 1943, the Polish Government suffered a heavy and irretrievable loss. On July fourth, the Prime Minister of the Polish Government and Commander in Chief of the Polish army, General Władysław Sikorski, who was returning to London from a tour of inspection of the Polish armed forces in the Near East, perished in an airplane accident at Gibraltar. Sikorski was succeeded in the premiership by the peasant leader, Stanisław Mikołajczyk, and General Casimir Sosnkowski became Commander in Chief of the Polish armed forces.

THE FUTURE

The problem of Poland's future is the logical result of the objectives which guided the Polish nation when, in 1939, it decided with unequal forces to resist German aggression. At this point there arises, perforce, the question: Was this war really necessary? Had there really been no opportunity to spare the Polish nation the untold measure of suffering, and mankind the utmost misery of war?

There was such an opportunity, without a doubt. In the period preceding the present war the Polish nation might have spared itself the catastrophe of war by one act of decision. A simple "yes," first to the tempting proposals and later to the threats of Germany would have sufficed. Had Poland, even as late as the fateful night of August 31, 1939, capitulated to Hitler's demands, there certainly would not have been a Polish-German war, and the history of the last five years would have taken a totally different course.

There is no anticipating the direction in which Hitler would have turned after having "peacefully coördinated Poland." Would he have turned eastward or westward? One point, however, definitely may be accepted as a fact. Had the Germans, after the losses suffered in Poland and the waste of eight months of time resulting from the campaign in Poland, been within a hair's breadth from winning in the west in 1940, and from smashing Russia in 1941, it does not require too much imagination to see what Hitler's "time table" would have looked like had it not been for the forced delay in Poland. The situation in which the democratic countries had to undertake the decisive struggle against the totalitarian countries would have been doubtful to say the least. The tempo and the force of the lightning-like strokes of the German military machine would have been speeded up by fully eight months. Without speculating too greatly within the bounds of calculated probabilities, one may quite safely aver that Poland's sacrificial resistance in 1939 decisively influenced the outcome of the present struggle.

But even while the war was raging, the Poles had the possibility of choosing the road of political opportunism and, after the pattern of other nations of seeking safety from both sides through the expedient of a Quisling. The theorists of Naziism had openly formulated the program of destroying the Polish nation. However, the Germans, on several occasions while already occupying Poland, made overtures to the Poles, for tactical reasons, concerning a compromise, promising in return various concessions. As early as October, 1939, the Germans approached Professor St. Estreicher at Cracow, suggesting a compromise and promising the establishment of an independent Polish state out of the General Government. The second time, in July, 1941, they made a similar proposal to Professor C. Bartel at Lwów. They repeated the selfsame proposal once more in December, 1941, and in January, 1942, and, at the same time, demanded the formation of anti-Bolshevist legions in Poland, promising in return their agreement to an extension of Poland's boundaries in the easterly direction. Although the rejection of these successive proposals brought ever-increasing terrorism and death to thousands of people, the Polish nation scorned all German proposals of compromise.

The question therefore arises as to what objective Poland had in view when, in September, 1939, it decided in favor of an unequal war, offering no chance of victory whatever and subsequently rejecting any and all proposals of compromise, in full realization of the fact that such irreconcilable attitude would only intensify the terrorism and the persecutions. There are people who have tried to prove that the Poles simply failed to realize the tremendous disproportion of power—that had they known they were to face an enemy twenty times stronger, without any doubt they would have thought better of their decision. Still others think that the resistance of the Poles had been and still is an act of desperate folly, that they plunged into the war because of a romantic impulse or, to express it in political terms, because of a lack of mental equilibrium.

Such opinions are wrong. Those who hold these opinions maintain that, in the game of politics, only what pays in the materialistic sense of the term has any value. Accordingly, the war certainly did not constitute for Poland a paying proposition nor did the Poles resist Germany on the basis of a materialistic calculation of probable profits and losses.

The source from which the Polish-German war sprang was neither a miscalculation of the ratio of power nor an impulse of desperate folly. The Polish nation entered the war fully aware of the disastrous consequences, and it drew the strength for the decision to enter the war solely and exclusively from its faith in the future. In September, 1939, entering into a war to the death with its enemy, the Polish nation deeply believed that beneath the veneer of political opportunism and inertia there still was a conscience left in the world at large, which conscience it was necessary to awaken by a determined struggle and by sacrifice.

Furthermore, Poland believed that the present war would decide the liberty and equality of nations, collective security, and an equal chance to prosperity for all peoples. Poland also believed that the struggle was against overt as well as covert methods of imposition and exploitation of individuals by individuals and of one nation by another. It had learned from dire experience that the world, for all time to come, would repudiate the basic principle of the pernicious German philosophy which distinguished between the rights allowed master nations and those of slave nations which were small and indigent.

Poland believed that the foundations of the future peace would be based on principles and rights equal and uniform for all nations, that the new peace would become an organized international coöperation and exchange on the largest scale possible of all achievements of human minds and of material gains. And Poland also believed that the crimes committed by the totalitarian states would meet with an exemplary punishment and that world peace would be safeguarded not only by a system of collective security, but also by a system of planned control over the aggressor nations as well as their reëducation. The great English statesman, Sir Edward Grey, said once after the First World War: "The postwar world must either learn or perish." The world did not learn, but men of good will did not lose faith.

Having been first among all the nations of the world to rise against totalitarianism and having for more than five years fought against it in furious battle at the price of appalling sacrifices, Poland gave and still gives, day in and day out, proof positive of her deep faith that the tremendous sacrifice of this war will not have been made in vain, and that the world at large will learn a lesson.

Even today many Americans do not realize that one of the decisive factors which sustains the vigor of Polish resistance is the Polish nation's faith in America's idealism. In September, 1939, when talking to an old Polish peasant the writer heard him say: "We will not be able to defend ourselves against both Germany and Russia. Bad times are coming over Poland. This will be a long war, but in the end American soldiers will come along and Wilson's sons will bring justice into the world." That was not an attempt at prophesying, but a very primitively expressed faith in the world's conscience as personified in the American ideals of justice. The Poles, both at home and abroad, are fighting for the freedom of their mother country and their conception of freedom is the same as that of Jefferson and Wilson, of Roosevelt and Churchill, the drafters of the "Atlantic Charter."

In the history of Poland the idea of federation on the basis of the principle of "equals with equals" has played a greater role than in that of other countries. Poland made a union with Lithuania for reasons of "mutual fraternal affection and of perennial defense of both countries." Poland was one of the first countries—two hun-

STANISŁAW MIKOŁAJCZYK

PRIME MINISTER, 1943–1944

dred years before England—to guarantee to the individual the inviolability of his liberty, assuring, at the same time, full freedom to all religious beliefs. The same Poles who have been accused of anti-Semitism were the only nation at the time of the most atrocious massacres and persecutions of Jews all over Europe which extended hospitality to them and thus probably saved Jewry from complete extermination. Such was Poland's way of interpreting liberty, whereas other European nations discharged their surplus energy on conquests of neighboring peoples or on colonial expeditions.

The historical destiny which plunged Poland and the entire world into the war lies not in mechanical imperatives nor in the impossibility of saving one's life by means of compromise with the enemy, but in a love of true liberty, untrammeled by any "spheres of influence." And this desire for liberty is why the Second World War should not and cannot end in a peace which would split the world's map into a chessboard dictated by consideration imposed through force of influence.

When reading some of the comments made by statesmen and scholars on the subject of the postwar world, one cannot prevent a sense of apprehension. They oppose President Roosevelt's inspiring ideas when suggesting for instance that the world be divided into several large areas (*Grossräume*), or that the postwar organization of the world be handled by the Great Powers combined into a permanent group. And one of the Great Powers registers its claims to a large "sphere of influence" of its own in Europe, justifying its demands by consideration of strategical nature, while, at the same time, even a purely defensive nationalism by the smaller and the small nations is severely condemned.

Such differentiation of nations into numerically large and numerically small nations is of doubtful value. One hundred years ago, France occupied second place in Europe after Russia; at present it is fifth. The biological strength of Germany has been declining so abruptly for the last twenty years that, according to calculations made by Germans, Germany will have, around the year 2000, a population of 68,000,000 people, whereas the Poles will have 58,000,000. What is more, the demographers presage the occurrence, within the next thirty years, of a real revolution in the numerical strength of the European nations.

As may be seen from the above statement, it is not possible, when planning for a long period of time, to speak of large and of small nations; nor is it logical to believe that Hitler based his entire doctrine on such brittle differentiations. And who knows but what the virus of Hitler's large space notions has penetrated the Allied camp because of the differentiation, as a matter of principle, betwen large and small nations.

The Polish nation went to war because it refused to be subservient to German power politics. And when the war is over, the Polish nation will not agree to live under any tutelage of a neighboring Great Power, be it western or eastern. The objectives which dictated the deliberate sacrifice by the present generation of Poles had, at the same time, staked out the goal which the nation expects to attain by fighting this war.

Epilogue

BY ROBERT J. KERNER

THE SUMMER OF 1944 OPENED in Europe with the end of the Second World War in sight. The great armies of the United Nations began bearing down on Nazi Germany from three sides. Inevitable defeat and catastrophe faced the German people. The dawn of the liberation of the subjugated peoples of Europe had at last broken.

In an otherwise triumphant course of events, the unsettled Polish-Soviet rift became ominous. Great Britain and the United States had sought for over a year, since the break in April, 1943, to secure a resumption of diplomatic relations between the Polish and Soviet governments as a preliminary to at least a provisional arrangement for the administration of parts of Poland about to be liberated by advancing Soviet armies. Rightly or wrongly, they hoped to postpone decisions on final frontiers between the two countries until after hostilities had ceased. Rightly or wrongly, the Soviet Union took a stand for the speediest settlement possible of the frontier during the war along the so-called Curzon Line.

On the Russian side, it should be remembered that Marshal Stalin announced publicly that he unquestionably desired to see a strong, independent, but friendly Poland, preferably in alliance with the Soviet Union. Such an arrangement was foreseen in the protocol attached to the Soviet-Czechoslovak Pact of December 12, 1943.

On the Polish side, there appeared to be little or no confidence in the public statements of Marshal Stalin or in the hints which emanated from time to time from Soviet Russia as to modifications of its boundary claims, particularly with reference to the inclusion of Lwów in Poland.

In June, 1944, Prime Minister Stanisław Mikołajczyk conferred with President Roosevelt, at the latter's invitation, as Soviet armies stood poised for the summer offensive and the armies of the United States and Britain had embarked upon the liberation of France. Authentic reports of what actually happened are lacking. It became evident, however, that a new atmosphere for the resumption of relations was being created. Premier Mikołajczyk next conferred with Premier Stalin in Moscow early in August. At the same time, President Władysław Raczkiewicz appointed Tomasz Arciszewski, the socialist leader, President-Designate in the place of General Casimir Sosnkowski, who was then also Commander in Chief of the Polish Armed Forces and to whom objections had been raised from the Russian side.

The Polish Committee of National Liberation in the meanwhile had been established at Lublin in Russian-occupied territory. On February 12th the Union of Polish Patriots in the Soviet Union had created a national council which, in turn, established the Polish Committee of National Liberation with its seat at Lublin. On July 26th the Soviet Union made an agreement in Moscow with the Polish Committee at Lublin concerning the relations between the Soviet Commander in Chief and the Polish administration after the entry of Soviet troops into Polish territory.

During his first visit to Moscow in August, Premier Mikołajczyk held conversations with the Polish Committee of National Liberation as a result of which the Polish Government in London offered to form a five-party coalition cabinet in which the Peasant, Social Democratic, National Democratic, Christian Labor, and Polish Workers parties were to be equally represented. On its side the Polish Committee let it be known that it stood for the substitution of the Constitution of 1921 for that of 1935 and that it accepted the so-called Curzon Line as Poland's eastern frontier. Later it announced that it favored also the cession of East Prussia, Pomorze, and Silesia from Germany to Poland.

In the meanwhile the situation of the Polish uprising in Warsaw, which had begun early in August and which was led by Lieutenant General Tadeusz Komorowski (General Bor), had become critical when Soviet armies before Warsaw were checked by reinforced German forces. At the same time the Soviet High Command decided, for obvious strategic reasons, to drive the Germans out of the Baltic region and the Balkans. It was at this juncture of affairs (September 30th) that the Polish Government in London announced the appointment of General Komorowski in Warsaw

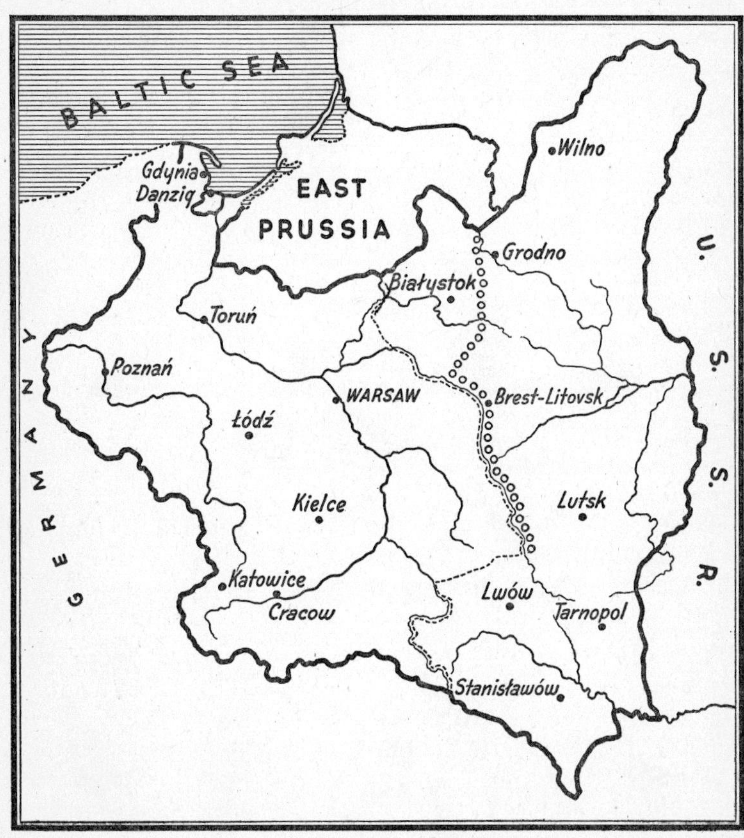

FRONTIERS OF POLAND

Solid line: frontiers, August 31, 1939. Broken line, German-Soviet Demarcation line, September 28, 1939. Line of circles, Curzon Line.

as Commander in Chief of Polish Armed Forces in place of General Sosnkowski. This conciliatory step was opposed by the Polish Committee of National Liberation in Lublin.

Relief in sufficient measure did not come to General Komorowski, who, obliged to surrender to the Germans on October 2d, indicated that "all supplies of food and ammunition" had been exhausted "on the sixty-third day of fighting in the face of overwhelming superiority." Thus ended one of the great tragedies of this war.

Just before these developments came to a head, Prime Minister Winston Churchill addressed the House of Commons on September 28th as follows:

> Territorial changes there will have to be. Russia has the right to our support in this matter because it is Russian Armies that can alone deliver Poland from the German talons and because, as I said before, after all the Russian people have suffered at the hands of Germany, they are entitled to safe frontiers and to have friendly neighbors on their western flank.
>
> All the more do I trust that the Soviet Government will make it possible for us to act unitedly with them in this solution of the Polish problem and that we shall not witness the unhappy spectacle of rival governments in Poland, one recognized by the Soviet Union and the other firmly adhered to by the Western Powers.
>
> I have good hope of Mr. Mikołajczyk, a worthy successor of General Sikorski and a man of real desire for friendly understanding with Russia and settlement with Russia. I hope that he and his colleagues may shortly resume those important conversations at Moscow which were interrupted some months ago.

British policy, as a result of this statement, limited the problem of Russo-Polish relations to the creation of a coalition government to be arranged between the Polish Government in London and the Polish National Committee of Liberation at Lublin and to the agreement of the Polish Government in London to an eastern frontier west of the boundary of 1939. On October 9th Prime Minister Churchill and Foreign Secretary Eden arrived in Moscow to be followed three days later by Premier Mikołajczyk, Polish Foreign Minister Tadeusz Romer, and Dr. Stanisław Grabski, Speaker of the Polish Assembly in London. Representatives of the Polish Committee of National Liberation, headed by Chairman Edward B. Osubka-Morawski and composed of President Bolesław Berut and Colonel General Michał Rola-Żymierski, were also called to Moscow. Serious discussions followed. Reports indicated that the Russians and the Lublin Committee stood firmly for the so-called Curzon Line, including the cession to the Soviet Union of Wilno and Lwów and that they demanded greater participation of the Lublin Committee in the proposed coalition government.

The discussions were suspended on October 19th, after Premier Mikołajczyk left for London to confer with his colleagues. Other discussions between the British and the Russians fared better because it was believed that some sort of agreement about the Balkans was reached. Pessimism reigned in the headquarters of the Polish Government in London, which apparently refused to accept the Russians demands and was reported to be awaiting the outcome of the national election in the United States to be held on November 7th. Some Poles are said to have had hope for a different policy, if the Republican party won the election.

If this hope were entertained, the election turned out otherwise. The idea then gained ground in the London Polish Government that the demands of the Russians could be acceptable only if the pact, which would embody a Soviet-Polish agreement, were guaranteed by the Big Three as to specific promises of Polish independence and of the territories to be obtained from Germany on the northern and western borders.

On November 20th Premier Mikołajczyk appealed to the United States for intervention in Poland's difficulties with the Soviet Union. However, the fact that the Polish Government in London would be obliged to accept the main terms laid down by the Soviet Union became evident, because two of the Big Three appeared to be in agreement upon them. Unable to obtain the consent of his Government to a policy which would result in agreement with the Soviet Union along the lines indicated above, Premier Mikołajczyk resigned on November 24th. On the next day the Department of State issued the following statement: "The specific question of the guarantee of Polish frontiers by this Government was not and could not have been an issue since this Government's traditional policy of not guaranteeing specific frontiers in Europe is well known." In the meanwhile, President Raczkiewicz asked Jan Kwapiński, a socialist, and Deputy Premier, to form a new cabinet. Kwapiński was unable to do this. However, on November 30th, Tomasz Arciszewski, the President-Designate and socialist leader, succeeded in forming a cabinet, in which, however, the largest political party—the Peasant party—which was led by Mikołajczyk, was not represented, although it declared it would "support sincerely" the Polish Government in London as the legal government.

In 1939 the Polish nation as a whole chose to fight for its existence against overwhelming odds. It did so with the undaunted faith that it would regain its complete independence. The despair of having lost its freedom a second time in a century and a half has not overcome its irresistible hope for the future. And, if the suffering the nation has endured has given it a fierce defiance, it has not deprived it of its resourcefulness and self-reliance. Poland is not yet lost, nor will it be lost.

Few nations have endured what has been the lot of the Polish people since 1939. Neither catastrophic defeat, nor ruthless terror by occupying forces, nor torture and murder in concentration camp, nor forced emigration have broken the nation. On the contrary, they have only steeled it. Through five long years—the blackest in history for any nation—the Poles have refused to bow to the conqueror. They have proved themselves unconquerable. Without yielding or cringing, they have fought back in every conceivable way with the means at their disposal. They have earned the imperishable right to be free and independent again.

In the two brief decades of its existence the Republic of Poland carried out a truly formidable task, a task which fate willed should be left unfinished. After more than a century of domination by the three Partitioning Powers, who did everything they could to destroy the nation, the Republic had to bring the nation together territorially and weld it together politically. It had to unify it economically. It had to fuse it spiritually. It had to teach its citizens to work together, after they had learned for more than a century how to oppose the governments which had ruled them. But the time vouchsafed the Polish nation—two decades—was too short in which to complete these vital labors. The difficulties of re-creating a nation in a world largely in chaos are not always understood by nations which were spared this dolorous experience. After this war, there may be a greater and more widespread understanding of what this means in the life of a nation.

Like all nations, the Poles made mistakes. The real issue of the future will be whether they and all other nations have learned from their mistakes. There are signs that they have. The Poland of the future—as the Underground pictures it—will work together better, have a keener appreciation of how a democracy must function in practice, and will be more willing to coöperate and compromise with neighbors for the common aims. All these qualities were in the picture before the war, but now they have been strengthened and purified until they are becoming irresistible.

No one who has reflected upon the history of the Polish nation and tried to understand its achievements in the past and in recent times can fail to observe its inexhaustible energy, its unquenchable spirit, its abundant resources. What a great and costly mistake it would be for anyone to believe that such a nation could be deprived of its freedom, that it could be kept long under subjugation, that it might lose its identity! The Polish nation can be ruled only by its own kind and by its own choice in line with its historic and cultural traditions. Otherwise, there can be no peace in eastern Europe, nor for that matter in Europe as a whole.

A SELECTED BIBLIOGRAPHY

A Selected Bibliography

THE FOLLOWING WORKS have been selected by the authors and arranged by topics for readers who desire to continue their study of Poland.

On the anthropology of Poland (chap. ii), see: (1) V. G. Childe, *The Danube in Prehistory,* Oxford, 1929; and *The Dawn of European Civilization,* New York, 1939; (2) J. G. D. Clark, *The Mesolithic Settlement of Northern Europe,* Cambridge, England, 1936, pp. 1–52, 62–66, 86–132, 190–217; (3) C. S. Coon, *The Races of Europe,* New York, 1939, pp. 104–109, 168, 186–220, 241–296, 563–572, 642–646; (4) Max Ebert, *Reallexikon der Vorgeschichte,* Berlin, 1924–1932 (R. Beltz, XII, pp. 251–273, P. Diels, XII, pp. 273–291, J. Kostrzewski, I, pp. 408–409; IV[2], pp. 363–364; VI, pp. 131–132; IX, pp. 214–217, 217–221, 244–246; X, pp. 177–200; XII, pp. 230–232; XIV, pp. 542–543, W. La Baume, IV[1], pp. 295–302, H. Obermaier, X, pp. 177–200); (5) D. A. E. Garrod, "The Upper Paleolithic in the Light of Recent Discovery," *Proceedings of the Prehistoric Society,* IV, 1938, pp. 1–26; (6) C. F. C. Hawkes, *The Prehistoric Foundations of Europe to the Mycenaean Age,* London, 1940; (7) Henri Hubert, *The Rise of the Celts* (trans. by M. R. Dobie), New York, 1914, pp. 68–71, 251; (8) E. W. Janczewski, B. Ginet-Piłsudski, and St. Dobrzycki, *Encyclopédie Polonaise,* II, Partie I, Lausaune, 1920, pp. 5–57; (9) M. J. Kostrozewski, "Nouvelles fouilles et découvertes en Pomeranie Polonaise," *Révue Anthropologique,* XXXIX, 1929, pp. 383–397; (10) L. Kozłowski, "L'Epoque Mésolithique en Pologne," *L'Anthropologie,* XXXVI, 1926, pp. 47–74; (11) L. Niederle, *Manuel de l'antiquité slave,* Paris, 1923; (12) I. Schwidetzky, "Die Rassenforschung in Polen," *Zeitschrift für Rassenkunde,* I, 1935, pp. 76–83, 136–204, 289–314; (13) K. Stołyhwo, "Czaszki z Jackowicz," *Swiatowit,* VI, 1905, pp. 74–80; (14) F. E. Zeuner, "The Climate of Countries Adjoining the Ice Sheet of the Pleistocene," *Proceedings of Geologists' Association,* XLVIII, 1937, pp. 378–395; (15) *Polska* (Odbitka z XIII., tomu *Wielkiej Illustrowanej Encyklopedji Powszechnej*), Cracow, 1931.

For the major bibliographical works on Polish history, see: (16) W. H. Allison et al, *A Guide to Historical Literature,* New York, 1931; and for further materials: (17) Karol J. T. Estreicher, *Bibliografia Polska,* Cracow, 1870–1929, 27 vols.; and (18) Ludwik Finkel, *Bibliografia historyi polskiej,* Cracow, 1891–1906, 1 vol. in 3, *Dodatek* I (1906) *Dodatek* II (1914); both to be supplemented by the Polish historical quarterlies: (19) *Kwartalnik historyczny,* Lwów, 1887 ff.; and (20) *Przegląd historyczny,* Warsaw, 1905 ff.

For general accounts of Polish history to the year 1386 (chap. iii), see: (21) "Historya polityczna Polski," in *Encyclopedja Polska,* t.V., Cracow, 1920; (22)

R. Grodecki and St. Zachorowski, *Dzieje Polski średniowiecznej,* Cracow, 1926; (23) J. Dąbrowski, *Dzieje Polski średniowiecznej,* Cracow, 1926; (24) R. Röpell and J. Caro, *Geschichte Polens,* Hamburg, 1840; vol. 1 (Röpell); vols. 2–5 (Caro), Gotha, 1863–1888; (25) H. Grappin, *Histoire de la Pologne des origines à 1922,* Paris, 1922; (26) St. Kutrzeba, *Historja ustroju Polski w zarysie,* Lwów, 1925; (27) Oscar Halecki, *A History of Poland,* New York, 1943.

For the ninth and tenth centuries, see: (28) H. Zeissberg, *Miseco I, der erste christliche Beherrscher der Polen,* Wien, 1867; (29) St. Zakrzewski, *Mieszko I, jako budowniczy państwa polskiego,* Warsaw, 1922; (30) K. Rawer, *Polityczne znaczenie zjazdu gnieźnieńskiego w r. 1000,* Lwów, 1882.

For the eleventh and twelfth centuries, see: (31) F. Duda, *Rozwoj terytorjalny Pomorza polskiego, Wiek XI–XIII,* Cracow, 1909; (32) E. Sieniawski, *Dzieje Słowian zachodnio-północnych,* Poznań, 1920; (33) St. Zakrzewski, *Bolesław Chrobry Wielki,* Lwów, 1925; (34) St. Smolka, *Mieszko Stary i jego wiek,* Warsaw, 1881.

For the thirteenth century, see: (35) Władysław Abraham, *Organizacya kościola w Polsce do połowy w. XIII,* Lwów, 1893; (36) K. Krotoski, *Sw. Stanisław i jego zatarg z krolem Bolesławem Smiałym,* Lwów, 1905; (37) St. Smolka, *Henryk Brodaty,* Lwów, 1872; (38) Fr. Bujak, "Studja nad osadnictwem Małopolski," Cracow, 1905 (*Rozpr. Ak. Um.* t.XLVII); (39) R. Grodecki, *Studja nad dziejami gospodarczemi Polski XII w.,* Lwów, 1915; (40) Z. Wojciechowski, *Ze studjów nad organizacją państwa polskiego za Piastów,* Lwów, 1924; (41) Strakosch-Grossmann, *Der Einfall der Mongolen in Mitteleuropa in den Jahren 1241 und 1242,* Innsbruck, 1893.

For the fourteenth century, see: (42) J. Kochanowski, *Kazimierz Wielki,* Warsaw, 1900; (43) A. Prochaska, *Król Władysław Jagiełło,* Cracow, 1908; (44) Oscar Halecki, *Dzieje Unii Jagiellońskiej,* Cracow, 1919–1920, 2 vols.; (45) M. Kukiel, *Zarys historji wojskowości w Polsce,* Warsaw, 1922; (46) T. Korzon, *Dzieje wojen i wojskowości w Polsce,* Lwów, 1923.

For the period from the fourteenth to the eighteenth century (chap. iv), see, besides Nos. 24 and 44, above, (47) E. Zivier, *Neuere Geschichte Polens,* Gotha, 1915 (vol. 1, 1506–1572); (48) Charlotte Kellogg, *Jadwiga: Poland's Great Queen,* New York, 1931; (49) L. Kolankowski, *Polska Jagiellonów,* Warsaw, 1937; (50) W. Konopczyński, *Dzieje Polski nowożytnej* (1506–1795), Cracow, 1937, 2 vols.; (51) J. B. Morton, *Sobieski, King of Poland,* London, 1932; (52) W. T. Reddaway, J. H. Penson, Oscar Halecki, and R. Dyboski, eds., *The Cambridge History of Poland; from Augustus II to Piłsudski, 1697–1935,* Cambridge, 1941; (53) R. H. Bain, *The Last King of Poland and His Contemporaries,* New York, 1909; (54) R. H. Lord, *The Second Partition of Poland,* Cambridge, Mass., 1915; (55) B. Dembiński, *Polska na przełomie,* Lwów, 1913; (56) Monica M. Gardner, *Kościuszko: A. Biography,* New York, 1920.

For the history of Poland from the partitioning to the First World War (chap. v), see, besides Nos. 25, 27, and 52 above, (57) M. Bobrzyński, *Dzieje Polski w zarysie,* Cracow, 1931, Vol. 3; (58) W. Sobieski, *Dzieje Polski,* 1938, 3 vols.; (59) Roman Dyboski, *Outlines of Polish History,* New York, 1931; (60) A. Bruce Boswell, *Poland and the Poles,* London, 1919; (61) St. Kozicki, *Social Evolution of Poland in the 19th Century,* London, 1918; (62) S. Askenazy, "Poland and the Polish Revolution," in *Cambridge Modern History,* London, 1907, Vol. X, Chap. XIV; (63) M. Handelsman, *Francja-Polska, 1795–1845,* Warsaw, 1926; (64) Monica M. Gardner, *Poland: A Study in National Idealism,* London, 1915; (65) M. Handelsman, "Prince Adam Czartoryski," in *Polski Słownik Biograficzny* (*Dictionary of Polish Biography*), 1938, Vol. IV, pp. 257–269; (66) E. Buzek, *Historja polityki narodowościowej rządu pruskiego, 1815–1908*) (*History of Prussian Policy in Poland, 1815–1908*), Lwów, 1909; (67) Roman Dmowski, *La question polonaise,* Paris, 1909; (68) T. Chrzanowski and W. Konsperynski, "Roman Dmowski," in *Polski Słownik Biograficzny,* 1939, Vol. V, pp. 213–225.

Useful for English readers on some topics in this and following chapters is: (69) Eleanor E. Ledbetter, *Polish Literature in English Translation: A Bibliography with a List of Books About Poland and the Poles,* New York, 1932.

For the period from the First World War to 1923 (chap. vi), in addition to Nos. 19, 20, 52, 57, and 58 above, see: (70) Wilhelm Arenz, *Polen und Russland, 1918–1920,* Leipzig, 1939; (71) S. Askenazy, *Dantzig and Poland* (trans. by W. J. Rose), London, 1922; (72) Michał Bobrzyński, *Wskrzeszenie państwa polskiego,* Cracow, 1920–1925, 2 vols.; (73) Joseph Blociszewski, *La restauration de la Pologne et la diplomatie européenne,* Paris, 1927; (74) Albert Brackmann, ed., *Germany and Poland in Their Historical Relations,* Munich, 1934; (75) Eldon R. Burke, *Polish Policy of the Central Powers during the World War,* Chicago, 1936; (76) Carlo Capasso, *La Polonia e la Guerra Mondiale,* Rome, 1927; (77) Viscount d'Abernon, *The Eighteenth Decisive Battle of the World,* London, 1931; (78) Roman Dmowski, *Polityka Polska i odbudowanie państwa,* Warsaw, 1925; (79) S. Filasiewicz, *La question polonaise pendant la guerre mondiale. Recueil des actes diplomatiques, traités et documents concernant la Pologne,* Paris, 1920, Vol. II; (80) C. T. Firich, *Polish Character of Upper Silesia According to Official Prussian Sources and the Results of the Plebiscite,* London, 1921; (81) Marcel Handelsmann, *La Pologne. Sa vie économique et sociale pendant la guerre,* New Haven, 1933; (82) Kazimierz Kumaniecki, *Odbudowa państwowości polskiej,* Warsaw, 1924; (83) Stanisław Kutrzeba, *Polska odrodzona,* Cracow, 1922; (84) Albert Geouffre de Lapradelle, *La loi polonaise de 1920 sur la nationalité et les traités de Versailles,* Paris, 1924; (85) R. Landau, *Piłsudski and Poland,* New York, 1929; (86) Lithuanian Information Bureau, *The Lithuanian-Polish Dispute,* London, 1921–1923, 3 vols.; (87) Robert Machray, *The Polish-German Problem: Poland's Western Provinces Are the Condition of Her Independence,* London, 1941; (88) David Hunter Miller, *My Diary at the Conference of Paris* (privately printed), 1928, 20 vols.; (89) Ian F. D. Morrow, *The Peace Settlement in the German and Polish Borderlands,* New York, 1936; (90) G. Moresthe, *Vilna et le problème de l'Est Européen, Paris,* 1922; (91) Sidney Osborne, ed., *The Problem of Upper Silesia,* London, 1921; (92) Charles J. M. Phillips, *Paderewski: The Story of a Modern Immortal,* New York, 1933; (93) Józef Piłsudski, *Joseph Piłsudski: Memories of a Polish Revolutionary Soldier* (trans. and ed. by D. R. Gillie), London, 1931; also his *Pisma zbiorowe,* Warsaw, 1931–38, 20 vols.; *L'année, 1920,* Paris, 1929; and *Du révolutionnaire au chef d'état, 1893–1935,* Paris, 1935; (94) Paul Roth, *Die politische Entwicklung in Kongresspolen während der deutschen Okkupation,* Leipzig, 1919; also *Die Entstehung des polnischen Staates,* Berlin, 1926; (95) Count Aleksander Józef Skrzyński, *Poland and Peace,* London, 1923; (96) Casimir Smogorzewski, *L'union sacrée polonaise. Le gouvernement de Varsovie et le "gouvernement" polonais de Paris (1918–1919),* Paris, 1929; also his *Joseph Pilsudski et les activistes polonais pendant la guerre,* Paris, 1931; and *La guerre polono-soviétique, d'après les livres des chefs polonais,* Paris, 1928; (97) H. W. V. Temperley, ed., *A History of the Peace Conference of Paris,* London, 1920–1924, 6 vols.; (98) Deputy A. Wierzbicki, *The Truth About Upper Silesia: A Speech Made in the Polish Diet on January 28, 1921,* Warsaw: Diet of the Polish Republic, 1921; (99) Stanisław Mackiewicz, *Historja Polski od 11 listopada 1918 do 17 września 1939 r.,* London, 1941.

The reader is referred to other literature listed under Nos. 217–266.

For the constitutional development of Poland (chap. vii), in addition to No. 71 above, see: (100) Stanisław Kutrzeba, *Historja ustroju Polski w zarysie,* Lwów, 1911–1917, 4 vols., 1st ed. 1905, of which *Grundriss der polnischen Verfassungsgeschichte,* Berlin, 1912, is a translation of Vol. 1 of 3d ed.; (101) Michał Potulicki, *Constitution de la république de Pologne du 17 mars 1921, contenant le texte du projet de la Commission constitutionelle de la Diète du 8 juillet 1920, et les amendements de la minorité,* Varsovie: Societé de publication internationales, 1921; and *Constitution of the Republic of Poland* (April 23, 1935), (preface by Stanisław Car. Outline of legislation on presidential and parliamentary elections. Warsaw: Polish Commission for International Law Coöperation, 1935); (102) Juljan Makowski, *Konstytucja Rzecyzpospolitej Polskiej,* Warsaw, 1924; (103) Charles Crozat, *Les constitutions de la Pologne et de Dantzig* (Etude et documents), Toulouse, 1923; (104) Władysław Leopold Jaworski, *Uwagi prawnicze a projekcie konstytucji (Legal Importance of the Proposed Constitution),* Cracow, 1921; (105) Şeweryn Różycki, *L'influence du constitutionalisme français sur la Constitution polonaise de 17 mars 1921,* Paris, 1930; (106) Czesław Znamierowski, *Konstytucja Rzeczypospolitej Polskiej,* Warsaw, 1938; (107) Agnes Headlam-Morley, *The New Democratic Constitutions of Europe,* London, 1929.

For materials on Polish political parties see the footnotes to chaps. viii and ix.

In addition to the works already cited on the minorities problems in the footnotes (chap. x), the following may be found useful: (108) G. Horace Alexander, *The League of Nations and the Working of the Minority Treaties,* London, 1926; (109) Raymond Leslie Buell, *Poland: Key to Europe,* New York, 1939; (110) Sir Robert Donald, *The Polish Corridor and the Consequences,* London, 1929; (111) M. Felinski, *The Ukrainians in Poland,* London, 1931; (112) A. L. Goodhardt, *Poland and the Minority Races,* New York, 1922; (113) Konstanty Jezioranski, *National Minorities in Europe,* Warsaw: The Polish Institute for Collaboration with Foreign Countries, 1933; (114) Georges Kaeckenbeeck, *The International Experiment of Upper Silesia,* New York, 1943; (115) V. J. Kurshnir, *Polish Atrocities in the West Ukraine,* Jersey City: United Ukrainian Organizations of the United States, 1931; (116) Roman Lutman, *The Truth About the "Corridor,"* Toruń: The Baltic Institute, n.d.; (117) Henryk Strasburger, *German Designs on Pomerania,* n.d.; (118) Stanisław Srokowski, *East Prussia,* 1934; (119) Florjan

Znaniecki, *The Sociology of the Struggle for Pomerania,* n.d.; (120) S. J. Paprocki, *Minority Affairs and Poland,* Warsaw: Nationality Research Institute, 1935; (121) Casimir Smorgorzewski, *Poland's Access to the Sea,* London, 1934; (122) W. J. Thomas and Florjan Znaniecki, *The Polish Peasant in Europe and America,* New York, 1927, 2 vols.; (123) Arthur Ruppin, *Jewish Fate and Future,* New York, 1940; (124) Abraham Leon Sacher, *Sufferance Is the Badge,* New York, 1939, and (125) Simon Segal, *The New Poland and the Jews,* New York, 1938.

For further reading on the general economic situation in Poland between the two wars (chap. xi), see: (126) Sir John Russell, "Reconstruction and Development in Eastern Poland, 1930–1939," *Geographical Journal,* Vol. 98 (November–December, 1941), pp. 273–291; (127) Gestor (pseud.), "Poland's Economic Development, 1919–1939," *Public Administration,* London, 1941, Vol. 19 (October, 1941), pp. 249–264; (128) *Ku przebudowie gospodarczej: wytyczne inwestycji państowowych (Towards an Economic Reorganization: Outline of the State's Policy of Investments),* Warsaw, 1937; (128) Henryk Strasburger, *The Core of a Continent,* Philadelphia, 1943; (130) Chief Bureau of Statistics, Republic of Poland, *Concise Statistical Year Book of Poland* (Annually since 1918 at Warsaw); (131) *Eastern Poland* (Edited by the Polish Research Center), London, December, 1941; (132) J. H. Retinger, *All About Poland: Facts, Figures, and Documents,* London, 1940; (133) E. Kwiatkowski, *Postęp gospodarczy Polski, (Poland's Economic Progress),* Warsaw, 1928; (134) H. Liepmann, *Tariff Levels and the Economic Unity of Europe,* New York, 1938; (135) *Poland* (Official Catalogue of the Polish Pavilion at the World's Fair in New York), New York, 1939; (136) Stanisław Aleksander Kempner, *Rozwoj gospodarczy Polski,* Warsaw, 1924; (137) Franciszek Bujak, *Poland's Economic Development,* London, 1926; (138) Władysław Studnicki, *Die wirtschaftliche und kulturelle Entwicklung des wiederauferstandenen Polens,* Berlin, 1930; (139) Mieczysław Szawleski, *Polska na tle gospodarski światowej,* Warsaw, 1928.

For additional data on industry, foreign trade, communications and public utilities (chap. xii), see: Nos. 109, 130, and 132 above, and (140) R. Dyboski, *Poland,* London, 1938; (141) Dr. Roman Gorecki, *Poland and Her Economic Development,* London, 1935; (142) Leopold Wellisz, *Foreign Capital in Poland,* London, 1938.

For material on Poland's financial policy (chap. xiii), in addition to No. 142 above, see: (143) *Statistical Bulletin of the Ministry of Finance,* Warsaw, 1924–1939; (144) *Annual Reports of the Bank of Poland,* Warsaw, 1924–1938; (145) *Quarterly Bulletins of the Bank of Poland,* Warsaw, 1928–1939; (146) *Quarterly Reports of the Financial Adviser to the Polish Government,* Warsaw, 1927–1930; (147) M. A. Halperin, *Le problème monetaire d'après guerre et sa solution en Pologne,* Paris, 1931; (148) F. J. Młynarski, *The International Significance of the Depreciation of the Złoty in 1925,* Warsaw, 1926.

For further reading on the agricultural problems of Poland (chap. xiv), in addition to Nos. 127–137 above, see: (149) Polish Ministry of Agriculture, *L'agriculture polonaise,* Warsaw, 1929; (150) Zdisł. Ludkiewicz, *Ustroj rolny Polski i jego niedomagania,* Warsaw, 1936; (151) Władysław Grabski, *Parcelacja agrarna wobec struktury, koniunktury, i chivili dziejowej Polski,* Warsaw (Reprint from

Ekonomista), 1937; (152) Zygmunt Chojecki, *Produkcja rolnicza i przemysł rolniczy w Polsce współczesnej,* Warsaw, 1938; (153) Józef Poniatowski, *Przeludnienie wsi i rolnictwa,* Warsaw, 1936; (154) Wincenty Styś, *Wpływ uprzemysłowienia na ustroj rolny,* Lwów, 1936.

Those who desire to read further on the development of social policy in Poland (chap. xv), in addition to No. 130 above, see: (155) *Workmen's Protective Legislation in Poland* (preface by Jan Stanczyk, Polish Minister of Labor), London: Congress of Polish Trade Unions, 1941; (156) F. Sokal, *Social Insurance in Poland,* Warsaw, 1926 (by the first Polish Delegate to the Administration Council of the International Labor Organization and the head of the Polish Ministry of Labor); (157) *The Protection of Women Workers and Minors in Poland,* London: Polish Women's Committee, 1941; (158) Zofia Zaleska, *The Welfare of Mothers and Children in Poland,* London, 1941; (159) *Polityka społeczna państwa polskiego, 1918–1935,* Warsaw, Ministerstwo Opieki Społecznej, 1935; (160) *10 lat polityki społecznej państwa polskiego, 1918–1927,* Warsaw: Ministerstwo Opieki Społecznej, 1928; (161) M. Lesniewska, *Rozwoj ochrony macierzynstwa robotnicy w przemysle polskim,* Warsaw, 1931; (162) *Dwadziescia lat publicznej słuzby zdrowia w Polsce, 1918–1938,* Warsaw: Ministerstwo Opieki Społecznej, 1939.

For materials on religion in Poland (chap. xvi), see the forthcoming work by K. Symonolewicz and: (163) *The Protestant Churches in Poland* (ed. by the Polish Research Center, with preface by William J. Rose), London, 1944; (164) J. Woliński, *Polska a Kościół prawosławny,* Lwów, 1936; and (165) numerous articles in *Przegląd powszechny* (a monthly edited by the Jesuits in Cracow to 1934 and in Warsaw from that date), *Kultura* (a weekly edited by the Catholic Action in Poznań), and *Prąd* (a monthly edited by the Association of Catholic Intellectuals in Lublin).

For materials on education (chap. xvii), besides No. 130 above, see: (166) *Oświata i Wychowanie,* Warsaw: Ministry of Education, 1936, pp. 1–25, 93–112, 443–445, 819–831; 1939, pp. 161–193, 245–255; (167) *Poland's Institutions of Higher Education,* Washington, United States Department of Interior, 1936, no. 14; (169) Grace Humphrey, *Poland Today,* Warsaw, 1935, pp. 36–60; (169) "Main Problems in Schools of Higher Education," *Przegląd Techniczny,* 1921; (170) *Przegląd Akademicki,* 1932, pp. 157–162; (171) *Nauka Polska,* Warsaw, 1918–1939: 1927, Vol. VIII, pp. 6–15; (172) *Journal of Chemical Education,* 1929, Vol. VI, pp. 451–457; on science (chap. xviii), besides Nos. 130 and 169 (Vol. X, 1928, pp. 1–11) above, see: (173) "Obowiązki pracowników naukowych względem państwa i społeczeństwa," *Księga Pamiatkowa XIII Zjazdu Lekarzy i Przyrodników (1929);* (174) "O organizacji pracy twórczej i wynalazczej," *Nauka Polska,* Vol. XVII, 1937.

Further reading in recent Polish literature (chap. xix), may be found in the following: (175) Wilhelm Feldman, *Wspolczesna literatura polska (Contemporary Polish Literature),* Warsaw, 1930, 8th ed.; (176) Kazimierz Czachowski, *Polska literatura wspolczesna (Contemporary Polish Literature),* Warsaw, 1933; (177) Wacław Borowy, "Fifteen Years of Polish Literature, 1918–1933," *Slavonic Review,* 1933–1934, XII, pp. 670–690; (178) F. Goetel, *From Day to Day* (foreword by John Galsworthy), London and New York, 1931; also "Back to Civilization," *Poland, Journal of the American-Polish Chamber of Commerce and Industry,* November-December, 1927; "Samson and Dalilah," *ibid,* March, 1927; and *The Messenger of the Snow* (preface by G. K. Chesterton), London, 1931; (179) Z. Kossak-Szczucka, *The Blaze: Reminiscences of Volhynia, 1917–1919,* London, 1927; and *The Troubles of a Gnome,* London, 1928; (180) J. Kaden-Bandrowski, "The Sentence," in Else C. M. Benecke and Marie Busch, *Selected Polish Tales,* London and New York, 1925; (181) Z. Rygier Nałkowska, "Women," in P.P.C., Else C. M. Benecke, *Selected Polish Tales,* New York, 1920; (182) W. Perzynski, "Three Tales," *Poland,* October, 1926; (183) L. Staff, "The Strange Shrine," "The Goblet of My Heart," in Paul Selver, *Anthology of Modern Slavonic Literature in Prose and Verse,* London and New York, 1919; (184) B. Winawer, *The Book of Job* (trans. by Joseph Conrad), London, 1931; (185) J. Wittlin, *Salt of the Earth,* New York, 1941; (186) S. Żeromski, *Ashes,* London, 1928; "Forebodings," in Else C. M. Benecke, *Selected Polish Tales,* New York, 1920; "The Stronger Sex," in Else C. M. Benecke and Marie Busch, *More Tales by Polish Authors,* New York, 1916; "Twilight," "Temptation," in Else C. M. Benecke, *Tales by Polish Authors,* New York, 1915.

Material on the fine arts in recent times in Poland (chap. xx), may be found in No. 135 above, and: (187) Wacław Borowy, "The Genius of Poland," *The Studio,* London, April, 1934; (188) Henryk Gotlib, *Polish Painting* (preface by R. H. Wilenski), London, 1942; (189) Polish number, *Art and Archaeology,* Washington, May, 1928; (190) Polish number, *Design,* Syracuse, April, 1932; (191) Polish number, *The School Arts Magazine,* January, 1935.

The following may give further light on recent Polish music (chap. xxi): (192) Henryk Opieński, *La musique polonaise,* Paris, 1929; (193) Zdzisław Tachimecki, *Polska, jej dzieje i kultura,* Warsaw, 1930, Vol. 26.

On the Polish national spirit (chap. xxii), see No. 59 above, and: (194) Paul Super, *The Polish Tradition,* London, 1940; (195) Monica M. Gardner, *Adam Mickiewicz, the National Poet of Poland,* New York, 1911; (196) Stephen P. Mizwa, ed., *Great Men and Women of Poland,* New York, 1942; (197) Ignacy Chrzanowski, *Literatura a naród,* Lwów, 1935.

There is no single book or even a worthwhile monograph dealing directly and exclusively with Polish-American cultural relationships (chap. xxiii). The best single source of information is the monthly magazine (198) *Poland,* published in New York from 1920 to 1933 inclusive, 14 vols.; however, a reader desiring further information with suggestive bibliographies will find useful, besides Nos. 69 and 192 above, the following books, lectures, and articles: (199) H. H. Fisher, *America and the New Poland,* New York, 1928; (200) Mieczysław Haiman, *Polish Past in America,* Chicago: The Polish Roman Catholic Union Archives and Museum, 1939; (201) *Poles in America: Their Contribution to a Century of Progress* (a commemorative souvenir book, compiled and published on the occasion of the Century of Progress, International Exposition in 1933), Chicago: Polish Day Association, 1933; (202) Mieczysław Haiman, "Nauka polska w Stanach Zjednoczonych Ameryki Północnej" ("Polish Learning in the United States of North America"), *Nauka Polska,* 1936, Vol. XXI, pp. 203–234; (203) Stephen P. Mizwa,

The Spirit of Polish Culture, New York: The Kościuszko Foundation, 1940; also "Americanization of the Educational System in Poland," *School and Society,* August 31, 1935, Vol. 42, No. 1079, pp. 1–4; and *Why Teach or Learn Polish?* New York: The Kościuszko Foundation, 1936, 2d ed., 12 pp.; (204) Isaac F. Marcosson, "America in Poland," *Saturday Evening Post,* December 11, 1926; (205) Roman Dyboski, *Immigration and the Interchange of Cultures* (an address delivered at the Immigrants' Protective League on February 28, 1929), Chicago, 1939, 8 pp.; (206) *Polish American Chamber of Commerce 15th Anniversary Commemorative Book,* Warsaw, 1936, 199 pp.; (207) Joseph S. Roucek, "Poles in the United States of America," *Baltic and Scandinavian Countries* (a journal published for Gdynia by the Baltic Institute), January, 1937, Vol. III, pp. 57–70.

For further reading on Polish-American relations (chap. xxiv), besides No. 130 above, see: (208) *Reports Submitted by the Commission of the Financial Experts Headed by E. W. Kemmerer,* Warsaw: Printing Office of Ministry of War, 1926; (209) Department of State, *Papers Relating to Foreign Relations of the United States, 1919. The Paris Peace Conference,* Washington: Government Printing Office, 1942, Vol. II, pp. 408–434; *Papers Relating to the Foreign Relations of the United States. 1920,* Vol. 1, pp. 36–73; *1921,* Vol. II, pp. 685–700; *1927,* Vol. III, pp. 600–630; *1928,* Vol. III, pp. 751–767, Washington: Government Printing Office, 1935–1943; (210) Sidney Brooks, "America and Poland, 1915–1925," *American Relief Administration Bulletin,* Series 2 (April, 1925), No. 44, pp. 1–111; (211) "Continuation of Child Feeding in Poland," *American Relief Administration Bulletin,* Series 2 (May, 1922), No. 24, pp. 34–54; (212) Dana E. Durand, "Food Situation and Policy of Poland, 1920–1921," *American Relief Administration Bulletin,* Series 2 (Oct. 1, 1920), pp. 15–23; (213) W. P. Fuller, Jr., "A Survey of Operations in Poland," *American Relief Administration Bulletin,* Series 2 (Dec. 15, 1920), No. 6, pp. 12–16; (214) "The Polish American Children's Relief Committee Foundation," *American Relief Administration Bulletin,* Series 2 (April 1, 1921), No. 11, pp. 15–39; (215) "A Polish Calendar of Relief," *American Relief Administration Bulletin,* Series 2 (January, 1923), No. 32, pp. 75–79; (216) *Relief Deliveries and Relief Loans, 1919–1923,* Geneva, League of Nations, 1943; (217) "Special Poland Number," *American Relief Administration Bulletin,* Series 1 (April 22, 1919), No. 6; (218) Edwin B. Parker, *Final Report of the United States Liquidation Commission,* Washington: Government Printing Office, 1920.

For the foreign policy of Poland (chap. xxv), besides Nos. 70–99, and 109 above, see: (219) Royal Institute of International Affairs, *Baltic States,* Oxford, 1938; (220) Józef Beck, *Przemówienia, deklaracje, wywiady, 1931–1937,* Warsaw, 1938; and *Mowy,* Warsaw, 1939; (221) Alexandre Bregman, *La politique de la Pologne dans la Société des Nations,* Paris, 1932; (222) *Dantzig et quelques aspects du problème germano-polonais,* Paris: Carnegie Endowment for International Peace, 1932; (223) J. W. Wheeler-Bennett and S. Heald, eds., *Documents on International Affairs,* London and New York, 1928 to date; (224) *Documents diplomatiques. Conflict polono-lithuanien, 1918–1924,* Kaunas, 1924; (225) Raphaël Gaston, *Allemagne et Pologne,* Paris, 1932; (226) A. Giannini, *The Problem of Danzig,* Rome, 1931; (227) Gorzuchowski, *Les rapports politiques de la Pologne et de la Lithuanie,* Paris, 1927; (228) C. Granzinis, *La question de Vilna,* Paris,

1927; (229) H. A. Harder, *Danzig, Polen und der Völkerbund,* Berlin, 1928; (230) Otto Hoetzsch, *Osteuropa und deutscher Osten,* Berlin, 1934; (231) A. de Lapradelle, et al., *The Vilna Question. Consultations,* London, 1929; (232) H. L. Leonhardt, *Nazi Conquest of Danzig,* Chicago, 1942; (233) Stanisław Lukasik, *Pologne et Roumanie,* Paris, 1937; (234) G. Kaeckenbeeck, *The International Experiment of Upper Silesia,* New York, 1942; (235) Robert Machray, *Poland, 1914–1931,* London, 1932 (reworked into his *The Poland of Piłsudski,* London and New York, 1937); (236) René Martel, *The Eastern Frontiers of Germany,* London, 1930; (237) Henri de Montfort, *L'aspect européen de la question de la Prusse Orientale,* Paris, 1933; (238) Ladas Natkevičius, *L'aspect politique et juridique du différend polono-lithuanien,* Paris, 1930; (239) Hermann Rauschning, *Die Entdeutschung Westpreussens und Posens,* Berlin, 1930; (240) W. J. Rose, *Poland,* London, 1939; (241) Friedrich Schinkel, *Polen, Preussen, und Deutschland als Problem der preussisch-deutschen Nationalstaats Entwicklung,* Breslau, 1931; (242) Władysław Sikorski, *Polska i Francja,* Lwów, 1931 (much of the material appeared in his *Le problème de la paix. Le jeu des forces politiques,* Paris, 1931); (243) Stanisław Slawski, *Poland's Access to the Sea,* London, 1925; (244) Casimir Smogorzewski, *Poland's Access to the Sea,* London, 1934; (245) A. J. Toynbee, ed., *Survey of International Affairs,* London and New York (annually), 1925 to date; (246) T. A. Taracouzio, *War and Peace in Soviet Diplomacy,* New York, 1940; (247) Victor Tapié, *Le pays de Teschen et les rapports entre la Pologne et la Tchécoslovaquie,* Paris, 1936; (248) F. J. Vondracek, *Foreign Policy of Czechoslovakia, 1918–1935,* New York, 1937.

Two Polish official publications of great importance are the periodicals: (249) *Polityka Zagranyczna (Foreign Policy)* and (250) *Przegląd Współczesnej (Contemporary Review);* the foreign affairs of Poland have been discussed frequently in numerous European and American periodicals: (251) *Foreign Affairs,* (252) *Slavonic Review,* (253) *Nineteenth Century,* (254) *L'Europe Nouvelle,* (255) *L'Esprit International,* (256) *Foreign Policy Reports,* (257) *Central European Observer,* (258) *American Political Science Review;* newspapers of most use and availability to western Europeans are: (259) Paris *Le Temps,* (260) *The Times* of London, (261) the *Manchester Guardian,* and (262) *The New York Times.*

The last phase of Poland's foreign affairs, the descent to war, can still be most profitably studied from a close reading of the official publications of the various Foreign Offices: (263) *The Polish White Book. Official Documents concerning Polish-German and Polish-Soviet Relations, 1933–1939,* London, 1940; (264) *The German White Book. Documents on the Events preceding the Outbreak of the War,* New York, 1940; (265) *The French Yellow Book,* New York, n.d. (the French edition was dated 1939); (266) *The British Blue Book, Documents concerning German-Polish Relations and the Outbreak of Hostilities between Great Britain and Germany on September 3, 1939,* London, 1939 (Command Paper 6106); (267) Sir Nevile Henderson's *Final Report* was published as Command Paper 6115. Much of this report was incorporated into the latter part of his book, (268) *Failure of a Mission, 1937–1939,* New York, 1940.

For further reading on Poland in the Second World War (chap. xxvi), see: Nos. 130, 263 above, and (269) Norwid Neugebauer, *Kampania wrześniowa 1939 w Polsce,* London, 1941; (270) *Polish White Book. German Occupation of Poland,* (Polish Ministry for Foreign Affairs), New York: The Greystone Press, 1942; (271) *L'Occupation Allemande et Soviétique de la Pologne.* (Note adressée le 3 Mai 1941 aux Puissances alliées et neutres.) Polish Ministry for Foreign Affairs, London: M. I. Kolin, Ltd., 1941; (272) *The Black Book of Poland* (Polish Ministry of Information, New York: G. P. Putnam's Sons, 1942; (273) *Documents Relating to the Administration of Occupied Countries in Eastern Europe,* New York: Polish Information Center, May, 1941; (274) *Polish-Soviet Relations, 1918–1943* (Documents), New York: Polish Information Center, 1943; (275) S. Segal, *The New Order in Poland,* New York, 1942; (276) Stanisław Strzetelski, *Where the Storm Broke,* New York, 1942; (277) *Poland Three Years After,* New York: Polish Information Center, 1942; (278) *Bestiality* (unknown in any previous record of history), London: Polish Ministry of Information, 1942; (279) Anna Maclaren, *Poland at Arms,* London, 1942; (280) Michał Kwiatkowski, *Rząd i rada narodowa R. P.,* London, 1942; (281) *War and Peace Aims,* New York: United Nations Information Office, 1943; (282) *Za waszą i naszą wolność,* New York; Polish Information Center, 1941; (283) Peter Jordan, *First to Fight,* London, 1943; (284) Ann Su Cardwell, *Poland and Russia: The Last Quarter Century,* New York, 1944; (285) Jan Karski, *The Story of a Secret State,* New York, 1944; (286) *Polish Facts and Figures* (appearing monthly), New York, 1944–; (287) Stanisław Grabski, *The Polish-Soviet Frontier,* New York, Polish Information Center, n.d.; (288) Wacław Lednicki, *Russo-Polish Relations, Their Historical, Cultural, and Political Background,* Chicago: Polish National Alliance Education Department, n.d.; and *Life and Culture of Poland* (as reflected in Polish literature), New York, 1944.

A recent and useful compilation is to be found in "Books on Poland," Supplement to *The Polish Review,* New York, 1944.

INDEX

Index

Academy of Arts and Sciences, 278
Academy of Technical Sciences, 280
Adalbert, Bishop, 35
Adamski, Monsignor, 251
Adriatic, 31
Aestii (Balts ?), 20
"Agricultural Reconstruction in Poland," by Jerzy Radwan, xiv, 219–231
Agriculture: Tripolye, 16; scratch-plough period of, 19; efficient plough, 20; enfranchisement of peasants, 62, 220; education of peasants in, 65; agrarian radicalism in Galicia, 107; agrarian reforms, 115, 116, 144, 162, 180; protectionism impeded, 175; predominant, 180; overpopulation on arable land, 181, 220, 221, 229, 231; advance in, in 1919–1939 period, 204; exports, 210; nobility owned land, 219, 230; strip system in, 219, 221–223 *passim;* primitive forms of, abolished, 220; parceling of large estates, 221, 224, 225, 229; unsound rural structure, 221, 224, 229; crop rotation, 223; structure changed, 223, 227, 230; commassation of, 225, 231; usufructs abolished, 225; common property lands divided, 226; few small tenancies, 227; dwarf farms, 228, 230; financing reconstruction of, 228, 229, 231; increase in production, 230, 231; under Reich, 437
Agudas Israel, 256
Albert of Hohenzollern, 42
Alexander I, Tsar: recognized Duchy of Warsaw, 50, 51; liberal sentiments of, 52, 56; interest of, in Poland, 53; treaty of, with King of Prussia, 54; death of, 56
Alexander of Jugoslavia, 382
Allenstein, 77, 78
Alpine type, 23–27 *passim*
America-Poland (*Ameryka-Polska*), 354
American Relief Administration, 368
Ancylus Lake, 11, 15
Angel, John Lawrence, "Anthropology of Poland: Prehistory and Race," ii, 10–28
Anthropology: evidence for Paleolithic man, 13, 16; Mousterian strata, 13; Upper Paleolithic, 13; Solutrean interlude in, 14; Gravettian sites, 14; Magdalenian influence, 14; Neanderthal man, 23; Lwów school of, 23
"Anthropology of Poland: Prehistory and Race," by John Lawrence Angel, ii, 10–28
Anti-Comintern Pact, 415
Appleget, Thomas B., 359
Architecture: in partitioned Poland, 311; international eclecticism in, 311, 312; opportunities for, in Republic, 312; modernistic, 312
Arciszewski, Tomasz, President-Designate, 458, 461
Arct, Eugeniusz, 320
Armenian Catholics, 253
Armenoid, 25, 27
Army: on French pattern, 52; Piłsudski's "legionaries" nucleus of, 67, 70, 74, 90; Central Powers plan for, 72
Art (*Sztuka*), 317
August Laws, 137
Augustus II of Saxony, 47
Augustus III, 47
Aunjetitz Bronze Age, 18
Aurignacian-Gravettian-Magdalenian sequence, 14

Austerlitz, 50
Austria: Galicia to, in First Partition, 48; annexed Cracow, 48, 67; Napolean defeated, 50, 51; a constitutional state, 68; with Prussia in First World War, 70, 90; proclaimed Polish Kingdom, 90; Poles in Dual Monarchy of, 106

Baltic: access to, 8, 46; Ancylus Lake on, 11; Litorina Sea in, 12; settlers on, 33, 37, 43
Banaczyk, 429
Bank of Poland. *See* Bank Polski
Bank Polski: created, 208; reserves of, 211; discount rate of, 215
Barber, A. B., 370
Barnagium Angliae, 37
Bartel, Casimir: transitional regime of, 117; premier, 137, 396; represented civilian element, 138; last civilian cabinet of, 139; German proposal to, 452
Barthou, Jean Louis, 402, 403
Bartłomiejczyk, Edmund, 321
Basil III of Moscow, 42
Bastarni (Peucini), 20
Báthory, Stephen, 43
Batu Khan, 37
Beck, Józef: Foreign Minister, 143, 390; cited on minorities, 153; against Four Power Pact, 399; quoted on honor, 340, 417; policy of, 402, 403, 405; visited Germany, 404; in Danzig crisis, 407; for bilateralism, 409; with Mussolini, 410; cited on League, 411; plans for Teschen, 412; for free Danzig, 414; reversed pro-German policy, 416
Bell-Beaker people, 17
Bem, General, 58
Beneš, Eduard, 382, 383, 384, 403
Berent, Wacław, 298
Berut, Bolesław, 460
Beskids, 10, 26; West, 20
Bessarabia, 75, 379, 432
Best, W., quoted, 430
Białystok, 51, 83, 154, 155
Bismarck, Otto, 64
Biuletyn Informacyjny, 439
Black Earth country, 10, 16
Black Sea: access to, 4; cut off from, 7; expedition to, 42
Blandowski, Constantine, 350
Boguszewska, Helen, 302
Bohemia, 7, 11; metal trade with, 17, 18; Slavic, 31, 33; Christianized, 34, 42; under Bolesław, 36; Silesia given to, 38; under Casimir, 41
Bohumín, 164, 412
Bolesław the Brave, 34
Bolesław II, 36
Bolesław III, 36
Books of the Polish Nation and of the Polish Pilgrimage, 59; quoted, 336, 338, 339
Bor, General. *See* Komorowski, Tadeusz
Borowski, Wacław, 318
Borowy, Wacław, quoted, 305
Borreby type, 23, 24, 27
Bourdelle, Emile-Antoine, 315
Boy-Zeleński, Tadeusz, 296
Boznańska, Olga, 317
Brandenburg, Mark of: formed part of Prussia, 7, 47, 63; migrations from, 11; culture of, 14; created for, 63
Bratianu, Ion, cited, 150
Brest-Litovsk, 48; negotiations at, 75; religious union concluded at, 253
Briand, 389, 397, 398
Broniewski, Władysław, 292
Brueckner, Alexander, 288
Brüning, Chancellor Heinrich, 398
Brünn-Předmost *Homo sapiens,* 23
Bug River: boundary, 10, 17, 18, 21, 34, 48; migration route, 11, 26
Burckhardt, Karl J., 422
Burke, Eldon R., "Polish-American Political and Economic Relations," xxiv, 365–374
Bursche, Juliusz, 255
Bydgoszcz (Bromberg), 430
Byzantine Greek: influence, 20; Orthodox tradition, 33

Cahals, 161
Camp of Great Poland, 137
Carol, King, 408
Carpathian Mountains: boundary, 4, 8, 10, 21, 26, 27, 31, 77, 157, 377; dwellings in, 11, 14

Casimir the Great, 38, 40
Casimir, John, 45
Castlereagh, Lord Robert Stewart, 55
Catherine II, 47, 52, 53, 153
Catholic Action, 250
Cattegat, 12
Celts, 21
Central Europe, 4
Centro-Lew coalition, 139
Chamberlain, Neville, 419
Charlemagne, 31, 32
Charles X Gustavus, 46
Charles XII of Sweden, 47
Chatelperronian (Early Aurignacian), 13
Chełm, 75
Children's Relief, 369
Chopin, 335, 350
Choromański, Michał, 301
Christian League of National Union (*Chrześcijański Związek Jedności Narodowej*), 112
Christian Nationalist Labor Club (*Narodowe Chrześcijańskie Stronnictwo Pracy*), 113
Churchill, Winston, quoted, 429, 460
Cieślewski, Tadeusz, Jr., 321
Cieszyn. *See* Teschen
Climate: in Würm glaciation, 11; Boreal, 12; oceanic for northern Europe, 12; sub-Boreal, 12, 17; sub-Atlantic, 12; present, 12; reduction of forests by, 17
Code Napoléon, 51
"Collaborationist" group (*Chliboroby*). *See* Ukrainian Peasant party
Comb-pottery hunters, 17, 21
Concentration camps: at Rajsk, 431; at Oswięcim, 431, 436; Soviet labor, 443; in Kazakhstan, 445
Concise Statistical Year Book of Poland, 267, 269
Confederation of Bar, 47
Conference of Ambassadors, 385, 386
Congress Kingdom: Tsar created, 54, 55; industries expanded in, 220
Congress of Vienna: Polish question for, 54, 377; treaties of, 57
Conquests: temporary, from 1308–1454, 4; First Partition, 4, 47; first German invasion, 6; Tartar invasions, 7; by Teutonic Knights, 37; Mongol, 37; Swedish and Turkish aggressions, 45; second and third partitions, 48; by Russia's *Organic Statute*, 57; by Bismarck, 64; in First World War, 70; Second World War, 147
Conrad, Duke of Mazovia, 36
Conrad, Joseph, 202, 299, 309
Constantine, Grand Duke, 56
Constituent Diet (*Sejm Ustawodawcy*): declaration of, 91; tasks of, 91, 132; nationalist tradition in, 112; tactics of party groups in, 131; nine ministries in, 132; period of, significant, 133
Constitutional development: federal constitution recognized status of Poland and Lithuania, 41; shortcomings of federal constitution, 44; cessation of, cause of decline, 45; constitution of Duchy of Warsaw, 51; Alexander's constitution for Kingdom, 55; five periods of, 89; preconstitution period in, 89; Little Constitution, 91, 131; Constitution of March 17, 1921, 92; Amended Constitution, 95; Constitution of April 23, 1935, 97; Republic to uphold Constitution, 100; future, 101
"Constitutional Development of Poland," Joseph C. Gidyński, vii, 89–103
Constitution of April 23, 1935: increased power of President, 97; Council of Ministers, 98; legislative power in, 98; rights of citizens in, 99; new electoral law, 99
Constitution of March 17, 1921: democratic, 92; executive powers by, 92; legislative powers, 93; membership of Diet, 94; Senate, 94; judicial power, 94; rights of citizens, 94; powers of President in Amended Constitution, 95; social problems considered, 236
Constitution of May Third, 1791: reformed public life, 48; social reforms in, 219, 233; spiritual regeneration in, 334; last great achievement of Republic, 336; national spirit in, 339

Coon, C. S., 23
Copernicus, Nikolaus, 43, 281, 363
Corded-ware people, 17, 18, 21, 24
Cossacks, 45, 46
Cotini, 21
Coulondre, 423
Council of Basel, 41
Council of Constance, 41, 332, 338
Council of Regency: Central Powers appointed, 74, 90; proclaimed independent Poland, 76; dissolved, 76; 91; failed to fill posts, 124; Kakowski headed, 250
Council of Trent, 248
Cracow (Kraków): Paleolithic man found at, 13: university of, 38, 43, 268; Austria annexed, 48, 67; added to Duchy of Warsaw, 51; Republic of, 54; conservative activity in, 107; *Times* quoted, 145; Populist meeting in, 145; party strength in, 147; archbishopric of, 250, 251; Academy of Arts and Sciences in, 278, 279, 317; Wawel Castle in, 314
Crimea, 41
Croatia, 31
Culture, anthropological: of Latin western Europe, 3, 43, 247; geographical influences on, 10; distribution, 11; communal hunting, 12; northward shift of, 13; Mousterian, 13, 23; Gravettian, 14; Swiderian, 14, 15; Maglemosean, 15; Microlithic, 15; Danubian, 16; Tripolye, 16, 21; Megalithic, 17; Danordic in west Poland, 17; Corded-ware invasion modified, 17, 21; northern, 18; Złota, 18, 22; Aunjetitz Bronze Age crystallized diverse, 18, 22; development of Lausitz, 18, 21, 22; Hallstatt derived, 19; Ivanovič, 19, 21; Scythian Iron-Age influence on, 19; LaTène, 19, 21; Burgundian link, 20; assumed continuity of language with, 21; Germanic-Celtic-Scythian contact with, 21, 22; Tardenoisian, 23.
Culture, social: influence of Greco-Roman civilization, 32, 33, 34, 43; cultural unity under Casimir, 38; Cracow University advance in, 38, 43; "golden age" of, 43; representatives of, 44; disastrous influence of "Deluge" on, 46; revival of, 47; Emigration poets expression of Romanticism in, 59; homogeneous tradition of, 232; trend of religious thought in, 252; present catastrophe in, 277; expressed in: literature, 284, architecture, 311, sculpture, 314, painting, 316, graphic arts, 320, interior decoration, 322, music, 323; of Tatras, 324; relations with America in, 348 ff.; work of Rockefeller Foundation in, 359; Kościusko Foundation aid to, 360; under Reich, 436
Curie, Maria Skłodowska, 281, 356
Curzon Line, 81, 82, 130, 366, 457, 459
Cwojdziński, Antoni, 309
Cybis, Bolesław, 319
Cybulski, Jan, 314
Czajkowski, Jósef, 313
Czapski, Józef, 320, 326
Czartoryski, Prince Adam, 53, 57, 59
Czechoslovakia: reconstituted, 9; Teschen to, 77, 80, 190; Russophile, 83; lost Teschen, 130; partitioned, 146, 161; German minority pact with, 151; gave autonomy to Ruthenia, 159; cordial relations with Poland, 382; absorption of rump of, 415
Czechowicz, Józef, 295
Czekanowski, Jan, 23
Czermański, Zdzisław, 321
Częstochowa: resisted Swedes, 46; shrine at, 251; pilgrimages to, 252
Czuchnowski, Marjan, 295
Czyzewski, Tytus, 317

Dąbrowska, Maria, 303
Dacia, 20
Dalbor, Cardinal, 250
Danube, migration routes along, 11, 31
Danubians, 16, 17, 21, 24, 25
Danzig: Teutonic Knights seized, 37; Casimir regained, 41; made free city, 51, 78, 149; Great Powers commission awarded, to Poland, 77; anti-Polish agitation in, 83, 407, 417; relations between Poland and, 151, 395, 404; minorities in, 164, 166; port of, modernized, 196, 201;

USS "Pittsburgh" entered, 367; Germany and, 391; demanded independence from League, 406; dispute over Polish customs inspectors in, 418
Daszyński, Ignacy: Socialist leader, 76; proclaimed Provisional Government, 125; coadjutor of Piłsudski, 126
Davout, Marshal, 52
Dawes Committee, 370
"Dawn," 60
Dawn of People's group (*Ludowcy Zaraniarze*), 115
Delbos, Yvon, 409
"Deluge," 46
Deutscher Volksbund, 394, 396
Dewey, Charles S., 372
Didur, Adam, 356–357
Diet (*Sejm*): 44, 51, 92, 125
Dinaric, 25–27 *passim*
Dionysius, Archbishop, 254
Dmowski, Roman: against Germany, 66, 106; *La question polonaise* by, 66; leader of National Democrats, 73, 75, 105; headed Polish National Committee, 74, 77, 365, 366; in National People's Union, 113; at Paris, 130; organized Camp of Great Poland, 137
Dnieper, a boundary, 8, 20, 31, 36, 42, 45, 157
Dniester, 8, 10, 157
Dogger Bank, 12, 15
Donets Basin, 190
Drang nach Osten, 35, 37, 66, 411
Drohobycz, 81
Dubravka, 34
Dunikowski, Ksawery, 314
Dunkirk, 448
Durand, E. D., 370
Dvina, 8, 445
Dzierożyński, Father Francis, 356

Economy: early phases in: food gathering, 12; farming, 12, 16; metalworking techniques in, 12; parasitism on herbivores, 14; Early Iron Age, 19; defense a drain on resources, 37; prosperity under Casimir, 38; decline from position as European power, 45; modern democratic state, 61 ff., 101; coöperative credit association, 65; Poznań richest in Poland, 65; "Organic Work," 65; despoiled by First World War, 71, 206; economic boundaries troublesome, 148; part of Jews in, 159; differences in, under Partitioning Powers, 169, 184, 198, 206; no part in industrial development, 170, 171; no post-war boom, 171; plan to adjust, of three provinces, 172; currency chaos, 172; budget, 172; little international capital, 173, 179, 195, 203; tariffs hampered trade, 174, 175; 1933 income dropped, 177, 210, 211; free trade, 177; occupational structure basic problem in, 180, 181; symptoms of progress, 182, 342; two lessons from Second World War, 195; future of, 196; export items, 194, 197; increase in foreign trade, 196; imports, 197; communications and transportation, 198 ff.; results of union with Pomorze and Danzig, 200; electrification, 203; housing, 204; improvement in, with Second World War, 212; usufructs harmful, 226; food and supplies, 369; credits, 369; bond issues, 369, 371, 372; American investments, 369, 373; tariff war with Germany, 394; agreements with Soviet Russia, 415; objective of German policy, 437. *See also* Industry
"Education," by Wojciech Świętosławski, xvii, 257–273
Education: under Russia, 57; until 1873 in hands of clergy, 64; Bismarck put, under state control, 64; underground system of, 65, 439; in agriculture, 65; separate school system for Galician Poles, 68; schools for minorities, 155; Jewish, 161, 256; illiteracy in Russian Poland, 172; compulsory after First World War, 193, 257, 258; eighteenth century reforms in, 233; Konarski's reorganization of, 248; Jesuit schools, 249, 256; Warsaw Catholic Action school, 250; Catholic university at Lublin,

Education (*Continued*)
251; growing influence of Catholicism in, 252; faculties of theology in universities, 252; differences under Partitioning Powers, 257; Alma Mater (*Macierz Szkolna*), 257; primitive buildings for, 258; problem of teachers for, 258, 259, 260; elementary system of, 258; migration a problem in, 259; Depression curtailed, 259; rural problems in, 260; free public schools, 261; religious, in schools, 261; nationalism in, 262; for minorities, 262, 267; secondary, 263; vocational, 264; continuation, 266; university, 268; professional schools, 269; teacher organizations, 271; student organizations, 272; number of professors for, 274; research, 276, 277; duties of scholar, 276; academic societies, 278; achievements in, 342; under Reich, 435; in Soviet-occupied Poland, 442
Eden, Anthony, 403
Eger, 23
Elbe River, 18, 31, 33, 36
Electoral Law of June, 1935, 154
Engraving (*Ryt*), 321
"Epilogue," by Robert J. Kerner, 457–463
Estonia, 15, 42, 127
Ethnography: ecologic zones, 10; influence of three geographical features on, 10; climatic zoning, 11, 14; defined by language, 20; blood groups, 26; average Pole, 26; German frontier justified by, 77; ethnic boundaries troublesome in 1919, 148
Etymological Dictionary of the Polish Language, 288
Expropriation Act of 1908, 64

Fałat, Juljan, 316
Fenn, Sereno P., 358
Fenni (Finns ?), 20
Ferdinand, King, 379
Fifth Partition, 123, 141, 144
Filipowicz, Tytus, 350
Financial policy: unification of currency, 207; stabilization of currency, 207, 208, 209; hyperinflation, 208; second period in, 209; effect of world banking crisis on, 210, 214; foreign credits withdrawn, 210; foreign exchange control, 212, 213; gold parity of złoty, 211, 212, 371; third period of, 212; bank runs counteracted, 214; interest rates, 215; decrease in debt, 216 ff.; American, in Poland, 370 ff.; Kemmerer Financial Mission, 371; bonds of Republic offered, 369, 370, 372
"Fine Arts, The," by Irena Piotrowska, xx, 311–322
Finno-Ugrians, 22
First Partition: deprived Poland of Baltic, 4; halved size, 8, 47; shock of, 334
Fitelberg, Grzegorz, 323, 327
Florentine Union of 1439, 253
Foch, Marshal Ferdinand, 76, 83
"Foreign Relations," by S. Harrison Thomson, xxv, 377–424
Foreign relations: frontier struggle with Germany, 32; Mieszko's alliance with Holy Roman Empire, 33; with Bohemia, 34, 36; Casimir's, 38, 40; fruit of eastern orientation of, 39; Polish-Lithuanian union of 1386, 39, 40; personal union with Hungary, 40; settlement with Germany, 42; closer contacts with France and England, 42; hope for Scandinavian coöperation, 43; Swedish and Turkish aggressions, 45; with Muscovite Russia, 46; plan of partitions, 47, 48; temporary alliance with Prussia, 48; conciliation toward Russia, 66; supported imperial policies in Reichsrat, 68; no compromise with Ukrainian nationalism, 69; looked on France as future ally, 78; bitterness toward Czechoslovakia, 80; toward Lithuania, 82, 380; to neighbors of new Poland, 378; Franco-Polish alliance, 378, 389; mutual assistance pact with Rumania, 379, 408; collaboration with Latvia, 380; relations with Baltic states, 380, 385; pro-Hungarian, 385; Helsinki conference, 381; boundary dispute with Czechoslovakia, 382, 383; collabo-

rated with Little Entente, 385; toward Soviet Russia, 387 ff.; nonaggression pact, 388, 389, 390, 398, 400–404 *passim;* League cornerstone of, 392, 393; negotiations over property expropriations of German nationals, 391, 394; regarding Danzig, 395, 405, 414; toward German militarism, 397; anti-Polish campaign in Germany, 397; Mussolini's suggestion, 399; objections to Four Power Pact, 399; anti-Czechoslovak, 401, 403; tariff war ended, 404; other sources of Polish-German friction, 408; "Colonial Week," 411; willingness to negotiate, 420; demand for Teschen, 412; rebuffed on frontier with Hungary, 413; overt phase of German-Polish crisis, 415
"Formation of the Polish State, The," by Frank T. Nowak, iii, 31–39
Forster, Albert, Danzig Nazi leader, 406, 430
Foundation of National Culture: aided students, 269; Piłsudski created, 275
Four-Power Pact: Mussolini suggested, 399; Little Entente signed, 401
Francis Joseph, Emperor, 70, 72, 107
Frank, Governor General, 433, 436
Frederick the Great, 47
Fredro, Aleksander, 307
Friedland, 50

Galicia: location of, 10; prehistoric man found in, 13, 23; hunters of, 14; migrations into, 16; copper prospectors from, 17, 18; agricultural, 67, 68; First Partition gave to Austria, 48; backward, 67, 68; began economic reform, 68; developed government, 68; intellectual center, 69; Supreme National Committee formed in, 70, 71; Austrian administration of, supplanted, 76; Allies awarded, to Poland, 80; gentry in, 106; concessions in, 107; industries undeveloped in, 186
Galicia, Eastern: Casimir regained, 39; racially Ukrainian, 69, 76, 80, 157; Uniate, 69; Allied compromise for, 81; Poland occupied, 81
Galinowski, Jan, 314
Gamelin, General Marie Gustave, 404
Gdynia, 196, 200, 201, 281, 342, 395, 405
General Review (Przegląd Powszechny), 252
Geneva: Disarmament Conference at, 390, 391; Protocol, 392
Genghis Khan, 37
Genoa Conference, 383, 384
Geography: belongs to eastern Europe, 3; key position, 4; from Baltic to Carpathians, 4, 8; unity shaped by rivers, 4, 5; access to sea important, 4; frontiers source of weakness, 5; frontiers persistent, 6, 377; neighbors, 6, 8, 378; Prussia encircled two sides, 7; possibilities of regional cooperation, 8; 1939 frontiers, 8; ecologic zones, 10, 16; three features of, influencing migrations, 10; glacier periods, 11; Slav territory, 20, 31; transitional area between cultures, 22; largest monarchy, 41, 42; territorial losses in Deluge, 46; partitioned, 48; boundaries of Duchy of Warsaw, 51; frontiers after First World War, 76, 79, 85, 148, 149, 377
German-Polish Non-Aggression Pact: signed, 400, 401; Prague press, 402
Germany: peaceful penetration policy of, 63; Bismarck's colonization policy, 64; real enemy of Poland, 66, 105; Prussia excluded Austria from, 68; army of, administered Poland, 71; Ludendorff's plan of independent Polish state, 72; withdrew from Poznań and West Prussia, 76; aims of, frustrated, 90; treatment of minorities by, 165; Hitler government of, 398, 402; wooed Poland, 399; German-Czechoslovak crisis, 410; nonaggression pact with Russia, 419; demands of, 421; beastiality of, 428; issued penal code, 431; policy in, 437
Gibson, Hugh, 366
Gidyński, Joseph C., "Constitutional Development of Poland," vii, 89–103
Głogoviensis, Joannes, 347
Gniezno: first capital, 33, 36; shrine at, 35; archbishops of, 250

Goering, General Hermann, 433
Goetel, Ferdinand, 301
Gojawiczyńska, Maria, 303
Goluchowski, Agenor, 68
Gömbös, General, 404
Goremykin, 71
Gorlice, 71
Goths, 20
Gotlib, Henryk, 317
Government Bloc, 137–140 *passim*, 142; liquidated, 143
G.P.U., 443
Grabski, Stanisław, 74, 460
Grabski, W., 230
Grabski, Władysław, 132, 135
Graham, Malbone W.: "Polish Political Parties," viii, 104–122; "Polish Politics, 1918–1939," ix, 123–147
Graphic arts, 320; foremost artists in, 320; woodcut technique in, 320; folk expression in, 321; Engraving (*Ryt*) society, 321
Gravette, La, 13
Gravettian: East (Upper Aurignacian), 13; hunters, 21; Late, 23
Great Diet, 48
Greek Orthodox Church, 44
Greiser, 406, 407; quoted, 431
Grey, Sir Edward, quoted, 454
Grodno, 48, 82, 83
Groener, General Wilhelm, 397
Grottgier, 335
Grudziądz, 422
Grünewald (Tannenberg), 332
Gruszecka, Aniela (Jan Powalski), 303
Gustavus Adolphus, 46

Habsburgs: alliance with Jagellonians, 42; Dual Monarchy of, collapsed, 123
Haiman, Miecislaus, 355
Halecki, Oscar: "Poland and Europe: Geographical Position," i, 3–9; "Poland as a European Power," iv, 40–48; "Religious Life," xvi, 247–256
Halich, 69
Haller, General Józef, 74, 81, 357, 367
Hallstatt, 19
Harpe, Frédéric César de la, 53
Hawley-Smoot Tariff Act, 176
Henderson, Sir Nevile, 419, 420, 421
Henri of Valois, 43
Henry II, Emperor, 35
Henry II of England, 38
Henry VII of England, 42
Herodotus, 21
Herriot, Édouard, 391
Hertling, Count Georg von, 75
Himmler, Heinrich, 436
History: conquests, 4, 6, 7; strong political state until invasions, 6; Holy Roman Empire danger to, 7; neighbors danger to, 7; community of interests in region, 9; migrations, 11, 131; three economic phases, 12; three major Lausitz phases, 18; western Slavs founded Poland, 31; origin of name, 33; first capital, 33; pact with Otto I, 33; in Patrimony of St. Peter, 34; first king of, 34; Gniezno conference, 35; national unity begun, 33, 36; German invasion, 36; Teutonic Knights on border, 37; Mongol inroads, 37; nobility powerful, 37, 44; beginning of constitutional government, 37; German settlers assimilated, 37; a European power under Casimir, 38, 45; union with Lithuania, 39, 40, 332; political system of Jagellonians, 40, 42; contacts with western Europe, 42; eastern frontier defended, 42; "Common Republic," 43; "golden age" in, 43; causes of decline, 45; Swedish and Turkish aggressions, 45; "Deluge," 46; renounced Kiev, 46; Peter the Great limited armaments, 47; First Partition, 47; a parliamentary monarchy, 48; second and third partitions, 48, 50; "the captivity," 49; no united state, 49, 50; with Napoleon, 50; Duchy of Warsaw recognized, 50, 51, 52; army on French basis, 52; Russia took Duchy, 52; Alexander's attitude, 53; after the Congress of Vienna, 54, 55; Congress Kingdom, 54, 55, 108; insurrection, 56, 61; under Russia, 57; Great Emigration, 58; revolution of 1863, 61; nationalism, 62, 104, 110, 128, 332; "Organic Work" period, 63, 66; Prussia's harsh policy, 63, 64; Bismarck's war against church, 64; Bis-

marck's policy of colonization, 64; army, 67; unprepared for First World War, 70, 108; devastation by retreating Russians, 71; on military basis, 71; "independent" state, 72, 74, 75, 83, 85, 89, 90, 91; as Allied power, 74, 76; Council of Regency, 74, 76, 90, 109; formally recognized, 77; claims of, 77; France supported, 78; signed minorities treaty, 78; Russians entered Congress Poland, 83; constitutional development, 89 ff.; 1926 regime ended, 100; principles for Polish Republic, 100; administration, 101; sixteen provinces, 101; self-government for, 102; state supervision, 103; Poles in Prussia, 104, in Russia, 105; political status in Austria, 105; political manipulation in Galicia, 107; party formation, 109; four ideologies, 110; populism, 114, 123, 169; four periods in political history after 1918, 123 ff.; socialist interlude, 123; Lublin regime, 124; incorporation or federalism, 129, 130; period of Constituent Diet, 131; First Parliament, 134; Piłsudski era, 136; military intimidation of Parliament, 138; pretorianism, 139; presidential government, 141; Second World War entombed independence, 147; dismemberment, 169; postwar economy, 171, 182; war with Russia, 171; patriotism, 328, 329, 330, 331, 340; anthem, 328, 335, 336; characteristics of people, 331; social consciousness, 334; relations with America, 347, 348; part of American Poles, 348, 349, 352; attack against Soviets, 366; new division, 429; General Government, 430, 432, 433, 437; underground government, 438; organized sabotage, 439; Soviet-occupied, 440; Government in Exile, 445; army, 446; choice of war, 453, 455

Hitler: advent of, 151; self-determination of, 152; fifth columnists of, 153, 162; denounced German-Polish pact, 417; tirade of, against England, 419; reply to British, 420; October 6, 1939, speech of, 427

Hlond, Cardinal Augustus, 250

Hofmann, Józef, 356

Hohenzollern: Albert of, 42; dynasty, 46; succeeded to Duchy of Prussia, 63; collapse of, Reich, 123

Holy Roman Empire, 33

Homo sapiens: Brünn-Předmost, 23; Borreby type of, 23; Alpinoid, 23

Hoover, Herbert: relief administrator, 351, 368, 369; suggested Technical Advisers Mission, 370

House, Edward M., 73, 351, 352

Huberman, Bronisław, 356

Hughes, Charles Evans, 353

Hundred Years' War, 41

Hungarian State: founded, 32; Teutonic Knights from, 37; friction with Poland, 40, 70, 159; kings of, 41, 42; Dmowski claimed part of, 77

Iłłakowicz, Kazimiera, 291

Imperial Manifesto of October 16, 1918, 124

Industry: Micoquian core, 13; Microlith, 15; industrial movement, 62; origins of, 184; developed under Partitioning Powers, 184, 220; condition of, when independence restored, 185; Russia prevented, 185; few Polish, in Poznań and Pomorze, 186; German heavy, in Upper Silesia, 186; undeveloped in Galicia, 186; progress in, 187 ff.; foundation of, 187; coal mining, 188; iron and steel, 190; metalworking, 190; textile, 192; paper, 192; raw materials for chemical, 193; machine tool, 193; meat-products, 194; state monopoly of potassium-salts, 194; miscellaneous, 194; advances in, to prewar level, 195; lack of capital for, 195; lessons of Second World War, 195. *See also* Metallurgy

"Industry, Foreign Trade, and Communications," by Leopold Wellisz, xii, 184–205

Institution of Labor Inspectors, 234

International Chamber of Commerce figures on world trade, 178

International Economic Conference in London, 211

Iranians, 31
Ivan the Terrible, Tsar, 42, 43
Ivanovič culture, 19, 21
Iwaszkiewicz, Jarosław, 302
Izvestiia, 403

Jackowski, Maximilian, 65
Jadwiga, Queen, 39, 40
Jagiełło, Władysław: marriage of, 39, 40; founder of dynasty, 41; statue of, 314
Jagiellonian dynasty, 40–43 *passim*
Jagiellonian University and Library, 278
Jankowski, Karol, 312
Jarecki, Henryk, 324
Jarecki, Tadeusz, 326
Jarema, Józef, 320
Jarocki, Władysław, 317
Jasiński, Monsignor, 251
Jaworzyna, territorial dispute over, 383
Jędrzejewicz, Janusz, 140, 141
Jena, 50, 51
Jewish Democratic party (*Żydowska Demokratyczna Partja*), 122
Jewish People's party (*Żydowska Partja Ludowa*), 121
Jews: variable in type, 27; protected under Casimir, 38, 488; in Eastern Galicia, 81; minority rights for, 100, 150; core of Zionist movement, 121; anti-Semitism, 143, 161, 272; migration of, urged, 143; Sabbath of, protected, 150; population, 159, 255; economic situation of, 160; school system of, 161, 162; Jewish Community Law, 256; in Reich, 431, 436
Jonescu, Take, 379, 382
Jordanes, 20
Jugoslavia, nucleus of Serbian kingdom, 169
Jutland, 17

Kaden-Bandrowski, Juliusz, 305
Kakowski, Alexander, 250
Kaniow, 75
Karge, Józef, 350
Karny, Alfons, 315
Karpiński, Zygmunt, "Poland's Monetary and Financial Policy, 1919–1939," xiii, 206–218
Kasprowicz, Jan, 295
Kasprzak, Jan K., "Social Progress in Poland, 1918–1939," xv, 232–244
Katowice, radio station at, 401
Kaunas. *See* Kowno
Kellogg-Briand Pact, 388, 392; Polish proposal to outlaw war in, 396
Kelly, Eric P., 362
Kemmerer, Edwin W., 371
Kerner, Robert J., "Epilogue," 457–463
Khazar, 27
Kielce: region, 10, 15, 18, 26; Forster's speech in, 430
Kiepura, Jan, 356
Kiev: Kievan Russia, 7, 8; Bolesław attacked, 36; Poland renounced, 46; captured, 83
Kleeberg, General, 427
Klonowicz, Sebastian, quoted, 347
Knights of the Sword, 63
Knokowski, Józef, 350
Koc, Adam, 144; quoted, 145
Kochański, Paul, 356
Kock, Battle of, 427
Komorowski, Tadeusz, 458, 459
Konarska, Janina, 321
Konarski, Stanisław, 233, 248
Kondracki, Michał, 325, 326
Königsberg, 392
"Korfanty line," 79
Kornacki, George, 302–303
Kościałkowski, Marjan Zyndram, 142, 144
Kościuszko, Tadeusz: insurrection, 48; cited on Napoleon, 50; proclamation of May 7, 1794, 219; social leader also, 233; as symbol of Polish-American relationship, 350; tributes to, 352, 353; squadron, 367; Foundation, 357, 360 ff.
Kossak-Szczucka, Zofja, 303
Kostiuchnowka, 71
Kovno. *See* Kowno
Kowarski, Felicjan, 319
Kowel, 71
Kowno, 48, 84, 386
Kozłowski, 140, 141
Krakau. *See* Cracow
Kraków. *See* Cracow
Krasiński, Zygmunt, 59, 60
Krasnodębska, Bogna, 321

Kridl, Manfred, "Polish Literature," xix, 284–310
Kruczkowski, Leon, 302
Krueger, Wilhelm, 439
Kruszwica, 33
Krysiński, A., 157
Krzyżanowski, Vladimir, 350
Kubina, Monsignor, 251
Kucharzewski, Jan, 75
Kujavian: graves, 17; people, 33
Kulisiewicz, Tadeusz, 321
Kultura, 252
Kumans, 27
Kuna, Henryk, 315, 318
Kuncewicz, Maria, 303
Kurek, Jalu, 295
Kurjer Warszawski, 393
Kwapiński, Jan, 461
Kwaśniewski, General, 411
Kwiatkowski, Eugeniusz, 146

Labuński, Felix Roderick: "Music," xxi, 323–327; a founder of Association of Young Polish Musicians, 326
Lachert, Bohdan, 313
Ladogans, 23–27 *passim*
Landowska, Wanda, 356
Landtag, Prussian, 104, 105
Lappish types, 23
LaTène influences, 19; metalwork, 19; imports, 20; Celtic in origin, 21
Latvia, 9; in federation, 42; political groupings in, 127; collaboration with Poland, 380; Soviet-Latvian pact, 388
Lausitz culture, 18, 19, 22
Laval, Pierre, 403
League of Nations: attempt of, to guarantee security, 7; as referee, 78, 79; decision of, on Polish boundaries, 79, 80, 81; Poland appealed to, 84; Danzig subject to, 149; minorities system of, 150, and failure of, 151; Germany in, 152; Russia member of, 153; on Ukraine, 158; report of, on loans, 177; interest of, in public health studies, 243; inadequate to guarantee peace, 392; Poland in, 393; resigned, 411
Lechon, Jan, 286, 289
Lednicka, Maryla, 315
Lednicki, Aleksander, 73
Legionaries, Piłsudski's. *See* Army
Leopold, King, 419
Leszczyński, Stanisław, 47
Letters from a Journey in America, 356
Libernum veto, 45; abolished, 48, 335
Liberation (*Wyzwolenie*) branch of Polish People's party, 115
Lignica, 37
Lipski, Józef, 410, 413, 414, 415
"Literature," by Manfred Kridl, xix, 284–310
Literature: under Sigismunds, 43; great names in, 44, 59; publication prohibited, 57; poets of Emigration saved Poland, 59; Christian spirit of, 249; influence of Catholicism in, 252; association of Catholic writers, 252; era of "Young Poland" in, 284; in Republic, 284 ff.; poetry, 284 ff.; novel, 297 ff.; realism in novels, 306; drama weak spot in, 307; comedy, 309; realism in drama, 310
Lithuania, Grand Duchy of: geography of, 8, 9, 14; union with Poland, 8, 39, 247, 332; Christianized, 39, 41; under Sigismunds, 42; White-Russian lands to, 43; culture of, 44; modeled government on Polish, 44; Bolshevik troops in, 82, 84; Wilno dispute, 84, 164, 385; political groupings in, 127; minority, 167; Polish reprisals against, 386; quarrel over Memel, 387, 409; diplomatic normality with Poland, 409; Soviet sympathetic to, 410
Litorina Sea, 12, 16
Little Entente: friendly relations of Poland and, 383, 384; anti-Hungarian aims of, 385; Danubian interests of, 385; objected to new Directory of Europe, 399
Litvinov, Maxim: Protocol, 389, 391; Commissar for Foreign Affairs, 413
Livonia, German Order of, 42; conquered by Swedes, 46
Lloyd George, David, 78, 366
Locarno: treaties, 380; Pact, 392, 393; treaties of 1925, 402; Eastern, Pact, 402, 403; Hitler denounced, Pact, 405

Łódź: industrial center, 117, 192; Populist-Socialist strength in, 147; Germans in, opposed Hitler, 162; social work of bishop of, 251
Lombardy, 50
Lord, R. H., 77
Louis of Anjou, 40
Louis XV, 47
Louis XVIII, 54
Lublin: -Sandomierz, 26; Diet of, 42; Union, 44; radical government in, 76, 125; Catholic university at, 251; Committee of National Liberation, 458, 459, 460
Łuck (Lutsk), 440
Ludendorff, General Erich von, 72
Lugano, 386
Lusatia, 18, 36
Luther, Chancellor Hans, 392
Lwów: school of anthropology at, 23; Ukrainians, seized, 76; Polish population of, 82; minority rights for Ukrainians in, 154, 155, 157; cultural leadership of, 158; three archbishops in, 253; universities of, 268; academic societies in, 279; arrests at, 440

MacCracken, Henry Noble, 361
MacDonald, Ramsay, 391, 399
Mączeński, Zdzisław, 313
"Magdalenian," 15
Magdeburg, 74, 76, 91
Maglemosean culture, 15
Maklakiewicz, Jan, 325
Makowski, Tadeusz, 318
Malczewski, Jacek, 317
Malczewski, Rafał, 319
Malhomme, Leon, 401
Maliszewski, Witold, 323
Marek, Czesław, 327
Marie-Louise, Archduchess, 51
Marie of Rumania, 382
Marienwerder, 78
Masaryk, Thomas G., 106
Mazovia: people of, 32; in Third Partition, 48
Mediterranean race, 23, 24
Memel: German-Lithuanian dispute over, 387, 409, 413; incorporated in Reich, 415
Mémoires de l'Académie des Sciences Techniques, 280
Mesolithic, 22, 23
Messianism: mystic nationalism in, 59; two fundamental ideas of, 60; Prussian Poland lost, 104; extreme, 249; a source of spiritual strength, 337; thread of, snapped, 340
Metallurgy: new techniques in, 12, 13, 19; copper and silver, 16, 17; Slovakian-Bohemian trade in, 18; bronze, 18; Iron-Age influence on, 19; La-Tène, 19; Germans looted, industry, 191; reëquipment begun, 191; technical perfection and low costs in, 192; scope of, 192; developed, 281
Mickiewicz, Adam: greatest poet, 59, 289; quoted, 331, 336; sustained national spirit, 335, 340
Microliths, 14, 15
Mieszko: ruled Slavic state, 23, 33, 36; Christianized Poland, 34
Mikołajczyk, Premier Stanisław, 458, 460, 461
Miłosz, Czesław, 295
"Minorities," by Joseph S. Roucek, x, 148–166
Minorities: four principal groups of, 118; political bloc of, 118, 120, 121, 122, 134, 154; Ukrainian, 118, 154; White-Russian, 120, 164; Jewish, 121, 159, 161; unavoidable, 149; better position of German, 149, 162, 163, 394; Upper Silesia Convention protected, 151, 154, 163; bilateral pact with Nazi Germany for, 151; system under league, 151; one cause of Second World War, 151; Treaty, 151, 154, 161; German, fifth columnists, 152, 162, 163; dominance-submission relationship, 152; Germany championed, 152, 153; right of, to petition League, 153; difficulties regarding, 165; democratic ideal of, 166; religious, 253
Mizrachi, 256
Mizwa, Stephen P.: "Polish-American Cultural Relations," xxiii, 347–364; helped organize Kościuszko Foundation, 361
Młynarski, Emil, 323

Modrzewski, Andrzej Frycz, 44; advocated protection for homeless, 232
Mohács, Battle of, 42
Mojeska, Helena (Modrzejewska), 356
Mołotkowa, 71
Molotov: cited, 423; quoted, 427
Moltke, Hans, German Ambassador to Poland, 412, 414, 416
Mongoloid invaders, 31
Moraczewski, Jędrzej; premier, 76, 91, 126; program of, 127; arrested, 128; lost control, 131
Moravia: migrations from 11, 16, 21; Bronze Age in, 18; Šipka jaw found in, 23; Polish rulers of, 34, 36
Morawski, Eugeniusz, 323
Mościcki, I., inventor, 281
Mościcki, Ignacy: President of Republic, 95, 136; fled, 100; ordinance power of, 137, 140; signed Constitution, 141; personal prestige of, 142; ordered new elections, 146; relinquished powers, 446
Most favored nation principle, 383, 415
Mousterian strata: hand axes in, 13; culture, 23
Mrozewski, Stefan, 321
Munich, 146, 159: Poland not a party to, Agreement, 412
Murmansk, 75
Muscovy, 7, 8, 41
Music: Polish contribution to European, 323; inspiration from folk, 325; two groups among composers, 325; neoclassicism in, 325, 326; Association of Young Polish Musicians, 326; emotionalism in, 326
"Music," by Felix Roderick Labuński, xxi, 323–327
Mussolini, Benito, 399

Nałkowska, Zofja, 299, 308
Napoleon: against Austrians in Italy, 50; Poles in army of "liberation" of, 50; defeated Partitioning Powers, 50; gave Warsaw to Poland, 51; retreat of, 52
Narutowicz, Gabriel, 134, 281
Narvik campaign, 446
National Assembly (*Zgromadzenie Narodowe*), 92
National Democratic party: Polish League became, 66; Dmowski leader of, 71, 73; against Regency Council, 75; frontier policy of, 82, 83; nationalism in, 106, 108; in Galicia, 107; fused into National People's Union, 112; principles of, 113; leaders of, 113; anti-Russian, 114; Right, 131; excesses against Jews by, 162
National League (*Liga Narodowa*), 66, 105
National Peasant Union (*Narodowy Związek Chłopski*), 114
National People's Union (*Związek Ludowo Narodowy*), 112, 113, 131, 138
National Radical Camp (*Nara*), 162
National Socialism in Germany, 389
National Workers party (*Narodowa Partja Robotnicza*), 112
Neolithic period, 21–25 *passim*
Neurath, Baron von, 400
Neuri, 21
Nicholas, Grand Duke, quoted, 71
Nicholas I, 56, 57
Nicholas II, 72
Niederle, L., 20
Niemcewicz, Juljan Ursyn, 356
Niemen: boundary, 8, 48; interview at Tilsit on, 50; opening of, 386
Niewiadomski, Stanisław, 324
Noakowski, Stanisław, 317
Nobles: 1374 charter to, 40; power of, 44; political rights to, 219
Nordic type, 24–26 *passim*
North Sea, 12
Northern War, 47
Notec (Netze), 11
Novosiltsov, Nicholas, 56
Nowaczyński, Adolf, 309
Nowak, Frank T., "The Formation of the Polish State," iii, 31–39
Nowogródek: minorities rights in, 154, 155; Lithuanians in, 164
Nowowiejski, Archbishop, 252
Nowowiejski, Felix, composer, 324
Nowy Dvor, 366

Oder: boundary, 4, 8, 11; farming along, 16; Slavic tribes on, 32, 33
Odo, Margrave, 34
Odrodzenie, 251

Official Journal of Laws of the Polish State, 101
Olszewski, K., 281
Opieński, Henryk, 323
Orava, 80, 382
Organic Statute, 57
"Organic Work," 66, 68
Orvis, Julia Swift, "Partitioned Poland, 1795–1914," v, 49–69
Ostoja-Chrostowski, Stanisław, 321
Ostrowski, Stanisław, 314
Osubka-Morawski, Edward, 460
Ottawa Imperial Preference Agreement, 176
Otto I, 33
Otto II, 34
Otto III, 34, 35
OZON (Camp of National Union), 144, 145; defections from, 146

Paderewski, Ignacy Jan: converted Wilson to Polish cause, 73, 351, 365; premier, 77, 131; resigned, 81; in Poznań, 89; cabinet of, 128, 132; in National People's Union, 113; at Paris, 130; cause of downfall, 130; resented League discrimination, 150
Painting: leading fine art, 316; appreciation of color in, 316, 317; formism in, 316–318 *passim;* Art society, 317; influence of French cubism on, 318; neoclassicism in, 317, 319; Brotherhood of St. Luke, 319; national influences on, 320
Paleolithic, 22, 24
Palester, Roman, 325, 326
Pankiewicz, Józef, 317, 320
Pan-Slavism: object of, 68; Poles opposed, 68
Papacy, 33
Papen, Franz von, 398
Paprocki, S. J., quoted, 155
Paris Committee, 366
Paris Pact, 389
Paris Peace Conference, 128, 130, 133; made Danzig a free city, 149; illusory hopes of, 151
Paris *Temps,* 389
Parker, Edwin B., 368
"Partitioned Poland, 1795–1914," by Julia Swift Orvis, v, 49–69
Partitioning Powers, 49; defeated by Napoleon, 50; not agreed, 72; collapse of, 76, 169; statutes of, abrogated, 101; policy of, 169, 172; industries under, 184; deferred social reform, 220
Partitions: crisis led to, 46; interest of Russia and Prussia in, 47; First, 47; Second, 48; Third, 48
Paskievich, Ivan, 57
Pautsch, Fryderyk, 317
Pawlikowska, Maria, 292
Peiper, Tadeusz, 293
Perkowski, Piotr, 325, 326
Perzyński, Włodzimierz, 298, 309
Petchenegs, 27
Peter the Great, 46, 47
Petlura, Hetman, 82, 83
Piarists, 249
Piast: name appropriated, 107; moderate Populist, 131. *See also* Polish People's party
Piast family, 33, 36, 40
Piedmont, 116
Pierachi, M., 158
Pilica, 14, 16, 48
Piłsudski, Józef: leader Socialist party, 66, 70, 106, 116; fled to Austria, 70; anti-Russian, 70, 77, 136, 388; created Polish Legion, 70, 71, 90, 136; resigned from Legion, 72, 74; confined in Magdeburg, 74, 365; released, 76, 91; minister of war, 76; favored federation with Lithuania, 82; maneuver of, and Weygand sent Russians eastward, 83; Chief of Polish State, 91, 132; refused presidency of Republic, 95; personal authority of, 96, 117, 136; *coup d'état* of, 95, 117, 126, 386; quoted on Lublin regime, 126; new cabinet of, 128; advocated federalist principle, 129; 1920 policy of expansion of, 130; character of, 135; era, 136 ff.; death of, 141, 161; Foundation for National Culture, 269; quoted on defeat, 329; policy of, of active struggle, 365; quoted to Ferdinand, 379; anti-Czech, 384; query of, to Hitler, 398; skeptical of Polish-German pact, 400
Piłsudski's "legionaries." *See* Army

Piotrowska, Irena, "The Fine Arts," xx, 311–322
Plebiscite(s): recommended for East Prussia, 77; stipulated for Upper Silesia, 78, 163; in Allenstein and Marienwerder, 78, 79; Lithuanians refused, for Wilno, 84; procedure, 146
Pleistocene period, 12, 13
Płock, 252
Pniewski, Bohdan, 313
Podhale Valley, 311, 315, 321
Podolia, 10
Poetry, 285 ff.; lyricism dominated, 285; Scamander group, 286; urban theme for, 286; changes in versification, 287; leaders in, 287 ff.; accomplishments of Vanguard in, 294; of bygone era, 295; spiritual leadership of poets, 340
Poland, 354
"Poland and Europe: Geographical Position," by Oscar Halecki, i, 3–9
"Poland and the War," by Stanisław Strzetelski, xxvi, 427–456
"Poland as a European Power," by Oscar Halecki, iv, 40–48
"Poland's Economy between Two World Wars," by Henryk Zieliński, xi, 169–183
"Poland's Monetary and Financial Policy, 1919–1939," by Zygmunt Karpiński, xiii, 206–218
Polanie, 32, 33
Polesie, minorities rights in, 154, 155
"Polish-American Cultural Relationships," by Stephen P. Mizwa, xxiii, 347–364
"Polish-American Political and Economic Relations," by Eldon R. Burke, xxiv, 365–374
Polish Committee of National Liberation, 458, 459, 460
Polish Corridor. *See* Pomorze
Polish-Czechoslovak federation, 448
Polish League. *See* National League
"Polish Literature," by Manfred Kridl, xix, 284–310
Polish-Lithuanian-Ruthenian Commonwealth, 333, 337
Polish-Lithuanian Union of 1386, 6, 8, 39, 40, 247, 332
Polish National Committee, 74
Polish National Revolution, 76, 89
"Polish National Spirit, The," by Edmund Zawacki, xix, 328–343
Polish People's party (*Polskie Stronnictwo Ludowe*), 114, 115, 116
"Polish Political Parties," by Malbone W. Graham, viii, 104–122
"Polish Politics, 1918–1939," by Malbone W. Graham, ix, 123–147
Polish Science, 275
Polish-Soviet Pact of July 30, 1941, 443–445 *passim*
Polish Word, 113
Political parties: Polish League, 66, National Democratic, 66; Socialist, 66; nationalism in, 105; socialism in, 106, 112, 116; forces to organize public opinion, 108; geopolitical fact of conquest, 108; formation of, began simultaneously, 109; crystallized at extraordinary moments, 109; four major ideologies in, 110; nationalist ideology, 110; and tradition, 111; democratic ideology in, 111; catalogue of, 112 ff.; Christian Democratic, 111, 114; Social Democratic, 111; National Workers, 112; National People's Union, 112, 131, 138; *NARAS* (National Radicals), 112; Catholic People's, 114; Christian League of National Union, 112, 114; National Peasant Union, 114; People's, 114; populism in, 114, 115; of minorities, 118 ff.; in Constituent Diet, 131. *See also* National Democratic, Socialist, White-Russian parties.
Pomerania: Kujavian graves in, 17; people of, 32; Mieszko ruled, 34; Teutonic Knights seized, 37, 38; Casimir regained, 41; to Prussia, 48. *See also* Pomorze
Pomorze (Pomerania): Polish policy to incorporate, 130; national party in, 147; German minority in, 149, 162; to Poland by Treaty of Versailles, 149; Germans prohibited industrialization of, 185; in Reich, 429
Poniatowski, Stanisław Augustus, 47
Ponikowski, 132, 136

Population: in 1939, 8; increases in, after economic phases, 12; accelerated by metallurgical techniques, 13; of Duchy of Warsaw, 51; after First World War, 85, 257; of minorities, 156, 159, 162, 164, 255; decrease in rural, 220; rural over-, 231; enormous growth in, 232, 237; Protestant, 255; prophecies concerning, 455
Populist party (*Polskie Stronnictwo Ludowe*): agrarian radicalism of, 107; rejected Left support, 124; rejected *OZON*, 145
Porembka, 200
Posen. *See* Poznań
Potemkin, Vladimir, 417
Pottery: from north Caucasian source, 17; for burial urns, 18; polychrome painting on, 19; face-urn complex in, 19; Roman, 20
Potworowski, Tadeusz, 320
Poznań (Posen): bishopric at, 34; ceded to Prussia, 54; richest state, 65; "supreme council of people" in, 76; awarded to Poland, 77; a loss to Germany, 80; Paderewski in, 89; *Courier*, 113; policy of "incorporation" for, 130; national party strength in, 147; German minority in, 149; industrialization of, prevented, 185; university in, 269; Polish National Exposition in, 313; Conservatory, 323; bombed, 422; in Reich, 429
Prague, Warsaw's ultimatum to, 165
Pravda, 403, 413
Pre-Boreal period, 14
Pripet marshes, 10, 20, 31
Problems of Central and Eastern Europe, 74
Prussia: origin of, 7, 46; plains of, 10; fief of Poland, 41; freed, 46; Pomerania to, 48; Napoleon defeated, 50; gained access to Baltic, 51; harsh policy of, 63; in First World War, 70; plans of Polish National Committee for East, 74, 77; West, lost to Germany, 77, 80; Prussian Poland anti-German, 104
Pruszkowski, Tadeusz, 318, 319
Prystor, Premier Aleksander, 140, 141
Przemyśl, 34
Przybos, Juljan, 295
Przybylski, Czesław, 312
Pułaski(s): leaders of Confederation of Bar, 47; in American Revolution, 349, 350; quoted, 350; tributes to, 350, 352

Quadragesimo anno, 251
Question polonaise, La, 66
Quo Vadis, 356

Race: origin of, 3; Slavic, 3, 20, 31, 32; ethnic complexity, 12, 17, 18, 22, 32; ethnic movements, 12, 13; four ethnic elements in Mesolithic Poland, 17; Złota contribution to, 18; ethnic amalgam, 22; heredity basic factor in, 22; ten types in post-Mesolithic Poland, 23; average Pole, 26; blood groups, 26; unity of, 28; German settlers assimilated, 37, 38; Halich, with Ukraine, 69; ethnic boundaries difficult, 148, 149, 366
Raczkiewicz, President Władysław, 100, 446, 458, 461
Raczyński, Count Edward, quoted, 391
Radwan, Jerzy, "Agricultural Reconstruction in Poland," xiv, 219–231
Rafajłowa, 71
Ragunda, 12
Rapallo Treaty, 387, 388, 392
Rathaus, Karol, 327
Ratti, Achilles (Pius XI), 249
Rauschning, Hermann, collaboration policy of, 405
Realist party, 71
"Rebirth of Poland, 1914–1923," by Bernadotte E. Schmitt, vi, 70–85
Religion: pagan, 33; Christianized, 34, 35, 39, 42; Catholicism predominant in Republic, 44, 64, 247, 248, 253; Bismarck's attack on church, 64; Uniate in Eastern Galicia, 69, 253; peasant Lutherans in Allenstein, 78; in Galicia, 106; church as political force, 110, 247; church against socialism, 117; Jewish Cahals, 161; influence of Reformation, 247; tolerance in, 248, 254, 333; Warsaw Confederation granted peace to, 248; Protestants, 248, 254, 255; bigotry in, 248;

tie between nationalism and, 249, 250, 251; skepticism before First World War, 249; Constitution recognized Church, 249; Concordat settled Church-State relations, 250; Catholic Action important in, 250; growing influence of Catholicism, 252; of minorities, 253; Ukrainian movement in, 253; Orthodox Church, 254; Jews not religious problem, 255; Mohammedans, 256; under Reich, 436; in Soviet-occupied Poland, 443

"Religious Life," by Oscar Halecki, xvi 247–256

Renaissance: influence of Italian, 43; culture, 44

Rerum novarum, 251

Rezke, Jean and Edouard de, 356

Reymont, Władysław, 356

Ribbentrop, Joachim von: asked Polish collaboration, 406; suggestions of, for Danzig problem, 413; veiled demand for Danzig, 17; assured Hitler of Britain's stand, 418; "concrete proposals" of, 421, 422; -Molotov pact, 427, 451

Riga, Treaty of: signed, 83, 131; Polish gains from, 83, 149, 164; provisions for minorities in, 151, 154; financial conditions of, never carried out, 207; ended struggle for political independence, 236; ended Polish-Russian war, 387

Rhythm (*Rytm*), 318

Rockefeller Foundation, 356, 359 ff., 361

Rodziński, Artur, 357

Rogowski, Ludomir, 323

Rola-Żymierski, Michał, 460

Romer, Tadeusz, 460

Roosevelt, Franklin D.: appealed to Poland and Germany, 419; formulated rights of man, 448; suggestion of *Grossräume* by, 455 conferred with Mikołajczyk

Ropice, 164

Rostworowski, Karol Hubert, 307

Roucek, Joseph S., "Minorities," x, 148–166

Rousseau, 50

Rovno (Równe), 13

Roznow, 200

Rożycki, Ludomir, 324

Rubinstein, Artur, 356

Rumania: Polish frontier, 9; Mościcki interned in, 100; beneficiary of Allied victory, 379; potential enemies of, 379; common cause with Poland, 379

Runnymede, 37

Russia: political unit of Slavic tribes, 6; Kievan, 7, 8; Muscovy transformed into, 7; USSR, 9; pottery in, 17; conquest of, by Batu Khan, 37; invaded beyond Dnieper, 42; Empire of Peter the Great, 46; interest of, in partitions, 47, 48; Napoleon defeated, 50; Alexander Tsar of, 51; defeated Napoleon, 52; Poland part of, 57; harsh to Poles, 63; devastated Poland, 71; negative attitude of, 72; recognized independence of Poland, 73; promised autonomy to Polish territories, 90; gains for Poles in Revolution of 1905, 105, 116; nationalism in Russian Poland, 105, 106; boundaries fixed, 387; German *rapprochement,* 387; Soviet-Latvian pact, 388; Litvinov Protocol, 389; Polish-Soviet Pact, 388, 390; Stalin, 419

Russians, White: Slavic, 31; Catholic, 82; indifferent to rule, 84; minorities rights for, 154, 155; population of, 164; status of, 164. *See also* White Russian parties

Ruthenian provinces: to Poland, 40; autonomy for, 41, 159; Orthodox, 45; question of Eastern Galicia, 69; minorities in, 80, 156; union between Greek and Roman church possible in, 247, 253

Rydzewski, Stanisław, 350

Saale River, 31

Sacrobosco, Joannes, 347

Sahm, Heinrich, 395

St. Croix Mountains, 10

St. Estreicher, 452

Salonica, 123

San River, 10, 16

Sandomierz, 16; -Kielce region, 18, 26; Holy Spirit Insurance at, 241

Sapieha, Bishop Adam, 251
Sapieha, Prince Eustache, 128
Saunders, George, quoted, 447
Saxony: King of, 51; constitution of, 51; Alexander's plan for, 54; to Prussia, 54
Saxo-Thuringia, 18
Scamander group: flamed national spirit, 285; credo of, 285; poets of contemporary life in, 286; urban theme for poetry of, 286; conservative, 293
Scandinavia, 16, 17
Schmitt, Bernadotte E., "Rebirth of Poland, 1914–1923," vi, 70–85
Schulz, Bruno, 307
Science: research publications in, 276; Academy of Arts and Sciences, 278; Academy of Technical Sciences, 280; background of, 281; scientists, 281, 282
"Science and Scientific Institutions," by Wojciech Świętosławski, xviii, 274–283
Schleicher, General Kurt von, 398
Sculpture, 314
Scythian(s): Iron Age, 19; people, 21, 25
Second Partition, 48
Sejm. See Diet
Sejm Ustawodawcy. See Constituent Diet
Sembrich-Kochanska, Marcella, 356
Serbia, 31
Settlement Act of 1886, 64
Seyda, Marjan, 73, 113
Sichulski, Kazimierz, 317
Sidor, Karol, 411
Sienkiewicz, Henryk, 356
Sigismund, Emperor, 41
Sigismund I, 42
Sigismund Augustus, 42, 43
Sigismund of Sweden, Prince, 43
Sikorski, Kazimierz, 325
Sikorski, Władysław: Prime Minister and Commander in Chief, 100, 135, 446; to U.S. for lend-lease, 448; quoted, 448; Sikorski-Stalin Declaration, 449; killed, 451
Silesia (Sląsk): migration route, 11; in Aunjetitz culture, 18; Ślęzanie in, 32; frontier, 37; to Bohemia, 38; Prussian conquest of, 47; "incorporation" policy for, 130; loan for, 209; in Reich, 429
Šipka jaw, 23
Skagerrak, 12
Skarga, Father, 232
Skaryce, 13
Sketches in Charcoal, 356
Skirmunt, Konstanty, 113, 380, 382, 383
Skoczylas, Władysław, 319, 321
Skrzyński, Aleksander, 135, 383
Skulski, Leopold, Prime Minister, 132
Skwarszyński, Stanisław, 145
Slavs: territory, 20, 21, 31; proto-, 21; founded various nations, 31, 32; overflowed central Europe, 31; major disaster to, 32; under Greco-Roman civilization, 32; Polish group of, 68
Slawek, Walery: headed Government Bloc, 138, 140; premier, 141; cabinet of, resigned, 142; liquidated Government Bloc, 143
Sławoj-Składkowski, Felicjan, 144, 446
Slendziński, Ludomir, 319
Slęza River, 32
Slęzanie, 42
Słiwiński, 132
Słonimski, Antoni, 288, 309
Słowacki, Juliusz, 59, 60, 307, 335, 340
Śmigły-Rydz, Edward: supported all-Socialist combination, 125; Piłsudski's choice as successor, 136; Marshal, 145; benevolent neutrality policy of, 404; order of, to Polish army, 420
Smolensk, 42
Smoluchowski, Marjan, 279
Sniadeckis, J. and V., 281
Sobieski, Jan (John III), 45, 46, 47, 337, 363
Social Democratic party, 111
Social progress: Renaissance statesmen interested in, 44; democratic liberties limited to nobles, 44, 51; serfs freed, 62, 219; rise of socialism, 62; class chasms bridged, 63; ancient tradition of, 232; labor insurance, 233; advanced at end of eighteenth century, 233; political struggles also for,

233; 1918 active measures in, 233; six diverse laws for social insurance, 234, 235, 238, 239, 240; electoral law, 234; eight-hour day, 234; subsidies to unemployed, 235, 237, 239; labor laws, 235, 236, 237; for women and children, 235, 236, 237, 238, 241, 243; collective bargaining, 235, 239; in health, 235, 240, 241, 242; private foundations for medical aid, 235; work of bishops in, 251; achievements, 342; annulled in Soviet-occupied Poland, 442
"Social Progress in Poland, 1918–1939," by Jan K. Kasprzak, xv, 232–244
Socialism: rise of, 62; nationalist, 106; persistent force in party politics, 116; urban, 117; in Catholic country, 117
Socialist party (*Polska Partja Socjalistyczna*): Piłsudski leader of, 66, 67, 70; aloof from Council of Regency, 75; impotent as partisan force, 106; center of, in Galicia, 107; opposed Piłsudski, 117, 118; reasons for decline of, 117; party rejected, Left, 124; Ministry of Social Welfare instigated by, 233
Solutrean interlude, 14
Somme, Battle of, 72
Sosnkowski, General Casimir, 74, 458
Soviet-Czechoslovak Pact, 457
Spisz (Spiš): claimed by Poland and Czechoslovakia, 80; minority, 164; boundary dispute in, 382
Staff, Leopold, 295
Stakhanov system, 442
Stalin, Premier Joseph, 419
Stanisławów, 154, 155, 157
Stankiewicz, Adam, 120
Starosta, 102
Starostwa, 101
Staszyc, Stanisław, 233
Statkowski, Roman, 324
Stochód River, 71
Stokowski, Leopold, 356
Stresemann, Gustav, 152, 393, 396, 397
Strug, Andrzej (Tadeusz Gałecki), 298
Stryjeńska, Zofia, 319
Strzetelski, Stanisław, "Poland and the War," xxvi, 427–456
Student Brotherhood (*Bratnia Pomoc*), 272
Stürmer, Boris Vladimirovich, 72
Styr River, 71
Subalyuk cave, 23
Sub-Boreal period, 12
Sudetens, 10
Super, Paul, 358; quoted, 359
Supreme National Committee, 70, 71
Suvorov, 48
Suwalki, armistice of, 84
Swedes: invasions by, 7; conquered Livonia, 46; Peter the Great defeated, 47
Swiderian: culture, 14; hunters, 21
Swidry, 14
Świerczyński, Rudolf, 313
Świętosławski, Wojciech: "Education," xvii, 257–273; "Science and Scientific Institutions," xviii, 274–283
Switalski, Casimir, 138, 139
Sylvester II, Pope, 35
Syrkus, Szymon, 313
Szalowski, Antoni, 325, 326
Szanajca, Józef, 313
Szaniawski, Klemens, 308
Szczepkowski, Jan, 314, 319
Szelburg-Zarembina, Eva, 303
Szeligowski, Tadeusz, 325, 326
Szeptycki, Archbishop Andrzy Count, 253
Szeptycki, General, 75
Szlagowski, Bishop, 252
Szopski, Felicjan, 324
Szukalski, Stanisław, 315
Szyk, Artur, 321
Szymanowski, Karol, 323, 324
Szyszko-Bohusz, Adolf, 314

Tacitus, 20
Tannenberg, 41. *See also* Grünewald
Tansman, Aleksander, 326
Tardenoisian: hunters, 15, 16, 17, 21; culture, 23
Tarnopol, 19, 154, 155, 157
Tarnów, 71
Tartars, 40, 41, 46
Tass, 450
Tatras, 10, 27; mountaineer culture of, 311, 324
Teodorowicz, Józef, 253

Teschen (Cieszyn): Dmowski claimed, 74, 77; Allied Powers divided, 80; Polish, 130; Poland retained, 146; Warsaw demanded evacuation of, 164; boundary dispute over, 382, 384; anti-Czechoslovak campaign in, 401; ultimatum to Prague concerning, 412

Teutonic Order (Knights), 7, 37, 41, 42, 63, 332, 377

Thames-Rhine valley, 12

Thietmar, quoted, 35

Third Partition: total dismemberment, 48, 50; Austro-Russian convention arranged, 50

Thirty Years' War, 45

Thomson, S. Harrison, "Foreign Relations," xxv, 377–424

Thorn. *See* Toruń

Thugutt, Stanisław: leader of Liberation movement, 115; displaced, 116

Thuringia, 17

Tilsit, 50

Tobruk, 447

Tools: new metallurgical techniques for, 13; from flakes, 13, 14; "core industries" for, 13; "stepped" retouch of edges of, 13; "gravers," 13

Topolski, Felix, 321

Toruń (Thorn), 154

Trade. *See* Economy

Transylvanians, 46

Treaty of Berlin, 388

Treaty of Versailles: Poland signed, 78; intended partition of Upper Silesia, 79, 163; article 87 of, on frontiers, 81; left some frontiers vague, 148; gave Pomorze to Poland, 149; Germany attacked, 149; Luther denounced, 392; German impression on eastern frontiers according to, 394

Trentowski, Bronisław, 330

Treviranus, 397

Tripolye: culture, 16; farmers, 17

Trumpeter of Kraków, The, 362

Turco-Tartar, 31

Turkey: invasions, 41, 45; supported Cossack insurrections, 46

Turosienski, S. K., 269

Tuwim, Juljan: in Scamander group, 287; text for "Slopiewnie" by, 324

Ukraine: in USSR, 9; immigration route, 10; Swiderian culture in, 14; Tripolye culture from, 16; burial urns in, 18; types in, 27; Ruthenian, 40; to Poland, 43; devastation of, 45; to Tsar, 45; Chełm to, 75; Galicia to, 82; political groups in, 118; Poland demanded, 158; terrorist activities in, 158; annexation of, 441

Ukrainian Christian Socialist party (*Ukraińska Partja Chrześcijańsko-Społeczna*), 118

Ukrainian Club (*Klub Ukraiński*), 118

Ukrainian National Labor League (*Ukraińska Konfederacja Pracy Narodowej*), 118

Ukrainian National Labor party (*Ukraińska Narodowa Trudowa Partja*), 119

Ukrainian National party (*Ukraińska Narodowa Partja*), 119

Ukrainian Peasant party, Parliamentary Club of (*Klub Sejmowy Ukrainskiej Włościańskiej Partji* or *Chliboroby*), 118

Ukrainian Radical party (*Ukraińska Radykalna Partja*), 119

Ukrainian Social Democratic party (*Ukraińska Socjal-Demokratyczna Partja*), 120

Ukrainian Social Revolutionary party (*Ukraińska Partja Socjalistów-Rewolucjonistów* or *"Es-erzy"*), 119

Ukrainian Socialist deputies (*Ukraińskie Socjalistyczne Zjednoczenie "Selanskyj Sojusz"*), 119

Ukrainian Socialist party (*Ukraińska Socjalistyczna Partja*), 120

Ukrainians: Slavic, 31, 157; in Halich Uniate, 69; a minority group, 148, 156 ff.; franchise rights of, 154; language rights of, 154; educational facilities for, 155; schools, 155; home of, 157; Russian in sympathies, 157, 158; cultural leadership of, in Lwów, 158; national movement of, 158; Orthodox, 254

Uniate Church, 69, 253

Union of Polish Patriots, 458

Union of the People (*Jednośći Ludowa*), 116

United States: intervention of, 73; formally recognized Poland, 77; Poland indebted to, 90, 368; policy of, toward expansion, 366; nonintervention policy of, 367; supplies from, 368
Upper Silesia: a frontier, 10, 74; hunters from, 15; Dmowski claimed, 77; rebellion in, 78; plebiscite for, 79, 163; Convention in force, 151, 154, 163; language rights in, 154; educational rights in, 155; controversy over, 163; under Treaty of Versailles, 163; German heavy industries in, 186

Vanguard, 293, 294
Varangians, 6
Varna, 41
Vasas: kingdom of, 43; kings, 44, 45
Vauclain, Samuel M., 361
Veneti (Wends), 20
Vienna Congress of 1515, 42
Vilna. *See* Wilno
Vilnius. *See* Wilno
Vistula (Wisła): boundary, 4, 8, 10, 14, 16, 18, 19, 21, 22, 32, 51; Upper, 10, 32; migration route, 11, 17, 20, 26; Reservoirs, 200, 314
Vitold, 41
Vladimir of Kiev, 34
Voice of Lublin, The, 113
Voldemaras, Augustine, 386, 387
Volhynia (Wołyn): Upper Paleolithic in, 13; flint axes found in, 13, 16; hunters from, 15; inhuming group in, 18; Złota culture of, 22; Nordic type in, 26; Ukrainians in, 155, 157; German minority in, 162; Czechs in, 164
Völkerwanderung Germans, 25

Waag-Vistula valley, 11
Wagram, 51
Waliszewski, Zygmunt, 320
Warsaw (Warszawa): temporary liberation of, 48; Duchy of, organized, 50, 51; Russia seized, 52; Alexander's attitude toward, 53 ff.; "Congress Kingdom," 54; German armies captured, 71; *Warsaw Gazette,* 113; socialism in, 117; Regency Council at, 124; and Berlin minorities pact, 151, 163; German minority in, 162; bank of issue in, 207; loan for, 209; Confederation, 248; Archbishop of, 250; Academy of Technical Sciences, 280; school of theology in University of, 254, 255; Ministry of Education in, 258; University, 268, 269; *Literary News,* 288; center of architecture, 312; "School of," 319–320; Academy of Fine Arts, 321; Polytechnic Institute, 317; conference at, 380; *Kurier Poranny,* 412
Warta River: migration route, 11; culture along, 18; boundary, 20, 33; Polanie on, 32
Warta-Pilica region, 16
Wasilewski, Leon, 129
Wąsowicz, Wacław, 317
Wawrzyniak, Piotr, 65
Weimar Republic, 175
Weiss, Wojciech, 317
Wellisz, Leopold, "Industry, Foreign Trade, and Communications," xii, 184–205
Wengierski, Tomasz Kajetan, 356
Wertheim, Juliusz, 324
Wesep, H. B. von, 360
Westerplatte, 422
Weygand, Maxim, 83
White Book, 409
White-Russian Democratic Council (*Białoruska Rada Demokratyczna*), 120
White-Russian Independent Socialist party (*Białoruska Partja Niezależnych Socjalistów*), 121
White-Russian Party of Social Revolutionaries *(Partja Białoruskich Socjalistów-Rewolucjonistów)*, 121
White-Russian Populist party (*Białoruska Partja Ludowa*), 120
White-Russian Social Democratic party (*Białoruska Socjalno-Demokratyczna Partja*), 121
White-Russians, Christian Democratic Union of (*Chrześcijańsko Demokratyczny Związek Białorusinów*), 120
Wichman, Count, 32, 34
Widukind, 32
Wiechowicz, Stanisław, 325, 326

Wieniawski, Adam, 323
Wierzyński, Kazimierz, 290
Wilhelmstrasse, 418, 419
William II, 72
Wilno (Vilna, Vilnius): temporary liberation of, 48; in hands of Bolsheviks, 76, 83; Lithuanians claimed, 82; question of, 84, 164; in Polish State, 85, 385; *Wilno Daily,* 113; Ukrainian minority in, 154, 155; White Russians in, 164; University, 269
Wilson, Woodrow: quoted, 73, 348; "Fourteen Points" of, 75, 90, 351, 365; Central Powers accepted "Points" of, 124; headed minorities system, 151; a symbol to Poles, 351; efforts of, to secure ethnic boundaries, 366; first great American friend, 368
Winawer, Bruno, 309
Wisła. *See* Vistula
Wisńiowiecki, Michał, 45
Witkiewicz, Stanisław Ignacy, 306, 317
Witos, Wincenty: cabinet of, 113, 132; leader of Piast, 114, 131, 135; clashed with Thugutt, 115; ousted, 136; debacle, 137
Wittig, Edward, 315, 318–319
Wittlin, Józef, 304
Władysław III, 41
Władysław IV, 45
Wojciechowski, Stanisław, 116, 135, 136
Wojewoda, 101
Województwa, 101
Wołyn. *See* Volhynia
Workman, The (*Robotnik*), 67
World War I: cruel decisions for Poland in, 70; Piłsudski's legions in Austrian army in, 71; Central Powers administered Poland, 71; Poland after, 72, 85, 148 ff.
World War II, 100; minorities problem a cause of, 151, 152
Woytowicz, Bolesław, 325, 326
Wroblewski, Z., 281
Würm glaciation, 11–14 *passim*
Wyczołkowski, Leon, 316, 320
Wysocki, 400
Wyspiański, Stanisław, 307, 311, 313
Wyzwolenie. See Liberation . . .

Y.M.C.A. in Poland, 357
"Young Poland" group, 284

Żak, Eugeniusz, 318
Zakopane, 311
Zaleski, August, 152, 384, 387–390 *passim,* 396
Zaliński, Edmund L., 350
Zamoyski, August, 315, 318
Zamoyski, John, 44
Zamoyski, Maurycy, 113
Zawacki, Edmund, "The Polish National Spirit," xxii, 328–343
Zbrucz River, 81
Żeleński, Władysław, 324
Żeligowski, Lucjan, 84, 385
Żeromski, Stefan, 297, 308; quoted, 329, 341
Zieliński, Henryk, "Poland's Economy between Two World Wars," xi, 169–183
Złota culture, 18, 22
Złoty: new monetary unit, 208; rate of exchange for, 208, 209. *See also* Financial policy.